W9-CTY-308

PRAISE FOR DAVID GRAEBER AND
DEBT: THE FIRST 5,000 YEARS

Winner of 2012 Bread and Roses Award for Radical Publishing

Winner of 2012 Gregory Bateson book prize, awarded by
the Society for Cultural Anthropology

"A brilliant, deeply original political thinker."
—Rebecca Solnit, author of *A Paradise Built in Hell*

"Fresh ... fascinating ... Graeber's book is not just thought-provoking, but also exceedingly timely. His sweeping narrative history essentially argues that many of our existing ideas about money and credit are limited, if not wrong."
—Gillian Tett, *The Financial Times*

"A lengthy field report on the state of our economic and moral disrepair. In the best tradition of anthropology, Graeber treats debt ceilings, subprime mortgages and credit default swaps as if they were the exotic practices of some self-destructive tribe. Written in a brash, engaging style, the book is also a philosophical inquiry into the nature of debt—where it came from and how it evolved."
—Thomas Meaney, *The New York Times Book Review*

"An alternate history of the rise of money and markets, a sprawling, erudite, provocative work."
—*Bloomberg Businessweek*

"The book is more readable and entertaining than I can indicate ... It is a meditation on debt, tribute, gifts, religion and the false history of money. Graeber is a scholarly researcher, an activist and a public intellectual. His field is the whole history of social and economic transactions."
—Peter Carey, *The Observer*

"An engaging book. Part anthropological history and part provocative political argument, it's a useful corrective to what passes for contemporary conversation about debt and the economy."
—*The Boston Globe*

DEBT

DEBT

THE FIRST 5,000 YEARS

DAVID GRAEBER

10TH ANNIVERSARY
EDITION WITH A PREFACE
BY THOMAS PIKETTY

MELVILLE HOUSE
BROOKLYN • LONDON

DEBT: THE FIRST 5,000 YEARS
TENTH ANNIVERSARY EDITION

© 2011, 2012 David Graeber

First published in hardcover in May 2011

First Melville House paperback printing: October 2012

Preface copyright 2021 by Thomas Piketty

Melville House Publishing
46 John Street
Brooklyn, NY 11201

and

Suite 2000
16/18 Woodford Road
London E7 0HA

www.mhpbooks.com

ISBN: 978-1-61219-933-7

Manufactured in the United States of America
2 3 4 5 6 7 8 9 10

The Library of Congress has cataloged the hardcover edition as follows:

Graeber, David.
 Debt : the first 5,000 years / David Graeber.
     p. cm.
 Includes bibliographical references and index.
 ISBN 978-1-933633-86-2 (alk. paper)
 1. Debt--History. 2. Money--History. 3. Financial crises--History. I. Title.
 HG3701.G73 2010
 332--dc22
                            2010044508

CONTENTS

Preface

DEBT AND IDEOLOGY

I AM BOTH happy and sad to write this preface for the new edition of David Graeber's magnificent book, *Debt: The First 5000 Years*, first published in 2011, just ten years ago.

Sad, because David's untimely death in September 2020 left a huge void. An "anarchist" social anthropologist, David was above all one of those social scientists who transcended disciplines and audiences. I had the pleasure of debating his book with David in September 2013 in Paris, in a slightly unreal bucolic country setting. I wish I could repeat that experience today.

Happy too, because as I immerse myself in these memories and this book, I rediscover the joy and intellectual happiness I experienced when reading *Debt: The First 5000 Years* for the first time. This book is fundamental, because for the first time it sets the long history of the cycles of debt and debt abolition that have punctuated human destiny since the invention of writing and the first tablets recording the assets and liabilities of creditors and debtors in a multi-millennium perspective. Above all, David Graeber shows that this story is also to a large extent that of equality and inequality, because there is a fundamental link between debt, power, and extreme forms of social domination, especially between debt and slavery.

David is certainly not the first to insist on the profound anthropological link between debt and slavery. A debt without limit amounts to placing all one's work, all one's existence, in the hands of one's creditor. It is not by chance that in English the terms *bond* and *bondage* refer to both monetary debts and relationships of extreme dependence and forced labor. In studies widely quoted by Graeber, the social anthropologist Alain Testart, has shown how societies that allow slavery for debt (or the sale of children, wives, or nephews, another major form of internal slavery) correspond to societies pushing inequalities of wealth to their extreme. At any given time, the ordinary inequalities between the poor and the rich can turn into absolute social exclusion and unlimited personal power. On the other hand, the prohibition of slavery for debt, or at least the limitation of the penalty that a creditor can impose on a debtor unable to repay his debts (a penalty which for example can be reduced to a limited number of years of work, or to a disciplinary treatment which is not too inhumane), enables the extent of the internal fracturing of a society, to be kept under control; examples include the abolitions of debt[*] decreed by Solon in Greece in the 7th century BCE, or the laws of the Han Empire, or those of the Ashanti or Dahomey kingdoms.[1]

In *Debt: The First 5000 Years*, David Graeber takes the thinking further. He is familiar with the terrain of slavery and post-slavery, which he studied in Madagascar by analyzing, in his doctoral thesis, the conflicting relations between former owners and former slaves in rural Malagasy communities.[†] But he is equally familiar with the world of post-slavery modern debt and the power relations it maintains, the world of Wall Street (he participated in the occupation of Wall Street) and the IMF (which he ridicules ironically in the first pages of the book). The strength of Graeber's book is precisely to allow us to think about the link between the two worlds: the old world of forced labor relations and debt cancellation, for example the liberation of slaves, and the new world of international financial markets and monetary debts and the resulting power relations.

For if modernity is characterized everywhere by the end of the intergenerational transmission of debts, and with it the family perpetuation of absolute dependence, there is nevertheless a debt that can still be passed down from generation to generation for ever: I am referring to the public debt. Those who were born in Greece or Argentina at the wrong time may find themselves suffering from austerity forever and having to repay interest infinitely. This book on the "first 5000 years" of debt was published in 2011, at a time when the 2008 financial crisis was about to turn into a public debt crisis in Europe and elsewhere; it had no difficulty in finding an audience. Published in 2021, at a time when the debate on the cancellation of the Covid debt and the need to resort to private billionaires is likely to return in force, this updated reissue of the book should probably do the same.

When confronted with owners of wealth and property, whose ideologies of debt sanctification and repayment are expressed today with

---

[*] See Alain Testart, *L'esclave, la dette et le pouvoir. Essais de sociologie comparative,* Errance 2001. See also by the same author *L'institution de l'esclavage. Une approche mondiale,* Gallimard 2018.

[†] See D. Graeber, *Lost People: Magic and the Legacy of Slavery in Madagascar,* Indiana University Press, 2007.

the same ease as in the past, one of our best antidotes remains the anthropological and historical analysis of David Graeber. Whatever the creditors' efforts to naturalize their domination, the fact is that human history is made up of multiple phases of consolidation and cancellation of debts, depending on the relationship of socio-political forces and historically located trajectories.

In this case, taking a very long-term perspective, David Graeber clearly distinguishes over the last five millennia two phases in which debt and dependency relations have been pushed to a climax, and which also correspond to phases of sacralization of metal currency: a first phase ranging from about 800 BCE to around the year 600 AD (the pivotal age); then a second phase where slavery and the power of the owners took off again on a global scale, and which began around 1450 AD with the development of the great Western colonial empires. The beginning of the end of this second phase can be situated as commencing with the two world wars of 1914–1945 and the fall of European colonialism in the 1950s–1960s. For Graeber, the symbolic date marking the true end of this "age of the great capitalist empires" was the abandonment of the gold-dollar convertibility in 1971. This elimination of the metal reference, which had played a central role during the period 1450–1971 and embodied the sacralization-naturalization of debt and property, could pave the way, according to Graeber, for a new period of radical questioning of the power of creditors, provided that adequate social mobilizations succeed in challenging the forces and institutions (such as the IMF) that have made the protection of creditors of all countries their primary mission.

However, not all theoretical and historical debates have been decided; far from it, starting with the question of the political forms on which future transformations will be based. In his work, Alain Testart hypothesizes that centralized states have historically tended to abolish slavery for debts and to regulate the relations of extreme dependence between the possessed and possessor: not out of greatness of soul or out of a taste for equality, but simply to avoid a fatal fracturing of the community into scattered sovereignties, in other words to establish their own political, fiscal and military sovereignty, at least in the territory they control directly, and then on a global scale. David Graeber is naturally of a different opinion; in his last writings* he insisted on the need to rethink human history by plac-

---

* Voir D., Graeber, D., Wengrow, "How to change the course of human history (at least, the part that's already happened)," *Eurozine*, 2018.

ing at the center of the analysis the multiple neglected experiences of egalitarian decentralization and horizontal federalism, which an official history centered on the coercive and hierarchical central state has always tried to forget. Unfortunately, these discussions will have to continue without David. Let us try to pursue them and prolong his flame with the same vigor.

—Thomas Piketty
February 2021
Translated from the French by Kristin Couper

Chapter One

ON THE EXPERIENCE OF MORAL CONFUSION

debt
• noun ɪ a sum of money owed. 2 the
state of owing money. 3 a feeling of
gratitude for a favour or service.
—*Oxford English Dictionary*

If you owe the bank a hundred thousand dollars, the bank owns you. If
you owe the bank a hundred million
dollars, you own the bank.
—American Proverb

TWO YEARS AGO, by a series of strange coincidences, I found myself
attending a garden party at Westminster Abbey. I was a bit uncomfortable. It's not that other guests weren't pleasant and amicable, and
Father Graeme, who had organized the party, was nothing if not a gra-
cious and charming host. But I felt more than a little out of place. At
one point, Father Graeme intervened, saying that there was someone
by a nearby fountain whom I would certainly want to meet. She turned
out to be a trim, well-appointed young woman who, he explained, was
an attorney—"but more of the activist kind. She works for a foundation that provides legal support for anti-poverty groups in London.
You'll probably have a lot to talk about."

We chatted. She told me about her job. I told her I had been
involved for many years with the global justice movement—"anti-
globalization movement," as it was usually called in the media. She
was curious: she'd of course read a lot about Seattle, Genoa, the tear
gas and street battles, but . . . well, had we really accomplished anything by all of that?

"Actually," I said, "I think it's kind of amazing how much we did
manage to accomplish in those first couple of years."

"For example?"

"Well, for example, we managed to almost completely destroy the IMF."

As it happened, she didn't actually know what the IMF was, so I offered that the International Monetary Fund basically acted as the world's debt enforcers—"You might say, the high-finance equivalent of the guys who come to break your legs." I launched into historical background, explaining how, during the '70s oil crisis, OPEC countries ended up pouring so much of their newfound riches into Western banks that the banks couldn't figure out where to invest the money; how Citibank and Chase therefore began sending agents around the world trying to convince Third World dictators and politicians to take out loans (at the time, this was called "go-go banking"); how they started out at extremely low rates of interest that almost immediately skyrocketed to 20 percent or so due to tight U.S. money policies in the early '80s; how, during the '80s and '90s, this led to the Third World debt crisis; how the IMF then stepped in to insist that, in order to obtain refinancing, poor countries would be obliged to abandon price supports on basic foodstuffs, or even policies of keeping strategic food reserves, and abandon free health care and free education; how all of this had led to the collapse of all the most basic supports for some of the poorest and most vulnerable people on earth. I spoke of poverty, of the looting of public resources, the collapse of societies, endemic violence, malnutrition, hopelessness, and broken lives.

"But what was *your* position?" the lawyer asked.

"About the IMF? We wanted to abolish it."

"No, I mean, about the Third World debt."

"Oh, we wanted to abolish that too. The immediate demand was to stop the IMF from imposing structural adjustment policies, which were doing all the direct damage, but we managed to accomplish that surprisingly quickly. The more long-term aim was debt amnesty. Something along the lines of the biblical Jubilee. As far as we were concerned," I told her, "thirty years of money flowing from the poorest countries to the richest was quite enough."

"But," she objected, as if this were self-evident, "they'd borrowed the money! Surely one has to pay one's debts."

It was at this point that I realized this was going to be a very different sort of conversation than I had originally anticipated.

Where to start? I could have begun by explaining how these loans had originally been taken out by unelected dictators who placed most of it directly in their Swiss bank accounts, and ask her to contemplate the justice of insisting that the lenders be repaid, not by the dictator, or even by his cronies, but by literally taking food from the mouths of hungry children. Or to think about how many of these poor countries had actually already paid back what they'd borrowed three or four times now, but that through the miracle of compound interest, it still hadn't made a significant dent in the principal. I could also observe that there was a difference between refinancing loans, and demanding that in order to obtain refinancing, countries have to follow some orthodox free-market economic policy designed in Washington or Zurich that their citizens had never agreed to and never would, and that it was a bit dishonest to insist that countries adopt democratic constitutions and then also insist that, whoever gets elected, they have no control over their country's policies anyway. Or that the economic policies imposed by the IMF didn't even work. But there was a more basic problem: the very assumption that debts *have* to be repaid.

Actually, the remarkable thing about the statement "one has to pay one's debts" is that even according to standard economic theory, it isn't true. A lender is supposed to accept a certain degree of risk. If all loans, no matter how idiotic, were still retrievable—if there were no bankruptcy laws, for instance—the results would be disastrous. What reason would lenders have not to make a stupid loan?

"Well, I know that sounds like common sense," I said, "but the funny thing is, economically, that's not how loans are actually supposed to work. Financial institutions are supposed to be ways of directing resources toward profitable investments. If a bank were guaranteed to get its money back, plus interest, no matter what it did, the whole system wouldn't work. Imagine I were to walk into the nearest branch of the Royal Bank of Scotland and say 'You know, I just got a really great tip on the horses. Think you could lend me a couple million quid?' Obviously they'd just laugh at me. But that's just because they know if my horse didn't come in, there'd be no way for them to get the money back. But, imagine there was some law that said they were guaranteed to get their money back no matter what happens, even if that meant, I don't know, selling my daughter into slavery or harvesting my organs or something. Well, in that case, why not? Why bother waiting for someone to walk in who has a viable plan to set up a laundromat or some such? Basically, that's the situation the IMF created on a global level—which is how you could have all those banks willing to fork over billions of dollars to a bunch of obvious crooks in the first place."

I didn't get quite that far, because at about that point a drunken financier appeared, having noticed that we were talking about money, and began telling funny stories about moral hazard—which somehow,

before too long, had morphed into a long and not particularly engross-
ing account of one of his sexual conquests. I drifted off.

In retrospect I was never quite sure what to make of that conversation. Could an activist lawyer really have never heard of the IMF, or was
she just gently playing me? But it didn't really matter one way or the other.
For several days afterward, that phrase kept resonating in my head.

"Surely one has to pay one's debts."

The reason it's so powerful is that it's not actually an economic
statement: it's a moral statement. After all, isn't paying one's debts
what morality is supposed to be all about? Giving people what is due
them. Accepting one's responsibilities. Fulfilling one's obligations to
others, just as one would expect them to fulfill their obligations to you.
What could be a more obvious example of shirking one's responsibilities than reneging on a promise, or refusing to pay a debt?

It was that very apparent self-evidence, I realized, that made the
statement so insidious. This was the kind of line that could make terrible things appear utterly bland and unremarkable. This may sound
strong, but it's hard not to feel strongly about such matters once you've
witnessed the effects. I had. For almost two years, I had lived in the
highlands of Madagascar. Shortly before I arrived, there had been an
outbreak of malaria. It was a particularly virulent outbreak because
malaria had been wiped out in highland Madagascar many years before, so that, after a couple of generations, most people had lost their
immunity. The problem was, it took money to maintain the mosquito
eradication program, since there had to be periodic tests to make sure
mosquitoes weren't starting to breed again and spraying campaigns if it
was discovered that they were. Not a lot of money. But owing to IMF-
imposed austerity programs, the government had to cut the monitoring
program. Ten thousand people died. I met young mothers grieving for
lost children. One might think it would be hard to make a case that the
loss of ten thousand human lives is really justified in order to ensure
that Citibank wouldn't have to cut its losses on one irresponsible loan
that wasn't particularly important to its balance sheet anyway. But
here was a perfectly decent woman—one who worked for a charitable
organization, no less—who took it as self-evident that it was. After all,
they owed the money, and surely one has to pay one's debts.

■ ■ ■ ■ ■

For the next few weeks, that phrase kept coming back at me. Why debt?
What makes the concept so strangely powerful? Consumer debt is the
lifeblood of our economy. All modern nation-states are built on deficit

spending. Debt has come to be the central issue of international politics. But nobody seems to know exactly what it is, or how to think about it.

The very fact that we don't know what debt is, the very flexibility of the concept, is the basis of its power. If history shows anything, it is that there's no better way to justify relations founded on violence, to make such relations seem moral, than by reframing them in the language of debt—above all, because it immediately makes it seem that it's the victim who's doing something wrong. Mafiosi understand this. So do the commanders of conquering armies. For thousands of years, violent men have been able to tell their victims that those victims owe them something. If nothing else, they "owe them their lives" (a telling phrase) because they haven't been killed.

Nowadays, for example, military aggression is defined as a crime against humanity, and international courts, when they are brought to bear, usually demand that aggressors pay compensation. Germany had to pay massive reparations after World War I, and Iraq is still paying Kuwait for Saddam Hussein's invasion in 1990. Yet the Third World debt, the debt of countries like Madagascar, Bolivia, and the Philippines, seems to work precisely the other way around. Third World debtor nations are almost exclusively countries that have at one time been attacked and conquered by European countries—often, the very countries to whom they now owe money. In 1895, for example, France invaded Madagascar, disbanded the government of then–Queen Ranavalona III, and declared the country a French colony. One of the first things General Gallieni did after "pacification," as they liked to call it then, was to impose heavy taxes on the Malagasy population, in part so they could reimburse the costs of having been invaded, but also, since French colonies were supposed to be fiscally self-supporting, to defray the costs of building the railroads, highways, bridges, plantations, and so forth that the French regime wished to build. Malagasy taxpayers were never asked whether they wanted these railroads, highways, bridges, and plantations, or allowed much input into where and how they were built.[1] To the contrary: over the next half century, the French army and police slaughtered quite a number of Malagasy who objected too strongly to the arrangement (a hundred thousand, by some reports, during one revolt in 1947). It's not as if Madagascar has ever done any comparable damage to France. Despite this, from the beginning, the Malagasy people were told they owed France money, and to this day, the Malagasy people are still held to owe France money, and the rest of the world accepts the justice of this arrangement. When the "international community" does perceive a moral issue, it's usually when they feel the Malagasy government is being slow to pay their debts.

But debt is not just victor's justice; it can also be a way of punishing winners who weren't supposed to win. The most spectacular example of this is the history of the Republic of Haiti—the first poor country to be placed in permanent debt peonage. Haiti was a nation founded by former plantation slaves who had the temerity not only to rise up in rebellion, amidst grand declarations of universal rights and freedoms, but to defeat Napoleon's armies sent to return them to bondage. France immediately insisted that the new republic owed it 150 million francs in damages for the expropriated plantations, as well as the expenses of outfitting the failed military expeditions, and all other nations, including the United States, agreed to impose an embargo on the country until it was paid. The sum was intentionally impossible (equivalent to about 18 billion dollars), and the resultant embargo ensured that the name "Haiti" has been a synonym for debt, poverty, and human misery ever since.[2]

Sometimes, though, debt seems to mean the very opposite. Starting in the 1980s, the United States, which insisted on strict terms for the repayment of Third World debt, itself accrued debts that easily dwarfed those of the entire Third World combined—mainly fueled by military spending. The U.S. foreign debt, though, takes the form of treasury bonds held by institutional investors in countries (Germany, Japan, South Korea, Taiwan, Thailand, the Gulf States) that are in most cases, effectively, U.S. military protectorates, most covered in U.S. bases full of arms and equipment paid for with that very deficit spending. This has changed a little now that China has gotten in on the game (China is a special case, for reasons that will be explained later), but not very much—even China finds that the fact it holds so many U.S. treasury bonds makes it to some degree beholden to U.S. interests, rather than the other way around.

So what is the status of all this money continually being funneled into the U.S. treasury? Are these loans? Or is it tribute? In the past, military powers that maintained hundreds of military bases outside their own home territory were ordinarily referred to as "empires," and empires regularly demanded tribute from subject peoples. The U.S. government, of course, insists that it is not an empire—but one could easily make a case that the only reason it insists on treating these payments as "loans" and not as "tribute" is precisely to deny the reality of what's going on.

Now, it's true that, throughout history, certain sorts of debt, and certain sorts of debtor, have always been treated differently than others. In the 1720s, one of the things that most scandalized the British public when conditions at debtors' prisons were exposed in the popular press was the fact that these prisons were regularly divided into two sections. Aristocratic inmates, who often thought of a brief stay in Fleet or Marshalsea as something of a fashion statement, were wined and dined by liveried servants and allowed to receive regular visits from prostitutes. On the "common side," impoverished debtors were shackled together in tiny cells, "covered with filth and vermin," as one report put it, "and suffered to die, without pity, of hunger and jail fever."[3]

In a way you can see current world economic arrangements as a much larger version of the same thing: the U.S. in this case being the Cadillac debtor, Madagascar the pauper starving in the next cell— while the Cadillac debtor's servants lecture him on how his problems are due to his own irresponsibility.

But there's something more fundamental going on here, too, a philosophical question, even, that we might do well to contemplate. What is the difference between a gangster pulling out a gun and demanding you give him a thousand dollars of "protection money," and that same gangster pulling out a gun and demanding you provide him with a thousand-dollar "loan"? In most ways, obviously, there is no difference. But in certain ways there is As in the case of the U.S. debt to Korea or Japan, were the balance of power at any point to shift, were America to lose its military supremacy, were the gangster to lose his henchmen, that "loan" might start being treated very differently. It might become a genuine liability. But the crucial element would still seem to be the gun.

There's an old vaudeville gag that makes the same point even more elegantly—here, as improved on by Steve Wright:

> I was walking down the street with a friend the other day and a guy with a gun jumps out of an alley and says "Stick 'em up."
> As I pull out my wallet, I figure, "Shouldn't be a total loss." So I pull out some money, turn to my friend and say, "Hey, Fred, here's that fifty bucks I owe you."
> The robber was so offended he took out a thousand dollars of his own money, forced Fred to lend it to me at gunpoint, and then took it back again.

In the final analysis, the man with the gun doesn't have to do anything he doesn't want to do. But in order to be able to run even a regime based on violence effectively, one needs to establish some kind of set of rules. The rules can be completely arbitrary. In a way it doesn't even matter what they are. Or, at least, it doesn't matter at first. The problem is, the moment one starts framing things in terms of debt, people will inevitably start asking who really owes what to whom.

Arguments about debt have been going on for at least five thousand years. For most of human history—at least, the history of states and empires—most human beings have been told that they are debtors.[4] Historians, and particularly historians of ideas, have been oddly reluctant to consider the human consequences, especially since this situation—more than any other—has caused continual outrage and resentment. Tell people they are inferior, they are unlikely to be pleased, but this surprisingly rarely leads to armed revolt. Tell people that they are potential equals who have failed and that therefore, even what they do have they do not deserve, that it isn't rightly theirs, and you are much more likely to inspire rage. Certainly this is what history would seem to teach us. For thousands of years, the struggle between rich and poor has largely taken the form of conflicts between creditors and debtors—of arguments about the rights and wrongs of interest payments, debt peonage, amnesty, repossession, restitution, the sequestering of sheep, the seizing of vineyards, and the selling of debtors' children into slavery. By the same token, for the last five thousand years, with remarkable regularity, popular insurrections have begun the same way: with the ritual destruction of the debt records—tablets, papyri, ledgers, whatever form they might have taken in any particular time and place. (After that, rebels usually go after the records of landholding and tax assessments.) As the great classicist Moses Finley often liked to say, in the ancient world, all revolutionary movements had a single program: "Cancel the debts and redistribute the land."[5]

Our tendency to overlook this is all the more peculiar when you consider how much of our contemporary moral and religious language originally emerged directly from these very conflicts. Terms like "reckoning" or "redemption" are only the most obvious, since they're taken directly from the language of ancient finance. In a larger sense, the same can be said of "guilt," "freedom," "forgiveness," and even "sin." Arguments about who really owes what to whom have played a central role in shaping our basic vocabulary of right and wrong.

The fact that so much of this language did take shape in arguments about debt has left the concept strangely incoherent. After all, to argue with the king, one has to use the king's language, whether or not the initial premises make sense.

If one looks at the history of debt, then, what one discovers first of all is profound moral confusion. Its most obvious manifestation is that most everywhere, one finds that the majority of human beings hold simultaneously that (1) paying back money one has borrowed is a simple matter of morality, and (2) anyone in the habit of lending money is evil.

It's true that opinions on this latter point do shift back and forth. One extreme possibility might be the situation the French anthropologist Jean-Claude Galey encountered in a region of the eastern Himalayas where as recently as the 1970s, the low-ranking castes—they were referred to as "the vanquished ones," since they were thought to be descended from a population once conquered by the current landlord caste many centuries before—lived in a situation of permanent debt dependency. Landless and penniless, they were obliged to solicit loans from the landlords simply to find a way to eat—not for the money, since the sums were paltry, but because poor debtors were expected to pay back the interest in the form of work, which meant they were at least provided with food and shelter while they cleaned out their creditors' outhouses and rerofed their sheds. For the "vanquished"—as for most people in the world, actually—the most significant life expenses were weddings and funerals. These required a good deal of money, which always had to be borrowed. In such cases it was common practice, Galey explains, for high-caste moneylenders to demand one of the borrower's daughters as security. Often, when a poor man had to borrow money for his daughter's marriage, the security would be the bride herself. She would be expected to report to the lender's household after her wedding night, spend a few months there as his concubine, and then, once he grew bored, be sent off to some nearby timber camp, where she would have to spend the next year or two working as a prostitute to pay off her father's debt. Once accounts were settled, she return to her husband and begin her married life.[6]

This seems shocking, outrageous even, but Galey does not report any widespread feeling of injustice. Everyone seemed to feel that this was just the way things worked. Neither was there much concern voiced among the local Brahmins, who were the ultimate arbiters in matters of morality—though this is hardly surprising, since the most prominent moneylenders were often Brahmins themselves.

Even here, of course, it's hard to know what people were saying behind closed doors. If a group of Maoist rebels were to seize control of the area (some do operate in this part of rural India) and round up the local usurers for trial, we might suddenly hear all sorts of views expressed.

Still, what Galey describes represents, as I say, one extreme of possibility: one in which the usurers themselves are the ultimate moral authorities. Compare this with, say, medieval France, where the moral status of moneylenders was seriously in question. The Catholic Church had always forbidden the practice of lending money at interest, but the rules often fell into desuetude, causing the Church hierarchy to authorize preaching campaigns, sending mendicant friars to travel from town to town warning usurers that unless they repented and made full restitution of all interest extracted from their victims, they would surely go to Hell.

These sermons, many of which have survived, are full of horror stories of God's judgment on unrepentant lenders: stories of rich men struck down by madness or terrible diseases, haunted by deathbed nightmares of the snakes or demons who would soon rend or eat their flesh. In the twelfth century, when such campaigns reached their heights, more direct sanctions began to be employed. The papacy issued instructions to local parishes that all known usurers were to be excommunicated; they were not to be allowed to receive the sacraments, and under no conditions could their bodies be buried on hallowed ground. One French cardinal, Jacques de Vitry, writing around 1210, recorded the story of a particularly influential moneylender whose friends tried to pressure their parish priest to overlook the rules and allow him to be buried in the local churchyard:

> Since the dead usurer's friends were very insistent, the priest yielded to their pressure and said, "Let us put his body on a donkey and see God's will, and what He will do with the body. Wherever the donkey takes it, be it a church, a cemetery, or elsewhere, there will I bury it." The body was placed upon the donkey which without deviating either to right or left, took it straight out of town to the place where thieves are hanged from the gibbet, and with a hearty buck, sent the cadaver flying into the dung beneath the gallows.[7]

Looking over world literature, it is almost impossible to find a single sympathetic representation of a moneylender—or anyway, a professional moneylender, which means by definition one who charges interest. I'm not sure there is another profession (executioners?) with such a consistently bad image. It's especially remarkable when one considers that unlike executioners, usurers often rank among the richest and most powerful people in their communities. Yet the very name, "usurer," evokes images of loan sharks, blood money, pounds of flesh, the selling of souls, and behind them all, the Devil, often represented as himself a kind of usurer, an evil accountant with his books and ledgers, or alternately, as the figure looming just behind the usurer, biding his

time until he can repossess the soul of a villain who, by his very occupation, has clearly made a compact with Hell.

Historically, there have been only two effective ways for a lender
to try to wriggle out of the opprobrium: either shunt off responsibility
onto some third party, or insist that the borrower is even worse. In medieval Europe, for instance, lords often took the first approach, employing Jews as surrogates. Many would even speak of "our" Jews—that is,
Jews under their personal protection—though in practice this usually
meant that they would first deny Jews in their territories any means
of making a living except by usury (guaranteeing that they would be
widely detested), then periodically turn on them, claiming they were
detestable creatures, and take the money for themselves. The second
approach is of course more common. But it usually leads to the conclusion that both parties to a loan are equally guilty; the whole affair is a
shabby business; and most likely, both are damned.

Other religious traditions have different perspectives. In medieval
Hindu law codes, not only were interest-bearing loans permissible (the
main stipulation was that interest should never exceed principal), but
it was often emphasized that a debtor who did not pay would be
reborn as a slave in the household of his creditor—or in later codes,
reborn as his horse or ox. The same tolerant attitude toward lenders,
and warnings of karmic revenge against borrowers, reappear in many
strands of Buddhism. Even so, the moment that usurers were thought
to go too far, exactly the same sort of stories as found in Europe would
start appearing. A Medieval Japanese author recounts one—he insists
it's a true story—about the terrifying fate of Hiromushime, the wife
of a wealthy district governor around 776 AD. An exceptionally greedy
woman,

> she would add water to the rice wine she sold and make a
> huge profit on such diluted saké. On the day she loaned some-
> thing to someone she would use a small measuring cup, but
> on the day of collection she used a large one. When lending
> rice her scale registered small portions, but when she received
> payment it was in large amounts. The interest that she forcibly
> collected was tremendous—often as much as ten or even one
> hundred times the amount of the original loan. She was rigid
> about collecting debts, showing no mercy whatsoever. Because
> of this, many people were thrown into a state of anxiety; they
> abandoned their households to get away from her and took to
> wandering in other provinces.[8]

After she died, for seven days, monks prayed over her sealed coffin. On the seventh, her body mysteriously sprang to life:

> Those who came to look at her encountered an indescribable stench. From the waist up she had already become an ox with four-inch horns protruding from her forehead. Her two hands had become the hooves of an ox, her nails were now cracked so that they resembled an ox hoof's instep. From the waist down, however, her body was that of a human. She disliked rice and preferred to eat grass. Her manner of eating was rumination. Naked, she would lie in her own excrement.[9]

Gawkers descended. Guilty and ashamed, the family made desperate attempts to buy forgiveness, canceling all debts owed to them by anybody, donating much of their wealth to religious establishments. Finally, mercifully, the monster died.

The author, himself a monk, felt that the story represented a clear case of premature reincarnation—the woman was being punished by the law of karma for her violations of "what is both reasonable and right." His problem was that Buddhist scriptures, insofar as they explicitly weighed in on the matter, didn't provide a precedent. Normally, it was debtors who were supposed to be reborn as oxen, not creditors. As a result, when it came time to explain the moral of the story, his exposition grew decidedly confusing:

> It is as one sutra says: "When we do not repay the things that we have borrowed, our payment becomes that of being reborn as a horse or ox." "The debtor is like a slave, the creditor is like a master." Or again: "a debtor is a pheasant and his creditor a hawk." If you are in a situation of having granted a loan, do not put unreasonable pressure on your debtor for repayment. If you do, you will be reborn as a horse or an ox and be put to work for him who was in debt to you, and then you will repay many times over.[10]

So which will it be? They can't both end up as animals in each other's barns.

All the great religious traditions seem to bang up against this quandary in one form or another. On the one hand, insofar as all human relations involve debt, they are all morally compromised. Both parties are probably already guilty of something just by entering into the relationship; at the very least they run a significant danger of becoming guilty if repayment is delayed. On the other hand, when we say someone acts like they "don't owe anything to anybody," we're hardly describing that person as a paragon of virtue. In the secular world, morality consists largely of fulfilling our obligations to others, and we have a stubborn tendency to imagine those obligations as debts. Monks, perhaps, can avoid the dilemma by detaching themselves from the secular world entirely, but the rest of us appear condemned to live in a universe that doesn't make a lot of sense.

■ ■ ■ ■ ■

The story of Hiromushime is a perfect illustration of the impulse to throw the accusation back at the accuser—just as in the story about the dead usurer and the donkey, the emphasis on excrement, animals, and humiliation is clearly meant as poetic justice, the creditor forced to experience the same feelings of disgrace and degradation that debtors are always made to feel. It's all a more vivid, more visceral way of asking that same question: "Who really owes what to whom?"

It's also a perfect illustration of how the moment one asks the question "Who really owes what to whom?," one has begun to adopt the creditor's language. Just as if we don't pay our debts, "our payment becomes that of being reborn as a horse or an ox"; so if you are an unreasonable creditor, you too will "repay." Even karmic justice can thus be reduced to the language of a business deal.

Here we come to the central question of this book: What, precisely, does it mean to say that our sense of morality and justice is reduced to the language of a business deal? What does it mean when we reduce moral obligations to debts? What changes when the one turns into the other? And how do we speak about them when our language has been so shaped by the market? On one level the difference between an obligation and a debt is simple and obvious. A debt is the obligation to pay a certain sum of money. As a result, a debt, unlike any other form of obligation, can be precisely quantified. This allows debts to become simple, cold, and impersonal—which, in turn, allows them to be transferable. If one owes a favor, or one's life, to another human being, it is owed to that person specifically. But if one owes forty thousand dollars at 12-percent interest, it doesn't really matter who the creditor is; neither does either of the two parties have to think much about what the other party needs, wants, is capable of doing—as they certainly would if what was owed was a favor, or respect, or gratitude. One does not need to calculate the human effects; one need only calculate principal, balances, penalties, and rates of interest. If you end up having to abandon your home and wander in other provinces, if your daughter ends up in a mining camp working as a prostitute, well, that's unfortunate, but incidental to the creditor. Money is money, and a deal's a deal.

From this perspective, the crucial factor, and a topic that will be explored at length in these pages, is money's capacity to turn morality into a matter of impersonal arithmetic—and by doing so, to justify things that would otherwise seem outrageous or obscene. The factor of violence, which I have been emphasizing up until now, may appear secondary. The difference between a "debt" and a mere moral obligation is not the presence or absence of men with weapons who can enforce that obligation by seizing the debtor's possessions or threatening to break his legs. It is simply that a creditor has the means to specify, numerically, exactly how much the debtor owes.

However, when one looks a little closer, one discovers that these two elements—the violence and the quantification—are intimately linked. In fact it's almost impossible to find one without the other. French usurers had powerful friends and enforcers, capable of bullying even Church authorities. How else could they have collected debts that were technically illegal? Hiromushime was utterly uncompromising with her debtors—"showing no mercy whatsoever"—but then, her husband was the governor. She didn't have to show mercy. Those of us who do not have armed men behind us cannot afford to be so exacting.

The way violence, or the threat of violence, turns human relations into mathematics will crop up again and again over the course of this book. It is the ultimate source of the moral confusion that seems to float around everything surrounding the topic of debt. The resulting dilemmas appear to be as old as civilization itself. We can observe the process in the very earliest records from ancient Mesopotamia; it finds its first philosophical expression in the Vedas, reappears in endless forms throughout recorded history, and still lies underneath the essential fabric of our institutions today—state and market, our most basic conceptions of the nature of freedom, morality, sociality—all of which have been shaped by a history of war, conquest, and slavery in ways we're no longer capable of even perceiving because we can no longer imagine things any other way.

■ ■ ■ ■ ■

There are obvious reasons why this is a particularly important moment to reexamine the history of debt. September 2008 saw the beginning of a financial crisis that almost brought the world economy screeching to a halt. In many ways the world economy did: ships stopped moving across the oceans and thousands lay idle or were even broken up for scrap metal.[11] Building cranes were dismantled, as no more buildings were being put up. Banks largely ceased making loans. In the wake of this, there was not only public rage and bewilderment, but the beginning of an actual public conversation about the nature of debt, of money, of the financial institutions that have come to hold the fate of nations in their grip.

But that was just a moment. The conversation never ended up taking place.

The reason that people were ready for such a conversation was that the story everyone had been told for the last decade or so had just been revealed to be a colossal lie. There's really no nicer way to say it. For years, everyone had been hearing of a whole host of new, ultra-sophisticated financial innovations: credit and commodity derivatives, collateralized mortgage obligation derivatives, hybrid securities, debt swaps, and so on. These new derivative markets were so incredibly sophisticated, that—according to one persistent story—a prominent investment house had to employ astrophysicists to run trading programs so complex that even the financiers couldn't begin to understand them. The message was transparent: leave these things to the professionals. You couldn't possibly get your minds around this. Even if you don't like financial capitalists very much (and few seemed inclined to argue that there was much to like about them), they were nothing if not capable, in fact so preternaturally capable that democratic oversight of financial markets was simply inconceivable. (Even a lot of academics fell for it. I well remember going to conferences in 2006 and 2007 where trendy social theorists presented papers arguing that these new forms of securitization, linked to new information technologies, heralded a looming transformation in the very nature of power, time, possibility—reality itself. I remember thinking: "Suckers!" And so they were.)

Then, when the rubble had stopped bouncing, it turned out that many if not most of them had been nothing more than very elaborate scams. They consisted of operations like selling poor families mortgages crafted in such a way as to make eventual default inevitable; taking bets on how long it would take the holders to default; packaging mortgage and bet together and selling them to institutional investors (representing, perhaps, the mortgage-holders' retirement accounts) claiming that it would make money no matter what happened, and allow said investors to pass such packages around as if they were money; turning over responsibility for paying off the bet to a giant insurance conglomerate that, were it to sink beneath the weight of its resultant debt (which certainly would happen), would then have to be bailed out by taxpayers (as such conglomerates were indeed bailed out).[12] In other words, it looked very much like an unusually elaborate version of what banks were doing when they lent money to dictators in Bolivia and Gabon in the late '70s: making utterly irresponsible loans with the full knowledge that, once it became known they had done so, politicians and bureaucrats would scramble to ensure that they'd still be reimbursed anyway, no matter how many human lives had to be devastated and destroyed in order to do it.

The difference, though, was that this time, the bankers were doing it on an inconceivable scale: the total amount of debt they had run up was larger than the combined Gross Domestic Products of every country in the world—and it threw the world into a tailspin and almost destroyed the system itself.

Armies and police quickly geared up to combat the expected riots and unrest, but at first, none materialized. But neither did any significant changes in how the system was run. At the time, everyone assumed that, with the very defining institutions of capitalism (Lehman Brothers, Citibank, General Motors) crumbling, and all claims to superior wisdom revealed to be false, we would at least restart a broader conversation about the nature of debt and credit institutions. And not just a conversation.

It seemed that most Americans were open to radical solutions. Surveys showed that an overwhelming majority of Americans felt that the banks should not be rescued, *whatever the economic consequences*, but that ordinary citizens stuck with bad mortgages should be bailed out. In the United States this is quite extraordinary. Since colonial days, Americans have been the population least sympathetic to debtors. In a way this is odd, since America was settled largely by absconding debtors, but it's a country where the idea that morality is a matter of paying one's debts runs deeper than almost any other. In colonial days, an insolvent debtor's ear was often nailed to a post. The United States was one of the last countries in the world to adopt a law of bankruptcy: despite the fact that in 1787, the Constitution specifically charged the new government with creating one, all attempts were rejected, or quickly reversed, on "moral grounds" until 1898.[13] The change was epochal. For this very reason, perhaps, those in charge of moderating debate in the media and legislatures decided that this was not the time. The United States government effectively put a three-trillion-dollar Band-Aid over the problem and changed nothing. The bankers were rescued; small-scale debtors—with a paltry few exceptions—were not.[14] To the contrary, in the middle of the greatest economic recession since the '30s, we are already beginning to see a backlash against them—driven by financial corporations who have now turned to the same government that bailed them out to apply the full force of the law against ordinary citizens in financial trouble. "It's not a crime to owe money," reports the Minneapolis-St. Paul *StarTribune*, "But people are routinely being thrown in jail for failing to pay debts." In Minnesota, "the use of arrest warrants against debtors has jumped 60 percent over the past four years, with 845 cases in 2009 . . . In Illinois and southwest Indiana, some judges jail debtors for missing court-ordered debt payments. In extreme cases, people stay in jail until they raise a minimum payment. In January [2010], a judge sentenced a Kenney, Ill., man 'to indefinite incarceration' until he came up with $300 toward a lumber yard debt."[15]

In other words, we are moving toward a restoration of something much like debtors' prisons. Something had to break eventually. In 2011, after a wave of popular movements swept out of the Middle East and found echoes all over the world, thousands across Europe and North America also began insisting some kind of conversation about the basic questions raised in 2008 be addressed. They were met with a brief spate of attention, and then violent suppression and media blackout. And all this despite the fact that the world economy appears to be tumbling inexorably toward the next great financial catastrophe—the only real question being just how long it will take.

We have reached the point where even some of the central institutions have been forced to admit, however quietly, that this is indeed the case. In America, the Federal Reserve floated a plan for mass mortgage relief in the summer of 2012, only to discover the political class was simply unwilling to consider it. For a while, even the IMF, under Dominique Strauss-Kahn, began trying to reposition itself as the conscience of global capitalism, issuing warnings that if the economy continues on the present course, some kind of crash is inevitable, and the next time, no bailout is likely to be forthcoming: the public simply will not stand for it, and as a result, everything really will come apart. "IMF Warns Second Bailout Would 'Threaten Democracy,'" reads one headline.[16] (Of course by "democracy" they mean "capitalism.") Surely it means something that even those who feel they are responsible for keeping the current global economic system running, who just a few years ago acted as if they could simply assume the current system would be around forever, are now seeing apocalypse everywhere.

■ ■ ■ ■ ■

In this case, the IMF had a point. We have every reason to believe that we do indeed stand on the brink of epochal changes.

Admittedly, the usual impulse is to imagine everything around us as absolutely new. Nowhere is this so true as with money. How many times have we been told that the advent of virtual money, the dematerialization of cash into plastic and dollars into blips of electronic information, has brought us to an unprecedented new financial world? The assumption that we were in such uncharted territory, of course, was one of the things that made it so easy for the likes of Goldman Sachs and AIG to convince people that no one could possibly understand their dazzling new financial instruments. The moment one casts matters on a broad historical scale, though, the first thing one learns is that there's nothing new about virtual money. Actually, this was the original form of money. Credit system, tabs, even expense accounts, all existed long before cash. These things are as old as civilization itself. True, we also find that history tends to move back and forth between periods dominated by bullion—where it's assumed that gold and silver *are* money—and periods where money is assumed to be an abstraction, a virtual unit of account. But historically, credit money comes first, and what we are witnessing today is a return of assumptions that would have been considered obvious common sense in, say, the Middle Ages—or even ancient Mesopotamia.

But history does provide fascinating hints of what we might expect. For instance: in the past, ages of virtual credit money almost invariably involve the creation of institutions designed to prevent everything going haywire—to stop the lenders from teaming up with bureaucrats and politicians to squeeze everybody dry, as they seem to be doing now. They are accompanied by the creation of institutions designed to protect debtors. The new age of credit money we are in seems to have started precisely backwards. It began with the creation of global institutions like the IMF designed to protect not debtors, but creditors. At the same time, on the kind of historical scale we're talking about here, a decade or two is nothing. We have very little idea what to expect.

■ ■ ■ ■ ■

This book is a history of debt, then, but it also uses that history as a way to ask fundamental questions about what human beings and human society are or could be like—what we actually do owe each other, what it even means to ask that question. As a result, the book begins by attempting to puncture a series of myths—not only the Myth of Barter, which is taken up in the first chapter, but also rival myths about primordial debts to the gods, or to the state—that in one way or another form the basis of our common-sense assumptions about the nature of economy and society. In that common-sense view, the State and the Market tower above all else as diametrically opposed principles. Historical reality reveals, however, that they were born together and have always been intertwined. The one thing that all these misconceptions have in common, we will find, is that they tend to reduce all human relations to exchange, as if our ties to society, even to the cosmos itself, can be imagined in the same terms as a business deal. This leads to another question: If not exchange, then what? In Chapter Five, I will begin to answer the question by drawing on the fruits of anthropology to describe a view of the moral basis of economic life, then return to the question of the origins of money to demonstrate how the very principle of exchange emerged largely as an effect of violence—that the real origins of money are to be found in crime and recompense, war and slavery, honor, debt, and redemption. That, in turn, opens the way to starting, with Chapter Eight, an actual history of the last five thousand years of debt and credit, with its great alternations between ages of virtual and physical money. Many of the discoveries here are profoundly unexpected: from the origins of modern conceptions of rights and freedoms in ancient slave law, to the origins of investment capital in medieval Chinese Buddhism, to the fact that many of Adam Smith's most famous arguments appear to have been cribbed from the works of free-market theorists from medieval Persia (a story which, incidentally, has interesting implications for understanding the current appeal of political Islam). All of this sets the stage for a fresh approach to the last five hundred years, dominated by capitalist empires, and allows us to at least begin asking what might really be at stake in the present day.

For a very long time, the intellectual consensus has been that we can no longer ask Great Questions. Increasingly, it's looking like we have no other choice.

Chapter Two

THE MYTH OF BARTER

> *For every subtle and complicated question, there is a perfectly simple and straightforward answer, which is wrong.*
> —H. L. Mencken (slightly rephrased)

WHAT IS THE DIFFERENCE between a mere obligation, a sense that one ought to behave in a certain way, or even that one owes something to someone, and a *debt*, properly speaking? The answer is simple: money. The difference between a debt and an obligation is that a debt can be precisely quantified. This requires money.

Not only is it money that makes debt possible: money and debt appear on the scene at exactly the same time. Some of the very first written documents that have come down to us are Mesopotamian tablets recording credits and debits, rations issued by temples, money owed for rent of temple lands, the value of each precisely specified in grain and silver. Some of the earliest works of moral philosophy, in turn, are reflections on what it means to imagine morality as debt—that is, in terms of money.

A history of debt, then, is thus necessarily a history of money—and the easiest way to understand the role that debt has played in human society is simply to follow the forms that money has taken, and the way money has been used, across the centuries—and the arguments that inevitably ensued about what all this means. Still, this is necessarily a very different history of money than we are used to. When economists speak of the origins of money, for example, debt is always something of an afterthought. First comes barter, then money; credit only develops later. Even if one consults books on the history of money in, say, France, India, or China, what one generally gets is a history of coinage, with barely any discussion of credit arrangements at all. For almost a century, anthropologists like me have been pointing out that there is something very wrong with this picture. The standard economic history version has little to do with anything we observe when we examine how economic life is actually conducted, in real communities and marketplaces, almost anywhere—where one is much more likely to discover everyone is in debt to everyone else in a dozen different ways, and that most transactions take place without the use of currency.

Why the discrepancy?

Some of it is just the nature of the evidence: coins are preserved in the archeological record; credit arrangements usually are not. Still, the problem runs deeper. The existence of credit and debt has always been something of a scandal for economists, since it's almost impossible to pretend that those lending and borrowing money are acting on purely "economic" motivations (for instance, that a loan to a stranger is the same as a loan to one's cousin); it seems important, therefore, to begin the story of money in an imaginary world from which credit and debt have been entirely erased. Before we can apply the tools of anthropology to reconstruct the real history of money, we need to understand what's wrong with the conventional account.

Economists generally speak of three functions of money: medium of exchange, unit of account, and store of value. All economic textbooks treat the first as primary. Here's a fairly typical extract from *Economics*, by Case, Fair, Gärtner, and Heather (1996):

> Money is vital to the working of a market economy. Imagine what life would be like without it. The alternative to a monetary economy is barter, people exchanging goods and services for other goods and services directly instead of exchanging via the medium of money.
>
> How does a barter system work? Suppose you want croissants, eggs and orange juice for breakfast. Instead of going to the grocer's and buying these things with money, you would have to find someone who has these items and is willing to trade them. You would also have to have something the baker, the orange juice purveyor and the egg vendor want. Having pencils to trade will do you no good if the baker and the orange juice and egg sellers do not want pencils.
>
> A barter system requires a double coincidence of wants for trade to take place. That is, to effect a trade, I need not only have to find someone who has what I want, but that person must also want what I have. Where the range of traded goods is small, as it is in relatively unsophisticated economies, it is

not difficult to find someone to trade with, and barter is often used.[1]

This latter point is questionable, but it's phrased in so vague a way that it would be hard to disprove.

> In a complex society with many goods, barter exchanges involve an intolerable amount of effort. Imagine trying to find people who offer for sale all the things you buy in a typical trip to the grocer's, and who are willing to accept goods that you have to offer in exchange for their goods.
>   Some agreed-upon medium of exchange (or means of payment) neatly eliminates the double coincidence of wants problem.[2]

It's important to emphasize that this is not presented as something that actually happened, but as a purely imaginary exercise. "To see that society benefits from a medium of exchange" write Begg, Fischer and Dornbuch (*Economics*, 2005), "imagine a barter economy." "Imagine the difficulty you would have today," write Maunder, Myers, Wall, and Miller (*Economics Explained*, 1991), "if you had to exchange your labor directly for the fruits of someone else's labor." "Imagine," write Parkin and King (*Economics*, 1995), "you have roosters, but you want roses."[3] One could multiply examples endlessly. Just about every economics textbook employed today sets out the problem the same way. Historically, they note, we know that there was a time when there was no money. What must it have been like? Well, let us imagine an economy something like today's, except with no money. That would have been decidedly inconvenient! Surely, people must have invented money for the sake of efficiency.

The story of money for economists always begins with a fantasy world of barter. The problem is where to locate this fantasy in time and space: Are we talking about cave men, Pacific Islanders, the American frontier? One textbook, by economists Joseph Stiglitz and John Driffill, takes us to what appears to be an imaginary New England or Midwestern town:

> One can imagine an old-style farmer bartering with the blacksmith, the tailor, the grocer, and the doctor in his small town. For simple barter to work, however, there must be a double coincidence of wants . . . Henry has potatoes and wants shoes, Joshua has an extra pair of shoes and wants potatoes. Bartering

can make them both happier. But if Henry has firewood and
Joshua does not need any of that, then bartering for Joshua's
shoes requires one or both of them to go searching for more
people in the hope of making a multilateral exchange. Money
provides a way to make multilateral exchange much simpler.
Henry sells his firewood to someone else for money and uses
the money to buy Joshua's shoes.[4]

Again this is just a make-believe land much like the present, except
with money somehow plucked away. As a result it makes no sense:
Who in their right mind would set up a grocery in such a place? And
how would they get supplies? But let's leave that aside. There is a
simple reason why everyone who writes an economics textbook feels
they have to tell us the same story. For economists, it is in a very real
sense the most important story ever told. It was by telling it, in the
significant year of 1776, that Adam Smith, professor of moral philosophy at the University of Glasgow, effectively brought the discipline of
economics into being.

He did not make up the story entirely out of whole cloth. Already
in 330 BC, Aristotle was speculating along vaguely similar lines in his
treatise on politics. At first, he suggested, families must have produced
everything they needed for themselves. Gradually, some would presumably have specialized, some growing corn, others making wine, swapping one for the other.[5] Money, Aristotle assumed, must have emerged
from such a process. But, like the medieval schoolmen who occasionally repeated the story, Aristotle was never clear as to how.[6]

In the years after Columbus, as Spanish and Portuguese adventurers were scouring the world for new sources of gold and silver,
these vague stories disappear. Certainly no one reported discovering a
land of barter. Most sixteenth- and seventeenth-century travelers in the
West Indies or Africa assumed that all societies would necessarily have
their own forms of money, since all societies had governments and all
governments issued money.[7]

Adam Smith, on the other hand, was determined to overturn the
conventional wisdom of his day. Above all, he objected to the notion
that money was a creation of government. In this, Smith was the intellectual heir of the Liberal tradition of philosophers like John Locke,
who had argued that government begins in the need to protect private
property and operated best when it tried to limit itself to that function.
Smith expanded on the argument, insisting that property, money, and
markets not only existed before political institutions but were the very
foundation of human society. It followed that insofar as government

should play any role in monetary affairs, it should limit itself to guaranteeing the soundness of the currency. It was only by making such an argument that he could insist that economics is itself a field of human inquiry with its own principles and laws—that is, as distinct from, say ethics or politics.

Smith's argument is worth laying out in detail because it is, as I say, the great founding myth of the discipline of economics.

What, he begins, is the basis of economic life, properly speaking? It is "a certain propensity in human nature . . . the propensity to truck, barter, and exchange one thing for another." Animals don't do this. "Nobody," Smith observes, "ever saw a dog make a fair and deliberate exchange of one bone for another with another dog."[8] But humans, if left to their own devices, will inevitably begin swapping and comparing things. This is just what humans do. Even logic and conversation are really just forms of trading, and as in all things, humans will always try to seek their own best advantage, to seek the greatest profit they can from the exchange.[9]

It is this drive to exchange, in turn, which creates that division of labor responsible for all human achievement and civilization. Here the scene shifts to another one of those economists' faraway fantasylands— it seems to be an amalgam of North American Indians and Central Asian pastoral nomads:[10]

> In a tribe of hunters or shepherds a particular person makes bows and arrows, for example, with more readiness and dexterity than any other. He frequently exchanges them for cattle or for venison with his companions; and he finds at last that he can in this manner get more cattle and venison, than if he himself went to the field to catch them. From a regard to his own interest, therefore, the making of bows and arrows grows to be his chief business, and he becomes a sort of armourer. Another excels in making the frames and covers of their little huts or moveable houses. He is accustomed to be of use in this way to his neighbours, who reward him in the same manner with cattle and with venison, till at last he finds it his interest to dedicate himself entirely to this employment, and to become a sort of house-carpenter. In the same manner a third becomes a smith or a brazier; a fourth a tanner or dresser of hides or skins, the principal part of the clothing of savages . . .

It's only once we have expert arrow-makers, wigwam-makers, and so on that people start realizing there's a problem. Notice how, as in so many examples, we have a tendency to slip from imaginary savages to small-town shopkeepers.

> But when the division of labor first began to take place, this power of exchanging must frequently have been very much clogged and embarrassed in its operations. One man, we shall suppose, has more of a certain commodity than he himself has occasion for, while another has less. The former consequently would be glad to dispose of, and the latter to purchase, a part of this superfluity. But if this latter should chance to have nothing that the former stands in need of, no exchange can be made between them. The butcher has more meat in his shop than he himself can consume, and the brewer and the baker would each of them be willing to purchase a part of it. But they have nothing to offer in exchange . . .
>
> [. . .]
>
> In order to avoid the inconveniency of such situations, every prudent man in every period of society, after the first establishment of the division of labor, must naturally have endeavored to manage his affairs in such a manner, as to have at all times by him, besides the peculiar produce of his own industry, a certain quantity of some one commodity or other, such as he imagined that few people would be likely to refuse in exchange for the produce of their industry.[11]

So everyone will inevitably start stockpiling something they figure that everyone else is likely to want. This has a paradoxical effect, because at a certain point, rather than making that commodity less valuable (since everyone already has some) it becomes more valuable (because it becomes, effectively, currency):

> Salt is said to be the common instrument of commerce and exchanges in Abyssinia; a species of shells in some parts of the coast of India; dried cod at Newfoundland; tobacco in Virginia; sugar in some of our West India colonies; hides or dressed leather in some other countries; and there is at this day a village in Scotland where it is not uncommon, I am told, for a workman to carry nails instead of money to the baker's shop or the ale-house.[12]

Eventually, of course, at least for long-distance trade, it all boils down to precious metals, since these are ideally suited to serve as currency, being durable, portable, and able to be endlessly subdivided into identical portions.

> Different metals have been made use of by different nations for this purpose. Iron was the common instrument of commerce among the ancient Spartans; copper among the ancient Romans; and gold and silver among all rich and commercial nations.
>
> [. . .]
>
> Those metals seem originally to have been made use of for this purpose in rude bars, without any stamp or coinage . . .
>
> [. . .]
>
> The use of metals in this rude state was attended with two very considerable inconveniencies; first with the trouble of weighing; and, secondly, with that of assaying them. In the precious metals, where a small difference in the quantity makes a great difference in the value, even the business of weighing, with proper exactness, requires at least very accurate weights and scales. The weighing of gold in particular is an operation of some nicety . . .[13]

It's easy to see where this is going. Using irregular metal ingots is easier than barter, but wouldn't standardizing the units—say, stamping pieces of metal with uniform designations guaranteeing weight and fineness, in different denominations—make things easier still? Clearly it would, and so was coinage born. True, issuing coinage meant governments had to get involved, since they generally ran the mints; but in the standard version of the story, governments have only this one limited role—to guarantee the money supply—and tend to do it badly, since throughout history, unscrupulous kings have often cheated by debasing the coinage and causing inflation and other sorts of political havoc in what was originally a matter of simple economic common sense.

Tellingly, this story played a crucial role not only in founding the discipline of economics, but in the very idea that there was something called "the economy," which operated by its own rules, separate from moral or political life, that economists could take as their field of study.

"The economy" is where we indulge in our natural propensity to truck and barter. We are still trucking and bartering. We always will be. Money is simply the most efficient means.

Economists like Karl Menger and Stanley Jevons later improved on the details of the story, most of all by adding various mathematical equations to demonstrate that a random assortment of people with random desires could, in theory, produce not only a single commodity to use as money but a uniform price system. In the process, they also substituted all sorts of impressive technical vocabulary (e.g., "inconveniences" became "transaction costs"). The crucial thing, though, is that by now, this story has become simple common sense for most people. We teach it to children in schoolbooks and museums. Everybody knows it. "Once upon a time, there was barter. It was difficult. So people invented money. Then came the development of banking and credit." It all forms a perfectly simple, straightforward progression, a process of increasing sophistication and abstraction that has carried humanity, logically and inexorably, from the Stone Age exchange of mastodon tusks to stock markets, hedge funds, and securitized derivatives.[14]

It really has become ubiquitous. Wherever we find money, we also find the story. At one point, in the town of Arivonimamo, in Madagascar, I had the privilege of interviewing a Kalanoro, a tiny ghostly creature that a local spirit medium claimed to keep hidden away in a chest in his home. The spirit belonged to the brother of a notorious local loan shark, a horrible woman named Nordine, and to be honest I was a bit reluctant to have anything to do with the family, but some of my friends insisted—since, after all, this was a creature from ancient times. The creature spoke from behind a screen in an eerie, otherworldly quaver. But all it was really interested in talking about was money. Finally, slightly exasperated by the whole charade, I asked, "So, what did you use for money back in ancient times, when you were still alive?"

The mysterious voice immediately replied, "No. We didn't use money. In ancient times we used to barter commodities directly, one for the other . . ."

■ ■ ■ ■ ■

The story, then, has become the founding myth of our system of economic relations. It is so deeply established in common sense, even in places like Madagascar, that most people on earth couldn't imagine any other way that money possibly could have come about.

The problem is there's no evidence that it ever happened, and an enormous amount of evidence suggesting that it did not.

For centuries now, explorers have been trying to find this fabled land of barter—none with success. Adam Smith set his story in aboriginal North America (others preferred Africa or the Pacific). In Smith's defense, at least it could be said that in his time, reliable information on Native American economic systems was unavailable in Scottish libraries. His successors have no excuse. By mid-century, Lewis Henry Morgan's descriptions of the Six Nations of the Iroquois, among others, were widely published—and they made clear that the main economic institution among the Iroquois nations were longhouses where most goods were stockpiled and then allocated by women's councils, and no one ever traded arrowheads for slabs of meat. Economists simply ignored this information.[15] Stanley Jevons, for example, who in 1871 wrote what has come to be considered the classic book on the origins of money, took his examples straight from Smith, with Indians swapping venison for elk and beaver hides, and made no use of actual descriptions of Indian life that made it clear that Smith had simply made this up. Around that same time, missionaries, adventurers, and colonial administrators were fanning out across the world, many bringing copies of Smith's book with them, expecting to find the land of barter. None ever did. They discovered an almost endless variety of economic systems. But to this day, no one has been able to locate a part of the world where the ordinary mode of economic transaction between neighbors takes the form of "I'll give you twenty chickens for that cow."

The definitive anthropological work on barter, by Caroline Humphrey, of Cambridge, could not be more definitive in its conclusions: "No example of a barter economy, pure and simple, has ever been described, let alone the emergence from it of money; all available ethnography suggests that there never has been such a thing."[16]

Now, all this hardly means that barter does not exist—or even that it's never practiced by the sort of people that Smith would refer to as "savages." It just means that it's almost never employed, as Smith imagined, between fellow villagers. Ordinarily, it takes place between strangers, even enemies. Let us begin with the Nambikwara of Brazil. They would seem to fit all the criteria: they are a simple society without much in the way of division of labor, organized into small bands that traditionally numbered at best a hundred people each. Occasionally if one band spots the cooking fires of another in their vicinity, they will send emissaries to negotiate a meeting for purposes of trade. If the offer is accepted, they will first hide their women and children in the forest, then invite the men of the other band to visit camp. Each band has a chief; once everyone has been assembled, each chief gives a formal speech praising the other party and belittling his own; everyone puts aside their weapons to sing and dance together—though the dance is one that mimics military confrontation. Then, individuals from each side approach each other to trade:

> If an individual wants an object he extols it by saying how fine it is. If a man values an object and wants much in exchange for it, instead of saying that it is very valuable he says that it is no good, thus showing his desire to keep it. "This axe is no good, it is very old, it is very dull," he will say, referring to his axe which the other wants.
>
> This argument is carried on in an angry tone of voice until a settlement is reached. When agreement has been reached each snatches the object out of the other's hand. If a man has bartered a necklace, instead of taking it off and handing it over, the other person must take it off with a show of force. Disputes, often leading to fights, occur when one party is a little premature and snatches the object before the other has finished arguing.[17]

The whole business concludes with a great feast at which the women reappear, but this too can lead to problems, since amidst the music and good cheer, there is ample opportunity for seductions.[18] This sometimes led to jealous quarrels. Occasionally, people would get killed.

Barter, then, for all the festive elements, was carried out between people who might otherwise be enemies and hovered about an inch away from outright warfare—and, if the ethnographer is to be believed—if one side later decided they had been taken advantage of, it could very easily lead to actual wars.

To shift our spotlight halfway around the world to Western Arnhem Land in Australia, where the Gunwinggu people are famous for entertaining neighbors in rituals of ceremonial barter called the *dzamalag*. Here the threat of actual violence seems much more distant. Partly, this is because things are made easier by the existence of a moiety system that embraces the whole region: no one is allowed to marry, or even have sex with, people of their own moiety, no matter where they come from, but anyone from the other is technically a potential match. Therefore, for a man, even in distant communities, half the women are strictly forbidden, half of them fair game. The region is also united by local specialization: each people has its own trade product to be bartered with the others.

What follows is from a description of a *dzamalag* held in the 1940s, as observed by an anthropologist named Ronald Berndt.

Once again, it begins as strangers, after some initial negotiations, are invited into the hosts' main camp. The visitors in this particular example were famous for their "much-prized serrated spears"—their hosts had access to good European cloth. The trading begins when the visiting party, which consisted of both men and women, enters the camp's dancing ground, or "ring place," and three of them begin to entertain their hosts with music. Two men start singing, a third accompanies them on the *didjeridu*. Before long, women from the hosts' side come and attack the musicians:

> Men and women rise and begin to dance. The *dzamalag* opens when two Gunwinggu women of the opposite moiety to the singing men "give *dzamalag*" to the latter. They present each man with a piece of cloth, and hit or touch him, pulling him down on the ground, calling him a *dzamalag* husband, and joking with him in an erotic vein. Then another woman of the opposite moiety to the pipe player gives him cloth, hits and jokes with him.
>
> This sets in motion the *dzamalag* exchange. Men from the visiting group sit quietly while women of the opposite moiety come over and give them cloth, hit them, and invite them to copulate; they take any liberty they choose with the men, amid amusement and applause, while the singing and dancing continue. Women try to undo the men's loin coverings or touch their penises, and to drag them from the "ring place" for coitus. The men go with their *dzamalag* partners, with a show of reluctance, to copulate in the bushes away from the fires which light up the dancers. They may give the women tobacco or beads. When the women return, they give part of this tobacco to their own husbands, who have encouraged them to go *dzamalag*. The husbands, in turn, use the tobacco to pay their own female *dzamalag* partners . . .[19]

New singers and musicians appear, are again assaulted and dragged off to the bushes; men encourage their wives "not to be shy," so as to maintain the Gunwinggu reputation for hospitality; eventually those men also take the initiative with the visitors' wives, offering cloth, hitting them, and leading them off into the bushes. Beads and tobacco circulate. Finally, once participants have all paired off at least once, and the guests are satisfied with the cloth they have acquired, the women stop dancing and stand in two rows and the visitors line up to repay them.

> Then visiting men of one moiety dance towards the women
> of the opposite moiety, in order to "give them *dzamalag*."
> They hold shovel-nosed spears poised, pretending to spear the
> women, but instead hit them with the flat of the blade. "We
> will not spear you, for we have already speared you with our
> penises." They present the spears to the women. Then visiting
> men of the other moiety go through the same actions with the
> women of their opposite moiety, giving them spears with ser-
> rated points. This terminates the ceremony, which is followed
> by a large distribution of food.[20]

This is a particularly dramatic case, but dramatic cases are revealing. What the Gunwinggu hosts appear to have been able to do here,
owing to the relatively amicable relations between neighboring peoples
in Western Arnhem Land, is to take all the elements in Nambikwara
barter (the music and dancing, the potential hostility, the sexual in-
trigue) and turn it all into a kind of festive game—one not, perhaps,
without its dangers, but (as the ethnographer emphasizes) considered
enormous good fun by everyone concerned.

What all such cases of trade through barter have in common is that
they are meetings with strangers who will, likely as not, never meet
again, and with whom one certainly will not enter into any ongoing relations. This is why a direct one-on-one exchange is appropriate: each
side makes their trade and walks away. It's all made possible by laying
down an initial mantle of sociability in the form of shared pleasures,
music, and dance—the usual base of conviviality on which trade must
always be built. Then comes the actual trading, where both sides make
a great display of the latent hostility that necessarily exists in any exchange of material goods between strangers—where neither party has
no particular reason *not* to take advantage of the other—by playful
mock aggression, though in the Nambikwara case, where the mantle
of sociability is extremely thin, mock aggression is in constant danger
of slipping over into the real thing. The Gunwinggu, with their more
relaxed attitude toward sexuality, have quite ingeniously managed to
make the shared pleasures and aggression into exactly the same thing.

Recall here the language of the economics textbooks: "Imagine a
society without money." "Imagine a barter economy." One thing these
examples make abundantly clear is just how limited the imaginative
powers of most economists turn out to be.[21]

Why? The simplest answer would be: for there to even be a discipline called "economics," a discipline that concerns itself first and foremost with how individuals seek the most advantageous arrangement

for the exchange of shoes for potatoes, or cloth for spears, it must assume that the exchange of such goods need have nothing to do with war, passion, adventure, mystery, sex, or death. Economics assumes a division between different spheres of human behavior that, among people like the Gunwinngu and the Nambikwara, simply does not exist. These divisions in turn are made possible by very specific institutional arrangements—the existence of lawyers, prisons, and police—to ensure that even people who don't like each other very much, who have no interest in developing any kind of ongoing relationship, but are simply interested in getting their hands on as much of the others' possessions as possible, will nonetheless refrain from the most obvious expedient (theft). This in turn allows us to assume that life is neatly divided between the marketplace, where we do our shopping, and the "sphere of consumption," where we concern ourselves with music, feasts, and seduction. In other words, the vision of the world that forms the basis of the economics textbooks, which Adam Smith played so large a part in promulgating, has by now become so much a part of our common sense that we find it hard to imagine any other possible arrangement.

From these examples, it begins to be clear why there are no societies based on barter. Such a society could only be one in which everybody was an inch away from everybody else's throat; but nonetheless hovering there, poised to strike but never actually striking, forever. True, barter does sometimes occur between people who do not consider each other strangers, but they're usually people who might as well be strangers—that is, who feel no sense of mutual responsibility or trust, or the desire to develop ongoing relations. The Pukhtun of Northern Pakistan, for instance, are famous for their open-handed hospitality. Barter is what you do with those to whom you are *not* bound by ties of hospitality (or kinship, or much of anything else):

A favorite mode of exchange among men is barter, or *adal-badal* (give and take). Men are always on the alert for the possibility of bartering one of their possessions for something better. Often the exchange is like for like: a radio for a radio, sunglasses for sunglasses, a watch for a watch. However, unlike objects can also be exchanged, such as, in one instance, a bicycle for two donkeys. *Adal-badal* is always practiced with non-relatives and affords men a great deal of pleasure as they attempt to get the advantage over their exchange partner. A good exchange, in which a man feels he has gotten the better of the deal, is cause for bragging and pride. If the exchange is bad, the recipient tries to renege on the deal or, failing that, to palm off the faulty object on someone unsuspecting. The best partner in *adal-badal* is someone who is distant spatially and will therefore have little opportunity to complain.[22]

Neither are such unscrupulous motives limited to Central Asia. They seem inherent to the very nature of barter—which would explain the fact that in the century or two before Smith's time, the English words "truck and barter," like their equivalents in French, Spanish, German, Dutch, and Portuguese, literally meant "to trick, bamboozle, or rip off."[23] Swapping one thing directly for another while trying to get the best deal one can out of the transaction is, ordinarily, how one deals with people one doesn't care about and doesn't expect to see again. What reason is there *not* to try to take advantage of such a person? If, on the other hand, one cares enough about someone—a neighbor, a friend—to wish to deal with her fairly and honestly, one will inevitably also care about her enough to take her individual needs, desires, and situation into account. Even if you do swap one thing for another, you are likely to frame the matter as a gift.

■ ■ ■ ■ ■

To illustrate what I mean by this, let's return to the economics text-books and the problem of the "double coincidence of wants." When we left Henry, he needed a pair of shoes, but all he had lying around were some potatoes. Joshua had an extra pair of shoes, but he didn't really need potatoes. Since money has not yet been invented, they have a problem. What are they to do?

The first thing that should be clear by now is that we'd really have to know a bit more about Joshua and Henry. Who are they? Are they related? If so, how? They appear to live in a small community. Any two people who have been living their lives in the same small community will have some sort of complicated history with each other. Are they friends, rivals, allies, lovers, enemies, or several of these things at once?

The authors of the original example seem to assume two neighbors of roughly equal status, not closely related, but on friendly terms—that is, as close to neutral equality as one can get. Even so, this doesn't say much. For example, if Henry was living in a Seneca longhouse and needed shoes, Joshua would not even enter into it; he'd simply mention it to his wife, who'd bring up the matter with the other matrons, and, if the matter were approved, fetch materials from the longhouse's collective storehouse, and sew him some. Alternately, to find a scenario fit for an imaginary economics textbook, we might place Joshua and

Henry together in a small, intimate community like a Nambikwara or Gunwinggu band:

SCENARIO 1

Henry walks up to Joshua and says, "Nice shoes!"

Joshua says, "Oh, they're not much, but since you seem to like them, by all means take them."

Henry takes the shoes.

Henry's potatoes are not at issue since both parties are perfectly well aware that if Joshua were ever short of potatoes, Henry would give him some.

And that's about it. Of course it's not clear, in this case, how long Henry will actually get to keep the shoes. It probably depends on how nice they are. If they were just ordinary shoes, this might be the end of the matter. If they are in any way unique or beautiful, they might end up being passed around. There's a famous story that John and Lorna Marshall, who carried out a study of Kalahari Bushmen in the '6os, once gave a knife to one of their favorite informants. They left and came back a year later, only to discover that pretty much everyone in the band had been in possession of the knife at some point in between. On the other hand, several Arab friends confirm to me that in less strictly egalitarian contexts, there is an expedient. If a friend praises a bracelet or bag, you are normally expected to immediately say, "Take it"—but if you are really determined to hold on to it, you can always say, "Yes, isn't it beautiful? It was a gift."

But clearly, the authors of the textbook have a slightly more impersonal transaction in mind. The authors seem to imagine the two men as the heads of patriarchal households, on good terms with each other, but who keep their own supplies. Perhaps they live in one of those Scottish villages with the butcher and the baker in Adam Smith's examples, or a colonial settlement in New England. Except for some reason they've never heard of money. It's a peculiar fantasy, but let's see what we can do:

SCENARIO 2

Henry walks up to Joshua and says, "Nice shoes!"

Or, perhaps—let's make this a bit more realistic—Henry's wife is chatting with Joshua's and strategically lets slip that the state of Henry's shoes is getting so bad he's complaining about corns.

The message is conveyed, and Joshua comes by the next day to offer his extra pair to Henry as a present, insisting that this is just a neighborly gesture. He would certainly never want anything in return.

It doesn't matter whether Joshua is sincere in saying this. By doing so, Joshua thereby registers a credit. Henry owes him one.

How might Henry pay Joshua back? There are endless possibilities. Perhaps Joshua really does want potatoes. Henry waits a discrete interval and drops them off, insisting that this too is just a gift. Or Joshua doesn't need potatoes now, but Henry waits until he does. Or maybe a year later, Joshua is planning a banquet, so he comes strolling by Henry's barnyard and says, "Nice pig . . ."

In any of these scenarios, the problem of "double coincidence of wants," so endlessly invoked in the economics textbooks, simply disappears. Henry might not have something Joshua wants right now. But if the two are neighbors, it's obviously only a matter of time before he will.[24]

This in turn means that the need to stockpile commonly acceptable items in the way that Smith suggested disappears as well. With it goes the need to develop currency. As with so many actual small communities, everyone simply keeps track of who owes what to whom.

There is just one major conceptual problem here—one the attentive reader might have noticed. Henry "owes Joshua one." One what? How do you quantify a favor? On what basis do you say that this many potatoes, or this big a pig, seems more or less equivalent to a pair of shoes? Because even if these things remain rough-and-ready approximations, there must be *some* way to establish that X is roughly equivalent to Y, or slightly worse or slightly better. Doesn't this imply that something like money, at least in the sense of a unit of account by which one can compare the value of different objects, already has to exist?

In most gift economies, there actually is a rough-and-ready way to solve the problem. One establishes a series of ranked categories of *types* of thing. Pigs and shoes may be considered objects of roughly equivalent status: one can give one in return for the other. Coral necklaces are quite another matter; one would have to give back another necklace, or at least another piece of jewelry—anthropologists are used to referring to these as creating different "spheres of exchange."[25] This does simplify things somewhat. When cross-cultural barter becomes a regular and unexceptional thing, it tends to operate according to similar principles: there are only certain things traded for certain others (cloth for spears, for example), which makes it easy to work out traditional equivalences. However, this doesn't help us at all with the problem of the origin of money. Actually, it makes it infinitely worse. Why stockpile salt or gold or fish if they can only be exchanged for some things and not others?

In fact, there is good reason to believe that barter is not a particularly ancient phenomenon at all, but has only really become widespread in modern times. Certainly in most of the cases we know about, it takes place between people who are familiar with the use of money but, for one reason or another, don't have a lot of it around. Elaborate barter systems often crop up in the wake of the collapse of national economies: most recently in Russia in the '90s and in Argentina around 2002, when rubles in the first case, and dollars in the second, effectively disappeared.[26] Occasionally one can even find some kind of currency beginning to develop: for instance, in POW camps and many prisons, inmates have indeed been known to use cigarettes as a kind of currency, much to the delight and excitement of professional economists.[27] But here too we are talking about people who grew up using money and now have to make do without it—exactly the situation "imagined" by the economics textbooks with which I began.

The more frequent solution is to adopt some sort of credit system. When much of Europe "reverted to barter" after the collapse of the Roman Empire, and then again after the Carolingian Empire likewise fell apart, this seems to be what happened. People continued keeping accounts in the old imperial currency, even if they were no longer using coins.[28] Similarly, the Pukhtun men who like to swap bicycles for donkeys are hardly unfamiliar with the use of money. Money has existed in that part of the world for thousands of years. They just prefer direct exchange between equals—in this case, because they consider it more manly.[29]

The most remarkable thing is that even in Adam Smith's examples of fish and nails and tobacco being used as money, the same sort of thing was happening. In the years following the appearance of *The Wealth of Nations*, scholars checked into most of those examples and discovered that in just about every case, the people involved were quite familiar with the use of money and, in fact, *were* using money—as a unit of account.[30] Take the example of dried cod, supposedly used as money in Newfoundland. As the British diplomat A. Mitchell-Innes pointed out almost a century ago, what Smith describes was really an illusion, created by a simple credit arrangement:

In the early days of the Newfoundland fishing industry, there was no permanent European population; the fishers went there for the fishing season only, and those who were not fishers were traders who bought the dried fish and sold to the fishers their daily supplies. The latter sold their catch to the traders at the market price in pounds, shillings and pence, and obtained in return a credit on their books, with which they paid for their supplies. Balances due by the traders were paid for by drafts on England or France.[31]

It was quite the same in the Scottish village. It's not as if anyone actually walked into the local pub, plunked down a roofing nail, and asked for a pint of beer. Employers in Smith's day often lacked coin to pay their workers; wages could be delayed by a year or more; in the meantime, it was considered acceptable for employees to carry off either some of their own products or leftover work materials, lumber, fabric, cord, and so on. The nails were de facto interest on what their employers owed them. So they went to the pub, ran up a tab, and when occasion permitted, brought in a bag of nails to charge off against the debt. The law making tobacco legal tender in Virginia seems to have been an attempt by planters to oblige local merchants to accept their products as a credit around harvest time. In effect, the law forced all merchants in Virginia to become middlemen in the tobacco business, whether they liked it or not; just as all West Indian merchants were obliged to become sugar dealers, since that's what all their wealthier customers brought in to write off against their debt.

The primary examples, then, were ones in which people were improvising credit systems because actual money—gold and silver coinage—was in short supply. But the most shocking blow to the conventional version of economic history came with the translation, first of Egyptian hieroglyphics, and then of Mesopotamian cuneiform, which pushed back scholars' knowledge of written history almost three millennia, from the time of Homer (circa 800 BC), where it had hovered in Smith's time, to roughly 3500 BC. What these texts revealed was that credit systems of exactly this sort actually *preceded* the invention of coinage by thousands of years.

The Mesopotamian system is the best documented, more so than that of Pharaonic Egypt (which appears similar), Shang China (about which we know little), or the Indus Valley civilization (about which we know nothing at all). As it happens, we know a great deal about Mesopotamia, since the vast majority of cuneiform documents were financial in nature.

The Sumerian economy was dominated by vast temple and palace complexes. These were often staffed by thousands: priests and officials, craftspeople who worked in their industrial workshops, farmers and shepherds who worked their considerable estates. Even though ancient Sumer was usually divided into a large number of independent city-states, by the time the curtain goes up on Mesopotamian civilization around 3500 BC, temple administrators already appear to have developed a single, uniform system of accountancy—one that is in some ways still with us, actually, because it's to the Sumerians that we owe such things as the dozen, 60-minute hour, or the 24-hour day.[32] The basic monetary unit was the silver shekel. One shekel's weight in silver was established as the equivalent of one gur, or bushel of barley. A shekel was subdivided into 60 minas, corresponding to one portion of barley—on the principle that there were 30 days in a month, and Temple workers received two rations of barley every day. It's easy to see that "money" in this sense is in no way the product of commercial transactions. It was actually created by bureaucrats in order to keep track of resources and move things back and forth between departments.

Temple bureaucrats used the system to calculate debts (rents, fees, loans, etc.) in silver. Silver was, effectively, money. And it did indeed circulate in the form of unworked chunks, "rude bars" as Smith had put it.[33] In this he was right. But it was almost the only part of his account that was right. For one thing, silver did not circulate very much. Most of it just sat around in Temple and Palace treasuries, some of which remained, carefully guarded, in the same place for literally thousands of years. It would have been easy enough to standardize the ingots, stamp them, create some authoritative system to guarantee their purity. The technology existed. Yet no one saw any particular need to do so. One reason was that while debts were calculated in silver, they did not have to be *paid* in silver—in fact, they could be paid in more or less anything one had around. Peasants who owed money to the Temple or Palace, or to some Temple or Palace official, seem to have settled their debts mostly in barley, which is why fixing the ratio of silver to barley was so important. But it was perfectly acceptable to show up with goats, or furniture, or lapis lazuli. Temples and Palaces were huge industrial operations—they could find a use for almost anything.[34]

In the marketplaces that cropped up in Mesopotamian cities, prices were also calculated in silver, and the prices of commodities that weren't entirely controlled by the Temples and Palaces would tend to fluctuate according to supply and demand. But even here, such evidence as we have suggests that most transactions were based on credit. Merchants (who sometimes worked for the Temples, sometimes operated independently) were among the few people who did, often, use silver in transactions; but even they mostly did much of their dealings on credit, and ordinary people buying beer from "ale women," or local innkeepers, once again, did so by running up a tab, to be settled at harvest time in barley or anything they might have had at hand.[35]

At this point, just about every aspect of the conventional story of the origins of money lay in rubble. Rarely has an historical theory been so absolutely and systematically refuted. By the early decades of the twentieth century, all the pieces were in place to completely rewrite the history of money. The groundwork was laid by Mitchell-Innes— the same one I've already cited on the matter of the cod—in two essays that appeared in New York's *Banking Law Journal* in 1913 and 1914. In these, Mitchell-Innes matter-of-factly laid out the false assumptions on which existing economic history was based and suggested that what was really needed was a history of debt:

> One of the popular fallacies in connection with commerce is that in modern days a money-saving device has been introduced called *credit* and that, before this device was known, all purchases were paid for in cash, in other words in coins. A careful investigation shows that the precise reverse is true. In olden days coins played a far smaller part in commerce than they do to-day. Indeed so small was the quantity of coins, that they did not even suffice for the needs of the [Medieval English] Royal household and estates which regularly used tokens of various kinds for the purpose of making small payments. So unimportant indeed was the coinage that sometimes Kings did not hesitate to call it all in for re-minting and re-issue and still commerce went on just the same.[36]

In fact, our standard account of monetary history is precisely backwards. We did not begin with barter, discover money, and then eventually develop credit systems. It happened precisely the other way around. What we now call virtual money came first. Coins came much later, and their use spread only unevenly, never completely replacing credit systems. Barter, in turn, appears to be largely a kind of accidental byproduct of the use of coinage or paper money: historically, it has mainly been what people who are used to cash transactions do when for one reason or another they have no access to currency.

The curious thing is that it never happened. This new history was never written. It's not that any economist has ever refuted Mitchell-Innes. They just ignored him. Textbooks did not change their story—even if all the evidence made clear that the story was simply wrong. People still write histories of money that are actually histories of coinage, on the assumption that in the past these were necessarily the same thing; periods when coinage largely vanished are still described as times when the economy "reverted to barter," as if the meaning of this phrase is self-evident, even though no one actually knows what it means. As a result we have next to no idea how, say, the inhabitant of a Dutch town in 950 AD actually went about acquiring cheese or spoons or hiring musicians to play at his daughter's wedding—let alone how any of this was likely to be arranged in Pemba or Samarkand.[37]

Chapter Three

PRIMORDIAL DEBTS

> *In being born every being is born as*
> *debt owed to the gods, the saints, the*
> *Fathers and to men. If one makes a sac-*
> *rifice, it is because of a debt owing to*
> *the gods from birth . . . If one recites a*
> *sacred text, it is because of a debt owing*
> *to the saints . . . If one wishes for off-*
> *spring, it is because of a debt due to the*
> *fathers from birth . . . And if one gives*
> *hospitality, it is because it is a debt ow-*
> *ing to men.*
> —Satapatha Brahmana 1.7.12, 1–6

> *Let us drive away the evil effects of bad*
> *dreams, just as we pay off debts.*
> —Rig Veda 8.47.17

THE REASON THAT economics textbooks now begin with imaginary villages is because it has been impossible to talk about real ones. Even some economists have been forced to admit that Smith's Land of Barter doesn't really exist.[1]

The question is why the myth has been perpetuated anyway. Mainstream economists have been happy to jettison other elements of *The Wealth of Nations*—for instance, Smith's labor theory of value and disapproval of joint-stock corporations.[2] Why not simply write off the myth of barter as a quaint Enlightenment parable and instead attempt to understand primordial credit arrangements—or anyway, something more in keeping with the historical evidence?

The answer seems to be that the Myth of Barter cannot go away because it is central to the entire discourse of economics.

Recall here what Smith was trying to do when he wrote *The Wealth of Nations*. Above all, the book was an attempt to establish the newfound discipline of economics as a science. This meant that not only did economics have its own peculiar domain of study—what we now call "the economy," though the idea that there even was something called an "economy" was very new in Smith's day—but that this economy operated according to laws of much the same sort as Sir Isaac Newton had so recently identified as governing the physical world. Newton had represented God as a cosmic watchmaker who had created the physical machinery of the universe in such a way that it would operate for the ultimate benefit of humans, and then let it run on its own. Smith was trying to make a similar, Newtonian argument.[3] God—or Divine Providence, as he put it—had arranged matters in such a way that our pursuit of self-interest would nonetheless, given an unfettered market, be guided "as if by an invisible hand" to promote the general welfare. Smith's famous invisible hand was, as he says in his *Theory of Moral Sentiments*, the agent of Divine Providence. It was literally the hand of God.[4]

Once economics had been established as a discipline, the theological arguments no longer seemed necessary or important. People continue to argue about whether an unfettered free market really will produce the results that Smith said it would; but no one questions whether "the market" naturally exists. The underlying assumptions that derive from this came to be seen as common sense—so much so that, as I've noted, we simply assume that when valuable objects change hands, it will normally be because two individuals have both decided they would gain a material advantage by swapping them. One interesting corollary is that, as a result, economists have come to see the very question of the presence or absence of money as not especially important, since money is just a commodity, chosen to facilitate exchange, and which we use to measure the value of other commodities. Otherwise, it has no special qualities. In 1958, Paul Samuelson, one of the leading lights of the neoclassical school that still predominates in modern economic thought, could still express disdain for what he called "the social contrivance of money." "Even in the most advanced industrial economies," he insisted, "if we strip exchange down to its barest essentials and peel off the obscuring layer of money, we find that trade between individuals and nations largely boils down to barter."[5] Others spoke of a "veil of money" obscuring the nature of the "real economy" in which people produced real goods and services and swapped them back and forth.[6]

Call this the final apotheosis of economics as common sense. Money is unimportant. Economies—"real economies"—are really vast barter systems. The problem is that history shows that without money, such vast barter systems do not occur. Even when economies "revert to barter," as Europe was said to do in the Middle Ages, they don't actually abandon the use of money. They just abandon the use of cash. In the Middle Ages, for instance, everyone continued to assess the value of tools and livestock in the old Roman currency, even if the coins themselves had ceased to circulate.[7]

It's money that had made it possible for us to imagine ourselves in the way economists encourage us to do: as a collection of individuals and nations whose main business is swapping things. It's also clear that the mere existence of money, in itself, is not enough to allow us see the world this way. If it were, the discipline of economics would have been created in ancient Sumer, or anyway, far earlier than 1776, when Adam Smith's *The Wealth of Nations* appeared.

The missing element is in fact exactly the thing Smith was attempting to downplay: the role of government policy. In England, in Smith's day, it became possible to see the market, the world of butchers, iron-mongers, and haberdashers, as its own entirely independent sphere of human activity because the British government was actively engaged in fostering markets. This required laws and police, but also specific monetary policies which liberals like Smith were (successfully) advocating.[8] It required pegging the value of the currency to silver, but at the same time greatly increasing the money supply, and particularly the amount of small change in circulation. This, in turn, not only required huge amounts of tin and copper, but also the careful regulation of the banks that were, at that time, the only source of paper money. The century before *The Wealth of Nations* had seen at least two attempts to create state-supported central banks, in France and Sweden, that had proven to be spectacular failures. In each case, the would-be central bank issued notes based largely on speculation that collapsed the moment investors lost faith. Smith supported the use of paper money, but like Locke before him, he also believed that the relative success of the Bank of England and Bank of Scotland had been due to their policy of pegging paper money firmly to precious metals. This became the mainstream economic view, so much so that alternative theories of money as credit—the one that Mitchell-Innes advocated—were quickly relegated to the margins, their proponents written off as cranks. They were dismissed as the very sort of thinking that led to bad banks and speculative bubbles in the first place.

It might be helpful, then, to consider what these alternative theories actually were.

State and Credit Theories of Money

Mitchell-Innes was an exponent of what came to be known as the Credit Theory of money, a position that over the course of the nineteenth century had its most avid proponents not in Mitchell-Innes's native Britain but in the two up-and-coming rival powers of the day, the United States and Germany. Credit Theorists insisted that money is not a commodity but an accounting tool. In other words, it is not a "thing" at all. For a Credit Theorist can no more touch a dollar or a deutschmark than you can touch an hour or a cubic centimeter. Units of currency are merely abstract units of measurement, and as the credit theorists correctly noted, historically, such abstract systems of accounting emerged long before the use of any particular token of exchange.[9]

The obvious next question is: If money is a just a yardstick, what then does it measure? The answer was simple: debt. A coin is, effectively, an IOU. Whereas conventional wisdom holds that a banknote is, or should be, a promise to pay a certain amount of "real money" (gold, silver, whatever that might be taken to mean), Credit Theorists argued that a banknote is simply the promise to pay *something* of the same value as an ounce of gold. But that's all that money ever is. There's no fundamental difference in this respect between a silver dollar, a Susan B. Anthony dollar coin made of a copper-nickel alloy designed to look vaguely like gold, a green piece of paper with a picture of George Washington on it, or a digital blip on some bank's computer. Conceptually, the idea that a piece of gold is really just an IOU is always rather difficult to wrap one's head around, but something like this must be true, because even when gold and silver coins were in use, they almost never circulated at their bullion value.

How could credit money come about? Let us return to the economics professors' imaginary town. Say, for example, that Joshua were to give his shoes to Henry, and, rather than Henry owing him a favor, Henry promises him something of equivalent value.[10] Henry gives Joshua an IOU. Joshua could wait for Henry to have something useful and then redeem it. In that case Henry would rip up the IOU and the story would be over. But say Joshua were to pass the IOU on to a third party—Sheila—to whom he owes something else. He could tick it off against his debt to a fourth party, Lola—now Henry will owe that amount to her. Hence, money is born, because there's no logical end to it. Say Sheila now wishes to acquire a pair of shoes from Edith; she can just hand Edith the IOU and assure her that Henry is good for it. In principle, there's no reason that the IOU could not continue circulating around town for years—provided people continue to have faith in Henry. In fact, if it goes on long enough, people might forget about the issuer entirely. Things like this do happen. The anthropologist Keith Hart once told me a story about his brother, who in the '50s was a British soldier stationed in Hong Kong. Soldiers used to pay their bar tabs by writing checks on accounts back in England. Local merchants would often simply endorse them over to each other and pass them around as currency: once, he saw one of his own checks, written six months before, on the counter of a local vendor covered with about forty different tiny inscriptions in Chinese.

What credit theorists like Mitchell-Innes were arguing is that even if Henry gave Joshua a gold coin instead of a piece of paper, the situation would be essentially the same. A gold coin is a promise to pay something else of equivalent value to a gold coin. After all, a gold coin is not actually useful in itself. One only accepts it because one assumes other people will.

In this sense, the value of a unit of currency is not the measure of the value of an object, but the measure of one's trust in other human beings.

This element of trust of course makes everything more complicated. Early banknotes circulated via a process almost exactly like what I've just described, except that, like the Chinese merchants, each recipient added his or her signature to guarantee the debt's legitimacy. But generally, the difficulty in the Chartalist position—this is what it came to be called, from the Latin *charta*, or token—is to establish why people would continue to trust a piece of paper. After all, why couldn't anyone just sign Henry's name on an IOU? True, this sort of debt-token system might work within a small village where everyone knew one another, or even among a more dispersed community like sixteenth-century Italian or twentieth-century Chinese merchants, where everyone at least had ways of keeping track of everybody else. But systems like these cannot create a full-blown currency system, and there's no evidence that they ever have. Providing a sufficient number of IOUs to allow everyone even in a medium-sized city to be able to carry out a significant portion of their daily transactions in such currency would require millions of tokens.[11] To be able to guarantee all of them, Henry would have to be almost unimaginably rich.

All this would be much less of a problem, however, if Henry were, say, Henry II, King of England, Duke of Normandy, Lord of Ireland, and Count of Anjou.

The real impetus for the Chartalist position, in fact, came out of what came to be known as the "German Historical School," whose most famous exponent was the historian G.F. Knapp, whose *State Theory of Money* first appeared in 1905.[12] If money is simply a unit of measure, it makes sense that emperors and kings should concern themselves with such matters. Emperors and kings are almost always concerned to established uniform systems of weights and measures throughout their kingdoms. It is also true, as Knapp observed, that once established, such systems tend to remain remarkably stable over time. During the reign of the actual Henry II (1154–1189), just about everyone in Western Europe was still keeping their accounts using the monetary system established by Charlemagne some 350 years earlier—that is, using pounds, shillings, and pence—despite the fact that some of these coins had never existed (Charlemagne never actually struck a silver pound), none of Charlemagne's actual shillings and pence remained in circulation, and those coins that did circulate tended to vary enormously in size, weight, purity, and value.[13] According to the Chartalists, this doesn't really matter. What matters is that there is a uniform system for measuring credits and debts, and that this system remains stable over time. The case of Charlemagne's currency is particularly dramatic because his actual empire dissolved quite quickly, but the monetary system he created continued to be used for keeping accounts within his former territories for more than 800 years. It was referred to, in the sixteenth century, quite explicitly as "imaginary money," and derniers and livres were only completely abandoned as units of account around the time of the French Revolution.[14]

According to Knapp, whether or not the actual, physical money stuff in circulation corresponds to this "imaginary money" is not particularly important. It makes no real difference whether it's pure silver, debased silver, leather tokens, or dried cod—provided the state is willing to accept it in payment of taxes. Because whatever the state was willing to accept, for that reason, became currency. One of the most important forms of currency in England in Henry's time were notched "tally sticks" used to record debts. Tally sticks were quite explicitly IOUs: both parties to a transaction would take a hazelwood twig, notch it to indicate the amount owed, and then split it in half. The creditor would keep one half, called "the stock" (hence the origin of the term "stock holder") and the debtor kept the other, called "the stub" (hence the origin of the term "ticket stub.") Tax assessors used such twigs to calculate amounts owed by local sheriffs. Often, though, rather than wait for the taxes to come due, Henry's exchequer would often sell the tallies at a discount, and they would circulate, as tokens of debt owed to the government, to anyone willing to trade for them.[15]

Modern banknotes actually work on a similar principle, except in reverse.[16] Recall here the little parable about Henry's IOU. The reader might have noticed one puzzling aspect of the equation: the IOU can operate as money only as long as Henry never pays his debt. In fact this is precisely the logic on which the Bank of England—the first successful modern central bank—was originally founded. In 1694, a consortium of English bankers made a loan of £1,200,000 to the king. In return they received a royal monopoly on the issuance of banknotes. What this meant in practice was they had the right to advance IOUs for a portion of the money the king now owed them to any inhabitant of the kingdom willing to borrow from them, or willing to deposit their own money in the bank—in effect, to circulate or "monetize" the newly created royal debt. This was a great deal for the bankers (they got to charge the king 8 percent annual interest for the original loan and simultaneously charge interest on the same money to the clients who borrowed it), but it only worked as long as the original loan remained outstanding. To this day, this loan has never been paid back. It cannot be. If it ever were, the entire monetary system of Great Britain would cease to exist.[17]

If nothing else, this approach helps solve one of the obvious mysteries of the fiscal policy of so many early kingdoms: Why did they make subjects pay taxes at all? This is not a question we're used to asking. The answer seems self-evident. Governments demand taxes because they wish to get their hands on people's money. But if Smith was right, and gold and silver became money through the natural workings of the market completely independently of governments, then wouldn't the obvious thing be to just grab control of the gold and silver mines? Then the king would have all the money he could possibly need. In fact, this is what ancient kings would normally do. If there were gold and silver mines in their territory, they would usually take control of them. So what exactly was the point of extracting the gold, stamping one's picture on it, causing it to circulate among one's subjects—and then demanding that those same subjects give it back again?

This does seem a bit of a puzzle. But if money and markets do not emerge spontaneously, it actually makes perfect sense. Because this is the simplest and most efficient way to bring markets into being. Let us take a hypothetical example. Say a king wishes to support a standing army of fifty thousand men. Under ancient or medieval conditions, feeding such a force was an enormous problem. Such a force would likely consume anything edible within ten miles of their camp in as many days; unless they were on the march, one would need to employ almost as many men and animals just to locate, acquire, and transport the necessary provisions.[18] On the other hand, if one simply hands out coins to the soldiers and then demands that every family in the kingdom was obliged to pay one of those coins back to you, one would, in one blow, turn one's entire national economy into a vast machine for the provisioning of soldiers, since now every family, in order to get their hands on the coins, must find some way to contribute to the general effort to provide soldiers with things they want. Markets are brought into existence as a side effect.

This is a bit of a cartoon version, but it is very clear that markets did spring up around ancient armies; one need only take a glance at Kautilya's *Arthasasatra*, the Sassanian "circle of sovereignty," or the Chinese "Discourses on Salt and Iron" to discover that most ancient rulers spent a great deal of their time thinking about the relation between mines, soldiers, taxes, and food. Most concluded that the creation of markets of this sort was not just convenient for feeding soldiers, but useful in all sorts of ways, since it meant officials no longer had to requisition everything they needed directly from the populace or figure out a way to produce it on royal estates or royal workshops. In other words, despite the dogged liberal assumption—again, coming from Smith's legacy—that the existence of states and markets are somehow opposed, the historical record implies that exactly the opposite is the case. Stateless societies tend also to be without markets.

As one might imagine, state theories of money have always been anathema to mainstream economists working in the tradition of Adam Smith. In fact, Chartalism has tended to be seen as a populist underside of economic theory, favored mainly by cranks.[19] The curious thing is that the mainstream economists often ended up actually working for governments and advising such governments to pursue policies much like those the Chartalists described—that is, tax policies designed to create markets where they had not existed before—despite the fact that they were in theory committed to Smith's argument that markets develop spontaneously of their own accord.

This was particularly true in the colonial world. To return to Madagascar for a moment: I have already mentioned that one of the first things that the French general Gallieni, conqueror of Madagascar, did when the conquest of the island was complete in 1901 was to impose a head tax. Not only was this tax quite high, it was also only payable in newly issued Malagasy francs. In other words, Gallieni did indeed print money and then demand that everyone in the country give some of that money back to him.

Most striking of all, though, was language he used to describe this tax. It was referred to as the "*impôt moralisateur*," the "educational" or "moralizing tax." In other words, it was designed—to adopt the language of the day—to teach the natives the value of work. Since the "educational tax" came due shortly after harvest time, the easiest way for farmers to pay it was to sell a portion of their rice crop to the Chinese or Indian merchants who soon installed themselves in small towns across the country. However, harvest was when the market price of rice was, for obvious reasons, at its lowest; if one sold too much of one's crop, that meant one would not have enough left to feed one's family for the entire year, and thus be forced to buy one's own rice back, on credit, from those same merchants later in the year when prices were much higher. As a result, farmers quickly fell hopelessly into debt (the merchants doubling as loan sharks). The easiest way to pay back the debt was either to find some kind of cash crop to sell—to start growing coffee, or pineapples—or else to send one's children off to work for wages in the city or on one of the plantations that French colonists were establishing across the island. The whole project might seem no more than a cynical scheme to squeeze cheap labor out of the peasantry, and it was that, but it was also something more. The colonial government was also quite explicit (at least in their own internal policy documents) about the need to make sure that peasants had at least some money of their own left over, and to ensure that they became accustomed to the minor luxuries—parasols, lipstick, cookies—available at the Chinese shops. It was crucial that they develop new tastes, habits, and expectations; that they lay the foundations of a consumer demand that would endure long after the conquerors had left, and keep Madagascar forever tied to France.

Most people are not stupid, and most Malagasy understood exactly what their conquerors were trying to do to them. Some were determined to resist. More than sixty years after the invasion, a French anthropologist, Gerard Althabe, was able to observe villages on the east coast of the island whose inhabitants would dutifully show up at the coffee plantations to earn the money for their poll tax and then, having paid it, studiously ignore the wares for sale at the local shops and instead turn over any remaining money to lineage elders, who would then use it to buy cattle for sacrifice to their ancestors.[20] Many were quite open in saying that they saw themselves as resisting a trap.

Still, such defiance rarely lasts forever. Markets did gradually take shape, even in those parts of the island where none had previously existed. With them came the inevitable network of little shops. And by the time I got there, in 1990, a generation after the poll tax had finally been abolished by a revolutionary government, the logic of the market had become so intuitively accepted that even spirit mediums were reciting passages that might as well have come from Adam Smith.

Such examples could be multiplied endlessly. Something like this occurred in just about every part of the world conquered by European arms where markets were not already in place. Rather than discovering barter, they ended up using the very techniques that mainstream economics rejected to bring something like the market into being.

In Search of a Myth

Anthropologists have been complaining about the Myth of Barter for almost a century. Occasionally, economists point out with slight exasperation that there's a fairly simple reason why they're still telling the same story despite all the evidence against it: anthropologists have never come up with a better one.[21] This is an understandable objection, but there's a simple answer to it. The reasons why anthropologists haven't been able to come up with a simple, compelling story for the origins of money is because there's no reason to believe there could be one. Money was no more ever "invented" than music or mathematics or jewelry. What we call "money" isn't a "thing" at all; it's a way of comparing things mathematically, as proportions: of saying one of X is equivalent to six of Y. As such it is probably as old as human thought. The moment we try to get any more specific, we discover that there are any number of different habits and practices that have converged in the stuff we now call "money," and this is precisely the reason why economists, historians, and the rest have found it so difficult to come up with a single definition.

Credit Theorists have long been hobbled by the lack of an equally compelling narrative. This is not to say that all sides in the currency debates that ranged between 1850 and 1950 were not in the habit of deploying mythological weaponry. This was true particularly, perhaps, in the United States. In 1894, the Greenbackers, who pushed for detaching the dollar from gold entirely to allow the government to spend freely on job-creation campaigns, invented the idea of the March on Washington—an idea that was to have endless resonance in U.S. history. L. Frank Baum's book *The Wonderful Wizard of Oz*, which appeared in 1900, is often held to be a parable for the Populist campaign of William Jennings Bryan, who twice ran for president on the Free Silver platform—vowing to replace the gold standard with a bimetallic system that would allow the free creation of silver money alongside gold.[22] As with the Greenbackers, one of the main constituencies for the movement was debtors: particularly, Midwestern farm families such as

Dorothy's, who had been facing a massive wave of foreclosures during the severe recession of the 1890s. According to the Populist reading, the Wicked Witches of the East and West represent the East and West Coast bankers (promoters of and benefactors from the tight money supply), the Scarecrow represented the farmers (who didn't have the brains to avoid the debt trap), the Tin Woodsman was the industrial proletariat (who didn't have the heart to act in solidarity with the farmers), the Cowardly Lion represented the political class (who didn't have the courage to intervene). The yellow brick road, silver slippers, emerald city, and hapless Wizard presumably speak for themselves.[23] "Oz" is of course the standard abbreviation for "ounce."[24] As an attempt to create a new myth, Baum's story was remarkably effective. As political propaganda, less so. William Jennings Bryan failed in three attempts to win the presidency, the silver standard was never adopted, and few nowadays even remember what *The Wonderful Wizard of Oz* was originally supposed to be about.[25]

For state-money theorists in particular, this has been a problem. Stories about rulers using taxes to create markets in conquered territories, or to pay for soldiers or other state functions, are not particularly inspiring. German ideas of money as the embodiment of national will did not travel very well.

Every time there was a major economic meltdown, however, conventional laissez-faire economics took another hit. The Bryan campaigns were born as a reaction to the Panic of 1893. By the time of the Great Depression of the 1930s, the very notion that the market could regulate itself, so long as the government ensured that money was safely pegged to precious metals, was completely discredited. From roughly 1933 to 1979, every major capitalist government reversed course and adopted some version of Keynesianism. Keynesian orthodoxy started from the assumption that capitalist markets would not really work unless capitalist governments were willing effectively to play nanny: most famously, by engaging in massive deficit "pump-priming" during downturns. While in the '80s, Margaret Thatcher in Britain and Ronald Reagan in the United States made a great show of rejecting all of this, it's unclear how much they really did.[26] And in any case, they were operating in the wake of an even greater blow to previous monetary orthodoxy: Richard Nixon's decision in 1971 to unpeg the dollar from precious metals entirely, eliminate the international gold standard, and introduce the system of floating currency regimes that has dominated the world economy ever since. This meant in effect that all national currencies were henceforth, as neoclassical economists like to put it, "fiat money" backed only by the public trust.

Now, John Maynard Keynes himself was much more open to what he liked to call the "alternative tradition" of credit and state theories than any economist of that stature (and Keynes is still arguably the single most important economic thinker of the twentieth century) before or since. At certain points he immersed himself in it: he spent several years in the 1920s studying Mesopotamian cuneiform banking records to try to ascertain the origins of money—his "Babylonian madness," as he would later call it.[27] His conclusion, which he set forth at the very beginning of his *Treatise on Money*, was more or less the only conclusion one could come to if one started not from first principles but from a careful examination of the historical record: that the lunatic fringe was, essentially, right. Whatever its earliest origins, for the last four thousand years money has been effectively a creature of the state. Individuals, he observed, make contracts with one another. They take out debts, and they promise payment.

> The State, therefore, comes in first of all as the authority of law which enforces the payment of the thing which corresponds to the name or description in the contract. But it comes doubly when, in addition, it claims the right to determine and declare *what thing* corresponds to the name, and to vary its declaration from time to time—when, that is to say it claims the right to re-edit the dictionary. This right is claimed by all modern States and has been so claimed for some four thousand years at least. It is when this stage in the evolution of Money has been reached that Knapp's Chartalism—the doctrine that money is peculiarly a creation of the State—is fully realized . . . To-day all civilized money is, beyond the possibility of dispute, chartalist.[28]

This does not mean that the state necessarily *creates* money. Money is credit, it can be brought into being by private contractual agreements (loans, for instance). The state merely enforces the agreement and dictates the legal terms. Hence Keynes' next dramatic assertion: that banks create money, and that there is no intrinsic limit to their ability to do so: since however much they lend, the borrower will have no choice but to put the money back into some bank again, and thus, from the perspective of the banking system as a whole, the total number of debits and credits will always cancel out.[29] The implications were radical, but Keynes himself was not. In the end, he was always careful to frame the problem in a way that could be reintegrated into the mainstream economics of his day.

Neither was Keynes much of a mythmaker. Insofar as the alternative tradition has come up with an answer to the Myth of Barter, it was not from Keynes' own efforts (Keynes ultimately decided that the origins of money were not particularly important) but in the work of some contemporary neo-Keynesians, who were not afraid to follow some of his more radical suggestions as far as they would go.

The real weak link in state-credit theories of money was always the element of taxes. It is one thing to explain why early states demanded taxes (in order to create markets). It's another to ask "By what right?" Assuming that early rulers were not simply thugs and that taxes were not simply extortion—and no Credit Theorist, to my knowledge, took such a cynical view even of early government—one must ask how they justified this sort of thing.

Nowadays, we all think we know the answer to this question. We pay our taxes so that the government can provide us with services. This starts with security services—military protection being about the only service many early states were really able to provide. By now, of course, the government provides all sorts of things. All of this is said to go back to some sort of original "social contract" that everyone somehow agreed on, though no one really knows exactly when or by whom, or why we should be bound by the decisions of distant ancestors on this one matter when we don't feel particularly bound by the decisions of our distant ancestors on anything else.[30] It all makes sense if you assume that markets come before governments, but the whole argument totters quickly once you realize that they don't.

There is an alternative explanation, one created to be in keeping with the state-credit theory approach. It's referred to as "primordial debt theory," and it has been developed largely in France by a team of researchers—not only economists but anthropologists, historians, and classicists—originally assembled around the figures of Michel Aglietta and Andre Orléans,[31] and more recently, Bruno Théret, and it has since been taken up by some neo-Keynesians in the United States and the United Kingdom as well.[32]

It's a position that has emerged quite recently and at first, largely amidst debates about the nature of the euro. The creation of a common European currency sparked not only all sorts of intellectual debates (Does a common currency necessarily imply the creation of a common European state? Or of a common European economy or society? Are these ultimately the same thing?) but dramatic political ones as well. The creation of the euro zone was spearheaded above all by Germany, whose central banks still see their main goal as combating inflation. What's more, tight money policies and the need to balance budgets having been used as the main weapon to chip away welfare-state policies in Europe, it has necessarily become the stake of political struggles between bankers and pensioners, creditors and debtors, just as heated as those of 1890s America.

The core argument is that any attempt to separate monetary policy from social policy is ultimately wrong. Primordial-debt theorists insist that these have always been the same thing. Governments use taxes to create money, and they are able to do so because they have become the guardians of the debt that all citizens have to one another. This debt is the essence of society itself. It exists long before money and markets, and money and markets themselves are simply ways of chopping pieces of it up.

At first, the argument goes, this sense of debt was expressed not through the state but through religion. To make the argument, Aglietta and Orléans fixed on certain works of early Sanskrit religious literature: the hymns, prayers, and poetry collected in the Vedas, and the Brahmanas, priestly commentaries composed over the centuries that followed, texts that are now considered the foundations of Hindu thought. It's not as odd a choice as it might seem. These texts constitute the earliest known historical reflections on the nature of debt.

Actually, even the very earliest Vedic poems, composed sometime between 1500 and 1200 BC, evince a constant concern with debt—which is treated as synonymous with guilt and sin.[33] There are numerous prayers pleading with the gods to liberate the worshipper from the shackles or bonds of debt. Sometimes these seem to refer to debt in the literal sense—Rig Veda 10.34, for instance, has a long description of the sad plight of gamblers who "wander homeless, in constant fear, in debt, and seeking money." Elsewhere it's clearly metaphorical.

In these hymns, Yama, the god of death, figures prominently. To be in debt was to have a weight placed on you by Death. To be under any sort of unfulfilled obligation, any unkept promise, to gods or to men, was to live in the shadow of Death. Often, even in the very early texts, debt seems to stand in for a broader sense of inner suffering, from which one begs the gods—particularly Agni, who represents the sacrificial fire—for release. It was only with the Brahmanas that commentators started trying to weave all this together into a more comprehensive philosophy. The conclusion: that human existence is itself a form of debt.

> A man, being born, is a debt; by his own self he is born to Death, and only when he sacrifices does he redeem himself from Death.[34]

Sacrifice (and these early commentators were themselves sacrificial priests) is thus called "tribute paid to Death." Or such was the manner of speaking. In reality, as the priests knew better than anyone, sacrifice was directed to all the gods, not just Death—Death was just the intermediary. Framing things this way, though, did immediately raise the one problem that always comes up, whenever anyone conceives human life through such an idiom. If our lives are on loan, who would actually wish to repay such a debt? To live in debt is to be guilty, incomplete. But completion can only mean annihilation. In this way, the "tribute" of sacrifice could be seen as a kind of interest payment, with the life of the animal substituting temporarily for what's really owed, which is ourselves—a mere postponement of the inevitable.[35]

Priestly commentators proposed different ways out of the dilemma. Some ambitious Brahmins began telling their clients that sacrificial ritual, if done correctly, promised a way to break out of the human condition entirely and achieve eternity (since, in the face of eternity, all debts become meaningless).[36] Another way was to broaden the notion of debt, so that all social responsibilities become debts of one sort or another. Thus two famous passages in the Brahmanas insist that we are born as a debt not just to the gods, to be repaid in sacrifice, but also to the Sages who created the Vedic learning to begin with, which we must repay through study; to our ancestors ("the Fathers"), who we must repay by having children; and finally, "to men"—apparently meaning humanity as a whole, to be repaid by offering hospitality to strangers.[37] Anyone, then, who lives a proper life is constantly paying back existential debts of one sort or another; but at the same time, as the notion of debt slides back into a simple sense of social obligation, it becomes something far less terrifying than the sense that one's very existence is a loan taken against Death.[38] Not least because social obligations always cut both ways. After all, once one has oneself fathered children, one is just as much a debtor as a creditor.

What primordial-debt theorists have done is to propose that the ideas encoded in these Vedic texts are not peculiar to a certain intellectual tradition of early Iron Age ritual specialists in the Ganges valley, but that they are essential to the very nature and history of human thought. Consider for example this statement, from an essay by French economist Bruno Théret with the uninspiring title "The Socio-Cultural Dimensions of the Currency: Implications for the Transition to the Euro," published in the *Journal of Consumer Policy* in 1999:

> At the origin of money we have a "relation of representation" of death as an invisible world, before and beyond life—a

representation that is the product of the symbolic function proper to the human species and which envisages birth as an original debt incurred by all men, a debt owing to the cosmic powers from which humanity emerged.

Payment of this debt, which can however never be settled on earth—because its full reimbursement is out of reach—takes the form of sacrifices which, by replenishing the credit of the living, make it possible to prolong life and even in certain cases to achieve eternity by joining the Gods. But this initial belief-claim is also associated with the emergence of sovereign powers whose legitimacy resides in their ability to represent the entire original cosmos. And it is these powers that invented money as a means of settling debts—a means whose abstraction makes it possible to resolve the sacrificial paradox by which putting to death becomes the permanent means of protecting life. Through this institution, belief is in turn transferred to a currency stamped with the effigy of the sovereign—a money put in circulation but whose return is organized by this other institution which is the tax/settlement of the life debt. So money also takes on the function of a means of payment.[39]

If nothing else, this provides a neat illustration of how different are standards of debate in Europe from those current in the Anglo-American world. One can't imagine an American economist of any stripe writing something like this. Still, the author is actually making a rather clever synthesis here. Human nature does not drive us to "truck and barter." Rather, it ensures that we are always creating symbols—such as money itself. This is how we come to see ourselves in a cosmos surrounded by invisible forces; as in debt to the universe.

The ingenious move of course is to fold this back into the state theory of money—since by "sovereign powers" Théret actually means "the state." The first kings were sacred kings who were either gods in their own right or stood as privileged mediators between human beings and the ultimate forces that governed the cosmos. This sets us on a road to the gradual realization that our debt to the gods was always, really, a debt to the society that made us what we are.

The "primordial debt," writes British sociologist Geoffrey Ingham, "is that owed by the living to the continuity and durability of the society that secures their individual existence."[40] In this sense it is not just criminals who owe a "debt to society"—we are all, in a certain sense, guilty, even criminals.

For instance, Ingham notes that, while there is no actual proof that money emerged in this way, "there is considerable indirect etymological evidence":

> In all Indo-European languages, words for "debt" are synonymous with those for "sin" or "guilt," illustrating the links between religion, payment and the mediation of the sacred and profane realms by "money." For example, there is a connection between money (German *Geld*), indemnity or sacrifice (Old English *Geild*), tax (Gothic *Gild*) and, of course, guilt.[41]

Or, to take another curious connection: Why were cattle so often used as money? The German historian Bernard Laum long ago pointed out that in Homer, when people measure the value of a ship or suit of armor, they always measure it in oxen—even though when they actually exchange things, they never pay for anything in oxen. It is hard to escape the conclusion that this was because an ox was what one offered the gods in sacrifice. Hence oxen represented absolute value. From Sumer to Classical Greece, silver and gold were dedicated as offerings in temples. Everywhere, money seems to have emerged from the thing most appropriate for giving to the gods.[42]

If the king has simply taken over guardianship of that primordial debt we all owe to society for having created us, this provides a very neat explanation for why the government feels it has the right to make us pay taxes. Taxes are just a measure of our debt to the society that made us. But this doesn't really explain how this kind of absolute life-debt can be converted into *money*, which is by definition a means of measuring and comparing the value of *different* things. This is just as much a problem for credit theorists as for neoclassical economists, even if the problem for them is somewhat differently framed. If you start from the barter theory of money, you have to resolve the problem of how and why you would come to select one commodity to measure just how much you want each of the other ones. If you start from a credit theory, you are left with the problem I described in the first chapter: how to turn a moral obligation into a specific sum of money, how the mere sense of owing someone else a favor can eventually turn into a system of accounting in which one is able to calculate exactly how many sheep or fish or chunks of silver it would take to repay the debt. Or in this case, how do we go from that absolute debt we owe to God to the very specific debts we owe our cousin, or the bartender?

The answer provided by primordial-debt theorists is, again, ingenious. If taxes represent our absolute debt to the society that created us, then the first step toward creating real money comes when we start calculating much more specific debts to society, systems of fines, fees, and penalties, or even debts we owe to specific individuals who we have wronged in some way, and thus to whom we stand in a relation of "sin" or "guilt."

This is actually much less implausible than it might sound. One of the puzzling things about all the theories about the origins of money that we've been looking at so far is that they almost completely ignore the evidence of anthropology. Anthropologists do have a great deal of knowledge of how economies within stateless societies actually worked—how they still work in places where states and markets have been unable to completely break up existing ways of doing things. There are innumerable studies of, say, the use of cattle as money in eastern or southern Africa, of shell money in the Americas (wampum being the most famous example) or Papua New Guinea, bead money, feather money, the use of iron rings, cowries, spondylus shells, brass rods, or woodpecker scalps.[43] The reason that this literature tends to be ignored by economists is simple: "primitive currencies" of this sort are only rarely used to buy and sell things, and even when they are, never primarily to buy and sell everyday items such as chickens or eggs or shoes or potatoes. Rather than being employed to acquire things, they are mainly used to rearrange relations between people. Above all, to arrange marriages and to settle disputes, particularly those arising from murders or personal injury.

There is every reason to believe that our own money started the same way—even the English word "to pay" is originally derived from a word for "to pacify, appease"—as in, to give someone something precious, for instance, to express just how badly you feel about having just killed his brother in a drunken brawl, and how much you would really like to avoid this becoming the basis for an ongoing blood-feud.[44]

Debt theorists are especially concerned with this latter possibility. This is partly because they tend to skip past the anthropological literature and look at early law codes—taking inspiration here from the groundbreaking work of one of the twentieth century's greatest numismatists, Philip Grierson, who in the '70s first suggested that money might first have emerged from early legal practice. Grierson was an expert in the European Dark Ages, and he became fascinated by what have come to be known as the "Barbarian Law Codes," established by many Germanic peoples after the destruction of the Roman Empire in the 600s and 700s—Goths, Frisians, Franks, and so on—soon followed by similar codes published everywhere from Russia to Ireland. Certainly, they are fascinating documents. On the one hand, they make it abundantly clear just how wrong are conventional accounts of Europe around this time "reverting to barter." Almost all of the Germanic law codes use Roman money to make assessments; penalties for theft, for instance, are almost always followed by demands that the thief not only return the stolen property but pay any outstanding rent (or in the event of stolen money, interest) owing for the amount of time it has been in his possession. On the other hand, these were soon followed by law codes by people living in territories that had never been under Roman rule—in Ireland, Wales, Nordic countries, Russia—and these are if anything even more revealing. They could be remarkably creative, both in what could be used as a means of payment and on the precise breakdown of injuries and insults that required compensation:

> Compensation in the Welsh laws is reckoned primarily in cattle and in the Irish ones in cattle or bondmaids (*cumal*), with considerable use of precious metals in both. In the Germanic codes it is mainly in precious metal . . . In the Russian codes it was silver and furs, graduated from marten down to squirrel. Their detail is remarkable, not only in the personal injuries envisioned—specific compensations for the loss of an arm, a hand, a forefinger, a nail, for a blow on the head so that the brain is visible or bone projects—but in the coverage some of them gave to the possessions of the individual household. Title II of the Salic Law deals with the theft of pigs, Title III with cattle, Title IV with sheep, Title V with goats, Title VI with dogs, each time with an elaborate breakdown differentiating between animals of different age and sex.[45]

This does make a great deal of psychological sense. I've already remarked how difficult it is to imagine how a system of precise equivalences—one young healthy milk cow is equivalent to exactly thirty-six chickens—could arise from most forms of gift exchange. If Henry gives Joshua a pig and feels he has received an inadequate counter-gift, he might mock Joshua as a cheapskate, but he would have little occasion to come up with a mathematical formula for precisely how cheap he feels Joshua has been. On the other hand, if Joshua's pig just destroyed Henry's garden, and especially, if that led to a fight in which Henry lost a toe, and Henry's family is now hauling Joshua up in front of the village assembly—this is precisely the context where people are most likely to become petty and legalistic and express outrage if they feel they have received one groat less than was their rightful due. That means exact mathematical specificity: for instance, the capacity to measure the exact value of a two-year-old pregnant sow. What's more, the levying of penalties must have constantly required the calculation of equivalences. Say the fine is in marten pelts but the culprit's clan doesn't have any martens. How many squirrel skins will do? Or pieces of silver jewelry? Such problems must have come up all the time and led to at least a rough-and-ready set of rules of thumb over what sorts of valuable were equivalent to others. This would help explain why, for instance, medieval Welsh law codes can contain detailed breakdowns not only of the value of different ages and conditions of milk cow, but of the monetary value of every object likely to be found in an ordinary homestead, down to the cost of each piece of timber—despite the fact that there seems no reason to believe that most such items could even be purchased on the open market at the time.[46]

■ ■ ■ ■ ■

There is something very compelling in all this. For one thing, the premise makes a great deal of intuitive sense. After all, we do owe everything we are to others. This is simply true. The language we speak and even think in, our habits and opinions, the kind of food we like to eat, the knowledge that makes our lights switch on and toilets flush, even the style in which we carry out our gestures of defiance and rebellion against social conventions—all of this we learned from other people, most of them long dead. If we were to imagine what we owe them as a debt, it could only be infinite. The question is: Does it really make sense to think of this as a debt? After all, a debt is by definition something that we could at least imagine paying back. It is strange enough to wish to be square with one's parents—it rather implies that one does not wish to think of them as parents anymore. Would we really want to be square with all humanity? What would that even mean? And is this desire really a fundamental feature of all human thought?

Another way to put this would be: Are primordial-debt theorists *describing* a myth, have they discovered a profound truth of the human condition that has always existed in all societies, and is it simply spelled out particularly clearly in certain ancient texts from India—or are they *inventing* a myth of their own?

Clearly it must be the latter. They are inventing a myth.

The choice of the Vedic material is significant. The fact is, we know almost nothing about the people who composed these texts and little about the society that created them.[47] We don't even know if interest-bearing loans existed in Vedic India—which obviously has a bearing on whether priests really saw sacrifice as the payment of interest on a loan we owe to Death.[48] As a result, the material can serve as a kind of empty canvas, or a canvas covered with hieroglyphics in an unknown language, on which we can project almost anything we want to. If we look at other ancient civilizations in which we do know something about the larger context, we find that no such notion of sacrifice as payment is in evidence.[49] If we look through the work of ancient theologians, we find that most were familiar with the idea that sacrifice was a way by which human beings could enter into commercial relations with the gods, but that they felt it was patently ridiculous: If the gods already have everything they want, what exactly do humans have to bargain with?[50] We've seen in the last chapter how difficult it is to give gifts to kings. With gods (let alone God) the problem is magnified infinitely. Exchange implies equality. In dealing with cosmic forces, this was simply assumed to be impossible from the start.

The notion that debts to gods were appropriated by the state, and thus became the bases for taxation systems, can't really stand up either. The problem here is that in the ancient world free citizens didn't usually pay taxes. Generally speaking, tribute was levied only on conquered populations. This was already true in ancient Mesopotamia, where the inhabitants of independent cities did not usually have to pay direct taxes at all. Similarly, as Moses Finley noted, "Classical Greeks looked upon direct taxes as tyrannical and avoided them whenever possible."[51] Athenian citizens did not pay direct taxes of any sort, though the city did sometimes distribute money to its citizens, a kind of reverse taxation—either directly, as with the proceeds of the Laurium silver mines, and indirectly, through generous fees for jury duty or attending the assembly. Subject cities, however, did have to pay tribute. Even within the Persian Empire, Persians did not have to pay tribute to the Great King, but the inhabitants of conquered provinces did.[52] The same was true in Rome, where for a very long time Roman citizens not only paid no taxes but had a right to a share of the tribute levied on others, in the form of the dole—the "bread" part of the famous "bread and circuses."[53]

In other words, Benjamin Franklin was wrong when he said that in this world nothing is certain except death and taxes. This obviously makes the idea that the debt to one is just a variation on the other much harder to maintain.

None of this, however, deals a mortal blow to the state theory of money, since even those states that did not demand taxes did levy fees, penalties, tariffs, and fines of one sort or another. But it *is* very hard to reconcile with any theory that claims states were first conceived as guardians of some sort of cosmic, primordial debt.

It's curious that primordial-debt theorists never have much to say about Sumer or Babylonia, despite the fact that Mesopotamia is where the practice of loaning money at interest was first invented, probably two thousand years before the Vedas were composed—and that it was also the home of the world's first states. But if we look into Mesopotamian history, it becomes a little less surprising. Again, what we find there is in many ways the exact opposite of what such theorists would have predicted.

The reader will recall here that Mesopotamian city-states were dominated by vast Temples: gigantic, complex industrial institutions often staffed by thousands—including everyone from shepherds and barge-pullers to spinners and weavers to dancing girls and clerical administrators. By at least 2700 BC, ambitious rulers had begun to imitate them by creating palace complexes organized on similar terms—with the exception that where the Temples centered on the sacred chambers of a god or goddess, represented by a sacred image who was fed and clothed and entertained by priestly servants as if he or she were a living person. Palaces centered on the chambers of an actual live king. Sumerian rulers rarely went so far as to declare themselves gods, but they often came very close. However, when they did interfere in the lives of their subjects in their capacity as cosmic rulers, they did not do it by imposing public debts, but rather by canceling private ones.[54]

We don't know precisely when and how interest-bearing loans originated, since they appear to predate writing. Most likely, Temple administrators invented the idea as a way of financing the caravan trade. This trade was crucial because while the river valley of ancient Mesopotamia was extraordinarily fertile and produced huge surpluses of grain and other foodstuffs, and supported enormous numbers of livestock, which in turn supported a vast wool and leather industry, it was almost completely lacking in anything else. Stone, wood, metal, even the silver used as money, all had to be imported. From quite early times, then, Temple administrators developed the habit of advancing goods to local merchants—some of them private, others themselves Temple functionaries—who would then go off and sell it overseas. Interest was just a way for the Temples to take their share of the resulting profits.[55] However, once established, the principle seems to have quickly spread. Before long, we find not only commercial loans, but also consumer loans—usury in the classical sense of the term. By c. 2400 BC it already appears to have been common practice on the part of local officials, or wealthy merchants, to advance loans to peasants who were in financial trouble on collateral and begin to appropriate their possessions if they were unable to pay. It usually started with grain, sheep, goats, and furniture, then moved on to fields and houses, or, alternately or ultimately, family members. Servants, if any, went quickly, followed by children, wives, and in some extreme occasions, even the borrower himself. These would be reduced to debt-peons: not quite slaves, but very close to that, forced into perpetual service in the lender's household—or, sometimes, in the Temples or Palaces themselves. In theory, of course, any of them could be redeemed whenever the borrower repaid the money, but for obvious reasons, the more a peasant's resources were stripped away from him, the harder that became.

The effects were such that they often threatened to rip society apart. If for any reason there was a bad harvest, large proportions of the peasantry would fall into debt peonage; families would be broken up. Before long, lands lay abandoned as indebted farmers fled their homes for fear of repossession and joined semi-nomadic bands on the desert fringes of urban civilization. Faced with the potential for complete social breakdown, Sumerian and later Babylonian kings periodically announced general amnesties: "clean slates," as economic historian Michael Hudson refers to them. Such decrees would typically declare all outstanding consumer debt null and void (commercial debts were not affected), return all land to its original owners, and allow all debt-peons to return to their families. Before long, it became more or less a regular habit for kings to make such a declaration on first assuming power, and many were forced to repeat it periodically over the course of their reigns.

In Sumer, these were called "declarations of freedom"—and it is significant that the Sumerian word *amargi*, the first recorded word for "freedom" in any known human language, literally means "return to mother"—since this is what freed debt-peons were finally allowed to do.[56]

Michael Hudson argues that Mesopotamian kings were only in a position to do this because of their cosmic pretensions: in taking power, they saw themselves as literally recreating human society, and so were in a position to wipe the slate clean of all previous moral obligations. Still, this is about as far from what primordial-debt theorists had in mind as one could possibly imagine.[57]

■ ■ ■ ■ ■

Probably the biggest problem in this whole body of literature is the initial assumption: that we begin with an infinite debt to something called "society." It's this debt to society that we project onto the gods. It's this same debt that then gets taken up by kings and national governments.

What makes the concept of society so deceptive is that we assume the world is organized into a series of compact, modular units called "societies," and that all people know which one they're in. Historically, this is very rarely the case. Imagine I am a Christian Armenian merchant living under the reign of Genghis Khan. What is "society" for me? Is it the city where I grew up, the society of international merchants (with its own elaborate codes of conduct) within which I conduct my daily affairs, other speakers of Armenian, Christendom (or maybe just Orthodox Christendom), or the inhabitants of the Mongol empire itself, which stretched from the Mediterranean to Korea? Historically, kingdoms and empires have rarely been the most important reference points in people's lives. Kingdoms rise and fall; they also strengthen and weaken; governments may make their presence known in people's lives quite sporadically, and for many people in history, it was not at all clear whose government they were actually in. Even until quite recently, many of the world's inhabitants were not quite sure of what country they were citizens, or why it should matter. My mother, who was born a Jew in Poland, once told me a joke from her childhood:

> There was a small town located along the frontier between Russia and Poland; no one was ever quite sure to which it belonged. One day an official treaty was signed and not long after, surveyors arrived to draw a border. Some villagers approached them where they had set up their equipment on a nearby hill.
>
> "So where are we, Russia or Poland?"
>
> "According to our calculations, your village now begins exactly thirty-seven meters into Poland."
>
> The villagers immediately began dancing for joy.
>
> "Why?" the surveyors asked. "What difference does it make?"
>
> "Don't you know what this means?" they replied. "It means we'll never have to endure another one of those terrible Russian winters!"

However, if we are born with an infinite debt to all those people who made our existence possible, but there is no natural unit called "society"—then who or what exactly do we really owe it to? Everyone? Everything? Some people or things more than others? And how do we pay a debt to something so diffuse? Or, perhaps more to the point, who exactly can claim the authority to tell us how we can repay it, and on what grounds?

If we frame the problem that way, the authors of the Brahmanas are offering a quite sophisticated reflection on a moral question that no one has really ever been able to answer any better before or since. As I say, we can't know much about the conditions under which those texts were composed, but such evidence as we do have suggests that the crucial documents date from sometime between 500 and 400 BC—that is, roughly the time of Socrates—which in India appears to have been just around the time that a commercial economy and institutions like coined money and interest-bearing loans were beginning to become features of everyday life. The intellectual classes of the time were, much as they were in Greece and China, grappling with the implications. In their case, this meant asking: What does it mean to imagine our responsibilities as debts? To whom do we owe our existence?

It's significant that their answer did not make any mention either of "society" or states (though kings and governments certainly existed in early India). Instead, they fixed on debts to gods, to sages, to fathers, and to "men." It wouldn't be at all difficult to translate their formulation into more contemporary language. We could put it this way. We owe our existence above all:

- To the universe, cosmic forces, as we would put it now, to Nature. The ground of our existence. To be repaid through ritual: ritual being an act of respect and recognition towards all that beside which we are small.[58]
- To those who have created the knowledge and cultural accomplishments that we value most, that give our existence its form, its meaning, but also its shape. Here we would include not only the philosophers and scientists who created our intellectual tradition but everyone from William Shakespeare to that long-since-forgotten woman, somewhere in the Middle East, who created leavened bread. We repay them by becoming learned ourselves and contributing to human knowledge and human culture.
- To our parents, and their parents—our ancestors. We repay them by becoming ancestors.
- To humanity as a whole. We repay them by generosity to strangers, by maintaining that basic communistic ground of sociality that makes human relations, and hence life, possible.

Set out this way, though, the argument begins to undermine its very premise. These are nothing like commercial debts. After all, one might repay one's parents by having children, but one is not generally thought to have repaid one's creditors if one lends the cash to someone else.[59]

Myself, I wonder: Couldn't that really be the point? Perhaps what the authors of the Brahmanas were really demonstrating was that, in the final analysis, our relation with the cosmos is ultimately nothing like a commercial transaction, nor could it be. That is because commercial transactions imply both equality and separation. These examples are all about overcoming separation: you are free from your debt to your ancestors when you become an ancestor; you are free from your debt to the sages when you become a sage, you are free from your debt to humanity when you act with humanity. All the more so if one is speaking of the universe. If you cannot bargain with the gods because they already have everything, then you certainly cannot bargain with the universe, because the universe *is* everything—and that everything necessarily includes yourself. One could in fact interpret this list as a subtle way of saying that the only way of "freeing oneself" from the debt was not literally repaying debts, but rather showing that these debts do not exist because one is not in fact separate to begin with, and hence that the very notion of canceling the debt and achieving a separate, autonomous existence was ridiculous from the start. Or even that the very presumption of positing oneself as separate from humanity or the cosmos, so much so that one can enter into one-to-one dealings with it, is itself the crime that can be answered only by death. Our guilt is not due to the fact that we cannot repay our debt to the universe. Our guilt is our presumption in thinking of ourselves as being in any sense an equivalent to Everything Else that Exists or Has Ever Existed, so as to be able to conceive of such a debt in the first place.[60]

Or let us look at the other side of the equation. Even if it is possible to imagine ourselves as standing in a position of absolute debt to the cosmos, or to humanity, the next question becomes: Who exactly has a right to speak for the cosmos, or humanity, to tell us how that debt must be repaid? If there's anything more preposterous than claiming to stand apart from the entire universe so as to enter into negotiations with it, it is claiming to speak for the other side.

If one were looking for the ethos for an individualistic society such as our own, one way to do it might well be to say: we all owe an infinite debt to humanity, society, nature, or the cosmos (however one prefers to frame it), but no one else could possibly tell us how we are to pay it. This at least would be intellectually consistent. If so, it would actually be possible to see almost all systems of established authority—religion, morality, politics, economics, and the criminal-justice system—as so many different fraudulent ways to presume to calculate what cannot be calculated, to claim the authority to tell us how some aspect of that unlimited debt ought to be repaid. Human freedom would then be our ability to decide for ourselves how we want to do so.

No one, to my knowledge, has ever taken this approach. Instead, theories of existential debt always end up becoming ways of justifying—or laying claim to—structures of authority. The case of the Hindu intellectual tradition is telling here. The debt to humanity appears only in a few early texts and is quickly forgotten. Almost all later Hindu commentators ignore it and instead put their emphasis on a man's debt to his father.[61]

■ ■ ■ ■ ■

Primordial-debt theorists have other fish to fry. They are not really interested in the cosmos, but actually, in "society."

Let me return again to that word, "society." The reason that it seems like such a simple, self-evident concept is because we mostly use it as a synonym for "nation." After all, when Americans speak of paying their debt to society, they are not thinking of their responsibilities to people who live in Sweden, or Gabon. It's only the modern state, with its elaborate border controls and social policies, that enables us to imagine "society" in this way, as a single bounded entity. This is why projecting that notion backwards into Vedic or Medieval times will always be deceptive, even though we don't really have another word.

It seems to me that this is exactly what the primordial-debt theorists are doing: projecting such a notion backwards.

Really, the whole complex of ideas they are talking about—the notion that there is this thing called society, that we have a debt to it, that governments can speak for it, that it can be imagined as a sort of secular god—all of these ideas emerged together around the time of the French Revolution, or in its immediate wake. In other words, it was born alongside the idea of the modern nation-state.

We can already see them coming together clearly in the work of Auguste Comte, in early nineteenth-century France. Comte, a philosopher and political pamphleteer now most famous for having first coined the term "sociology," went so far, by the end of his life, as actually proposing a Religion of Society, which he called Positivism, broadly modeled on Medieval Catholicism, replete with vestments where all the buttons were on the back (so they couldn't be put on without the help of others). In his last work, which he called a "Positivist Catechism," he also laid down the first explicit theory of social debt. At one point someone asks an imaginary Priest of Positivism what he thinks of the notion of human rights. The priest scoffs at the idea. This is nonsense, he says, an error born of individualism. Positivism understands only duties. After all:

> We are born under a load of obligations of every kind, to our predecessors, to our successors, to our contemporaries. After our birth these obligations increase or accumulate before the point where we are capable of rendering anyone any service. On what human foundation, then, could one seat the idea of "rights"?[62]

While Comte doesn't use the word "debt," the sense is clear enough. We have already accumulated endless debts before we get to the age at which we can even think of paying them. By that time, there's no way to calculate to whom we even owe them. The only way to redeem ourselves is to dedicate ourselves to the service of Humanity as a whole.

In his lifetime, Comte was considered something of a crackpot, since he obviously was—but his ideas proved influential. His notion of unlimited obligations to society ultimately crystallized in the notion of the "social debt," a notion taken up among social reformers and, eventually, socialist politicians in many parts of Europe and abroad.[63] "We are all born as debtors to society": in France the notion of a social debt soon became something of a catchphrase, a slogan, and eventually a cliché.[64] The state, according to this view, was merely the administrator of an existential debt that all of us have to the society that created us, embodied not least in the fact that we all continue to be completely dependent on one another for our existence, even if we are not completely aware of how.

These are also the intellectual and political circles that shaped the thought of Emile Durkheim, the founder of the discipline of sociology that we know today, who in a way did Comte one better by arguing that all gods in all religions are always already projections of society— so an explicit religion of society would not even be necessary. All religions, for Durkheim, are simply ways of recognizing our mutual dependence on one another, a dependence that affects us in a million ways that we are never entirely aware of. "God" and "society" are ultimately the same.

The problem is that for several hundred years now, it has simply been assumed that the guardian of that debt we owe for all of this, the legitimate representatives of that amorphous social totality that has allowed us to become individuals, must necessarily be the state. Almost all socialist or socialistic regimes end up appealing to some version of this argument. To take one notorious example, this was how the Soviet Union used to justify forbidding their citizens from emigrating to other countries. The line was always: The USSR created these people, the USSR raised and educated them, made them who they are. What right do they have to take the product of our investment and transfer it to another country, as if they didn't owe us anything? Neither is this rhetoric restricted to socialist regimes. Nationalists appeal to exactly the same kind of arguments—especially in times of war. And all modern governments are nationalist to some degree.

One might even say that what we really have here, in the idea of primordial debt, is the ultimate nationalist myth. Once we owed our lives to the gods that created us, paid interest in the form of animal sacrifice, and ultimately paid back the principal with our lives. Now we owe it to the Nation that formed us, pay interest in the form of taxes, and when it comes time to defend the nation against its enemies, offer to pay it with our lives.

This is a great trap of the twentieth century: on one side is the logic of the market, where we like to imagine we all start out as individuals who don't owe each other anything. On the other is the logic of the state, where we all begin with a debt we can never truly pay. We are constantly told that they are opposites and that between them they contain the only real human possibilities. But it's a false dichotomy. States created markets. Markets require states. Neither could continue without the other, at least, in anything like the forms we would recognize today.

Chapter Four

CRUELTY AND REDEMPTION

*We will buy the poor for silver, the
needy for a pair of sandals.*

—*Amos* 2:6

THE READER MAY have noticed that there is an unresolved debate
between those who see money as a commodity and those who see it
as an IOU. So which one is it? By now, the answer should be obvious:
it's both. Keith Hart, probably the best-known current anthropological
authority on the subject, pointed this out many years ago. There are,
he famously observed, two sides to any coin:

> Look at a coin from your pocket. On one side is "heads"—the
> symbol of the political authority which minted the coin; on the
> other side is "tails"—the precise specification of the amount
> the coin is worth as payment in exchange. One side reminds us
> that states underwrite currencies and the money is originally a
> relation between persons in society, a token perhaps. The other
> reveals the coin as a thing, capable of entering into definite
> relations with other things.[1]

Clearly, money was not invented to overcome the inconveniences
of barter between neighbors—since neighbors would have no reason to
engage in barter in the first place. Still, a system of pure credit money
would have serious inconveniences as well. Credit money is based on
trust, and in competitive markets, trust itself becomes a scarce commodity. This is particularly true of dealings between strangers. Within
the Roman empire, a silver coin stamped with the image of Tiberius
might have circulated at a value considerably higher than the value of
the silver it contained. Ancient coins invariably circulated at a value
higher than their metal content.[2] This was largely because Tiberius's
government was willing to accept them at face value. However, the

Persian government probably wasn't, and the Mauryan and Chinese governments definitely would not. Very large numbers of Roman gold and silver coins did end up in India and even China; this is presumably the main reason that they were made of gold and silver to begin with.

What's true for a vast empire like Rome or China is obviously all the more true for a Sumerian or Greek city-state, let alone for the kind of broken checkerboard of kingdoms, towns, and tiny principalities that characterized most of Medieval Europe or India. As I've pointed out, often what was inside and what was outside were not especially clear. Within a community—a town, a city, a guild or religious society—pretty much anything could function as money, provided everyone knew there was *someone* willing to accept it to cancel out a debt. To offer one particularly striking example, in certain cities in nineteenth-century Siam, small change consisted entirely of porcelain Chinese gaming counters—basically, the equivalent of poker chips—issued by local casinos. If one of these casinos went out of business or lost its license, its owners would have to send a crier through the streets banging a gong and announcing that anyone holding such chits had three days to redeem them.[3] For major transactions, of course, currency that was also acceptable outside the community (usually silver or gold again) was ordinarily employed.

In a similar way, English shops, for many centuries, would issue their own wood or lead or leather token money. The practice was often technically illegal, but it continued until relatively recent times. Here is an example from the seventeenth century, by a certain Henry, who had a store at Stony Stratford, Buckinghamshire:

This is clearly a case of the same principle: Henry would provide small change in the form of IOUs redeemable at his store. As such, they might circulate broadly, at least among anyone who did regular business at that shop. But they were unlikely to travel very far from Stony Stratford—most tokens, in fact, never circulated more than a few blocks in any direction. For larger transactions, everyone, including Henry, expected money in a form that would be acceptable anywhere, including in Italy or France.[4]

Throughout most of history, even where we do find elaborate markets, we also find a complex jumble of different sorts of currency. Some of these may have originally emerged from barter between foreigners: the cacao money of Mesoamerica or salt money of Ethiopia are frequently cited examples.[5] Others arose from credit systems, or from arguments over what sort of goods should be acceptable to pay taxes or other debts. Such questions were often matters of endless contestation. One could often learn a lot about the balance of political forces in a given time and place by what sorts of things were acceptable as currency. For instance: in much the same way that colonial Virginia planters managed to pass a law obliging shopkeepers to accept their tobacco as currency, medieval Pomeranian peasants appear to have at certain points convinced their rulers to make taxes, fees, and customs duties, which were registered in Roman currency, payable in wine, cheese, peppers, chickens, eggs, and even herring—much to the annoyance of traveling merchants, who therefore had to either carry such things around in order to pay the tolls or buy them locally at prices that would have been more advantageous to their suppliers for that very reason.[6] This was in an area with a free peasantry, rather than serfs. They were in a relatively strong political position. In other times and places, the interests of lords and merchants prevailed instead.

Thus money is almost always something hovering between a commodity and a debt-token. This is probably why coins—pieces of silver or gold that are already valuable commodities in themselves but that, being stamped with the emblem of a local political authority, became even more valuable—still sit in our heads as the quintessential form of money. They most perfectly straddle the divide that defines what money is in the first place. What's more, the relation between the two was a matter of constant political contestation.

In other words, the battle between state and market, between governments and merchants, is not inherent to the human condition.

■ ■ ■ ■ ■

Our two origin stories—the myth of barter and the myth of primordial debt—may appear to be about as far apart as they could be, but in their own way, they are also two sides of the same coin. One assumes the other. It's only once we can imagine human life as a series of commercial transactions that we're capable of seeing our relation to the universe in terms of debt.

To illustrate, let me call a perhaps surprising witness, Friedrich Nietzsche, a man able to see with uncommon clarity what happens when you try to imagine the world in commercial terms.

Nietzsche's *On the Genealogy of Morals* appeared in 1887. In it, he begins with an argument that might well have been taken directly from Adam Smith—but he takes it a step further than Smith ever dared to, insisting that not just barter, but buying and selling itself, precede any other form of human relationship. The feeling of personal obligation, he observes,

> has its origin in the oldest and most primitive personal rela-
> tionship there is, in the relationship between seller and buyer,
> creditor and debtor. Here for the first time one person moved
> up against another person, here an individual *measured himself*
> against another individual. We have found no civilization still
> at such a low level that something of this relationship is not
> already perceptible. To set prices, to measure values, to think
> up equivalencies, to exchange things—that preoccupied man's
> very first thinking to such a degree that in a certain sense
> it's what thinking *itself* is. Here the oldest form of astuteness
> was bred; here, too, we can assume are the first beginnings of
> man's pride, his feeling of pre-eminence in relation to other
> animals. Perhaps our word "man" (*manas*) continues to ex-
> press directly something of *this* feeling of the self: the human
> being describes himself as a being which assesses values, which
> values and measures, as the "inherently calculating animal."
> Selling and buying, together with their psychological attributes,
> are even older than the beginnings of any form of social orga-
> nizations and groupings; out of the most rudimentary form of
> personal legal rights the budding feeling of exchange, contract,
> guilt, law, duty, and compensation was instead first *transferred*
> to the crudest and earliest social structures (in their relation-
> ships with similar social structures), along with the habit of
> comparing power with power, of measuring, of calculating.[7]

Smith, too, we will remember, saw the origins of language—and hence of human thought—as lying in our propensity to "exchange one thing for another," in which he also saw the origins of the market.[8] The urge to trade, to compare values, is the very thing that makes us intelligent beings, and different from other animals. Society comes later—which means our ideas about responsibilities to other people first take shape in strictly commercial terms.

Unlike with Smith, however, it never occurred to Nietzsche that you could have a world where all such transactions immediately cancel out. Any system of commercial accounting, he assumed, will produce creditors and debtors. In fact, he believed that it was from this very fact that human morality emerged. Note, he says, how the German word *schuld* means both "debt" and "guilt." At first, to be in debt was simply to be guilty, and creditors delighted in punishing debtors unable to repay their loans by inflicting "all sorts of humiliation and torture on the body of the debtor, for instance, cutting as much flesh off as seemed appropriate for the debt."[9] In fact, Nietzsche went so far as to insist that those original barbarian law codes that tabulated so much for a ruined eye, so much for a severed finger, were not originally meant to fix rates of monetary compensation for the loss of eyes and fingers, but to establish how much of the debtor's body creditors were allowed to take! Needless to say, he doesn't provide a scintilla of evidence for this (none exists).[10] But to ask for evidence would be to miss the point. We are dealing here not with a real historical argument but with a purely imaginative exercise.

When humans did begin to form communities, Nietzsche continues, they necessarily began to imagine their relationship to the community in these terms. The tribe provides them with peace and security. They are therefore in its debt. Obeying its laws is a way of paying it back ("paying your debt to society" again). But this debt, he says, is also paid—here too—in sacrifice:

> Within the original tribal cooperatives—we're talking about primeval times—the living generation always acknowledged a legal obligation to the previous generations, and especially to the earliest one which had founded the tribe [. . .] Here the reigning conviction is that the tribe only *exists* at all only because of the sacrifices and achievements of its ancestors—and that people have to *pay them back* with sacrifices and achievements. In this people recognize a *debt* which keeps steadily growing because these ancestors in their continuing existence as powerful spirits do not stop giving the tribe new advantages and lending them their power. Do they do this for free? But there is no "for free" for those raw and "spiritually destitute" ages. What can people give back to them? Sacrifices (at first as nourishment understood very crudely), festivals, chapels, signs of honor, above all, obedience—for all customs, as work of one's ancestors, are also their statutes and commands. Do people ever give them enough? This suspicion remains and grows.[11]

In other words, for Nietzsche, starting from Adam Smith's assumptions about human nature means we must necessarily end up with something very much along the lines of primordial-debt theory. On the one hand, it is because of our feeling of debt to the ancestors that we obey the ancestral laws: this is why we feel that the community has the right to react "like an angry creditor" and punish us for our transgressions if we break them. In a larger sense, we develop a creeping feeling that we could never really pay back the ancestors, that no sacrifice (not even the sacrifice of our first-born) will ever truly redeem us. We are terrified of the ancestors, and the stronger and more powerful a community becomes, the more powerful they seem to be, until finally, "the ancestor is necessarily transfigured into a god." As communities grow into kingdoms and kingdoms into universal empires, the gods themselves come to seem more universal, they take on grander, more cosmic pretentions, ruling the heavens, casting thunderbolts—culminating in the Christian god, who, as the maximal deity, necessarily "brought about the maximum feeling of indebtedness on earth." Even our ancestor Adam is no longer figured as a creditor, but as a transgressor, and therefore a debtor, who passes on to us his burden of Original Sin:

> Finally, with the impossibility of discharging the debt, people also come up with the notion that it is impossible to remove the penance, the idea that it cannot be paid off ("*eternal* punishment") . . . until all of a sudden we confront the paradoxical and horrifying expedient with which a martyred humanity found temporary relief, that stroke of genius of *Christianity*: God sacrificing himself for the guilt of human beings, God paying himself back with himself, God as the only one who can redeem man from what for human beings has become impossible to redeem—the creditor sacrificing himself for the debtor, out of *love* (can people believe that?), out of love for his debtor![12]

It all makes perfect sense if you start from Nietzsche's initial premise. The problem is that the premise is insane.

There is also every reason to believe that Nietzsche knew the premise was insane; in fact, that this was the entire point. What Nietzsche is doing here is starting out from the standard, common-sense assumptions about the nature of human beings prevalent in his day (and to a large extent, still prevalent)—that we are rational calculating machines, that commercial self-interest comes before society, that "society" itself is just a way of putting a kind of temporary lid on the resulting conflict. That is, he is starting out from ordinary bourgeois assumptions and driving them to a place where they can only shock a bourgeois audience.

It's a worthy game and no one has ever played it better; but it's a game played entirely within the boundaries of bourgeois thought. It has nothing to say to anything that lies beyond it. The best response to anyone who wants to take seriously Nietzsche's fantasies about savage hunters chopping pieces off each other's bodies for failure to remit are the words of an actual hunter-gatherer—an Inuit from Greenland made famous in the Danish writer Peter Freuchen's *Book of the Eskimo*. Freuchen tells how one day, after coming home hungry from an unsuccessful walrus-hunting expedition, he found one of the successful hunters dropping off several hundred pounds of meat. He thanked him. The man objected indignantly:

> "Up in our country we are human!" said the hunter. "And since we are human we help each other. We don't like to hear anybody say thanks for that. What I get today you may get tomorrow. Up here we say that by gifts one makes slaves and by whips one makes dogs."[13]

The last line is something of an anthropological classic, and similar statements about the refusal to calculate credits and debits can be found throughout the anthropological literature on egalitarian hunting societies. Rather than seeing himself as human because he could make economic calculations, the hunter insisted that being truly human meant *refusing* to make such calculations, refusing to measure or remember who had given what to whom, for the precise reason that doing so would inevitably create a world where we began "comparing power with power, measuring, calculating" and reducing each other to slaves or dogs through debt.

It's not that he, like untold millions of similar egalitarian spirits throughout history, was unaware that humans have a propensity to calculate. If he wasn't aware of it, he could not have said what he did. Of course we have a propensity to calculate. We have all sorts of propensities. In any real-life situation, we have propensities that drive us in several different contradictory directions simultaneously. No one is more real than any other. The real question is which we take as the foundation of our humanity and therefore, make the basis of our civilization. If Nietzsche's analysis of debt is helpful to us, then, it is because it reveals that when we start from the assumption that human thought is essentially a matter of commercial calculation, that buying and selling are the basis of human society—then, yes, once we begin to think about our relationship with the cosmos, we will necessarily conceive of it in terms of debt.

■ ■ ■ ■ ■

I do think Nietzsche helps us in another way as well: to understand the concept of redemption. Niezsche's account of "primeval times" might be absurd, but his description of Christianity—of how a sense of debt is transformed into an abiding sense of guilt, and guilt to self-loathing, and self-loathing to self-torture—all of this does ring very true.

Why, for instance, do we refer to Christ as the "redeemer"? The primary meaning of "redemption" is to buy something back, or to recover something that had been given up in security for a loan; to acquire something by paying off a debt. It is rather striking to think that the very core of the Christian message, salvation itself, the sacrifice of God's own son to rescue humanity from eternal damnation, should be framed in the language of a financial transaction.

Nietzsche might have been playfully adopting the same assumptions as Adam Smith, but clearly the early Christians were not. The roots of this thinking lie deeper than Smith's with his nation of shopkeepers. The authors of the Brahmanas were not alone in borrowing the language of the marketplace as a way of thinking about the human condition. Indeed, to one degree or another, all the major world religions did.

The reason is that all of them—from Zoroastrianism to Islam—arose amidst intense arguments about the role of money and the market in human life, and particularly about what these institutions meant for fundamental questions of what human beings owed to one another. The question of debt, and arguments about debt, ran through every aspect of the political life of the time. These arguments were set amidst revolts, petitions, and reformist movements. Some such movements gained allies in the temples and palaces. Others were brutally suppressed. Most of the terms, slogans, and specific issues being debated, though, have been lost to history. We just don't have any idea what a political argument in a Syrian tavern in, say, 750 BC was likely to have been like. As a result, we have spent thousands of years contemplating sacred texts full of political allusions that would have been instantly recognizable to any reader at the time when they were written, but whose meaning we now can only guess at.[14]

One of the unusual things about the Bible is that it preserves some bits of this larger context. To return to the notion of redemption: the Hebrew words *padah* and *goal*, both translated as "redemption," could be used for buying back anything one had sold to someone else, particularly the recovery of ancestral land, or to recovering some object held by creditors in way of a pledge.[15] The example foremost in the minds of prophets and theologians seems to have been the last: the redemption of pledges and especially, of family members held as debt-pawns. It would seem that the economy of the Hebrew kingdoms, by the time of the prophets, was already beginning to develop the same kinds of debt crises that had long been common in Mesopotamia: especially in years of bad harvests, as the poor became indebted to rich neighbors or to wealthy moneylenders in the towns, they would begin to lose title to their fields and to become tenants on what had been their own land, and their sons and daughters would be removed to serve as servants in their creditors' households, or even sold abroad as slaves.[16] The earlier prophets contain allusions to such crises, but the book of Nehemiah, written in Persian times, is the most explicit:[17]

> Some also there were that said, "We have mortgaged our lands, vineyards, and houses, that we might buy corn, because of the dearth."
>
> There were also those that said, "We have borrowed money for the king's tribute, and that upon our lands and vineyards.
>
> "Yet now our flesh is as the flesh of our brethren, our children as their children: and, lo, we bring into bondage our sons and our daughters to be servants, and some of our daughters are brought unto bondage already: neither is it in our power to redeem them; for other men have our lands and vineyards."
>
> And I was very angry when I heard their cry and these words.
>
> Then I consulted with myself, and I rebuked the nobles, and the rulers, and said unto them, "Ye exact usury, every one of his brother." And I set a great assembly against them.[18]

Nehemiah was a Jew born in Babylon, a former cup-bearer to the Persian emperor. In 444 BC, he managed to talk the Great King into appointing him governor of his native Judaea. He also received permission to rebuild the Temple in Jerusalem that had been destroyed by Nebuchadnezzar more than two centuries earlier. In the course of rebuilding, sacred texts were recovered and restored; in a sense, this was the moment of the creation of what we now consider Judaism.

But as soon as Nehemiah returned home, he found himself confronted with a social crisis. All around him, impoverished peasants were unable to pay their taxes; creditors were carrying off the children of the poor. His first response was to issue a classic Babylonian-style "clean

slate" edict—having himself been born in Babylon, he was clearly familiar with the general principle. All non-commercial debts were to be
forgiven. Maximum interest rates were set. At the same time, though,
Nehemiah managed to locate, revise, and reissue much older Jewish
laws, now preserved in Exodus, Deuteronomy, and Leviticus, which
in certain ways went even further, by institutionalizing the principle.[19]
The most famous of these is the Law of Jubilee: a law that stipulated
that all debts would be automatically canceled "in the Sabbath year"
(that is, after seven years had passed), and that all who languished in
bondage owing to such debts would be released.[20]

In the Bible, as in Mesopotamia, "freedom," came to refer above
all to release from the effects of debt. Over time, the history of the Jewish people itself came to be interpreted in this light: the liberation from
bondage in Egypt was God's first, paradigmatic act of redemption; the
historical tribulations of the Jews (defeat, conquest, exile) were seen
as misfortunes that would eventually lead to a final redemption with
the coming of the Messiah—though this could only be accomplished,
prophets such as Jeremiah warned them, after the Jewish people truly
repented of their sins (carrying each other off into bondage, whoring
after false gods, the violation of commandments).[21] In this light, the
adoption of the term by Christians is hardly surprising. Redemption
was a release from one's burden of sin and guilt, and the end of history
would be that moment when all slates are wiped clean and all debts
finally lifted, when a great blast from angelic trumpets will announce
the final Jubilee.

If so, "redemption" is no longer about buying something back.
It's really more a matter of destroying the entire system of accounting. In many Middle Eastern cities, this was literally true: one of the
common acts during debt cancellation was the ceremonial destruction
of the tablets on which financial records had been kept, an act to be
repeated, much less officially, in just about every major peasant revolt
in history.[22]

This leads to another problem: What is possible in the meantime,
before that final redemption comes? In one of his more disturbing
parables, the Parable of the Unforgiving Servant, Jesus seemed to be
explicitly playing with the problem:

> Therefore, the kingdom of heaven is like a king who wanted to
> settle accounts with his servants. As he began the settlement, a
> man who owed him ten thousand talents was brought to him.
> Since he was not able to pay, the master ordered that he and

his wife and his children and all that he had be sold to repay the debt.

The servant fell on his knees before him. "Be patient with me," he begged, "and I will pay back everything." The servant's master took pity on him, canceled the debt, and let him go.

But when that servant went out, he found one of his fellow servants who owed him a hundred denarii. He grabbed him and began to choke him. "Pay back what you owe me!" he demanded.

His fellow servant fell to his knees and begged him, "Be patient with me, and I will pay you back."

But he refused. Instead, he went off and had the man thrown into prison until he could pay the debt. When the other servants saw what had happened, they were greatly distressed and went and told their master everything that had happened.

Then the master called the servant in. "You wicked servant," he said, "I canceled all that debt of yours because you begged me to. Shouldn't you have had mercy on your fellow servant just as I had on you?" In anger his master turned him over to the jailers to be tortured, until he should pay back all he owed.[23]

This is quite an extraordinary text. On one level it's a joke; in others, it could hardly be more serious.

We begin with the king wishing to "settle accounts" with his servants. The premise is absurd. Kings, like gods, can't really enter into relations of exchange with their subjects, since no parity is possible. And this is a king who clearly *is* God. Certainly there can be no final settling of accounts.

So at best we are dealing with an act of whimsy on the king's part. The absurdity of the premise is hammered home by the sum the first man brought before him is said to owe. In ancient Judaea, to say someone owes a creditor "ten thousand talents" would be like now saying someone owes "a hundred billion dollars." The number is a joke, too; it simply stands in for "a sum no human being could ever conceivably repay."[24]

Faced with infinite, existential debt, the servant can only tell obvious lies: "A hundred billion? Sure, I'm good for it! Just give me a little more time." Then, suddenly, apparently just as arbitrarily, the Lord forgives him.

Yet, it turns out, the amnesty has a condition he is not aware of. It is incumbent on his being willing to act in an analogous way to other humans—in this particular case, another servant who owes him (to translate again into contemporary terms), maybe a thousand bucks. Failing the test, the human is cast into hell for all eternity, or "until he should pay back all he owed," which in this case comes down to the same thing.

The parable has long been a challenge to theologians. It's normally interpreted as a comment on the endless bounty of God's grace and how little He demands of us in comparison—and thus, by implication, as a way of suggesting that torturing us in hell for all eternity is not as unreasonable as it might otherwise seem. Certainly, the unforgiving servant is a genuinely odious character. Still, what is even more striking to me is the tacit suggestion that forgiveness, in this world, is ultimately impossible. Christians practically say as much every time they recite the Lord's Prayer and ask God to "forgive us our debts, as we also forgive our debtors."[25] It repeats the story of the parable almost exactly, and the implications are similarly dire. After all, most Christians reciting the prayer are aware that they do not generally forgive their debtors. Why then should God forgive them their sins?[26]

What's more, there is the lingering suggestion that we really couldn't live up to those standards even if we tried. One of the things that makes the Jesus of the New Testament such a tantalizing character is that it's never clear what he's telling us. Everything can be read two ways. When he calls on his followers to forgive all debts, refuse to cast the first stone, turn the other cheek, love their enemies, to hand over their possessions to the poor—is he really expecting them to do this? Or are such demands just a way of throwing in their faces that, since we are clearly not prepared to act this way, we are all sinners whose salvation can only come in another world—a position that can be (and has been) used to justify almost anything? This is a vision of human life as inherently corrupt, but it also frames even spiritual affairs in commercial terms: with calculations of sin, penance, and absolution, the Devil and St. Peter with their rival ledger books, usually accompanied by the creeping feeling that it's all a charade because the very fact that we are reduced to playing such a game of tabulating sins reveals us to be fundamentally unworthy of forgiveness.

World religions, as we shall see, are full of this kind of ambivalence. On the one hand they are outcries against the market; on the other, they tend to frame their objections in commercial terms—as if to argue that turning human life into a series of transactions is not a very good deal. What I think even these few examples reveal, though, is how much is being papered over in the conventional accounts of the origins and history of money. There is something almost touchingly naïve in the stories about neighbors swapping potatoes for an extra pair of shoes. When the ancients thought about money, friendly swaps were hardly the first thing that came to mind.

True, some might have thought about their tab at the local ale-house or, if they were a merchant or administrator, of storehouses, account books, exotic imported delights. For most, though, what was likely to come to mind was the selling of slaves and ransoming of prisoners, corrupt tax-farmers and the depredations of conquering armies, mortgages and interest, theft and extortion, revenge and punishment, and, above all, the tension between the need for money to create families, to acquire a bride so as to have children, and use of that same money to destroy families—to create debts that lead to the same wife and children being taken away. "Some of our daughters are brought unto bondage already: neither is it in our power to redeem them." One can only imagine what those words meant, emotionally, to a father in a patriarchal society in which a man's ability to protect the honor of his family was everything. Yet this is what money meant to the majority of people for most of human history: the terrifying prospect of one's sons and daughters being carried off to the homes of repulsive strangers to clean their pots and provide occasional sexual services, to be subject to every conceivable form of violence and abuse, possibly for years, conceivably forever, as their parents waited, helpless, avoiding eye contact with their neighbors, who knew exactly what was happening to those they were supposed to have been able to protect.[27] Clearly, this was the worst thing that could happen to anyone—which is why, in the parable, it could be treated as interchangeable with being "turned over to the jailors to be tortured" for life. And that's just from the perspective of the father. One can only imagine how it might have felt to be the daughter. Yet, over the course of human history, untold millions of daughters have known (and in fact many still know) exactly what it's like.

One might object that this was just assumed to be in the nature of things: like the imposition of tribute on conquered populations, it might have been resented, but it wasn't considered a moral issue, a matter of right and wrong. Some things just happen. This has been the most common attitude of peasants to such phenomena throughout human history. What's striking about the historical record is that in the case of debt crises, this was *not* how many reacted. Many actually did become indignant. So many, in fact, that most of our contemporary language of social justice, our way of speaking of human bondage and emancipation, continues to echo ancient arguments about debt.

It's particularly striking because so many other things do seem to have been accepted as simply in the nature of things. One does not see a similar outcry against caste systems, for example, or for that matter, the institution of slavery.[28] Surely slaves and untouchables often experienced at least equal horrors. No doubt many protested their condition. Why was it that the debtors' protests seemed to carry such greater moral weight? Why were debtors so much more effective in winning the ear of priests, prophets, officials, and social reformers? Why was it that officials like Nehemiah were willing to give such sympathetic consideration to their complaints, to inveigh, to summon great assemblies?

Some have suggested practical reasons: debt crises destroyed the free peasantry, and it was free peasants who were drafted into ancient armies to fight in wars.[29] Rulers thus had a vested interest in maintaining their recruitment base. No doubt this was a factor; clearly, it wasn't the only one. There is no reason to believe that Nehemiah, for instance, in his anger at the usurers, was primarily concerned with his ability to levy troops for the Persian king. It had to be something deeper.

What makes debt different is that it is premised on an assumption of equality.

To be a slave, or lower caste, is to be intrinsically inferior. These are relations of unadulterated hierarchy. In the case of debt, we are talking about two individuals who begin as equal parties to a contract. Legally, at least as far as the contract is concerned, they are the same.

We can add that, in the ancient world, when people who actually were more or less social equals loaned money to one another, the terms appear to have normally been quite generous. Often no interest was charged, or if it was, it was very low. "And don't charge me interest," wrote one wealthy Canaanite to another, in a tablet dated around 1200 BC, "after all, we are both gentlemen."[30] Between close kin, many "loans" were probably, then as now, just gifts that no one seriously expected to recover. Loans between rich and poor were something else again.

The problem was that, unlike status distinctions like caste or slavery, the line between rich and poor was never precisely drawn. One can imagine the reaction of a farmer who went up to the house of a wealthy cousin, on the assumption that "humans help each other," and ended up, a year or two later, watching his vineyard seized and his sons and daughters led away. Such behavior could be justified, in legal terms, by insisting that the loan was not a form of mutual aid but a commercial relationship—a contract is a contract. (It also required a certain reliable access to superior force.) But it could only have felt like a terrible betrayal. What's more, framing it as a breach of contract meant stating that this was, in fact, a moral issue: these two parties *ought* to be equals, but one had failed to honor the bargain. Psychologically, this can only have made the indignity of the debtor's condition all the more painful, since it made it possible to say that it was his own turpitude that sealed his daughter's fate. But that just made the motive all the more compelling to throw back the moral aspersions: "Our flesh is as the flesh of our brethren, our children as their children." We are all the same people. We have a responsibility to take account of one another's needs and interests. How, then, could my brother do such a thing to me?

In the Old Testament case, debtors were able to marshal a particularly powerful moral argument—as the authors of Deuteronomy constantly reminded their readers, were not the Jews all slaves in Egypt, and had they not all been redeemed by God? Was it right, when they had all been given this promised land to share, for some to take that land away from others? Was it right for a population of liberated slaves to go about enslaving one another's children?[31] But analogous arguments were being made in similar situations almost everywhere in the ancient world: in Athens, in Rome, and for that matter, in China—where legend had it that coinage itself was first invented by an ancient emperor to redeem the children of families who had been forced to sell them after a series of devastating floods.

Throughout most of history, when overt political conflict between classes did appear, it took the form of pleas for debt cancellation—the freeing of those in bondage and, usually, a more just reallocation of the land. What we see in the Bible and other religious traditions are traces of the moral arguments by which such claims were justified, usually subject to all sorts of imaginative twists and turns, but inevitably, to some degree, incorporating the language of the marketplace itself.

Chapter Five

A BRIEF TREATISE ON THE MORAL
GROUNDS OF ECONOMIC RELATIONS

TO TELL THE HISTORY of debt, then, is also necessarily to reconstruct how the language of the marketplace has come to pervade every aspect of human life—even to provide the terminology for the moral and religious voices raised against it. We have already seen how both Vedic and Christian teachings thus end up making the same curious move: first describing all morality as debt, but then, in their very manner of doing so, demonstrating that morality cannot really be reduced to debt, that it must be grounded in something else.[1]

But what? Religious traditions prefer vast, cosmological answers: the alternative to the morality of debt lies in recognition of continuity with the universe, or life in the expectation of the imminent annihilation of the universe, or absolute subordination to the deity, or withdrawal into another world. My own aims are more modest, so I will take the opposite approach. If we really want to understand the moral grounds of economic life and, by extension, human life, it seems to me that we must start instead with the very small things: the everyday details of social existence, the way we treat our friends, enemies, and children—often with gestures so tiny (passing the salt, bumming a cigarette) that we rarely stop to think about them at all. Anthropology has shown us just how different and numerous are the ways in which humans have been known to organize themselves. But it also reveals some remarkable commonalities—fundamental moral principles that appear to exist everywhere and that will always tend to be invoked wherever people transfer objects back and forth or argue about what other people owe them.

One of the reasons that human life is so complicated, in turn, is because many of these principles contradict one another. As we will see, they are constantly pulling us in different directions. The moral logic of exchange, and hence of debt, is only one; in any given situation, there are likely to be completely different principles that could be brought to bear. In this sense, the moral confusion discussed in the first chapter is hardly new; in a sense, moral thought is founded on this tension.

■ ■ ■ ■ ■

To really understand what debt is, then, it will be necessary to understand how it's different from other sorts of obligation that human beings might have to one another—which, in turn, means mapping out what those other sorts of obligation actually are. Doing so, however, poses peculiar challenges. Contemporary social theory—economic anthropology included—offers surprisingly little help in this regard. There's a vast anthropological literature on gifts, for instance, starting with the French anthropologist Marcel Mauss's essay "The Gift" in 1924, as well as on "gift economies" that operate on completely different principles than market economies—but in the end, almost all this literature concentrates on the exchange of gifts, assuming that whenever one gives a gift, this act incurs a debt, and the recipient must eventually reciprocate in kind. Much as in the case of the great religions, the logic of the marketplace has insinuated itself even into the thinking of those who are most explicitly opposed to it. As a result, I am going to have to start over here, to create a new theory, pretty much from scratch.

Part of the problem is the extraordinary place that economics currently holds in the social sciences. In many ways it is treated as a kind of master discipline. Just about anyone who runs anything important in America is expected to have some training in economic theory, or at least to be familiar with its basic tenets. As a result, those tenets have come to be treated as received wisdom, as basically beyond question (one knows one is in the presence of received wisdom when, if one challenges some tenet of it, the first reaction is to treat one as simply ignorant— "You obviously have never heard of the Laffer Curve"; "Clearly you need a course in Economics 101"—the theory is seen as so obviously true that no one exposed to it could possibly disagree). What's more, those branches of social theory that make the greatest claims to "scientific status"—"rational choice theory," for instance—start from the same assumptions about human psychology that economists do: that human beings are best viewed as self-interested actors calculating how to get the best terms possible out of any situation, the most profit or pleasure or happiness for the least sacrifice or investment—curious, considering experimental psychologists have demonstrated over and over again that these assumptions simply aren't true.[2]

From early on, there were those who wished to create a theory of social interaction grounded in a more generous view of human nature—who insisted that moral life comes down to something more than mutual advantage, that it is motivated above all by a sense of justice. The key term here became "reciprocity," the sense of equity, balance, fairness, and symmetry, embodied in our image of justice as a set of scales. Economic transactions were just one variant of the principle of balanced exchange—and one that had a notorious tendency to go awry. But if one examines matters closely, one finds that all human relations are based on some variation on reciprocity.

In the 1950s, '60s, and '70s, there was something of a craze for this sort of thing, in the guise of what was then called "exchange theory," developed in infinite variations, from George Homans' "Social Exchange Theory" in the United States to Claude Levi-Strauss's Structuralism in France. Levi-Strauss, who became a kind of intellectual god in anthropology, made the extraordinary argument that human life could be imagined as consisting of three spheres: language (which consisted of the exchange of words), kinship (which consisted of the exchange of women), and economics (which consisted of the exchange of things). All three, he insisted, were governed by the same fundamental law of reciprocity.[3]

Levi-Strauss's star is fallen now, and such extreme statements seem, in retrospect, a little bit ridiculous. Still, it's not as if anyone has proposed a bold new theory to replace all this. Instead, the assumptions have simply retreated into the background. Almost everyone continues to assume that in its fundamental nature, social life is based on the principle of reciprocity, and therefore that all human interaction can best be understood as a kind of exchange. If so, then debt really is at the root of all morality, because debt is what happens when some balance has not yet been restored.

But can all justice really be reduced to reciprocity? It's easy enough to come up with forms of reciprocity that don't seem particularly just. "Do unto others as you would wish others to do unto you" might seem like an excellent foundation for a system of ethics, but for most of us, "an eye for an eye" does not evoke justice so much as vindictive brutality.[4] "One good turn deserves another" is a pleasant sentiment, but "I'll scratch your back, you scratch mine" is shorthand for political corruption. Conversely, there are relationships that seem clearly moral but appear to have nothing to do with reciprocity. The relation between mother and child is an oft-cited example. Most of us learn our sense of justice and morality first from our parents. Yet it is extremely difficult to see the relation between parent and child as particularly reciprocal.

Would we really be willing to conclude that therefore it is not a moral relationship? That it has nothing to do with justice?

The Canadian novelist Margaret Atwood begins her recent book on debt with a similar paradox:

> Nature Writer Ernest Thompson Seton had an odd bill presented to him on his twenty-first birthday. It was a record kept by his father of all the expenses connected with young Ernest's childhood and youth, including the fee charged by the doctor for delivering him. Even more oddly, Ernest is said to have paid it. I used to think that Mr. Seton Senior was a jerk, but now I'm wondering.[5]

Most of us wouldn't wonder much. Such behavior seems monstrous, inhuman. Certainly Seton found it so: he paid the bill, but never spoke to his father again afterward.[6] And in a way, this is precisely why the presentation of such a bill seems so outrageous. Squaring accounts means that the two parties have the ability to walk away from each other. By presenting it, his father suggested he'd just as soon have nothing further to do with him.

In other words, while most of us can imagine what we owe to our parents as a kind of debt, few of us can imagine being able to actually pay it—or even that such a debt ever *should* be paid. Yet if it can't be paid, in what sense is it a "debt" at all? And if it is not a debt, what is it?

■ ■ ■ ■ ■

One obvious place to look for alternatives is in cases of human interaction in which expectations of reciprocity seem to slam into a wall. Nineteenth-century travelers' accounts, for instance, are full of this sort of thing. Missionaries working in certain parts of Africa would often be astounded by the reactions they would receive when they administered medicines. Here's a typical example, from a British missionary in Congo:

> A day or two after we reached Vana we found one of the natives very ill with pneumonia. Comber treated him and kept him alive on strong fowl-soup; a great deal of careful nursing and attention was visited on him, for his house was beside the camp. When we were ready to go on our way again, the man

was well. To our astonishment he came and asked us for a present, and was as astonished and disgusted as he had made us to be, when we declined giving it. We suggested that it was his place to bring us a present and to show some gratitude. He said to us, "Well indeed! You white men have no shame!"[7]

In the early decades of the twentieth century, the French philosopher Lucien Levy-Bruhl, in an attempt to prove that "natives" operated with an entirely different form of logic, compiled a list of similar stories: for instance, of a man saved from drowning who proceeded to ask his rescuer to give him some nice clothes to wear, or another who, on being nursed back to health after having been savaged by a tiger, demanded a knife. One French missionary working in Central Africa insisted that such things happened to him on a regular basis:

You save a person's life, and you must expect to receive a visit from him before long; you are now under an obligation to him, and you will not get rid of him except by giving him presents.[8]

Now, certainly, there is almost always felt to be something extraordinary about saving a life. Anything surrounding birth and death almost cannot help but partake of the infinite, and, therefore, throw all everyday means of moral calculation askew. This is probably why stories like this had become something of a cliché in America when I was growing up. I remember as a child several times being told that among the Inuit (or sometimes it was among Buddhists, or Chinese, but, curiously, never Africans)—that if one saves someone else's life, one is considered responsible for taking care of that person forever. It defies our sense of reciprocity. But, somehow, it also makes a weird kind of sense.

We have no way of knowing what was really going on in the minds of the patients in these stories, since we don't know who they were or what sort of expectations they had (how they normally interacted with their doctors, for example). But we can guess. Let's try a thought experiment. Imagine that we are dealing with a place where if one man saved another's life, the two became like brothers. Each was now expected to share everything and to provide for the other when he was in need. If so, the patient would surely notice that his new brother appeared to be extraordinarily wealthy, not in much need of anything, but that he, the patient, was lacking in many things the missionary could provide.

Alternately (and more likely), imagine that we are dealing not with a relationship of radical equality but the very opposite. In many parts of Africa, accomplished curers were also important political figures with extensive clienteles of former patients. A would-be follower thus arrives to declare his political allegiance. What complicates the matter in this case is that followers of great men, in this part of Africa, were in a relatively strong bargaining position. Good henchmen were hard to come by; important people were expected to be generous with followers to keep them from joining some rival's entourage instead. If so, asking for a shirt or knife would be a way of asking for confirmation that the missionary does wish to have the man as a follower. Paying him back, in contrast, would be, like Seton's gesture to his father, an insult: a way of saying that despite the missionary having saved his life, he would just as soon have nothing further to do with him.

This is a thought experiment—again, we don't really know what the African patients were thinking. My point is that such forms of radical equality and radical inequality do exist in the world, that each carries within it its own kind of morality, its own way of thinking and arguing about the rights and wrongs of any given situation, and these moralities are entirely different than that of tit-for-tat exchange. In the rest of the chapter, I will provide a rough-and-ready way to map out the main possibilities, by proposing that there are three main moral principles on which economic relations can be founded, all of which occur in any human society, and which I will call communism, hierarchy, and exchange.

Communism

I will define communism here as any human relationship that operates on the principles of "from each according to their abilities, to each according to their needs."

I admit that the usage here is a bit provocative. "Communism" is a word that can evoke strong emotional reactions—mainly, of course, because we tend to identify it with "communist" regimes. This is ironic, since the Communist parties that ruled over the USSR and its satellites, and that still rule China and Cuba, never described their own systems as "communist." They described them as "socialist." "Communism" was always a distant, somewhat fuzzy utopian ideal, usually to be accompanied by the withering away of the state—to be achieved at some point in the distant future.

Our thinking about communism has been dominated by a myth. Once upon a time, humans held all things in common—whether in the Garden of Eden, during the Golden Age of Saturn, or in Paleolithic hunter-gatherer bands. Then came the Fall, as a result of which we are now cursed with divisions of power and private property. The dream was that someday, with the advance of technology and general prosperity, with social revolution or the guidance of the Party, we would finally be in a position to put things back, to restore common ownership and common management of collective resources. Throughout the last two centuries, Communists and anti-Communists argued over how plausible this picture was and whether it would be a blessing or a nightmare. But they all agreed on the basic framework: communism was about collective property, "primitive communism" did once exist in the distant past, and someday it might return.

We might call this "mythic communism"—or even "epic communism"—a story we like to tell ourselves. Since the days of the French Revolution, it has inspired millions; but it has also done enormous damage to humanity. It's high time, I think, to brush the entire argument aside. In fact, "communism" is not some magical utopia, and neither does it have anything to do with ownership of the means of production. It is something that exists right now—that exists, to some degree, in any human society, although there has never been one in which *everything* has been organized in that way, and it would be difficult to imagine how there could be. All of us act like communists a good deal of the time. None of us act like a communist consistently. "Communist society"—in the sense of a society organized exclusively on that single principle—could never exist. But all social systems, even economic systems like capitalism, have always been built on top of a bedrock of actually-existing communism.

Starting, as I say, from the principle of "from each according to their abilities, to each according to their needs" allows us to look past the question of individual or private ownership (which is often little more than formal legality anyway) and at much more immediate and practical questions of who has access to what sorts of things and under what conditions.[9] Whenever it is the operative principle, even if it's just two people who are interacting, we can say we are in the presence of a sort of communism.

Almost everyone follows this principle if they are collaborating on some common project.[10] If someone fixing a broken water pipe says,

"Hand me the wrench," his co-worker will not, generally speaking, say, "And what do I get for it?"—even if they are working for Exxon-Mobil, Burger King, or Goldman Sachs. The reason is simple efficiency (ironically enough, considering the conventional wisdom that "communism just doesn't work"): if you really care about getting something done, the most efficient way to go about it is obviously to allocate tasks by ability and give people whatever they need to do them.[11] One might even say that it's one of the scandals of capitalism that most capitalist firms, internally, operate communistically. True, they don't tend to operate very democratically. Most often they are organized around military-style top-down chains of command. But there is often an interesting tension here, because top-down chains of command are not particularly efficient: they tend to promote stupidity among those on top and resentful foot-dragging among those on the bottom. The greater the need to improvise, the more democratic the cooperation tends to become. Inventors have always understood this, start-up capitalists frequently figure it out, and computer engineers have recently rediscovered the principle: not only with things like freeware, which everyone talks about, but even in the organization of their businesses.

This is presumably also why in the immediate wake of great disasters—a flood, a blackout, or an economic collapse—people tend to behave the same way, reverting to a rough-and-ready communism. However briefly, hierarchies and markets and the like become luxuries that no one can afford. Anyone who has lived through such a moment can speak to their peculiar qualities, the way that strangers become sisters and brothers and human society itself seems to be reborn. This is important, because it shows that we are not simply talking about cooperation. In fact, *communism is the foundation of all human sociability*. It is what makes society possible. There is always an assumption that anyone who is not an enemy can be expected to act on the principle of "from each according to their abilities," at least to an extent: for example, if one needs to figure out how to get somewhere and the other knows the way.

We so take this for granted, in fact, that the exceptions are themselves revealing. E.E. Evans-Pritchard, an anthropologist who in the 1920s carried out research among the Nuer, Nilotic pastoralists in southern Sudan, reports his discomfiture when he realized that someone had intentionally given him wrong directions:

> On one occasion I asked the way to a certain place and was
> deliberately deceived. I returned in chagrin to camp and asked

the people why they had told me the wrong way. One of them replied, "You are a foreigner, why should we tell you the right way? Even if a Nuer who was a stranger asked us the way we would say to him, 'You continue straight along that path,' but we would not tell him that the path forked. Why should we tell him? But you are now a member of our camp and you are kind to our children, so we will tell you the right way in future."[12]

The Nuer are constantly engaged in feuds; any stranger might well turn out to be an enemy there to scout out a good place for an ambush, and it would be unwise to give such a person useful information. What's more, Evans-Pritchard's own situation was obviously relevant, since he was an agent of the British government—the same government that had recently sent in the RAF to strafe and bomb the inhabitants of this very settlement before forcibly resettling them there. Under the circumstances, the inhabitants' treatment of Evans-Pritchard seems quite generous. The main point, though, is that it requires something on this scale—an immediate threat to life and limb, terror-bombing of civilian populations—before people will ordinarily consider not giving a stranger accurate directions.[13]

It's not just directions. Conversation is a domain particularly disposed to communism. Lies, insults, put-downs, and other sorts of verbal aggression are important—but they derive most of their power from the shared assumption that people do not ordinarily act this way: an insult does not sting unless one assumes that others will normally be considerate of one's feelings, and it's impossible to lie to someone who does not assume you would ordinarily tell the truth. When we genuinely wish to break off amicable relations with someone, we stop speaking to them entirely.

The same goes for small courtesies like asking for a light, or even for a cigarette. It seems more legitimate to ask a stranger for a cigarette than for an equivalent amount of cash, or even food; in fact, if one has been identified as a fellow smoker, it's rather difficult to refuse such a request. In such cases—a match, a piece of information, holding the elevator—one might say the "from each" element is so minimal that most of us comply without even thinking about it. Conversely, the same is true if another person's need—even a stranger's—is particularly spectacular or extreme: if he is drowning, for example. If a child has fallen onto the subway tracks, we assume that anyone who is capable of helping her up will do so.

I will call this "baseline communism": the understanding that, unless people consider themselves enemies, if the need is considered great enough, or the cost considered reasonable enough, the principle of "from each according to their abilities, to each according to their needs" will be assumed to apply. Of course, different communities apply very different standards. In large, impersonal urban communities, such a standard may go no further than asking for a light or directions. This might not seem like much, but it founds the possibility of larger social relations. In smaller, less impersonal communities—especially those not divided into social classes—the same logic will likely extend much further: for example, it is often effectively impossible to refuse a request not just for tobacco, but for food, sometimes even from a stranger, and certainly from anyone considered to belong to the community. Exactly one page after describing his difficulties in asking for directions, Evans-Pritchard notes that these same Nuer find themselves unable, when dealing with someone they have accepted as a member of their camp, to refuse a request for almost any item of common consumption. A man or woman known to have anything extra in the way of grain, tobacco, tools, or agricultural implements can be expected to see their stockpiles disappear almost immediately.[14] However, this baseline of openhanded sharing and generosity never extends to everything. Often, in fact, things freely shared are treated as trivial and unimportant for that very reason. Among the Nuer, true wealth takes the form of cattle. No one would freely share their cattle; in fact, young Nuer men learn that they are expected to defend their cattle with their lives; but for the same reason, neither are cattle ever bought or sold.

The obligation to share food, and whatever else is considered a basic necessity, tends to become the basis of everyday morality in a society whose members see themselves as equals. Another anthropologist, Audrey Richards, once described how Bemba mothers, "such lax disciplinarians in everything else," will scold their children harshly if they give one an orange or some other treat and the child does not immediately offer to share it with her friends.[15] But sharing is also, in such societies—in any, if we really think about it—a major focus of life's pleasures. As a result, the need to share is particularly acute in both the best of times and the worst of times: during famines, for example, but also during moments of extreme plenty. Early missionary accounts of native North Americans almost invariably include awestruck remarks on generosity in times of famine, often to total strangers.[16] At the same time,

> On returning from their fishing, their hunting, and their trading, they exchange many gifts; if they have thus obtained something unusually good, even if they have bought it, or if it has been given to them, they make a feast to the whole village with it. Their hospitality towards all sorts of strangers is remarkable.[17]

The more elaborate the feast, the more likely one is to see some combination of free sharing of some things (for instance, food and drink) and careful distribution of others: say, prize meat, whether from game or sacrifice, which is often parceled out according to very elaborate protocols or equally elaborate gift exchange. The giving and taking of gifts often takes on a distinctly gamelike quality, continuous often with the actual games, contests, pageants, and performances that also often mark popular festivals. As with society at large, the shared conviviality could be seen as a kind of communistic base on top of which everything else is constructed. It also helps to emphasize that sharing is not simply about morality, but also about pleasure. Solitary pleasures will always exist, but for most human beings, the most pleasurable activities almost always involve sharing something: music, food, liquor, drugs, gossip, drama, beds. There is a certain communism of the senses at the root of most things we consider fun.

The surest way to know that one is in the presence of communistic relations is that not only are no accounts taken, but it would be considered offensive, or simply bizarre, to even consider doing so. Each village, clan, or nation within the League of the Hodenosaunee, or Iroquois, for example, was divided into two "moieties," or halves.[18] This is a common pattern: in other parts of the world (Amazonia, Melanesia) too, there are arrangements in which members of one side can only marry someone from the other side, or only eat food grown on the other side; such rules are explicitly designed to make each side dependent on the other for some basic necessity of life. Among the Six Iroquois, each side was expected to bury the other's dead. Nothing would be more absurd than for one side to complain that, "Last year, we buried five of your dead, but you only buried two of ours."

Baseline communism might be considered the raw material of sociality, a recognition of our ultimate interdependence that is the ultimate substance of social peace. Still, in most circumstances, that minimal baseline is not enough. One always behaves in a spirit of solidarity more with some people than others, and certain institutions are specifically based on principles of solidarity and mutual aid. First among these are those we love, with mothers being the paradigm of selfless love.

Others include close relatives, wives and husbands, lovers, one's closest friends. These are the people with whom we share everything, or at least to whom we know we can turn in need, which is the definition of a true friend everywhere. Such friendships may be formalized by a ritual as "bond-friends" or "blood brothers" who cannot refuse each other anything. As a result, any community could be seen as criss-crossed with relations of "individualistic communism," one-to-one relations that operate, to varying intensities and degrees, on the basis of "from each according to their ability, to each according to their needs."[19]

This same logic can be, and is, extended within groups: not only cooperative work groups, but almost any in-group will define itself by creating its own sort of baseline communism. There will be certain things shared or made freely available within the group, others that anyone will be expected to provide for other members on request, that one would never share with or provide to outsiders: help in repairing one's nets in an association of fisherman, stationery supplies in an office, certain sorts of information among commodity traders, and so forth. Also, certain categories of people we can always call on in certain situations, such as harvesting or moving house.[20] One could go on from here to various forms of sharing, pooling, who gets to call on whom for help with certain tasks: moving, or harvesting, or even, if one is in trouble, providing an interest-free loan. Finally, there are the different sorts of "commons," the collective administration of common resources.

The sociology of everyday communism is a potentially enormous field, but one which, owing to our peculiar ideological blinkers, we have been unable to write about because we have been largely unable to see it. Rather than try to further outline it, I will limit myself to three final points.

First, we are not really dealing with reciprocity here—or at best, only with reciprocity in the broadest sense.[21] What is equal on both sides is the knowledge that the other person *would* do the same for you, not that they necessarily *will*. The Iroquois example brings home clearly what makes this possible: that such relations are based on a presumption of eternity. Society will always exist. Therefore, there will always be a north and a south side of the village. This is why no accounts need be taken. In a similar way, people tend to treat their mothers and best friends as if they will always exist, however well they know it isn't true.

The second point has to do with the famous "law of hospitality." There is a peculiar tension between a common stereotype of what are called "primitive societies" (people lacking both states and markets) as societies in which anyone not a member of the community is assumed to be an enemy, and the frequent accounts of early European travelers awestruck by the extraordinary generosity shown them by actual "savages." Granted, there is a certain truth to both sides. Wherever a stranger is a dangerous potential enemy, the normal way to overcome the danger is by some dramatic gesture of generosity whose very magnificence catapults them into that mutual sociality that is the ground for all peaceful social relations. True, when one is dealing with completely unknown quantities, there is often a process of testing. Both Christopher Columbus, in Hispaniola, and Captain Cook, in Polynesia, reported similar stories of islanders who either flee, attack, or offer everything—but who often later enter the boats and help themselves to anything they take a fancy to, provoking threats of violence from the crew, who then did their utmost to establish the principle that relations between strange peoples should be mediated instead by "normal" commercial exchange.

It's understandable that dealings with potentially hostile strangers should encourage an all-or-nothing logic, a tension preserved even in English in the etymology of the words "host," "hostile," "hostage," and indeed "hospitality," all of which are derived from the same Latin root.[22] What I want to emphasize here is that all such gestures are simply exaggerated displays of that very "baseline communism" that I have already argued is the ground of all human social life. This is why, for instance, the difference between friends and enemies is so often articulated through food—and often the most commonplace, humble, domestic sorts of food: as in the familiar principle, common in both Europe and the Middle East, that those who have shared bread and salt must never harm one another. In fact, those things that exist above all to be shared often become those things one *cannot* share with enemies. Among the Nuer, so free with food and everyday possessions, if one man murders another, a blood feud follows. Everyone in the vicinity will often have to line up on one side or another, and those on opposite sides are strictly forbidden to eat with anyone on the other, or even to drink from a cup or bowl one of their newfound enemies has previously used, lest terrible results ensue.[23] The extraordinary inconvenience this creates is a major incentive to try to negotiate some sort of settlement. By the same token, it is often said that people who have shared food, or the right, archetypal kind of food, are forbidden to harm one another, however much they might be otherwise inclined to do so. At times, this can take on an almost comical formality, as in the Arab story of the burglar who, while ransacking a house, stuck his finger in a jar to see if it was full of sugar, only to discover it was full of salt instead. Realizing that he had now eaten salt at the owner's table, he dutifully put back everything he'd stolen.

Finally, once we start thinking of communism as a principle of morality rather than just a question of property ownership, it becomes clear that this sort of morality is almost always at play to some degree in any transaction—even commerce. If one is on sociable terms with someone, it's hard to completely ignore their situation. Merchants often reduce prices for the needy. This is one of the main reasons why shopkeepers in poor neighborhoods are almost never of the same ethnic group as their customers; it would be almost impossible for a merchant who grew up in the neighborhood to make money, as they would be under constant pressure to give financial breaks, or at least easy credit terms, to their impoverished relatives and school chums. The opposite is true as well. An anthropologist who lived for some time in rural Java once told me that she measured her linguistic abilities by how well she could bargain at the local bazaar. It frustrated her that she could never get it down to a price as low as local people seemed to pay. "Well," a Javanese friend finally had to explain, "they charge rich Javanese people more, too."

Once again, we are back to the principle that if the needs (for instance, dire poverty) or the abilities (for instance, wealth beyond imagination) are sufficiently dramatic, then unless there is a complete absence of sociality, some degree of communistic morality will almost inevitably enter into the way people take accounts.[24] A Turkish folktale about the Medieval Sufi mystic Nasruddin Hodja illustrates the complexities thus introduced into the very concept of supply and demand:

> One day when Nasruddin was left in charge of the local teahouse, the king and some retainers, who had been hunting nearby, stopped in for breakfast.
> "Do you have quail eggs?" asked the king.
> "I'm sure I can find some," answered Nasruddin.
> The king ordered an omelet of a dozen quail eggs, and Nasruddin hurried out to look for them. After the king and his party had eaten, he charged them a hundred gold pieces.
> The king was puzzled. "Are quail eggs really that rare in this part of the country?"
> "It's not so much quail eggs that are rare around here," Nasruddin replied. "It's more visits from kings."

Exchange

Communism, then, is based neither in exchange nor in reciprocity—except, as I have observed, in the sense that it does involve mutual expectations and responsibilities. Even here, it seems better to use another word ("mutuality"?) so as to emphasize that exchange operates on entirely different principles, that it's a fundamentally different kind of moral logic.

Exchange is all about equivalence. It's a back-and-forth process involving two sides in which each side gives as good as it gets. This is why one can speak of people exchanging words (if there's an argument), blows, or even gunfire.[25] In these examples, it's not that there is ever an exact equivalence—even if there were some way to measure an exact equivalence—but more a constant process of interaction tending toward equivalence. Actually, there's something of a paradox here: each side in each case is trying to outdo the other, but, unless one side is utterly put to rout, it's easiest to break the whole thing off when both consider the outcome to be more or less even. When we move to the exchange of material goods, we find a similar tension. Often there is an element of competition; if nothing else, there's always that possibility. But at the same time, there's a sense that both sides are keeping accounts and that, unlike what happens in communism, which always partakes of a certain notion of eternity, the entire relationship can be canceled out, and either party can call an end to it at any time.

This element of competition can work in completely different ways. In cases of barter or commercial exchange, when both parties to the transaction are only interested in the value of goods being transacted, they may well—as economists insist they should—try to seek the maximum material advantage. On the other hand, as anthropologists have long pointed out, when the exchange is of gifts, that is, the objects passing back and forth are mainly considered interesting in how they reflect on and rearrange relations between the people carrying out the transaction, then insofar as competition enters in, it is likely to work precisely the other way around—to become a matter of contests of generosity, of people showing off who can give more away.

Let me take these one at a time.

What marks commercial exchange is that it's "impersonal": who it is that is selling something to us, or buying something from us, should in principle be entirely irrelevant. We are simply comparing the value of two objects. True, as with any principle, in practice, this is rarely completely true. There has to be some minimal element of trust for a transaction to be carried out at all and, unless one is dealing with a vending machine, that usually requires some outward display of sociality. Even in the most impersonal shopping mall or supermarket, clerks are expected to at least simulate personal warmth, patience, and other reassuring qualities; in a Middle Eastern bazaar, one might have to go through an elaborate process of establishing a simulated friendship, sharing tea, food, or tobacco, before engaging in similarly elaborate haggling—an interesting ritual that begins by establishing sociality through baseline communism—and continues with an often prolonged mock battle over prices. It's all done on the basis of the assumption that buyer and seller are, at least at that moment, friends (and thus each entitled to feel outraged and indignant at the other's unreasonable demands), but it's all a little piece of theater. Once the object changes hands, there is no expectation that the two will ever have anything to do with each other again.[26]

Most often this sort of haggling—in Madagascar the term for it literally means "to battle out a sale" (*miady varotra*)—can be a source of pleasure in itself.

The first time I visited Analakely, the great cloth market in Madagascar's capital, I came with a Malagasy friend intent on buying a sweater. The whole process took about four hours. It went something like this: my friend would spot a likely sweater hanging in some booth, ask the price, and then she would begin a prolonged battle of wits with the vendor, invariably involving dramatic displays of insult and indignation, and simulated walkings off in disgust. Often it seemed ninety percent of the argument was spent on a final, tiny difference of a few ariary—literally, pennies—that seemed to become a profound matter of principle on either side, since a merchant's failure to concede it could sink the entire deal.

The second time I visited Analakely I went with another friend, also a young woman, who had a list of measures of cloth to buy, supplied by her sister. At each booth she adopted the same procedure: she simply walked up and asked for the price.

The man would quote her one.

"All right," she then asked, "and what's your real final price?"

He'd tell her, and she'd hand over the money.

"Wait a minute!" I asked. "You can *do* that?"

"Sure," she said. "Why not?"

I explained what had happened with my last friend.

"Oh, yeah," she said. "Some people enjoy that sort of thing."

Exchange allows us to cancel out our debts. It gives us a way to call it even: hence, to end the relationship. With vendors, one is usually only pretending to have a relationship at all. With neighbors, one might for this very reason prefer *not* to pay one's debts. Laura Bohannan writes about arriving in a Tiv community in rural Nigeria; neighbors immediately began arriving bearing little gifts: "two ears corn, one vegetable marrow, one chicken, five tomatoes, one handful peanuts."[27] Having no idea what was expected of her, she thanked them and wrote down in a notebook their names and what they had brought. Eventually, two women adopted her and explained that all such gifts did have to be returned. It would be entirely inappropriate to simply accept three eggs from a neighbor and never bring anything back. One did not have to bring back eggs, but one should bring something back of approximately the same value. One could even bring money—there was nothing inappropriate in that—provided one did so at a discreet interval and above all, that one did not bring the exact cost of the eggs. It had to be either a bit more or a bit less. To bring back nothing at all would be to cast oneself as an exploiter or a parasite. To bring back an exact equivalent would be to suggest that one no longer wishes to have anything to do with the neighbor. Tiv women, she learned, might spend a good part of the day walking for miles to distant homesteads to return a handful of okra or a tiny bit of change, "in an endless circle of gifts to which no one ever handed over the precise value of the object last received"—and in doing so, they were continually creating their society. There was certainly a trace of communism here—neighbors on good terms could also be trusted to help each other out in emergencies—but unlike communistic relations, which are assumed to be permanent, this sort of neighborliness had to be constantly created and maintained, because any link can be broken off at any time.

There are endless variations on this sort of tit-for-tat, or almost tit-for-tat, gift exchange. The most familiar is the exchange of presents: I buy someone a beer; they buy me the next one. Perfect equivalence implies equality. But consider a slightly more complicated example: I take a friend out to a fancy restaurant for dinner; after a discreet interval, my friend does the same. As anthropologists have long been in the habit of pointing out, the very existence of such customs—especially, the feeling that one really *ought* to return the favor—can't be explained by standard economic theory, which assumes that any human interaction is ultimately a business deal and that we are all self-interested individuals trying to get the most for ourselves for the least cost or least amount of effort.[28] But this feeling is quite real, and it can cause genuine strain for those of limited means trying to keep up appearances. So: Why, if I took a free-market economic theorist out to an expensive dinner, would that economist feel somewhat diminished—uncomfortably in my debt—until he had been able to return the favor? Why, if he were feeling competitive with me, would he be inclined to take me to someplace even more expensive?

Recall the feasts and festivals alluded to above: here, too, there is a base of conviviality and playful (sometimes not so playful) competition.

On the one hand, everyone's pleasure is enhanced—after all, how many people would really want to eat a superb meal at a French restaurant all by themselves? On the other, things can easily slip into games of one-upmanship—and hence obsession, humiliation, rage . . . or, as we'll soon see, even worse. In some societies, these games are formalized, but it's important to stress that such games only really develop between people or groups who perceive themselves to be more or less equivalent in status.[29] To return to our imaginary economist: it's not clear that he would feel diminished if he received a present, or was taken out to dinner, by just anyone. He would be most likely to feel this way if the benefactor were someone he felt was of roughly equivalent status or dignity: a colleague, for example. If Bill Gates or George Soros took him out to dinner, he would likely conclude that he had indeed received something for nothing and leave it at that. If some ingratiating junior colleague or eager graduate student did the same, he'd be equally likely to conclude that he was doing the man a favor just by accepting the invitation—if indeed he did accept, which he probably wouldn't.

This, too, appears to be the case wherever we find society divided into fine gradations of status and dignity. Pierre Bourdieu has described the "dialectic of challenge and riposte" that governs all games of honor among Kabyle Berber men in Algeria, in which the exchange of insults, attacks (in feud or battles), thefts, or threats was seen to follow exactly the same logic as the exchange of gifts.[30] To give a gift is both an honor and a provocation. To respond to one requires infinite artistry. Timing is all-important. So is making the counter-gift just different enough, but also just slightly grander. Above all is the tacit moral principle that one must always pick on someone one's own size. To challenge someone obviously older, richer, and more honorable is to risk being snubbed, and hence humiliated; to overwhelm a poor but respectable man with a gift he couldn't possibly pay back is simply cruel, and will do equal damage to your reputation. There's an Indonesian story about that, too: a rich man sacrificed a magnificent ox to shame a penurious rival; the poor man utterly humiliated him, and won the contest, by calmly proceeding to sacrifice a chicken.[31]

Games like this become especially elaborate when status is to some degree up for grabs. When matters are *too* clear-cut, that introduces its own sorts of problems. Giving gifts to kings is often a particularly tricky and complicated business. The problem here is that one cannot really give a gift fit for a king (unless, perhaps, one is another king), since kings by definition already have everything. On the one hand, one is expected to make a reasonable effort:

Nasruddin was once called up to visit the king. A neighbor saw him hurrying along the road carrying a bag of turnips.

"What are those for?" he asked.

"I've been called to see the king. I thought it would be best to bring some kind of present."

"You're bringing him turnips? But turnips are peasant food! He's a king! You should bring him something more appropriate, like grapes."

Nasruddin agreed, and came to the king carrying a bunch of grapes. The king was not amused. "You're giving me grapes? But I'm a king! This is ridiculous. Take this idiot out and teach him some manners! Throw each and every one of the grapes at him and then kick him out of the palace."

The emperor's guards dragged Nasruddin into a side room and began pelting him with grapes. As they did so, he fell on his knees and began crying, "Thank you, thank you God, for your infinite mercy!"

"Why are you thanking God?" they asked. "You're being totally humiliated!"

Nasruddin replied, "Oh, I was just thinking, 'Thank God I didn't bring the turnips!'"

On the other hand, to give something that a king does not already have can get you in even greater trouble. One story circulating in the early Roman Empire concerned an inventor who, with great fanfare, presented a glass bowl as a gift to the emperor Tiberius. The emperor was puzzled: What was so impressive about a piece of glass? The man dropped it on the ground. Rather than shattering, it merely dented. He picked it up and simply pushed it back into its former shape.

"Did you tell anyone else how you made this thing?" asked a startled Tiberius.

The inventor assured him that he had not. The emperor therefore ordered him killed, since, if word of how to make unbreakable glass got out, his treasury of gold and silver would soon be worthless.[32]

The best bet when dealing with kings was to make a reasonable effort to play the game, but one that is still bound to fail. The fourteenth-century Arab traveler Ibn Battuta tells of the customs of the King of Sind, a terrifying monarch who took a particular delight in displays of arbitrary power.[33] It was customary for foreign worthies visiting the king to present him with magnificent presents; whatever the gift was, he would invariably respond by presenting the bearer with something many times its value. As a result, a substantial business developed where local bankers would lend money to such visitors to finance particularly spectacular gifts, knowing they could be well re-paid from the proceeds of royal one-upmanship. The king must have known about this. He didn't object—since the whole point was to show that his wealth exceeded all possible equivalence—anyway he knew if he really needed to, he could always expropriate the bankers. Kings knew that the really important game was not economic, but one of status, and theirs was absolute.

In exchange, the objects being traded are seen as equivalent. There-fore, by implication, so are the people: at least, at the moment when gift is met with counter-gift, or money changes hands; when there is no further debt or obligation and each of the two parties is equally free to walk away. This in turn implies autonomy. Both principles sit uncom-fortably with monarchs, which is the reason that kings generally dislike getting themselves entangled in any sort of exchange.[34] But within that overhanging prospect of potential cancellation, of ultimate equivalence, we find endless variations, endless games one can play. One can de-mand something from another person, knowing that by doing so, one is giving the other the right to demand something of equivalent value in return. In some contexts, even praising another's possession might be interpreted as a demand of this sort. In eighteenth-century New Zealand, English settlers soon learned that it was not a good idea to admire, say, a particularly beautiful jade pendant worn around the neck of a Maori warrior; the latter would inevitably insist on giving it, not take no for an answer, and then, after a discreet interval, return to praise the settler's coat or gun. The only way to head this off was to quickly give him a gift before he could ask for one. Sometimes gifts are offered in order for the giver to be able to make such a demand: if one accepts the present, one is tacitly agreeing to allow the giver to claim whatever he deems equivalent.[35]

All this, in turn, can shade into something very much like barter, directly swapping one thing for another—which as we've seen does oc-cur even in what Marcel Mauss liked to refer to as "gift economies," even if largely between strangers.[36] Within communities, there is almost always a reluctance, as the Tiv example so nicely illustrates, to allow things to cancel out—one reason that if there is money in common usage, people will often either refuse to use it with friends or relatives (which in a village society includes pretty much everyone) or alter-nately, like the Malagasy villagers in Chapter Three, use it in radically different ways.

Hierarchy

Exchange, then, implies formal equality—or, at least, the potential for it. This is precisely why kings have such trouble with it.

In contrast, relations of explicit hierarchy—that is, relations between at least two parties in which one is considered superior to the other—do not tend to operate by reciprocity at all. It's hard to see because the relation is often justified in reciprocal terms ("the peasants provide food, the lords provide protection"), but the principle by which they operate is exactly the opposite. In practice, hierarchy tends to work by a logic of precedent.

To illustrate what I mean by this, let us imagine a kind of continuum of one-sided social relations, ranging from the most exploitative to the most benevolent. At one extreme is theft, or plunder; on the other selfless charity.[37] Only at these two extremes is it is possible to have material interactions between people who otherwise have no social relation of any kind. Only a lunatic would mug his next-door neighbor. A band of marauding soldiers or nomadic horsemen falling on a peasant hamlet to rape and pillage also obviously have no intention of forming any ongoing relations with the survivors. But in a similar way, religious traditions often insist that the only true charity is anonymous—in other words, not meant to place the recipient in one's debt. One extreme form of this, documented in various parts of the world, is the gift by stealth, in a kind of reverse burglary: to literally sneak into the recipient's house at night and plant one's present so no one can know for sure who has left it. The figure of Santa Claus, or Saint Nicholas (who, it must be remembered, was not just the patron saint of children, but also the patron saint of thieves) would appear to be the mythological version of the same principle: a benevolent burglar with whom no social relations are possible and therefore to whom no one could possibly owe anything, in his case, above all, because he does not actually exist.

Observe, however, what happens when one moves just a little bit less far out on the continuum in either direction. I have been told that in some of the more lawless parts of the former Soviet Union, gangs prey so systematically on travelers on trains and buses that they have developed the habit of giving each victim a little token to confirm that the bearer has already been robbed. Obviously, one step toward the creation of a state. Actually, one popular theory of the origins of the state, which goes back at least to the fourteenth-century North African historian Ibn Khaldun, runs precisely along these lines: nomadic raiders eventually systematize their relations with sedentary villagers; pillage turns into tribute, rape turns into the "right of the first night" or the carrying off of likely candidates as recruits for the royal harem. Conquest, untrammeled force, becomes systematized, and thus framed not as a predatory relation but as a moral one, with the lords providing protection, and the villagers, their sustenance. But even if all parties assume they are operating by a shared moral code, that even kings cannot do whatever they want but must operate within limits, allowing peasants to argue about the rights and wrongs of just how much of their harvest a king's retainers are entitled to carry off, they are very unlikely to frame their calculation in terms of the quality or quantity of protection provided, but rather in terms of custom and precedent: How much did we pay last year? How much did our ancestors have to pay? The same is true on the other side. If charitable donations become the basis for any sort of social relation, it will not be one based on reciprocity. If you give some coins to a panhandler, and that panhandler recognizes you later, it is unlikely that he will give you any money—but he might well consider you more likely to give him money again. Certainly, this is true if one donates money to a charitable organization. (I gave money to the United Farm Workers once and I still haven't heard the end of it.) Such an act of one-sided generosity is treated as a precedent for what will be expected afterward.[38] It's quite the same if one gives candy to a child.

This is what I mean when I say that hierarchy operates by a principle that is the very opposite of reciprocity. Whenever the lines of superiority and inferiority are clearly drawn and accepted by all parties as the framework of a relationship, and relations are sufficiently ongoing that we are no longer simply dealing with arbitrary force, then relations will be seen as being regulated by a web of habit or custom. Sometimes the situation is assumed to have originated in some founding act of conquest. Or it might be seen as ancestral custom for which there is no need of explanation. But this introduces another complication to the problem of giving gifts to kings, or to any superior: there is always the danger that it will be treated as a precedent, added to the web of custom, and therefore considered obligatory thereafter. Xenophon claims that in the early days of the Persian Empire, each province vied to send the Great King gifts of its most unique and valuable products. This became the basis of the tribute system: each province was eventually expected to provide the same "gifts" every year.[39] Similarly, according to the great Medieval historian Marc Bloch:

[I]n the ninth century, when one day there was a shortage of wine in the royal cellars at Ver, the monks of Saint-Denis were asked to supply the two hundred hogs-heads required. This contribution was thenceforth claimed from them as of right every year, and it required an imperial charter to abolish it. At Ardres, we are told, there was once a bear, the property of the local lord. The inhabitants, who loved to watch it fight with dogs, undertook to feed it. The beast eventually died, but the lord continued to exact the loaves of bread."[40]

In other words, any gift to a feudal superior, "especially if repeated three or four times," was likely to be treated as a precedent and added to the web of custom. As a result, those giving gifts to superiors often insisted on receiving a "letter of non-prejudice" legally stipulating that such a gift would not be required in the future. While it is unusual for matters to become quite so formalized, any social relation that is assumed from the start to be unequal will inevitably begin to operate on an analogous logic—if only because, once relations are seen as based on "custom," the only way to demonstrate that one has a duty or obligation to do something is to show that one has done it before.

Often, such arrangements can turn into a logic of caste: certain clans are responsible for weaving the ceremonial garments, or bringing the fish for royal feasts, or cutting the king's hair. They thus come to be known as weavers or fishermen or barbers.[41] This last point can't be overemphasized because it brings home another truth regularly overlooked: that the logic of identity is, always and everywhere, entangled in the logic of hierarchy. It is only when certain people are placed above others, or where everyone is being ranked in relation to the king, or the high priest, or Founding Fathers, that one begins to speak of people bound by their essential nature: about fundamentally different kinds of human being. Ideologies of caste or race are just extreme examples. It happens whenever one group is seen as raising themselves above others, or placing themselves below others, in such a way that ordinary standards of fair dealing no longer apply.

In fact, something like this happens in a small way even in our most intimate social relations. The moment we recognize someone as a different *sort* of person, either above or below us, then ordinary rules of reciprocity become modified or are set aside. If a friend is unusually generous once, we will likely wish to reciprocate. If she acts this way repeatedly, we conclude she is a generous person, and are hence less likely to reciprocate.[42]

We can describe a simple formula here: a certain action, repeated, becomes customary; as a result, it comes to define the actor's essential nature. Alternately, a person's nature may be defined by how others have acted toward him in the past. To be an aristocrat is largely to insist that, in the past, others have *treated* you as an aristocrat (since aristocrats don't really do anything in particular: most spend their time simply existing in some sort of putatively superior state) and therefore should continue to do so. Much of the art of being such a person is that of treating oneself in such a manner that it conveys how you expect others to treat you: in the case of actual kings, covering oneself with gold so as to suggest that others do likewise. On the other end of the scale, this is also how abuse becomes self-legitimating. As a former student of mine, Sarah Stillman, pointed out: in the United States, if a middle-class thirteen-year-old girl is kidnapped, raped, and killed, it is considered an agonizing national crisis that everyone with a television is expected to follow for several weeks. If a thirteen-year-old girl is turned out as a child prostitute, raped systematically for years, and ultimately killed, all this is considered unremarkable—really just the sort of thing one can expect to end up happening to someone like that.[43]

When objects of material wealth pass back and forth between superiors and inferiors as gifts or payments, the key principle seems to be that the sorts of things given on each side should be considered fundamentally different in quality, their relative value impossible to quantify—the result being that there is no way to even conceive of a squaring of accounts. Even if Medieval writers insisted on imagining society as a hierarchy in which priests pray for everyone, nobles fight for everyone, and peasants feed everyone, it never even occurred to any of them to establish how many prayers or how much military protection was equivalent to a ton of wheat. Nor did anyone ever consider making such a calculation. Neither is it that "lowly" sorts of people are necessarily given lowly sorts of things and vice versa. Sometimes it is quite the opposite. Until recently, just about any notable philosopher, artist, poet, or musician was required to find a wealthy patron for support. Famous works of poetry or philosophy are often prefaced— oddly, to the modern eye—with gushing, sycophantic praise for the wisdom and virtue of some long-forgotten earl or count who provided a meager stipend. The fact that the noble patron merely provided room and board, or money, and that the client showed his gratitude by painting the *Mona Lisa*, or composing the *Toccata and Fugue in D Minor*, was in no way seen to compromise the assumption of the noble's intrinsic superiority.

There is one great exception to this principle, and that is the phenomenon of hierarchical redistribution. Here, though, rather than giving back and forth the same sorts of things, they give back and forth *exactly* the same thing: as, for instance, when fans of certain Nigerian pop stars throw money onto the stage during concerts, and the pop stars in question make occasional tours of their fans' neighborhoods tossing (the same) money from the windows of their limos. When this is all that's going on, we may speak of an absolutely minimal sort of hierarchy. In much of Papua New Guinea, social life centers on "big men," charismatic individuals who spend much of their time coaxing, cajoling, and manipulating in order to acquire masses of wealth to give away again at some great feast. One could, in practice, pass from here to, say, an Amazonian or indigenous North American chief. Unlike big men, their role is more formalized; but actually such chiefs have no power to compel anyone to do anything they don't want to (hence North American Indian chiefs' famous skill at oratory and powers of persuasion). As a result, they tended to give away far more than they received. Observers often remarked that in terms of personal possessions, a village chief was often the poorest man in the village, such was the pressure on him for constant supply of largesse.

Indeed, one could judge how egalitarian a society really was by exactly this: whether those ostensibly in positions of authority are merely conduits for redistribution, or able to use their positions to accumulate riches. The latter seems most likely in aristocratic societies that add another element: war and plunder. After all, just about anyone who comes into a very large amount of wealth will ultimately give at least part of it away—often in grandiose and spectacular ways to large numbers of people. The more of one's wealth that is obtained by plunder or extortion, the more spectacular and self-aggrandizing will be the forms in which it's given away.[44] And what is true of warrior aristocracies is all the more true of ancient states, where rulers almost invariably represented themselves as the protectors of the helpless, supporters of widows and orphans, and champions of the poor. The genealogy of the modern redistributive state—with its notorious tendency to foster identity politics—can be traced back not to any sort of "primitive communism" but ultimately to violence and war.

Shifting between Modalities

I should underline again that we are not talking about different types of society here (as we've seen, the very idea that we've ever been organized into discrete "societies" is dubious) but moral principles that always coexist everywhere. We are all communists with our closest friends, and feudal lords when dealing with small children. It is very hard to imagine a society where this would not be true.

The obvious question is: If we are all ordinarily moving back and forth between completely different systems of moral accounting, why hasn't anybody noticed this? Why, instead, do we continually feel the need to reframe everything in terms of reciprocity?

Here we must return to the fact that reciprocity is our main way of imagining justice. In particular, it is what we fall back on when we're thinking in the abstract, and especially when we're trying to create an idealized picture of society. I've already given examples of this sort of thing. Iroquois communities were based on an ethos that required everyone to be attentive to the needs of several different sorts of people: their friends, their families, members of their matrilineal clans, even friendly strangers in situations of hardship. It was when they had to think about society in the abstract that they started to emphasize the two sides of the village, each of which had to bury the other's dead. It was a way of imagining communism through reciprocity. Similarly, feudalism was a notoriously messy and complicated business, but whenever Medieval thinkers generalized about it, they reduced all its ranks and orders into one simple formula in which each order contributed its share: "Some pray, some fight, still others work."[45] Even hierarchy was seen as ultimately reciprocal, despite this formula having virtually nothing to do with how real relations between priests, knights, and peasants operated on the ground. Anthropologists are familiar with the phenomenon: it's only when people who have never had occasion to really think about their society or culture as a whole, who probably weren't even aware they were living inside something other people considered a "society" or a "culture," are asked to explain how everything works that they say things like, "This is how we repay our mothers for the pain of having raised us," or puzzle over conceptual diagrams in which clan A gives their women in marriage to clan B who gives theirs to clan C, who gives theirs back to A again, but which never seem to quite correspond to what real people actually do.[46] When trying to imagine a just society, it's hard not to evoke images of balance and symmetry, of elegant geometries where everything balances out.

The idea that there is something called "the market" is not so very different. Economists will often admit this, if you ask them in the right way. Markets aren't real. They are mathematical models, created by imagining a self-contained world where everyone has exactly the same motivation and the same knowledge and is engaged in the same self-interested calculating exchange. Economists are aware that reality is always more complicated; but they are also aware that to come up with a mathematical model, one always has to make the world into a bit of a cartoon. There's nothing wrong with this. The problem comes when it enables some (often these same economists) to declare that anyone who ignores the dictates of the market shall surely be punished—or that since we live in a market system, everything (except government interference) is based on principles of justice: that our economic system is one vast network of reciprocal relations in which, in the end, the accounts balance and all debts are paid.

These principles get tangled up in each other and it's thus often difficult to tell which predominates in a given situation—one reason that it's ridiculous to pretend we could ever reduce human behavior, economic or otherwise, to a mathematical formula of any sort. Still, this means that some degree of reciprocity can be detected as potentially present in any situation; so a determined observer can always find some excuse to say it's there. What's more, certain principles appear to have an inherent tendency to slip into others. For instance, a lot of extremely hierarchical relationships can operate (at least some of the time) on communistic principles. If you have a rich patron, you come to him in times of need, and he is expected to help you. But only to a certain degree. No one expects the patron to provide so much help that it threatens to undermine the underlying inequality.[47]

Likewise, communistic relations can easily start slipping into relations of hierarchical inequality—often without anyone noticing it. It's not hard to see why this happens. Sometimes different people's "abilities" and "needs" are grossly disproportionate. Genuinely egalitarian societies are keenly aware of this and tend to develop elaborate safeguards around the dangers of anyone—say, especially good hunters, in a hunting society—rising too far above themselves, just as they tend to be suspicious of anything that might make one member of the society feel in genuine debt to another. A member who draws attention to his own accomplishments will find himself the object of mockery. Often, the only polite thing to do if one has accomplished something significant is to instead make fun of oneself. The Danish writer Peter Freuchen, in his *Book of the Eskimo*, described how in Greenland, one could tell what a fine delicacy someone had to offer his guests by how much he belittled it beforehand:

> The old man laughed. "Some people don't know much. I am such a poor hunter and my wife a terrible cook who ruins everything. I don't have much, but I think there is a piece of meat outside. It might still be there as the dogs have refused it several times."

> This was such a recommendation in the Eskimo way of
> backwards bragging that everyone's mouths began to water . . .

The reader will recall the walrus hunter of the last chapter, who took offense when the author tried to thank him for giving him a share of meat—after all, humans help one another, and once we treat something as a gift, we turn into something less than human: "Up here we say that by gifts one makes slaves and by whips one makes dogs."[48]

"Gift" here does *not* mean something given freely, not mutual aid that we can ordinarily expect human beings to provide to one another. To thank someone suggests that he or she might *not* have acted that way, and that therefore the choice to act this way creates an obligation, a sense of debt—and hence, inferiority. Communes or egalitarian collectives in the United States often face similar dilemmas, and they have to come up with their own safeguards against creeping hierarchy. It's not that the tendency for communism to slip into hierarchy is inevitable—societies like the Inuit have managed to fend it off for thousands of years—but rather, that one must always guard against it.

In contrast, it's notoriously difficult—often downright impossible—to shift relations based on an assumption of communistic sharing to relations of equal exchange. We observe this all the time with friends: if someone is seen as taking advantage of your generosity, it's often much easier to break off relations entirely than to demand that they somehow pay you back. One extreme example is the Maori story about a notorious glutton who used to irritate fishermen up and down the coast near where he lived by constantly asking for the best portions of their catch. Since to refuse a direct request for food was effectively impossible, they would dutifully turn it over; until one day, people decided enough was enough and killed him.[49]

We've already seen how creating a ground of sociability among strangers can often require an elaborate process of testing the others' limits by helping oneself to their possessions. The same sort of thing can happen in peacemaking, or even in the creation of business partnerships.[50] In Madagascar, people told me that two men who are thinking of going into business together will often become blood brothers. Blood brotherhood, *fatidra*, consists of an unlimited promise of mutual aid. Both parties solemnly swear that they will never refuse any request from the other. In reality, partners to such an agreement are usually fairly circumspect in what they actually request. But, my friends insisted, when people first make such an agreement, they sometimes like to test it out. One may demand their new partner's pet dog, the shirt off their back, or (everyone's favorite example) the right to spend the night with their wife or husband. The only limit is the knowledge that anything one can demand, the other one can too.[51] Here, again, we are talking about an initial establishment of trust. Once the genuineness of the mutual commitment has been confirmed, the ground is prepared, as it were, and the two men can begin to buy and sell on consignment, advance funds, share profits, and otherwise trust that each will look after the other's commercial interests from then on. The most famous and dramatic moments, however, are those when relations of exchange threaten to break down into hierarchy: that is, when two parties are acting like equals, trading gifts, or blows, or commodities, or anything else, but one of them does something that completely flips the scale.

I've already mentioned the tendency of gift exchange to turn into games of one-upmanship, and how in some societies this potential is formalized in great public contests. This is typical, above all, of what are often called "heroic societies": those in which governments are weak or nonexistent and society is organized instead around warrior noblemen, each with his entourage of loyal retainers and tied to the others by ever-shifting alliances and rivalries. Most epic poetry—from the *Iliad* to the *Mahabharata* to *Beowulf*—harkens back to this sort of world, and anthropologists have discovered similar arrangements among the Maori of New Zealand and the Kwakiutl, Tlingit, and Haida of the American Northwest coast. In heroic societies, the throwing of feasts and resulting contests of generosity are often spoken of as mere extensions of war: "fighting with property" or "fighting with food." Those who throw such feasts often indulge in colorful speeches about how their enemies are thus crushed and destroyed by glorious feats of generosity aimed in their direction (Kwakiutl chiefs liked to speak of themselves as great mountains from which gifts rolled like giant boulders), and of how conquered rivals are thus reduced—much as in the Inuit metaphor—to slaves.

Such statements are not to be taken literally—another feature of such societies is a highly developed art of boasting.[52] Heroic chiefs and warriors tended to talk themselves up just as consistently as those in egalitarian societies talked themselves down. It's not as if someone who loses out in a contest of gift exchange is ever actually reduced to slavery, but he might end up feeling as if he were. And the consequences could be catastrophic. One ancient Greek source describes Celtic festivals where rival nobles would alternate between jousts and contests of generosity, presenting their enemies with magnificent gold and silver treasures. Occasionally this could lead to a kind of checkmate; someone would be faced with a present so magnificent that he could not possibly match it. In this case, the only honorable response was for him to cut his own throat, thus allowing his wealth to be distributed to his followers.[53] Six hundred years later, we find a case from an Icelandic saga of an aging Viking named Egil who befriended a younger man named Einar, who was still actively raiding. They liked to sit together composing poetry. One day Einar came by a magnificent shield "inscribed with old tales; and between the writing were overlaid spangles of gold with precious stones." No one had ever seen anything like it. He took it with him on a visit to Egil. Egil was not at home, so Einar waited three days, as was the custom, then hung the shield as a present in the mead-hall and rode off.

> Egil returned home, saw the shield, and asked who owned such a treasure. He was told that Einar had visited and given it to him. Then Egil said, "To hell with him! Does he think I'm going to stay up all night and compose a poem about his shield? Get my horse, I'm going to ride after him and kill him." As Einar's luck would have it he had left early enough to put sufficient distance between himself and Egil. So Egil resigned himself to composing a poem about Einar's gift.[54]

■ ■ ■ ■ ■

Competitive gift exchange, then, does not literally render anyone slaves; it is simply an affair of honor. These are people, however, for whom honor is everything.

The main reason that being unable to pay a debt, especially a debt of honor, was such a crisis was because this *was* how noblemen assembled their entourages. The law of hospitality in the ancient world, for instance, insisted that any traveler must be fed, given shelter, and treated as an honored guest—but only for a certain length of time. If a guest did not go away, he would eventually become a mere subordinate. The role of such hangers-on has been largely neglected by students of human history. In many periods—from imperial Rome to medieval China—probably the most important relationships, at least in towns and cities, were those of patronage. Anyone rich and important would find himself surrounded by flunkies, sycophants, perpetual dinner guests, and other sorts of willing dependents. Drama and poetry of the time are full of such characters.[55] Similarly, for much of human history, being respectable and middle-class meant spending one's mornings going from door to door, paying one's respects to important local patrons. To this day, informal patronage systems still crop up, whenever relatively rich and powerful people feel the need to assemble networks of supporters—a practice well documented in many parts of the Mediterranean, the Middle East, and Latin America. Such relationships seem to consist of a slapdash mix of all three principles that I've been mapping out over the course of this chapter; nevertheless, those observing them insist on trying to cast them in the language of exchange and debt.

A final example: in a collection called *Gifts and Spoils*, published in 1971, we find a brief essay by the anthropologist Lorraine Blaxter about a rural department in the French Pyrenees, most of whose inhabitants are farmers. Everyone places a great emphasis on the importance of mutual aid—the local phrase means "giving service" (*rendre service*). People living in the same community should look out for one another and pitch in when their neighbors are having trouble. This is the essence of communal morality; in fact, it's how one knows that any sort of community exists. So far so good. However, she notes, when someone does a particularly great favor, mutual aid can turn into something else:

> If a man in a factory went to the boss and asked for a job, and the boss found him one, this would be an example of someone giving service. The man who got the job could never repay the boss, but he could show him respect, or perhaps give him symbolic gifts of garden produce. If a gift demands a return, and no tangible return is possible, the repayment will be through support or esteem.[56]

Thus does mutual aid slip into inequality. Thus do patron-client relations come into being. We have already observed this. I chose this particular passage because the author's phrasing is so weird. It completely contradicts itself. The boss does the man a favor. The man cannot repay the favor. Therefore, the man repays the favor by showing up at the boss's house with the occasional basket of tomatoes and showing him respect. So which one is it? Can he repay the favor, or not?

Peter Freuchen's walrus hunter would, no doubt, think he knew exactly what was going on here. Bringing the basket of tomatoes was simply the equivalent of saying "thank you." It was a way of acknowledging that one owes a debt of gratitude, that gifts had in fact made slaves just as whips make dogs. The boss and the employee are now fundamentally different sorts of people. The problem is that in all other respects, they are not fundamentally different sorts of people. Most likely they are both middle-aged Frenchmen, fathers of families, citizens of the Republic with similar tastes in music, sports, and food. They *ought* to be equals. As a result, even the tomatoes, which are really a token of recognition of the existence of a debt that can never be repaid, has to be represented as if it was itself a kind of repayment—an interest payment on a loan that could, everyone agrees to pretend, someday be paid back, thus returning the two members to their proper equal status once again.[57]

(It's telling that the favor is finding the client a job in a factory, because what happens is not very different from what happens when you get a job in a factory to begin with. A wage-labor contract is, ostensibly, a free contract between equals—but an agreement between equals in which both agree that once one of them punches the time clock, they won't be equals any more.[58] The law does recognize a bit of a problem here; that's why it insists that you cannot sell off your equality permanently. Such arrangements are only acceptable if the boss's power is not absolute, if it is limited to work time, and if you have the legal right to break off the contract and thereby to restore yourself to full equality, at any time.)

It seems to me that this agreement between equals to no longer be equal (at least for a time) is critically important. It is the very essence of what we call "debt."

■ ■ ■ ■ ■

What, then, is debt?

Debt is a very specific thing, and it arises from very specific situations. It first requires a relationship between two people who do not consider each other fundamentally different sorts of being, who are at least potential equals, who *are* equals in those ways that are really important, and who are not currently in a state of equality—but for whom there is some way to set matters straight.

In the case of gift-giving, as we've seen, this requires a certain equality of status. That's why our economics professor didn't feel any sense of obligation—any debt of honor—if taken out to dinner by someone who ranked either much higher or much lower than himself. With money loans, all that is required is that the two parties be of equal legal standing. (You can't lend money to a child, or to a lunatic. Well, you can, but the courts won't help you get it back.) Legal—rather than moral—debts have other unique qualities. For instance, they can be forgiven, which isn't always possible with a moral debt.

This means that there is no such thing as a genuinely unpayable debt. If there was no conceivable way to salvage the situation, we wouldn't be calling it a "debt." Even the French villager could, conceivably, save his patron's life, or win the lottery and buy the factory. Even when we speak of a criminal "paying his debt to society," we are saying that he has done something so terrible that he has now been banished from that equal status under the law that belongs by natural right to any citizen of his country; however, we call it a "debt" because it *can* be paid, equality *can* be restored, even if the cost may be death by lethal injection.

During the time that the debt remains unpaid, the logic of hierarchy takes hold. There is no reciprocity. As anyone who has ever been in jail knows, the first thing the jailors communicate is that nothing that happens in jail has anything to do with justice. Similarly, debtor and creditor confront each other like a peasant before a feudal lord. The law of precedent takes hold. If you bring your creditor tomatoes from the garden, it never occurs to you that he would give something back. He might expect you to do it again, though. But always there is the assumption that the situation is somewhat unnatural, because the debt really ought to be paid.

This is what makes situations of effectively unpayable debt so difficult and so painful. Since creditor and debtor are ultimately equals, if the debtor cannot do what it takes to restore herself to equality, there is obviously something wrong with her; it must be her fault.

This connection becomes clear if we look at the etymology of common words for "debt" in European languages. Many are synonyms for "fault," "sin," or "guilt": just as a criminal owes a debt to society, a debtor is always a sort of criminal.[59] In ancient Crete, according to Plutarch, it was the custom for those taking loans to pretend to snatch the money from the lender's purse. Why, he wondered? Probably "so that, if they default, they could be charged with violence and punished all the more."[60] This is why in so many periods of history insolvent debtors could be jailed, or even—as in early Republican Rome—executed.

A debt, then, is just an exchange that has not been brought to completion.

It follows that debt is strictly a creature of reciprocity and has little to do with other sorts of morality (communism, with its needs and abilities; hierarchy, with its customs and qualities). True, if we were really determined, we could argue (as some do) that communism is a condition of permanent mutual indebtedness, or that hierarchy is constructed out of unpayable debts. But isn't this just the same old story, starting from the assumption that all human interactions must be, by definition, forms of exchange, and then performing whatever mental somersaults are required to prove it?

No. All human interactions are not forms of exchange. Only some are. Exchange encourages a particular way of conceiving human relations. This is because exchange implies equality, but it also implies separation. It's precisely when the money changes hands, when the debt is canceled, that equality is restored *and* both parties can walk away and have nothing further to do with each other.

Debt is what happens in between: when the two parties cannot yet walk away from each other, because they are not yet equal. But it is carried out in the shadow of eventual equality. Because achieving that equality, however, destroys the very reason for having a relationship, just about everything interesting happens in between.[61] In fact, just about everything human happens in between—even if this means that all such human relations bear with them at least a tiny element of criminality, guilt, or shame.

For the Tiv women whom I mentioned earlier in the chapter, this wasn't much of a problem. By ensuring that everyone was always slightly in debt to one another, they actually created human society, if a very fragile sort of society—a delicate web made up of obligations to return three eggs or a bag of okra, ties renewed and recreated, as any one of them could be canceled out at any time.

Our own habits of civility are not so very different. Consider the custom, in American society, of constantly saying "please" and "thank you." To do so is often treated as basic morality: we are constantly chiding children for forgetting to do it, just as the moral guardians of our society—teachers and ministers, for instance—do to everybody else. We often assume that the habit is universal, but as the Inuit hunter made clear, it is not.[62] Like so many of our everyday courtesies, it is a kind of democratization of what was once a habit of feudal deference: the insistence on treating absolutely everyone the way that one used only to have to treat a lord or similar hierarchical superior.

Perhaps this is not so in every case. Imagine we are on a crowded bus, looking for a seat. A fellow passenger moves her bag aside to clear one; we smile, or nod, or make some other little gesture of acknowledgment. Or perhaps we actually say, "thank you." Such a gesture is simply a recognition of common humanity: we are acknowledging that the woman who had been blocking the seat is not a mere physical obstacle but a human being, and that we feel genuine gratitude toward someone we will likely never see again. None of this is generally true when one asks someone across the table to "please pass the salt," or when the postman thanks you for signing for a delivery. We think of these simultaneously as meaningless formalities and as the very moral basis of society. Their apparent unimportance can be measured by the fact that almost no one would refuse, on principle, to say "please" or "thank you" in just about any situation—even those who might find it almost impossible to say "I'm sorry" or "I apologize."

In fact, the English "please" is short for "if you please," "if it pleases you to do this"—it is the same in most European languages (French *si il vous plait*, Spanish *por favor*). Its literal meaning is "You are under no obligation to do this." "Hand me the salt. Not that I am saying that you have to!" This is not true; there is a social obligation, and it would be almost impossible not to comply. But etiquette largely consists of the exchange of polite fictions (to use less polite language, lies). When you ask someone to pass the salt, you are also giving them an order; by attaching the word "please," you are saying that it is not an order. But, in fact, it is.

In English, "thank you" derives from "think." It originally meant, "I will remember what you did for me"—which is usually not true either—but in other languages (the Portuguese *obrigado* is a good example) the standard term follows the form of the English "much obliged"—it actually does mean, "I am in your debt." The French *merci* is even more graphic: it derives from "mercy," as in begging for mercy; by saying it you are symbolically placing yourself in your benefactor's power—since a debtor is, after all, a criminal.[63] Saying "you're welcome" or "it's nothing" (French *de rien*, Spanish *de nada*)—the latter has at least the advantage of often being literally true—is a way of reassuring the one to whom one has passed the salt that you are not actually inscribing a debit in your imaginary moral account book. So is saying "my pleasure"—you are saying, "No, actually, it's a credit, not a debit—you did *me* a favor because in asking me to pass the salt, you gave me the opportunity to do something I found rewarding in itself!"[64]

Decoding the tacit calculus of debt ("I owe you one," "No, you don't owe me anything," "Actually, if anything, it's me who owes you," as if inscribing and then scratching off so many infinitesimal entries in an endless ledger) makes it easy to understand why this sort of thing is often viewed not as the quintessence of morality, but as the quintessence of *middle-class* morality. True, by now middle-class sensibilities dominate society. But there are still those who find the practice odd. Those at the very top of society often still feel that deference is owed primarily to hierarchical superiors and find it slightly idiotic to watch postmen and pastry chefs taking turns pretending to treat each other like little feudal lords. At the other extreme, those who grew up in what in Europe are called "popular" environments—small towns, poor neighborhoods, any place where there is still an assumption that people who are not enemies will, ordinarily, take care of one another—will often find it insulting to be constantly told, in effect, that there is some chance they might *not* do their job as a waiter or taxi driver correctly, or provide house guests with tea. In other words, middle-class etiquette insists that we are all equals, but it does so in a very particular way. On the one hand, it pretends that nobody is giving anybody orders (think here of the burly security guard at the mall who appears before someone walking into a restricted area and says, "Can I help you?"); on the other, it treats every gesture of what I've been calling "baseline communism" as if it were really a form of exchange. As a result, like Tiv neighborhoods, middle-class society has to be endlessly recreated, as a kind of constant flickering game of shadows, the criss-crossing of an infinity of momentary debt relations, each one almost instantly canceled out.

All of this is a relatively recent innovation. The habit of always saying "please" and "thank you" first began to take hold during the commercial revolution of the sixteenth and seventeenth centuries—among those very middle classes who were largely responsible for it. It is the language of bureaus, shops, and offices, and over the course of the last five hundred years it has spread across the world along with them. It is also merely one token of a much larger philosophy, a set of assumptions of what humans are and what they owe one another, that have by now become so deeply ingrained that we cannot see them.

■ ■ ■ ■ ■

Sometimes, at the brink of a new historical era, some prescient soul can see the full implications of what is beginning to happen—sometimes in a way that later generations can't. Let me end with a text by such a person. In Paris, sometime in the 1540s, François Rabelais—lapsed monk, doctor, legal scholar—composed what was to become a famous mock eulogy, which he inserted in the third book of his great *Gargantua and Pantagruel*, and which came to be known as "In Praise of Debt."

Rabelais places the encomium in the mouth of one Panurge, a wandering scholar and man of extreme classical erudition who, he observes, "knew sixty-three ways of making money—the most honorable and most routine of which was stealing."[65] The good-natured giant Pantagruel adopts Panurge and even provides him with a respectable income, but it bothers him that Panurge continues to spend money like water and remains up to his ears in debt. Wouldn't it be better, Pantagruel suggests, to be able to pay his creditors?

Panurge responds with horror: "God forbid that I should ever be out of debt!" Debt is, in fact, the very basis of his philosophy:

Always owe somebody something, then he will be forever praying God to grant you a good, long and blessed life. Fearing to
lose what you owe him, he will always be saying good things
about you in every sort of company; he will be constantly acquiring new lenders for you, so that you can borrow to pay
him back, filling his ditch with other men's spoil.[66]

Above all else, they will always be praying that you come into
money. It's like those ancient slaves destined to be sacrificed at their
masters' funerals. When they wished their master long life and good
health, they genuinely meant it! What's more, debt can make you into a
kind of god, who can make something (money, well-wishing creditors)
out of absolutely nothing.

Worse still: I give myself to bonnie Saint Bobelin if all my life
I have not reckoned debts to be, as it were, a connection and
colligation between Heaven and Earth (uniquely preserving the
lineage of Man without which, I say, all human beings would
soon perish) and perhaps to be that great World Soul which,
according to the Academics, gives life to all things.
    That it really is so, evoke tranquilly in your mind the Idea
and Form of a world—take if you like the thirtieth of the
worlds imagined by Metrodorus—in which there were no debtors or lenders at all. A universe sans debts! Amongst the heavenly bodies there would be no regular course whatsoever: all
would be in disarray. Jupiter, reckoning that he owed no debt
to Saturn, would dispossess him of his sphere, and with his Homeric chain hold in suspension all the Intelligences, gods, heavens, daemons, geniuses, heroes, devils, earth, sea and all the
elements . . . The Moon would remain dark and bloody; why
should the Sun share his light with her? He is under no obligation. The Sun would never shine on their Earth; the heavenly
bodies would pour no good influences down upon it.
    Between the elements there will be no mutual sharing of
qualities, no alternation, no transmutation whatsoever, one
will not think itself obliged to the other; it has lent it nothing.
From earth no longer will water be made, nor water trans-
muted into air; from air fire will not be made, and fire will not
warm the earth. Earth will bring forth nothing but monsters,
Titans, giants. The rain will not rain, the light will shed no
light, the wind will not blow, and there will be no summer, no
autumn, Lucifer will tear off his bonds and, sallying forth from
deepest Hell with the Furies, the Vengeances and the horned

devils, will seek to turf the gods of both the greater and lesser nations out from their nests in the heavens.

And what's more, if human beings owed nothing to one another, life would "be no better than a dog-fight"—a mere unruly brawl.

> Amongst human beings none will save another; it will be no good a man shouting Help! Fire! I'm drowning! Murder! Nobody will come and help him. Why? Because he has lent nothing: and no one owes him anything. No one has anything to lose by his fire, his shipwreck, his fall, or his death. He has lent nothing. And: he would lend nothing either hereafter.
> In short, Faith, Hope and Charity would be banished from this world.

Panurge—a man without a family, alone, whose entire calling in life was getting large amounts of money and then spending it—serves as a fitting prophet for the world that was just beginning to emerge. His perspective of course is that of a *wealthy* debtor—not one liable to be trundled off to some pestiferous dungeon for failure to pay. Still, what he is describing is the logical conclusion, the *reductio ad absurdum*, which Rabelais as always lays out with cheerful perversity, of the assumptions about the world as exchange slumbering behind all our pleasant bourgeois formalities (which Rabelais himself detested—the book is basically a mixture of classical erudition and dirty jokes).

And what he says is true. If we insist on defining all human interactions as matters of people giving one thing for another, then any ongoing human relations can only take the form of debts. Without them, no one would owe anything to anybody. A world without debt would revert to primordial chaos, a war of all against all; no one would feel the slightest responsibility for one another; the simple fact of being human would have no significance; we would all become isolated planets who couldn't even be counted on to maintain our proper orbits.

Pantagruel will have none of it. His own feelings on the matter, he says, can be summed up with one line from the Apostle Paul: "Owe no man anything, save mutual love and affection."[67] Then, in an appropriately biblical gesture, he declares, "From your past debts I shall free you."

"What can I do but thank you?" Panurge replies.

Chapter Six

GAMES WITH SEX AND DEATH

WHEN WE RETURN to an examination of conventional economic history, one thing that jumps out is how much has been made to disappear. Reducing all human life to exchange means not only shunting aside all other forms of economic experience (hierarchy, communism), but also ensuring that the vast majority of the human race who are not adult males, and therefore whose day-to-day existence is relatively difficult to reduce to a matter of swapping things in such a way as to seek mutual advantage, melts away into the background.

As a result, we end up with a sanitized view of the way actual business is conducted. The tidy world of shops and malls is the quintessential middle-class environment, but at either the top or the bottom of the system, the world of financiers or of gangsters, deals are often made in ways not so completely different from ways that the Gunwinggu or Nambikwara make them—at least in that sex, drugs, music, extravagant displays of food, and the potential for violence do often play parts.

Consider the case of Neil Bush (George W.'s brother), who, during divorce proceedings with his wife, admitted to multiple infidelities with women who, he claimed, would mysteriously appear at his hotel-room door after important business meetings in Thailand and Hong Kong.

> "You have to admit it's pretty remarkable," remarked one of his wife's attorneys, "for a man to go to a hotel-room door and open it and have a woman standing there and have sex with her."
>
> "It was very unusual," Bush replied, admitting however that this had happened to him on numerous occasions.
>
> "Were they prostitutes?"
>
> "I don't know."[1]

In fact, such things seem almost par for the course when really big money comes into play.

In this light, the economists' insistence that economic life begins with barter, the innocent exchange of arrows for teepee frames, with no one in a position to rape, humiliate, or torture anyone else, and that it continues in this way, is touchingly utopian.

As a result, though, the histories we tell are full of blank spaces, and the women in them seem to appear out of nowhere, without explanation, much like the Thai women who appeared at Bush's door. Recall the passage cited in Chapter Three, from numismatist Philip Grierson, about money in the barbarian law codes:

> Compensation in the Welsh laws is reckoned primarily in cattle
> and in the Irish ones in cattle or bondmaids (cumal), with con-
> siderable use of precious metals in both. In the Germanic codes
> it is mainly in precious metal . . .[2]

How is it possible to read this passage without immediately stopping at the end of the first line? "Bondmaids"? Doesn't that mean "slaves"? (It does.) In ancient Ireland, female slaves were so plentiful and important that they came to function as currency? How did that happen? And if we are trying to understand the origins of money here, isn't the fact that people are using *one another* as currency at all interesting or significant?[3] Yet none of the sources on money remark much on it. It would seem that by the time of the law codes, slave girls were not actually traded, but just used as units of account. Still, they must have been traded at some point. Who were they? How were they enslaved? Were they captured in war, sold by their parents, or reduced to slavery through debt? Were they a major trade item? The answer to all these questions would seem to be yes, but it's hard to say more because the history remains largely unwritten.[4]

Or let's return to the parable of the ungrateful servant. "Since he was not able to pay, the master ordered that he and his wife and his children and all that he had be sold to repay the debt." How did that happen? Note that we're not even speaking of debt service here (he is already his creditor's servant), but outright slavery. How did a man's wife and children come to be considered no different than his sheep and crockery—as property to be liquidated on occasion of default? Was it normal for a man in first-century Palestine to be able to sell his wife? (It wasn't.)[5] If he didn't own her, why was someone else allowed to sell her if he couldn't pay his debts?

The same could be asked of the story in Nehemiah. It's hard not to empathize with the distress of a father watching his daughter taken off by strangers. On the other hand, one might also ask: Why weren't they taking *him*? The daughter hadn't borrowed any money.

It's not as if it is ordinary for fathers in traditional societies to be able to sell their children. This is a practice with a very specific history: it appears in the great agrarian civilizations, from Sumer to Rome to China, right around the time when we also start to see evidence of money, markets, and interest-bearing loans; later, more gradually, it also appears in those surrounding hinterlands that supplied those civilizations with slaves.[6] What's more, if we examine the historical evidence, there seems good reason to believe that the very obsession with patriarchal honor that so defines "tradition" in the Middle East and Mediterranean world *itself* arose alongside the father's power to alienate his children—as a reaction to what were seen as the moral perils of the market. All of this is treated as somehow outside the bounds of economic history.

Excluding all this is deceptive not only because it excludes the main purposes to which money was actually put in the past, but because it doesn't give us a clear vision of the present. After all, who were those Thai women who so mysteriously appeared at Neil Bush's hotel door? Almost certainly, they were children of indebted parents. Likely as not, they were contractual debt peons themselves.[7]

Focusing on the sex industry would be deceptive, though. Then as now, most women in debt bondage spend the vast majority of their time sewing, preparing soups, and scouring latrines. Even in the Bible, the admonition in the Ten Commandments not to "covet thy neighbor's wife" clearly referred not to lust in one's heart (adultery had already been covered in commandment number seven), but to the prospect of taking her as a debt-peon—in other words, as a servant to sweep one's yard and hang out the laundry.[8] In most such matters, sexual exploitation was at best incidental (usually illegal, sometimes practiced anyway, symbolically important). Again, once we remove some of our usual blinders, we can see that matters have changed far less, over the course of the last five thousand years or so, than we really like to think.

■ ■ ■ ■ ■

These blinders are all the more ironic when one looks at the anthropological literature on what used to be called "primitive money"— that is, the sort one encounters in places where there are no states or markets—whether Iroquois wampum, African cloth money, or Solomon Island feather money, and discovers that such money is used almost exclusively for the kinds of transactions that economists don't like to have to talk about.

In fact, the term "primitive money" is deceptive for this very reason, since it suggests that we are dealing with a crude version of the kind of currencies we use today. But this is precisely what we don't find. Often, such currencies are never used to buy and sell anything at all.[9] Instead, they are used to create, maintain, and otherwise reorganize relations between people: to arrange marriages, establish the paternity of children, head off feuds, console mourners at funerals, seek forgiveness in the case of crimes, negotiate treaties, acquire followers—almost anything but trade in yams, shovels, pigs, or jewelry.

Often, these currencies were extremely important, so much so that social life itself might be said to revolve around getting and disposing of the stuff. Clearly, though, they mark a totally different conception of what money, or indeed an economy, is actually about. I've decided therefore to refer to them as "social currencies," and the economies that employ them as "human economies." By this I mean not that these societies are necessarily in any way more humane (some are quite humane; others extraordinarily brutal), but only that they are economic systems primarily concerned not with the accumulation of wealth, but with the creation, destruction, and rearranging of human beings.

Historically, commercial economies—market economies, as we now like to call them—are a relative newcomer. For most of human history, human economies predominated. To even begin to write a genuine history of debt, then, we have to start by asking: What sort of debts, what sort of credits and debits, do people accumulate in human economies? And what happens when human economies begin to give away to or are taken over by commercial ones? This is another way of asking the question, "How do mere obligations turn into debts?"—but it means not just asking the question in the abstract, but examining the historical record to try to reconstruct what actually did happen.

This is what I will do over the course of the next two chapters. First I will look at the role of money in human economies, then describe what can happen when human economies are suddenly incorporated into the economic orbits of larger, commercial ones. The African slave trade will serve as a particularly catastrophic case in point. Then, in the next chapter, I will return to the first emergence of commercial economies in early civilizations of Europe and the Middle East.

Money as Inadequate Substitute

The most interesting theory of the origin of money is the one recently put forward by a French economist-turned-anthropologist named Philippe Rospabé. While his work is largely unknown in the English-speaking world, it's quite ingenious, and it bears directly on our problem. Rospabé's argument is that "primitive money" was not originally a way to pay debts of any sort. It's a way of recognizing the existence of debts that cannot possibly be paid. His argument is worth considering in detail.

In most human economies, money is used first and foremost to arrange marriages. The simplest and probably most common way of doing this was by being presented as what used to be called "bride-price": a suitor's family would deliver a certain number of dog teeth, or cowries, or brass rings, or whatever is the local social currency, to a woman's family, and they would present their daughter as his bride. It's easy to see why this might be interpreted as buying a woman, and many colonial officials in Africa and Oceania in the early part of the twentieth century did indeed come to that conclusion. The practice caused something of a scandal, and by 1926, the League of Nations was debating banning the practice as a form of slavery. Anthropologists objected. Really, they explained, this was nothing like the purchase of, say, an ox—let alone a pair of sandals. After all, if you buy an ox, you don't have any responsibilities *to* the ox. What you are really buying is the right to dispose of the ox in any way that pleases you. Marriage is entirely different, since a husband will normally have just as many responsibilities toward his wife as his wife will have toward him. It's a way of rearranging relations between people. Second of all, if you were really buying a wife, you'd be able to sell her. Finally, the ultimate significance of the payment concerns the status of the woman's children: if he's buying anything, it's the right to call her offspring his own.[10]

The anthropologists ended up winning the argument, and "bride-price" was dutifully redubbed "bridewealth." But they never really answered the question: What is actually happening here? When a Fijian suitor's family presents a whale tooth to ask for a woman's hand in marriage, is this an advance payment for the services the woman will provide in cultivating her future husband's gardens? Or is he purchasing the future fertility of her womb? Or is this a pure formality, the equivalent of the dollar that has to change hands in order to seal a contract? According to Rospabé, it's none of these. The whale tooth, however valuable, is not a form of payment. It is really an acknowledgment that one is asking for something so uniquely valuable that payment of any sort would be impossible. The only appropriate payment for the gift of a woman is the gift of another woman, in the meantime, all one can do is to acknowledge the outstanding debt.

■ ■ ■ ■ ■

There are places where suitors say this quite explicitly. Consider the Tiv of Central Nigeria, who we have already met briefly in the last chapter. Most of our information on the Tiv comes from mid-century, when they were still under British colonial rule.[11] Everyone at that time insisted that a proper marriage should take the form of an exchange of sisters. One man gives his sister in marriage to another, that man marries the sister of his newfound brother-in-law. This is the perfect marriage because the only thing one can really give in exchange for a woman is another woman.

Obviously, even if every family had exactly equal numbers of brothers and sisters, things couldn't always work this neatly. Say I marry your sister but you don't want to marry mine (because, say, you don't like her, or because she's only five years old). In that case, you become her "guardian," which means you can claim the right to dispose of her in marriage to someone else—for instance, someone whose sister you actually do wish to marry. This system quickly gave rise to a very complex set of arrangements in which most important men became guardians of numerous "wards," often scattered over wide areas; they would swap and trade them and in the process accumulate numerous wives for themselves, while less-fortunate men were only able to marry late in life, or not at all.[12]

There was one other expedient. The Tiv at that time used bundles of brass rods as their most prestigious form of currency. Brass rods were only held by men, and never used to buy things in markets (markets were dominated by women); instead, they were exchanged only for things that men considered of higher importance: cattle, horses, ivory, ritual titles, medical treatment, magical charms. It was possible, as one Tiv ethnographer, Akiga Sai, explains, to acquire a wife with brass rods, but it required quite a lot of them. You would need to give two or three bundles of them to her parents to establish yourself as a suitor; then, when you did finally make off with her (such marriages were always first framed as elopements), another few bundles to assuage her mother when she showed up angrily demanding to know what was going on. This would normally be followed by five more to get her guardian to at least temporarily accept the situation, and more still to her parents when she gave birth, if you were to have any chance of their accepting your claims to be the father of her children. That might get her parents off your back, but you'd have to pay off the guardian forever, because you could never really use money to acquire the rights to a woman. Everyone knew that the only thing you can legitimately give in exchange for a woman is another woman. In this case, everyone has to abide by the pretext that a woman will someday be forthcoming. In the meantime, as one ethnographer succinctly puts it, "the debt can never be fully paid."[13]

According to Rospabé, the Tiv are just making explicit the underlying logic of bridewealth everywhere. The suitor presenting bridewealth is never paying for a woman, or even for the rights to claim her children. That would imply that brass rods, or whale's teeth, cowrie shells, or even cattle are somehow the equivalent of a human being, which by the logic of a human economy is obviously absurd. Only a human could ever be considered equivalent to another human. All the more so since, in the case of marriage, we are speaking of something even more valuable than one human life: we are speaking of a human life that also has the capacity to generate new lives.

Certainly, many of those who pay bridewealth are, like the Tiv, quite explicit about all this. Bridewealth money is presented not to settle a debt, but as a kind of acknowledgment that there exists a debt that *cannot* be settled by means of money. Often the two sides will maintain at least the polite fiction that there will, someday, be a recompense in kind: that the suitor's clan will eventually provide one of its own women, perhaps even that very woman's daughter or granddaughter, to marry a man of the wife's natal clan. Or maybe there will be some arrangement about the disposition of her children; perhaps her clan will get to keep one for itself. The possibilities are endless.

■ ■ ■ ■ ■

Money, then, begins, as Rospabé himself puts it, "as a substitute for life."[14] One might call it the recognition of a life-debt. This, in turn, explains why it's invariably the exact same kind of money that's used to arrange marriages that is also used to pay wergeld (or "bloodwealth," as it's sometimes also called): money presented to the family of a murder victim so as to prevent or resolve a blood-feud. Here the sources are even more explicit. On the one hand, one presents whale teeth or brass rods because the murderer's kin recognize they owe a life to the victim's family. On the other, whale teeth or brass rods are in no sense, and can never be, compensation for the loss of a murdered relative.

Certainly no one presenting such compensation would ever be foolish enough to suggest that any amount of money could possibly be the "equivalent" to the value of someone's father, sister, or child.

So here again, money is first and foremost an acknowledgment that one owes something much more valuable than money.

In the case of a blood-feud, both parties will also be aware that even a revenge killing, while at least it conforms to the principle of a life for a life, won't really compensate for the victim's grief and pain either. This knowledge allows for some possibility of settling the matter without violence. But even here, there is often a feeling that, as in the case of marriage, the *real* solution to the problem is simply being temporarily postponed.

An illustration might be helpful. Among the Nuer, there is a special class of priestly figures who specialize in mediating feuds, referred to in the literature as "leopard-skin chiefs." If one man murders another, he will immediately seek out one of their homesteads, since such a homestead is treated as an inviolate sanctuary: even the dead man's family, who will be honor-bound to avenge the murder, will know that they cannot enter it, lest terrible consequences ensue. According to Evans-Pritchard's classic account, the chief will immediately start trying to negotiate a settlement between the murderer and victim's families, a delicate business, because the victim's family will always first refuse:

> The chief first finds out what cattle the slayer's people possess and what they are prepared to pay in compensation. . . . He then visits the dead man's people and asks them to accept cattle for the life. They usually refuse, for it is a point of honor to be obstinate, but their refusal does not mean that they are unwilling to accept compensation. The chief knows this and insists on their acceptance, even threatening to curse them if they do not give way . . .[15]

More-distant kin weigh in, reminding everyone of their responsibility to the larger community, of all the trouble that an outstanding feud will cause to innocent relatives, and after a great show of holding out, insisting that it is insulting to suggest that any number of cattle could possibly substitute for the life of a son or brother, they will usually grudgingly accept.[16] In fact, even once the matter has technically been settled, it really hasn't—it usually takes years to assemble the cattle, and even once they have been paid, the two sides will avoid each other, "especially at dances, for in the excitement they engender, merely bumping into a man whose kinsman has been slain may cause a fight to break out, because the offense is never forgiven and the score must finally be paid with a life."[17]

So it's much the same as with bridewealth. Money does not wipe out the debt. One life can only be paid for with another. At best those paying bloodwealth, by admitting the existence of the debt and insisting that they wish they could pay it, even though they know this is impossible, can allow the matter to be placed permanently on hold.

Halfway around the world, one finds Lewis Henry Morgan describing the elaborate mechanisms set up by the Six Nations of the Iroquois to avoid precisely this state of affairs. In the event one man killed another,

> Immediately on the commission of a murder, the affair was taken up by the tribes to which the parties belonged, and strenuous efforts were made to effect a reconciliation, lest private retaliation should lead to disastrous consequences.
>
> The first council ascertained whether the offender was willing to confess his crime, and to make atonement. If he was, the council immediately sent a belt of white wampum, in his name, to the other council, which contained a message to that effect. The latter then endeavored to pacify the family of the deceased, to quiet their excitement, and to induce them to accept the wampum as condonation.[18]

Much as in the case of the Nucr, there were complicated schedules of exactly how many fathoms of wampum were paid over, depending on the status of the victim and the nature of the crime. As with the Nuer, too, everyone insisted that this was *not* payment. The value of the wampum in no sense represented the value of the dead man's life:

> The present of white wampum was not in the nature of a compensation for the life of the deceased, but of a regretful confession of the crime, with a petition for forgiveness. It was a peace-offering, the acceptance of which was pressed by mutual friends . . .[19]

Actually, in many cases there was also some way to manipulate the system to turn payments meant to assuage one's rage and grief into ways of creating a new life that would in some sense substitute for the one that was lost. Among the Nuer, forty cattle were set as the standard fee for bloodwealth. But it was also the standard rate of bridewealth. The logic was this: if a man had been murdered before he was able to marry and produce offspring, it's only natural that his spirit would be angry. He had been, effectively, robbed of his eternity. The best solution would be to use the cattle paid in settlement to acquire what was called a "ghost-wife": a woman who would then be formally married to the dead man. Sometimes she was paired off with one of the victim's brothers, sometimes she was left to cohabit with anyone she liked; it didn't really matter too much who impregnated her, since he would be in no sense the father of her children. Any children she produced would be considered the children of the victim's ghost—and as a result, any boys among them were seen as having been born with a particular commitment to someday avenge his death.[20]

Nuer appear to have been unusually stubborn about feuds. Rospabé provides examples from other parts of the world that are even more telling. Among North African Bedouins, for instance, it sometimes happened that the only way to settle a feud was for the killer's family to turn over a daughter, who would then marry the victim's next of kin—his brother, say. If she bore him a male child, the boy was given the same name as his dead uncle and considered to be, at least in the broadest sense, a substitute for him.[21] The Iroquois, who traced descent in the female line, did not trade women in this fashion. However, they had another, more direct approach. If a man died—even of natural causes—his wife's relatives might "put his name upon the mat," sending off belts of wampum to commission a war party, which would then raid an enemy village to secure a captive. The captive could either be tortured to death, or, if the clan matrons were in a benevolent mood (one could never tell; the grief of mourning is tricky), adopted: this was signified by throwing a belt of wampum around his shoulders, whereon he would be given the name of the deceased and be considered, from that moment on, married to the victim's wife, the owner of his personal possessions, and in every way, effectively, the exact same person as the dead man used to be.[22]

All of this merely serves to underline Rospabé's basic point, which is that money can be seen, in human economies, as first and foremost the acknowledgment of the existence of a debt that *cannot* be paid.

In a way, it's all very reminiscent of primordial-debt theory: money emerges from the recognition of an absolute debt to that which has given you life. The difference is that instead of imagining such debts as between an individual and society, or perhaps the cosmos, here they are imagined as a kind of network of dyadic relations: almost everyone in such societies was in a relation of absolute debt to someone else. It's not that we owe "society." If there is any notion of "society" here—and it's not clear that there is—society *is* our debts.

Blood Debts (Lele)

Obviously, this leads us to the same familiar problem: How does a token of recognition that one cannot pay a debt turn into a form of payment by which a debt can be extinguished? If anything, the problem seems even worse than it was before.

In fact, it isn't. The African evidence clearly shows how such things can happen—though the answer is a bit unsettling. To demonstrate this, it will be necessary to look at one or two African societies with a closer focus.

I'll start with the Lele, an African people who had, at the time that Mary Douglas studied them in the 1950s, managed to turn the principle of blood debts into the organizing principle of their entire society.

The Lele were, at that time, perhaps ten thousand souls, living on a stretch of rolling country near the Kasai River in the Belgian Congo, and considered a rude backcountry folk by their richer and more cosmopolitan neighbors, the Kuba and Bushong. Lele women grew maize and manioc; the men thought of themselves as intrepid hunters but spent most of their time weaving and sewing raffia-palm cloth. This cloth was what the area was really known for. It was not only used for every sort of clothing, but also exported: the Lele considered themselves the clothiers of the region, and it was traded with surrounding people to acquire luxuries. Internally, it functioned as a sort of currency. Still, it was not used in markets (there were no markets), and, as Mary Douglas discovered to her great inconvenience, within a village, neither could one use it to acquire food, tools, tableware, or really much of anything else.[23] It was the quintessential social currency.

> Informal gifts of raffia cloth smooth all social relations: husband to wife, son to mother, son to father. They resolve occasions of tension, as peace-offerings; they make parting gifts, or convey congratulations. There are also formal gifts of raffia which are neglected only at risk of rupture of the social ties involved. A man, on reaching adulthood, should give 20 cloths to his father. Otherwise he would be ashamed to ask his father's help for raising his marriage dues. A man should give 20 cloths to his wife on each delivery of a child . . .[24]

Cloth was also used for various fines and fees, and to pay curers. So, for instance, if a man's wife reported a would-be seducer, it was customary to reward her with 20 cloths for her fidelity (it was not required, but not doing so was considered decidedly unwise); if an adulterer was caught, he was expected to pay 50 or 100 cloths to the woman's husband; if the husband and lover disturbed the peace of the village by fighting before the matter was settled, each would have to pay two in compensation, and so forth.

Gifts tended to flow upward. Young people were always giving little presents of cloth as marks of respect to fathers, mothers, uncles, and the like. These gifts were hierarchical in nature: that is, it never occurred to those receiving them that they should have to reciprocate in any way. As a result, elders, and especially elder men, usually had a few extra pieces lying around, and young men, who could never weave quite enough to meet their needs, would have to turn to them whenever time for some major payment rolled around: for instance, if they had to pay a major fine, or wished to hire a doctor to assist their wife in childbirth, or wanted to join a cult society. They were thus always slightly in debt, or at least slightly beholden, to their elders. But everyone also had a whole range of friends and relatives who they had helped out, and so could turn to for assistance.[25]

Marriage was particularly expensive, since the arrangements usually required getting one's hands on several bars of camwood. If raffia cloth was the small change of social life, camwood—a rare imported wood used for the manufacture of cosmetics—was the high-denomination currency. A hundred raffia cloths were equivalent to three to five bars. Few individuals owned much in the way of camwood, usually just little bits to grind up for their own use. Most was kept in each village's collective treasury.

This is not to say that camwood was used for anything like bridewealth—rather, it was used in marriage negotiations, in which all sorts of gifts were passed back and forth. In fact, there was no bridewealth. Men could not use money to acquire women; nor could they use it to claim any rights over children. The Lele were matrilineal. Children belonged not to their father's clan, but to their mother's.

There was another way that men gained control over women, however.[26] This was the system of blood debts.

It is a common understanding among many traditional African peoples that human beings do not simply die without a reason. If someone dies, someone must have killed them. If a Lele woman died in childbirth, for example, this was assumed to be because she had committed adultery. The adulterer was thus responsible for the death. Sometimes she would confess on her deathbed, otherwise the facts of the matter would have to be established through divination. It was the same if a baby died. If someone became sick, or slipped and fell while climbing a tree, their next of kin would check to see if they had been involved in any quarrel that could be said to have caused the misfortune. If all else failed, they could employ magical means to identify the sorcerer. Once the village was satisfied that a culprit had been identified, that person owed a blood-debt: that is, he owed the victim's next of kin a human life. The culprit would thus have to transfer over a young woman from his family, his sister or her daughter, to be the victim's ward, or "pawn."

As with the Tiv, the system quickly became immensely complicated. Pawnship was inherited. If a woman was someone's pawn, so would her children be, and so would her daughters' children. This meant that most males were also considered someone else's man. Still, no one would accept a male pawn in payment of blood-debts: the whole point was to get hold of a young woman, who would then go on to produce additional pawn children. Douglas's Lele informants emphasized that any man would naturally want to have as many of these as possible:

> Ask, "Why do you want to have more pawns?" and they invariably say, "The advantage of owning pawns is that if you incur a blood-debt, you can settle it by paying one of your pawns, and your own sisters remain free." Ask, "Why do you wish your own sisters to remain free?" and they reply, "Ah! then if I incur a blood-debt, I can settle it by giving one of them as a pawn . . ."
>
> Every man is always aware that at any time he is liable for a blood-debt. If any woman he has seduced confesses his name in the throes of child-birth, and subsequently dies, or if her child dies, or if anyone he has quarreled with dies of illness or accident, he may be held responsible . . . Even if a woman runs away from her husband, and fighting breaks out on her account, the deaths will be laid at her door, and her brother or mother's brother will have to pay up. Since only women are accepted as blood-compensation, and since compensation is demanded for all deaths, of men as well as of women, it is obvious that there can never be enough to go around. Men fall into arrears in their pawnship obligations, and girls used to be pledged before their birth, even before their mothers were of marriageable age.[27]

In other words, the whole thing turned into an endlessly complicated chess game—one reason, Douglas remarks, why the term "pawn" seems singularly apropos. Just about every adult Lele male was both someone else's pawn and engaged in a constant game of securing, swapping, or redeeming pawns. Every major drama or tragedy of village life would ordinarily lead to a transfer of rights in women. Almost all of those women would eventually get swapped again.

Several points need to be emphasized here. First of all, what were being traded were, quite specifically, human lives. Douglas calls them "blood-debts," but "life-debts" would be more appropriate. Say, for instance, a man is drowning, and another man rescues him. Or say he's deathly ill but a doctor cures him. In either case, we would likely say one man "owes his life" to the other. So would the Lele, but they meant it literally. Save someone's life, they owe you a life, and a life owed had to be paid back. The usual recourse was for a man whose life was saved to turn over his sister as a pawn—or if not that, a different woman; a pawn he had acquired from someone else.

The second point is that nothing could substitute for a human life. "Compensation was based on the principle of equivalence, a life for a life, a person for a person." Since the value of a human life was absolute, no amount of raffia cloth, or camwood bars, or goats, or transistor radios, or anything else could possibly take its place.

The third and most important point is that in practice, "human life" actually meant "woman's life"—or even more specifically, "young woman's life." Ostensibly this was to maximize one's holdings: above all, one wished for a human being who could become pregnant and produce children, since those children would also be pawns. Still, even Mary Douglas, who was in no sense a feminist, was forced to admit that the whole arrangement did seem to operate as if it were one gigantic apparatus for asserting male control over women. This was true above all because women themselves could not own pawns.[28] They could only be pawns. In other words: when it came to life-debts, only men could be either creditors *or* debtors (in fact, most men were both). Young women were thus the credits and the debits—the pieces being moved around the chessboard—while the hands that moved them were invariably male.[29]

Of course, since almost everyone was a pawn, or had been at some point in their lives, being one could not in itself be much of a tragedy. For male pawns it was in some ways quite advantageous, since one's "owner" had to pay most of one's fines and fees and even blood-debts. This is why, as Douglas's informants uniformly insisted, pawnship had nothing in common with slavery. The Lele did keep slaves, but never very many. Slaves were war captives, usually foreigners. As such they had no family, no one to protect them. To be a pawn, on the other hand, meant to have not one, but two different families to look after you: you still had your own mother and her brothers, but now you also had your "lord."

For a woman, the very fact that she was the stakes in a game that all men were playing afforded all sorts of opportunities to game the system. In principle, a girl might be born a pawn, assigned to some man for eventual marriage. In practice, Mary Douglas insists,

> a little Lele girl would grow up a coquette. From infancy she was the centre of affectionate, teasing, flirting attention. Her affianced husband never gained more than a very limited control over her . . . Since men competed with one another for women there was scope for women to manoeuvre and intrigue. Hopeful seducers were never lacking and no woman doubted that she could get another husband if it suited her.[30]

In addition, a young Lele woman had one unique and powerful card to play. Everyone was well aware that, if she completely refused to countenance her situation, she always had the option of becoming a "village-wife."[31]

The institution of village-wife was a peculiarly Lele one. Probably the best way to describe it is to imagine a hypothetical case. Let us say that an old, important man acquires a young woman as pawn through a blood-debt, and he decides to marry her himself. Technically, he has the right to do so, but it's no fun for a young woman to be an old man's third or fourth wife. Or, say he decides to offer her in marriage to one of his male pawns in a village far away from her mother and natal home. She protests. He ignores her protestations. She waits for an opportune moment and slips off at night to an enemy village, where she asks for sanctuary. This is always possible: all villages have their traditional enemies. Neither would an enemy village refuse a woman who came to them in such a situation. They would immediately declare her "wife of the village," who all men living there would then be obliged to protect.

It helps to understand that here, as in many parts of Africa, most older men had several wives. This meant that the pool of women available for younger men was considerably reduced. As our ethnographer explains, the imbalance was a source of considerable sexual tension:

> Everyone recognized that the young unmarried men coveted the wives of their seniors. Indeed, one of their pastimes was to plan seductions and the man who boasted of none was derided. Since the old men wished to remain polygynists, with two or

three wives, and since adulteries were thought to disrupt the peace of the village, Lele had to make some arrangement to appease their unmarried men.

Therefore, when a sufficient number of them reached the age of eighteen or so, they were allowed to buy the right to a common wife.[32]

After paying an appropriate fee in raffia cloth to the village treasury, they were permitted to build a collective house, and then they were either allotted a wife to put in it or allowed to form a party that would try to steal one from a rival village. (Or, alternately, if one showed up as a refugee, they would ask the rest of the village for the right to accept her: this was invariably granted.) This common wife is what's referred to as a "village wife." The position of village wife was more than respectable. In fact, a newly married village wife was treated very much like a princess. She was not expected to plant or weed in the gardens, fetch wood or water, or even to cook; all household chores were done by her eager young husbands, who provided the best of everything, spending much of their time hunting in the forest vying to bring her the choicest delicacies or plying her with palm wine. She could help herself to others' possessions and was expected to make all sorts of mischief to the bemused indulgence of all concerned. She was also expected to make herself sexually available to all members of the age-set—perhaps ten or twelve different men—at first, pretty much whenever they wanted her.[33]

Over time, a village wife would usually settle down with just three or four of her husbands, and finally, just one. The domestic arrangements were flexible. Nonetheless, in principle, she was married to the village as a whole. If she had children, the village was considered to be their father, and as such expected to bring them up, provide them with resources, and eventually, get them properly married off—which is why villages had to maintain collective treasuries full of raffia and camwood bars in the first place. Since at any time a village was likely to have several village wives, it would also have its own children and grandchildren, and therefore be in a position to both demand and pay blood-debts, and thus, to accumulate pawns.

As a result, villages became corporate bodies, collective groups that, like modern corporations, had to be treated as if they were individuals for purposes of law. There was one key difference, however. Unlike ordinary individuals, villages could back up their claims with force.

As Douglas emphasizes, this was crucial, because ordinary Lele men were simply not able to do this to one another.[34] In everyday affairs, there was an almost complete lack of any systematic means of coercion. This was the main reason, she notes, that pawnship was so innocuous. There were all sorts of rules, but with no government, no courts, no judges to make authoritative decisions, no group of armed men willing or able to employ the threat of force to back those decisions up, rules were there to be adjusted and interpreted. In the end, everyone's feelings had to be taken into account. In everyday affairs, Lele put great stock on gentle and agreeable behavior. Men might have been regularly seized with the urge to throw themselves at each other in fits of jealous rage (often they had good reason to), but they very rarely did. And if a fight did break out, everyone would immediately jump in to break it up and submit the affair to public mediation.[35]

Villages, in contrast, were fortified, and age-sets could be mobilized to act as military units. Here, and only here, did organized violence enter the picture. True, when villages fought, it was also always over women (everyone Douglas talked to expressed incredulity at the very idea that grown men, anywhere, could ever come to blows over anything else). But in the case of villages, it could come to an actual war. If another village's elders ignored one's claims to a pawn, one's young men might organize a raiding party and kidnap her, or carry off some other likely young women to be their collective wife. This might lead to deaths, and to further claims for compensation. "Since it had the backing of force," Douglas observes drily, "the village could afford to be less conciliatory towards the wishes of its pawns."[36]

It's at exactly this point, too, where the potential for violence enters, that the great wall constructed between the value of lives and money can suddenly come tumbling down.

> Sometimes when two clans were disputing a claim to blood compensation, the claimant might see no hope of getting satisfaction from his opponents. The political system offered no direct means for one man (or clan) to use physical coercion or to resort to superior authority to enforce claims against another. In such a case, rather than abandon his claim to a pawn-woman, he would be ready to take the equivalent in wealth, if he could get it. The usual procedure was to sell his case against the defendants to the only group capable of extorting a pawn by force, that is, to a village.
>
> The man who meant to sell his case to a village asked them for 100 raffia cloths or five bars of camwood. The village raised the amount, either from its treasury, or by a loan from one

of its members, and thereby adopted as its own his claim to
a pawn.[37]

Once he held the money, his claim was over, and the village, which had
now bought it, would proceed to organize a raid to seize the woman
in dispute.

   In other words, it was *only* when violence was brought into the
equation that there was any question of buying and selling people. The
ability to deploy force, to cut through the endless maze of preferences,
obligations, expectations, and responsibilities that mark real human
relationships, also made it possible to overcome what is otherwise the
first rule of all Lele economic relationships: that human lives can only
be exchanged for other human lives, and never for physical objects.
Significantly, the amount paid—a hundred cloths, or an equivalent
amount of camwood—was also the price of a slave.[38] Slaves were, as
I mentioned, war captives. There seem never to have been very many
of them; Douglas only managed to locate two descendants of slaves
in the 1950s, some twenty-five years after the practice had been abolished.[39] Still, the numbers were not important. The mere fact of their
existence set a precedent. The value of a human life could, sometimes,
be quantified; but if one was able to move from A = A (one life equals
another) to A = B (one life = one hundred cloths), it was only because
the equation was established at the point of a spear.

Flesh-Debt (Tiv)

I have dwelt on the Lele in such detail in part because I wanted to con-
vey some sense of why I was using the term "human economy," what
life is like inside one, what sort of dramas fill people's days, and how
money typically operates in the midst of all this. Lele currencies are,
as I say, quintessential social currencies. They are used to mark every
visit, every promise, every important moment in a man's or woman's
life. It is surely significant, too, what the objects used as currency here
actually were. Raffia cloth was used for clothing. In Douglas's day,
it was the main thing used to clothe the human body; camwood bars
were the source of a red paste that was used as a cosmetic—it was the
main substance used as makeup, by both men and women, to beautify
themselves each day. These, then, were the materials used to shape
people's physical appearance, to make them appear mature, decent, attractive, and dignified to their fellows. They were what turned a mere
naked body into a proper social being.

This is no coincidence. In fact, it's extraordinarily common in what I've been calling human economies. Money almost always arises first from objects that are used primarily as adornment of the person. Beads, shells, feathers, dog or whale teeth, gold, and silver are all well-known cases in point. All are useless for any purpose other than making people look more interesting, and hence, more beautiful. The brass rods used by the Tiv might seem an exception, but actually they're not: they were used mainly as raw material for the manufacture of jewelry, or simply twisted into hoops and worn at dances. There are exceptions (cattle, for instance), but as a general rule, it's only when governments, and then markets, enter the picture that we begin to see currencies like barley, cheese, tobacco, or salt.[40]

It also illustrates the peculiar progression of ideas that so often mark human economies. On the one hand, human life is the absolute value. There is no possible equivalent. Whether a life is given or taken, the debt is absolute. In places, this principle is indeed sacrosanct. More often, it is compromised by the elaborate games played by the Tiv, who treat the giving of lives, and the Lele, who treat the taking of lives, as creating debts that can only be paid by delivering another human being. In each case, too, the practice ends up engendering an extraordinarily complex game in which important men end up exchanging women, or at least, rights over their fertility.

But this is already a kind of opening. Once the game exists, once the principle of substitution comes in, there was always the possibility of extending it. When that begins to happen, systems of debt that were premised on creating people can—even here—suddenly become the means of destroying them.

As an example, let us once again return to the Tiv. The reader will recall that if a man did not have a sister or a ward to give in exchange for one's wife, it was possible to assuage her parents and guardians by gifts of money. However, such a wife would never be considered truly his. Here too, there was one dramatic exception. A man could buy a slave, a woman kidnapped in a raid from a distant country.[41] Slaves, after all, had no parents, or could be treated as if they didn't; they had been forcibly removed from all those networks of mutual obligation and debt in which ordinary people acquired their outward identities. This was why they could be bought and sold.

Once married, though, a purchased wife would quickly develop new ties. She was no longer a slave, and her children were perfectly legitimate—more so, in fact, than those of a wife who was merely acquired through the continual payment of brass rods.

We have perhaps a general principle: to make something saleable, in a human economy, one needs to first rip it from its context. That's what slaves are: people stolen from the community that made them what they are. As strangers to their new communities, slaves no longer had mothers, fathers, kin of any sort. This is why they could be bought and sold or even killed: because the *only* relation they had was to their owners. A Lele village's ability to organize raids and kidnap a woman from an alien community seems to have been the key to its ability to start trading women for money—even if in their case, they could do so only to a very limited extent. After all, her relatives were not very far away, and they would surely come around demanding an explanation. In the end, someone would have to come up with an arrangement that everyone could live with.[42]

Still, I would also insist that there is something more than this. One gets the distinct sense, in much of the literature, that many African societies were haunted by the awareness that these elaborate networks of debt could, if things went just slightly wrong, be transformed into something absolutely terrible. The Tiv are a dramatic case in point.

■ ■ ■ ■ ■

Among students of anthropology, the Tiv are mainly famous for the fact that their economic life was divided into what their best-known ethnographers, Paul and Laura Bohannan, referred to as three separate "spheres of exchange." Ordinary, everyday economic activity was mostly the affair of women. They were the ones who filled the markets, and who trod the paths giving and returning minor gifts of okra, nuts, or fish. Men concerned themselves with what they considered higher things: the kind of transactions that could be conducted using the Tiv currency, which, as with the Lele, consisted of two denominations, a kind of locally made cloth called *tugudu*, widely exported, and, for major transactions, bundles of imported brass rods.[43] These could be used to acquire certain flashy and luxurious things (cows, purchased foreign wives), but they were mainly for the give and take of political affairs, hiring curers, acquiring magic, gaining initiation into cult societies. In political matters, Tiv were even more resolutely egalitarian than the Lele: successful old men with their numerous wives might have lorded it over their sons and other dependants within their own house compounds, but beyond that, there was no formal political organization of any sort. Finally, there was the system of wards, which consisted entirely of men's rights in women. Hence, the notion of "spheres." In principle, these three levels—ordinary consumption goods, masculine prestige goods, and rights in women—were completely separate. No amount of okra could get you a brass rod, just as, in principle, no number of brass rods could give you full rights to a woman.

In practice, there were ways to game the system. Say a neighbor was sponsoring a feast but was short on supplies; one might come to his aid, then later, discreetly, ask for a bundle or two in repayment. To be able to wheel and deal, to "turn chickens into cows," as the saying went, and ultimately, broker one's wealth and prestige into a way of acquiring wives, required a "strong heart"—that is, an enterprising and charismatic personality.[44] But "strong heart" had another meaning too. There was believed to be a certain actual biological substance called *tsav* that grew on the human heart. This was what gave certain people their charm, their energy, and their powers of persuasion. *Tsav* therefore was both a physical substance and that invisible power that allows certain people to bend others to their will.[45]

The problem was—and most Tiv of that time appear to have believed that this was *the* problem with their society—that it was also possible to augment one's *tsav* through artificial means, and this could only be accomplished by consuming human flesh.

Now, I should emphasize right away that there is no reason to believe that any Tiv actually did practice cannibalism. The idea of eating human flesh appears to have disgusted and horrified the average Tiv as much as it would the average American. Yet for centuries, most appear to have been veritably obsessed by the suspicion that some of their neighbors—and particularly prominent men who became de facto political leaders—were, in fact, secret cannibals. Men who built up their *tsav* by such means, the stories went, attained extraordinary powers: the ability to fly, to become impervious to weapons, to be able to send out their souls at night to kill their victims in such a way that their victims did not even know that they were dead, but would wander about, confused and feckless, to be harvested for their cannibal feasts. They became, in short, terrifying witches.[46]

The *mbatsav*, or society of witches, was always looking for new members, and the way to accomplish this was to trick people into eating human flesh. A witch would take a piece of the body of one of his own close relatives, who he had murdered, and place it in the victim's food. If the man was foolish enough to eat it, he would contract a "flesh-debt," and the society of witches ensured that flesh-debts are always paid.

> Perhaps your friend, or some older man, has noticed that you
> have a large number of children, or brothers and sisters, and so

tricks you into contracting the debt with him. He invites you
to eat food in his house alone with him, and when you begin
the meal he sets before you two dishes of sauce, one of which
contains cooked human flesh . . .

If you eat from the wrong dish, but you do not have a "strong
heart"—the potential to become a witch—you will become sick and
flee from the house in terror. But if you have that hidden potential, the
flesh will begin to work in you. That evening, you will find your house
surrounded by screeching cats and owls. Strange noises will fill the air.
Your new creditor will appear before you, backed by his confederates
in evil. He will tell of how he killed his own brother so you two could
dine together, and pretend to be tortured by the thought of having lost
his own kin as you sit there, surrounded by your plump and healthy
relatives. The other witches will concur, acting as if all this is your own
fault. "You have sought for trouble, and trouble has come upon you.
Come and lie down on the ground, that we may cut your throat."[47]
There's only one way out, and that's to pledge a member of your
own family as substitute. This is possible, because you will find you
have terrible new powers, but they must be used as the other witches
demand. One by one, you must kill off your brothers, sisters, children;
their bodies will be stolen from their graves by the college of witches,
brought back to life just long enough to be properly fattened, tortured,
killed again, then carved and roasted for yet another feast.

> The flesh debt goes on and on. The creditor keeps on coming.
> Unless the debtor has men behind him who are very strong in
> *tsav*, he cannot free himself from the flesh debt until he has
> given up all his people, and his family is finished. Then he goes
> himself and lies down on the ground to be slaughtered, and so
> the debt is finally discharged.[48]

The Slave Trade

In one sense, it's obvious what's going on here. Men with "strong
hearts" have power and charisma; using it, they can manipulate debt
to turn extra food into treasures, and treasures into wives, wards, and
daughters, and thus become the heads of ever-growing families. But
that very power and charisma that allows them to do this also makes
them run the constant danger of sending the whole process jolting back

into a kind of horrific implosion, of creating flesh-debts whereby one's family is converted back into food.

Now, if one is simply trying to imagine the worst thing that could possibly happen to someone, surely, being forced to dine on the mutilated corpses of one's own children would, anywhere, be pretty high on the list. Still, anthropologists have come to understand, over the years, that every society is haunted by slightly different nightmares, and these differences are significant. Horror stories, whether about vampires, ghouls, or flesh-eating zombies, always turn out to reflect some aspect of the tellers' own social lives, some terrifying potential, in the way they are accustomed to interact with each other, that they do not wish to acknowledge or confront, but also cannot help but talk about.[49]

In the Tiv case, what would that be? Clearly, Tiv did have a major problem with authority. They lived in a landscape dotted with compounds, each organized around a single older man with his numerous wives, children, and assorted hangers-on. Within each compound, that man had near-absolute authority. Outside there was no formal political structure, and Tiv were fiercely egalitarian. In other words: all men aspired to become the masters of large families, but they were extremely suspicious of any other form of mastery. Hardly surprising, then, that Tiv men were so ambivalent about the nature of power that they became convinced that the very qualities that allow a man to rise to legitimate prominence could, if taken just a little bit further, turn him into a monster.[50] In fact, most Tiv seemed to assume that most male elders *were* witches, and that if a young person died, they were probably being paid off for a flesh-debt.

But this still doesn't answer the one obvious question: Why is all this framed in terms of debt?

■ ■ ■ ■ ■

Here a little history is in order. It would appear that the ancestors of the Tiv arrived in the Benue river valley and adjacent lands sometime around 1750—a time when all of what's now Nigeria was being torn apart by the Atlantic slave trade. Early stories relate how the Tiv, during their migrations, used to paint their wives and children with what looked like smallpox scars, so that potential raiders would be afraid to carry them off.[51] They established themselves in a notoriously inaccessible stretch of country and offered up ferocious defense against periodic raids from neighboring kingdoms to their north and west—with which they eventually came to a political rapprochement.[52]

The Tiv, then, were well aware of what was happening all around them. Consider, for example, the case of the copper bars whose use they were so careful to restrict, so as to avoid their becoming an all-purpose form of currency.

Now, copper bars had been used for money in this part of Africa for centuries, and at least in some places, for ordinary commercial transactions, as well. It was easy enough to do: one simply snapped them apart into smaller pieces, or pulled some of them into thin wires, twisted those around into little loops, and one had perfectly service-able small change for everyday market transactions.[53] Most of the ones current in Tivland since the late eighteenth century, on the other hand, were mass-produced in factories in Birmingham and imported through the port of Old Calabar, at the mouth of the Cross River, by slave-traders based in Liverpool and Bristol.[54] In all the country adjoining the Cross River—that is, in the region directly to the south of the Tiv territory—copper bars were used as everyday currency. This was presumably how they entered Tivland; they were either carried in by pedlars from the Cross River or acquired by Tiv traders on expeditions abroad. All this, however, makes the fact that the Tiv refused to use copper bars as such a currency doubly significant.

During the 1760s alone, perhaps a hundred thousand Africans were shipped down the Cross River to Calabar and nearby ports, where they were put in chains, placed on British, French, or other European ships, and shipped across the Atlantic—part of perhaps a million and a half exported from the Bight of Biafra during the whole period of the Atlantic slave trade.[55] Some of them had been captured in wars or raids, or simply kidnapped. The majority, though, were carried off because of debts.

Here, though, I must explain something about the organization of the slave trade.

The Atlantic Slave Trade as a whole was a gigantic network of credit arrangements. Ship-owners based in Liverpool or Bristol would acquire goods on easy credit terms from local wholesalers, expecting to make good by selling slaves (also on credit) to planters in the Antilles and America, with commission agents in the city of London ultimately financing the affair through the profits of the sugar and tobacco trade.[56] Ship-owners would then transport their wares to African ports like Old Calabar. Calabar itself was the quintessential mercantile city-state, dominated by rich African merchants who dressed in European clothes, lived in European-style houses, and in some cases even sent their children to England to be educated.

On arrival, European traders would negotiate the value of their cargoes in the copper bars that served as the currency of the port. In 1698, a merchant aboard a ship called the *Dragon* noted the following prices he managed to establish for his wares:

one bar iron	4 copper bars
one bunch of beads	4 copper bars
five rangoes[57]	4 copper bars
one basin No. 1	4 copper bars
one tankard	3 copper bars
one yard linen	1 copper bar
six knives	1 copper bar
one brass bell No. 1	3 copper bars[58]

By the height of the trade fifty years later, British ships were bringing in large quantities of cloth (both products of the newly created Manchester mills and calicoes from India) and iron and copper ware, along with incidental goods like beads, and also, for obvious reasons, substantial numbers of firearms.[59] The goods were then advanced to African merchants, again on credit, who assigned them to their own agents to move upstream.

The obvious problem was how to secure the debt. The trade was an extraordinarily duplicitous and brutal business, and slave raiders were unlikely to be dependable credit risks—especially when dealing with foreign merchants who they might never see again.[60] As a result, a system quickly developed in which European captains would demand security in the form of pawns.

These pawns are quite different from the kind we encountered among the Lele. In many of the kingdoms and trading towns of West Africa, the nature of pawnship appears to have already undergone profound changes by the time Europeans showed up on the scene around 1500—it had become, effectively, a kind of debt peonage. Debtors would pledge family members as surety for loans; the pawns would then become dependents in the creditors' households, working their fields and tending to their household chores—their persons acting as security while their labor, effectively, substituted for interest.[61] Pawns were not slaves; they were not, like slaves, cut off from their families; but neither were they precisely free.[62] In Calabar and other ports, masters of slaving ships, on advancing goods to their African counterparts, developed the custom of demanding pawns as security—for instance, two of the merchant's own dependents for every three slaves to be delivered, preferably including at least one member of the merchant's families.[63] This was in practice not much different than demanding the surrender of hostages, and at times it created major political crises when captains, tired of waiting for delayed shipments, decided to take off with a cargo of pawns instead.

Upriver, debt pawns also played a major part in the trade. In one way, the area was a bit unusual. In most of West Africa, the trade ran through major kingdoms such as Dahomey or Asante to make wars and impose draconian punishments—one very common expedient for rulers was to manipulate the justice system, so that almost any crime came to be punishable by enslavement, or by death with the enslavement of one's wife and children, or by outrageously high fines which, if one could not pay them, would cause the defaulter and his family to be sold as slaves. In another way, it is unusually revealing, since the lack of any larger government structures made it easier to see what was really happening. The pervasive climate of violence led to the systematic perversion of all the institutions of existing human economies, which were transformed into a gigantic apparatus of dehumanization and destruction.

In the Cross River region, the trade seems to have seen two phases. The first was a period of absolute terror and utter chaos, in which raids were frequent, and anyone traveling alone risked being kidnapped by roving gangs of thugs and sold to Calabar. Before long, villages lay abandoned; many people fled into the forest; men would have to form armed parties to work the fields.[64] This period was relatively brief. The second began when representatives of local merchant societies began to establish themselves in communities up and down the region, offering to restore order. The most famous of these was the Aro Confederacy, who called themselves "Children of God."[65] Backed by heavily armed mercenaries and the prestige of their famous Oracle at Arochukwu, they established a new and notoriously harsh justice system.[66] Kidnappers were hunted down and themselves sold as slaves. Safety was restored to roads and farmsteads. At the same time, Aro collaborated with local elders to create a code of ritual laws and penalties so comprehensive and severe that everyone was at constant risk of falling afoul of them.[67] Anyone who violated even the most apparently trivial of these laws and could not pay the fine would be turned over to the Aro for transport to the coast, with their accuser receiving their price in copper bars.[68] According to some contemporary accounts, a man who simply disliked his wife and was in need of brass rods could always come up with some reason to sell her, and the village elders—who received a share of the profits—would almost invariably concur.[69]

The most ingenious trick of the merchant societies, though, was to assist in the dissemination of a secret society, called Ekpe, which made its members complicit in their own potential enslavement. Ekpe was most famous for sponsoring magnificent masquerades and for initiating its members into arcane mysteries, but it also acted as a secret mechanism for the enforcement of debts.[70] In Calabar itself, for example, the Ekpe society had access to a whole range of sanctions, starting with boycotts (all members were forbidden to conduct trade with a defaulting debtor), fines, seizure of property, arrest, and finally, execution—with the most hapless victims left tied to trees, their lower jaws removed, as a warning to others.[71] It was ingenious, particularly, because such societies always allowed anyone to buy in, rising though the nine initiatory grades if they could pay the fee—these also exacted, of course, in the brass rods the merchants themselves supplied. In Calabar, the fee schedule for each grade looked like this:[72]

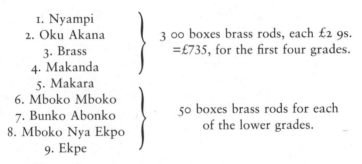

1. Nyampi
2. Oku Akana
3. Brass
4. Makanda
} 3 oo boxes brass rods, each £2 9s. =£735, for the first four grades.

5. Makara
6. Mboko Mboko
7. Bunko Abonko
8. Mboko Nya Ekpo
9. Ekpe
} 50 boxes brass rods for each of the lower grades.

In other words, it was quite expensive. But membership quickly became the chief mark of honor and distinction everywhere. Entry fees were no doubt less exorbitant in small, distant communities, but the effect was still the same: thousands ended up in debt to the merchants, whether for the fees required for joining, or for the trade goods they supplied (mostly cloth and metal put to use creating the gear and costumes for the Ekpe performances—debts that they thus themselves became responsible for enforcing on themselves. These debts, too, were regularly paid in people, ostensibly yielded up as pawns.)

How did it work in practice? It appears to have varied a great deal from place to place. In the Afikpo district, on a remote part of the upper Cross River, for instance, we read that everyday affairs—the acquisition of food, for example—was conducted, as among the Tiv, "without trade or the use of money." Brass rods, supplied by the merchant

societies, were used to buy and sell slaves, but otherwise mostly as a
social currency, "used for gifts and for payments in funerals, titles, and
other ceremonies."[73] Most of those payments, titles, and ceremonies
were tied to the secret societies that the merchants had also brought
to the area. All this does sound a bit like the Tiv arrangement, but the
presence of the merchants ensured that the effects were very different:

> In the old days, if anybody got into trouble or debt in the up-
> per parts of the Cross River, and wanted ready money, he used
> generally to "pledge" one or more of his children, or some
> other members of his family or household, to one of the Aku-
> nakuna traders who paid periodical visits to his village. Or he
> would make a raid on some neighboring village, seize a child,
> and sell him or her to the same willing purchaser.[74]

The passage only makes sense if one recognizes that debtors were
also, owing to their membership in the secret societies, collectors. The
seizing of a child is a reference to the local practice of "panyarring,"
current throughout West Africa, by which creditors despairing of repayment would simply sweep into the debtor's community with a group of
armed men and seize anything—people, goods, domestic animals—that
could be easily carried off, then hold it hostage as security.[75] It didn't
matter if the people or goods had belonged to the debtor, or even the
debtor's relatives. A neighbor's goats or children would do just as well,
since the whole point was to bring social pressure on whoever owed
the money. As William Bosman put it, "If the Debtor be an honest man
and the Debt just, he immediately endeavours by the satisfaction of his
Creditors to free his Countrymen."[76] It was actually a quite sensible
expedient in an environment with no central authority, where people
tended to feel an enormous sense of responsibility toward other members of their community and very little responsibility toward anyone
else. In the case of the secret society cited above, the debtor would,
presumably, be calling in his own debts—real or imagined—to those
outside the organization, in order not to have to send off members of
his own family.[77]

Such expedients were not always effective. Often debtors would be
forced to pawn more and more of their own children or dependents,
until finally there was no recourse but to pawn themselves.[78] And of
course, at the height of the slave trade, "pawning" had become little
more than a euphemism. The distinction between pawns and slaves
had largely disappeared. Debtors, like their families before them, ended
up turned over to the Aro, then to the British, and finally, shackled and

chained, crowded into tiny slaving vessels and sent off to be sold on plantations across the sea.[79]

■ ■ ■ ■ ■

If the Tiv, then, were haunted by the vision of an insidious secret organization that lured unsuspecting victims into debt traps, whereby they themselves became the enforcers of debts to be paid with the bodies of their children, and ultimately, themselves—one reason was because this was literally happening to people who lived a few hundred miles away. Nor is the use of the phrase "flesh-debt" in any way inappropriate. Slave-traders might not have been reducing their victims to meat, but they were certainly reducing them to nothing more than bodies. To be a slave was to be plucked from one's family, kin, friends, and community, stripped of one's name, identity, and dignity; of everything that made one a person rather than a mere human machine capable of understanding orders. Neither were most slaves offered much opportunity to develop enduring human relations. Most that ended up in Caribbean or American plantations were simply worked to death.

What is remarkable is that all this was done, the bodies extracted, through the very mechanisms of the human economy, premised on the principle that human lives are the ultimate value, to which nothing could possibly compare. Instead, all the same institutions—fees for initiations, means of calculating guilt and compensation, social currencies, debt pawnship—were turned into their opposite; the machinery was, as it were, thrown into reverse; and, as the Tiv also perceived, the gears and mechanisms designed for the creation of human beings collapsed on themselves and became the means for their destruction.

■ ■ ■ ■ ■

I do not want to leave the reader with the impression that what I am describing here is in any way peculiar to Africa. One could find the exact same things happening wherever human economies came into contact with commercial ones (and particularly, commercial economies with advanced military technology and an insatiable demand for human labor).

Remarkably similar things, for instance, can be observed throughout Southeast Asia, particularly amongst hill and island people living on the fringes of major kingdoms. As the premier historian of the region,

Anthony Reid, has pointed out, labor throughout Southeast Asia has long been organized above all through relations of debt bondage.

> Even in relatively simple societies little penetrated by money, there were ritual needs for substantial expenditures—the payment of bride-price for marriage and the slaughter of a buffalo at the death of a family member. It is widely reported that such ritual needs are the most common reason why the poor become indebted to the rich . . .[80]

One practice, noted from Thailand to Sulawesi, is for a group of poor brothers to turn to a rich sponsor to pay for the expenses of one brother's marriage. He's then referred to as their "master." This is more like a patron-client relation than anything else: the brothers might be obliged to do the occasional odd job or appear as his entourage on occasions when he has to make a good impression—not much more. Still, technically, he owns their children and "can also repossess the wife he provided if his bondsmen fail to carry out his obligations."[81]

Elsewhere, we hear similar stories to those in Africa—of peasants pawning themselves or members of their families, or even gambling themselves into bondage; of principalities where penalties invariably took the form of heavy fines. "Frequently, of course, these fines could not be paid, and the condemned man, often accompanied by his dependants, became the bondsman of the ruler, of the injured party, or of whoever was able to pay his fine for him."[82] Reid insists that most of this was relatively innocuous—in fact, poor men might take out loans for the express purpose of becoming debtors to some wealthy patron who could provide them with food during hard times, a roof, a wife. Clearly, this was not "slavery" in the ordinary sense. That is, unless the patron decided to ship some of his dependents off to creditors of his own in some distant city like Majapahit or Ternate, whereupon they could well find themselves toiling in some grandee's kitchen or pepper plantation like any other slave.

It's important to point this out because one of the effects of the slave trade is that people who don't actually live in Africa are often left with an image of that continent as an irredeemably violent, savage place—an image that has had disastrous effects on those who do live there. It might be fitting, then, to consider the history of one place that is usually represented as the polar opposite: Bali, the famous "land of ten thousand temples"—an island often pictured in anthropological texts and tourist brochures as if it were inhabited exclusively by placid, dreamy artists who spend their days arranging flowers and practicing synchronized dance routines.

In the seventeenth and eighteenth centuries, Bali had not yet obtained this reputation. At the time, it was still divided among a dozen tiny, squabbling kingdoms in an almost perpetual state of war. In fact, its reputation among the Dutch merchants and officials ensconced in nearby Java was almost exactly the opposite of what it is today. Balinese were considered a rude and violent people ruled by decadent, opium-addicted nobles whose wealth was based almost exclusively on their willingness to sell their subjects to foreigners as slaves. By the time the Dutch were fully in control in Java, Bali had been turned largely into a reservoir for the export of human beings—young Balinese women in particular being in great demand in cities through the region as both prostitutes and concubines.[83] As the island was drawn into the slave trade, almost the entire social and political system of the island was transformed into an apparatus for the forcible extraction of women. Even within villages, ordinary marriages took the form of "marriage by capture"—sometimes staged elopements, sometimes real forcible kidnappings, after which the kidnappers would pay a woman's family to let the matter drop.[84] If a woman was captured by someone genuinely important, though, no compensation would be offered. Even in the 1960s, elders recalled how attractive young women used to be hidden away by their parents,

> forbidden to bear towering offerings to temple festivals, lest they be espied by a royal scout and hustled into the closely protected female quarters of the palace, where the eyes of male visitors were restricted to foot level. For there was slim chance a girl would become a legitimate low-caste wife (*penawing*) of the raja . . . More likely after affording a few years' licentious satisfaction, she would degenerate into a slave-like servant.[85]

Or, if she did rise to such a position that the high-caste wives began to see her as a rival, she might be either poisoned or shipped off overseas to end up servicing soldiers at some Chinese-run bordello in Jogjakarta, or changing bedpans in the house of a French plantation-owner in the Indian Ocean island of Reunion.[86] Meanwhile, royal law codes were rewritten in all the usual ways, with the exception that here, the force of law was directed above all and explicitly against women. Not only were criminals and debtors to be enslaved and deported, but any married man was granted the power to renounce his wife, and by doing so to render her, automatically, property of the local ruler, to be disposed of as he wished. Even a woman whose husband died before she had produced male offspring could be handed over to the palace to be sold abroad.[87]

As Adrian Vickers explains, even Bali's famous cockfights—so familiar to any first-year anthropology student—were originally promoted by royal courts as a way of recruiting human merchandise:

> Kings even helped put people into debt by staging large cock-fights in their capitals. The passion and extravagance encouraged by this exciting sport led many peasants to bet more than they could afford. As with any gambling, the hope of great wealth and the drama of a contest fuelled ambitions which few could afford and at the end of the day, when the last spur had sunk into the chest of the last rooster, many peasants had no home and family to return to. They, and their wives and children, would be sold to Java.[88]

Reflections on Violence

I began this book by asking a question: How is it that moral obligations between people come to be thought of as debts and as a result, end up justifying behavior that would otherwise seem utterly immoral?

I began this chapter by beginning to propose an answer: by making a distinction between commercial economies and what I call "human economies"—that is, those where money acts primarily as a social currency, to create, maintain, or sever relations between people rather than to purchase things. As Rospabé so cogently demonstrated, it is the peculiar quality of such social currencies that they are never quite equivalent to people. If anything, they are a constant reminder that human beings can never be equivalent to anything—even, ultimately, to one another. This is the profound truth of the blood-feud. No one can ever really forgive the man who killed his brother because every brother is unique. Nothing could substitute—not even some other man given the same name and status as your brother, or a concubine who will bear a son who will be named after your brother, or a ghost-wife who will bear a child pledged to some day avenge his death.

In a human economy, each person is unique, and of incomparable value, because each is a unique nexus of relations with others. A woman may be a daughter, sister, lover, rival, companion, mother, age-mate, and mentor to many different people in different ways. Each relation is unique, even in a society in which they are sustained through the constant giving back and forth of generic objects such as raffia cloth or bundles of copper wire. In one sense, those objects make one who one is—a fact illustrated by the way the objects used as social currencies are so often things otherwise used to clothe or decorate the human body, that help make one who one is in the eyes of others. Still, just as our clothes don't really make us who we are, a relationship kept alive by the giving and taking of raffia is always something more than that.[89] This means that the raffia, in turn, is always something less. This is why I think Rospabé was right to emphasize the fact that in such economies, money can never substitute for a person: money is a way of acknowledging that very fact, that the debt cannot be paid. But even the notion that a person can substitute for a person, that one sister can somehow be equated with another, is by no means self-evident. In this sense, the term "human economy" is double-edged. These are, after all, *economies*: that is, systems of exchange in which qualities are reduced to quantities, allowing calculations of gain and loss—even if those calculations are simply a matter (as in sister exchange) of 1 equals 1, or (as in the feud) of 1 minus 1 equals 0.

How is this calculability effectuated? How does it become possible to treat people as if they are identical? The Lele example gave us a hint: to make a human being an object of exchange, one woman equivalent to another, for example, requires first of all ripping her from her context; that is, tearing her away from that web of relations that makes her the unique conflux of relations that she is, and thus, into a generic value capable of being added and subtracted and used as a means to measure debt. This requires a certain violence. To make her equivalent to a bar of camwood takes even more violence, and it takes an enormous amount of sustained and systematic violence to rip her so completely from her context that she becomes a slave.

I should be clear here. I am not using the word "violence" metaphorically. I am not speaking merely of conceptual violence, but of the literal threat of broken bones and bruised flesh; of punches and kicks; in much the same way that when the ancient Hebrews spoke of their daughters in "bondage," they were not being poetic, but talking about literal ropes and chains.

Most of us don't like to think much about violence. Those lucky enough to live relatively comfortable, secure lives in modern cities tend either to act as if it does not exist or, when reminded that it does, to write off the larger world "out there" as a terrible, brutal place, with not much that can be done to help it. Either instinct allows us not to have to think about the degree to which even our own daily existence is defined by violence or at least the threat of violence (as I've often

noted, think about what would happen if you were to insist on your
right to enter a university library without a properly validated ID), and
to overstate the importance—or at least the frequency—of things like
war, terrorism, and violent crime. The role of force in providing the
framework for human relations is simply more explicit in what we call
"traditional societies"—even if in many, actual physical assault by one
human on another occurs less often than in our own. Here's a story
from the Bunyoro kingdom, in East Africa:

> Once a man moved into a new village. He wanted to find out
> what his neighbors were like, so in the middle of the night he
> pretended to beat his wife very severely, to see if the neighbors
> would come and remonstrate with him. But he did not really
> beat her; instead he beat a goatskin, while his wife screamed
> and cried out that he was killing her. Nobody came, and the
> very next day the man and his wife packed up and left that vil-
> lage and went to find some other place to live.[90]

The point is obvious. In a proper village, the neighbors should have
rushed in, held him back, demanded to know what the woman could
possibly have done to deserve such treatment. The dispute would become a collective concern that ended in some sort of collective settlement. This is how people ought to live. No reasonable man or woman
would want to live in a place where neighbors don't look after one
another.

In its own way it's a revealing story, charming even, but one must
still ask: How would a community—even one the man in the story would have considered a proper community—have reacted if they
thought *she* was beating *him*?[91] I think we all know the answer. The
first case would have led to concern; the second would have led to ridi-
cule. In Europe in the sixteenth and seventeenth centuries, young villagers used to put on satirical skits making fun of husbands beaten by
their wives, even to parade them about the town mounted backwards
on an ass for everyone to jeer at.[92] No African society, as far as I know,
went quite this far. (Neither did any African society burn as many
witches—Western Europe at that time was a particularly savage place.)
Yet as in most of the world, the assumption that the one sort of brutality was at least potentially legitimate, and that the other was not, was
the framework within which relations between the sexes took place.[93]

What I want to emphasize is that there is a direct relation between that fact and the possibility of trading lives for one another.

Anthropologists are fond of making diagrams to represent preferential marriage patterns. Sometimes, these diagrams can be quite beautiful:[94]

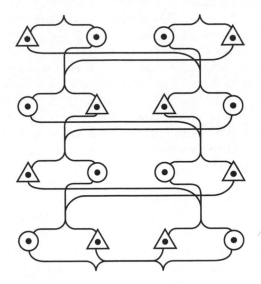

Ideal pattern of bilateral cross-cousin marriage

Sometimes they merely have a certain elegant simplicity, as in this diagram on an instance of Tiv sister exchange:[95]

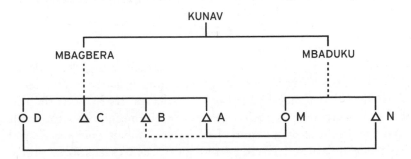

Human beings, left to follow their own desires, rarely arrange themselves in symmetrical patterns. Such symmetry tends to be bought at a terrible human price. In the Tiv case, Akiga is actually willing to describe it:

> Under the old system an elder who had a ward could always marry a young girl, however senile he might be, even if he

were a leper with no hands or feet; no girl would dare to refuse him. If another man were attracted by his ward he would
take his own and give her to the old man by force, in order
to make an exchange. The girl had to go with the old man,
sorrowfully carrying his goat-skin bag. If she ran back to her
home her owner caught her and beat her, then bound her and
brought her back to the elder. The old man was pleased, and
grinned till he showed his blackened molars. "Wherever you
go," he told her, "you will be brought back here to me; so
stop worrying, and settle down as my wife." The girl fretted,
till she wished the earth might swallow her. Some women even
stabbed themselves to death when they were given to an old
man against their will; but in spite of all, the Tiv did not care.[96]

The last line says everything. Citing it might seem unfair (the Tiv
did, evidently, care enough to elect Akiga to be their first parliamentary representative, knowing he supported legislation to outlaw such
practices), but it serves nicely to bring home the real point: that certain
sorts of violence *were* considered morally acceptable.[97] No neighbors
would rush in to intervene if a guardian was beating a runaway ward.
Or if they did, it would be to insist that he use more gentle means to
return her to her rightful husband. And it was because women knew
that this is how their neighbors, or even parents, would react that "exchange marriage" was possible.

This is what I mean by people "ripped from their contexts."

■ ■ ■ ■ ■

The Lele were fortunate enough to have largely escaped the devasta-
tions of the slave trade; the Tiv were sitting practically on the teeth
of the shark, and they had to make heroic efforts to keep the threat
at bay. Nonetheless, in both cases there were mechanisms for forcibly
removing young women from their homes, and it was precisely this
that made them exchangeable—though in each case, too, a principle
stipulated that a woman could only be exchanged for another woman.
The few exceptions, when women could be exchanged for other things,
emerged directly from war and slavery—that is, when the level of violence was significantly ratcheted up.

The slave trade, of course, represented violence on an exponen-
tially different scale. We are speaking here of destruction of genocidal
proportions, in world-historic terms, comparable only to events like
the destruction of New World civilizations or the Holocaust. Neither

do I mean in any way to blame the victims: we need only imagine what would be likely to happen in our own society if a group of space aliens suddenly appeared, armed with undefeatable military technology, infinite wealth, and no recognizable morality—and announced that they were willing to pay a million dollars each for human workers, no questions asked. There will always be at least a handful of people unscrupulous enough to take advantage of such a situation—and a handful is all it takes.

Groups like the Aro Confederacy represent an all-too-familiar strategy, deployed by fascists, mafias, and right-wing gangsters everywhere: first unleash the criminal violence of an unlimited market, in which everything is for sale and the price of life becomes extremely cheap; then step in, offering to restore a certain measure of order—though one which in its very harshness leaves all the most profitable aspects of the earlier chaos intact. The violence is preserved within the structure of the law. Such mafias, too, almost invariably end up enforcing a strict code of honor in which morality becomes above all a matter of paying one's debts.

Were this a different book, I might reflect here on the curious parallels between the Cross River societies and Bali, both of which saw a magnificent outburst of artistic creativity (Cross River Ekpe masks were a major influence on Picasso) that took the form, above all, of an efflorescence of theatrical performance, replete with intricate music, splendid costumes, and stylized dance—a kind of alternative political order as imaginary spectacle—at the exact moment that ordinary life became a game of constant peril in which any misstep might lead to being sent away. What was the link between the two? It's an interesting question, but not one we can really answer here. For present purposes, the crucial question has to be: How common was this? The African slave trade was, as I mentioned, an unprecedented catastrophe, but commercial economies had already been extracting slaves from human economies for thousands of years. It is a practice as old as civilization. The question I want to ask is: To what degree is it actually constitutive of civilization itself?

I am not speaking strictly of slavery here, but of that process that dislodges people from the webs of mutual commitment, shared history, and collective responsibility that make them what they are, so as to make them exchangeable—that is, to make it possible to make them subject to the logic of debt. Slavery is just the logical end-point, the most extreme form of such disentanglement. But for that reason it provides us with a window on the process as a whole. What's more, owing to its historical role, slavery has shaped our basic assumptions and

institutions in ways that we are no longer aware of and whose influence we would probably never wish to acknowledge if we were. If we
have become a debt society, it is because the legacy of war, conquest,
and slavery has never completely gone away. It's still there, lodged in
our most intimate conceptions of honor, property, even freedom. It's
just that we can no longer see that it's there.

In the next chapter, I will begin to describe how this happened.

Chapter Seven

HONOR AND DEGRADATION

OR, ON THE FOUNDATIONS OF CONTEMPORARY CIVILIZATION

> *ur₅ [HAR]: n., liver; spleen; heart, soul;*
> *bulk, main body; foundation; loan;*
> *obligation; interest; surplus, profit;*
> *interest-bearing debt; repayment; slave-*
> *woman.*
>   —early Sumerian dictionary[1]

> *It is just to give each what is owed.*
>   —Simonides

IN THE LAST CHAPTER, I offered a glimpse of how human economies, with their social currencies—which are used to measure, assess,
and maintain relationships between people, and only perhaps incidentally to acquire material goods—might be transformed into something
else. What we discovered was that we cannot begin to think about such
questions without taking into account the role of sheer physical violence. In the case of the African slave trade, this was primarily violence
imposed from outside. Nonetheless, its very suddenness, its very brutality, provides us with a sort of freeze-frame of a process that must have
occurred in a much slower, more haphazard fashion in other times and
places. This is because there is every reason to believe that slavery, with
its unique ability to rip human beings from their contexts, to turn them
into abstractions, played a key role in the rise of markets everywhere.

What happens, then, when the same process happens more slowly?
It would seem that much of this history is permanently lost—since in
both the ancient Middle East and the ancient Mediterranean, most of
the really critical moments seem to have occurred just before the advent of written records. Still, the broad outlines can be reconstructed.

The best way to do so, I believe, is to start from a single, odd, vexed concept: the concept of honor, which can be treated as a kind of artifact, or even as a hieroglyphic, a fragment preserved from history that seems to compress into itself the answer to almost everything we've been trying to understand. On the one hand, violence: men who live by violence, whether soldiers or gangsters, are almost invariably obsessed with honor, and assaults on honor are considered the most obvious justification for acts of violence. On the other, debt. We speak both of debts of honor, and honoring one's debts; in fact, the transition from one to the other provides the best clue to how debts emerge from obligations; even as the notion of honor seemed to echo a defiant insistence that financial debts are not really the most important ones; an echo, here, of arguments that, like those in the Vedas and the Bible, go back to the very dawn of the market itself. Even more disturbingly, since the notion of honor makes no sense without the possibility of degradation, reconstructing this history reveals how much our basic concepts of freedom and morality took shape within institutions—notably, but not only, slavery—that we'd sooner not have to think about at all.

■ ■ ■ ■ ■

To underscore some of the paradoxes surrounding the concept and bring home what's really at stake here, let us consider the story of one man who survived the Middle Passage: Olaudah Equiano, born sometime around 1745 in a rural community somewhere within the confines of the Kingdom of Benin. Kidnapped from his home at the age of eleven, Equiano was eventually sold to British slavers operating in the Bight of Biafra, from whence he was conveyed first to Barbados, then to a plantation in colonial Virginia.

Equiano's further adventures—and there were many—are narrated in his autobiography, *The Interesting Narrative of the Life of Olaudah Equiano: or, Gustavus Vassa, the African*, published in 1789. After spending much of the Seven Years' War hauling gunpowder on a British frigate, he was promised his freedom, denied his freedom, sold to several owners—who regularly lied to him, promising his freedom, and then broke their word—until he passed into the hands of a Quaker merchant in Pennsylvania, who eventually allowed him to purchase his liberty. Over the course of his later years he was to become a successful merchant in his own right, a best-selling author, an Arctic explorer, and eventually, one of the leading voices of English Abolitionism. His eloquence and the power of his life story played significant parts in the movement that led to the British abolition of the slave trade in 1807.

Readers of Equiano's book are often troubled by one aspect of the story: that for most of his early life, he was not opposed to the institution of slavery. At one point, while saving money to buy his freedom, he even briefly took a job that involved purchasing slaves in Africa. Equiano only came around to an abolitionist position after converting to Methodism and making common cause with religious activists against the trade. Many have asked: Why did it take him so long? Surely if anyone had reason to understand the evils of slavery, it was he.

The answer seems, oddly, to lie in the man's very integrity. One thing that comes through strikingly in the book is that this was not only a man of endless resourcefulness and determination, but above all, a man of honor. Yet this created a terrible dilemma. To be made a slave is to be stripped of any possible honor. Naturally, Equiano wished to regain what had been taken from him. His problem was that honor is, by definition, something that exists in the eyes of others. To be able to recover it, then, a slave must necessarily adopt the rules and standards of the society that surrounds him, and this means that, in practice at least, he cannot absolutely reject the institutions that deprived him of his honor in the first place.

It strikes me that this experience—of only being able to restore one's lost honor, to regain the ability to act with integrity by acting in accord with the terms of a system that one knows, through deeply traumatic personal experience, to be utterly unjust—is itself one of the most profoundly violent aspects of slavery. It is another example, perhaps, of the need to argue in the master's language, but here taken to insidious extremes.

All societies based on slavery tend to be marked by this agonizing double consciousness: the awareness that the highest things one has to strive for are also, ultimately, wrong; but at the same time, the feeling that this is simply the nature of reality. This might help explain why throughout most of history, when slaves did rebel against their masters, they rarely rebelled against slavery itself. But the flip side of this is that even slave-owners seemed to feel that the whole arrangement was somehow fundamentally perverse or unnatural. First-year Roman law students, for instance, were made to memorize the following definition:

> slavery
>   is an institution according to the law of nations whereby
> one person falls under the property rights of another, contrary
> to nature.[2]

At the very least, there was always seen to be something disreputable and ugly about slavery. Anyone too close to it was tainted. Slave-traders particularly were scorned as inhuman brutes. Throughout history, moral justifications for slavery are rarely taken particularly seriously even by those who espouse them. Instead, most people saw slavery much as we see war: a tawdry business, to be sure, but one would have to be naïve indeed to imagine it could simply be eliminated.

Honor Is Surplus Dignity

So what is slavery? I've already begun to suggest an answer in the last chapter. Slavery is the ultimate form of being ripped from one's context, and thus from all the social relationships that make one a human being. Another way to put this is that the slave is, in a very real sense, dead.

This was the conclusion of the first scholar to carry out a broad historical survey of the institution, an Egyptian sociologist named Ali 'Abd al-Wahid Wafi, in a dissertation he wrote in Paris in 1931.[3] Everywhere, he observes, from the ancient world to then–present-day South America, one finds the same list of possible ways whereby a free person might be reduced to slavery:

1) By the law of force
   a. By surrender or capture in war
   b. By being the victim of raiding or kidnapping
2) As legal punishment for crimes (including debt)
3) Through paternal authority (a father's sale of his children)
4) Through the voluntary sale of one's self[4]

Everywhere, too, capture in war is considered the only way that is considered absolutely legitimate. All the others were surrounded by moral problems. Kidnapping was obviously criminal, and parents would not sell children except under desperate circumstances.[5] We read of famines in China so severe that thousands of poor men would castrate themselves, in the hope that they might sell themselves as eunuchs at court—but this was also seen as the sign of total social breakdown.[6] Even the judicial process could easily be corrupted, as the ancients were well aware—especially when it came to enslavement for debt.

On one level, al-Wahid's argument is just an extended apologia for the role of slavery in Islam—widely criticized, since Islamic law never eliminated slavery, even when the institution largely vanished in the rest of the Medieval world. True, he argues, Mohammed did not forbid the practice, but still, the early Caliphate was the first government we know of that actually succeeded in eliminating all these practices (judicial abuse, kidnappings, the sale of offspring) that had been recognized as social problems for thousands of years, and to limit slavery strictly to prisoners of war.

The book's most enduring contribution, though, lay simply in asking: What do all these circumstances have in common? Al-Wahid's answer is striking in its simplicity: one becomes a slave in situations where one would otherwise have died. This is obvious in the case of war: in the ancient world, the victor was assumed to have total power over the vanquished, including their women and children; all of them could be simply massacred. Similarly, he argued, criminals were condemned to slavery only for capital crimes, and those who sold themselves, or their children, normally faced starvation.[7]

This is not just to say, though, that a slave was seen as owing his master his life since he would otherwise be dead.[8] Perhaps this was true at the moment of his or her enslavement. But after that, a slave could not owe debts, because in almost every important sense, a slave *was* dead. In Roman law, this was quite explicit. If a Roman soldier was captured and lost his liberty, his family was expected to read his will and dispose of his possessions. Should he later regain his freedom, he would have to start over, even to the point of remarrying the woman who was now considered his widow.[9]

In West Africa, according to one French anthropologist, the same principles applied:

> Once he had been finally removed from his own milieu through capture the slave was considered as socially *dead*, just as if he had been vanquished and killed in combat. Among the Mande, at one time, prisoners of war brought home by the conquerors were offered *dege* (millet and milk porridge)—because it was held that a man should not die on an empty stomach—and then presented with their arms so that they could kill themselves. Anyone who refused was slapped on the face by his abductor and kept as a captive: he had accepted the contempt which deprived him of personality.[10]

Tiv horror stories about men who are dead but do not know it or who are brought back from the grave to serve their murderers, and

Haitian zombie stories, all seem to play on this essential horror of slavery: the fact that it's a kind of living death.

In a book called *Slavery and Social Death*—surely the most profound comparative study of the institution yet written—Orlando Patterson works out exactly what it has meant to be so completely and absolutely ripped from one's context.[11] First of all, he emphasizes, slavery is unlike any other form of human relation because it is not a moral relation. Slave-owners might dress it up in all sorts of legalistic or paternalistic language, but really this is just window-dressing and no one really believes otherwise; really, it is a relation based purely on violence; a slave must obey because if he doesn't, he can be beaten, tortured, or killed, and everyone is perfectly well aware of this. Second of all, being socially dead means that a slave has no binding moral relations with anyone else: he is alienated from his ancestors, community, family, clan, city; he cannot make contracts or meaningful promises, except at the whim of his master, who could just as easily take it back; even if he acquires a family, it can be broken up at any time. The relation of pure force that attached him to his master was hence the only human relationship that ultimately mattered. As a result—and this is the third essential element—the slave's situation was one of utter degradation. Hence the Mande warrior's slap: the captive, having refused his one final chance to save his honor by killing himself, must recognize that he will now be considered an entirely contemptible being.[12]

Yet at the same time, this ability to strip others of their dignity becomes, for the master, the foundation of his honor. As Patterson notes, there have been places—the Islamic world affords numerous examples—where slaves are not even put to work for profit; instead, rich men make a point of surrounding themselves with battalions of slave retainers as tokens of their magnificence and nothing else.

It seems to me that this is precisely what gives honor its notoriously fragile quality. Men of honor tend to combine a sense of total ease and self-assurance, which comes with the habit of command, with a notorious jumpiness, a heightened sensitivity to slights and insults, the feeling that a man (and it is almost always a man) is somehow reduced, humiliated, if any "debt of honor" is allowed to go unpaid. This is because honor is not the same as dignity. One might even say: honor is surplus dignity. It is that heightened consciousness of power, and its dangers, that comes from having stripped away the power and dignity of others; or at the very least, from the knowledge that one is capable of doing so. At its simplest, honor is that excess dignity that must be defended with the knife or sword (violent men, as we all know, are almost invariably obsessed with honor). Hence the warrior's ethos, where almost anything that could possibly be seen as a sign of disrespect—in inappropriate word, an inappropriate glance—is considered a challenge, or can be treated as such. Yet even where overt violence has largely been put out of the picture, wherever honor is at issue, it comes with a sense that dignity *can* be lost, and therefore must be constantly defended.

The result is that to this day, "honor" has two contradictory meanings. On the one hand, we can speak of honor as simple integrity. Decent people honor their commitments. This is clearly what "honor" meant for Equiano: to be an honorable man meant to be one who speaks the truth, obeys the law, keeps his promises, is fair and conscientious in his commercial dealings.[13] His problem was that honor simultaneously meant something else, which had everything to do with the kind of violence required to reduce human beings to commodities to begin with.

The reader might be asking: But what does all this have to do with the origins of money? The answer is, surprisingly: everything. Some of the most genuinely archaic forms of money we know about appear to have been used precisely as measures of honor and degradation: that is, the value of money was, ultimately, the value of the power to turn others into money. The curious puzzle of the *cumal*—the slave-girl money of medieval Ireland—provides one dramatic illustration. Let us turn to it now.

Honor Price (Early Medieval Ireland)

For much of its early history, Ireland's situation was not very different than that of many of the African societies we looked at in the end of the last chapter. It was a human economy perched uncomfortably on the fringe of an expanding commercial one. What's more, at certain periods there was a very lively slave trade. As one historian put it, "Ireland has no mineral wealth, and foreign luxury goods could be bought by Irish kings mainly for two export goods, cattle and people."[14] Hardly surprising, perhaps, that cattle and people were the two major denominations of the currency. Still, by the time our earliest records kick in, around 600AD, the slave trade appears to have died off, and slavery itself was a waning institution, coming under severe disapproval from the Church.[15] Why, then, were cumal still being used as units of account, to tally up debts that were actually paid out in cows, in cups and brooches and other objects made of silver, or, in the case of minor transactions, sacks of wheat or oats? And there's an even more obvious question: Why *women*? There were plenty of male slaves in early Ireland, yet no one seems ever to have used them as money.

Most of what we know about the economy of early Medieval Ireland comes from legal sources—a series of law codes, drawn up by a powerful class of jurists, dating roughly from the seventh to ninth centuries AD. These, however, are exceptionally rich. Ireland at that time was still very much a human economy. It was also very much a rural one: people lived in scattered homesteads, not unlike the Tiv, growing wheat and tending cattle. The closest there were to towns were a few concentrations around monasteries. There appears to have been a near total absence of markets, except for a few on the coast—presumably, mainly slave or cattle markets—frequented by foreign ships.[16]

As a result, money was employed almost exclusively for social purposes: gifts; fees to craftsmen, doctors, poets, judges, and entertainers; various feudal payments (lords gave gifts of cattle to clients who then had to regularly supply them with food). The authors of the law codes didn't even know how to put a price on most goods of ordinary use—pitchers, pillows, chisels, slabs of bacon, and the like; no one seems ever to have paid money for them.[17] Food was shared in families or delivered to feudal superiors, who laid it out in sumptuous feasts for friends, rivals, and retainers. Anyone needing a tool or furniture or clothing either went to a kinsman with the relevant craft skills or paid someone to make it. The objects themselves were not for sale. Kings, in turn, assigned tasks to different clans: this one was to provide them with leather, this one poets, this one shields . . . precisely the sort of unwieldy arrangement that markets were later developed to get around.[18]

Money could be loaned. There was a highly complex system of pledges and sureties to guarantee that debtors delivered what they owed. Mainly, though, it was used for paying fines. These fines are endlessly and meticulously elaborated in the codes, but what really strikes the contemporary observer is that they were carefully graded by the injured party's rank. This is true of almost all the "Barbarian Law Codes"—the size of the penalties usually has at least as much do with the status of the victim as it does with the nature of the injury—but only in Ireland were things mapped out quite so systematically.

The key to the system was a notion of honor: literally "face."[19] One's honor was the esteem one had in the eyes of others, one's honesty, integrity, and character, but also one's power, in the sense of the ability to protect oneself, and one's family and followers, from any sort of degradation or insult. Those who had the highest degree of honor were literally sacred beings: their persons and possessions were sacrosanct. What was so unusual about Celtic systems—and the Irish one went further with this than any other—was that honor could be precisely quantified. Every free person had his or her "honor price": the price that one had to pay for an insult to the person's dignity. Here too there was a graded scale. The honor price of a king, for instance, was seven cumals, or seven slave girls—this was the standard honor price for any sacred being, the same as a bishop or master poet. Since (as all sources hasten to point out) slave girls were not normally paid as such, this would mean, in the case of an insult to such a person's dignity, one would have to pay twenty-one milk cows or twenty-one ounces of silver.[20] The honor price of a wealthy peasant was two and a half cows, of a minor lord, that, plus half a cow additionally for each of his free dependents—and since a lord, to remain a lord, had to have at least five of these, that brought him up to at least five cows total.[21]

Honor price is not to be confused with wergeld—the actual price of a man or woman's life. If one killed a man, one paid goods to the value of seven cumals, in recompense for killing him, to which one then added his honor price, for having offended against his dignity (by killing him). Interestingly, only in the case of a king are the blood price and his honor price the same.

There were also payments for injury: if one wounds a man's cheek, one pays his honor price plus the price of the injury. (A blow to the face was, for obvious reasons, particularly egregious.) The problem was how to calculate the injury, since this varied according to both the physical damage and status of the injured party. Here, Irish jurists developed the ingenious expedient of measuring different wounds with different varieties of grain: a cut on the king's cheek was measured in grains of wheat, on that of a substantial farmer in oats, on that of a smallholder merely in peas. One cow was paid for each.[22] Similarly, if one stole, say, a man's brooch or pig, one had to pay back three brooches or three pigs, plus his honor price, for having violated the sanctity of his homestead. Attacking a peasant under the protection of a lord was the same as raping a man's wife or daughter, a violation of the honor not of the victim, but of the man who should have been able to protect them.

Finally, one had to pay the honor price if one simply insulted someone of any importance: say, by turning the person away at a feast, inventing a particularly embarrassing nickname (at least, if it caught on), or humiliating the person through the use of satire.[23] Mockery was a refined art in Medieval Ireland, and poets were considered close to magicians: it was said that a talented satirist could rhyme rats to death, or at the very least, raise blisters on the faces of his victims. Any man publicly mocked would have no choice but to defend his honor; and, in Medieval Ireland, the value of that honor was precisely defined.

I should note that while twenty-one cows might not seem like much when we are dealing with the honor of kings, Ireland at the time had about 150 kings.[24] Most had only a couple of thousand subjects, though there were also higher-ranking, provincial kings for whom the honor price was double.[25] What's more, since the legal system was completely separate from the political one, jurists, in theory, had the right the demote anyone—including a king—who had committed a dishonorable act. If a nobleman turned a worthy man away from his door or feast, sheltered a fugitive, or ate steak from an obviously stolen cow, or even if he allowed himself to be satirized and did not take the offending poet to court, his price could be lowered to that of a commoner. But the same was true of a king who ran away in battle, or abused his powers, or even was caught working in the fields or otherwise engaging in tasks beneath his dignity. A king who did something utterly outrageous— murdered one of his own relatives, for example—might end up with no honor price at all, which meant not that people could say anything they liked about the king, without fear of recompense, but that he couldn't stand as surety or witness in court, as one's oath and standing in law were also determined by one's honor price. This didn't happen often, but it did happen, and legal wisdom made sure to remind people of it: the list, contained in one famous legal text, of the "seven kings who lost their honor price," was meant to ensure that everyone remembered that no matter how sacred and powerful, anyone could fall.

What's unusual about the Irish material is that it's all spelled out so clearly. This is partly because Irish law codes were the work of a class of legal specialists who seem to have turned the whole business almost into a form of entertainment, devoting endless hours to coming up with every possible ramification of existing legal principles, whether or not there was any real possibility such a case might end up in court. Some of the provisos are so whimsical ("if stung by another man's bee, one must calculate the extent of the injury, but also, if one swatted it in the process, subtract the replacement value of the bee") that one has to assume they were basically jokes. Still, as a result, the moral logic that lies behind any elaborate code of honor is laid out here in startling honesty. What about women? A free woman was honored at precisely 50 percent of the price of her nearest male relative (her father, if alive; if not, her husband). If she was dishonored, her price was payable to that relative. Unless, that is, she was an independent landholder. In that case, her honor price was the same as that of a man. Unless she was a woman of easy virtue, in which case it was zero, since she had no honor to outrage. What about marriage? A suitor paid the value of the wife's honor to her father and thus became its guardian. What about serfs? The same principle applied: when a lord acquired a serf, he bought out that man's honor price, presenting him with its equivalent in cows. From that moment on, if anyone insulted or injured the serf, it was seen an attack on the lord's honor, and it was up to the lord to collect the attendant fees. Meanwhile the lord's honor price was notched upward as a result of gathering another dependent: in other words, he literally absorbs his new vassal's honor into his own.[26]

All this, in turn, makes it possible to understand both something of the nature of honor, and why slave girls were kept as units for reckoning debts of honor even at a time when—owing no doubt to church influence—they no longer actually changed hands. At first sight it might seem strange that the honor of a nobleman or king should be measured in slaves, since slaves were human beings whose honor was zero. But if one's honor is ultimately founded on one's ability to extract the honor of others, it makes perfect sense. The value of a slave is that of the honor that has been extracted from them.

Sometimes, one comes upon a single haphazard detail that gives the entire game away. In this case it comes not from Ireland but from the Dimetian Code in Wales, written somewhat later but operating on much the same principles. At one point, after listing the honors due to the seven holy sees of the Kingdom of Dyfed, whose bishops and abbots were the most exalted and sacred creatures in the kingdom, the text specifies that

> Whoever draws blood from an abbot of any one of those principal seats before mentioned, let him pay seven pounds; and a female of his kindred to be a washerwoman, as a disgrace to the kindred, and to serve as a memorial to the payment of the honor price.[27]

A washerwoman was the lowest of servants, and the one turned over in this case was to serve for life. She was, in effect, reduced to slavery. Her permanent disgrace was the restoration of the abbot's honor. While we cannot know if some similar institution once lay behind the habit of reckoning the honor of Irish "sacred" beings in slave-women, the principle is clearly the same. Honor is a zero-sum game. A man's ability to protect the women of his family is an essential part of that honor. Therefore, forcing him to surrender a woman of his family to perform menial and degrading chores in another's household is the ultimate blow to his honor. This, in turn, makes it the ultimate reaffirmation of the honor of he who takes it away.

■ ■ ■ ■ ■

What makes Medieval Irish laws seem so peculiar from our perspective
is that their exponents had not the slightest discomfort with putting
an exact monetary price on human dignity. For us, the notion that the
sanctity of a priest or the majesty of a king could be held equivalent to
a million fried eggs or a hundred thousand haircuts is simply bizarre.
These are precisely the things that ought to be considered beyond all
possibility of quantification. If Medieval Irish jurists felt otherwise, it
was because people at that time did not use money to acquire eggs or
haircuts.[28] It was the fact that it was still a human economy, in which
money was used for social purposes, that made it possible to create such
an intricate system whereby it was possible not just to measure but to
add and subtract specific quantities of human dignity—and in doing so,
provide us with a unique window into the true nature of honor itself.

The obvious question is: What happens to such an economy when
people do begin to use the same money used to measure dignity to
acquire eggs and haircuts? As the history of ancient Mesopotamia and
the Mediterranean world reveals, the result was a profound—and enduring—moral crisis.

Mesopotamia (The Origins of Patriarchy)

In ancient Greek, the word for "honor" was *tīme*. In Homer's time, the
term appears to have been used much like the Irish term "honor price":
it referred both to the glory of the warrior and the compensation paid
as damages in case of injury or insult. Yet with the rise of markets
over the next several centuries, the meaning of the word *tīme* began to
change. On the one hand, it became the word for "price"—as in, the
price of something one buys in the market. On the other, it referred to
an attitude of complete contempt for markets.

Actually, this is still the case today:

> In Greece the word "timi" means honor, which has been typi-
> cally seen as the most important value in Greek village society.
> Honor is often characterized in Greece as an open-handed gen-
> erosity and blatant disregard for monetary costs and counting.
> And yet the same word also means "price" as in the price of a
> pound of tomatoes.[29]

The word "crisis" literally refers to a crossroads: it is the point where things could go either of two different ways. The odd thing about the crisis in the concept of honor is that it never seems to have been resolved. Is honor the willingness to pay one's monetary debts? Or is it the fact that one does not feel that monetary debts are really that important? It appears to be both at the same time.

There's also the question of what men of honor actually *do* think is important. When most of us think of a Mediterranean villager's sense of honor, we don't think so much of a casual attitude toward money as of a veritable obsession with premarital virginity. Masculine honor is caught up not even so much in a man's ability to protect his womenfolk as in his ability to protect their sexual reputations, to respond to any suggestion of impropriety on the part of his mother, wife, sister, or daughter as if it were a direct physical attack on his own person. This is a stereotype, but it's not entirely unjustified. One historian who went through fifty years of police reports about knife-fights in nineteenth-century Ionia discovered that virtually every one of them began when one party publicly suggested that the other's wife or sister was a whore.[30]

So, why the sudden obsession with sexual propriety? It doesn't seem to be there in the Welsh or Irish material. There, the greatest humiliation was to see your sister or daughter reduced to scrubbing someone else's laundry. What is it, then, about the rise of money and markets that cause so many men to become so uneasy about sex?[31]

This is a difficult question, but at the very least, one can imagine how the transition from a human economy to a commercial one might cause certain moral dilemmas. What happens, for instance, when the same money once used to arrange marriages and settle affairs of honor can also be used to pay for the services of prostitutes?

As we'll see, there is reason to believe that it is in such moral crises that we can find the origin not only of our current conceptions of honor, but of patriarchy itself. This is true, at least, if we define "patriarchy" in the strict sense, familiar from the book of Genesis: the rule of fathers, with all the familiar images of stern bearded men in robes, keeping a close eye over their sequestered wives and daughters, even as their children kept a close eye over their flocks and herds.[32] Readers of the Bible had always assumed that there was something primordial in all this; that this was simply the way desert people, and thus the earliest inhabitants of the Near East, had always behaved. This was why the translation of Sumerian, in the first half of the twentieth century, came as something of a shock.

In the very earliest Sumerian texts, particularly those from roughly 3000 to 2500 BC, women are everywhere. Early histories not only record the names of numerous female rulers, but make clear that women were well represented among the ranks of doctors, merchants, scribes, and public officials, and generally free to take part in all aspects of public life. One cannot speak of full gender equality: men still outnumbered women in all these areas. Still, one gets the sense of a society not so different than that which prevails in much of the developed world today. Over the course of the next thousand years or so, all this changes. The place of women in civic life erodes; gradually, the more familiar patriarchal pattern takes shape, with its emphasis on chastity and premarital virginity, a weakening and eventually wholesale disappearance of women's role in government and the liberal professions, and the loss of women's independent legal status, which renders them wards of their husbands. By the end of the Bronze Age, around 1200 BC, we begin to see large numbers of women sequestered away in harems and (in some places, at least) subjected to obligatory veiling.

In fact, this appears to reflect a much broader worldwide pattern. It has always been something of a scandal for those who like to see the advance of science and technology, the accumulation of learning, economic growth—"human progress," as we like to call it—as necessarily leading to greater human freedom, that for women, the exact opposite often seems to be the case. Or at least, has been the case until very recent times. A similar gradual restriction on women's freedoms can be observed in India and China. The question is, obviously, Why? The standard explanation in the Sumerian case has been the gradual infiltration of pastoralists from the surrounding deserts who, presumably, always had more patriarchal mores. There was, after all, only a narrow strip of land along the Tigris and Euphrates rivers that could support intensive irrigation, and hence, urban life. Civilization was thus from early times surrounded by a fringe of desert people, who lived much like those described in Genesis and spoke the same Semitic languages. It is undeniably true that, over the course of time, the Sumerian language was gradually replaced—first by Akkadian, then by Amorite, then by Aramaic languages, and finally, most recently of all, by Arabic, which was also brought to Mesopotamia and the Levant by desert pastoralists. While all this did, clearly, bring with it profound cultural changes as well, it's not a particularly satisfying explanation.[33] Former nomads appear to have been willing to adapt to urban life in any number of other ways. Why not that one? And it's very much a local explanation and does nothing, really, to explain the broader pattern. Feminist scholarship has instead tended to emphasize the growing scale and social importance of war, and the increasing centralization of the state that accompanied it.[34] This is more convincing. Certainly, the more militaristic the state, the harsher its laws tended to be toward women. But I would add another, complementary argument. As I have emphasized, historically, war, states, and markets all tend to feed off one another. Conquest leads to taxes. Taxes tend to be ways to create markets, which are convenient for soldiers and administrators. In the specific case of Mesopotamia, all of this took on a complicated relation to an explosion of debt that threatened to turn all human relations— and by extension, women's bodies—into potential commodities. At the same time, it created a horrified reaction on the part of the (male) winners of the economic game, who over time felt forced to go to greater and greater lengths to make clear that *their* women could in no sense be bought or sold.

A glance at the existing material on Mesopotamian marriage gives us a clue as to how this might have happened.

It is common anthropological wisdom that bridewealth tends to be typical of situations where population is relatively thin, land not a particularly scarce resource, and therefore, politics are all about controlling labor. Where population is dense and land at a premium, one tends to instead find dowry: adding a woman to the household is adding another mouth to feed, and rather than having to be paid off, a bride's father is expected to contribute something (land, wealth, money . . .) to help support his daughter in her new home.[35] In Sumerian times, for instance, the main payment at marriage was a huge gift of food paid by the groom's father to the bride's, destined to provide a sumptuous feast for the wedding.[36] Before long, however, this seems to have split into two payments, one for the wedding, another to the woman's father, calculated—and often paid—in silver.[37] Wealthy women sometimes appear to have ended up with the money: at least, many appear to have to worn silver arm and leg rings of identical denominations.

However, as time went on, this payment, called the *terhatum*, often began to take on the qualities of a simple purchase. It was referred to as "the price of a virgin"—not a mere metaphor, since the illegal deflowering of a virgin was considered a property crime against her father.[38] Marriage was referred to as "taking possession" of a woman, the same word one would use for the seizure of goods.[39] In principle, a wife, once possessed, owed her husband strict obedience, and often could not seek a divorce even in cases of physical abuse.

For women with wealthy or powerful parents, all this remained largely a matter of principle, modified considerably in practice. Merchants' daughters, for example, typically received substantial cash dowries, with which they could go into business in their own right, or act as partners to their husbands. However, for the poor—that is, most people—marriage came more and more to resemble a simple cash transaction.

Some of this must have been an effect of slavery: while actual slaves were rarely numerous, the very existence of a class of people with no kin, who were simply commodities, did make a difference. In Nuzi, for instance, "the brideprice was paid in domestic animals and silver amounting to a total value of 40 shekels of silver"'—to which the author drily adds, "there is some evidence that it was equal to the price of a slave girl."[40] This must have been making things uncomfortably obvious. It's in Nuzi, too, where we happen to have unusually detailed records, that we find examples of rich men paying cut-rate "brideprice" to impoverished families to acquire a daughter who they would then adopt, but who would in fact be either kept as a concubine or nurse-maid, or married to one of their slaves.[41]

Still, the really critical factor here was debt. As I pointed out in the last chapter, anthropologists have long emphasized that paying bride-wealth is not the same as buying a wife. After all—and this was one of the clinching arguments, remember, in the original 1930s League of Nations debate—if a man were really buying a woman, wouldn't he also be able to sell her? Clearly African and Melanesian husbands were not able to sell their wives to some third party. At most, they could send them home and demand back their bridewealth.[42]

A Mesopotamian husband couldn't sell his wife either. Or, normally he couldn't. Still, everything changed the moment he took out a loan. Since if he did, it was perfectly legal—as we've seen—to use his wife and children as surety, and if he was unable to pay, they could then be taken away as debt pawns in exactly the same way that he could lose his slaves, sheep, and goats. What this also meant was that honor and credit became, effectively, the same thing: at least for a poor man, one's creditworthiness was precisely one's command over one's household, and (the flip side, as it were) relations of domestic authority, relations that in principle involved a responsibility for care and protection, be-came property rights that could indeed be bought and sold.

Again, for the poor, this meant that family members became com-modities that could be rented or sold. Not only could one dispose of daughters as "brides" to work in rich men's households, tablets in Nuzi show that one could now hire out family members simply by taking out a loan: there are recorded cases of men sending their sons or even wives as "pawns" for loans that were clearly just advance payment for employment in the lender's farm or cloth workshop.[43]

The most dramatic and enduring crisis centered on prostitution. It's actually not entirely clear, from the sources, whether in the earliest period one can speak of "prostitution" at all. Sumerian temples do often appear to have hosted a variety of sexual activities. Some priestesses, for instance, were considered to be married to or otherwise dedicated to gods. What this meant in practice seems to have varied considerably. Much as in the case of the later *devadasis*, or "temple dancers," of Hindu India, some remained celibate; others were permitted to marry but were not to bear children; others were apparently expected to find wealthy patrons, becoming in effect courtesans to the elite. Still others lived in the temples and had the responsibility to make themselves sexually available to worshippers on certain ritual occasions.[44] One thing the early texts do make clear is that all such women were considered extraordinarily important. In a very real sense, they were the ultimate embodiments of civilization. After all, the entire machinery of the Sumerian economy ostensibly existed to support the temples, which were considered the households of the gods. As such, they represented the ultimate possible refinement in everything from music and dance to art, cuisine, and graciousness of living. Temple priestesses and spouses of the gods were the highest human incarnations of this perfect life.

It's also important to emphasize that Sumerian men do not appear, at least in this earliest period, to have seen anything troubling about the idea of their sisters having sex for money. To the contrary, insofar as prostitution did occur (and remember, it could not have been nearly so impersonal, cold-cash a relation in a credit economy), Sumerian religious texts identify it as among the fundamental features of human civilization, a gift given by the gods at the dawn of time. Procreative sex was considered natural (after all, animals did it). Non-procreative sex, sex for pleasure, was divine.[45]

The most famous expression of this identification of prostitute and civilization can be found in the story of Enkidu in the epic of Gilgamesh. In the beginning of the story, Enkidu is a monster—a naked and ferocious "wild man" who grazes with the gazelles, drinks at the watering place with wild cattle, and terrorizes the people of the city. Unable to defeat him, the citizens finally send out a courtesan who is also a priestess of the goddess Ishtar. She strips before him, and they make love for six days and seven nights. Afterward, Enkidu's former animal companions run away from him. After she explains that he has now learned wisdom and become like a God (she is, after all, a divine consort), he agrees to put on clothing and come to live in the city like a proper, civilized human being.[46]

Already, in the earliest version of the Enkidu story, though, one can detect a certain ambivalence. Much later, Enkidu is sentenced to death by the gods, and his immediate reaction is to condemn the courtesan for having brought him from the wilds in the first place: he curses her to become a common streetwalker or tavern keeper, living among vomiting drunks, abused and beaten by her clients. Then, later, he regrets his behavior and blesses her instead. But that trace of ambivalence was there from the beginning, and over time, it grew more powerful. From early times, Sumerian and Babylonian temple complexes were surrounded by far less glamorous providers of sexual services—indeed, by the time we know much about them, they were the center of veritable red-light districts full of taverns with dancing girls, men in drag (some of them slaves, some runaways), and an almost infinite variety of prostitutes. There is an endlessly elaborate terminology of types of sex worker whose subtleties are long since lost to us. Most seem to have doubled as entertainers: tavern-keepers doubled as musicians; male transvestites were not only singers and dancers, but often performed knife-throwing acts. Many were slaves put to work by their masters, or women working off religious vows or debts, or debt bondswomen, or, for that matter, women escaping debt bondage with no place else to go. Over time, many of the lower-ranking temple women were either bought as slaves or debt peons as well, and there might have often been a blurring of roles between priestesses who performed erotic rituals and prostitutes owned by the temple (and hence, in principle, by the god), sometimes lodged within the temple compound itself, whose earnings added to the temple treasuries.[47] Since most everyday transactions in Mesopotamia were not cash transactions, once has to assume that it was the same with prostitutes—like the tavern-keepers, many of whom seem to have been former prostitutes, they developed ongoing credit relations with their clients—and this must have meant that most were less like what we think of as streetwalkers and more like courtesans.[48] Still, the origins of commercial prostitution appear to have been caught up in a peculiar mixture of sacred (or once-sacred) practice, commerce, slavery, and debt.

■ ■ ■ ■ ■

"Patriarchy" originated, first and foremost, in a rejection of the great urban civilizations in the name of a kind of purity, a reassertion of paternal control against great cities like Uruk, Lagash, and Babylon, seen as places of bureaucrats, traders, and whores. The pastoral fringes, the deserts and steppes away from the river valleys, were the places to which displaced, indebted farmers fled. Resistance, in the ancient Middle East, was always less a politics of rebellion than a politics of exodus, of melting away with one's flocks and families—often before both were taken away.[49] There were always tribal peoples living on the fringes. During good times, they began to take to the cities; in hard times, their numbers swelled with refugees—farmers who effectively became Enkidu once again. Then, periodically, they would create their own alliances and sweep back into the cities once again as conquerors. It's difficult to say precisely how they imagined their situation, because it's only in the Old Testament, written on the other side of the Fertile Crescent, that one has any record of the pastoral rebels' points of view. But nothing there mitigates against the suggestion that the extraordinary emphasis we find there on the absolute authority of fathers, and the jealous protection of their fickle womenfolk, was made possible by, but at the same time was a protest against, this very commoditization of people in the cities that they fled.

The world's Holy Books—the Old and New Testaments, the Koran, religious literature from the Middle Ages to this day—echo this voice of rebellion, combining contempt for the corrupt urban life, suspicion of the merchant, and often, intense misogyny. One need only think of the image of Babylon itself, which has become permanently lodged in the collective imagination as not only the cradle of civilization, but also the Place of Whores. Herodotus echoed popular Greek fantasies when he claimed that every Babylonian maiden was obliged to prostitute herself at the temple, so as to raise the money for her dowry.[50] In the New Testament, Saint Peter often referred to Rome as "Babylon," and the Book of Revelation provides perhaps the most vivid image of what he meant by this when it speaks of Babylon, "the great whore," sitting "upon a scarlet colored beast, full of names of blasphemy":

> 17:4 And the woman was arrayed in purple and scarlet color, and decked with gold and precious stones and pearls, having a golden cup in her hand full of abominations and filthiness of her fornication:
>
> 17:5 And upon her forehead was a name written, MYSTERY, BABYLON THE GREAT, THE MOTHER OF HARLOTS AND ABOMINATIONS OF THE EARTH.[51]

Such is the voice of patriarchal hatred of the city, and of the angry millennial voices of the fathers of the ancient poor.

Patriarchy as we know it seems to have taken shape in a see-sawing battle between the newfound elites and newly dispossessed. Much of my own analysis here is inspired by the brilliant work of feminist historian Gerda Lerner, who, in an essay on the origins of prostitution, observed:

> Another source for commercial prostitution was the pauperization of farmers and their increasing dependence on loans in order to survive periods of famine, which led to debt slavery. Children of both sexes were given up for debt pledges or sold for "adoption." Out of such practices, the prostitution of female family members for the benefit of the head of the family could readily develop. Women might end up as prostitutes because their parents had to sell them into slavery or because their impoverished husbands might so use them. Or they might become self-employed as a last alternative to enslavement. With luck, they might in this profession be upwardly mobile through becoming concubines.
>
> By the middle of the second millennium B.C., prostitution was well established as a likely occupation for the daughters of the poor. As the sexual regulation of women of the propertied class became more firmly entrenched, the virginity of respectable daughters became a financial asset for the family. Thus, commercial prostitution came to be seen as a social necessity for meeting the sexual needs of men. What remained problematic was how to distinguish clearly and permanently between respectable and non-respectable women.

This last point is crucial. The most dramatic known attempt to solve the problem, Lerner observes, can be found in a Middle Assyrian law code dating from somewhere between 1400 and 1100 BC, which is also the first known reference to veiling in the history of the Middle East—and also, Lerner emphasizes, first to make the policing of social boundaries the responsibility of the state.[52] It is not surprising that this takes place under the authority of perhaps the most notoriously militaristic state in the entire ancient Middle East.

The code carefully distinguishes among five classes of women. Respectable women (either married ladies or concubines), widows, and daughters of free Assyrian men—"must veil themselves" when they go out on the street. Prostitutes and slaves (and prostitutes are now considered to include unmarried temple servants as well as simple harlots) are not allowed to wear veils. The remarkable thing about the laws is that the punishments specified in the code are not directed at respectable women who do not wear veils, but against prostitutes and slaves who do. The prostitute was to be publicly beaten fifty times with staves and have pitch poured on her head; the slave girl was to have her ears cut off. Free men proven to have knowingly abetted an impostor would also be thrashed and put to a month's forced labor.

Presumably in the case of respectable women, the law was assumed to be self-enforcing: as what respectable woman would wish to go out on the street in the guise of a prostitute?

When we refer to "respectable" women, then, we are referring to those whose bodies could not, under any conditions, be bought or sold. Their physical persons were hidden away and permanently relegated to some man's domestic sphere; when they appeared in public veiled, they were effectively still ostentatiously walking around, even in public, inside such a sphere.[53] Women who could be exchanged for money, on the other hand, must be instantly recognizable as such.

The Assyrian law code is one isolated instance; veils certainly did not become obligatory everywhere after 1300 BC. But it provides a window on developments that were happening, however unevenly, even spasmodically, across the region, propelled by the intersection of commerce, class, defiant assertions of male honor, and the constant threat of the defection of the poor. States seem to have played a complex dual role, simultaneously fostering commoditization and intervening to ameliorate its effects: enforcing the laws of debt and rights of fathers, and offering periodic amnesties. But the dynamic also led, over the course of millennia, to a systematic demotion of sexuality itself from a divine gift and embodiment of civilized refinement to one of its more familiar associations: with degradation, corruption, and guilt.

■ ■ ■ ■ ■

Here I think we have the explanation for that general decline of women's freedoms that may be observed in all the great urban civilizations for so much of their history. In all of them, similar things were happening, even if in each case, the pieces came together in different ways.

The history of China, for instance, saw continual and largely unsuccessful government campaigns to eradicate both brideprice and debt slavery, and periodic scandals over the existence of "markets in daughters," including the outright sale of girls as daughters, wives, concubines, or prostitutes (at the buyer's discretion) continue to this day.[54] In India, the caste system allowed what were elsewhere de facto differences between rich and poor to be made formal and explicit. Brahmins and other members of the upper castes jealously sequestered their daughters and married them off with lavish dowries, while the lower castes practiced brideprice, allowing members of the higher ("twice-born") castes to scoff at them for selling their daughters. The twice-born were likewise largely protected from falling into debt bondage, while for much of the rural poor, debt dependency was institutional-ized, with the daughters of poor debtors, predictably, often dispatched to brothels or to the kitchens or laundries of the rich.[55] In either case, between the push of commoditization, which fell disproportionally on daughters, and the pull of those trying to reassert patriarchal rights to "protect" women from any suggestion that they might be commod-itized, women's formal and practical freedoms appear to have been gradually but increasingly restricted and effaced. As a result, notions of honor changed too, becoming a kind of protest against the implications of the market, even as at the same time (like the world religions) they came to echo that market logic in endless subtle ways.

Nowhere, however, are our sources as rich and detailed as they are for ancient Greece. This is partly because a commercial economy arrived there so late, almost three thousand years later than in Sumer. As a result, Classical Greek literature gives us a unique opportunity to observe the transformation as it was actually taking place.

Ancient Greece (Honor and Debt)

The world of the Homeric epics is one dominated by heroic warriors who are disdainful of trade. In many ways, it is strikingly reminiscent of medieval Ireland. Money existed, but it was not used to buy any-thing; important men lived their lives in pursuit of honor, which took material form in followers and treasure. Treasures were given as gifts, awarded as prizes, carried off as loot.[56] This is no doubt how *timē* first came to mean both "honor" and "price"—in such a world, no one sensed any sort of contradiction between the two.[57]

All this was to change dramatically when commercial markets be-gan to develop two hundred years later. Greek coinage seems to have been first used mainly to pay soldiers, as well as to pay fines and fees and payments made to and by the government, but by about 600 BC, just about every Greek city-state was producing its own coins as a mark of civic independence. It did not take long, though, before coins were in common use in everyday transactions. By the fifth century, in

Greek cities, the *agora*, the place of public debate and communal assembly, also doubled as a marketplace.

One of the first effects of the arrival of a commercial economy was a series of debt crises, of the sort long familiar from Mesopotamia and Israel. "The poor," as the author of *Constitution of the Athenians* succinctly put it, "together with their wives and children, were enslaved to the rich."[58] Revolutionary factions emerged, demanding amnesties, and most Greek cities were at least for a while taken over by populist strongmen swept into power partly by the demand for radical debt relief. The solution most cities ultimately found, however, was quite different than it had been in the Near East. Rather than institutionalize periodic amnesties, Greek cities tended to adopt legislation limiting or abolishing debt peonage altogether, and then, to forestall future crises, they would turn to a policy of expansion, shipping off the children of the poor to found military colonies overseas. Before long, the entire coast from Crimea to Marseille was dotted with Greek cities, which served, in turn, as conduits for a lively trade in slaves.[59] The sudden abundance of chattel slaves, in turn, completely transformed the nature of Greek society. First and most famously, it allowed even citizens of modest means to take part in the political and cultural life of the city and have a genuine sense of citizenship. But this, in turn, drove the old aristocratic classes to develop more and more elaborate means of setting themselves off from what they considered the tawdriness and moral corruption of the new democratic state.

When the curtain truly goes up on Greece, in the fifth century, we find everybody arguing about money. For the aristocrats, who wrote most of the surviving texts, money was the embodiment of corruption. Aristocrats disdained the market. Ideally, a man of honor should be able to raise everything he needed on his own estates and never have to handle cash at all.[60] In practice, they knew this was impossible. Yet at every point they tried to set themselves apart from the values of the ordinary denizens of the marketplace: to contrast the beautiful gold and silver beakers and tripods they gave one another at funerals and weddings with the vulgar hawking of sausages or charcoal; the dignity of the athletic contests for which they endlessly trained with commoners' vulgar gambling; the sophisticated and literate courtesans who attended to them at their drinking clubs, and common prostitutes (*porne*)—slave-girls housed in brothels near the agora, brothels often sponsored by the democratic polis itself as a service to the sexual needs of its male citizenry. In each case, they placed a world of gifts, generosity, and honor above sordid commercial exchange.[61]

This resulted in a slightly different play of push and pull than we saw in Mesopotamia. On the one hand, we see a culture of aristocratic protest against what they saw as the lowly commercial sensibilities of ordinary citizens. On the other hand, we see an almost schizophrenic reaction on the part of the ordinary citizens themselves, who simultaneously tried to limit or even ban aspects of aristocratic culture and to imitate aristocratic sensibilities themselves. Pederasty is an excellent case in point here. On the one hand, man-boy love was seen as the quintessential aristocratic practice—it was the way, in fact, that young aristocrats would ordinarily become initiated into the privileges of high society. As a result, the democratic polis saw it as politically subversive and made sexual relations between male citizens illegal. At the same time, almost everyone began to practice it.

The famous Greek obsession with male honor that still informs so much of the texture of daily life in rural communities in Greece hearkens back not so much to Homeric honor but to this aristocratic rebellion against the values of the marketplace, which everyone, eventually, began to make their own.[62] The effects on women, though, were even more severe than they had been in the Middle East. Already by the age of Socrates, while a man's honor was increasingly tied to disdain for commerce and assertiveness in public life, a woman's honor had come to be defined in almost exclusively sexual terms: as a matter of virginity, modesty, and chastity, to the extent that respectable women were expected to be shut up inside the household and any woman who played a part in public life was considered for that reason a prostitute, or tantamount to one.[63] The Assyrian habit of veiling was not widely adopted in the Middle East, but it *was* adopted in Greece. As much as it flies in the face of our stereotypes about the origins of "Western" freedoms, women in democratic Athens, unlike those of Persia or Syria, were expected to wear veils when they ventured out in public.[64]

■ ■ ■ ■ ■

Money, then, had passed from a measure of honor to a measure of everything that honor was not. To suggest that a man's honor could be bought with money became a terrible insult—this despite the fact that, since men were often taken in war or even by bandits or pirates and held for ransom, they often did go through dramas of bondage and redemption not unlike those experienced by so many Middle Eastern women. One particularly striking way of hammering it home—actually, in this case, almost literally—was by branding ransomed prisoners with the mark of their own currency, much as if today some imaginary foreign kidnapper, after having received the ransom money for an American victim, made a point of burning a dollar sign onto the victim's forehead before returning him.[65]

One question that isn't clear from all this is, Why? Why had money, in particular, become such a symbol of degradation? Was it all because of slavery? One might be tempted to conclude that it was: perhaps the newfound presence of thousands of utterly degraded human beings in ancient Greek cities made any suggestion that a free man (let alone a free woman) might in any sense be bought or sold particularly insulting. But this is clearly not the case. Our discussion of the slave money of Ireland showed that the possibility of the utter degradation of a human being was in no sense a threat to heroic honor—in a way, it was its very essence. Homeric Greeks do not appear to have been any different. It seems hardly coincidental that the quarrel between Agamemnon and Achilles that sets off the action of the *Iliad*, generally considered to be the first great work of Western literature, is a dispute over honor between two heroic warriors on the occasion of the disposition of a slave girl.[66] Agamemnon and Achilles were also well aware that it would only take an unfortunate turn in battle, or perhaps a shipwreck, for either of them to wind up as a slave. Odysseus barely escapes being enslaved on several occasions in the *Odyssey*. Even in the third century AD, the Roman emperor Valerian (253–260 AD), defeated at the Battle of Edessa, was captured and spent the last years of his life as the footstool that the Sassanian emperor Shapur I used to mount his horse. Such were the perils of war. All this was essential to the nature of martial honor. A warrior's honor is his willingness to play a game on which he stakes everything. His grandeur is directly proportional to how far he can fall.

Was it, then, that the advent of commercial money threw traditional social hierarchies into disarray? Greek aristocrats often spoke this way, but the complaints seem rather disingenuous. Surely, it was money that allowed such a polished aristocracy to exist in the first place.[67] Rather, the thing that really seemed to bother them about money was simply that they wanted it so much. Since money could be used to buy just about anything, everyone desired it. That is: it was desirable *because* it was non-discriminating. One could see how the metaphor of the *porne* might seem particularly appropriate. A woman "common to the people"—as the poet Archilochos put it—is available to everyone. In principle, we shouldn't be attracted to such an undiscriminating creature. In fact, of course, we are.[68] And nothing was both so undiscriminating, and so desirable, as money. True, Greek aristocrats would ordinarily insist that they were not attracted to common *porne*, and that the courtesans, flute-girls, acrobats, and beautiful boys that frequented their symposia were not really prostitutes at all (though at times they also admitted that they really were). They also struggled with the fact that their own high-minded pursuits, such as chariot-racing, outfitting ships for the navy, and sponsoring tragic dramas, required the exact same coins as the ones used to buy cheap perfume and pies for a fisherman's wife—the only real difference being that their pursuits tended to require a lot more of them.[69]

We might say, then, that money introduced a democratization of desire. Insofar as everyone wanted money, everyone, high and low, was pursuing the same promiscuous substance. But even more: increasingly, they did not just want money. They needed it. This was a profound change. In the Homeric world, as in most human economies, we hear almost no discussion of those things considered necessary to human life (food, shelter, clothing) because it is simply assumed that everybody has them. A man with no possessions could, at the very least, become a retainer in some rich man's household. Even slaves had enough to eat.[70] Here too, the prostitute was a potent symbol for what had changed, since while some of the denizens of brothels were slaves, others were simply poor; the fact that their basic needs could no longer be taken for granted were precisely what made them submit to others' desires. This extreme fear of dependency on others' whims lies at the basis of the Greek obsession with the self-sufficient household.

All this lies behind the unusually assiduous efforts of the male citizens of Greek city-states—like the later Romans—to insulate their wives and daughters from both the dangers and the freedoms of the marketplace. Unlike their equivalents in the Middle East, they do not seem to have offered them as debt pawns. Neither, at least in Athens, was it legal for the daughters of free citizens to be employed as prostitutes.[71] As a result, respectable women became invisible, largely removed from the high dramas of economic and political life.[72] If anyone was enslaved for debt, it was normally the debtor. Even more dramatically, it was ordinarily *male* citizens who accused one another of prostitution—with Athenian politicians regularly asserting that their rivals, when they were young boys being plied with gifts from their male suitors, were really trading sex for money, and hence deserved to lose their civic freedoms.[73]

■ ■ ■ ■ ■

It might be helpful here to return to the principles laid out in Chapter Five. What we see above all is the erosion both of older forms of hierarchy—the Homeric world of great men with their retainers—and, at the same time, of older forms of mutual aid, with communistic relations increasingly being confined to the interior of the household.

It's the former—the erosion of hierarchy—that really seems to have been at stake in the "debt crises" that struck so many Greek cities around 600 BC, right around the time that commercial markets were first taking shape.[74] When the author of *Constitution of Athenians* spoke of the poor as falling slave to the rich, what he appears to have meant was that, in harsh years, many poor farmers fell into debt; as a result they ended up as sharecroppers on their own property, dependents. Some were even sold abroad as slaves. This led to unrest and agitation, and also to demands for clean slates, for the freeing of those held in bondage, and for the redistribution of agricultural land. In a few cases, it led to outright revolution. In Megara, we are told, a radical faction that seized power not only made interest-bearing loans illegal, but did so retroactively, forcing creditors to make restitution of all interest they had collected in the past.[75] In other cities, populist tyrants seized power on promises to abrogate agricultural debts.

On the face of it, all of this doesn't seem all that surprising: the moment when commercial markets developed, Greek cities quickly developed all the social problems that had been plaguing Middle Eastern cities for millennia: debt crises, debt resistance, political unrest. In reality, things are not so clear. For one thing, for the poor to be "enslaved to the rich," in the loose sense our author seems to be using, was hardly a new development. Even in Homeric society, it was assumed as a matter of course that rich men would live surrounded by dependents and retainers, drawn from the ranks of the dependent poor. The critical thing, though, about such relations of patronage is that they involved responsibilities on both sides. A noble warrior and his humble client were assumed to be fundamentally different sorts of people, but both were also expected to take account of each other's (fundamentally different) needs. Transforming patronage into debt relations—treating, say, an advance of seed corn as a *loan*, let alone an interest-bearing loan—changed all this.[76] What's more, it did so in two completely contradictory respects. On the one hand, a loan implies no ongoing responsibilities on the part of the creditor. On the other, as I have continually emphasized, a loan does assume a certain formal, legal equality between contractor and contractee. It assumes that they are, at least in some ways and on some level, fundamentally the same kind of person. This is certainly about the most ruthless and violent form of equality imaginable. But the fact that it was conceived as equality before the market made such arrangements even more difficult to endure.[77]

The same tensions can be observed between neighbors, who in farming communities tend to give, lend, and borrow things amongst themselves—anything from sieves and sickles to charcoal and cooking oil, to seed corn or oxen for plowing. On the one hand, such giving and lending were considered essential parts of the basic fabric of human sociability in farm communities, on the other, overly demanding neighbors were a notorious irritant—one that could only have grown worse when all parties are aware of precisely how much it would have cost to buy or rent the same items that were being given away. Again, one of the best ways to get a sense of what were considered everyday dilemmas for Mediterranean peasants is to look at jokes. Late stories from across the Aegean in Turkey echo exactly the same concerns:

> Nasruddin's neighbor once came by to ask if he could borrow his donkey for an unexpected errand. Nasruddin obliged, but the next day the neighbor was back again—he needed to take some grain to be milled. Before long he was showing up almost every morning, barely feeling he needed a pretext. Finally, Nasruddin got fed up, and one morning told him his brother had already come by and taken the donkey.
>
> Just as the neighbor was leaving he heard a loud braying sound from the yard.
>
> "Hey, I thought you said the donkey wasn't here!"
>
> "Look, who are you going to believe?" asked Nasruddin. "Me, or some animal?"

With the appearance of money, it could also become unclear what was a gift and what was a loan. On the one hand, even with gifts, it was always considered best to return something slightly better than one had received.[78] On the other hand, friends do not charge one another interest, and any suggestion that they might was sure to rankle. So what's the difference between a generous return gift and an interest payment? This is the basis of one of the most famous Nasruddin stories, one that appears to have provided centuries of amusement for peasants across the Mediterranean basin and adjoining regions. (It is also, I might note, a play on the fact that in many Mediterranean languages, Greek included, the word for "interest" literally means "offspring.")

> One day Nasruddin's neighbor, a notorious miser, came by to announce he was throwing a party for some friends. Could he borrow some of Nasruddin's pots? Nasruddin didn't have many but said he was happy to lend whatever he had. The next

day the miser returned, carrying Nasruddin's three pots, and one tiny additional one.

"What's that?" asked Nasrudddin.

"Oh, that's the offspring of the pots. They reproduced during the time they were with me."

Nasruddin shrugged and accepted them, and the miser left happy that he had established a principle of interest. A month later Nasruddin was throwing a party, and he went over to borrow a dozen pieces of his neighbor's much more luxurious crockery. The miser complied. Then he waited a day. And then another . . .

On the third day, the miser came by and asked what had happened to his pots.

"Oh, them?" Nasruddin said sadly. "It was a terrible tragedy. They died."[79]

In a heroic system, it is only debts of honor—the need to repay gifts, to exact revenge, to rescue or redeem friends or kinsmen fallen prisoner—that operate completely under a logic of tit-for-tat exchange. Honor is the same as credit; it's one's ability to keep one's promises, but also, in the case of a wrong, to "get even." As the last phrase implies, it was a monetary logic, but money, or anyway a money-like relation, is confined to this. Gradually, subtly, without anyone completely understanding the full implications of what was happening, what had been the essence of moral relations turned into the means for every sort of dishonest stratagem.

We know a little about it from trial speeches, many of which have survived. Here is one from the fourth century, probably around 365 BC. Apollodorus was a prosperous but low-born Athenian citizen (his father, a banker, had begun life as a slave) who, like many such gentlemen, had acquired a country estate. There he made a point of making friends with his closest neighbor, Nicostratus, a man of aristocratic origins, though currently of somewhat straitened means. They acted as neighbors normally did, giving and borrowing small sums, lending each other animals or slaves, minding each other's property when one was away. Then one day Nicostratus ran into a piece of terrible luck. While trying to track down some runaway slaves, he was himself captured by pirates and held for ransom at the slave market on the island of Aegina. His relatives could only assemble part of the price, so he was forced to borrow the rest from strangers in the market. These appear to have been professionals who specialized in such loans, and their terms were notoriously harsh: if not repaid in thirty days, the sum doubled; if not repaid at all, the debtor became the slave of the man who had put up the money for his redemption.

Tearfully, Nicostratus appealed to his neighbor. All his possessions were already pledged now to one creditor or another; he knew Apollodorus wouldn't have that much cash lying around, but could his dear friend possibly put up something of his own by way of security? Apollodorus was moved. He would be happy to forgive all debts Nicostratus already owed him, but the rest would be difficult. Still, he would do his best. In the end, he arranged to himself take a loan from an acquaintance of his, Arcesas, on the security of his town-house, at 16 percent annual interest, so as to be able to satisfy Nicostratus's creditors while Nicostratus himself arranged a friendly, no-interest *eranos* loan from his own relatives. But before long, Apollodorus began to realize that he had been set up. The impoverished aristocrat had decided to take advantage of his nouveau-riche neighbor; he was actually working with Arcesas and some of Apollodorus's enemies to have him falsely declared a "public debtor," that is, someone who had defaulted on an obligation to the public treasury. This would have first of all meant that he would lose his right to take anyone to court (i.e., his deceivers, to recover the money), and second, would give them a pretext to raid his house to remove his furniture and other possessions. Presumably, Nicostratus had never felt especially comfortable being in debt to a man he considered his social inferior. Rather like Egil the Viking, who would rather kill his friend Einar than have to compose an elegy thanking him for an overly magnificent gift, Nicostratus appears to have concluded that it was more honorable, or anyway more bearable, to try to extract the money from his lowly friend through force and fraud than to spend the rest of his life feeling beholden. Before long, things had indeed descended to outright physical violence, and the whole matter ended up in court.[80]

The story has everything. We see mutual aid: the communism of the prosperous, the expectation that if the need is great enough, or the cost manageable enough, friends and neighbors will help one another.[81] And most did, in fact, have circles of people who would pool money if a crisis did arise: whether a wedding, a famine, or a ransom. We also see the omnipresent danger of predatory violence that reduces human beings to commodities, and by doing so introduces the most cutthroat kinds of calculation into economic life—not just on the part of the pirates, but even more so, perhaps, on those moneylenders lurking by the market offering stiff credit terms to anyone who came to ransom their relatives but found themselves caught short, and who then could appeal to the state to allow them to hire men with weapons to enforce the contract. We see heroic pride, which sees too great an act of generosity as itself a kind of belittling assault. We see the ambiguity among gifts, loans, and commercial credit arrangements. Neither does the way things played out in this case seem particularly unusual, except perhaps for Nicostratus's extraordinary ingratitude. Prominent Athenians were always borrowing money to pursue their political projects; less-prominent ones were constantly worrying about their debts, or how to collect from their own debtors.[82] Finally, there is another, subtler element here. While everyday market transactions, at shops or stalls in the agora, were here as elsewhere typically conducted on credit, the mass production of coinage permitted a degree of anonymity for transactions that, in a pure credit regime, simply could not exist.[83] Pirates and kidnappers do business in cash—yet the loan sharks at Aegina's marketplace could not have operated without them. It is on this same combination of illegal cash business, usually involving violence, and extremely harsh credit terms, also enforced through violence, that innumerable criminal underworlds have been constructed ever since.

■ ■ ■ ■ ■

In Athens, the result was extreme moral confusion. The language of money, debt, and finance provided powerful—and ultimately irresistible—ways to think about moral problems. Much as in Vedic India, people started talking about life as a debt to the gods, of obligations as debts, about literal debts of honor, of debt as sin and of vengeance as debt collection.[84] Yet if debt was morality—and certainly at the very least it was in the interest of creditors, who often had little legal recourse to compel debtors to pay up, to insist that it was—what was one to make of the fact that money, that very thing that seemed capable of turning morality into an exact and quantifiable science, also seemed to encourage the very worst sorts of behavior?

It is from such dilemmas that modern ethics and moral philosophy begin. I think this is true quite literally. Consider Plato's *Republic*, another product of fourth-century Athens. The book begins when Socrates visits an old friend, a wealthy arms manufacturer, at the port of Piraeus. They get into a discussion of justice, which begins when the old man proposes that money cannot be a bad thing, since it allows those who have it to be just, and that justice consists in two things: telling the truth and always paying one's debts.[85] The proposal is easily demolished. What, Socrates asks, if someone lent you his sword, went violently insane, and then asked for it back (presumably, so he could kill someone)? Clearly, it can never be right to arm a lunatic whatever the circumstances.[86] The old man cheerfully shrugs the problem off and heads off to attend to some ritual, leaving his son to carry on the argument.

The son, Polemarchus, switches gears: clearly, his father hadn't meant "debt" in the literal sense of returning what one has borrowed. He meant it more in the sense of giving people what is owed to them; repaying good with good and evil with evil; helping one's friends and hurting one's enemies. Demolishing this one takes a little more work (Are we saying justice plays no part in determining who one's friends and enemies are? If so, wouldn't someone who decided he had no friends, and therefore tried to hurt everyone, be a just man? And even if you did have some way to say for certain that one's enemy really is an intrinsically bad person and deserves harm, by harming him, do you not thus make him worse? Can turning bad people into even worse people really be an example of justice?), but it is eventually accomplished. At this point, a Sophist, Thrasymachos, enters and denounces all of the debaters as milky-eyed idealists. In reality, he says, all talk of "justice" is mere political pretext, designed to justify the interests of the powerful. And so it should be, because insofar as justice exists, it is simply that: the interest of the powerful. Rulers are like shepherds. We like to think of them as benevolently tending their flocks, but what do shepherds ultimately *do* with sheep? They kill and eat them, or sell the meat for money. Socrates responds by pointing out that Thrasymachos is confusing the art of tending sheep with the art of profiting from them. The art of medicine aims to improve health, whether or not doctors get paid for practicing it. The art of shepherding aims to ensure the well-being of sheep, whether or not the shepherd (or his employer) is also a businessman who knows how to extract a profit from them. Just so with the art of governance. If such an art exists, it must have its own intrinsic aim apart from any profit one might also get from it, and what can this be other than the establishment of social justice? It's only the existence of money, Socrates suggests, that allows us to imagine that words like "power" and "interest" refer to universal realities that can be pursued in their own right, let alone that all pursuits are really ultimately the pursuit of power, advantage, or self-interest.[87] The question, he said, is how to ensure that those who hold political office will do so not for gain, but rather for honor.

I will leave off here. As we all know, Socrates eventually gets around to offering some political proposals of his own, involving philosopher kings; the abolition of marriage, the family, and private property; selective human breeding boards. (Clearly, the book was meant to annoy its readers, and for more than two thousand years, it has succeeded brilliantly.) What I want to emphasize, though, is the degree to which what we consider our core tradition of moral and political theory today springs from this question: What does it mean to pay one's debts? Plato presents us first with the simple, literal business-man's view. When this proves inadequate, he allows it to be reframed in heroic terms. Perhaps all debts are really debts of honor after all.[88] But heroic honor no longer works in a world where (as Apollodorus sadly discovered) commerce, class, and profit have so confused every-thing that people's true motives are never clear. How do we even know who our enemies are? Finally, Plato presents us with cynical realpolitik. Maybe nobody really owes anything to anybody. Maybe those who pursue profit for its own sake have it right after all. But even that does not hold up. We are left with a certainty that existing standards are incoherent and self-contradictory, and that *some* sort of radical break would be required in order to create a world that makes any logical sense. But most of those who seriously consider a radical break along the lines that Plato suggested have come to the conclusion that there might be far worse things than moral incoherence. And there we have stood, ever since, in the midst of an insoluble dilemma.

■ ■ ■ ■ ■

It's not surprising that these issues weighed on Plato's mind. Not seven years before, he had apparently taken an ill-fated sea cruise and wound up being captured and, like Nicostratus, offered for sale on the auction block at Aegina. However, Plato had better luck. A Libyan philoso-pher of the Epicurean school, one Annikeris, happened to be in the market at the time. He recognized Plato and ransomed him. Plato felt honor-bound to try to repay him, and his Athenian friends assembled twenty minas in silver with which to do so, but Annikeris refused to accept the money, insisting that it was his honor to be able to benefit a fellow lover of wisdom.[89] As indeed it was: Annikeris has been remem-bered, and celebrated, for his generosity ever since. Plato went on to use the twenty minas to buy land for a school, the famous Academy. And while he hardly showed the same ingratitude as Nicostratus, one does rather get the impression that even Plato wasn't especially happy about the fact that his subsequent career was, in a sense, made pos-sible by his debt to a man who he probably considered an extremely minor philosopher—and Annikeris wasn't even Greek! At least this would help explain why Plato, otherwise the inveterate name-dropper, never mentioned Annikeris. We know of his existence only from later biographers.[90]

Ancient Rome (Property and Freedom)

If Plato's work testifies to how profoundly the moral confusion introduced by debt has shaped our traditions of thought, Roman law reveals how much it has shaped even our most familiar institutions.

German legal theorist Rudolf von Jhering famously remarked that ancient Rome had conquered the world three times: the first time through its armies, the second through its religion, the third through its laws.[91] He might have added: each time more thoroughly. The Empire, after all, only spanned a tiny portion of the globe; the Roman Catholic Church has spread farther; Roman law has come to provide the language and conceptual underpinnings of legal and constitutional orders everywhere. Law students from South Africa to Peru are expected to spend a good deal of their time memorizing technical terms in Latin, and it is Roman law that provides almost all our basic conceptions about contract, obligation, torts, property, and jurisdiction—and, in a broader sense, of citizenship, rights, and liberties on which political life, too, is based.

Jhering claimed this was possible because the Romans were the first to turn jurisprudence into a genuine science. This may be true. But it remains the case that Roman law has a few notoriously quirky features, some so odd that they have confused and confounded jurists ever since Roman law was revived in Italian universities in the High Middle Ages. The most notorious of these is the unique way it defines property. In Roman law, property, or *dominium*, is a relation between a person and a thing, characterized by absolute power of that person over that thing. This definition has caused endless conceptual problems. First of all, it's not clear what it would even mean for a human to have a "relation" with an inanimate object. Human beings can have relations with one another. But such relations are always mutual. How could one have a mutual relation with a thing? And if one did, what would it mean to give that relation legal standing? A simple illustration will suffice: imagine a man trapped on a desert island. He might develop extremely personal relationships with, say, the palm trees growing on that island. If he's there too long, he might well end up giving them all names and spending half his time having imaginary conversations with them. Still, does he *own* them? The question is meaningless. There's no need to worry about property rights if no one else is there.

Clearly, then, property is not really a relation between a person and a thing. It's an understanding or arrangement between people concerning things. The only reason that we sometimes fail to notice this is that in many cases—particularly when we are talking about our rights over our shoes, or cars, or power tools—we are talking of rights held, as English law puts it, "against all the world"—that is, understandings between ourselves and everyone else on the planet, that they will all refrain from interfering with our possessions, and therefore allow us to treat them more or less any way we like. A relation between one person and everyone else on the planet is, understandably, difficult to conceive as such. It's easier to think of it as a relationship with a thing. But even here, in practice this freedom to do as one likes turns out to be fairly limited. To say that the fact that I own a chainsaw gives me an "absolute power" to do anything I want with it is obviously absurd. Almost anything I might think of doing with a chainsaw outside my own home or land is likely to be illegal, and there are only a limited number of things I can really do with it inside. The only thing "absolute" about my rights to a chainsaw is my right to prevent anyone *else* from using it.[92]

Nonetheless, Roman law does insist that the basic form of property is private property, and that private property is the owner's absolute power to do anything he wants with his possessions. Twelfth-century Medieval jurists came to refine this into three principles, *usus* (use of the thing), *fructus* (fruits, i.e., enjoyment of the products of the thing), and *abusus* (abuse or destruction of the thing), but Roman jurists weren't even interested in specifying that much, since, in a certain way, they saw the details as lying entirely outside the domain of law. In fact, scholars have spent a great deal of time debating whether Roman authors actually considered private property to be a right (*ius*),[93] for the very reason that rights were ultimately based on agreements between people, and one's power to dispose of one's property was not: it was just one's natural ability to do whatever one pleased when social impediments were absent.[94]

If you think about it, this really is an odd place to start in developing a theory of property law. It is probably fair to say that, in any part of the world, in any period of history, whether in ancient Japan or Machu Picchu, someone who had a piece of string was free to twist it, knot it, pull it apart, or toss it in the fire more or less as they had a mind to. Nowhere else did legal theorists appear to have found this fact in any way interesting or important. Certainly, no other tradition makes it the very basis of property law—since, after all, doing so made almost all actual law little more than a series of exceptions.

How did this come about? And why? The most convincing explanation I've seen is Orlando Patterson's: the notion of absolute private property is really derived from slavery. One can imagine property not as a relation between people, but as a relation between a person and a thing, if one's starting point is a relation between two people, one of whom is also a thing. (This is how slaves were defined in Roman law: they were people who were also a *res*, a thing.)[95] The emphasis on absolute power begins to make sense as well.[96]

The word *dominium*, meaning absolute private property, was not particularly ancient.[97] It only appears in Latin in the late Republic, right around the time when hundreds of thousands of captive laborers were pouring into Italy, and when Rome, as a consequence, was becoming a genuine slave society.[98] By 50 BC, Roman writers had come to simply assume that workers—whether the farmworkers harvesting peas in countryside plantations, the muleteers delivering those peas to shops in the city, or the clerks keeping count of them—were someone else's property. The existence of millions of creatures who were simultaneously persons and things created endless legal problems, and much of the creative genius of Roman law was spent in working out the endless ramifications. One need only flip open a casebook of Roman law to get a sense of these. This is from the second-century jurist Ulpian:

> Again, Mela writes that if some persons were playing ball and one of them, hitting the ball quite hard, knocked it against a barber's hands, and in this way the throat of a slave, whom the barber was shaving, was cut by a razor pressed against it, then who is the person with whom the culpability lay is liable under the Lex Aquilia [the law of civil damages]? Proclus says that the culpability lies with the barber; and indeed, if he was shaving at a place where games are normally played or where traffic was heavy, there is reason to fault him. But it would not be badly held that if someone entrusts himself to a barber who has a chair in a dangerous place, he should have himself to blame.[99]

In other words, the master cannot claim civil damages against the ballplayers or barber for destroying his property if the real problem was that he bought a stupid slave. Many of these debates might strike us as profoundly exotic (Could you be accused of theft for merely convincing a slave to run away? If someone killed a slave who was also your son, could you take your sentimental feelings toward him into account in assessing damages, or would you have to stick to his market value?), but our contemporary tradition of jurisprudence is founded directly on such debates.[100]

As for *dominium*, the word is derived from *dominus*, meaning "master" or "slave-owner," but ultimately from *domus*, meaning "house" or "household." It's of course related to the English term "domestic," which even now can be used either to mean "pertaining to private life," or to refer to a servant who cleans the house. *Domus* overlaps somewhat in meaning with *familia*, "family"—but, as proponents of "family values" might be interested to know, *familia* itself ultimately derives from the word *famulus*, meaning "slave." A family was originally all those people under the domestic authority of a *paterfamilias*, and that authority was, in early Roman law at least, conceived as absolute.[101] A man did not have total power over his wife, since she was still to some degree under the protection of her own father, but his children, slaves, and other dependents were his to do with as he wanted—at least in early Roman law, he was perfectly free to whip, torture, or sell them. A father could even execute his children, provided he found them to have committed capital crimes.[102] With his slaves, he didn't even need that excuse.

In creating a notion of *dominium*, then, and thus creating the modern principle of absolute private property, what Roman jurists were doing first of all was taking a principle of domestic authority, of absolute power over people, defining some of those people (slaves) as things, and then extending the logic that originally applied to slaves to geese, chariots, barns, jewelry boxes, and so forth—that is, to every other sort of thing that the law had anything to do with.

It was quite extraordinary, even in the ancient world, for a father to have the right to execute his slaves—let alone his children. No one is quite sure why the early Romans were so extreme in this regard. It's telling, though, that the earliest Roman debt law was equally unusual in its harshness, since it allowed creditors to execute insolvent debtors.[103] The early history of Rome, like the histories of early Greek city-states, was one of continual political struggle between creditors and debtors, until the Roman elite eventually figured out the principle that most successful Mediterranean elites learned: that a free peasantry means a more effective army, and that conquering armies can provide war captives who can do anything debt bondsmen used to do, and therefore, a social compromise—allowing limited popular representation, banning debt slavery, channeling some of the fruits of empire into social-welfare payments—was actually in their interest. Presumably, the absolute power of fathers developed as part of this whole constellation in the same way as we've seen elsewhere. Debt bondage reduced family relations to relations of property; social reforms retained the new power of fathers but protected them from debt. At the same time, the increasing influx of slaves soon meant that any even moderately prosperous household was likely to contain slaves. This, in turn, meant that the logic of conquest extended into the most intimate aspects of everyday life. Conquered people poured one's bath and combed one's hair. Conquered tutors taught one's children about poetry. Since slaves were sexually available to owners and their families, as well as to their friends and dinner guests, it is likely that most Romans' first sexual experience was with a boy or girl whose legal status was conceived as that of a defeated enemy.[104]

Over time, this became more and more of a legal fiction—actual slaves were much more likely to have been paupers sold by parents, unfortunates kidnapped by pirates or bandits, victims of wars or judicial process among barbarians at the fringes of the empire, or children of other slaves.[105] Still, the fiction was maintained.

What made Roman slavery so unusual, in historical terms, was a conjuncture of two factors. One was its very arbitrariness. In dramatic contrast with, say, plantation slavery in the Americas, there was no sense that certain people were naturally inferior and therefore destined to be slaves. Instead, slavery was seen as a misfortune that could happen to anyone.[106] As a result, there was no reason that a slave might not be in every way superior to his or her master: smarter, with a finer sense of morality, better taste, and a greater understanding of philosophy. The master might even be willing to acknowledge this. There was no reason not to, since it had no effect on the nature of the relationship, which was simply one of power.

The second was the absolute nature of this power. There are many places where slaves are conceived as war captives, and masters as conquerors with absolute powers of life and death—but usually, this is something of an abstract principle. Almost everywhere, governments quickly move to limit such powers. At the very least, emperors and kings will insist that they are the only ones with the power to order others put to death.[107] But under the Roman Republic there was no emperor; insofar as there was a sovereign body, it was the collective body of the slave-owners themselves. Only under the early Empire do we see any legislation limiting what owners could do to their (human) property: the first being a law of the time of the emperor Tiberius (dated 16 AD) stipulating that a master had to obtain a magistrate's permission before ordering a slave publicly torn apart by wild beasts.[108] However, the absolute nature of the master's power—the fact that in this context, he effectively *was* the state—also meant that there were also, at first, no restrictions on manumission: a master could liberate his slave, or even adopt him or her, whereby—since liberty meant nothing outside of membership in a community—that slave automatically became a Roman citizen. This led to some very peculiar arrangements. In the first century AD, for example, it was not uncommon for educated Greeks to have themselves sold into slavery to some wealthy Roman in need of a secretary, entrust the money to a close friend or family member, and then, after a certain interval, buy themselves back, thus obtaining Roman citizenship. This despite the fact that, during such time as they were slaves, if their owner decided to, say, cut one of his secretary's feet off, legally, he would have been perfectly free to do so.[109]

The relation of *dominus* and slave thus brought a relation of conquest, of absolute political power into the household (in fact, made it the essence of the household). It's important to emphasize that this was not a moral relation on either side. A well-known legal formula, attributed to a Republican lawyer named Quintus Haterius, brings this home with particular clarity. With the Romans as with the Athenians, for a male to be the object of sexual penetration was considered unbefitting to a citizen. In defending a freedman accused of continuing to provide sexual favors to his former master, Haterius coined an aphorism that was later to become something of a popular dirty joke: *impudicitia in ingenuo crimen est, in servo necessitas, in liberto officium* ("to be the object of anal penetration is a crime in the freeborn, a necessity for a slave, a duty for a freedman").[110] What is significant here is that sexual subservience is considered the "duty" only of the freedman. It is not considered the "duty" of a slave. This is because, again, slavery was not a moral relation. The master could do what he liked, and there was nothing the slave could do about it.

■ ■ ■ ■ ■

The most insidious effect of Roman slavery, however, is that through Roman law, it has come to play havoc with our idea of human freedom. The meaning of the Roman word *libertas* itself changed dramatically over time. As everywhere in the ancient world, to be "free" meant, first and foremost, not to be a slave. Since slavery means above all the annihilation of social ties and the ability to form them, freedom meant the capacity to make and maintain moral commitments to others. The English word "free," for instance, is derived from a German root meaning "friend," since to be free meant to be able to make friends, to keep promises, to live within a community of equals. This is why freed slaves in Rome became citizens: to be free, by definition, meant to be anchored in a civic community, with all the rights and responsibilities that this entailed.[111]

By the second century AD, however, this had begun to change. The jurists gradually redefined *libertas* until it became almost indistinguishable from the power of the master. It was the right to do absolutely anything, with the exception, again, of all those things one could not do. Actually, in the *Digest*, the definitions of freedom and slavery appear back to back:

> Freedom is the natural faculty to do whatever one wishes that is not prevented by force or law. Slavery is an institution according to the law of nations whereby one person becomes private property (*dominium*) of another, contrary to nature.[112]

Medieval commentators immediately noticed the problem here.[113] But wouldn't this mean that everyone is free? After all, even slaves are free to do absolutely anything they're actually permitted to do. To say a slave is free (except insofar as he isn't) is a bit like saying the earth is square (except insofar as it is round), or that the sun is blue (except insofar as it is yellow), or, again, that we have an absolute right to do anything we wish with our chainsaw (except those things that we can't).

In fact, the definition introduces all sorts of complications. If freedom is natural, then surely slavery is unnatural, but if freedom and slavery are just matters of degree, then, logically, would not *all* restrictions on freedom be to some degree unnatural? Would not that imply that society, social rules, in fact even property rights, are unnatural as well? This is precisely what many Roman jurists did conclude—that is, when they did venture to comment on such abstract matters, which was only rarely. Originally, human beings lived in a state of nature where all things were held in common; it was war that first divided up the world, and the resultant "law of nations," the common usages of mankind that regulate such matters as conquest, slavery, treaties, and borders, that was first responsible for inequalities of property as well.[114]

This in turn meant that there was no intrinsic difference between private property and political power—at least, insofar as that power was based in violence. As time went on, Roman emperors also began claiming something like *dominium*, insisting that within their dominions, they had absolute freedom—in fact, that they were not bound by laws.[115] At the same time, Roman society shifted from a republic of slave-holders to arrangements that increasingly resembled later feudal Europe, with magnates on their great estates surrounded by dependent peasants, debt servants, and an endless variety of slaves—with whom they could largely do as they pleased. The barbarian invasions that overthrew the empire merely formalized the situation, largely eliminating chattel slavery, but at the same time introducing the notion that the noble classes were really descendants of the Germanic conquerors, and that the common people were inherently subservient.

Still, even in this new Medieval world, the old Roman concept of freedom remained. Freedom was simply power. When Medieval political theorists spoke of "liberty," they were normally referring to a lord's right to do whatever he wanted within his own domains. This was, again, usually assumed to be not something originally established by agreement, but a mere fact of conquest: one famous English legend holds that when, around 1290, King Edward I asked his lords to produce documents to demonstrate by what right they held their franchises (or "liberties"), the Earl Warenne presented the king only with his rusty sword.[116] Like Roman *dominium*, it was a power exercised first and foremost over others—which is why in the Middle Ages it was common to speak of the "liberty of the gallows," meaning a lord's right to maintain his own private place of execution.

When Roman law began to be recovered and modernized in the twelfth century, the term *dominium* posed a particular problem, since, in ordinary church Latin of the time, it had come to be used equally for "lordship" and "private property." Medieval jurists spent a great deal of time and argument establishing whether there was indeed a difference between the two. It was a particularly thorny problem because, if property rights really were, as the *Digest* insisted, a form of absolute power, it was very difficult to see how anyone could have it but a king—or even, for certain jurists, God.[117]

This is not the place to describe the ensuing debate, but I feel it's important to end here because, in a way, it brings us full circle and allows us to understand precisely how Liberals like Adam Smith were able to imagine the world the way they did. This is a tradition that assumes that liberty is essentially the right to do what one likes with one's own property. In fact, not only does it make property a right, it treats rights themselves as a form of property. In a way, this is the greatest paradox of all. We are so used to the idea of "having" rights—that rights are something one can possess—that we rarely think about what this might actually mean. In fact (as Medieval jurists were well aware), one man's right is simply another's obligation. My right to free speech is others' obligation not to punish me for speaking; my right to a trial by a jury of my peers is the responsibility of others to maintain a system of jury duty. The problem is just the same as it was with property rights: when we are talking about obligations owed by everyone in the entire world, it's difficult to think about it that way. It's much easier to speak of "having" rights and freedoms. Still, if freedom is basically our right to own things, or to treat things as if we own them, then what would it mean to "own" a freedom—wouldn't it have to mean that our right to own property is *itself* a form of property? That does seem unnecessarily convoluted. What possible reason would one have to want to define it this way?[118]

Historically, there is a simple—if somewhat disturbing—answer to this. Those who have argued that we are the natural owners of our rights and liberties have been mainly interested in asserting that we should be free to give them away, or even to sell them.

Modern ideas of rights and liberties are derived from what came to be known as "natural rights theory"—from the time when Jean Gerson, Rector of the University of Paris, began to lay them out around 1400, building on Roman law concepts. As Richard Tuck, the premier historian of such ideas, has long noted, it is one of the great ironies of history that this was always a body of theory embraced not by the progressives of that time, but by conservatives. "For a Gersonian, liberty was property and could be exchanged in the same way and in the same terms as any other property"—sold, swapped, loaned, or otherwise voluntarily surrendered.[119] It followed that there could be nothing intrinsically wrong with, say, debt peonage, or even slavery. And this is exactly what natural-rights theorists came to assert. In fact, over the next centuries, these ideas came to be developed above all in Antwerp and Lisbon, cities at the very center of the emerging slave trade. After all, its exponents argued, we don't really know what's going on in the lands behind places like Calabar, but there is no intrinsic reason to assume that the vast majority of the human cargo conveyed to European ships had not sold themselves, or been disposed of by their legal guardians, or lost their liberty in some other perfectly legitimate fashion. No doubt some had not, but abuses will exist in any system. The important thing was that there was nothing inherently unnatural or illegitimate about the idea that freedom *could* be sold.[120]

Before long, similar arguments came to be employed to justify the absolute power of the state. Thomas Hobbes was the first to really develop this argument in the seventeenth century, but it soon became commonplace. Government was essentially a contract, a kind of business arrangement, whereby citizens had voluntarily given up some of their natural liberties to the sovereign. Finally, similar ideas have become the basis of that most basic, dominant institution of our present economic life: wage labor, which is, effectively, the renting of our freedom in the same way that slavery can be conceived as its sale.[121]

It's not only our freedoms that we own; the same logic has come to be applied even to our own bodies, which are treated, in such formulations, as really no different than houses, cars, or furniture. We own ourselves, therefore outsiders have no right to trespass on us.[122] Again, this might seem an innocuous, even a positive notion, but it looks rather different when we take into consideration the Roman tradition of property on which it is based. To say that we own ourselves is, oddly enough, to cast ourselves as both master and slave simultaneously. "We" are both owners (exerting absolute power over our property), and yet somehow, at the same time, the things being owned (being the object of absolute power). The ancient Roman household, far from having been forgotten in the mists of history, is preserved in our most basic conception of ourselves—and, once again, just as in property law, the result is so strangely incoherent that it spins off into endless paradoxes the moment one tries to figure out what it would actually mean in practice. Just as lawyers have spent a thousand years trying to make sense of Roman property concepts, so have philosophers spent centuries trying to understand how it could be possible for us to have a relation of domination over ourselves. The most popular solution—to say that each of us has something called a "mind" and that this is completely separate from something else, which we can call "the body," and that the first thing holds natural dominion over the second—flies in the face of just about everything we now know about cognitive science. It's obviously untrue, but we continue to hold onto it anyway, for the simple reason that none of our everyday assumptions about property, law, and freedom would make any sense without it.[123]

Conclusions

The first four chapters of this book describe a dilemma. We don't really know how to think about debt. Or, to be more accurate, we seem to be trapped between imagining society in the Adam Smith mode, as a collection of individuals whose only significant relations are with their own possessions, happily bartering one thing for another for the sake of mutual convenience, with debt almost entirely abolished from the picture, and a vision in which debt is everything, the very substance of all human relations—which, of course, leaves everyone with the uncomfortable sense that human relations are somehow an intrinsically tawdry business, that our very responsibilities to one another are already somehow necessarily based in sin and crime. It's not an appealing set of alternatives.

In the last three chapters I have tried to show that there is another way of looking at things, and then to describe how it is that we got here. This is why I developed the concept of human economies: ones in which what is considered really important about human beings is the fact that they are each a unique nexus of relations with others—therefore, that no one could ever be considered exactly equivalent to anything or anyone else. In a human economy, money is not a way of buying or trading human beings, but a way of expressing just how much one cannot do so.

I then went on to describe how all this can begin to break down: how humans can become objects of exchange: first, perhaps, women given in marriage; ultimately, slaves captured in war. What all these relations have in common, I observed, was violence. Whether it is Tiv girls being tied up and beaten for running away from their husbands, or husbands being herded into slave ships to die on faraway plantations, that same principle always applies: it is only by the threat of sticks, ropes, spears, and guns that one can tear people out of those endlessly complicated webs of relationship with others (sisters, friends, rivals . . .) that render them unique, and thus reduce them to something that can be traded.

All of this, it is important to emphasize, can happen in places where markets in ordinary, everyday goods—clothing, tools, foodstuffs—do not even exist. In fact, in most human economies, one's most important possessions could never be bought and sold for the same reasons that people can't: they are unique objects, caught up in a web of relationships with human beings.[124]

My old professor John Comaroff used to tell a story about carrying out a survey in Natal, in South Africa. He had spent most of a week driving from homestead to homestead in a jeep with a box full of questionnaires and a Zulu-speaking interpreter, driving past apparently endless herds of cattle. After about six days, his interpreter suddenly started and pointed into the middle of one herd. "Look!" he said. "That's the same cow! That one there—with the red spot on its back. We saw it three days ago in a place ten miles from here. I wonder what happened? Did someone get married? Or maybe there was a settlement to some dispute."

In human economies, when this ability to rip people from their contexts does appear, it is most often seen as an end in itself. One can already see a hint of this among the Lele. Important men would occasionally acquire war captives from far away as slaves, but it was almost always to be sacrificed at their funeral.[125] The squelching of one man's individuality was seen as somehow swelling the reputation, the social existence, of the other.[126] In what I've been calling heroic societies, of course, this kind of addition and subtraction of honor and disgrace is lifted from a somewhat marginal practice to become the very essence of politics. As endless epics, sagas, and eddas attest, heroes become heroes by making others small. In Ireland and Wales, we can observe how this very ability to degrade others, to remove unique human beings from their hearths and families and thus render them anonymous units of accounting—the Irish slave-girl currency, the Welsh washerwomen—is itself the highest expression of honor.

In heroic societies, the role of violence is not hidden—it's glorified. Often, it can form the basis of one's most intimate relations. In the *Iliad*, Achilles sees nothing shameful in his relation with his slave-girl, Briseis, whose husband and brothers he killed; he refers to her as his "prize of honor," but almost in the very same breath, he also insists that, just any decent man must love and care for his household dependents, "so I from my heart loved this one, even though I won her with my spear."[127]

That such relations of intimacy can often develop between men of honor and those they have stripped of their dignity, history can well attest. After all, the annihilation of any possibility of equality also eliminates any question of debt, of any relation other than power. It allows a certain clarity. This is presumably why emperors and kings have such a notorious tendency to enjoy the company of slaves or eunuchs.

There is something more here, though. If one looks across the expanse of history, one cannot help but notice a curious sense of identification between the most exalted and the most degraded; particularly, between emperors and kings, and slaves. Many kings surround themselves with slaves, appoint slave ministers—there have even been, as with the Mamluks in Egypt, actual dynasties of slaves. Kings surround themselves with slaves for the same reason that they surround themselves with eunuchs: because the slaves and criminals have no families or friends, no possibility of other loyalties—or at least, in principle, they shouldn't. But, in a way, kings should really be like that too. As many an African proverb emphasizes: a proper king has no relatives either, or at least, he acts as if he does not.[128] In other words, king and slave are mirror images, in that unlike normal human beings who are defined by their commitments to others, they are defined *only* by relations of power. They are as close to perfectly isolated, alienated beings as one can possibly become.

At this point, we can finally see what's really at stake in our peculiar habit of defining ourselves simultaneously as master and slave, reduplicating the most brutal aspects of the ancient household in our very concept of ourselves, as masters of our freedoms, or as owners of our very selves. It is the only way that we can imagine ourselves as completely isolated beings. There is a direct line from the new Roman conception of liberty—not as the ability to form mutual relationships with others, but as the kind of absolute power of "use and abuse" over the conquered chattel who make up the bulk of a wealthy Roman man's household—to the strange fantasies of liberal philosophers like Hobbes, Locke, and Smith about the origins of human society in some collection of thirty- or forty-year-old males who seem to have sprung from the earth fully formed, who then must decide whether to kill each other or to swap beaver pelts.[129]

European and American intellectuals, it is true, have spent much of the last two hundred years trying to flee from the more disturbing implications of this tradition of thought. Thomas Jefferson, that owner of many slaves, chose to begin the Declaration of Independence by directly contradicting the moral basis of slavery, writing "We hold these truths to be self-evident, that all men are created equal, and that they are endowed by their Creator with certain inalienable Rights . . ."—thus undercutting simultaneously any argument that Africans were racially inferior, and also that they or their ancestors could ever have been justly and legally deprived of their freedom. In doing so, however, he did not propose some radically new conception of rights and liberties. Neither have subsequent political philosophers. For the most part, we've just kept the old ones, but with the word "not" inserted here and there. Most of our most precious rights and freedoms are a series of exceptions to an overall moral and legal framework that suggests we shouldn't really have them in the first place.

Formal slavery has been eliminated, but (as anyone who works from nine to five can testify) the idea that you can alienate your liberty, at least temporarily, endures. In fact, it determines what most of us have to do for most of our waking hours, except, usually, on weekends. The violence has been largely pushed out of sight.[130] But this is largely because we're no longer able to imagine what a world based on social arrangements that did not require the continual threat of tasers and surveillance cameras would even look like.

Chapter Eight

CREDIT VERSUS BULLION

AND THE CYCLES OF HISTORY

> *Bullion is the accessory of war, and not of peaceful trade.*
> —Geoffrey W. Gardiner

ONE MIGHT WELL ASK: If our political and legal ideas really are founded on the logic of slavery, then how did we ever abolish it? Of course, a cynic might argue that we haven't really abolished slavery; we've just relabeled it. The cynic would have a point: an ancient Greek would certainly have seen the distinction between a slave and an indebted wage laborer as, at best, a legalistic nicety.[1] Still, even the elimination of formal chattel slavery has to be considered a remarkable achievement, and it is worthwhile to wonder how it was accomplished. Especially since it was not just accomplished once. The truly remarkable thing, if one consults the historical record, is that slavery has been eliminated—or effectively eliminated—many times in human history.

In Europe, for instance, the institution largely vanished in the centuries following the collapse of the Roman empire—an historical achievement rarely recognized by those of us used to referring to these events as the beginning of "the Dark Ages."[2] No one is quite sure how it happened. Most agree that the spread of Christianity must have had something to do with it, but that can't have been the direct cause, since the Church itself was never explicitly opposed to the institution and in many cases defended it. Instead, the abolition appears to have happened *despite* the attitudes of both the intellectuals and the political authorities of the time. Yet it did happen, and it had lasting effects. On the popular level, slavery remained so universally detested that even a thousand years later, when European merchants started trying to revive the trade, they discovered that their compatriots would not countenance slaveholding in their own countries—one reason why planters were eventually obliged to acquire their slaves in Africa and set up plantations in the New World.[3] It is one of the great ironies of history that modern racism—probably the single greatest evil of our last two centuries—had to be invented largely because Europeans continued to refuse to listen to the arguments of the intellectuals and jurists and did not accept that anyone they believed to be a full and equal human being could ever be justifiably enslaved.

What's more, the demise of ancient slavery was not limited to Europe. Remarkably, right around the same time—in the years around 600 AD—we find almost exactly the same thing happening in India and China, where, over the course of centuries, amidst much unrest and confusion, chattel slavery largely ceased to exist. What all this suggests is that moments of historical opportunity—moments when meaningful change is possible—follow a distinct, even a cyclical pattern, one that has long been far more coordinated across geographical space than we would ever have imagined. There is a shape to the past, and it is only by understanding it that we can begin to have a sense of the historical opportunities that exist in the present.

■ ■ ■ ■ ■

The easiest way to make these cycles visible is to reexamine exactly the phenomenon we've been concerned with over the course of this book: the history of money, debt, and credit. The moment we begin to map the history of money across the last five thousand years of Eurasian history, startling patterns begin to emerge. In the case of money, one event stands out above all others: the invention of coinage. Coinage appears to have arisen independently in three different places, almost simultaneously: on the Great Plain of northern China, in the Ganges river valley of northeast India, and in the lands surrounding the Aegean Sea, in each case, between roughly 600 and 500 BC. This wasn't due to some sudden technological innovation: the technologies used in making the first coins were, in each case, entirely different.[4] It was a social transformation. Why this happened in exactly this way is an historical mystery. But this much we know: for some reason, in Lydia, India, and China, local rulers decided that whatever longstanding credit systems had existed in their kingdoms were no longer adequate, and they began to issue tiny pieces of precious metals—metals that had previously been used largely in international commerce, in ingot form—and to encourage their subjects to use them in day-to-day transactions.

From there, the innovation spread. For more than a thousand years, states everywhere started issuing their own coinage. But then, right around 600 AD, about the time that slavery was disappearing, the whole trend was suddenly thrown into reverse. Cash dried up. Everywhere, there was a movement back to credit once again.

If we look at Eurasian history over the course of the last five thousand years, what we see is a broad alternation between periods dominated by credit money and periods in which gold and silver come to dominate—that is, those during which at least a large share of transactions were conducted with pieces of valuable metal being passed from hand to hand.

Why? The single most important factor would appear to be war. Bullion predominates, above all, in periods of generalized violence. There's a very simple reason for that. Gold and silver coins are distinguished from credit arrangements by one spectacular feature: they can be stolen. A debt is, by definition, a record, as well as a relation of trust. Someone accepting gold or silver in exchange for merchandise, on the other hand, need trust nothing more than the accuracy of the scales, the quality of the metal, and the likelihood that someone else will be willing to accept it. In a world where war and the threat of violence are everywhere—and this appears to have been an equally accurate description of Warring States China, Iron Age Greece, and pre-Mauryan India—there are obvious advantages to making one's transactions simple. This is all the more true when dealing with soldiers. On the one hand, soldiers tend to have access to a great deal of loot, much of which consists of gold and silver, and will always seek a way to trade it for the better things in life. On the other, a heavily armed itinerant soldier is the very definition of a poor credit risk. The economists' barter scenario might be absurd when applied to transactions between neighbors in the same small rural community, but when dealing with a transaction between the resident of such a community and a passing mercenary, it suddenly begins to make a great deal of sense.

For much of human history, then, an ingot of gold or silver, stamped or not, has served the same role as the contemporary drug dealer's suitcase full of unmarked bills: an object without a history, valuable because one knows it will be accepted in exchange for other goods just about anywhere, no questions asked. As a result, while credit systems tend to dominate in periods of relative social peace, or across networks of trust (whether created by states or, in most periods, transnational institutions like merchant guilds or communities of faith), in periods characterized by widespread war and plunder, they tend to be replaced by precious metal. What's more, while predatory lending goes on in every period of human history, the resulting debt crises appear to have the most damaging effects at times when money is most easily convertible into cash.

As a starting point to any attempt to discern the great rhythms that define the current historical moment, let me propose the following breakdown of Eurasian history according to the alternation between periods of virtual and metal money. The cycle begins with the Age of the First Agrarian Empires (3500–800 BC), dominated by virtual credit money. This is followed by the Axial Age (800 BC–600 AD), which will be covered in the next chapter, and which saw the rise of coinage and a general shift to metal bullion. The Middle Ages (600–1450 AD), which saw a return to virtual credit money, will be covered in Chapter Ten; Chapter Eleven will cover the next turn of the cycle, the Age of Capitalist Empires, which began around 1450 with a massive planetary switch back to gold and silver bullion, and which could only really be said to have ended in 1971, when Richard Nixon announced that the U.S. dollar would no longer be redeemable in gold. This marked the beginning of yet another phase of virtual money, one which has only just begun, and whose ultimate contours are, necessarily, invisible. Chapter Twelve, the final chapter, will be devoted to applying the insights of history to understanding what it might mean and the opportunities it might throw open.

Mesopotamia

(3500–800 BC)

We have already had occasion to note the predominance of credit money in Mesopotamia, the earliest urban civilization that we know about. In the great temple and palace complexes, not only did money serve largely as an accounting measure rather than physically changing hands, merchants and tradespeople developed credit arrangements of their own. Most of these took the physical form of clay tablets, inscribed with some obligation of future payment, that were then sealed inside clay envelopes and marked with the borrower's seal. The creditor would keep the envelope as a surety, and it would be broken open on repayment. In some times or places, at least, these *bullae* appear to have become what we would now call negotiable instruments, since the tablet inside did not simply record a promise to pay the original lender, but was designated "to the bearer"—in other words, a tablet recording a debt of five shekels of silver (at prevailing rates of interest) could circulate as the equivalent of a five-shekel promissory note—that is, as money.[5]

We don't know how often this happened, how many hands such tablets would typically pass through, how many transactions were based on credit, how often merchants actually did weigh out silver in rough chunks to buy and sell their merchandise, or when they were most likely to do so. No doubt all this varied over time. Promissory notes usually circulated within merchant guilds, or between inhabitants of the relatively well-off urban neighborhoods where people knew their neighbors well enough to trust them to be accountable, but not so well that they could rely on one another for more traditional forms of mutual aid.[6] We know even less about the marketplaces frequented by ordinary Mesopotamians, except that tavern-keepers operated on credit, and hawkers and operators of market stalls probably did as well.[7]

The origins of interest will forever remain obscure, since they preceded the invention of writing. The terminology for interest in most ancient languages is derived from some word for "offspring," causing some to speculate that it originates in loans of livestock, but this seems a bit literal-minded. More likely, the first widespread interest-bearing loans were commercial: temples and palaces would forward wares to merchants and commercial agents, who would then trade them in nearby mountain kingdoms or on trading expeditions overseas.[8]

The practice is significant because it implies a fundamental lack of trust. After all, why not simply demand a share in the profits? This seems more fair (a merchant who came back bankrupt would probably have little means of repaying a loan anyway), and profit-sharing partnerships of this sort became common practice in the later Middle East.[9] The answer seems to be that profit-sharing partnerships were typically contracted between merchants, or anyway people of similar background and experience who had ways of keeping track of one another. Palace or temple bureaucrats and world-roaming merchant adventurers had little in common, and the bureaucrats seem to have concluded that one could not normally expect a merchant adventurer returned from a far-off land to be entirely honest about his adventures. A fixed interest rate would render irrelevant whatever elaborate tales of robbery, shipwreck, or attacks by winged snakes or elephants a creative trader might have concocted. The return was fixed in advance.

This connection between borrowing and lying, incidentally, is an important one to history. Herodotus remarked about the Persians: "To tell a lie is considered by them the greatest disgrace, and next to that to be in debt . . . especially because they think that one in debt must of necessity tell lies."[10] (Later, Herodotus reported a story told to him by a Persian about the origins of the gold that the Persians had acquired in India: they stole it from the nests of giant ants.)[11] Jesus's parable of the unforgiving servant makes a joke out of the matter ("Ten thousand talents? No problem. Just give me a little more time"), but even here, one can see how such endless falsehoods contributed to a broader sense that a world in which moral relations are conceived as debts is also, while in certain ways entertaining, necessarily a world of corruption, guilt, and sin.

By the time of the earliest Sumerian documents, this world may not yet have arrived. Still, the principle of lending at interest, even compound interest, was already familiar to everyone. In 2402 BC, for instance, a royal inscription by King Enmetena of Lagash—one of the earliest we have—complains that his enemy, the King of Umma, had been, for decades, occupying a huge stretch of farmland that had rightfully belonged to Lagash. He announces: if one were to calculate the rental fees for all that land, then the interest that would have been due on that rent, compounded annually, it would reveal that Umma now owes Lagash four and a half trillion liters of barley. The sum was, as in the parable, intentionally preposterous.[12] It was just an excuse to start a war. Still, he wanted everyone to know that he knew exactly how to do the math.

Usury—in the sense of interest-bearing consumer loans—was also well established by Enmetena's time. The king ultimately had his war and won it, and two years later, fresh off his victory, he was forced to publish another edict: this one a general debt cancellation within his kingdom. As he later boasted, "He instituted freedom (*amargi*) in Lagash. He restored the child to its mother, and the mother to her child; he canceled all interest due."[13] This was, in fact, the very first such declaration we have on record—and the first time in history that the word "freedom" appears in a political document.

Enmetena's text is a bit vague on the details, but a half-century later, when his successor Uruinimgina declared a general amnesty during the New Year's ceremonies of 2350 BC, the terms are all spelled out, and they conform to what was to become typical of such amnesties: canceling not only all outstanding loans, but all forms of debt servitude, even those based on failure to pay fees or criminal penalties—the only thing excepted being commercial loans.

Similar declarations are to be found again and again, in Sumerian and later Babylonian and Assyrian records, and always with the same theme: the restoration of "justice and equity," the protection of widows and orphans, to ensure—as Hammurabi was to put it when he abolished debts in Babylon in 1761 BC—"that the strong might not op-press the weak."[14] In the words of Michael Hudson,

> The designated occasion for clearing Babylonia's financial slate was the New Year festival, celebrated in the spring. Babylo-nian rulers oversaw the ritual of "breaking the tablets," that is, the debt records, restoring economic balance as part of the calendrical renewal of society along with the rest of nature. Hammurabi and his fellow rulers signaled these proclamations by raising a torch, probably symbolizing the sun-god of justice Shamash, whose principles were supposed to guide wise and fair rulers. Persons held as debt pledges were released to rejoin their families. Other debtors were restored cultivation rights to their customary lands, free of whatever mortgage liens had accumulated.[15]

Over the next several thousand years, this same list—canceling the debts, destroying the records, reallocating the land—was to become the standard list of demands of peasant revolutionaries everywhere. In Mesopotamia, rulers appear to have headed off the possibility of unrest by instituting such reforms themselves, as a grand gesture of cosmic renewal, a recreation of the social universe—in Babylonia, dur-ing the same ceremony in which the king reenacts his god Marduk's creation of the physical universe. The history of debt and sin was wiped out, and it was time to begin again. But it's also clear what they saw as the alternative: the world plunged into chaos, with farmers defecting to swell the ranks of nomadic pastoralists, and ultimately, if the breakdown continued, returning to overrun the cities and destroy everything.

Egypt

(2650–716 BC)

Egypt represents an interesting contrast, since, for most of its history, it managed to avoid the development of interest-bearing debt entirely.

Egypt was, like Mesopotamia, extraordinarily rich by ancient stan-dards, but it was also a self-contained society, a river running through a desert, and far more centralized than Mesopotamia. The pharaoh was a god, and the state and temple bureaucracies had their hands in everything: there were a dazzling array of taxes and a continual distribution of allotments, wages, and payments from the state. Here, too, money clearly arose as a means of account. The basic unit was the *deben*, or "measure"—originally referring to measures of grain, and later of copper or silver. A few records make clear the catch-as-catch-can nature of most transactions:

> In the 15th year of Ramses II [c. 1275 BC] a merchant offered the Egyptian lady Erenofre a Syrian slave girl whose price, no doubt after bargaining, was fixed at 4 *deben* 1 *kite* [about 373 grams] of silver. Erenofre made up a collection of clothes and blankets to the value of 2 *deben* 2 1/3 *kite*—the details are set out in the record—and then borrowed a miscellany of objects from her neighbors—bronze vessels, a pot of honey, ten shirts, ten *deben* of copper ingots—till the price was made up.[16]

Most merchants were itinerant, either foreigners or commercial agents for the owners of large estates. There's not much evidence for commercial credit, however; loans in Egypt were still more likely to take the form of mutual aid between neighbors.[17]

To state the matter simply: in Mesopotamia, interest-bearing loans by palace and temple officials largely substituted for the lack of a comprehensive system of taxation. In Egypt this was not necessary.

Substantial, legally enforceable loans, the kind that can lead to the loss of lands or family members, are documented, but they appear to have been rare—and much less pernicious, as the loans did not bear interest. Similarly, we do occasionally hear of debt-bondservants, and even debt slaves, but these seem to have been unusual phenomena and there's no suggestion that their numbers ever reached crisis proportions, as they so regularly did in Mesopotamia and the Levant.[18]

In fact, for the first several thousand years, we seem to be in a somewhat different world, where debt really was a matter of "guilt" and treated largely as a criminal matter:

> When a debtor failed to repay his debt on time, his creditor could take him to court, where the debtor would be required to promise to pay in full by a specific date. As part of his promise—which was under oath—the debtor also pledged to undergo 100 blows and/or repay twice the amount of the original loan if he failed to pay by the date specified.[19]

The "and/or" is significant. There was no formal distinction between a fine and a beating. In fact, the entire purpose of the oath (rather like the Cretan custom of having a borrower pretend to snatch the money) seems to have been to create the justification for punitive action: so the debtor could be punished as *either* a perjurer or a thief.[20]

By the time of the New Kingdom (1550–1070), there is more evidence for markets, but it's only by the time we reach the Iron Age, just before Egypt was absorbed into the Persian empire, that we begin to see evidence for Mesopotamian-style debt crises. Greek sources, for instance, record that the Pharaoh Bakenranef (reigned 720–715 BC) issued a decree abolishing debt bondage and annulling all outstanding liabilities, since "he felt it would be absurd for a soldier, perhaps at the moment when he was setting forth to fight for his fatherland, to be hauled off to prison by his creditor for an unpaid loan"—which, if true, is also one of the earliest mentions of a debt prison.[21] Under the Ptolemies, the Greek dynasty that ruled Egypt after Alexander, periodic clean slates had become institutionized. It's well known that the Rosetta Stone, written both in Greek and Egyptian, proved to be the key that made it possible to translate Egyptian hieroglyphics. Few are aware of what it actually says. The stela was originally raised to announce an amnesty, both for debtors and for prisoners, declared by Ptolemy V in 196 BC.[22]

China

(2200–771 BC)

We can say almost nothing about Bronze Age India, since its writing remains indecipherable, and not much more about Early China. What little we do know—mainly culled from dribs and drabs in later literary sources—suggests that the earliest Chinese states were far less bureaucratic than their western cousins.[23] There being no centralized temple or palace system with priests and administrators managing the storerooms and recording inputs and outputs, there was also little incentive to create a single, uniform unit of account. Instead, the evidence suggests a different path, with social currencies of various sorts still holding sway in the countryside and being converted to commercial purposes in dealings between strangers.

Later sources recall that early rulers "used pearls and jade as their superior method of payment, gold as their middle method of payment, and knives and spades as their lower method of payment."[24] The author can only be talking about gifts here, and hierarchical ones at that: kings and great magnates rewarding their followers for services in theory rendered voluntarily. In most places, long strings of cowrie shells figure prominently, but even here, though we often hear of "the cowrie money of early China," and it's easy enough to find texts in which the value of sumptuous gifts are *measured* in cowries, it's never clear whether people were really carrying them around to buy and sell things in the marketplace.[25]

The most likely interpretation is that they were carrying the shells, but for a long time marketplaces themselves were of minor significance, so this use was not nearly as important as the usual uses for social currencies: marriage presents, fines, fees, and tokens of honor.[26] At any rate, all sources insist that there was a wide variety of currencies in circulation. As David Scheidel, one of the premier contemporary scholars of early money, notes:

> In pre-imperial China, money took the form of cowrie shells, both originals and—increasingly—bronze imitations, tortoise shells, weighed gold and (rarely) silver bars, and most notably—from at least 1000 BC onward—utensil money in the shape of spade blades and knives made of bronze.[27]

These were most often used between people who didn't know each other very well. For tabulating debts between neighbors, with local vendors, or with anything having to do with the government, people appear to have employed a variety of credit instruments: later Chinese historians claimed that the earliest of these were knotted strings, rather like the Inca *khipu* system, and then later, notched strips of wood or bamboo.[28] As in Mesopotamia, these appear to have long predated writing.

We don't really know when the practice of lending at interest first reached China either, or whether Bronze Age China came to see the same sorts of debt crises as occurred in Mesopotamia, but there are tantalizing hints in later documents.[29] For instance, later Chinese legends about the origin of coinage ascribed the invention to emperors trying to relieve the effects of natural disasters. One early Han text reports:

> In ancient times, during the floods of Yu and the droughts of Tang, the common people became so exhausted that they were forced to borrow from one another in order to obtain food and clothing. [Emperor] Yu coined money for his people from the gold of Mount Li and [Emperor] Tang did likewise from

the copper of Mount Yan. Therefore the world called them benevolent.[30]

Other versions are a little more explicit. The *Guanzi*, a collection that in early imperial China became the standard primer on political economy, notes, "There were people who lacked even gruel to eat, and who were forced to sell their children. To rescue these people, Tang coined money."[31]

The story is clearly fanciful (the real origins of coined money were at least a thousand years later), and it is very hard to know what to make of it. Could this reflect a memory of children being taken away as debt sureties? On the face of it, it seems more like starving people selling their children outright—a practice that was to become commonplace in later periods of Chinese history.[32] But the juxtaposition of loans and the sale of children is suggestive, especially considering what was happening on the other side of Asia at exactly the same time. The *Guanzi* later goes on to explain that these same rulers instituted the custom of retaining 30 percent of the harvest in public granaries for redistribution in emergencies, so as to ensure that no one would ever be reduced to such desperate straits again. In other words, they began to set up just the kind of bureaucratic storage facilities that, in places like Egypt and Mesopotamia, had been responsible for creating money as a unit of account to begin with.

Chapter Nine

THE AXIAL AGE

(800 BC – 600 AD)

> Let us designate this period as the "axial age." Extraordinary events are crowded into this period. In China lived Confucius and Lao Tse, all the trends in Chinese philosophy arose . . . In India it was the age of the Upanishads and of Buddha; as in China, all philosophical trends, including skepticism and materialism, sophistry and nihilism, were developed.
>
> —Karl Jaspers, *Way to Wisdom*

THE PHRASE "THE AXIAL AGE" was coined by the German existentialist philosopher Karl Jaspers.[1] In the course of writing a history of philosophy, Jaspers became fascinated by the fact that figures like Pythagoras (570–495 BC), the Buddha (563–483 BC), and Confucius (551–479 BC) were all contemporaries, and that Greece, India, and China, in that period, all saw a sudden efflorescence of debate between contending intellectual schools, each group apparently unaware of the others' existence. Like the simultaneous invention of coinage, why this happened had always been a puzzle. Jaspers wasn't entirely sure himself. To some extent, he suggested, it must have been an effect of similar historical conditions. For most of the great urban civilizations of the time, the early Iron Age was a kind of pause between empires, a time when political landscapes were broken into a checkerboard of often diminutive kingdoms and city-states, most often at constant war externally and locked in constant political debate within. Each case witnessed the development of something akin to a drop-out culture, with ascetics and sages fleeing to the wilderness or wandering from town to town seeking wisdom; in each, too, they were eventually reabsorbed into the political order as a new kind of intellectual or spiritual elite, whether as Greek sophists, Jewish prophets, Chinese sages, or Indian holy men.

Whatever the reasons, the result, Jaspers argued, was the first period in history in which human beings applied principles of reasoned inquiry to the great questions of human existence. He observed that all these great regions of the world, China, India, and the Mediterranean, witnessed the emergence of almost exactly the same collection of philosophical tendencies, from skepticism to idealism—in fact, that philosophers in each managed to simultaneously develope all the major positions on the nature of cosmos, mind, action, and the ends of human existence that have remained the stuff of philosophical debate ever since. As one of Jaspers' disciples later put it—overstating only slightly—"no really new ideas have been added since that time."[2]

For Jaspers, the period begins with the Persian prophet Zoroaster, around 800 BC, and ends around 200 BC, to be followed by a Spiritual Age that centers on figures like Jesus and Mohammed. For my own purposes, I find it more useful to combine the two. Let us define the Axial Age, then, as running from 800 BC to 600 AD.[3] This makes the Axial Age the period that saw the birth not only of all the world's major philosophical tendencies, but also all of today's major world religions: Zoroastrianism, Prophetic Judaism, Buddhism, Jainism, Hinduism, Confucianism, Taoism, Christianity, and Islam.[4]

The attentive reader may have noticed that the core period of Jasper's Axial age—the lifetimes of Pythagoras, Confucius, and the Buddha—corresponds almost exactly to the period in which coinage was invented. What's more, the three parts of the world where coins were first invented were also the very parts of the world where those sages lived; in fact, they became the epicenters of Axial Age religious and philosophical creativity: the kingdoms and city-states around the Yellow River in China, the Ganges valley in northern India, and the shores of the Aegean Sea.

What was the connection? We might start by asking: What is a coin? The normal definition is that a coin is a piece of valuable metal, shaped into a standardized unit, with some emblem or mark inscribed to authenticate it. The world's first coins appear to have been created within the kingdom of Lydia, in western Anatolia (now Turkey), sometime around 600 BC.[5] These first Lydian coins were basically just round lumps of electrum—a gold-silver alloy that occurred naturally in the nearby Pactolus River—that had been heated, then hammered with some kind of insignia. The very first, stamped only with a few letters, appear to have been manufactured by ordinary jewelers, but these disappeared almost instantly, replaced by coins manufactured in a newly established royal mint. Greek cities on the Anatolian coast soon began to strike their own coins, and they came to be adopted in Greece itself; the same thing occurred in the Persian Empire after it absorbed Lydia in 547 BC.

In both India and China, we can observe the same pattern: invented by private citizens, coinage was quickly monopolized by the state. The first Indian money, which seems to have appeared at some point in the sixth century, consisted of bars of silver trimmed down to uniform weights, then punch-marked with some kind of official symbol.[6] Most of the examples discovered by archaeologists contain numerous additional counter-punches, presumably added much in the way that a check or other credit instrument is endorsed before being transferred. This strongly suggests that they were being handled by people used to dealing with more abstract credit instruments.[7] Much early Chinese coinage also shows signs of having evolved directly from social currencies: some were in fact cast bronze in the shape of cowries, though others took the shape of diminutive knives, disks, or spades. In every case, local governments quickly stepped in—presumably within the space of about a generation.[8] However, since in each of the three areas there was a plethora of tiny states, this meant that each ended up with a wide variety of different currency systems. For example, around 700 BC, northern India was still divided into Janapadas or "tribal territories," some of them monarchies and some republics, and in the sixth century there were still at least sixteen major kingdoms. In China, this was the period where the old Zhou Empire first devolved into vying principalities (the "Spring and Autumn" period, 722–481 BC), then splintered into the chaos of the "Warring States" (475–221 BC). Like the Greek city-states, all of the resulting kingdoms, no matter how diminutive, aspired to issue their own official currency.

Recent scholarship has shed a great deal of light on how this must have happened. Gold, silver, and bronze—the materials from which coins were made—had long been the media of international trade; but until that time, only the rich actually had much in their possession. A typical Sumerian farmer may well have never had occasion to hold a substantial piece of silver in his hand, except perhaps at his wedding. Most precious metals took the form of wealthy women's anklets and heirloom chalices presented by kings to their retainers, or it was simply stockpiled in temples, in ingot form, as sureties for loans. Somehow, during the Axial Age, all this began to change. Large amounts of silver, gold, and copper were dethesaurized, as the economic historians like to say; it was removed from the temples and houses of the rich and placed in the hands of ordinary people, was broken into tinier pieces, and began to be used in everyday transactions.

How? Israeli Classicist David Schaps provides the most plausible suggestion: most of it was stolen. This was a period of generalized warfare, and it is in the nature of war that precious things are plundered.

> Soldiers who plunder may indeed go first for the women, the alcoholic drinks, or the food, but they will also be looking around for things of value that are easily portable. A long-term standing army will tend to accumulate many things that are valuable and portable—and the most valuable and portable items are precious metals and precious stones. It may well have been the protracted wars among the states of these areas that first produced a large population of people with precious metal in their possession and a need for everyday necessities . . .
>
> Where there are people who want to buy there will be people willing to sell, as innumerable tracts on black markets, drug dealing, and prostitution point out . . . The constant warfare of the archaic age of Greece, of the Janapadas of India, of the Warring States of China, was a powerful impetus for the development of market trade, and in particular for market trade based on the exchange of precious metal, usually in small amounts. If plunder brought precious metal into the hands of the soldiers, the market will have spread it through the population.[9]

Now, one might object: but surely, war and plunder were nothing new. The Homeric epics, for instance, show a well-nigh obsessive interest in the division of the spoils. True, but what the Axial Age also saw—again, equally in China, India, and the Aegean—was the rise of a new kind of army, made up not of aristocratic warriors and their retainers, but trained professionals. The period when the Greeks began to use coinage, for instance, was also the period when they developed their famous phalanx tactics, which required constant drill and training of the hoplite soldiers. The results were so extraordinarily effective that Greek mercenaries were soon being sought after from Egypt to Crimea. But unlike the Homeric retainers, who could simply be ignored, an army of trained mercenaries needs to be rewarded in some meaningful way. One could perhaps provide them all with livestock, but livestock are hard to transport; or with promissory notes, but these would be worthless in the mercenaries' own country. Allowing each a tiny share of the plunder does seem an obvious solution.

These new armies were, directly or indirectly, under the control of governments, and it took governments to turn these chunks of metal into genuine currency. The main reason for this is simple capacity: to create enough coins that the people could begin to use them in everyday transactions required mass production on a scale far beyond the abilities of local merchants or smiths.[10] Of course, we have already seen why governments might have incentive to do so: the existence of markets was highly convenient for governments, and not just because it made it so much easier for them to provision large standing armies. By insisting that only their own coins were acceptable as fees, fines, or taxes, governments were able to overwhelm the innumerable social currencies that already existed in their hinterlands, and to establish something like uniform national markets.

Actually, one theory is that the very first Lydian coins were invented explicitly to pay mercenaries.[11] This might help explain why the Greeks, who supplied most of the mercenaries, so quickly became accustomed to the use of coins, and why the use of coinage spread so quickly across the Hellenic world, so that by 480 BC there were at least one hundred mints operating in different Greek cities, even though at that time, none of the great trading nations of the Mediterranean had as yet showed the slightest interest in them. The Phoenicians, for example, were considered the consummate merchants and bankers of antiquity.[12] They were also great inventors, having been the first to develop both the alphabet and the abacus. Yet for centuries after the invention of coinage, they preferred to continue conducting business as they always had, with unwrought ingots and promissory notes.[13] Phoenician cities struck no coins until 365 BC, and while Carthage, the great Phoenician colony in North Africa that came to dominate commerce in the Western Mediterranean, did so a bit earlier, it was only when "forced to do so to pay Sicilian mercenaries; and its issues were marked in Punic, 'for the people of the camp.'"[14]

On the other hand, in the extraordinary violence of the Axial Age, being a "great trading nation" (rather than, say, an aggressive military power like Persia, Athens, or Rome) was not, ultimately, a winning proposition. The fate of the Phoenician cities is instructive. Sidon, the wealthiest, was destroyed by the Persian emperor Artaxerxes III after a revolt in 351 BC. Forty thousand of its inhabitants are said to have committed mass suicide rather than surrender. Nineteen years later, Tyre was destroyed after a prolonged siege by Alexander: ten thousand died in battle, and the thirty thousand survivors were sold into slavery.

Carthage lasted longer, but when Roman armies finally destroyed the city in 146 BC, hundreds of thousands of Carthaginians were said to have been raped and slaughtered, and fifty thousand captives put on the auction block, after which the city itself was razed and its fields sowed with salt.

All this may bring home something of the level of violence amidst which Axial Age thought developed.[15] But it also leaves us asking: What exactly was the ongoing relation among coinage, military power, and this unprecedented outpouring of ideas?

The Mediterranean

Here again our best information is from the Mediterranean world, and I have already provided some of its outlines. Comparing Athens—with its far-flung naval empire—and Rome, we can immediately detect striking similarities. In each city, history begins with a series of debt crises. In Athens, the first crisis, the one that culminated in Solon's reforms of 594 BC, was so early that coinage could hardly have been a factor. In Rome, too, the earliest crises seem to have proceeded the advent of currency. Rather, in each case, coinage became a solution. In brief, one might say that these conflicts over debt had two possible outcomes. The first was that the aristocrats could win, and the poor remain "slaves of the rich"—which in practice meant that most people would end up clients of some wealthy patron. Such states were generally militarily ineffective.[16] The second was that popular factions could prevail, institute the usual popular program of redistribution of lands and safeguards against debt peonage, and thus create the basis for a class of free farmers whose children would, in turn, be free to spend much of their time training for war.[17]

Coinage played a critical role in maintaining this kind of free peasantry—secure in their landholding, not tied to any great lord by bonds of debt. In fact, the fiscal policies of many Greek cities amounted to little more than elaborate systems for the distribution of loot. It's important to emphasize that few ancient cities, if any, went so far as to outlaw predatory lending, or even debt peonage, entirely. Instead, they threw money at the problem. Gold, and especially silver, were acquired in war, or mined by slaves captured in war. Mints were located in temples (the traditional place for depositing spoils), and city-states developed endless ways to distribute coins, not only to soldiers, sailors, and those producing arms or outfitting ships, but to the populace generally, as jury fees, fees for attending public assemblies, or sometimes just as outright distributions, as Athens did most famously when they discovered a new vein of silver in the mines at Laurium in 483 BC. At the same time, insisting that the same coins served as legal tender for all payments due to the state guaranteed that they would be in sufficient demand that markets would soon develop.

Many of the political crises in ancient Greek cities similarly turned on the distribution of the spoils. Here is an incident recorded in Aristotle, who provides a conservative take on the origins of a coup in the city of Rhodes around 391 BC ("demagogues" here refers to the leaders of the democracy):

> The demagogues needed money to pay the people for attending the assembly and serving on juries; for if the people did not attend, the demagogues would lose their influence. They raised at least some of the money they needed by preventing the disbursement of the money due the trireme [warship] commanders under their contracts with the city to build and fit triremes for the Rhodian navy. Since the trireme commanders were not paid, they were unable in turn to pay their suppliers and workers, who sued the trireme commanders. To escape these lawsuits the trireme commanders banded together and overthrew the democracy.[18]

It was slavery, though, that made all this possible. As the figures concerning Sidon, Tyre, and Carthage suggest, enormous numbers of people were being enslaved in many of these conflicts, and, of course, many slaves ended up working in the mines, producing even more gold, silver, and copper. (The mines in Laurium reportedly employed ten to twenty thousand of them.)[19]

Geoffrey Ingham calls the resulting system a "military-coinage complex"—though I think it would be even better to call it a "military-coinage-slavery complex."[20] Anyway, that describes rather nicely how it worked in practice. When Alexander set out to conquer the Persian Empire, he borrowed much of the money with which to pay and provision his troops, and he minted his first coins, used to pay his creditors and continue to support the money, by melting down gold and silver plundered after his initial victories.[21] However, an expeditionary force needed to be paid, and paid well: Alexander's army, which numbered some 120,000 men, required half a ton of silver a day just for wages. For this reason, conquest meant that the existing Persian system of mines and mints had to be reorganized around providing for the invading army; and ancient mines, of course, were worked by slaves. In turn, most slaves in mines were war captives. Presumably most of the unfortunate survivors of the siege of Tyre ended up working in such mines. One can see how this process might feed upon itself.[22]

Alexander was also the man responsible for destroying what remained of the ancient credit systems, since not only the Phoenicians but also the old Mesopotamian heartland had resisted the new coin economy. His armies not only destroyed Tyre; they also dethesaurized the gold and silver reserves of Babylonian and Persian temples, the security on which their credit systems were based, and insisted that all taxes to his new government be paid in his own money. The result was to "release the accumulated specie of century onto the market in a matter of months," something like 180,000 talents, or in contemporary terms, an estimated $285 billion.[23]

The Hellenistic successor kingdoms established by Alexander's generals, from Greece to India, employed mercenaries rather than national armies, but the story of Rome is, again, similar to that of Athens. Its early history, as recorded by official chroniclers like Livy, is one of continual struggles between patricians and plebians, and of continual crises over debt. Periodically, these would lead to what were called moments of "the secession of the plebs," when the commoners of the city abandoned their fields and workshops, camped outside the city, and threatened mass defection—an interesting halfway point between the popular revolts of Greece and the strategy of exodus typically pursued in Egypt and Mesopotamia. Here, too, the patricians were ultimately faced with a decision: they could use agricultural loans to gradually turn the plebian population into a class of bonded laborers on their estates, or they could accede to popular demands for debt protection, preserve a free peasantry, and employ the younger sons of free farm families as soldiers.[24] As the prolonged history of crises, secessions, and reforms makes clear, the choice was made grudgingly.[25] The plebs practically had to force the senatorial class to take the imperial option. Still, they did, and over time the senate gradually legislated into being a welfare system that recycled at least a share of the spoils to soldiers, veterans, and their families.

It seems significant, in this light, that the traditional date of the first Roman coinage—338 BC—is almost exactly the date when debt bondage was finally outlawed (326 BC).[26] Again, coinage, minted from war spoils, didn't cause the crisis. It was used as a solution.

In fact, the entire Roman empire, at its height, could be understood as a vast machine for the extraction of precious metals and their coining and distribution to the military—combined with taxation policies designed to encourage conquered populations to adopt coins in their everyday transactions. Even so, for most of its history, use of coins was heavily concentrated in two zones within the empire: Italy and a few big cities, and along the frontiers, where the legions were actually stationed. In areas where there were neither mines nor military operations, older credit systems would appear to have continued largely as before.

I will add one final note here. In Greece, as in Rome, attempts to solve the debt crisis through military expansion were always, ultimately, just ways of fending off the problem—and they only worked for a limited period of time. When expansion stopped, everything returned to as it had been before. Actually, it's not clear that all forms of debt bondage were ever entirely eliminated even in cities like Athens and Rome. In cities that were not successful military powers, without any source of income to set up welfare policies, debt crises continued to flare up every century or so—and they often became far more acute than they ever had in the Middle East, because there was no mechanism, short of outright revolution, to declare a Mesopotamian-style clean slate. Large populations, even in the Greek world, did, in fact, sink to the rank of serfs and clients.[27]

Athenians, as we've seen, seemed to assume that a gentleman normally lived a step or two ahead of his creditors. Roman politicians were little different. Of course, much of the debt was owed by members of the senatorial class to each other: in a way, this was just the usual communism of the rich, extending easy credit to one another on terms that they would never think to offer others. Still, under the late Republic, history records many intrigues and conspiracies hatched by desperate debtors, often aristocrats driven by relentless creditors to make common cause with the poor.[28] If we hear less about this sort of thing happening under the emperors, it's probably because there were fewer opportunities for protest; what evidence we have suggests that, if anything, the problem got much worse.[29] Around 100 AD, Plutarch wrote about his own country as if it were under foreign invasion:

> And as King Darius sent to the city of Athens his lieutenants Datis and Artaphernes with chains and cords, to bind the prisoners they should take; so these usurers, bringing into Greece boxes full of schedules, bills, and obligatory contracts, as so many irons and fetters for the shackling of poor criminals . . .
>
> For at the very delivery of their money, they immediately ask it back, taking it up at the same moment they lay it down; and they let out that again to interest which they take for the use of what they have before lent.

> So that they laugh at those natural philosophers who hold
> that nothing can be made of nothing and of that which has no
> existence; but with them usury is made and engendered of that
> which neither is nor ever was.[30]

The works of the early Christian fathers likewise resound with endless descriptions of the misery and desperation of those caught in rich lenders' webs. In the end, through this means, that small window of freedom that had been created by the plebs was undone, and the free peasantry largely eliminated. By the waning days of the empire, most people in the countryside who weren't outright slaves had become, effectively, debt peons to some rich landlord, a situation in the end legally formalized by imperial decrees binding peasants to the land.[31] Without a free peasantry to form the basis for the army, the state was forced to rely more and more on arming and employing Germanic barbarians from across the imperial frontiers—with results that need hardly be recalled here.

India

In most ways, India could not be more different as a civilization than the ancient Mediterranean—but to a remarkable degree, the same basic pattern repeats itself there as well.

The Bronze Age civilization of the Indus Valley collapsed sometime around 1600 BC; it would be about a thousand years before India saw the emergence of another urban civilization. When it did, that civilization was centered on the fertile plains that surrounded the Ganges farther east. Here too we observe, at first, a checkerboard of different sorts of government, from the famous "Ksatriya republics" with a populace in arms and urban democratic assemblies, to elective monarchies, to centralized empires like Kosala and Magadha.[32] Both Gautama (the future Buddha) and Mahavira (the founder of Jainism) were born in one of these republics, though both ultimately found themselves teaching within the great empires, whose rulers often became patrons of wandering ascetics and philosophers.

Both kingdoms and republics produced their own silver and copper coinage, but in some ways the republics were more traditional, since the self-governing "populace in arms" consisted of the traditional Ksatriya or warrior caste, who typically held their lands in common and had them worked by serfs or slaves.[33] The kingdoms, on the other hand, were founded on a fundamentally new institution: a trained, professional army, open to young men of a wide variety of back-grounds, their equipment supplied by central authorities (soldiers were obliged to check their arms and armor when they entered cities), and provided with generous salaries.

Whatever their origins, here too, coins and markets sprung up above all to feed the machinery of war. Magadha, which ultimately came out on top, did so largely because it controlled most of the mines. Kautilya's *Arthasastra*, a political treatise written by one of the chief ministers for the Mauryan dynasty that succeeded it (321–185 BC), stated the matter precisely: "The treasury is based upon mining, the army upon the treasury; he who has army and treasury may conquer the whole wide earth."[34] The government drew its personnel first of all from a landed class, which provided trained administrators, but even more, full-time soldiers: the salaries of each rank of soldier and administrator were carefully stipulated. These armies could be huge. Greek sources report that Magadha could put to the field a force of 200,000 infantry, 20,000 horses, and about 4,000 elephants—and that Alexander's men mutinied rather than have to face them. Whether on campaign or in garrison, they were inevitably accompanied by a range of different sorts of camp followers—petty traders, prostitutes, and hired servants—which, with the soldiers, seems to have been the very medium through which a cash economy had originally taken form.[35] By Kautilya's time, a few hundred years later, the state was inserting itself into every aspect of the process: Kautilya suggests paying sol-diers apparently generous wages, then secretly replacing hawkers with government agents who could charge them twice the normal rates for supplies. He also recommends organizing prostitutes under a ministry in which they could be trained as spies, so as to make detailed reports on their clients' loyalties.

Thus was the market economy, born of war, gradually taken over by government. Rather than stifle the spread of currency, the process seems to have doubled and even tripled it: the military logic was ex-tended to the entire economy, the government systematically setting up its granaries, workshops, trading houses, warehouses, and jails, staffed by salaried officials, and all selling products on the market so as to col-lect the pieces of silver paid off to soldiers and officials and put them back into the royal treasuries again.[36] The result was a monetarization of daily life unlike anything India was to see for another two thousand years.[37]

Something similar seems to have happened with chattel slavery, which became quite commonplace at the time of the rise of the great armies—again, unlike almost any other point in Indian history—but was gradually brought under government control.[38] By Kautilya's time, most war captives were not sold in marketplaces but relocated to government villages on newly reclaimed land. They were not allowed to leave. These government villages were, at least according to the regulations, remarkably dreary places: veritable work camps, with all forms of festive entertainment officially prohibited. Slave hirelings were mostly convicts, rented by the state during their terms.

With their armies, spies, and administrators controlling everything, the new Indian kings evinced little interest in the old priestly caste and its Vedic ritual, though many kept up a lively interest in the new philosophical and religious ideas that seem to have been cropping up everywhere at the time. As time went on, however, the war machine began to sputter. It's not clear exactly why this happened. By the time of emperor Aśoka (273–232 BC), the Mauryan dynasty controlled almost all of present-day India and Pakistan, but the Indian version of the military-coinage-slavery complex was showing definite signs of strain. Perhaps the clearest sign was the debasement of the coinage, which over the course of two centuries or so had gone from almost pure silver to about fifty percent copper.[39]

Aśoka, famously, began his reign in conquest: in 265 BC, destroying the Kalingas, one of the last remaining Indian republics, in a war in which hundreds of thousands of human beings were, according to his own account, killed or carried off into slavery. The king later claimed to have been so disturbed and haunted by the carnage that he renounced war altogether, embraced Buddhism, and declared that from that time on, his kingdom would be governed by principles of *ahimsa*, or nonviolence. "Here in my kingdom," he declared in an edict inscribed on one of the great granite pillars in his capital of Patna, which so dazzled the Greek ambassador Megasthenes, "no living being must be killed or sacrificed."[40] Such a statement obviously can't be taken literally: Aśoka might have replaced sacrificial ritual with vegetarian feasts, but he didn't abolish the army, abandon capital punishment, or even outlaw slavery. But his rule marked a revolutionary shift in ethos. Aggressive war was abandoned, and much of the army does seem to have been demobilized, along with the network of spies and state bureaucrats, with the new, proliferating mendicant orders (Buddhists, Jains, and also world-renouncing Hindus) given official state support to preach to the villages on questions of social morality. Aśoka and his successors diverted substantial resources to these religious orders, with the result that, over the next centuries, thousands of stupas and monasteries were built across the subcontinent.[41]

Aśoka's reforms are useful to contemplate here because they help reveal just how mistaken some of our basic assumptions are: particularly, that money equals coins, and that more coins in circulation means more commerce and a greater role for private merchants. In reality, the Magadha state promoted markets but had been suspicious of private merchants, seeing them largely as competitors.[42] Merchants had been among the earliest and most ardent supporters of the new religions (Jains, owing to their rigorous enforcement of rules against harm to any living creature, were obliged to become, effectively, a mercantile caste). Mercantile interests fully supported Aśoka's reforms. Yet the result was not an increase in the use of cash in everyday affairs but exactly the opposite.

Early Buddhist economic attitudes have long been considered something of a puzzle. On the one hand, monks could not own property as individuals; they were expected to live an austere communistic life with little more than a robe and begging bowl as personal possessions, and they were strictly forbidden to so much as touch anything made of gold or silver. On the other hand, however suspicious of precious metals, Buddhism had always had a liberal attitude toward credit arrangements. It is one of the few of the great world religions that has never formally condemned usury.[43] Taken in the context of the times, however, there's nothing particularly mysterious about any of this. It makes perfect sense for a religious movement that rejected violence and militarism, but that was in no way opposed to commerce.[44] As we shall see, while Aśoka's own empire was not long to endure, soon to be replaced by a succession of ever weaker and mostly smaller states, Buddhism took root. The decline of the great armies eventually led to the near-disappearance of coinage, but also to a veritable efflorescence of increasingly sophisticated forms of credit.

China

Until about 475 BC, northern China was still nominally an empire, but the emperors had devolved into figureheads and a series of de facto kingdoms had emerged. The period from 475 to 221 BC is referred to as the "Warring States period"; at that point, even the pretense of unity was cast aside. Ultimately, the country was reunited by the state of Qin, who established a dynasty that was then immediately overthrown by a series of massive popular insurrections, ushering in the Han dynasty (206 BC–220 AD), founded by a previously obscure rural constable and peasant leader named Liu Bao, who was the first Chinese leader to adopt the Confucian ideology, exam system, and pattern of civil administration that were to continue for almost two thousand years.

Still, the golden age of Chinese philosophy was the period of chaos that preceded unification, and this followed the typical Axial Age pattern: the same fractured political landscape, the same rise of trained, professional armies, and the creation of coined money largely in order to pay them.[45] We also see the same government policies designed to encourage the development of markets, chattel slavery on a scale not seen before or since in Chinese history, the appearance of itinerant philosophers and religious visionaries, battling intellectual schools, and eventually, attempts by political leaders to transform the new philosophies into religions of state.[46]

There were also significant differences, starting with the currency system. China never minted gold or silver coins. Merchants used precious metals in the form of bullion, but the coins in actual circulation were basically small change: cast bronze disks, usually with a hole in the middle so that they could be strung together. Such strings of "cash" were produced in extraordinary numbers, and very large amounts had to be assembled for large-scale transactions: when wealthy men wished to make donations to temples, for instance, they had to use oxcarts to carry the money. The most plausible explanation is that, especially after unification, Chinese armies were enormous—some Warring States armies numbered up to a million—but not nearly as professional or well paid as those of kingdoms farther west, and from Qin and Han times on, rulers were careful to ensure that this remained the case, to make sure their armies never became an independent power base.[47]

There was also a notable difference in that the new religious and philosophical movements in China were from their very beginnings also social movements. Elsewhere, they only gradually became so. In ancient Greece, philosophy began with cosmological speculation; philosophers were more likely to be individual sages, perhaps surrounded by a few ardent disciples, than founders of movements.[48] Under the Roman empire, schools of philosophy like the Stoics, Epicureans, and Neo-Platonists did become movements of a sort: at least in the sense that they had thousands of educated adherents who "practiced" philosophy not only by reading, writing, and debating, but even more by meditation, diet, and exercise. Still, philosophical movements were basically confined to the civic elite; it was only with the rise of Christianity and other religious movements that philosophy moved beyond it.[49] One can observe a similar evolution in India, from individual Brahman world-renouncers, forest sages, and wandering mendicants with theories about the nature of the soul or the composition of the material universe; to philosophical movements of the Buddhists, Jains, Ājīvika, and others mostly long forgotten; to, finally, mass religious movements with thousands of monks, shrines, schools, and networks of lay supporters.

In China, while many of the founders of the "hundred schools" of philosophy that blossomed under the Warring States were wandering sages who spent their days moving from city to city trying to catch the ears of princes, others were leaders of social movements from the very start. Some of these movements didn't even have leaders, like the School of the Tillers, an anarchist movement of peasant intellectuals who set out to create egalitarian communities in the cracks and fissures between states.[50] The Mohists, egalitarian rationalists whose social base seems to have been urban artisans, not only were philosophically opposed to war and militarism, but organized battalions of military engineers who would actively discourage conflicts by volunteering to fight in any war against the side of the aggressor. Even the Confucians, for all the importance they attached to courtly ritual, were in their early days mainly known for their efforts in popular education.[51]

Materialism I:

The Pursuit of Profit

What is one to make of all this? The popular education campaigns of the period perhaps provide a clue. The Axial Age was the first time in human history when familiarity with the written word was no longer limited to priests, administrators, and merchants, but had become necessary to full participation in civic life. In Athens, it was taken for granted that only a country bumpkin would be entirely illiterate.

Without mass literacy, neither the emergence of mass intellectual movements nor the spread of Axial Age ideas would have been possible. By the end of the period, these ideas had produced a world where even the leaders of barbarian armies descending on the Roman empire felt obliged to take a position on the question of the Mystery of the Trinity, and where Chinese monks could spend time debating the relative merits of the eighteen schools of Classical Indian Buddhism.

No doubt the growth of markets played a role too, not only helping to free people from the proverbial shackles of status or community, but encouraging a certain habit of rational calculation, of measuring inputs and outputs, means and ends, all of which must inevitably have found some echoes in the new spirit of rational inquiry that begins to appear in all the same times and places. Even the word "rational" is telling: it derives, of course, from "ratio"—how many of X go into Y—a sort of mathematical calculation previously used mainly by architects and engineers, but which, with the rise of markets, everyone who didn't want to get cheated at the marketplace had to learn how to do. Still, we must be careful here. After all, money in itself was nothing new. Sumerian farmers and tradesmen were already perfectly capable of making such calculations in 3500 BC; but none, as far as we know, were so impressed that they concluded, like Pythagoras, that mathematical ratios were the key to understanding the nature of the universe and the movement of celestial bodies, and that all things were ultimately composed of numbers—and they certainly hadn't formed secret societies based on sharing this understanding, debating and purging and excommunicating one another.[52]

To understand what had changed, we have to look, again, at the particular *kind* of markets that were emerging at the beginning of the Axial Age: impersonal markets, born of war, in which it was possible to treat even neighbors as if they were strangers.

Within human economies, motives are assumed to be complex. When a lord gives a gift to a retainer, there is no reason to doubt that it is inspired by a genuine desire to benefit that retainer, even if it is also a strategic move designed to ensure loyalty, and an act of magnificence meant to remind everyone else that he is great and the retainer small. There is no sense of contradiction here. Similarly, gifts between equals are usually fraught with many layers of love, envy, pride, spite, communal solidarity, or any of a dozen other things. Speculating on such matters is a major form of daily entertainment. What's missing, though, is any sense that the most selfish ("self-interested") motive is necessarily the real one: those speculating on hidden motives are just as likely to assume that someone is secretly trying to help a friend or harm an enemy as to acquire some advantage for him- or herself.[53] Neither is any of this likely to have changed much in the rise of early credit markets, where the value of an IOU was as much dependent on assessments of its issuer's character as on his disposable income, and motives of love, envy, pride, etc., could never be completely set aside.

Cash transactions between strangers were different, and all the more so when trading is set against a background of war and emerges from disposing of loot and provisioning soldiers; when one often had best not ask where the objects traded came from, and where no one is much interested in forming ongoing personal relationships anyway. Here, transactions really do become simply a figuring-out of how many of X will go for how many of Y, of calculating proportions, estimating quality, and trying to get the best deal for oneself. The result, during the Axial Age, was a new way of thinking about human motivation, a radical simplification of motives that made it possible to begin speaking of concepts like "profit" and "advantage"—and imagining that this is what people are *really* pursuing, in every aspect of existence, as if the violence of war or the impersonality of the marketplace has simply allowed them to drop the pretense that they ever cared about anything else. It was this, in turn, that allowed human life to seem like it could be reduced to a matter of means-to-end calculation, and hence something that could be examined using the same means that one used to study the attraction and repulsion of celestial bodies.[54] If the underlying assumption very much resembles those of contemporary economists, it's no coincidence—but with the difference that, in an age when money, markets, states, and military affairs were all intrinsically connected, money was needed to pay armies to capture slaves to mine gold to produce money; when "cutthroat competition" often did involve the literal cutting of throats, it never occurred to anyone to imagine that selfish ends could be pursued by peaceful means. Certainly, this picture of humanity does begin to appear, with startling consistency, across Eurasia, wherever we also see coinage and philosophy appear.

China provides an unusually transparent case in point. Already in Confucius's time, Chinese thinkers were speaking of the pursuit of profit as the driving force in human life. The actual term used was *li*, a word first used to refer to the increase of grain one harvests from a field over and above what one originally planted (the pictogram represents a sheaf of wheat next to a knife).[55] From there it came to mean commercial profit, and thence, a general term for "benefit" or "payback." The following story, which purports to tell the reaction of a merchant's son named Lü Buwei on learning that an exiled prince was living nearby, illustrates the progression nicely:

> On returning home, he said to his father, "What is the profit on investment that one can expect from plowing fields?"
> "Ten times the investment," replied his father.
> "And the return on investment in pearls and jades is how much?"
> "A hundredfold."
> "And the return on investment from establishing a ruler and securing the state would be how much?"
> "It would be incalculable."[56]

Lü adopted the prince's cause and eventually contrived to make him King of Qin. He went on to became first minister for the king's son, Qin Shi Huang, helping him defeat the other Warring States to became the first Emperor of China. We still have a compendium of political wisdom that Lü commissioned for the new emperor, which contains such military advice as the following:

> As a general principle, when an enemy's army comes, it seeks some profit. Now if they come and find the prospect of death instead, they will consider running away the most profitable thing to do. When all one's enemies consider running to be the most profitable thing to do, no blades will cross.
> This is the most essential point in military matters.[57]

In such a world, heroic considerations of honor and glory, vows to gods or desire for vengeance, were at best weaknesses to be manipulated. In the numerous manuals on statecraft produced at the time, everything was cast as a matter of recognizing interest and advantage, calculating how to balance that which will profit the ruler against that which will profit the people, determining when the ruler's interests are the same as the people's and when they contradict.[58] Technical terms drawn from politics, economics, and military strategy ("return on investment," "strategic advantage") blended and overlapped.

The predominant school of political thought under the Warring States was that of the Legalists, who insisted that in matters of statecraft, a ruler's interests were the only consideration, even if rulers would be unwise to admit this. Still, the people could be easily manipulated, since they had the same motivations: the people's pursuit of profit, wrote Lord Shang, is utterly predictable, "just like the tendency of water to flow downhill."[59] Shang was harsher than most of his fellow Legalists in that he believed that widespread prosperity would ultimately harm the ruler's ability to mobilize his people for war, and therefore that terror was the most efficient instrument of governance, but even he insisted that this regime be clothed as a regime of law and justice.

Wherever the military-coinage-slavery complex began to take hold, we find political theorists propounding similar ideas. Kautilya was no different: the title of his book, the *Arthasastra*, is usually translated as "manual of statecraft," since it consists of advice to rulers, but its more literal translation is "the science of material gain."[60] Like the Legalists, Kautilya emphasized the need to create a pretext that governance was a matter of morality and justice, but in addressing the rulers themselves, he insisted that "war and peace are considered solely from the point of view of profit"—of amassing wealth to create a more effective army, of using the army to dominate markets and control resources to amass more wealth, and so on.[61] In Greece we've already met Thrasymachos. True, Greece was slightly different. Greek city-states did not have kings, and the collapse of private interests and affairs of state was in principle universally denounced as tyranny. Still, in practice, what this meant was that city-states, and even political factions, ended up acting in precisely the same coldly calculating way as Indian or Chinese sovereigns. Anyone who has ever read Thucydides' Melian dialogue—in which Athenian generals present the population of a previously friendly city with elegantly reasoned arguments for why the Athenians have determined that it is to the advantage of their empire to threaten them with collective massacre if they are not willing to become tribute-paying subjects, and why it is equally in the interests of the Melians to submit—will be aware of the results.[62]

Another striking feature of this literature is its resolute materialism. Goddesses and gods, magic and oracles, sacrificial ritual, ancestral cults, even caste and ritual status systems all either disappear or are sidelined, no longer treated as ends in themselves but as yet mere tools to be used for the pursuit of material gain.

That intellectuals willing to produce such theories should win the ears of princes is hardly surprising. Neither is it particularly surprising that other intellectuals should have been so offended by this sort of cynicism that they began to make common cause with the popular movements that inevitably began to form against those princes. But as is so often the case, oppositional intellectuals were faced with two choices: either adopt the reigning terms of debate, or try to come up with a diametrical inversion. Mo Di, the founder of Mohism, took the first approach. He turned the concept of *li*, profit, into something more like "social utility," and then he attempted to demonstrate that war itself is, by definition, an unprofitable activity. For example, he wrote, campaigns can only be fought in spring and autumn, and each had equally deleterious effects:

> If in the spring then the people miss their sowing and planting, if in the autumn, they miss their reaping and harvesting. Even if they miss only one season, then the number of people who will die of cold and hunger is incalculable. Now let us calculate the army's equipment, the arrows, standards, tents, armor, shields, and sword hilts; the number of these which will break and perish and not come back . . . So also with oxen and horses . . .[63]

His conclusion: if one could add up the total costs of aggression in human lives, animal lives, and material damage, one would be forced to the conclusion that they never outweighed the benefits—even for the victor. In fact, Mo Di took this sort of logic so far that he ended up arguing that the only way to optimize the overall profit of humanity was to abandon the pursuit of private profit entirely and adopt a principle of what he called "universal love"—essentially arguing that if one takes the principle of market exchange to its logical conclusion, it can only lead to a kind of communism.

The Confucians took the opposite approach, rejecting the initial premise. A good example is most of the opening of Mencius' much-remembered conversation with King Hui:

> "Venerable Sir," the King greeted him, "since you have not counted a thousand miles too far to come here, may I suppose that you also have something with which you may profit my kingdom?"
> Mencius replied:
> "Why must Your Majesty necessarily use this word 'profit'? What I have are only these two topics: benevolence and righteousness, and nothing else."[64]

Still, the end-point was roughly the same. The Confucian ideal of *ren*, of humane benevolence, was basically just a more complete inversion of profit-seeking calculation than Mo Di's universal love; the main difference was that the Confucians added a certain aversion to calculation itself, preferring what might almost be called an art of decency. Taoists were later to take this even further with their embrace of intuition and spontaneity. All were so many attempts to provide a mirror image of market logic. Still, a mirror image is, ultimately, just that: the same thing, only backwards. Before long in each case we end up with an endless maze of paired opposites—egoism versus altruism, profit versus charity, materialism versus idealism, calculation versus spontaneity—none of which could ever have been imagined except by someone starting out from pure, calculating, self-interested market transactions.[65]

Materialism II:

Substance

> *As in the near presence of death, despise poor flesh, this refuse of blood and bones, this web and tissue of nerves and veins and arteries.*
> —Marcus Aurelius, *Meditations* 2.2

> *Taking pity on the hungry wolf, Wenshuang announced, "I do not covet this filthy bag of meat. I give it over to you that I may quickly acquire a body of more enduring strength. This donation will help benefit us both."*
> —*Discourse on the Pure Land* 21.12

As I've already observed, China was unusual because philosophy there began with debates about ethics and only later turned to speculations about the nature of the cosmos. In both Greece and India, cosmological speculation came first. In each, too, questions about the nature of the physical universe quickly give way to speculation about mind, truth, consciousness, meaning, language, illusion, world-spirits, cosmic intelligence, and the fate of the human soul.

This particular maze of mirrors is so complex and dazzling that it's extraordinarily difficult to discern the starting point—that is, what, precisely, is being reflected back and forth. Here anthropology can be helpful, as anthropologists have the unique advantage of being able to observe how human beings who have not previously been part of these conversations react when first exposed to Axial Age concepts. Every now and then too, we are presented with moments of exceptional clarity: ones that reveal the essence of our own thought to be almost exactly the opposite of what we thought it to be.

Maurice Leenhardt, a Catholic missionary who had spent many long years teaching the Gospel in New Caledonia, experienced such a moment in the 1920s, when he asked one of his students, an aged sculptor named Boesoou, how he felt about having been introduced to spiritual ideas:

> Once, waiting to assess the mental progress of the Canaques I
> had taught for many years, I risked the following suggestion:
> "In short, we introduced the notion of the spirit to your way
> of thinking?"
>
>   He objected, "Spirit? Bah! You didn't bring us the spirit.
> We already knew the spirit existed. We have always acted in
> accord with the spirit. What you've brought us is the body."[66]

The notion that humans had souls appeared to Boesoou to be self-
evident. The notion that there was such a thing as the body, apart from
the soul, a mere material collection of nerves and tissues—let alone
that the body is the prison of the soul; that the mortification of the
body could be a means to the glorification or liberation of the soul—all
this, it turns out, struck him as utterly new and exotic.

Axial Age spirituality, then, is built on a bedrock of materialism.
This is its secret; one might almost say, the thing that has become
invisible to us.[67] But if one looks at the very beginnings of philosophical inquiry in Greece and India—the point when there was as yet no
difference between what we'd now call "philosophy" and what we'd
now call "science"—this is exactly what one finds. "Theory," if we can
call it that, begins with the questions: "What substance is the world
made of?" "What is the underlying material behind the physical forms
of objects in the world?" "Is everything made up of varying combina-
tions of certain basic elements (earth, air, water, fire, stone, motion,
mind, number . . .), or are these basic elements just the forms taken by
some even more elementary substance (for instance, as Nyāya and later
Democritus proposed, atomic particles . . .)"[68] In just about every case,
some notion of God, Mind, Spirit, some active organizing principle
that gave form to and was not itself substance, emerged as well. But
this was the kind of spirit that, like Leenhardt's God, only emerges in
relation to inert matter.[69]

To connect this impulse, too, with the invention of coinage might
seem like pushing things a bit far, but, at least for the Classical world,
there is an emerging scholarly literature—first set off by Harvard literary theorist Marc Shell, and more recently set forth by British classicist
Richard Seaford in a book called *Money and the Early Greek Mind*—
that aims to do exactly that.[70]

In fact, some of the historical connections are so uncannily close
that they are very hard to explain any other way. Let me give an example. After the first coins were minted around 600 BC in the kingdom
of Lydia, the practice quickly spread to Ionia, the Greek cities of the
adjacent coast. The greatest of these was the great walled metropolis of

Miletus, which also appears to have been the first Greek city to strike its own coins. It was Ionia, too, that provided the bulk of the Greek mercenaries active in the Mediterranean at the time, with Miletus their effective headquarters. Miletus was also the commercial center of the region and, perhaps, the first city in the world where everyday market transactions came to be carried out primarily in coins instead of credit.[71] Greek philosophy, in turn, begins with three men: Thales, of Miletus (c. 624 BC–c. 546 BC), Anaximander, of Miletus (c. 610 BC–c. 546 BC), and Anaximenes, of Miletus (c. 585 BC–c. 525 BC)—in other words, men who were living in that city at exactly the time that coinage was first introduced.[72] All three are remembered chiefly for their speculations on the nature of the physical substance from which the world ultimately sprang. Thales proposed water, Anaximenes, air. Anaximander made up a new term, *apeiron*, "the unlimited," a kind of pure abstract substance that could not itself be perceived but was the material basis of everything that could be. In each case, the assumption was that this primal substance, by being heated, cooled, combined, divided, compressed, extended, or set in motion, gave rise to the endless particular stuffs and substances that humans actually encounter in the world, from which physical objects are composed—and was also that into which all those forms would eventually dissolve.

It was something that could turn into everything. As Seaford emphasizes, so was money. Gold, shaped into coins, is a material substance that is also an abstraction. It is both a lump of metal and something more than a lump of metal—it's a drachma or an obol, a unit of currency which (at least if collected in sufficient quantity, taken to the right place at the right time, turned over to the right person) could be exchanged for absolutely any other object whatsoever.[73]

For Seaford, what was genuinely new about coins was their double-sidedness: the fact that they were both valuable pieces of metal and, at the same time, something more. At least within the communities that created them, ancient coins were always worth more than the gold, silver, or copper of which they were composed. Seaford refers to this extra value by the inelegant term "fiduciarity," which comes from the term for public trust, the confidence a community places in its currency.[74] True, at the height of Classical Greece, when there were hundreds of city-states producing different currencies according to a number of different systems of weights and denominations, merchants often did carry scales and treat coins—particularly foreign coins—like so many chunks of silver, just as Indian merchants seem to have treated Roman coins; but within a city, that city's currency had a special status, since it was always acceptable at face value when used to pay taxes, public fees, or legal penalties. This is, incidentally, why ancient governments were so often able to introduce base metal into their coins without leading to immediate inflation; a debased coin might have lost value when traded overseas, but at home, it was still worth just as much when purchasing a license, or entering the public theater.[75] This is also why, during publc emergencies, Greek city-states would occasionally strike coins made entirely of bronze or tin, which everyone would agree, while the emergency lasted, to treat as if they were really made of silver.[76]

This is the key to Seaford's argument about materialism and Greek philosophy. A coin was a piece of metal, but by giving it a particular shape, stamped with words and images, the civic community agreed to make it something more. But this power was not unlimited. Bronze coins could not be used forever; if one debased the coinage, inflation would eventually set in. It was as if there was a tension there between the will of the community and the physical nature of the object itself. Greek thinkers were suddenly confronted with a profoundly new type of object, one of extraordinary importance—as evidenced by the fact that so many men were willing to risk their lives to get their hands on it—but whose nature was a profound enigma.

Consider this word, "materialism." What does it mean to adopt a "materialist" philosophy? What is "material," anyway? Normally, we speak of "materials" when we refer to objects that we wish to make into something else. A tree is a living thing. It only becomes "wood" when we begin to think about all the other things you could carve out of it. And of course you can carve a piece of wood into almost anything. The same is true of clay, or glass, or metal. They're solid and real and tangible, but also abstractions, because they have the potential to turn into almost anything else—or, not precisely that; one can't turn a piece of wood into a lion or an owl, but one can turn it into an image of a lion or an owl—it can take on almost any conceivable form. So already in any materialist philosophy, we are dealing with an opposition between form and content, substance and shape; a clash between the idea, sign, emblem, or model in the creator's mind, and the physical qualities of the materials on which it is to be stamped, built, or imposed, from which it will be brought into reality.[77] With coins this rises to an even more abstract level because that emblem can no longer be conceived as the model in one person's head, but is rather the mark of a collective agreement. The images stamped on Greek coins (Miletus' lion, Athens' owl) were typically the emblems of the city's god, but they were also a kind of collective promise, by which citizens assured one another that not only would the coin be acceptable in payment of public debts, but in a larger sense, that everyone would accept them, for any debts, and thus, that they could be used to acquire anything anyone wanted.

The problem is that this collective power is not unlimited. It only really applies within the city. The farther you go outside, into places dominated by violence, slavery, and war—the sort of place where even philosophers taking a cruise might end up on the auction block—the more it turns into a mere lump of precious metal.[78]

The war between Spirit and Flesh, then, between the noble Idea and ugly Reality, the rational intellect versus stubborn corporeal drives and desires that resist it, even the idea that peace and community are not things that emerge spontaneously but that need to be stamped onto our baser material natures like a divine insignia stamped into base metal—all those ideas that came to haunt the religious and philosophical traditions of the Axial Age, and that have continued to surprise people like Boesoou ever since—can already be seen as inscribed in the nature of this new form of money.

It would be foolish to argue that all Axial Age philosophy was simply a meditation on the nature of coinage, but I think Seaford is right to argue that this is a critical starting place: one of the reasons that the pre-Socratic philosophers began to frame their questions in the peculiar way they did, asking (for instance): What are Ideas? Are they merely collective conventions? Do they exist, as Plato insisted, in some divine domain beyond material existence? Or do they exist in our minds? Or do our minds themselves ultimately partake of that divine immaterial domain? And if they do, what does this say about our relation to our bodies?

■ ■ ■ ■ ■

In India and China, the debate took different forms, but materialism was always the starting point. We only know the ideas of most truly materialist thinkers from the works of their intellectual enemies: as is the case with the Indian king Pāyāsi, who enjoyed debating Buddhist and Jain philosophers, taking the position that the soul does not exist, that human bodies are nothing but particular configurations of air, water, earth, and fire, their consciousness the result of the elements' mutual interaction, and that when we die, the elements simply dissolve.[79] Clearly, though, such ideas were commonplace. Even the Axial Age religions are often startlingly lacking in the plethora of supernatural forces seen before and after: as witnessed by continued debates over whether Buddhism even *is* a religion, since it rejects any notion of a supreme being, or whether Confucius' admonitions that one should continue to venerate one's ancestors was merely a way of encouraging filial piety, or based on a belief that dead ancestors did, in some sense, continue to exist. The fact that we have to ask says everything. Yet at the same time, what endures, above all, from that age—in institutional terms—are what we call the "world religions."

What we see then is a strange kind of back-and-forth, attack and riposte, whereby the market, the state, war, and religion all continually separate and merge with one another. Let me summarize it as briefly as I can:

1) Markets appear to have first emerged, in the Near East at least, as a side effect of government administrative systems. Over time, however, the logic of the market became entangled in military affairs, where it became almost indistinguishable from the mercenary logic of Axial Age warfare, and then, finally, that logic came to conquer government itself, to define its very purpose.

2) As a result, everywhere we see the military-coinage-slavery complex emerge, we also see the birth of materialist philosophies. They are materialist, in fact, in both senses of the term: in that they envision a world made up of material forces, rather than divine powers, and in that they imagine the ultimate end of human existence to be the accumulation of material wealth, with ideals like morality and justice being reframed as tools designed to satisfy the masses.

3) Everywhere, too, we find philosophers who react to this by exploring ideas of humanity and the soul, attempting to find a new foundation for ethics and morality.

4) Everywhere, some of these philosophers made common cause with social movements that inevitably formed in the face of these new and extraordinarily violent and cynical elites. The result was something new to human history: popular movements that were also intellectual movements, due to the assumption that those opposing existing power arrangements did so in the name of some kind of theory about the nature of reality.

5) Everywhere, these movements were also first and foremost peace movements, in that they rejected the new conception of violence, and especially aggressive war, as the foundation of politics.

6) Everywhere, too, there seems to have been an initial impulse to use the new intellectual tools provided by impersonal markets to come up with a new basis for morality, and everywhere, it foundered. Mohism, with its notion of social profit, flourished briefly and then collapsed. It was replaced by Confucianism, which rejected such ideas outright. We have already seen that reimagining moral

responsibility in terms of debt—an impulse that cropped up in both Greece and India—while almost inevitable given the new economic circumstances, seems to prove uniformly unsatisfying.[80] The stronger impulse is to imagine another world where debt—and with it, all other worldly connections—can be entirely annihilated, where social attachments are seen as forms of bondage, just as the body is a prison.

7) Rulers' attitudes changed over time. At first, most appear to have affected an attitude of bemused tolerance toward the new philosophical and religious movements while privately embracing some version of cynical realpolitik. But as warring cities and principalities were replaced by great empires and especially, as those empires began to reach the limits of their expansion, sending the military-coinage-slavery complex into crisis, all this changed. In India, Aśoka tried to re-found his kingdom on Buddhism; in Rome, Constantine turned to the Christians; in China, the Han emperor Wu-Ti (157–87 BC), faced with a similar military and financial crisis, adopted Confucianism as the philosophy of state. Of the three, only Wu Ti was ultimately successful: the Chinese empire endured, in one form or another, for two thousand years, almost always with Confucianism as its official ideology. In Constantine's case the Western empire fell apart, but the Roman church endured. Aśoka's project could be said to be the least successful. Not only did his empire fall apart, replaced by an endless series of weaker, usually fragmentary kingdoms, but Buddhism itself was largely driven out of his one-time territories, though it did establish itself much more firmly in China, Nepal, Tibet, Sri Lanka, Korea, Japan, and much of Southeast Asia.

8) The ultimate effect was a kind of ideal division of spheres of human activity that endures to this day: on the one hand the market, on the other, religion. To put the matter crudely: if one relegates a certain social space simply to the selfish acquisition of material things, it is almost inevitable that soon someone else will come to set aside another domain in which to preach that, from the perspective of ultimate values, material things are unimportant, that selfishness—or even the self—are illusory, and that to give is better than to receive. If nothing else, it is surely significant that all the Axial Age religions emphasized the importance of charity, a concept that had barely existed before. Pure greed and pure generosity are complementary concepts; neither could really be imagined without the other; both could only arise in institutional contexts that insisted on such pure and single-minded behavior; and both seem to have appeared together wherever impersonal, physical, cash money also appeared on the scene.

As for the religious movements: it would be easy enough to write them off as escapist, as promising the victims of the Axial Age empires liberation in the next world as a way of letting them accept their lot in this one, and convincing the rich that all they really owed the poor were occasional charitable donations. Radical thinkers almost invariably do write them off in this way. Surely, the willingness of the governments themselves to eventually embrace such religions would seem to support this conclusion. But the issue is more complicated. First of all, there is something to be said for escapism. Popular uprisings in the ancient world usually ended in the massacre of the rebels. As I've already observed, physical escape, such as via exodus or defection, has always been the most effective response to oppressive conditions since the earliest times we know about. Where physical escape is not possible, what, exactly, is an oppressed peasant supposed to do? Sit and contemplate her misery? At the very least, otherworldly religions provided glimpses of radical alternatives. Often they allowed people to create other worlds within this one, liberated spaces of one sort or another. It is surely significant that the only people who succeeded in abolishing slavery in the ancient world were religious sects, such as the Essenes—who did so, effectively, by defecting from the larger social order and forming their own utopian communities.[81] Or, in a smaller but more enduring example: the democratic city-states of northern India were all eventually stamped out by the great empires (Kautilya provides extensive advice on how to subvert and destroy democratic constitutions), but the Buddha admired the democratic organization of their public assemblies and adopted it as the model for his followers.[82] Buddhist monasteries are still called *sangha*, the ancient name for such republics, and continue to operate by the same consensus-finding process to this day, preserving a certain egalitarian democratic ideal that would otherwise have been entirely forgotten.

Finally, the larger historical achievements of these movements are not, in fact, insignificant. As they took hold, things began to change. Wars became less brutal and less frequent. Slavery faded as an institution, to the point at which, by the Middle Ages, it had become insignificant or even nonexistent across most of Eurasia. Everywhere too, the new religious authorities began to seriously address the social dislocations introduced by debt.

Chapter Ten

THE MIDDLE AGES

(600 AD – 1450 AD)

> *Artificial wealth comprises the things*
> *which of themselves satisfy no natu-*
> *ral need, for example money, which is a*
> *human contrivance.*
> —St. Thomas Aquinas

IF THE AXIAL AGE saw the emergence of complementary ideals of commodity markets and universal world religions, the Middle Ages were the period in which those two institutions began to merge.

Everywhere, the age began with the collapse of empires. Eventually, new states formed, but in these new states, the nexus between war, bullion, and slavery was broken; conquest and acquisition for their own sake were no longer celebrated as the end of all political life. At the same time, economic life, from the conduct of international trade to the organization of local markets, came to fall increasingly under the regulation of religious authorities. One result was a widespread movement to control, or even forbid, predatory lending. Another was a return, across Eurasia, to various forms of virtual credit money.

Granted, this is not the way we're used to thinking of the Middle Ages. For most of us, "medieval" remains a synonym for superstition, intolerance, and oppression. Yet for most of the earth's inhabitants, it could only be seen as an extraordinary improvement over the terrors of the Axial Age.

One reason for our skewed perception is that we're used to thinking of the Middle Ages as something that happened primarily in Western Europe, in territories that had been little more than border outposts of the Roman Empire to begin with. According to the conventional wisdom, with the collapse of the empire, the cities were largely abandoned and the economy "reverted to barter," taking at least five centuries to recover. Even for Europe, though, this is based on a series of unquestioned assumptions that, as I've said, crumble the moment one starts seriously poking at them. Chief among them is the idea that the absence of coins means the absence of money. True, the destruction of the Roman war machine also meant that Roman coins went out of circulation, and the few coins produced within the Gothic or Frankish kingdoms that established themselves over the ruins of the old empire were largely fiduciary in nature.[1] Still, a glance at the "barbarian law codes" reveals that even at the height of the Dark Ages, people were still carefully keeping accounts in Roman money as they calculated interest rates, contracts, and mortgages. Again, cities shriveled, and many were abandoned, but even this was something of a mixed blessing. Certainly, it had a terrible effect on literacy; but one must also bear in mind that ancient cities could only be maintained by extracting resources from the countryside. Roman Gaul, for instance, had been a network of cities, connected by the famous Roman roads to an endless succession of slave plantations, which were owned by the urban grandees.[2] After around 400 AD, the population of the towns declined radically, but the plantations also disappeared. In the following centuries, many came to be replaced by manors, churches, and even later, castles—where new local lords extracted their own dues from the surrounding farmers. But one need only do the math: since medieval agriculture was no less efficient than ancient agriculture (in fact, it rapidly became a great deal more so), the amount of work required to feed a handful of mounted warriors and clergymen could not possibly have been anything like that required to feed entire cities. However oppressed medieval serfs might have been, their plight was nothing compared with that of their Axial Age equivalents.

Still, the Middle Ages proper are best seen as having begun not in Europe but in India and China, between 400 and 600 AD, and then sweeping across much of the western half of Eurasia with the advent of Islam. They only really reached Europe four hundred years later. Let us begin our story, then, in India.

Medieval India

(Flight into Hierarchy)

I left off in India with Aśoka's embrace of Buddhism, but I noted that, ultimately, his project foundered. Neither his empire nor his church was to endure. It took a good deal of time, however, for this failure to occur.

The Mauryans represented a high watermark of empire. The next five hundred years saw a succession of kingdoms, most of them strongly supportive of Buddhism. Stupas and monasteries sprang up everywhere, but the states that sponsored them grew weaker and weaker; centralized armies dissolved; soldiers, like officials, increasingly came to be paid by land grants rather than salaries. As a result, the number of coins in circulation steadily declined.[3] Here too, the early Middle Ages witnessed a dramatic decline of cities: where the Greek ambassador Megasthenes described Aśoka's capital of Patna as the largest city in the world of his day, medieval Arab and Chinese travelers described India as a land of endless tiny villages.

As a result, most historians have come to write, much as they do in Europe, of a collapse of the money economy, of commerce becoming a "reversion to barter." Here too, this appears to be simply untrue. What vanished were the military means to extract resources from the peasants. In fact, Hindu law-books written at the time show increasing attention to credit arrangements, with a sophisticated language of sureties, collateral, mortgages, promissory notes, and compound interest.[4] One need only consider how the Buddhist establishments popping up all over India during these centuries were funded. While the earliest monks were wandering mendicants, owning little more than their begging bowls, early medieval monasteries were often magnificent establishments with vast treasuries. Still, in principle, their operations were financed almost entirely through credit.

The key innovation was the creation of what were called the "perpetual endowments" or "inexhaustible treasuries." Say a lay supporter wished to make a contribution to her local monastery. Rather than offering to provide candles for a specific ritual, or servants to attend to the upkeep of the monastic grounds, she would provide a certain sum of money—or something worth a great deal of money—that would then be loaned out in the name of the monastery, at the accepted 15-percent annual rate. The interest on the loan would then be earmarked for that specific purpose.[5] An inscription discovered at the Great Monastery of Sanci sometime around 450 AD provides a handy illustration. A woman named Harisvamini donates the relatively modest sum of twelve *dinaras* to the "Noble Community of Monks."[6] The text carefully inscribes how the income is to be divided up: the interest on five of the dinaras was to provide daily meals for five different monks, the interest from another three would pay to light three lamps for the Buddha, in memory of her parents, and so forth. The inscription ends by saying that this was a permanent endowment, "created with a document in stone to last as long as the moon and the sun": since the principal would never be touched, the contribution would last forever.[7]

Some of these loans presumably went to individuals, others were commercial loans to "guilds of bamboo-workers, braziers, and potters," or to village assemblies.[8] We have to assume that in most cases the money is an accounting unit: what were really being transacted were animals, wheat, silk, butter, fruit, and all the other goods whose appropriate rates of interest were so carefully stipulated in the law-codes of the time. Still, large amounts of gold did end up flowing into monastic coffers. When coins go out of circulation, after all, the metal doesn't simply disappear. In the Middle Ages—and this seems to have been true across Eurasia—the vast majority of it ended up in religious establishments, churches, monasteries, and temples, either stockpiled in hoards and treasuries or gilded onto or cast into altars, sanctums, and sacred instruments. Above all, it was shaped into images of gods. As a result, those rulers who did try to put an Axial Age–style coin-age system back into circulation—invariably, to fund some project of military expansion—often had to pursue self-consciously anti-religious policies in order to do so. Probably the most notorious was one Harsa, who ruled Kashmir from 1089 to 1101 AD, who is said to have appointed an officer called the "Superintendent for the Destruction of the Gods." According to later histories, Harsa employed leprous monks to systematically desecrate divine images with urine and excrement, thus neutralizing their power, before dragging them off to be melted down.[9] He is said to have destroyed more than four thousand Buddhist establishments before being betrayed and killed, the last of his dynasty—and his miserable fate was long held out as an example of where the revival of the old ways was likely to lead one in the end.

For the most part, then, the gold remained sacrosanct, laid up in the sacred places—though in India, over time, these were increasingly Hindu ones, not Buddhist. What we now see as traditional Hindu-village India appears to have been largely a creation of the early Middle Ages. We do not know precisely how it happened. As kingdoms continued to rise and fall, the world inhabited by kings and princes became increasingly distant from that of most people's everyday affairs. During much of the period immediately following the collapse of the Mauryan empire, for instance, much of India was governed by foreigners.[10] Apparently, this increasing distance allowed local Brahmins to begin reshaping the new—increasingly rural—society along strictly hierarchical principles.

They did it above all by seizing control of the administration of law. The Dharmaśāstra, law-codes produced by Brahmin scholars between roughly 200 BC and 400 AD, give us a good idea of the new vision of society. In it, old ideas like the Vedic conception of a debt to gods, sages, and ancestors were resuscitated—but now, they applied only and specifically to Brahmins, whose duty and privilege it was to stand in for all humanity before the forces that controlled the universe.[11] Far from being required to attain learning, members of the inferior classes were forbidden to do so: the Laws of Manu, for instance, set down that any Sudra (the lowest caste, assigned to farming and material production) who so much as listened in on the teaching of the law or sacred texts should have molten lead poured into their ears; on the occasion of a repeat offense, they should have their tongues cut out.[12] At the same, time Brahmins, however ferociously they guarded their privileges, also adopted aspects of once-radical Buddhist and Jain ideas like karma, reincarnation, and *ahimsa*. Brahmins were expected to refrain from any sort of physical violence, and even to become vegetarians. In alliance with representatives of the old warrior caste, they also managed to win title to most of the land in the ancient villages. Artisans and craftsmen fleeing the decline or destruction of cities often ended up as suppliant refugees and, gradually, low-caste clients. The result was increasingly complex local patronage systems in the countryside—*jajmani* systems, as they came to be known—where the refugees provided services for the landowning castes, who took on many of the roles once held by the state, providing protection and justice, extracting labor dues, and so on—but also protected local communities from actual royal representatives.[13]

This latter function is crucial. Foreign visitors were later to be awed by the self-sufficiency of the traditional Indian village, with its elaborate system of landowning castes, farmers, and such "service castes" as barbers, smiths, tanners, drummers, and washermen, all arranged in hierarchical order, each seen as making its own unique and necessary contribution to their little society, all of it typically operating entirely without the use of metal currency. It was only possible for those reduced to the status of Sudras and Untouchables to have a chance of accepting their lowly position because the exaction of local landlords was, again, on nothing like the same scale as that under earlier governments—under which villagers had to support cities of upwards of a million people—and because the village community became an effective means of holding the state and its representatives at least partially at bay.

We don't know the mechanisms that brought this world about, but the role of debt was surely significant. The creation of thousands of Hindu temples alone must have involved hundreds of thousands, even millions, of interest-bearing loans—since, while Brahmins were themselves forbidden to lend money at interest, temples were not. We can already observe, in the earliest of the new law-codes, the Laws of Manu, local authorities struggling to reconcile old customs like debt peonage and chattel slavery with the desire to establish an overarching hierarchical system in which everyone knew their place. The Laws of Manu carefully classify slaves into seven types depending on how they were reduced to slavery (war, debt, self-sale . . .) and explain the conditions under which each might be emancipated—but then go on to say that Sudras can never really be emancipated, since, after all, they were created to serve the other castes.[14] Similarly, where earlier codes had established a 15-percent annual rate of interest, with exceptions for commercial loans,[15] the new codes organized interest by caste: stating that one could charge a maximum of 2 percent a month for a Brahmin, 3 percent for a Ksatriya (warrior), 4 percent for a Vaisya (merchant), and 5 percent for a Sudra—which is the difference between 24 percent annually on the one extreme and a hefty 60 percent on the other.[16] The laws also identify five different ways interest can be paid, of which the most significant for our concerns is "bodily interest": physical labor in the creditor's house or fields, to be rendered until such time as the principal is cleared. Even here, though, caste considerations were paramount. No one could be forced into the service of anyone of lower caste; moreover, since debts were enforceable on a debtor's children and even grandchildren, "until the principal is cleared" could mean quite some time—as the Indian historian R.S. Sharma notes, such stipulations "remind us of the present practice according to which several generations of the same family have been reduced to the position of hereditary ploughmen in consideration of some paltry sum advanced to them."[17]

Indeed, India has become notorious as a country in which a very large part of the working population is laboring in effective debt peonage to a landlord or other creditor. Such arrangements became even easier over time. By about 1000 AD, restrictions on usury by members of the upper castes in Hindu law-codes largely disappeared. On the other hand, 1000 AD was about the same time that Islam appeared in India—a religion dedicated to eradicating usury altogether. So at the very least we can say that these things never stopped being contested. And even Hindu law of that time was far more humane than almost anything found in the ancient world. Debtors were not, generally speaking, reduced to slavery, and there is no widespread evidence of the selling of women or children. In fact, overt slavery had largely vanished from the countryside by this time. And debt peons were not even pawns, exactly; by law, they were simply paying interest on a freely contracted agreement. Paying the principlet might take generations, but the law stipulated that even if it was never paid, in the third generation, they would be freed.

There is a peculiar tension here, a kind of paradox. Debt and credit arrangements may well have played a crucial role in creating the Indian village system, but they could never really become their basis. It might have made a certain sense to declare that, just as Brahmins had to dispatch their debts to the gods, everyone should be, in a certain sense, in debt to those above them. But in another sense, that would have completely subverted the very idea of caste, which was that the universe was a vast hierarchy in which different sorts of people were assumed to be of fundamentally different natures, that these ranks and grades were fixed forever, and that when goods and services moved up and down the hierarchy, they followed not principles of exchange at all but (as in all hierarchical systems) custom and precedent. The French anthropologist Louis Dumont made the famous argument that one cannot even really talk about "inequality" here, because to use that phrase implies that one believes people should or could be equal, and this idea was completely alien to Hindu conceptions.[18] For them to have imagined their responsibilities as debts would have been profoundly subversive, since debts are by definition arrangements between equals—at least in the sense that they are equal parties to a contract—that could and should be repaid.[19]

Politically, it is never a particularly good idea to first tell people they are your equals, and then humiliate and degrade them. This is presumably why peasant insurrections, from Chiapas to Japan, have so regularly aimed to wipe out debts, rather than focus on more structural issues like caste systems, or even slavery.[20] The British Raj discovered this to their occasional chagrin when they used debt peonage—superimposed on the caste system—as the basis of their labor system in colonial India. Perhaps the paradigmatic popular insurrection was the Deccan riots of 1875, when indebted farmers rose up to seize and systematically destroy the account books of local money-lenders. Debt peonage, it would appear, is far more likely to inspire outrage and collective action than is a system premised on pure inequality.

——————

China:

Buddhism (the Economy of Infinite Debt)

By medieval standards, India was unusual for resisting the appeal of the great Axial Age religions, but we observe the basic pattern: the decline of empire, armies, and cash economy, the rise of religious authorities, independent of the state, who win much of their popular legitimacy through their ability to regulate emerging credit systems.

China might be said to represent the opposite extreme. This was the one place where a late Axial Age attempt to yoke empire and religion together was a complete success. True, here as elsewhere, there was an initial period of breakdown: after the collapse of the Han dynasty around 220 AD, the central state broke apart, cities shrank, coins disappeared, and so on. But in China this was only temporary. As Max Weber long ago pointed out, once one sets up a genuinely effective bureaucracy, it's almost impossible to get rid of it. And the Chinese bureaucracy was uniquely effective. Before long, the old Han system reemerged: a centralized state, run by Confucian scholar-gentry trained in the literary classics, selected through a national exam system, working in meticulously organized national and regional bureaus where the money supply, like other economic matters, was continually monitored and regulated. Chinese monetary theory was always chartalist. This was partly just an effect of size: the empire and its internal market were so huge that foreign trade was never especially important; therefore, those running the government were well aware that they could turn pretty much anything into money, simply by insisting that taxes be paid in that form.

The two great threats to the authorities were always the same: the nomadic peoples to the north (who they systematically bribed, but who nonetheless periodically swept over and conquered sections of China) and popular unrest and rebellion. The latter was almost constant, and on a scale unknown anywhere else in human history. There were decades in Chinese history when the rate of recorded peasant uprisings was roughly 1.8 *per hour*.[21] What's more, such uprisings were frequently successful. Most of the most famous Chinese dynasties that were not the product of barbarian invasion (the Yuan or Qing) were originally peasant insurrections (the Han, Tang, Song, and Ming). In no other part of the world do we see anything like this. As a result, Chinese statecraft ultimately came down to funneling enough resources to the cities to feed the urban population and keep the nomads at bay, without causing a notoriously contumacious rural population to rise up in arms. The official Confucian ideology of patriarchal authority, equal opportunity, promotion of agriculture, light taxes, and careful government control of merchants seemed expressly designed to appeal to the interests and sensibilities of a (potentially rebellious) rural patriarch.[22]

One need hardly add that in these circumstances, limiting the depredations of the local village loan shark—the traditional bane of rural families—was a constant government concern. Over and over we hear the same familiar story: peasants down on their luck, whether due to natural disaster or the need to pay for a parent's funeral—would fall into the hands of predatory lenders, who would seize their fields and houses, forcing them to work or pay rent in what had once been their own lands; the threat of rebellion would then drive the government to institute a dramatic program of reforms. One of the first we know about came in the form of a coup d'état in 9 AD, when a Confucian official named Wang Mang seized the throne to deal (so he claimed) with a nationwide debt crisis. According to proclamations made at the time, the practice of usury had caused the effective tax rate (that is, the amount of the average peasant's harvest that ended up being carried off by someone else) to rise from just over 3 percent, to 50 percent.[23] In reaction, Wang Mang instituted a program reforming the currency, nationalizing large estates, promoting state-run industries—including public granaries—and banning private holding of slaves. Wang Mang also established a state loan agency that would offer interest-free funeral loans for up to ninety days for those caught unprepared by the death of relatives, as well as long-term loans of 3 percent monthly or 10 percent annual income rates for commercial or agricultural investments.[24] "With this scheme," one historian remarks, "Wang was confident that all business transactions would be under his scrutiny and the abuse of usury would be forever eradicated."[25]

Needless to say, it was not, and later Chinese history is full of similar stories: widespread inequality and unrest followed by the appointment of official commissions of inquiry, regional debt relief (either blanket amnesties or annulments of all loans in which interest had exceeded the principal), cheap grain loans, famine relief, laws against the selling of children.[26] All this became the standard fare of government policy. It was very unevenly successful; it certainly did not create an egalitarian peasant utopia, but it prevented any widespread return to Axial Age conditions.

We are used to thinking of such bureaucratic interventions—particularly the monopolies and regulations—as state restriction on "the market"—owing to the prevailing prejudice that sees markets as quasi-natural phenomena that emerge by themselves, and governments as having no role other than to squelch or siphon from them. I have repeatedly pointed out how mistaken this is, but China provides a particularly striking example. The Confucian state may have been the world's greatest and most enduring bureaucracy, but it actively promoted markets, and as a result, commercial life in China soon became far more sophisticated, and markets more developed, than anywhere else in the world.

This despite the fact that Confucian orthodoxy was overtly hostile to merchants and even the profit motive itself. Commercial profit was seen as legitimate only as compensation for the labor that merchants expended in transporting goods from one place to another, but never as fruits of speculation. What this meant in practice was that they were pro-market but anti-capitalist.

Again, this seems bizarre, since we're used to assuming that capitalism and markets are the same thing, but, as the great French historian Fernand Braudel pointed out, in many ways they could equally well be conceived as opposites. While markets are ways of exchanging goods through the medium of money—historically, ways for those with a surplus of grain to acquire candles and vice versa (in economic shorthand, C-M-C', for commodity-money-other commodity)—capitalism for Braudel is first and foremost the art of using money to get more money (M-C-M'). Normally, the easiest way to do this is by establishing some kind of formal or de facto monopoly. For this reason, capitalists, whether merchant princes, financiers, or industrialists, invariably try to ally themselves with political authorities to limit the freedom of the market, so as to make it easier for them to do so.[27] From this perspective, China was for most of its history the ultimate anti-capitalist market state.[28] Unlike later European princes, Chinese rulers systematically refused to team up with would-be Chinese capitalists (who always existed). Instead, like their officials, they saw them as destructive parasites—though, unlike the usurers, ones whose fundamentally selfish and antisocial motivations could still be put to use in certain ways. In Confucian terms, merchants were like soldiers. Those drawn to a career in the military were assumed to be driven largely by a love of violence. As individuals, they were not good people, but they were also necessary to defend the frontiers. Similarly, merchants were driven by greed and basically immoral; yet if kept under careful administrative supervision, they could be made to serve the public good.[29] Whatever one might think of the principles, the results are hard to deny. For most of its history, China maintained the highest standard of living in the world—even England only really overtook it in perhaps the 1820s, well past the time of the Industrial Revolution.[30]

Confucianism is not precisely a religion, perhaps; it is usually considered more an ethical and philosophical system. So China too could be considered something of a departure from the common medieval pattern, whereby commerce was, almost everywhere, brought under the control of religion. But it wasn't a complete departure. One need only consider the remarkable economic role of Buddhism in this same period. Buddhism had arrived in China through the Central Asia caravan routes and in its early days was largely a religion promoted by merchants, but in the chaos following the collapse of the Han dynasty in 220 AD, it began to take popular roots. The Liang (502–557) and Tang (618–907) dynasties saw outbreaks of passionate religious fervor, in which thousands of rural young people across China would renounce their farms, shops, and families to seek ordination as Buddhist monks and nuns; where merchants or landed magnates pledged their entire fortunes to the propagation of the Dharma; building projects hollowed out whole mountains to create bodhisattvas and giant statues of the Buddha; and pageants where monks and devotees ritually burned their heads and hands or, in some instances, set themselves on fire. By the mid–fifth century, there were dozens of such spectacular suicides; they became, as one historian put it, "a macabre kind of fashion."[31]

Historians differ over their meaning. Certainly the passions unleashed provided a dramatic alternative to the staid orthodoxy of the Confucian literati, but it's also surprising, to say the least, to see this in a religion promoted above all by the commercial classes. The French Sinologist Jacques Gernet observes:

> It is clear that these suicides, so contrary to traditional morality, aimed to redeem the sins of all beings, to compel the gods and men at one and the same time. And they were staged: usually, in the fifth century, a pyre was erected on a mountain. The suicide took place in the presence of a large crowd uttering lamentations and bringing forward rich offerings. People of all social ranks attended the spectacle together. After the fire had burned out, the ashes of the monk were collected and a stupa, a new place of worship, was created to house them.[32]

Gernet's picture of dozens of Christ-like redeemers seems overstated, but the precise meaning of these suicides was unclear—and widely debated—even in the Middle Ages. Some contemporaries saw them as the ultimate expression of contempt for the body; others as recognition of the illusory nature of the self and all material attachments; yet others, as the ultimate form of charity, the giving of that which can only be most precious, one's very physical existence, as a sacrifice to the benefit of all living things; a sentiment that one tenth-century biographer expressed in the following verses:

> To give away the thing that is difficult to part with,
> Is the best offering amongst the alms.
> Let this impure and sinful body,
> Turn into something like a diamond.[33]

That is, an object of eternal value, an investment that can bear fruit for all eternity.

I draw attention to this because this sentiment provides an elegant illustration of a problem that seems to have first appeared in the world with notions of pure charity that always seemed to accompany Axial Age religions, and which provided endless philosophical conundrums. In human economies, it does not appear to have occurred to anyone that any act *could* be either purely selfish or purely altruistic. As I noted in Chapter Five, an act of absolute selfless giving can only also be absolutely antisocial—hence, in a way, inhuman. It is merely the mirror image of an act of theft or even murder; hence, it makes a certain sort of sense that suicide be conceived as the ultimate selfless gift. Yet this is the door that necessarily opens as soon as one develops a notion of "profit" and then tries to conceive its opposite.

This tension seems to hang over the economic life of medieval Chinese Buddhism, which, true to its commercial origins, retained a striking tendency to employ the language of the marketplace. "One purchases felicity, and sells one's sins," wrote one monk, "just as in commercial operations."[34] Nowhere was this so true as in those schools, such as the School of the Three Stages, that adopted the notion of "karmic debt"—that each of the sins of one's accumulated past lives continues as a debt needing to be discharged. An obscure and unusual view in classical Indian Buddhism, the notion of karmic debt took on a powerful new life in China.[35] As one Three Stages text puts it, we all know that insolvent debtors will be reborn as animals or slaves; but in reality, we are all insolvent debtors, because acquiring the money to repay our temporal debts necessarily means acquire new, spiritual ones, since every means of acquiring wealth will necessarily involve exploiting, damaging, and causing suffering to other living beings.

> Some use their power and authority as officials in order to bend the law and seize wealth. Some prosper in the marketplace . . .

> They engage in an excess of lies and cheat and extort prof-
> its from others. Still others, farmers, burn the mountains and
> marshes, flood the fields, plough and mill, destroying the nests
> and burrows of animals . . .
>
> There is no avoiding the fact of our past debts, and it is
> difficult to comprehend the number of separate lives it would
> require if you wanted to pay them one by one.[36]

As Gernet remarks, the idea of life as an endless burden of debt would surely have struck a chord with Chinese villagers, for whom this was all too often literally true; but, as he also points out, like their counterparts in ancient Israel, they were also familiar with that sense of sudden liberation that came with official amnesties. There was a way to achieve that too. All that was required was to make regular donations to some monastery's Inexhaustible Treasury. The moment one does so, the debts from every one of one's past lives are instantly blotted out. The author even provides a little parable, not unlike Jesus's parable of the ungrateful servant, but far more optimistic. How, it might be asked, would a poor man's tiny contribution possibly have such cosmic effects?

> Answer: In a parable it is like a poor man burdened by a debt
> of one thousand strings of coins to another person. He always
> suffers from his debt, and the poor man is afraid whenever the
> debt-master comes to collect.
>
> He visits the rich man's house and confesses he is beyond
> the time-limit and begs forgiveness for his offense—he is poor
> and without a station in life. He tells him that each day he
> makes a single coin he will return it to the rich man. On hear-
> ing this, the rich man is very pleased and forgives him for being
> overdue; moreover, the poor man is not dragged away to jail.
>
> Giving to the Inexhaustible Storehouse is also like this.[37]

One might almost call this salvation on the installment plan—but the implication is that the payments shall be made, like the interest payments on the wealth when it is subsequently loaned out, for all eternity.

Other schools concentrated not on karmic debt, but on one's debt to one's parents. Where Confucians built their system of morality above all on filial piety to fathers, Chinese Buddhists were primarily concerned with mothers, with the care and suffering required in raising, feeding, and educating children. A mother's kindness is unlimited, her selflessness absolute; this was seen to be embodied above all in the

act of breastfeeding, the fact that mothers transform their very flesh
and blood into milk; they feed their children with their own bodies. In
doing so, however, they allow unlimited love to be precisely quantified.
One author calculated that the average infant absorbs precisely 180
pecks of mother's milk in its first three years of life, and this consti-
tutes its debt as an adult. The figure soon became canonical. To repay
this milk debt, or indeed one's debt to one's parents more generally,
was simply impossible. "If you stacked up jewels from the ground up
to the twenty-eighth heaven," wrote one Buddhist author, "it would
not compare" with the value of your parent's nurturance.[38] Even if you
were to "cut your own flesh to offer her three times a day for four billion years," wrote another, "it would not pay back even a single day"
of what your mother did for you.[39]

The solution, however, is the same: donating money to the Inexhaustible Treasuries. The result was an elaborate cycle of debts and
forms of redemption. A man begins with an unpayable milk-debt. The
only thing of comparable value is the Dharma, the Buddhist truth itself. One can thus repay one's parents by bringing them to Buddhism;
indeed, this can be done even after death, when one's mother will otherwise wind up as a hungry ghost in hell. If one makes a donation to
the Inexhaustible Treasuries in her name, sutras will be recited for her;
she will be delivered; the money, in the meantime, will be put partly to
work as charity, as pure gift, but partly, too, as in India, as interest-
bearing loans, earmarked for specific purposes for the furtherance of
Buddhist education, ritual, or monastic life.

The Chinese Buddhist approach to charity was nothing if not mul-
tifaceted. Festivals often led to vast outpourings of contributions, with
wealthy adherents vying with one another in generosity, often driving
their entire fortunes to the monasteries, in the forms of oxcarts laden
with millions of strings of cash—a kind of economic self-immolation
that paralleled the spectacular monastic suicides. Their contributions
swelled the Inexhaustible Treasuries. Some would be given to the needy,
particularly in times of hardship. Some would be loaned. One practice
that hovered between charity and business was providing peasants with
alternatives to the local moneylender. Most monasteries had attendant
pawnshops where the local poor could place some valuable possession—a robe, a couch, a mirror—in hock in exchange for low-interest
loans.[40] Finally, there was the business of the monastery itself: that portion of the Inexhaustible Treasury turned over to the management of
lay brothers, and either put out at loan or invested. Since monks were
not allowed to eat the products of their own fields, the fruit or grain
had to be put on the market, further swelling monastic revenues. Most

monasteries came to be surrounded not only by commercial farms but veritable industrial complexes of oil presses, flour mills, shops, and hostels, often with thousands of bonded workers.[41] At the same time, the Treasuries themselves became—as Gernet was perhaps the first to point out—the world's first genuine forms of concentrated finance capital. They were, after all, enormous concentrations of wealth managed by what were in effect monastic corporations, which were constantly seeking new opportunities for profitable investment. They even shared the quintessential capitalist imperative of continual growth; the Treasuries had to expand, since according to Mahayana doctrine, genuine liberation would not be possible until the whole world embraced the Dharma.[42]

This was precisely the situation—huge concentrations of capital interested in nothing more than profit—that Confucian economic policy was supposed to prevent. Still, it took some time for Chinese governments to recognize the threat. Government attitudes veered back and forth. At first, especially in the chaotic years of the early Middle Ages, monks were welcomed—even given generous land grants and provided with convict laborers to reclaim forests and marshes, and tax-exempt status for their business enterprises.[43] A few emperors converted, and while most of the bureaucracy kept the monks at arm's length, Buddhism became especially popular with court women, as well as with eunuchs and many scions of wealthy families. As time went on, though, administrators turned from seeing monks as a boon to rural society to its potential ruination. Already, by 511 AD, there were decrees condemning monks for diverting grain that was supposed to be used for charitable purposes to high-interest loans, and altering debt contracts—a government commission had to be appointed to review the accounts and nullify any loans in which interest was found to have exceeded principal. In 713 AD we have another decree, confiscating two Inexhaustible Treasuries of the Three Stages sect, whose members they accused of fraudulent solicitation.[44] Before long there were major campaigns of government repression, at first often limited to certain regions, but over time, more often empire-wide. During the most severe, carried out in 845 AD, a total of 4,600 monasteries were razed along with their shops and mills, 260,000 monks and nuns forcibly defrocked and returned to their families—but at the same time, according to government reports, 150,000 temple serfs released from bondage.

Whatever the real reasons behind the waves of repression (and these were no doubt many), the official reason was always the same: a need to restore the money supply. The monasteries were becoming so large, and so rich, administrators insisted, that China was simply running out of metal:

> The great repressions of Buddhism under the Chou emperor Wu between 574 and 577, under Wu-tsung in 842–845, and finally in 955, presented themselves primarily as measures of economic recovery: each of them provided an opportunity for the imperial government to procure the necessary copper for the minting of new coins.[45]

One reason is that monks appear to have been systematically melting down strings of coins, often hundreds of thousands at a time, to build colossal copper or even gilded copper statues of the Buddha— along with other objects such as bells and copper chimes, or even such extravagances as mirrored halls or gilded copper roof tiles. The result, according to official commissions of inquiry, was economically disastrous: the price of metals would soar, coinage disappear, and rural marketplaces cease to function, even as those rural people whose children had not become monks often fell deeper into debt to the monasteries.

■ ■ ■ ■ ■

It perhaps stands to reason that Chinese Buddhism, a religion of merchants that then took popular roots, should have developed in this direction: a genuine theology of debt, even perhaps a practice of absolute self-sacrifice, of abandoning everything, one's fortune or even one's life, that ultimately led to collectively managed finance capital. The reason that the result seems so weird, so full of paradoxes, is that it is again an attempt to apply the logic of exchange to questions of Eternity.

Recall an idea from earlier in the book: exchange, unless it's an instantaneous cash transaction, creates debts. Debts linger over time. If you imagine all human relations as exchange, then insofar as people do have ongoing relations with one another, those relations are laced with debt and sin. The only way out is to annihilate the debt, but then social relations vanish too. This is quite in accord with Buddhism, whose ultimate aim is indeed the attainment of "emptiness," absolute liberation, the annihilation of all human and material attachments, since these are all ultimately causes of suffering. For Mahayana Buddhists, however, absolute liberation cannot be achieved by any one being independently; the liberation of each depends on all the others; therefore, until the end of time, such matters are in a certain sense always in suspension.

In the meantime, exchange dominates: "One purchases felicity, and sells one's sins, just as in commercial operations." Even acts of charity and self-sacrifice are not purely generous; one is purchasing "merit" from the bodhisattvas.[46] The notion of infinite debt comes in when this logic slams up against the Absolute, or, one might perhaps better say, against something that utterly defies the logic of exchange. Because there are things that do. This would explain, for instance, the odd urge to first quantify the exact amount of milk one has absorbed at one's mother's breast, and then to say that there is no conceivable way to repay it. Exchange implies interaction between equivalent beings. Your mother, on the other hand, is not an equivalent being. She created you out of her own flesh. This is exactly the point that I suggested the Vedic authors were subtly trying to make when they talked about "debts" to the gods: of course you cannot really "pay your debt to the universe"—that would imply that (1) you and (2) everything that exists (including you) are in some sense equivalent entities. This is clearly absurd. The closest you can come to repayment is to simply recognize that fact. Such recognition is the true meaning of sacrifice. Like Rospabé's original money, a sacrificial offering is not a way to pay a debt, but a way to acknowledge the impossibility of the idea that there could ever be repayment:

> The parallel was not missed in certain mythological traditions. According to one famous Hindu myth, two gods, the brothers Kartikeya and Ganesha, had a quarrel over who should be the first to marry. Their mother Parvati suggested a contest: the winner would be the one to most quickly circle the entire universe. Kartikeya set off on the back of a giant peacock. It took him three years to transverse the limits of the cosmos. Ganesha bided his time, then, finally, walked in a circle around his mother, remarking, "You are the universe to me."

I've also argued that any system of exchange is always necessarily founded on something else, something that, in its social manifestation at least, is ultimately communism. With all those things that we treat as eternal, that we assume will always be there—our mother's love, true friendship, sociality, humanity, belonging, the existence of the cosmos—no calculation is necessary, or even ultimately possible; insofar as there is give and take, they follow completely different principles. What, then, happens to such absolute and unlimited phenomena when one tries to imagine the world as a set of transactions—as exchange? Generally, one of two things. We either ignore or deify them. (Mothers, and caregiving women in general, are a classic case in point.) Or we do both. What we treat as eternal in our actual relations with one another vanishes and reappears as an abstraction, an absolute.[47] In the case of Buddhism, this was framed as the inexhaustible merit of bodhisattvas, who exist, in a certain sense, outside of time. They are at once the model for the Inexhaustible Treasuries and also their practical foundation: one can only repay one's endless karmic debt, or one's infinite milk-debt, by drawing on this equally infinite pool of redemption, which, in turn, becomes the basis for the actual material funds of the monasteries, which are equally eternal—a pragmatic form of communism, in fact, since they were vast pools of wealth collectively owned and collectively managed: the center of vast projects of human cooperation, which were assumed to be similarly eternal. Yet at the same time—here I think Gernet is right—this communism became the basis, in turn, of something very much like capitalism. The reason was, above all, the need for constant expansion. Everything—even charity—was an opportunity to proselytize; the Dharma had to grow, ultimately, to encompass everyone and everything, in order to effect the salvation of all living beings.

■ ■ ■ ■ ■

The Middle Ages were marked by a general move toward abstraction: real gold and silver ended up largely in churches, monasteries, and temples, money became virtual again, and at the same time, the tendency everywhere was to set up overarching moral institutions meant to regulate the process and, in particular, to establish certain protections for debtors.

China was unusual in that it was one place where an Axial Age empire managed to survive—though, at first, only barely. Chinese governments did manage to keep coins in circulation in most places most of the time. This was made easier by their reliance exclusively on small-denomination coins made of bronze. Even so, it clearly took enormous efforts.

As usual, we don't know a lot about how everyday economic transactions took place, but what we do know suggests that in small-scale transactions, coins were probably most often used in dealing with strangers. As elsewhere, local shopkeepers and merchants extended credit. Most accounts seem to have been kept through the use of tally sticks, strikingly similar to those used in England, except that rather than hazelwood they were usually made of a split piece of notched bamboo. Here, too, the creditor took one half, and the debtor held the other; they were joined at the moment of repayment, and often broken afterward to mark the cancellation of the debt.[48] To what degree were they transferable? We don't really know. Most of what we do know is from casual references in texts that are mainly about something else: anecdotes, jokes, and poetic allusions. The great collection of Taoist wisdom, the *Leizi*, probably written during the Han dynasty, contains one such:

> There was a man of Sung who was strolling in the street and picked up a half tally someone had lost. He took it home and stored it away, and secretly counted the indentations of the broken edge. He told a neighbor: "I shall be rich any day now."[49]

Rather like someone who finds a key and figures "just as soon as I can figure out which lock . . ."[50] Another story tells of how Liu Bang, a bibulous local constable and future founder of the Han dynasty, used to go on all-night drinking binges, running up enormous tabs. Once, while he lay collapsed in a drunken stupor in a wine-shop, the owner saw a dragon hovering over his head—a sure sign of future greatness—and immediately "broke the tally," forgiving him his accumulated drinking debts.[51]

Tallies weren't just used for loans, but for any sort of contract—which is why early paper contracts also had to be cut in half and one half kept by each party.[52] With paper contracts, there was a definite tendency for the creditor's half to function as an IOU and thus become transferable. By 806 AD, for instance, right around the apogee of Chinese Buddhism, merchants moving tea over long distances from the far south of the country and officials transporting tax payments to the capital, all of them concerned with the dangers of carrying bullion over long distances, began to deposit their money with bankers in the capital and devised a system of promissory notes. They were called "Flying Cash," also divided in half, like tallies, and redeemable for cash in their branches in the provinces. They quickly started passing from hand to hand and operated something like currency. The government first tried to forbid their use, then a year or two later—and this became a familiar pattern in China—when it realized that it could not suppress them, switched gears and established a bureau empowered to issue such notes themselves.[53]

By the early Song dynasty (960–1279 AD), local banking operations all over China were running similar operations, accepting cash and bullion for safekeeping and allowing depositors to use their receipts as promissory notes, as well as trading in government coupons for salt and tea. Many of these notes came to circulate as de facto money.[54] The government, as usual, first tried to ban the practice, then control it (granting a monopoly to sixteen leading merchants), then, finally, set up a government monopoly—the Bureau of Exchange Medium, established in 1023—and before long, aided by the newly invented printing press, was operating factories in several cities employing thousands of workers and producing literally millions of notes.[55]

At first, this paper money was meant to circulate for a limited time (notes would expire after two, then three, then seven years) and was redeemable in bullion. Over time, especially as the Song came under increasing military pressure, the temptation to simply print money with little or no backup became overwhelming—and, moreover, Chinese governments were rarely completely willing to accept their own paper money for tax purposes. Combine this with the fact that the bills were worthless outside China, and it's rather surprising that the system worked at all. Certainly, inflation was a constant problem and the money would periodically have to be recalled and reissued. Occasionally, the whole system would break down, but then people would resort to their own expedients: "privately issued tea checks, noodle checks, bamboo tallies, wine tallies, etc."[56] Still, the Mongols, who ruled China from 1271 to 1368 AD, chose to maintain the system, and it was only abandoned in the seventeenth century.

This is important to note because the conventional account tends to represent China's experiment with paper money as a failure, even, for Metallists, proof that "fiat money," backed only by state power, will always eventually collapse.[57] This is especially odd, since the centuries when paper money was in use are usually considered the most economically dynamic in Chinese history. Surely, if the United States government is ultimately forced to abandon the use of federal reserve notes in 2400 AD, no one would thereby conclude paper money was always intrinsically unworkable. Nonetheless, the main point I'd like to emphasize here is that terms like "fiat money," however common, are deceptive. Almost all of the new forms of paper money that emerged were not originally created by governments at all; they were simply ways of recognizing and expanding the use of credit instruments that emerged from everyday economic transactions. If it was only China that developed paper money in the Middle Ages, this was largely because only in China was there a government large and powerful enough, but also, sufficiently suspicious of its mercantile classes, to feel it had to take charge of such operations itself.

The Near West:

Islam (Capital as Credit)

> *Prices depend on the will of Allah; it is*
> *he who raises and lowers them.*
>
> —Attributed to the
> Prophet Mohammed

> *The profit of each partner must be in*
> *proportion to the share of each in the*
> *adventure.*
>
> —Islamic legal precept

For most of the Middle Ages, the economic nerve center of the world economy and the source of its most dramatic financial innovations was neither China nor India, but the West, which, from the perspective of the rest of the world, meant the world of Islam. During most of this period, Christendom, lodged in the declining empire of Byzantium and the obscure semi-barbarous principalities of Europe, was largely insignificant.

Since people who live in Western Europe have so long been in the habit of thinking of Islam as the very definition of "the East," it's easy to forget that, from the perspective of any other great tradition, the difference between Christianity and Islam is almost negligible. One need only pick up a book on, say, medieval Islamic philosophy to discover disputes between the Baghdad Aristoteleans and the neo-Pythagoreans in Basra, or Persian Neo-Platonists—essentially, scholars doing the same work of trying to square the revealed religion tradition beginning with Abraham and Moses with the categories of Greek philosophy, and doing so in a larger context of mercantile capitalism, universalistic missionary religion, scientific rationalism, poetic celebrations of romantic love, and periodic waves of fascination with mystical wisdom from the East.

From a world-historical perspective, it seems much more sensible to see Judaism, Christianity, and Islam as three different manifestations of the same great Western intellectual tradition, which for most of human history has centered on Mesopotamia and the Levant, extending into Europe as far as Greece and into Africa as far as Egypt, and sometimes farther west across the Mediterranean or down the Nile. Economically, most of Europe was until perhaps the High Middle Ages in exactly the same situation as most of Africa: plugged into the larger world economy, if at all, largely as an exporter of slaves, raw materials, and the occasional exotica (amber, elephant tusks . . .), and importer of manufactured goods (Chinese silks and porcelain, Indian calicoes, Arab steel). To get a sense of comparative economic development (even if the examples are somewhat scattered over time), consider the following table:[58]

Populations and Tax Revenue, 350 BC–1200 AD

	Population	Revenue	Revenue per Head
	Millions	*Tons of Silver*	*Grams of Silver*
Persia, c. BC 350	17	697	41
Egypt, c. BC 200	7	384	55
Rome, c. 1 AD	50	825	17
Rome, c. 150 AD	50	1,050	21
Byzantium, c. 850 AD	10	150	15
Abbasids, c. 850 AD	26	1,260	48
Tang, c. 850 AD	50	2,145	43
France, 1221 AD	8.5	20.3	2.4
England, 1203 AD	2.5	11.5	4.6

What's more, for most of the Middle Ages, Islam was not only the core of Western civilization; it was its expansive edge, working its way into India, expanding in Africa and Europe, sending missionaries and winning converts across the Indian Ocean.

The prevailing Islamic attitude toward law, government, and economic matters was the exact opposite of that prevalent in China. Confucians were suspicious of governance through strict codes of law, preferring to rely on the inherent sense of justice of the cultivated scholar—a scholar who was simply assumed to also be a government official. Medieval Islam, on the other hand, enthusiastically embraced law, which was seen as a religious institution derived from the Prophet, but tended to view government, more often than not, as an unfortunate necessity, an institution that the truly pious would do better to avoid.[59]

In part, this was because of the peculiar nature of Islamic government. The Arab military leaders who, after Mohammed's death in 632 AD, conquered the Sassanian empire and established the Abbasid Caliphate, always continued to see themselves as people of the desert, and never felt entirely part of the urban civilizations they had come to rule. This discomfort took a long time to overcome—on either side. It took the bulk of the population several centuries to convert to the conqueror's religion, and even when they did, they never seem to have really identified with their rulers. Government was seen as military power—necessary, perhaps, to defend the faith, but fundamentally exterior to society.

In part, too, it was because of the peculiar alliance between merchants and common folk that came to be aligned against them. After Caliph al-Ma'mum's abortive attempt to set up a theocracy in 832 AD, the government took a hands-off position on questions of religion. The various schools of Islamic law were free to create their own educational institutions and maintain their own separate system of religious justice. Crucially, it was the *ulema*, the legal scholars, who were the principal agents in the conversion of the bulk of the empire's population to Islam in Mesopotamia, Syria, Egypt, and North Africa in those same years.[60] But—like the elders in charge of guilds, civic associations, commercial sodalities, and religious brotherhoods—they did their best to keep the government, with its armies and ostentation, at arm's length.[61] "The best princes are those who visit religious teachers," one proverb put it, "the worst religious teachers are the those who allow themselves to be visited by princes."[62] A medieval Turkish story brings it home even more pointedly:

> The king once summoned Nasruddin to court.
>
> "Tell me," said the king, "you are a mystic, a philosopher, a man of unconventional understandings. I have become interested in the issue of value. It's an interesting philosophical question. How does one establish the true worth of a person, or an object? Take me for example. If I were to ask you to estimate my value, what would you say?"
>
> "Oh," Nasruddin said, "I'd say about two hundred dinars."
>
> The emperor was flabbergasted. "What?! But this belt I'm wearing is worth two hundred dinars!"
>
> "I know," said Nasruddin. "Actually, I was taking the value of the belt into consideration."

This disjuncture had profound economic effects. It meant that the Caliphate, and later Muslim empires, could operate in many ways much like the old Axial Age empires—creating professional armies, waging wars of conquest, capturing slaves, melting down loot and distributing it in the form of coins to soldiers and officials, demanding that those coins be rendered back as taxes—but at the same time, without having nearly the same effects on ordinary people's lives.

Over the course of the wars of expansion, for example, enormous quantities of gold and silver were indeed looted from palaces, temples, and monasteries and stamped into coinage, allowing the Caliphate to produce gold dinars and silver dirhams of remarkable purity—that is, with next to no fiduciary element, the value of each coin corresponding almost precisely to its weight in precious metal.[63] As a result, they were able to pay their troops extraordinarily well. A soldier in the Caliph's army, for example, received almost four times the wages once received by a Roman legionary.[64] We can, perhaps, speak of a kind of "military-coinage-slavery" complex here—but it existed in a kind of bubble. Wars of expansion, and trade with Europe and Africa, did produce a fairly constant flow of slaves, but in dramatic contrast to the ancient world, very few of them ended up laboring in farms or workshops. Most ended up as decoration in the houses of the rich or, increasingly over time, as soldiers. Over the course of the Abbasid dynasty (750–1258 AD), in fact, the empire came to rely, for its military forces, almost exclusively on Mamluks, highly trained military slaves captured or purchased from the Turkish steppes. The policy of employing slaves as soldiers was maintained by all of the Islamic successor states, including the Mughals, and culminated in the famous Mamluk sultanate in Egypt in the thirteenth century, but historically, it was unprecedented.[65] In most times and places, slaves are, for obvious reasons, the very last people to be allowed anywhere near weapons. Here it was systematic. But, in a strange way, it also made perfect sense: if slaves are, by definition, people who have been severed from society, this was the logical consequence of the wall created between society and the medieval Islamic state.[66]

Religious teachers appear to have done everything they could to prop up the wall. One reason for the recourse to slave soldiers was their tendency to discourage the faithful from serving in the military (since it might mean fighting fellow believers). The legal system that they created also ensured that it was effectively impossible for Muslims—or for that matter Christian or Jewish subjects of the Caliphate—to be reduced to slavery. Here al-Wahid seems to have been largely correct. Islamic law took aim at just about all the most notorious abuses of earlier, Axial Age societies. Slavery through kidnapping, judicial punishment, debt, and the exposure or sale of children, even through the voluntary sale of one's own person—all were forbidden, or rendered unenforceable.[67] Likewise with all the other forms of debt peonage that had loomed over the heads of poor Middle Eastern farmers and their families since the dawn of recorded history. Finally, Islam strictly forbade usury, which it interpreted to mean any arrangement in which money or a commodity was lent at interest, for any purpose whatsoever.[68]

In a way, one can see the establishment of Islamic courts as the ultimate triumph of the patriarchal rebellion that had begun so many thousands of years before; a universal embrace of the ethos of the desert or the steppe, real or imagined, even as the faithful did their best to keep the heavily armed descendants of actual nomads confined to their camps and palaces. It was made possible by a profound shift in class alliances. The great urban civilizations of the Middle East had always been dominated by a de facto alliance between administrators and merchants, both of whom kept the rest of the population either in debt peonage or in constant peril of falling into it. In converting to Islam, the commercial classes, so long the arch-villains in the eyes of ordinary farmers and townsfolk, effectively agreed to change sides, abandon all their most hated practices, and become instead the leaders of a society that now defined itself against the state.

It was possible because, from the beginning, Islam had a positive view toward commerce. Mohammed himself had begun his adult life as a merchant, and no Islamic thinker ever treated the honest pursuit of profit as itself intrinsically immoral or inimical to faith. Neither in practice did the prohibitions against usury—which for the most part were scrupulously enforced, even in the case of commercial loans—in any sense mitigate against the growth of commerce, or even the development of complex credit instruments.[69] To the contrary, the early centuries of the Caliphate saw an immediate efflorescence in both.

Profits were still possible because Islamic jurists were careful to allow for certain service fees and other considerations—notably, allowing goods bought on credit to be priced slightly higher than those bought for cash—that ensured that bankers and traders still had an incentive to provide credit services.[70] Still, these incentives were never enough to allow banking to become a full-time occupation: instead, almost any merchant operating on a sufficiently large scale could be expected to combine banking with a host of other moneymaking activities. As a result, credit instruments soon became so essential to trade that almost anyone of prominence was expected to keep most of his or her wealth on deposit and to make everyday transactions not by counting out coins, but by inkpot and paper. Promissory notes were called *sakk*, "checks," or *ruq'a*, "notes." Checks could bounce. One German historian, picking through a multitude of old Arabic literary sources, recounts that:

About 900 a great man paid a poet in this way, only the banker refused the check, so that the disappointed poet composed a verse to the effect that he would gladly pay a million on the same plan. A patron of the same poet and singer (936) during a concert wrote a check in his favor on a banker for five hundred dinars. When paying, the banker gave the poet to understand that it was customary to charge one dirham discount on each dinar, i.e., about ten per cent. Only if the poet would spend the afternoon and evening with him, he would make no deduction . . .

By about 1000 the banker had made himself indispensable in Basra: every trader had his banking account, and paid only in checks on his bank in the bazaar. . . .[71]

Checks could be countersigned and transferred, and letters of credit (*suftaja*) could travel across the Indian Ocean or the Sahara.[72] If they did not turn into de facto paper money, it was because, since they operated completely independent of the state (they could not be used to pay taxes, for instance), their value was based almost entirely on trust and reputation.[73] Appeal to the Islamic courts was generally voluntary or mediated by merchant guilds and civic associations. In such a context, having a famous poet compose verses making fun of you for bouncing a check was probably the ultimate disaster.

When it came to finance, instead of interest-bearing investments, the preferred approach was partnerships, where (often) one party would supply the capital, the other carry out the enterprise. Instead of fixed return, the investor would receive a share of the profits. Even labor arrangements were often organized on a profit-sharing basis.[74] In all such matters, reputation was crucial—in fact, one lively debate in early commercial law was over the question of whether reputation could (like land, labor, money, or other resources) itself be considered a form of capital. It sometimes happened that merchants would form partnerships with no capital at all, but only their good names. This was called "partnership of good reputation." As one legal scholar explained:

As for the credit partnership, it is also called the "partnership of the penniless" (*sharika al-mafalis*). It comes about when two people form a partnership without any capital in order to buy on credit and then sell. It is designated by this name partnership of good reputations because their capital consists of their status and good reputations; for credit is extended only to him who has a good reputation among people.[75]

Some legal scholars objected to the idea that such a contract could be considered legally binding, since it was not based on an initial outlay of material capital; others considered it legitimate, provided the partners make an equitable partition of the profits—since reputation cannot be quantified. The remarkable thing here is the tacit recognition that, in a credit economy that operates largely without state mechanisms of enforcement (without police to arrest those who commit fraud, or bailiffs to seize a debtor's property), a significant part of the value of a promissory note is indeed the good name of the signatory. As Pierre Bourdieu was later to point out in describing a similar economy of trust in contemporary Algeria: it's quite possible to turn honor into money, almost impossible to convert money into honor.[76]

These networks of trust, in turn, were largely responsible for the spread of Islam over the caravan routes of Central Asia and the Sahara, and especially across the Indian Ocean, the main conduit of medieval world trade. Over the course of the Middle Ages, the Indian Ocean effectively became a Muslim lake. Muslim traders appear to have played a key role in establishing the principle that kings and their armies should keep their quarrels on dry land; the seas were to be a zone of peaceful commerce. At the same time, Islam gained a toehold in trade emporia from Aden to the Moluccas because Islamic courts were so perfectly suited to provide those functions that made such ports attractive: means of establishing contracts, recovering debts, creating a banking sector capable of redeeming or transferring letters of credit.[77] The level of trust thereby created between merchants in the great Malay entrepôt Malacca, gateway to the spice islands of Indonesia, was legendary. The city had Swahili, Arab, Egyptian, Ethiopian, and Armenian quarters, as well as quarters for merchants from different regions of India, China, and Southeast Asia. Yet it was said that its merchants shunned enforceable contracts, preferring to seal transactions "with a handshake and a glance at heaven."[78]

In Islamic society, the merchant became not just a respected figure, but a kind of paragon: like the warrior, a man of honor able to pursue far-flung adventures; unlike him, able to do so in a fashion damaging to no one. The French historian Maurice Lombard draws a striking, if perhaps rather idealized, picture of him "in his stately town-house, surrounded by slaves and hangers-on, in the midst of his collections of books, travel souvenirs, and rare ornaments," along with his ledgers, correspondence, and letters of credit, skilled in the arts of double-entry book-keeping along with secret codes and ciphers, giving alms to the poor, supporting places of worship, perhaps, dedicating himself to the writing of poetry, while still able to translate his general creditworthiness into great capital reserves by appealing to family and partners.[79] Lombard's picture is to some degree inspired by the famous *Thousand and One Nights* description of Sindbad, who, having spent his youth in perilous mercantile ventures to faraway lands, finally retired, rich beyond dreams, to spend the rest of his life amidst gardens and dancing girls, telling tall tales of his adventures. Here's a glimpse, from the eyes of a humble porter (also named Sindbad) when first summoned to see him by the master's page:

> He found it to be a goodly mansion, radiant and full of majesty, till he brought him to a grand sitting room wherein he saw a company of nobles and great lords seated at tables garnished with all manner of flowers and sweet-scented herbs, besides great plenty of dainty viands and fruits dried and fresh and confections and wines of the choicest vintages. There also were instruments of music and mirth and lovely slave girls playing and singing. All the company was ranged according to rank, and in the highest place sat a man of worshipful and noble aspect whose bearded sides hoariness had stricken, and he was stately of stature and fair of favor, agreeable of aspect and full of gravity and dignity and majesty. So Sindbad the Porter was confounded at that which he beheld and said in himself, "By Allah, this must be either some king's palace, or a piece of Paradise!"[80]

It's worth quoting not only because it represents a certain ideal, a picture of the perfect life, but because there's no real Christian parallel. It would be impossible to conceive of such an image appearing in, say, a medieval French romance.

The veneration of the merchant was matched by what can only be called the world's first popular free-market ideology. True, one should be careful not to confuse ideals with reality. Markets were ever entirely independent from the government. Islamic regimes did employ all the usual strategies of manipulating tax policy to encourage the growth of markets, and they periodically tried to intervene in commercial law.[81] Still, there was a very strong popular feeling that they shouldn't. Once freed from its ancient scourges of debt and slavery, the local bazaar had become, for most, not a place of moral danger, but the very opposite:

the highest expression of the human freedom and communal solidarity, and thus to be protected assiduously from state intrusion.

There was a particular hostility to anything that smacked of price-fixing. One much-repeated story held that the Prophet himself had refused to force merchants to lower prices during a shortage in the city of Medina, on the grounds that doing so would be sacrilegious, since, in a free-market situation, "prices depend on the will of God."[82] Most legal scholars interpreted Mohammed's decision to mean that any government interference in market mechanisms should be considered similarly sacrilegious, since markets were designed by God to regulate themselves.[83]

If all this bears a striking resemblance to Adam Smith's "invisible hand" (which was also the hand of Divine Providence), it might not be a complete coincidence. In fact, many of the specific arguments and examples that Smith uses appear to trace back directly to economic tracts written in medieval Persia. For instance, not only does his argument that exchange is a natural outgrowth of human rationality and speech already appear both in both Ghazali (1058–1111 AD) and Tusi (1201–1274 AD); both use exactly the same illustration: that no one has ever observed two dogs exchanging bones.[84] Even more dramatically, Smith's most famous example of division of labor, the pin factory, where it takes eighteen separate operations to produce one pin, already appears in Ghazali's *Ihya*, in which he describes a needle factory, where it takes twenty-five different operations to produce a needle.[85]

The differences, however, are just as significant as the similarities. One telling example: like Smith, Tusi begins his treatise on economics with a discussion of the division of labor; but where for Smith, the division of labor is actually an outgrowth of our "natural propensity to truck and barter" in pursuit of individual advantage, for Tusi, it was an extension of mutual aid:

> Let us suppose that each individual were required to busy himself with providing his own sustenance, clothing, dwelling-place and weapons, first acquiring the tools of carpentry and the smith's trade, then readying thereby tools and implements for sowing and reaping, grinding and kneading, spinning and weaving . . . Clearly, he would not be capable of doing justice to any one of them. But when men render aid to each other, each one performing one of these important tasks that are beyond the measure of his own capacity, and observing the law of justice in transactions by giving greatly and receiving in exchange of the labor of others, then the means of livelihood

are realized, and the succession of the individual and the survival of the species are assured.[86]

As a result, he argues, divine providence has arranged us to have
different abilities, desires, and inclinations. The market is simply one
manifestation of this more general principle of mutual aid, of the
matching of abilities (supply) and needs (demand)—or, to translate it
into my own earlier terms, it is not only founded on, but is itself an
extension of the kind of baseline communism on which any society
must ultimately rest.

All this is not to say that Tusi was in any sense a radical egalitarian. Quite the contrary. "If men were equal," he insists, "they would
all perish." We need differences between rich and poor, he insisted, just
as much as we need differences between farmers and carpenters. Still,
once you start from the initial premise that markets are primarily about
cooperation rather than competition—and while Muslim economic
thinkers did recognize and accept the need for market competition,
they never saw competition as its essence[87]—the moral implications are
very different. Nasruddin's story about the quail eggs might have been
a joke, but Muslim ethicists did often enjoin merchants to drive a hard
bargain with the rich so they could charge less, or pay more, when
dealing with the less fortunate.[88]

Ghazali's take on the division of labor is similar, and his account
of the origins of money is if anything even more revealing. It begins
with what looks much like the myth of barter, except that, like all
Middle Eastern writers, he starts not with imaginary primitive tribes-
men, but with strangers meeting in an imaginary marketplace.

> Sometimes a person needs what he does not own and he owns
> what he does not need. For example, a person has saffron but
> needs a camel for transportation and one who owns a camel
> does not presently need that camel but he wants saffron. Thus,
> there is the need for an exchange. However, for there to be an
> exchange, there must be a way to measure the two objects, for
> the camel-owner cannot give the whole camel for a quantity
> of saffron. There is no similarity between saffron and camel
> so that equal amount of that weight and form can be given.
> Likewise is the case of one who desires a house but owns some
> cloth or desires a slave but owns socks, or desires flour but
> possesses a donkey. These goods have no direct proportional-
> ity so one cannot know how much saffron will equal a camel's
> worth. Such barter transactions would be very difficult.[89]

Ghazali also notes that there might also be a problem of one person not even needing what the other has to offer, but this is almost an afterthought; for him, the real problem is conceptual. How do you compare two things with no common qualities? His conclusion: it can only be done by comparing both to a third thing with no qualities at all. For this reason, he explains, God created dinars and dirhams, coins made out of gold and silver, two metals that are otherwise no good for anything:

> Dirhams and dinars are not created for any particular purpose; they are useless by themselves; they are just like stones. They are created to circulate from hand to hand, to govern and to facilitate transactions. They are symbols to know the value and grades of goods.[90]

They can be symbols, units of measure, because of this very lack of usefulness, indeed lack of any particular feature other than value:

> A thing can only be exactly linked to other things if it has no particular special form or feature of its own—for example, a mirror that has no color can reflect all colors. The same is the case with money—it has no purpose of its own, but it serves as medium for the purpose of exchanging goods.[91]

From this it also follows that lending money at interest must be illegitimate, since it means using money as an end in itself: "Money is not created to earn money." In fact, he says, "in relation to other goods, dirhams and dinars are like prepositions in a sentence," words that, as the grammarians inform us, are used to give meaning to other words, but can only do so because they have no meaning in themselves. Money is thus a unit of measure that provides a means of assessing the value of goods, but also one that operates as such only if it stays in constant motion. To enter into monetary transactions in order to obtain even more money, even if it's a matter of M-C-M', let alone M-M', would be, according to Ghazali, the equivalent of kidnapping a postman.[92]

Whereas Ghazali speaks only of gold and silver, what he describes— money as symbol, as abstract measure, having no qualities of its own, whose value is only maintained by constant motion—is something that would never have occurred to anyone were it not in an age when it was perfectly normal for money to be employed in purely virtual form.

■ ■ ■ ■ ■

Much of our free-market doctrine, then, appears to have been originally borrowed piecemeal from a very different social and moral universe.[93] The mercantile classes of the medieval Near West had pulled off an extraordinary feat. By abandoning the usurious practices that had made them so obnoxious to their neighbors for untold centuries before, they were able to become—alongside religious teachers—the effective leaders of their communities: communities that are still seen as organized, to a large extent, around the twin poles of mosque and bazaar.[94] The spread of Islam allowed the market to become a global phenomenon, operating largely independent of governments, according to its own internal laws. But the very fact that this was, in a certain way, a genuine free market, not one created by the government and backed by its police and prisons—a world of handshake deals and paper promises backed only by the integrity of the signer—meant that it could never really become the world imagined by those who later adopted many of the same ideas and arguments: one of purely self-interested individuals vying for material advantage by any means at hand.

The Far West:

Christendom (Commerce, Lending, and War)

> *Where there is justice in war, there is also justice in usury.*
>
> —Saint Ambrose

Europe, as I mentioned, came rather late to the Middle Ages and for most of it was something of a hinterland. Still, the period began much as it did elsewhere, with the disappearance of coinage. Money retreated into virtuality. Everyone continued to calculate costs in Roman currency, then, later, in Carolingian "imaginary money"—the purely conceptual system of pounds, shillings, and pence used across Western Europe to keep accounts well into the seventeenth century.

Local mints did gradually come back into operation, producing coins in an endless variety of weight, purity, and denominations. How these related to the pan-European system, though, was a matter of manipulation. Kings regularly issued decrees revaluing their own coins in relation to the money of account, "crying up" the currency by, say, declaring that, henceforth, one of their *ecus* or *escudos* would no longer be worth $1/_{12}$ but now $1/_8$ of a shilling (thus effectively raising taxes) or "crying down" the value of their coins by doing the reverse (thus effectively reducing their debts).[95] The real gold or silver content of coins was endlessly readjusted, and currencies were frequently called in for re-minting. Meanwhile, most everyday transactions dispensed with cash entirely, operating through tallies, tokens, ledgers, or transactions in kind. As a result, when the Scholastics came to address economic questions in the thirteenth century, they quickly adopted Aristotle's position that money was a mere social convention: that it was, basically, whatever human beings decided that it was.[96]

All this fit the broader medieval pattern: actual gold and silver, such of it as was still around, was increasingly laid up in sacred places; as centralized states disappeared, the regulation of markets was increasingly in the hands of the Church.

At first, the Catholic attitudes toward usury were just as harsh as Muslim ones, and attitudes toward merchants, considerably harsher. In the first case, they had little choice, as many Biblical texts were quite explicit. Consider Exodus 22:25:

> If you lend money to My people, to the poor among you, you are not to act as a creditor to him; you shall not charge him interest.

Both the Psalms (15:5, 54:12) and Prophets (Jeremiah 9.6, Nehemiah 5:11) were explicit in assigning usurers to death and hellfire. What's more, the early Christian Fathers, who laid the foundation of Church teachings on social issues in the waning years of the Roman empire, were writing amidst the ancient world's last great debt crisis, one that was effectively in the process of destroying the empire's remaining free peasantry.[97] While few were willing to condemn slavery, all condemned usury.

Usury was seen above all as an assault on Christian charity, on Jesus's injunction to treat the poor as they would treat the Christ himself, giving without expectation of return and allowing the borrower to decide on recompense (Luke 6:34–35). In 365 AD, for instance, St. Basil delivered a sermon on usury in Cappadocia that set the standard for such issues:

> The Lord gave His own injunction quite plainly in the words, "from him that would borrow of thee turn not thou away."[98]
>
> But what of the money lover? He sees before him a man under stress of necessity bent to the ground in supplication. He sees him hesitating at no act, no words, of humiliation. He sees him suffering undeserved misfortune, but he is merciless. He does not reckon that he is a fellow-creature. He does not give in to his

entreaties. He stands stiff and sour. He is moved by no prayers; his resolution is broken by no tears. He persists in refusal . . ."[99]

That is, until the suppliant mentions "interest."

Basil was particularly offended by the crass dishonesty by which moneylenders operated, their abuse of Christian fellowship. The man in need comes seeking a friend, the rich man pretends to be one. In fact, he's a secret enemy, and everything he says is a lie. Witness, St. Basil said, how the rich man will always at first swear mighty oaths that he has no money to his name:

> Then the suppliant mentions interest, and utters the word security. All is changed. The frown is relaxed; with a genial smile he recalls old family connection. Now it is "my friend."
>
> "I will see," says he, "if I have any money by me. Yes, there is that sum which a man I know has left in my hands on deposit for profit. He stipulated a very heavy rate of interest. However, I shall certainly take something off, and give it to you on better terms." With pretences of this kind and talk like this he fawns on the wretched victim, and induces him to swallow the bait. Then he binds him with a written security, adds loss of liberty to the trouble of his pressing poverty, and is off. The man who has made himself responsible for interest that he cannot pay has accepted voluntary slavery for life.[100]

The borrower, coming home with his newfound money, at first rejoices. But quickly, "the money slips away," interest accumulates, and his possessions are sold off. Basil grows poetic in describing the debtor's plight. It's as if time itself has become his enemy. Every day and night conspires against him, as they are the parents of interest. His life becomes a "sleepless daze of anxious uncertainty," as he is humiliated in public; while at home, he is constantly hiding under the couch at every unexpected knock on the door and can barely sleep, startled awake by nightmare visions of his creditor standing over his pillow.[101]

Probably the most famous ancient homily on usury, though, was Saint Ambrose's *De Tobia*, pronounced over several days in Milan in 380 BC. He reproduces the same vivid details as Basil: fathers forced to sell their children, debtors who hanged themselves out of shame. Usury, he observes, must be considered a form of violent robbery, even murder.[102] Ambrose, though, added one small proviso that was later to have enormous influence. His sermon was the first to carefully examine every Biblical reference to moneylending, which meant that he had to address the one problem later authors always had to struggle with—the fact that, in the Old Testament, usury is not quite forbidden to everyone. The key sticking point is always Deuteronomy 23:19–20:

> Thou shalt not lend upon usury to thy brother; usury of money, usury of victuals, usury of any thing that is lent upon usury.
>   Unto a stranger thou mayest lend upon usury; but unto thy brother thou shalt not lend upon usury.

So who then is this "stranger" or, a better translation of the Hebrew *nokri*, "foreigner"? Presumably, Ambrose concluded, one against whom robbery and murder would have been justified as well. After all, the ancient Jews lived amidst tribes like the Amalekites, on whom God had specifically instructed them to make war. If by extracting interest one is, as he puts it, fighting without a sword, then it is only legitimate to do so from those "whom it would not be a crime to kill."[103] For Ambrose, living in Milan, all this was something of a technicality. He included all Christians and all those subject to Roman law as "brothers"; there weren't, then, a lot of Amalekites around.[104] Later, the "Exception of St. Ambrose," as it came to be known, was to become extremely important.

All of these sermons—and there were many of them—left certain critical questions unanswered. What *should* the rich man do when receiving a visit from his troubled neighbor? True, Jesus had said to give without expectation of return, but it seemed unrealistic to expect most Christians to do that. And even if they did, what sort of ongoing relationships would that create? St. Basil took the radical position. God had given us all things in common, and he had specifically instructed the rich to give their possessions to the poor. The communism of the Apostles—who pooled all their wealth and took freely what they needed—was thus the only proper model for a truly Christian society.[105] Few of the other Christian Fathers were willing to take things this far. True, they admitted, communism was the ideal, but in this fallen and temporary world, it was simply unrealistic. The Church must accept existing property arrangements, but also come up with spiritual arguments to encourage the rich to nonetheless act with Christian charity. Many of these employed distinctly commercial metaphors. Even Basil was willing to indulge in this sort of thing:

> Whenever you provide for the destitute on account of the Lord, it is both a gift and a loan. It is a gift because you entertain no

hope in recovering it, a loan because of our Lord's munificence in paying you back on his behalf, when, having taken a small sum for the poor, he will give you back a vast sum in return. "For he who takes pity on the poor, lends to God."[106]

Since Christ is in the poor, a gift of charity is a loan to Jesus, to be repaid in heaven with interest inconceivable on earth.

Charity, however, is a way of maintaining inequality, not undermining it. What Basil is talking about here really has nothing to do with debt, and playing with such metaphors seems ultimately to serve only to underline the fact that the rich man doesn't *owe* the poor suppliant anything, any more than God is in any way legally bound to save the soul of anyone who feeds a beggar. "Debt" here dissolves into a pure hierarchy (hence, "the Lord") where utterly different beings provide each other utterly different kinds of benefit. Later theologians were to explicitly confirm this: human beings live in time, noted St. Thomas Aquinas, so it makes sense to say that sin is a debt of punishment we owe to God. But God lives outside of time. By definition, he cannot owe anything to anyone. His grace can therefore only be a gift given with no obligation.[107]

This, in turn, provides an answer to the question: What are they really asking the rich man to do? The Church opposed usury, but it had little to say about relations of feudal dependency, where the rich man provides charity and the poor suppliant shows his gratitude in other ways. Neither, when these kinds of arrangements began to emerge across the Christian West, did the Church offer any significant objections.[108] Former debt peons were gradually transformed into serfs or vassals. In some ways, the relationship was not much different, since vassalage was, in theory, a voluntary, contractual relationship. Just as a Christian has to be able to freely choose to submit himself to "the Lord," so did a vassal have to agree to make himself someone else's man. All this proved perfectly consonant with Christianity.

Commerce, on the other hand, remained a problem. There was not much of a leap between condemning usury as the taking of "whatever exceeds the amount loaned" and condemning any form of profit-taking. Many—Saint Ambrose among them—were willing to take that leap. Where Mohammed declared that an honest merchant deserved a place by the seat of God in heaven, men like Ambrose wondered if an "honest merchant" was not a contradiction in terms. Many held that one simply could not be both a merchant and a Christian.[109] In the early Middle Ages, this was not a pressing issue—especially since so much commerce was conducted by foreigners. The conceptual problems, however, were never resolved. What did it mean that one could only lend to "strangers"? Was it just usury, or was even commerce tantamount to war?

■ ■ ■ ■ ■

Probably the most notorious, and often catastrophic, way that this problem worked itself out in the High Middle Ages was in relations between Christians and Jews. In the years since Nehemiah, Jewish attitudes toward lending had themselves changed. In the time of Augustus, Rabbi Hillel had effectively rendered the sabbatical year a dead letter by allowing two parties to place a rider on any particular loan contract agreeing that it would not apply. While both the Torah and the Talmud stand opposed to loans on interest, exceptions were made in dealing with Gentiles—particularly as, over the course of the eleventh and twelfth centuries, European Jews were excluded from almost any other line of work.[110] This in turn made it harder to contain the practice, as witnessed in the common joke, current in twelfth-century ghettos to justify usury between Jews. It consisted, it is said, of reciting Deuteronomy 23:20 in interrogative tones to make it mean the opposite of its obvious sense: "Unto a foreigner thou mayest lend upon usury, but unto thy brother thou shalt not lend upon usury?"[111]

On the Christian side, in 1140 AD the "Exception of Saint Ambrose" found its way into Gratian's *Decretum*, which came to be considered the definitive collection of canon law. At the time, economic life fell very much under the jurisdiction of the Church. While that might appear to leave Jews safely outside the system, in reality, matters were more complicated. For one thing, while both Jews and Gentiles would occasionally attempt to make recourse to the Exception, the prevailing opinion was that it only really applied to Saracens or others with whom Christendom was literally at war. After all, Jews and Christians lived in the same towns and villages. If one were to concede that the Exception allowed Jews and Christians the right to lend to each other at interest, it would also mean that they had the right to murder one another.[112] No one really wanted to say that. On the other hand, real relations between Christians and Jews often did seem to skate perilously close to this unfortunate ideal—though obviously the actual murder (apart from mere economic aggression) was all on one side.

In part, this was due to the habit of Christian princes of exploiting, for their own purposes, the fact that Jews did sit slightly outside the system. Many encouraged Jews to operate as moneylenders, under their protection, simply because they also knew that protection could be withdrawn at any time. The kings of England were notorious in this regard. They insisted that Jews be excluded from merchant and craft guilds, but granted them the right to charge extravagant rates of interest, backing up the loans by the full force of law.[113] Debtors in medieval England were regularly thrown in prisons until their families settled with the creditor.[114] Yet the same thing regularly happened to the Jews themselves. In 1210 AD, for example, King John ordered a tallage, or emergency levy, to pay for his wars in France and Ireland. According to one contemporary chronicler, "All the Jews throughout England, of both sexes, were seized, imprisoned, and tortured severely, in order to do the king's will with their money." Most who where put to torture offered all they had and more—but on that occasion, one particularly wealthy merchant, a certain Abraham of Bristol, who the king decided owed him ten thousand marks of silver (a sum equivalent to about a sixth of John's total annual revenue), became famous for holding out. The king therefore ordered that one of his molars be pulled out daily, until he paid. After seven had been extracted, Abraham finally gave in.[115]

John's successor, Henry III (1216–1272 AD), was in the habit of turning over Jewish victims to his brother the Earl of Cornwall, so that, as another chronicler put it, "those whom one brother had flayed, the other might embowel."[116] Such stories about the extraction of Jewish teeth, skin, and intestines are, I think, important to bear in mind when thinking about Shakespeare's imaginary Merchant of Venice demanding his "pound of flesh."[117] It all seems to have been a bit of a guilty projection of terrors that Jews had never really visited on Christians, but that had been directed the other way around.

The terror inflicted by kings carried in it a peculiar element of identification: the persecutions and appropriations were an extension of the logic whereby kings effectively treated debts owed to Jews as ultimately owed to themselves, even setting up a branch of the Treasury ("the Exchequer of the Jews") to manage them.[118] This was of course much in keeping with the popular English impression of their kings as themselves a group of rapacious Norman foreigners. But it also gave the kings the opportunity to periodically play the populist card, dramatically snubbing or humiliating their Jewish financiers, turning a blind eye or even encouraging pogroms by townsfolk who chose to take the Exception of Saint Ambrose literally and treat moneylenders as enemies of Christ who could be murdered in cold blood. Particularly gruesome massacres occurred in Norwich in 1144 AD, and in Blois, France, in 1171. Before long, as Norman Cohn put it, "What had once been a flourishing Jewish culture had turned into a terrorized society locked in perpetual warfare with the greater society around it."[119]

One mustn't exaggerate the Jewish role in lending. Most Jews had nothing to do with the business, and those who did were typically bit players, making minor loans of grain or cloth for a return in kind. Others weren't even really Jews. Already in the 1190s, preachers were complaining about lords who would work hand in glove with Christian moneylenders claiming they were "our Jews"—and thus under their special protection.[120] By the 1100s, most Jewish moneylenders had long since been displaced by Lombards (from Northern Italy) and Cahorsins (from the French town of Cahors)—who established themselves across Western Europe and became notorious rural usurers.[121]

The rise of rural usury was itself a sign of a growing free peasantry (there had been no point in making loans to serfs, since they had nothing to repossess). It accompanied the rise of commercial farming, urban craft guilds, and the "commercial revolution" of the High Middle Ages, all of which finally brought Western Europe to a level of economic activity comparable to that long since considered normal in other parts of the world. The Church quickly came under considerable popular pressure to do something about the problem, and at first, it did try to tighten the clamps. Existing loopholes in the usury laws were systematically closed, particularly the use of mortgages. These latter began as an expedient: as in medieval Islam, those determined to dodge the law could simply present the money, claim to be buying the debtor's house or field, and then "rent" the same house or field back to the debtor until the principal was repaid. In the case of a mortgage, the house was in theory not even purchased but pledged as security, but any income from it accrued to the lender. In the eleventh century, this became a favorite trick of monasteries. In 1148, it was made illegal: henceforth, all income was to be subtracted from the principal. Similarly, in 1187, merchants were forbidden to charge higher prices when selling on credit—the Church thereby going much further than any school of Islamic law ever had. In 1179, usury was made a mortal sin, and usurers were excommunicated and denied Christian burial.[122] Before long, new orders of itinerant friars like the Franciscans and Dominicans organized preaching campaigns, traveling town to town, village to village, threatening moneylenders with the loss of their eternal souls if they did not make restitution to their victims.

All this was echoed by a heady intellectual debate in the newly founded universities, not so much as to whether usury was sinful and illegal, but precisely why. Some argued that it was theft of another's material possessions; others that it constituted a theft of time, charging others for something that belonged only to God. Some held that it embodied the sin of Sloth, since like the Confucians, Catholic thinkers usually held that a merchant's profit could only be justified as payment for his labor (i.e., in transporting goods to wherever they were needed), whereas interest accrued even if the lender did nothing at all. Soon the rediscovery of Aristotle, who returned in Arabic translation, and the influence of Muslim sources like Ghazali and Ibn Sina, added new arguments: that treating money as an end in itself defied its true purpose, that charging interest was unnatural, in that it treated mere metal as if it were a living thing that could breed or bear fruit.[123]

But as the Church authorities soon discovered, when one opens up such debates, it's very hard to keep a lid on them. Soon, new popular religious movements were appearing everywhere, and many took up the same direction so many had in late Antiquity, not only challenging commerce but questioning the very legitimacy of private property. Most of these movements were labeled heresies and violently suppressed, but some of their arguments were taken up by members of the mendicant orders themselves. By the thirteenth century, the great intellectual debate was between the Franciscans and the Dominicans over "apostolic poverty"—basically, over whether Christianity could be reconciled with property of any sort.

At the same time, the revival of Roman law—which, as we've seen, began from the assumption of absolute private property—put new intellectual weapons in the hands of those who wished to argue that, at least in the case of commercial loans, usury laws should be relaxed. The great discovery in this case was the notion of *interesse*, which is where our word "interest" originally comes from: a compensation for loss suffered because of late payment.[124] The argument soon became that if a merchant made a commercial loan even for some minimal period (say, a month), it was not usurious for him to charge a percentage for each month afterward, since this was a penalty, not rental for the money, and it was justified as compensation for the profit he *would* have made, had he placed it in some profitable investment, as any merchant would ordinarily be expected to do.[125]

■ ■ ■ ■ ■

The reader may be wondering how it could have been possible for usury laws to move in two opposite directions simultaneously. The answer would seem to be that politically, the situation in Western Europe was remarkably chaotic. Most kings were weak, their holdings fractured and uncertain; the Continent was a checkerboard of baronies, principalities, urban communes, manors, and church estates. Jurisdictions were constantly being renegotiated—usually by war. Merchant

capitalism of the sort long familiar in the Muslim Near West only really managed to establish itself—quite late, compared with the situation
in the rest of the medieval world—when merchant capitalists managed
to secure a political foothold in the independent city-states of northern
Italy—most famously, Venice, Florence, Genoa, and Milan—followed
by the German cities of the Hanseatic League.[126] Italian bankers ultimately managed to free themselves from the threat of expropriation by
themselves taking over governments and by doing so, acquiring their
own court systems (capable of enforcing contracts) and, even more
critically, their own armies.[127]

What jumps out, in comparison with the Muslim world, are these
links of finance, trade, and violence. Whereas Persian and Arab thinkers assumed that the market emerged as an extension of mutual aid,
Christians never completely overcame the suspicion that commerce was
really an extension of usury, a form of fraud only truly legitimate when
directed against one's mortal enemies. Debt was, indeed, sin—on the
part of both parties to the transaction. Competition was essential to the
nature of the market, but competition was (usually) nonviolent warfare. There was a reason why, as I've already observed, the words for
"truck and barter" in almost all European languages were derived from
terms meaning "swindle," "bamboozle," or "deceive." Some disdained
commerce for that reason. Others embraced it. Few would have denied
that the connection was there.

One need only examine the way that Islamic credit instruments—
or for that matter, the Islamic ideal of the merchant adventurer—were
eventually adopted to see just how intimate this connection really was.

It is often held that the first pioneers of modern banking were the
Military Order of the Knights of the Temple of Solomon, commonly
known as the Knights Templar. A fighting order of monks, they played
a key role in financing the Crusades. Through the Templars, a lord in
southern France might take out a mortgage on one of his tenements
and receive a "draft" (a bill of exchange, modeled on the Muslim *suftaja*, but written in a secret code) redeemable for cash from the Temple
in Jerusalem. In other words, Christians appear to have first adopted
Islamic financial techniques to finance attacks against Islam.

The Templars lasted from 1118 to 1307, but they finally went the
way of so many medieval trading minorities: King Phillip IV, deep
in debt to the order, turned on them, accusing them of unspeakable
crimes; their leaders were tortured and ultimately killed, and their
wealth was expropriated.[128] Much of the problem was that they lacked
a powerful home base. Italian banking houses such as the Bardi, Pe-
ruzzi, and Medici did much better. In banking history, the Italians are

most famous for their complex joint-stock organization and for spear-heading the use of Islamic-style bills of exchange.[129] At first these were simple enough: basically just a form of long-distance money-changing. A merchant could present a certain amount in florins to a banker in Italy and receive a notarized bill registering the equivalent in the international money of account (Carolingian derniers), due in, say, three months' time, and then after it came due, either he or his agent could cash it for an equivalent amount of local currency in the Champagne fairs, which were both the great yearly commercial emporia and great financial clearing houses of the European High Middle Ages. But they quickly morphed into a plethora of new, creative forms, mainly a way of navigating—or even profiting from—the endlessly complicated European currency situation.[130]

Most of the capital for these banking enterprises derived from the Mediterranean trade in Indian Ocean spices and Eastern luxuries. Yet, unlike the Indian Ocean, the Mediterranean was a constant war zone. Venetian galleys doubled as both merchant vessels and warships, replete with cannon and marines, and the differences between trade, crusade, and piracy often depended on the balance of forces at any given moment.[131] The same was true on land: where Asian empires tended to separate the sphere of warriors and merchants, in Europe they often overlapped:

> All up and down Central Europe, from Tuscany to Flanders, from Brabant to Livonia, merchants not only supplied warriors—as they did all over Europe—they sat in governments that made war and, sometimes, buckled on armor and went into battle themselves. Such places make a long list: not only Florence, Milan, Venice, and Genoa, but also Augsburg, Nuremberg, Strasbourg, and Zurich; not only Lübeck, Hamburg, Bremen, and Danzig, but also Bruges, Ghent, Leiden, and Cologne. Some of them—Florence, Nuremberg, Siena, Bern, and Ulm come to mind—built considerable territorial states.[132]

The Venetians were only the most famous in this regard. They created a veritable mercantile empire over the course of the eleventh century, seizing islands like Crete and Cyprus and establishing sugar plantations that eventually—anticipating a pattern eventually to become all too familiar in the New World—came to be staffed largely by African slaves.[133] Genoa soon followed suit; one of their most lucrative businesses was raiding and trading along the Black Sea to acquire slaves to sell to the Mamluks in Egypt or to work mines leased from the Turks.[134] The Genoese republic was also the inventor of a unique mode of military financing, which might be known as war by subscription, whereby those planning expeditions sold shares to investors in exchange for the rights to an equivalent percentage of the spoils. It was precisely the same galleys, with the same "merchant adventurers" aboard, who would eventually pass through the pillars of Hercules to follow the Atlantic coast to Flanders or the Champagne fairs, carrying cargoes of nutmeg or cayenne, silks and woolen goods—along with the inevitable bills of exchange.[135]

■ ■ ■ ■ ■

It would be instructive, I think, to pause a moment to think about this term, "merchant adventurer." Originally, it just meant a merchant who operated outside of his own country. It was around this same time, however, at the height of the fairs of Champagne and the Italian merchant empires, between 1160 and 1172, that the term "adventure" began to take on its contemporary meaning. The man most responsible for it was the French poet Chretien de Troyes, author of the famous Arthurian romances—most famous, perhaps, for being the first to tell the story of Sir Percival and the Holy Grail. The romances were a new sort of literature featuring a new sort of hero, the "knight-errant," a warrior who roamed the world in search of, precisely, "adventure"—in the contemporary sense of the word: perilous challenges, love, treasure, and renown. Stories of knightly adventure quickly became enormously popular, Chretein was followed by innumerable imitators, and the central characters in the stories—Arthur and Guinevere, Lancelot, Gawain, Percival, and the rest—became known to everyone, as they are still. This courtly ideal of the gallant knight, the quest, the joust, romance and adventure, remains central to our image of the Middle Ages.[136]

The curious thing is that it bears almost no relation to reality. Nothing remotely like a real "knight-errant" ever existed. "Knights" had originally been a term for freelance warriors, drawn from the younger or, often, bastard sons of the minor nobility. Unable to inherit, they were often forced to band together to seek their fortunes. Many of these bands became little more than roving gangs of thugs, in an endless pursuit of plunder—precisely the sort of people who made merchants' lives so dangerous. Culminating in the twelfth century, there was a concerted effort to bring this dangerous population under the control of the civil authorities: not only the code of chivalry, but the tournament, the joust—all these were more than anything else ways of keeping them out of trouble, as it were, in part by setting knights against each other, in part by turning their entire existence into a kind of stylized game.[137] The ideal of the lone wandering knight, in search of some gallant adventure, on the other hand, seems to have come out of nowhere.

This is important, since it lies at the very heart of our image of the Middle Ages—and the explanation, I think, is revealing. We have to recall that merchants had begun to achieve unprecedented social and even political power around this time, but that, in dramatic contrast to Islam, where a figure like Sindbad—the successful merchant adventurer—could serve as a fictional exemplar of the perfect life, merchants, unlike warriors, were never seen as paragons of much of anything.

It's likely no coincidence that Chretien was living in Troyes, at the very heartland of the Champagne fairs that had become, in turn, the commercial hub of Western Europe.[138] While he appears to have modeled his vision of Camelot on the elaborate court life under his patron Henri the Liberal (1152–1181), Count of Champagne, and his wife Marie, daughter of Eleanor of Aquitaine, the real court was staffed by low-born *commerçants*, who served as serjeants of the fairs—leaving most real knights in the role of onlookers, guards, or—at tournaments—entertainers.

This is not to say that tournaments did not become a kind of economic focus in their own right, according to one early twentieth-century medievalist, Amy Kelly:

> The biographer of Guillaume le Marechal gives an idea of how this rabble of courtly routiers amused itself on the jousting fields of western Europe. To the tournaments, occurring in a brisk season about twice a month from Pentecost to the feast of St John, flocked the young bloods, sometimes three thousand strong, taking possession of the nearest town. Thither also flocked horse dealers from Lombardy and Spain, from Brittany and the Low Countries, as well as armorers, haberdashers for man and beast, usurers, mimes and story-tellers, acrobats, necromancers, and other gentlemen of the lists, the field, the road. Entertainers of every stripe found liberal patronage . . . There were feasts in upper chambers, and forges rang in the smithies all night long. Brawls with grisly incidents—a cracked skull, a gouged eye—occurred as the betting progressed and the dice flew. To cry up their champions in the field came ladies of fair name and others of no name at all.
>
> The hazards, the concourse, the prizes, keyed men to the pitch of war. The stakes were magnificent, for the victor held

his prize, horse and man, for ransom. And for these ransoms fiefs went in gage or the hapless victim fell into the hands of usurers, giving his men, and in extremity, himself, as hostages. Fortunes were made and lost on the point of a lance and many a mother's son failed to ride home.[139]

So, it was not only that the merchants supplied the materials that made the fairs possible; since vanquished knights technically owed their lives to the victors, merchants ended up, in their capacity as money-lenders, making good business out of liquidating their assets. Alternately, a knight might borrow vast sums to outfit himself in magnificence, hoping to impress some fair lady (with handsome dowry) with his victories; others, to take part in the continual whoring and gambling that always surrounded such events. Losers would end up having to sell their armor and horses, and this created the danger that they would go back to being highwaymen, foment pogroms (if their creditors were Jews) or, if they had lands, make new fiscal demands on those unfortunate enough to live on them.

Others turned to war, which itself tended to drive the creation of new markets.[140] In one of the most dramatic of such incidents, in November 1199, a large number of knights at a tournament at the castle of Écry in Champagne, sponsored by Henry's son, Theobald, were seized by a great religious passion, abandoned their games, and swore a vow to instead retake the Holy Land. The crusader army then proceeded to commission the Venetian fleet for transport in exchange for a promise of a 50-percent share in all resulting profits. In the end, rather than proceeding to the Holy Land, they ended up sacking the (much wealthier, Orthodox) Christian city of Constantinople after a prolonged and bloody siege. A Flemish count named Baldwin was installed as "Latin Emperor of Constantinople," but attempting to govern a city that had been largely destroyed and stripped of everything of value ensured that he and his barons soon ended up in great financial difficulties. In a gigantic version of what was happening on the small scale in so many tournaments, they were ultimately reduced to stripping the metal off the church roofs and auctioning holy relics to pay back their Venetian creditors. By 1259, Baldwin had sunk to the point of taking out a mortgage on his own son, who was taken back to Venice as security for a loan.[141]

All this does not really answer the question: Whence, then, this image of the solitary knight-errant, wandering the forests of a mythic Albion, challenging rivals, confronting ogres, fairies, wizards, and mysterious beasts? The answer should be clear by now. Really, this is just a sublimated, romanticized image of the traveling merchants themselves: men who did, after all, set off on lonely ventures through wilds and forests, whose outcome was anything but certain.[142]

And what of the Grail, that mysterious object that all the knights-errant were ultimately seeking? Oddly enough, Richard Wagner, composer of the opera *Parzifal*, first suggested that the Grail was a symbol inspired by the new forms of finance.[143] Where earlier epic heroes sought after, and fought over, piles of real, concrete gold and silver—the Nibelung's hoard—these new ones, born of the new commercial economy, pursued purely abstract forms of value. No one, after all, knew precisely what the Grail was. Even the epics disagree: sometimes it's a plate, sometimes a cup, sometimes a stone. (Wolfram von Eschenbach imagined it to be a jewel knocked from Lucifer's helmet in a battle at the dawn of time.) In a way, it doesn't matter. The point is that it's invisible, intangible, but at the same time of infinite, inexhaustible value, containing everything, capable of making the wasteland flower, feeding the world, providing spiritual sustenance, and healing wounded bodies. Marc Shell even suggested that it would best be conceived as a blank check, the ultimate financial abstraction.[144]

What, Then, Were the Middle Ages?

> Each of us is a mere symbolon of a man, the result of bisection, like the flat fish, two out of one, and each of us is constantly searching for his corresponding symbolon.
> —Plato, *The Symposium*

There is one way that Wagner got it wrong: the introduction of financial abstraction was not a sign that Europe was leaving the Middle Ages, but that it was finally, belatedly, entering it.

Wagner's not really to blame here. Almost everyone gets this wrong, because the most characteristic medieval institutions and ideas arrived so late in Europe that we tend to mistake them for the first stirrings of modernity. We've already seen this with bills of exchange, already in use in the East by 700 or 800 AD, but only reaching Europe several centuries later. The independent university—perhaps the quintessential medieval institution—is another case in point. Nalanda was founded in 427 AD, and there were independent institutions of higher learning all over China and the Near West (from Cairo to Constantinople) centuries before the creation of similar institutions in Oxford, Paris, and Bologna.

If the Axial Age was the age of materialism, the Middle Ages were above all else the age of transcendence. The collapse of the ancient empires did not, for the most part, lead to the rise of new ones.[145] Instead, once-subversive popular religious movements were catapulted into the status of dominant institutions. Slavery declined or disappeared, as did the overall level of violence. As trade picked up, so did the pace of technological innovation; greater peace brought greater possibilities not only for the movement of silks and spices, but also of people and ideas. The fact that monks in medieval China could devote themselves to translating ancient treatises in Sanskrit, and that students in madrasas in medieval Indonesia could debate legal terms in Arabic, is testimony to the profound cosmopolitanism of the age.

Our image of the Middle Ages as an "age of faith"—and hence, of blind obedience to authority—is a legacy of the French Enlightenment. Again, it makes sense only if you think of the "Middle Ages" as something that happened primarily in Europe. Not only was the Far West an unusually violent place by world standards, the Catholic Church was extraordinarily intolerant. It's hard to find many medieval Chinese, Indian, or Islamic parallels, for example, to the burning of "witches" or the massacre of heretics. More typical was the pattern that prevailed in certain periods of Chinese history, when it was perfectly acceptable for a scholar to dabble in Taoism in his youth, become a Confucian in middle age, then turn to Buddhism on retirement. If there is an essence to medieval thought, it lies not in blind obedience to authority, but rather in a dogged insistence that the values that govern our ordinary daily affairs—particularly those of the court and marketplace—are confused, mistaken, illusory, or perverse. True value lay elsewhere, in a domain that cannot be directly perceived, but only approached through study or contemplation. But this in turn made the faculties of contemplation, and the entire question of knowledge, an endless problem. Consider for example the great conundrum, pondered by Muslim, Christian, and Jewish philosophers alike: What does it mean to simultaneously say that we can only know God through our faculties of Reason, but that Reason itself partakes of God? Chinese philosophers were struggling with similar conundrums when they asked, "Do we read the classics or do the classics read us?" Almost all the great intellectual debates of the age turned on this question in one way or another. Is the world created by our minds, or our minds by the world?

We can see the same tensions within predominant theories of money. Aristotle had argued that gold and silver had no intrinsic value in themselves, and that money therefore was just a social convention, invented by human communities to facilitate exchange. Since it had "come about by agreement, therefore it is within our power to change it or render it useless" if we all decide that that's what we want to do.[146] This position gained little traction in the materialist intellectual environment of the Axial Age, but by the later Middle Ages, it had become standard wisdom. Ghazali was among the first to embrace it. In his own way, he took it even further, insisting that the fact that a gold coin has no intrinsic value *is* the basis of its value as money, since this very lack of intrinsic value is what allows it to "govern," measure, and regulate the value of other things. But, at the same time, Ghazali denied that money was a social convention. It was given to us by God.[147]

Ghazali was a mystic and a political conservative, so one might argue that he ultimately shied away from the most radical implications of his own ideas. But one could also ask whether, in the Middle Ages, arguing that money was an arbitrary social convention was really all that radical a position. After all, when Christian and Chinese thinkers insisted that it was, it was almost always as a way of saying that money is whatever the king or the emperor wished it to be. In that sense, Ghazali's position was perfectly consonant with the Islamic desire to protect the market from political interference by saying that it fell properly under the aegis of religious authorities.

■ ■ ■ ■ ■

The fact that medieval money took such abstract, virtual forms—checks, tallies, paper money—meant that questions like these ("What does it mean to say that money is a symbol?") cut to the core of the philosophical issues of the day. Nowhere is this so true as in the history of the word "symbol" itself. Here we encounter some parallels so extraordinary that they can only be described as startling.

When Aristotle argued that coins are merely social conventions, the term he used was *symbolon*—from which our own word "symbol" is derived. Symbolon was originally the Greek word for "tally"—an object broken in half to mark a contract or agreement, or marked and broken to record a debt. So our word "symbol" traces back originally to objects broken to record debt contracts of one sort or another. This is striking enough. What's really remarkable, though, is that the contemporary Chinese word for "symbol," *fu*, or *fu hao*, has almost exactly the same origin.[148]

Let's start with the Greek term "*symbolon.*" Two friends at dinner might create a symbolon if they took some object—a ring, a knuckle-bone, a piece of crockery —and broke it in half. Any time in the future when either of them had need of the other's help, they could bring their halves as reminders of the friendship. Archeologists have found hundreds of little broken friendship tablets of this sort in Athens, often made of clay. Later they became ways of sealing a contract, the object standing in the place of witnesses.[149] The word was also used for tokens of every sort: those given to Athenian jurors entitling them to vote, or tickets for admission to the theater. It could be used to refer to money too, but only if that money had no intrinsic value: bronze coins whose value was fixed only by local convention.[150] Used for written documents, a symbolon could also be passport, contract, commission, or receipt. By extension, it came to mean: omen, portent, symptom, or finally, in the now-familiar sense, symbol.

The path to the latter appears to have been twofold. Aristotle fixed on the fact that a tally could be anything: what the object was didn't matter; all that mattered was that there was a way to break it in half. It is exactly so with language: words are sounds we use to refer to objects, or to ideas, but the relation is arbitrary: there's no particular reason, for example, that English-speakers should choose "dog" to refer to an animal and "god" to refer to a deity, rather than the other way around. The only reason is social convention: an agreement between all speakers of a language that this sound shall refer to that thing. In this sense, all words were arbitrary tokens of agreement.[151] So, of course, is money—for Aristotle, not only worthless bronze coins that we agree to treat as if they were worth a certain amount, but all money, even gold, is just a symbolon, a social convention.[152]

All this came to seem almost commonsensical in the thirteenth century of Thomas Aquinas, when rulers could change the value of currency simply by issuing a decree. Still, medieval theories of symbols derived less from Aristotle than from the Mystery Religions of Antiquity, where "symbolon" came to refer to certain cryptic formulae or talismans that only initiates could understand.[153] It thus came to mean a concrete token, perceptible to the senses, that could only be understood in reference to some hidden reality entirely beyond the domain of sensory experience.[154]

The theorist of the symbol whose work was most widely read and respected in the Middle Ages was a sixth-century Greek Christian mystic whose real name has been lost to history, but who has come to be known by his pseudonym Dionysius the Areopagite.[155] Dionysius took up the notion in this latter sense to confront what was to become the

great intellectual problem of the age: How is it possible for humans to
have knowledge of God? How can we, whose knowledge is confined to
what our senses can perceive of the material universe, have knowledge
of a being whose nature is absolutely alien to that material universe—
"that infinity beyond being," as he puts it, "that oneness that is beyond
intelligence"?[156] It would be impossible were it not for the fact that God,
being all-powerful, can do anything, and therefore, just as he places
his own body in the Eucharist, so can he reveal himself to our minds
through an endless variety of material shapes. Intriguingly, Dionysius
warns us that we cannot begin to understand how symbols work until
we rid ourselves of the notion that divine things are likely to be beautiful. Images of luminous angels and celestial chariots are only likely to
confuse us, since we will be tempted to imagine that that's what heaven
is actually like, and in fact we cannot possibly conceive of what heaven
is like. Instead, effective symbols are, like the original symbolon, homely objects selected apparently at random; often, ugly, ridiculous things,
whose very incongruity reminds us that they are *not* God, of the fact
that God "transcends all materiality," even as, in another sense, they
are God.[157] But the notion that they are in any sense tokens of agreement between equals is gone entirely. Symbols are gifts, absolute, free,
hierarchical gifts, presented by a being so far above us that any thought
of reciprocity, debt, or mutual obligation is simply inconceivable.[158]

Compare the Greek dictionary above to the following, from a Chinese dictionary:

> FU. To agree with, to tally. The two halves of a tally.
> - evidence; proof of identity, credentials
> - to fulfill a promise, to keep one's word
> - to reconcile
> - the mutual agreement between Heaven's appointment and
>   human affairs
> - a tally, a check
> - an imperial seal or stamp
> - a warrant, a commission, credentials
> - like fitting the two halves of a tally, in exact agreement
>   - a symbol, a sign . . .[159]

The evolution is almost exactly the same. Like *symbola*, *fu* can be
tallies, contracts, official seals, warrants, passports, or credentials. As
promises, they can embody an agreement, a debt contract, or even a
relation of feudal vassalage—since a minor lord agreeing to become

another man's vassal would split a tally just as he would if borrowing grain or money. The common feature seems to be a contract between two parties that begin as equal in which one agrees to become subordinate. Later, as the state became more centralized, we mainly hear about fu presented to officials as a means of conveying order: the official would take the left half with him when posted to the provinces, and when the emperor wished to send an important command, he would send the right half with the messenger to make sure that the official knew it was actually the imperial will.[160]

We've already seen how paper money seems to have developed from paper versions of such debt contracts, ripped in half and reunited. For Chinese theorists, of course, Aristotle's argument that money was simply a social convention was hardly radical; it was simply assumed. Money was whatever the emperor established it to be. Though even here there was a slight proviso, as evidenced in the entry above, that "fu" could also refer to "the mutual agreement between heaven's appointment and human affairs." Just as officials were appointed by the emperor, the emperor was ultimately appointed by a higher power, and he could only rule effectively as long as he kept its mandate, which is why propitious omens were called "fu," signs that heaven approved of the ruler, just as natural disasters were a sign that he had strayed.[161]

Here Chinese ideas did grow a bit closer to the Christian ones. But Chinese conceptions of the cosmos had one crucial difference: since there was no emphasis on the absolute gulf between our world and the one beyond it, contractual relations with the gods were by no means out of the question. This was particularly true in medieval Taoism, where monks were ordained through a ceremony called "rending the tally," ripping apart a piece of paper that represented a contract with heaven.[162] It was the same with the magical talismans, also called "fu," which an adept might receive from his master. These were literally tallies: the adept kept one; the other half was said to be retained by the gods. Such talismanic fu took the form of diagrams, said to represent a form of celestial writing, comprehensible only to the gods, which committed them to assist the bearer, often giving the adept the right to call on armies of divine protectors with whose help he could slay demons, cure the sick, or otherwise attain miraculous powers. But they could also become, like Dionysius' symbola, objects of contemplation, by which one's mind can ultimately attain some knowledge of the invisible world beyond our own.[163]

Many of the most compelling visual symbols to emerge from medieval China trace back to such talismans: the River Symbol or, for that matter, the yin-yang symbol that seems to have developed out of it.[164] Just looking at a yin-yang symbol, it is easy enough to imagine the left and right (sometimes, too, called "male" and "female") halves of a tally.

■ ■ ■ ■

A tally does away with the need for witnesses; if the two surfaces agree, then everyone knows that the agreement between the contracting parties exists as well. This is why Aristotle saw it as a fit metaphor for words: word A corresponds to concept B because there is a tacit agreement that we shall act as if it does. The striking thing about tallies is that even though they might begin as simple tokens of friendship and solidarity, in almost all the later examples, what the two parties actually agree to create is a relation of inequality: of debt, obligation, subordination to another's orders. This is in turn what makes it possible to use the metaphor for the relation between the material world and that more powerful world that ultimately gives it meaning. The two sides are the same. Yet what they create is absolute difference. Hence, for a medieval Christian mystic, as for medieval Chinese magicians, symbols could be literal fragments of heaven—even if, for the first, they provided a language whereby one could have some understanding of beings one could not possibly interact with, while for the second, they provided a way of interacting, even making practical arrangements, with beings whose language one could not possibly understand.

On one level, this is just another version of the dilemmas that always arise when we try to reimagine the world through debt—that peculiar agreement between two equals that they shall no longer be equals, until such time as they become equals once again. Still, the problem took on a peculiar piquancy in the Middle Ages, when the economy became, as it were, spiritualized. As gold and silver migrated to holy places, ordinary transactions everywhere came to be carried out primarily through credit. Inevitably, arguments about wealth and markets became arguments about debt and morality, and arguments about debt and morality became arguments about the nature of our place in the universe. As we've seen, the solutions varied considerably. Europe and India saw a return to hierarchy: society became a ranked order of Priests, Warriors, Merchants, and Farmers (or in Christendom, just Priests, Warriors, and Farmers). Debts between the orders were considered threatening because they implied the potential of equality, and they often led to outright violence. In China, in contrast, the principle of debt often became the governing principle of the cosmos: karmic debts, milk-debts, debt contracts between human beings and celestial powers. From the point of view of the authorities, all these led to excess, and potentially to vast concentrations of capital that might throw the entire social order out of balance. It was the responsibility of government to intervene constantly to keep markets running smoothly and equitably, thus avoiding new outbreaks of popular unrest. In the world of Islam, where theologians held that God recreated the entire universe at every instant, market fluctuations were instead seen as merely another manifestation of divine will.

The striking thing is that the Confucian condemnation of the merchant and the Islamic celebration of the merchant ultimately led to the same thing: prosperous societies with flourishing markets, but where the elements never came together to create the great merchant banks and industrial firms that were to become the hallmark of modern capitalism. It's especially striking in the case of Islam. Certainly, the Islamic world produced figures who would be hard to describe as anything but capitalists. Large-scale merchants were referred to as *sāhib al-māl*, "owners of capital," and legal theorists spoke freely about the creation and expansion of capital funds. At the height of the Caliphate, some of these merchants were in possession of millions of dinars and seeking profitable investment. Why did nothing like modern capitalism emerge? I would highlight two factors. First, Islamic merchants appear to have taken their free-market ideology seriously. The marketplace did not fall under the direct supervision of the government; contracts were made between individuals—ideally, "with a handshake and a glance at heaven"—and thus honor and credit became largely indistinguishable. This is inevitable: you can't have cutthroat competition where there is no one stopping people from literally cutting one another's throats. Second, Islam also took seriously the principle, later enshrined in classical economic theory but only unevenly observed in practice, that profits are the reward for risk. Trading enterprises were assumed to be, quite literally, adventures, in which traders exposed themselves to the dangers of storm and shipwreck, savage nomads, forests, steppes, and deserts, exotic and unpredictable foreign customs, and arbitrary governments. Financial mechanisms designed to avoid these risks were considered impious. This was one of the objections to usury: if one demands a fixed rate of interest, the profits are guaranteed. Similarly, commercial investors were expected to share the risk. This made most of the forms of finance and insurance that were to later develop in Europe impossible.[165]

In this sense, the Buddhist monasteries of early medieval China represent the opposite extreme. The Inexhaustible Treasuries were inexhaustible because, by continually lending their money out at interest and never otherwise touching their capital, they could guarantee effectively risk-free investments. That was the entire point. By doing so, Buddhism, unlike Islam, produced something very much like what we now call "corporations"—entities that, through a charming legal fiction, we imagine to be persons, just like human beings, but immortal, never having to go through all the human untidiness of marriage, reproduction, infirmity, and death. To put it in properly medieval terms, they are very much like angels.

Legally, our notion of the corporation is very much a product of the European High Middle Ages. The legal idea of a corporation as a "fictive person" (*persona ficta*)—a person who, as Maitland, the great British legal historian, put it, "is immortal, who sues and is sued, who holds lands, has a seal of his own, who makes regulations for those natural persons of whom he is composed"[166]—was first established in canon law by Pope Innocent IV in 1250 AD, and one of the first kinds of entities it applied to were monasteries—as also to universities, churches, municipalities, and guilds.[167]

The idea of the corporation as an angelic being is not mine, incidentally. I borrowed it from the great medievalist Ernst Kantorowicz, who pointed out that all this was happening right around the same time that Thomas Aquinas was developing the notion that angels were really just the personification of Platonic Ideas.[168] "According to the teachings of Aquinas," he notes, "every angel represented a species."

> Little wonder then that finally the personified collectives of the jurists, which were juristically immortal species, displayed all the features otherwise attributed to angels . . . The jurists themselves recognized that there was some similarity between their abstractions and the angelic beings. In this respect, it may be said that the political and legal world of thought of the later Middle Ages began to be populated by immaterial angelic bodies, large and small: they were invisible, ageless, sempiternal, immortal, and sometimes even ubiquitous; and they were endowed with a *corpus intellectuale* or *mysticum* [an intellectual or mystical body] which could stand any comparison with the "spiritual bodies" of the celestial beings.[169]

All this is worth emphasizing because while we are used to assuming that there's something natural or inevitable about the existence of corporations, in historical terms, they are actually strange, exotic creatures. No other great tradition came up with anything like it.[170] They are the most peculiarly European addition to that endless proliferation of metaphysical entities so characteristic of the Middle Ages—as well as the most enduring.

They have, of course, changed a great deal over time. Medieval corporations owned property, and they often engaged in complex financial arrangements, but in no case were they profit-seeking enterprises in the modern sense. The ones that came closest were, perhaps unsurprisingly, monastic orders—above all, the Cistercians—whose monasteries became something like the Chinese Buddhist ones, surrounded by mills and smithies, practicing rationalized commercial agriculture with a workforce of "lay brothers" who were effectively wage laborers, spinning and exporting wool. Some even talk about "monastic capitalism."[171] Still, the ground was only really prepared for capitalism in the familiar sense of the term when the merchants began to organize themselves into eternal bodies as a way to win monopolies, legal or de facto, and avoid the ordinary risks of trade. An excellent case in point was the Society of Merchant Adventurers, charted by King Henry IV in London in 1407, who, despite the romantic-sounding name, were mainly in the business of buying up British woolens and selling them in the Flanders fairs. They were not a modern joint-stock company, but a rather old-fashioned medieval merchant guild, but they provided a structure whereby older, more substantial merchants could provide loans to younger ones, and they managed to secure enough of an exclusive control over the woolen trade that substantial profits were pretty much guaranteed.[172] When such companies began to engage in armed ventures overseas, though, a new era of human history might be said to have begun.

Chapter Eleven

AGE OF THE GREAT CAPITALIST EMPIRES

(1450 - 1971 AD)

"Eleven pesos, then; and as you can't pay me the eleven pesos, that makes another eleven pesos—twenty-two in all: eleven for the serape and the petate and eleven because you can't pay. Is that right, Crisiero?"

Crisiero had no knowledge of figures, so it was very natural that he said, "That is right, patrón."

Don Arnulfo was a decent, honorable man. Other landowners were a good deal less softhearted with their peons.

"The shirt is five pesos. Right? Very well. And as you can't pay for it, that's five pesos. And as you remain in my debt for the five pesos, that's five pesos. And as I shall never have the money from you, that's five pesos. So that makes five and five and five and five. That's twenty pesos. Agreed?"

"Yes, patrón, agreed."

The peon can get the shirt nowhere else when he needs one. He can get credit nowhere but from his master, for whom he works and from whom he can never get away as long as he owes him a centavo.

—B. Traven, The Carreta

THE EPOCH THAT BEGAN with what we're used to calling the "Age of Exploration" was marked by so many things that were genuinely new—the rise of modern science, capitalism, humanism, the nation-state—that it may seem odd to frame it as just another turn of an historical cycle. Still, from the perspective I've been developing in this book, that is what it was.

The era begins around 1450 with a turn away from virtual currencies and credit economies and back to gold and silver. The subsequent flow of bullion from the Americas sped the process immensely, sparking a "price revolution" in Western Europe that turned traditional society upside-down. What's more, the return to bullion was accompanied by the return of a whole host of other conditions that, during the Middle Ages, had been largely suppressed or kept at bay: vast empires and professional armies, massive predatory warfare, untrammeled usury and debt peonage, but also materialist philosophies, a new burst of scientific and philosophical creativity—even the return of chattel slavery. It was in no way a simple repeat performance. All the Axial Age pieces reappeared, but they came together in an entirely different way.

■ ■ ■ ■ ■

The 1400s are a peculiar period in European history. It was a century of endless catastrophe: large cities were regularly decimated by the Black Death; the commercial economy sagged and in some regions collapsed entirely; whole cities went bankrupt, defaulting on their bonds; the knightly classes squabbled over the remnants, leaving much of the countryside devastated by endemic warfare. Even in geopolitical terms Christendom was staggering, with the Ottoman Empire not only scooping up what remained of Byzantium but pushing steadily into central Europe, its forces expanding on land and sea.

At the same time, from the perspective of many ordinary farmers and urban laborers, times couldn't have been much better. One of the perverse effects of the bubonic plague, which killed off about one-third of the European workforce in the years after it first struck in 1347, was that wages increased dramatically. It didn't happen immediately, but this was largely because the first reaction of the authorities was to enact legislation freezing wages, or even attempting to tie free peasants back to the land again. Such efforts were met with powerful resistance, culminating in a series of popular uprisings across Europe—the famous English peasant revolt of 1381 being only the most famous example. All these were squelched, but the authorities were also forced to compromise.

Before long, so much wealth was flowing into the hands of ordinary people that governments had to start introducing new laws forbidding the lowborn to wear silks and ermine, and to limit the number of feast days, which, in many towns and parishes, began eating up one-third or even half of the year. The fifteenth century is, in fact, considered the heyday of medieval festive life, with its floats and dragons, maypoles and church ales, its Abbots of Unreason and Lords of Misrule.[1]

Over the next centuries, all this was to be destroyed. In England, the festive life was systematically attacked by Puritan reformers, then eventually by reformers everywhere, Catholic and Protestant alike. At the same time its economic basis in popular prosperity dissolved.

Why this happened has been a matter of intense historical debate for centuries. This much we know: it began with a massive inflation. Between 1500 and 1650, for instance, prices in England increased 500 percent, but wages rose much more slowly, so that in five generations, real wages fell to perhaps 40 percent of what they had been. The same thing happened everywhere in Europe.

Why? The favorite explanation, ever since a French lawyer named Jean Bodin first proposed it in 1568, was the vast influx of gold and silver that came pouring into Europe after the conquest of the New World. As the value of precious metals collapsed, the argument went, the price of everything else skyrocketed, and wages simply couldn't keep up.[2] There is some evidence to support this. The height of popular prosperity around 1450 did correspond to a period when bullion—and therefore, coin—was in particularly short supply.[3] The lack of cash sometimes played havoc with international trade; in the 1460s, we hear of ships full of wares forced to turn back from major ports, as no one had any cash on hand to buy from them. The problem only started to turn around later in the decade, with a sudden burst of silver mining in Saxony and the Tirol, followed by the opening of new sea routes to the Gold Coast of West Africa. Then came the conquests of Cortés and Pizarro. Between 1520 and 1640, untold tons of gold and silver from Mexico and Peru were transported across the Atlantic and Pacific in Spanish treasure ships.

The problem with the conventional story is that very little of that gold and silver lingered very long in Europe. Most of the gold ended up in temples in India, and the overwhelming majority of the silver bullion was ultimately shipped off to China. The latter is crucial. If we really want to understand the origins of the modern world economy, the place to start is not in Europe at all. The real story is of how China abandoned the use of paper money. It's a story worth telling briefly, because very few people know it.

■ ■ ■ ■ ■

After the Mongols conquered China in 1271, they kept the system of paper money in place, and even made occasional (if usually disastrous) attempts to introduce it in the other parts of their empire. In 1368, however, they were overthrown by another of China's great popular insurrections, and a former peasant leader was once again installed in power.

During their century of rule, the Mongols had worked closely with foreign merchants, who became widely detested. Partly as a result, the former rebels, now the Ming dynasty, were suspicious of commerce in any form, and they promoted a romantic vision of self-sufficient agrarian communities. This had some unfortunate consequences. For one thing, it meant the maintenance of the old Mongol tax system, paid in labor and in kind; especially since that, in turn, was based on a quasi-caste system in which subjects were registered as farmers, craftsmen, or soldiers and forbidden to change their jobs. This proved extraordinarily unpopular. While government investment in agriculture, roads, and canals did set off a commercial boom, much of this commerce was technically illegal, and taxes on crops were so high that many indebted farmers began to flee their ancestral lands.[4]

Typically, such floating populations can be expected to seek just about anything but regular industrial employment; here, as in Europe, most preferred a combination of odd jobs, peddling, entertainment, piracy, or banditry. In China, many also turned prospector. There was a minor silver rush, with illegal mines cropping up everywhere. Uncoined silver ingots, instead of official paper money and strings of bronze coins, soon became the real money of the off-the-books informal economy. When the government attempted to shut down illegal mines in the 1430s and 1440s, their efforts sparked local insurrections in which miners would make common cause with displaced peasants, seize nearby cities, and sometimes threaten entire provinces.[5]

In the end, the government gave up even trying to suppress the informal economy. Instead, they swung the other way entirely: they stopped issuing paper money, legalized the mines, allowed silver bullion to become the recognized currency for large transactions, and even gave private mints the authority to produce strings of cash.[6] This, in turn, allowed the government to gradually abandon the system of labor exactions and substitute a uniform tax system payable in silver.

Effectively, the Chinese government had gone back to its old policy of encouraging markets and merely intervening to prevent any undue concentrations of capital. It quickly proved spectacularly successful, and Chinese markets boomed. Indeed, many speak of the Ming as having accomplished something almost unique in world history: this was a time when the Chinese population was exploding, but living standards markedly improved.[7] The problem was that the new policy meant that the regime had to ensure an abundant supply of silver in the country, so as to keep its price low and minimize popular unrest—but, as it turned out, the Chinese mines were very quickly exhausted. In the 1530s, new silver mines were discovered in Japan, but these were exhausted in a decade or two as well. Before long, China had to turn to Europe and the New World.

Now, since Roman times, Europe had been exporting gold and silver to the East: the problem was that Europe had never produced much of anything that Asians wanted to buy, so it was forced to pay in specie for silks, spices, steel, and other imports. The early years of European expansion were largely attempts to gain access either to Eastern luxuries or to new sources of gold and silver with which to pay for them. In those early days, Atlantic Europe really had only one substantial advantage over its Muslim rivals: an active and advanced tradition of naval warfare, honed by centuries of conflict in the Mediterranean. The moment when Vasco da Gama entered the Indian Ocean in 1498, the principle that the seas should be a zone of peaceful trade came to an immediate end. Portuguese flotillas began bombarding and sacking every port city they came across, then seizing control of strategic points and extorting protection money from unarmed Indian Ocean merchants for the right to carry on their business unmolested.

At almost exactly the same time, Christopher Columbus—a Genoese mapmaker seeking a short-cut to China—touched land in the New World, and the Spanish and Portuguese empires stumbled into the greatest economic windfall in human history: entire continents full of unfathomable wealth, whose inhabitants, armed only with Stone Age weapons, began conveniently dying almost as soon as they arrived. The conquest of Mexico and Peru led to the discovery of enormous new sources of precious metal, and these were exploited ruthlessly and systematically, even to the point of largely exterminating the surrounding populations to extract as much precious metal as quickly as possible. As Kenneth Pomeranz has recently pointed out, none of this would have been possible were it not for the practically unlimited Asian demand for precious metals.

> Had China in particular not had such a dynamic economy that changing its metallic base could absorb the staggering quantities of silver mined in the New World over three centuries,

those mines might have become unprofitable within a few decades. The massive inflation of silver-denominated prices in Europe from 1500 to 1640 indicates a shrinking value for the metal there even with Asia draining off much of the supply.[8]

By 1540, a silver glut caused a collapse in prices across Europe; the American mines would, at this point, simply have stopped functioning, and the entire project of American colonization foundered, had it not been for the demand from China.[9] Treasure galleons moving toward Europe soon refrained from unloading their cargoes, instead rounding the horn of Africa and proceeding across the Indian Ocean toward Canton. After 1571, with the foundation of the Spanish city of Manila, they began to move directly across the Pacific. By the late sixteenth century, China was importing almost fifty tons of silver a year, about 90 percent of its silver, and by the early seventeenth century, 116 tons, or over 97 percent.[10] Huge amounts of silk, porcelain, and other Chinese products had to be exported to pay for it. Many of these Chinese products, in turn, ended up in the new cities of Central and South America. This Asian trade became the single most significant factor in the emerging global economy, and those who ultimately controlled the financial levers—particularly Italian, Dutch, and German merchant bankers—became fantastically rich.

But how exactly did the new global economy cause the collapse of living standards in Europe? One thing we do know: it clearly was *not* by making large amounts of precious metal available for everyday transactions. If anything, the effect was the opposite. While European mints were stamping out enormous numbers of rials, thalers, ducats, and doubloons, which became the new medium of trade from Nicaragua to Bengal, almost none found their way into the pockets of ordinary Europeans. Instead, we hear constant complaints about the shortage of currency. In England:

> For much of the Tudor period the circulating medium was so small that the taxable population simply did not have sufficient coin in which to pay the benevolences, subsidies, and tenths levied upon them, and time and time again household plate, the handiest near money that most people possessed, had to be surrendered.[11]

This was the case in most of Europe. Despite the massive influx of metal from the Americas, most families were so low on cash that they were regularly reduced to melting down the family silver to pay their taxes.

This was because taxes *had* to be paid in metal. Everyday business, in contrast, continued to be transacted much as it had in the Middle Ages, by means of various forms of virtual credit money: tallies, promissory notes, or, within smaller communities, simply by keeping track of who owed what to whom. What really caused the inflation is that those who ended up in control of the bullion—governments, bankers, large-scale merchants—were able to use that control to begin changing the rules, first by insisting that gold and silver *were* money, and second by introducing new forms of credit-money for their own use while slowly undermining and destroying the local systems of trust that had allowed small-scale communities across Europe to operate largely without the use of metal currency.

This was a political battle, even if it was also a conceptual argument about the nature of money. The new regime of bullion money could only be imposed through almost unparalleled violence—not only overseas, but at home as well. In much of Europe, the first reaction to the "price revolution" and accompanying enclosures of common lands was not very different from what had so recently happened in China: thousands of one-time peasants fleeing or being forced out of their villages to become vagabonds or "masterless men," a process that culminated in popular insurrections. The reaction of European governments, however, was entirely different. The rebellions were crushed, and this time, no subsequent concessions were forthcoming. Vagabonds were rounded up, exported to the colonies as indentured laborers, and drafted into colonial armies and navies—or, eventually, set to work in factories at home.

Almost all of this was carried out through a manipulation of debt. As a result, the very nature of debt, too, became once again one of the principal bones of contention.

Part I:

Greed, Terror, Indignation, Debt

No doubt scholars will never stop arguing about the reasons for the great "price revolution"—largely because it's not clear what kind of tools can be applied. Can we really use the methods of modern economics, which were designed to understand how contemporary economic institutions operate, to describe the political battles that led to the creation of those very institutions?

This is not just a conceptual problem. There are moral dangers here. To take what might seem an "objective" economic approach to the origins of the world economy would be to treat the behavior of early European explorers, merchants, and conquerors as if they were simply rational responses to opportunities—as if this were just what anyone would have done in the same situation. This is what the use of equations so often does: make it seem perfectly natural to assume that, if the price of silver in China is twice what it is in Seville, and inhabitants of Seville are capable of getting their hands on large quantities of silver and transporting it to China, then clearly they will, even if doing so requires the destruction of entire civilizations. Or if there is a demand for sugar in England, and enslaving millions is the easiest way to acquire labor to produce it, then it is inevitable that some will enslave them. In fact, history makes it quite clear that this is not the case. Any number of civilizations have probably been in a position to wreak havoc on the scale that the European powers did in the sixteenth and seventeenth centuries (Ming China itself was an obvious candidate), but almost none actually did so.[12]

Consider, for instance, how the gold and silver from the American mines were extracted. Mining operations began almost immediately upon the fall of the Aztec capital of Tenochtitlán in 1521. While we are used to assuming that the Mexican population was devastated simply as an effect of newly introduced European diseases, contemporary observers felt that the dragooning of the newly conquered natives to work in the mines was at least equally responsible.[13] In *The Conquest of America*, Tzvetan Todorov offers a compendium of some of the most chilling reports, mostly from Spanish priests and friars who, even when committed in principle to the belief that the extermination of the Indians was the judgment of God, could not disguise their horror at scenes of Spanish soldiers testing the blades of their weapons by eviscerating random passers-by and tearing babies off their mother's backs to be eaten by dogs. If these were just sporadic incidents, they might be written off as what one would expect when a collection of heavily armed men—many of violent criminal background—are given absolute impunity; but the reports from the mines imply something far more systematic. When Fray Toribio de Motolinia wrote of the ten plagues that he believed God had visited on the inhabitants of Mexico, he listed smallpox, war, famine, labor exactions, taxes (which caused many to sell their children to moneylenders, others to be tortured to death in cruel prisons), and the thousands who died in the building of the capital city. Above all, he insisted, were the uncountable numbers who died in the mines:

> The eighth plague was the slaves whom the Spaniards made in order to put them to work in the mines. At first those who were already slaves of the Aztecs were taken; then those who had given evidence of insubordination; finally all those who could be caught. During the first years after the conquest, the slave traffic flourished, and slaves often changed master. They produced so many marks on their faces, in addition to the royal brand, that they had their faces covered with letters, for they bore the marks of all who had bought and sold them.
>
> The ninth plague was the service in the mines, to which the heavily laden Indians traveled sixty leagues or more to carry provisions . . . When their food gave out they died, either at the mines or on the road, for they had no money to buy food and there was no one to give it to them. Some reached home in such a state that they died soon after. The bodies of those Indians and of the slaves who died in the mines produced such a stench that it caused a pestilence, especially at the mines of Oaxaca. For half a league around these mines and along a great part of the road one could scarcely avoid walking over dead bodies or bones, and the flocks of birds and crows that came to fatten themselves upon the corpses were so numerous that they darkened the sun."[14]

Similar scenes were reported in Peru, where whole regions were depopulated by forced service in the mines, and Hispaniola, where the indigenous population was eradicated entirely.[15]

When dealing with conquistadors, we are speaking not just of simple greed, but greed raised to mythic proportions. This is, after all, what they are best remembered for. They never seemed to get enough. Even after the conquest of Tenochtitlán or Cuzco, and the acquisition of hitherto-unimaginable riches, the conquerors almost invariably regrouped and started off in search of more treasure.

Moralists throughout the ages have inveighed against the endlessness of human greed, just as they have against our supposedly endless lust for power. What history actually reveals, though, is that while humans may be justly accused of having a proclivity to accuse *others* of acting like conquistadors, few really act this way themselves. Even for the most ambitious of us, our dreams are more like Sindbad's: to have adventures, to acquire the means to settle down and live an enjoyable life, and then, to enjoy it. Max Weber of course argued that the essence of capitalism is the urge—which he thought first appeared in Calvinism—never to settle down, but to engage in endless expansion. But the conquistadors were good medieval Catholics, even if ones usually drawn from the most ruthless and unprincipled elements of Spanish society. Why the unrelenting drive for more and more and more?

It might help, I think, to go back to the very onset of Hernán Cortés's conquest of Mexico: What were his immediate motives? Cortés had migrated to the colony of Hispaniola in 1504, dreaming of glory and adventure, but for the first decade and a half, his adventures had largely consisted of seducing other people's wives. In 1518, however, he managed to finagle his way into being named commander of an expedition to establish a Spanish presence on the mainland. As Bernal Díaz del Castillo, who accompanied him, later wrote, around this time:

> He began to adorn himself and be more careful of his appearance than before. He wore a plume of feathers, with a medallion and a gold chain, and a velvet cloak trimmed with loops of gold. In fact he looked like a bold and gallant Captain. However, he had no money to defray the expenses I have spoken about, for at the time he was very poor and much in debt, despite the fact that he had a good estate of Indians and was getting gold from the mines. But all this he spent on his person, on finery for his wife, whom he had recently married, and on entertaining guests . . .
>
> When some merchant friends of his heard that he had obtained his command as Captain General, they lent him four thousand gold pesos in coin and another four thousand in goods secured on his Indians and estates. He then ordered two standards and banners to be made, worked in gold with the royal arms and a cross on each side with a legend which said, "Comrades, let us follow the sign of the Holy Cross with true faith, and through it we shall conquer."[16]

In other words, he'd been living beyond his means, got himself in trouble, and decided, like a reckless gambler, to double down and go for broke. Unsurprising, then, that when the governor at the last minute decided to cancel the expedition, Cortés ignored him and sailed for the mainland with six hundred men, offering each an equal share in the expedition's profits. On landing he burned his boats, effectively staking everything on victory.

Let us skip, then, from the beginning of Díaz's book to its final chapter. Three years later, through some of the most ingenious, ruthless, brilliant, and utterly dishonorable behavior by a military leader ever recorded, Cortés had his victory. After eight months of grueling house-to-house warfare and the death of perhaps a hundred thousand Aztecs, Tenochtitlán, one of the greatest cities of the world, lay entirely destroyed. The imperial treasury was secured, and the time had come, then, for it to be divided in shares amongst the surviving soldiers.

Yet, according to Díaz, the result among the men was outrage. The officers connived to sequester most of the gold, and when the final tally was announced, the troops learned that they would be receiving only fifty to eighty pesos each. What's more, the better part of their shares was immediately seized again by the officers in their capacity of creditors—since Cortés had insisted that the men be billed for any replacement equipment and medical care they had received during the siege. Most found they had actually lost money on the deal. Díaz writes:

> We were all very deeply in debt. A crossbow was not to be purchased for less than forty or fifty pesos, a musket cost one hundred, a sword fifty, and a horse from 800 to 1000 pesos, and above. Thus extravagantly did we have to pay for everything! A surgeon, who called himself Mastre Juan, who had tended some very bad wounds, charged wildly inflated fees, and so did a quack named Murcia, who was an apothecary and a barber and also treated wounds, and there were thirty other tricks and swindles for which payment was demanded of our shares as soon as we received them.
>
> Serious complaints were made about this, and the only remedy that Cortés provided was to appoint two trustworthy persons who knew the prices of goods and could value anything that we had bought on credit. An order went out that whatever price was placed on our purchases or the surgeon's cures must be accepted, but that if we had no money, our creditors must wait two years for payment.[17]

Spanish merchants soon arrived charging wildly inflated prices for basic necessities, causing further outrage, until:

> Our general becoming weary of the continual reproaches which were thrown out against him, saying he had stolen everything for himself, and the endless petitions for loans and advance

in pay, determined at once to get rid of the most troublesome
fellows, by forming settlements in those provinces which appeared most eligible for this purpose.[18]

These were the men who ended up in control of the provinces and
who established local administration, taxes, and labor regimes. Which
makes it a little easier to understand the descriptions of Indians with
their faces covered by names like so many counter-endorsed checks,
or the mines surrounded by miles of rotting corpses. We are not dealing with a psychology of cold, calculating greed, but of a much more
complicated mix of shame and righteous indignation, and of the frantic
urgency of debts that would only compound and accumulate (these
were, almost certainly, interest-bearing loans), and outrage at the idea
that, after all they had gone through, they should be held to owe anything to begin with.

And what of Cortés? He had just pulled off perhaps the greatest
act of theft in world history. Certainly, his original debts had now
been rendered inconsequential. Yet he somehow always seemed to find
himself in new ones. Creditors were already starting to repossess his
holdings while he was off on an expedition to Honduras in 1526; on his
return, he wrote the Emperor Charles V that his expenses were such
that "all I have received has been insufficient to relieve me from misery
and poverty, being at the moment I write in debt for upwards of five
hundred ounces of gold, without possessing a single peso towards it."[19]
Disingenuous, no doubt (Cortés at the time owned his own personal
palace), but only a few years later, he was reduced to pawning his
wife's jewelry to help finance a series of expeditions to California, hoping to restore his fortunes. When those failed to turn a profit, he ended
up so besieged by creditors that he had to return to Spain to petition
the emperor in person for relief.[20]

■ ■ ■ ■ ■

If all this seems suspiciously reminiscent of the fourth Crusade, with its
indebted knights stripping whole foreign cities of their wealth and still
somehow winding up only one step ahead of their creditors, there is a
reason. The financial capital that backed these expeditions came from
more or less the same place (if in this case Genoa, not Venice). What's
more, that relationship, between the daring adventurer on the one
hand, the gambler willing to take any sort of risk, and on the other,
the careful financier, whose entire operations are organized around

producing steady, mathematical, inexorable growth of income, lies at the very heart of what we now call "capitalism."

As a result, our current economic system has always been marked by a peculiar dual character. Scholars have long been fascinated by debates that ensued in Spanish universities like Santander about the humanity of the Indians (Did they have souls? Could they have legal rights? Was it legitimate to forcibly enslave them?), just as they have argued about the real attitudes of the conquistadors (Was it contempt, revulsion, or even grudging admiration for their adversaries?)[21] The real point is that at the key moments of decision, none of this mattered. Those making the decisions did not feel they were in control anyway; those who were in control did not particularly care to know the details. To take a telling example: after the earliest years of the gold and silver mines described by Motolinia, where millions of Indians were simply rounded up and marched off to their deaths, colonists settled on a policy of debt peonage: the usual trick of demanding heavy taxes, lending money at interest to those who could not pay, and then demanding that the loans be repaid with work. Royal agents regularly attempted to forbid such practices, arguing that the Indians were now Christian and that this violated their rights as loyal subjects of the Spanish crown. But as with almost all such royal efforts to act as protector of the Indians, the result was the same. Financial exigencies ended up taking precedence. Charles V himself was deeply in debt to banking firms in Florence, Genoa, and Naples, and gold and silver from the Americas made up perhaps one-fifth of his total revenue. In the end, despite a lot of initial noise and the (usually quite sincere) moral outrage on the part of the king's emissaries, such decrees were either ignored or, at best, enforced for a year or two before being allowed to slip into abeyance.[22]

■ ■ ■ ■ ■

All of this helps explain why the Church had been so uncompromising in its attitude toward usury. It was not just a philosophical question; it was a matter of moral rivalry. Money always has the potential to become a moral imperative unto itself. Allow it to expand and it can quickly become a morality so imperative that all others seem frivolous in comparison. For the debtor, the world is reduced to a collection of potential dangers, potential tools, and potential merchandise.[23] Even human relations become a matter of cost-benefit calculation. Clearly, this is the way the conquistadors viewed the worlds that they set out to conquer.

It is a peculiar feature of modern capitalism to create social arrangements that essentially force us to think this way. The structure of the corporation is a telling case in point—and it is no coincidence that the first major joint-stock corporations in the world were the English and Dutch East India companies, ones that pursued that very same combination of exploration, conquest, and extraction as did the conquistadors. It is a structure designed to eliminate all moral imperatives but profit. The executives who make decisions can argue—and regularly do—that, if it were their own money, of course they would not fire lifelong employees a week before retirement, or dump carcinogenic waste next to schools. Yet they are morally bound to ignore such considerations, because they are mere employees whose only responsibility is to provide the maximum return on investment for the company's stockholders. (The stockholders, of course, are not given any say.)

The figure of Cortés is instructive for another reason. We are speaking of a man who, in 1521, had conquered a kingdom and was sitting atop a vast pile of gold. Neither did he have any intention of giving it away—even to his followers. Five years later, he was claiming to be a penniless debtor. How was this possible?

The obvious answer would be: Cortés was not a king; he was a subject of the King of Spain, living within the legal structure of a kingdom that insisted that, if he were not good at managing his money, he would lose it. Yet, as we've seen, the king's laws could be ignored in other cases. What's more, even kings were not entirely free agents. Charles V was continually in debt, and when his son Philip II—his armies fighting on three different fronts at once—attempted the old medieval trick of defaulting, all his creditors, from the Genoese Bank of St. George to the German Fuggers and Welsers, closed ranks to insist that he would receive no further loans until he started honoring his commitments.[24]

Capital, then, is not simply money. It is not even just wealth that can be turned into money. But neither is it just the use of political power to help one use one's money to make more money. Cortés was trying to do exactly that: in classical Axial Age fashion, he was attempting to use his conquests to acquire plunder, and slaves to work the mines, with which he could pay his soldiers and suppliers cash to embark on even further conquests. It was a tried-and-true formula. But for all the other conquistadors, it provided a spectacular failure.

This would seem to mark the difference. In the Axial Age, money was a tool of empire. It might have been convenient for rulers to promulgate markets in which everyone would treat money as an end in itself; at times, rulers might have even come to see the whole apparatus of government as a profit-making enterprise; but money always remained a political instrument. This is why when the empires collapsed and armies were demobilized, the whole apparatus could simply melt away. Under the newly emerging capitalist order, the logic of money was granted autonomy; political and military power were then gradually reorganized around it. True, this was a financial logic that could never have existed without states and armies behind it in the first place. As we have seen in the case of medieval Islam, under genuine free-market conditions—in which the state is not involved in regulating the market in any significant way, even in enforcing commercial contracts—purely competitive markets will not develop, and loans at interest will become effectively impossible to collect. It was *only* the Islamic prohibition against usury, really, that made it possible for them to create an economic system that stood so far apart from the state.

Martin Luther was making this very point in 1524, right around the time that Cortés was first beginning to have trouble with his creditors. It is all very well, Luther said, for us to imagine that all might live as true Christians, in accordance with the dictates of the Gospel. But in fact there are few who are really capable of acting this way:

> Christians are rare in this world; therefore the world needs a strict, hard, temporal government that will compel and constrain the wicked not to rob and to return what they borrow, even though a Christian ought not to demand it, or even hope to get it back. This is necessary in order that the world not become a desert, peace may not perish, and trade and society not be utterly destroyed; all of which would happen if we were to rule the world according to the Gospel and not drive and compel the wicked, by laws and the use of force, to do what is right . . . Let no one think that the world can be ruled without blood; the sword of the ruler must be red and bloody; for the world will and must be evil, and the sword is God's rod and vengeance upon it.[25]

"Not to rob and to return what they borrow"—a telling juxtaposition, considering that in Scholastic theory, lending money at interest had itself been considered theft.

And Luther *was* referring to interest-bearing loans here. The story of how he got to this point is telling. Luther began his career as a reformer in 1520 with fiery campaigns against usury; in fact, one of his objections to the sale of Church indulgences was that it was itself a form of spiritual usury. These positions won him enormous popular

support in towns and villages. However, he soon realized that he'd unleashed a genie that threatened to turn the whole world upside-down.
More radical reformers appeared, arguing that the poor were not morally obliged to repay the interest on usurious loans, and proposing the
revival of Old Testament institutions like the sabbatical year. They
were followed by outright revolutionary preachers who began once
again questioning the very legitimacy of aristocratic privilege and private property. In 1525, the year after Luther's sermon, there was a massive uprising of peasants, miners, and poor townsfolk across Germany:
the rebels, in most cases, representing themselves as simple Christians
aiming to restore the true communism of the Gospels. Over a hundred
thousand were slaughtered. Already in 1524, Luther had a sense that
matters were spilling out of control and that he would have to choose
sides: in that text, he did so. Old Testament laws like the Sabbatical
year, he argued, are no longer binding; the Gospel merely describes
ideal behavior; humans are sinful creatures, so law is necessary; while
usury is a sin, a four to five-percent rate of interest is currently legal
under certain circumstances; and while collecting that interest is sinful,
under *no* circumstances is it legitimate to argue that for that reason,
borrowers have the right to break the law.[26]

The Swiss Protestant reformer Zwingli was even more explicit.
God, he argued, gave us the divine law: to love thy neighbor as thyself.
If we truly kept this law, humans would give freely to one another, and
private property would not exist. However, Jesus excepted, no human
being has ever been able to live up to this pure communistic standard.
Therefore, God has also given us a second, inferior, human law, to be
enforced by the civil authorities. While this inferior law cannot compel us to act as we really ought to act ("the magistrate can force no
one to lend out what belongs to him without hope of recompense or
profit")—at least it can make us follow the lead of the apostle Paul,
who said: "Pay all men what you owe."[27]

Soon afterward, Calvin was to reject the blanket ban on usury
entirely, and by 1650, almost all Protestant denominations had come to
agree with his position that a reasonable rate of interest (usually five
percent) was not sinful, provided the lenders act in good conscience,
do not make lending their exclusive business, and do not exploit the
poor.[28] (Catholic doctrine was slower to come around, but it did ultimately accede by passive acquiescence.)

If one looks at how all this was justified, two things jump out.
First, Protestant thinkers all continued to make the old medieval argument about *interesse*: that "interest" is really compensation for the
money that the lender *would* have made had he been able to place his

money in some more profitable investment. Originally, this logic had only been applied to commercial loans. Increasingly, it was now applied to all loans. Far from being unnatural, then, the growth of money was now treated as completely expected. All money was assumed to be capital.[29] Second, the assumption that usury is something that one properly practices on one's enemies, and therefore, by extension, that all commerce partakes something of the nature of war, never entirely disappears. Calvin, for instance, denied that Deuteronomy only referred to the Amalekites; clearly, he said, it meant that usury was acceptable when dealing with Syrians or Egyptians; indeed with all nations with whom the Jews traded.[30] The result of opening the gates was, at least tacitly, to suggest that one could now treat *anyone*, even a neighbor, as a foreigner.[31] One need only observe how European merchant adventurers of the day actually were treating foreigners, in Asia, Africa, and the Americas, to understand what this might mean in practice.

Or, one might look closer to home. Take the story of another well-known debtor of the time, the Margrave Casimir of Brandenburg-Ansbach (1481–1527), of the famous Hohenzollern dynasty:

Casimir was the son of Margrave Friedrich the Elder of Brandenburg, who has come to be known as one of the "mad princes" of the German Renaissance. Sources differ on just how mad he actually was. One contemporary chronicle describes him as "somewhat deranged in his head from too much racing and jousting." Most agree that he was given to fits of inexplicable rage, as well as to the sponsorship of wild, extravagant festivals, said often to have degenerated into bacchanalian orgies.[32]

All agree, however, that he was poor at managing his money. At the beginning of 1515, Friedrich was in such financial trouble—he is said to have owed 200,000 guilders—that he alerted his creditors, mostly fellow nobles, that he might soon be forced to temporarily suspend interest payments on his debts. This seems to have caused a crisis of faith, and within a matter of weeks, his son Casimir staged a palace coup—moving, in the early hours of February 26, 1515, to seize control of the castle of Plassenburg while his father was distracted with the celebration of Carnival, then forcing him to sign papers abdicating for reason of mental infirmity. Friedrich spent the rest of his life confined in Plassenburg, denied all visitors and correspondence. When at one point his guards requested that the new Margrave provide a couple guilders so he could pass the time gambling with them, Casimir made a great public show of refusal, stating (ridiculously, of course) that his father had left his affairs in such disastrous shape that he could not possibly afford to.[33]

Casimir dutifully doled out governorships and other prize offices to his father's creditors. He tried to get his house in order, but this proved surprisingly difficult. His enthusiastic embrace of Luther's reforms in 1521 clearly had as much to do with the prospect of getting his hands on Church lands and monastic assets than with any particular religious fervor. Yet, at first, the disposition of Church property remained moot, and Casimir himself compounded his problems by running up gambling debts of his own, said to have amounted to nearly 50,000 guilders.[34]

Placing his creditors in charge of the civil administration had predictable effects: increasing exactions on his subjects, many of whom became hopelessly indebted themselves. Unsurprisingly, Casimir's lands in the Tauber Valley in Franconia became one of the epicenters of the revolt of 1525. Bands of armed villagers assembled, declaring they would obey no law that did not accord with "the holy word of God." At first, the nobles, isolated in their scattered castles, offered little resistance. The rebel leaders—many of them local shopkeepers, butchers, and other prominent men from nearby towns—began with a largely orderly campaign of tearing down castle fortifications, their knightly occupants being offered guarantees of safety if they cooperated, agreed to abandon their feudal privileges, and swore oaths to abide by the rebels' Twelve Articles. Many complied. The real venom of the rebels was reserved for cathedrals and monasteries, dozens of which were sacked, pillaged, and destroyed.

Casimir's reaction was to hedge his bets. At first, he bided his time, assembling an armed force of about two thousand experienced soldiers but refusing to intervene as rebels pillaged several nearby monasteries; in fact, he negotiated with the various rebel bands in such apparent good faith that many believed he was preparing to join them "as a Christian brother."[35] In May, however, after the knights of the Swabian League defeated the rebels of the Christian Union to the south, Casimir swung into action, his forces brushing aside poorly disciplined rebel bands to sweep through his own territories like a conquering army, burning and pillaging villages and towns, slaughtering women and children. In every town he set up punitive tribunals and seized all looted property, which he kept, even as his men also expropriated any wealth still to be found in the region's cathedrals, ostensibly as emergency loans to pay his troops.

It seems significant that Casimir was, of all the German princes, both the longest to waver before intervening and the most savagely vengeful once he did. His forces became notorious not only for executing accused rebels, but systematically chopping off the fingers of accused collaborators, his executioner keeping a grim ledger of amputated body parts for later reimbursement—a kind of carnal inversion of the account ledgers that had caused him so much trouble in his life. At one point, in the town of Kitzingen, Casimir ordered the gouging out of the eyes of fifty-eight burghers who had, he declared, "refused to look at him as their lord." Afterward, he received the following bill:[36]

80 beheaded

69 eyes put out or fingers cut off	114 ½ fl.
from this to deduct	
received from the Rothenburgers	10 fl.
received from Ludwig von Hutten	2 fl.
Remainder	
Plus 2 months' pay at 8 fl. per month	16 fl.
Total	118 ½ fl.

[Signed] Augustin, the executioner, who the Kitzingers call "Master Ouch."

The repression eventually inspired Casimir's brother Georg (later known as "the Pious") to write a letter asking him if Casimir was intending to take up a trade—since, as Georg gently reminded him, he could not very well continue to be a feudal overlord if his peasants were all dead.[37]

With such things happening, it is hardly surprising that men like Thomas Hobbes came to imagine the basic nature of society as a war of all against all, from which only the absolute power of monarchs could save us. At the same time, Casimir's behavior—combining as it does a general attitude of unprincipled, cold-blooded calculation with outbursts of almost inexplicably vindictive cruelty—seems, like that of Cortés's angry foot soldiers when unleashed on the Aztec provinces, to embody something essential about the psychology of debt. Or, more precisely, perhaps, about the debtor who feels he has done nothing to deserve being placed in his position: the frantic urgency of having to convert everything around oneself into money, and rage and indignation at having been reduced to the sort of person who would do so.

─────────

Part II:

The World of Credit and the World of Interest

> *Of all the beings that have existence*
> *only in the minds of men, nothing is*
> *more fantastical and nice than Credit;*
> *it is never to be forced; it hangs upon*
> *opinion; it depends upon our passions*
> *of hope and fear; it comes many times*
> *unsought-for, and often goes away*
> *without reason; and once lost, it is*
> *hardly to be quite recovered.*
>
> —Charles Davenant, 1696

> *He that has lost his credit is dead to*
> *the world.*
>
> —English and German Proverb

The peasants' visions of communistic brotherhood did not come out of nowhere. They were rooted in real daily experience: of the maintenance of common fields and forests, of everyday cooperation and neighborly solidarity. It is out of such homely experience of everyday communism that grand mythic visions are always built.[38] Obviously, rural communities were also divided, squabbling places, since communities always are—but insofar as they are communities at all, they are necessarily founded on a ground of mutual aid. The same, incidentally, can be said of members of the aristocracy, who might have fought endlessly over love, land, honor, and religion, but nonetheless still cooperated remarkably well with one another when it really mattered (most of all, when their position as aristocrats was threatened); just as the merchants and bankers, much as they competed with one another, managed to close ranks when it really mattered too. This is what I refer to as the "communism of the rich," and it is a powerful force in human history.[39]

The same, as we've seen repeatedly, applies to credit. There are always different standards for those one considers friends or neighbors. The inexorable nature of interest-bearing debt, and the alternately savage and calculating behavior of those enslaved to it, are typical above all of dealings between strangers: it's unlikely that Casimir felt much more kinship with his peasants than Cortés did with the Aztecs (in fact, most likely less, since Aztec warriors were at least aristocrats). Inside the small towns and rural hamlets, where the state was mostly far away, medieval standards survived intact, and "credit" was just as much a matter of honor and reputation as it had ever been. The great untold story of our current age is of how these ancient credit systems were ultimately destroyed.

Recent historical research, notably that of Craig Muldrew, who has sifted through thousands of inventories and court cases from sixteenth- and seventeenth-century England, has caused us to revise almost all our old assumptions about what everyday economic life at that time was like. Of course, very little of the American gold and silver that reached Europe actually ended up in the pockets of ordinary farmers, mercers, or haberdashers.[40] The lion's share stayed in the coffers of either the aristocracy or the great London merchants, or else in the royal treasury.[41] Small change was almost nonexistent. As I've already pointed out, in the poorer neighborhoods of cities or large towns, shopkeepers would issue their own lead, leather, or wooden token money; in the sixteenth century, this became something of a fad, with artisans and even poor widows producing their own currency as a way to make ends meet.[42] Elsewhere, those frequenting the local butcher, baker, or shoemaker would simply put things on the tab. The same was true of those attending weekly markets, or selling neighbors milk or cheese or candle-wax. In a typical village, the only people likely to pay cash were passing travelers, and those considered riff-raff: paupers and ne'er-do-wells so notoriously down on their luck that no one would extend credit to them. Since everyone was involved in selling something, however, just about everyone was both creditor and debtor; most family income took the form of promises from other families; everyone knew and kept count of what their neighbors owed one another; and every six months or year or so, communities would hold a general public "reckoning," canceling debts out against each other in a great circle, with only those differences then remaining when all was done being settled by use of coin or goods.[43]

The reason that this upends our assumptions is that we're used to blaming the rise of capitalism on something vaguely called "the market"—the breakup of older systems of mutual aid and solidarity, and the creation of a world of cold calculation, where everything had its price. Really, English villagers appear to have seen no contradiction between the two. On the one hand, they believed strongly in the collective stewardship of fields, streams, and forests, and the need to help neighbors in difficulty. On the other hand, markets were seen as a kind of attenuated version of the same principle, since they were entirely founded on trust. Much like the Tiv women with their gifts of yams and okra, neighbors assumed they ought to be constantly slightly in debt to one another. At the same time, most appear to have been quite comfortable with the idea of buying and selling, or even with market fluctuations, provided things didn't get to the point of threatening honest families' livelihoods.[44] When loans at interest began to be legalized in 1545, that did not ruffle too many feathers, either, provided such loans took place within that same larger moral framework: lending was considered an appropriate vocation, for example, for widows with no other source of income, or as a way for neighbors to share in the profits from some minor commercial venture. William Stout, a Quaker merchant from Lancashire, spoke glowingly of Henry Coward, the tradesman in whose shop he first apprenticed:

> My master then had a full trade of groceries, ironmongerware, and several other goods, and very much respected and trusted, not only by the people of his own religious profession, but by all others of all professions and circumstances . . . His credit was so much, that any who had money to dispose of lodged it with him to put out to interest or to make use of it.[45]

In this world, trust was everything. Most money literally was trust, since most credit arrangements were handshake deals. When people used the word "credit," they referred above all to a reputation for honesty and integrity; and a man or woman's honor, virtue, and respectability, but also, reputation for generosity, decency, and good-natured sociability, were at least as important considerations when deciding whether to make a loan as were assessments of net income.[46] As a result, financial terms became indistinguishable from moral ones. One could speak of others as "worthies," as "a woman of high estimation" or "a man of no account," and equally of "giving credit" to someone's words when one believes what they say ("credit" is from the same root as "creed" or "credibility"), or of "extending credit" to them, when you take them at their word that they will pay you back.

One should not idealize the situation. This was a highly patriarchal world: a man's wife or daughter's reputation for chastity was as much a part of his "credit" as his own reputation for kindness or piety. What's more, almost all people below the age of thirty, male or female, were employed as servants in someone else's household—as farmhands, milkmaids, apprentices—and as such, were of "no account" at all.[47] Finally, those who lost credibility in the eyes of the community became, effectively, pariahs, and descended into the criminal or semi-criminal

classes of rootless laborers, beggars, harlots, cutpurses, hawkers, pedlars, fortune-tellers, minstrels, and other such "masterless men" or
"women of ill repute."[48]

Cold cash was employed largely between strangers, or when paying rents, tithes, and taxes to landlords, bailiffs, priests, and other
superiors. The landed gentry and wealthy merchants, who eschewed
handshake deals, would often use cash with one another, especially
to pay off bills of exchange drawn on London markets.[49] Above all,
gold and silver were used by the government to purchase arms and
pay soldiers, and amongst the criminal classes themselves. This meant
that coins were most likely to be used both by the sort of people who
ran the legal system—the magistrates, constables, and justices of the
peace—and by those violent elements of society they saw it as their
business to control.

■ ■ ■ ■ ■

Over time, this led to an increasing disjuncture of moral universes.
For most, who tried to avoid entanglement in the legal system just as
much as they tried to avoid the affairs of soldiers and criminals, debt
remained the very fabric of sociability. But those who spent their working lives within the halls of government and great commercial houses
gradually began to develop a very different perspective, whereby cash
exchange was normal and it was debt that came to be seen as tinged
with criminality.

Each perspective turned on a certain tacit theory of the nature of
society. For most English villagers, the real font and focus of social
and moral life was not so much the church as the local ale-house—and
community was embodied above all in the conviviality of popular festivals like Christmas or May Day, with everything that such celebrations
entailed: the sharing of pleasures, the communion of the senses, all the
physical embodiment of what was called "good neighborhood." Society
was rooted above all in the "love and amity" of friends and kin, and it
found expression in all those forms of everyday communism (helping
neighbors with chores, providing milk or cheese for old widows) that
were seen to flow from it. Markets were not seen as contradicting this
ethos of mutual aid. It was, much as it was for Tusi, an extension of
mutual aid—and for much the same reason: because it operated entirely through trust and credit.[50]

England might not have produced a great theorist like Tusi, but
one can find the same assumptions echoed in most of the Scholastic
writers, as for instance in Jean Bodin's *De Republica*, widely circulated

in English translation after 1605. "Amity and friendship," Bodin wrote, "are the foundation of all human and civil society"—they constitute that "true, natural justice" on which the whole legal structure of contracts, courts, and even government must necessarily be built.[51] Similarly, when economic thinkers reflected on the origins of the money, they spoke of "trusting, exchanging, and trading."[52] It was simply assumed that human relations came first.

As a result, all moral relations came to be conceived as debts. "Forgive us our debts"—this was the period, the very end of the Middle Ages, that this translation of the Lord's Prayer gained such universal popularity. Sins are debts to God: unavoidable, but perhaps manageable, since at the end of time our moral debts and credits will be all canceled out against each other in God's final Reckoning. The notion of debt inserted itself into even the most intimate of human relations. Like the Tiv, medieval villagers would sometimes refer to "flesh debts," but the notion was completely different: it referred to the right of either partner in a marriage to demand sex from the other, which in principle either could do whenever he or she desired. The phrase "paying one's debts" thus developed connotations, much as the Roman phrase "doing one's duty" had, centuries before. Geoffrey Chaucer even makes a pun out of "tally" (French: *taille*) and "tail" in the Shipman's Tale, a story about a woman who pays her husband's debts with sexual favors: "and if so I be faille, I am youre wyf, score it upon my taille."[53]

Even London merchants would occasionally appeal to the language of sociability, insisting that in the final analysis, all trade is built on credit, and credit is really just an extension of mutual aid. In 1696, for instance, Charles Davenant wrote that even if there were a general collapse of confidence in the credit system, it could not last long, because eventually, when people reflected on the matter and realized that credit is simply an extension of human society,

> They will find, that no trading nation ever did subsist, and carry on its business by real stock [that is, just coin and merchandise]; that trust and confidence in each other, are as necessary to link and hold a people together, as obedience, love, friendship, or the intercourse of speech. And when experience has taught man how weak he is, depending only on himself, he will be willing to help others, and call upon the assistance of his neighbors, which of course, by degrees, must set credit again afloat.[54]

Davenant was an unusual merchant (his father was a poet). More typical of his class were men like Thomas Hobbes, whose *Leviathan*, published in 1651, was in many ways an extended attack on the very idea that society is built on any sort of prior ties of communal solidarity.

Hobbes might be considered the opening salvo of the new moral perspective, and it was a devastating one. When *Leviathan* came out, it's not clear what scandalized its readers more: its relentless materialism (Hobbes insisted that humans were basically machines whose actions could be understood by one single principle: that they tended to move toward the prospect of pleasure and away from the prospect of pain), or its resultant cynicism (if love, amity, and trust are such powerful forces, Hobbes asked, why is it that even within our families, we lock our most valuable possessions in strongboxes?) Still, Hobbes' ultimate argument—that humans, being driven by self-interest, cannot be trusted to treat each other justly of their own accord, and therefore that society only emerges when they come to realize that it is to their long-term advantage to give up a portion of their liberties and accept the absolute power of the King—differed little from arguments that theologians like Martin Luther had been making a century earlier. Hobbes simply substituted scientific language for biblical references.[55]

I want to draw particular attention to the underlying notion of "self-interest."[56] It is in a real sense the key to the new philosophy. The term first appears in English right around Hobbes' time, and it is, indeed, directly borrowed from *interesse*, the Roman law term for interest payments. When it was first introduced, most English authors seemed to view the idea that all human life can be explained as the pursuit of self-interest as a cynical, foreign, Machiavellian idea, one that sat uncomfortably with traditional English mores. By the eighteenth century, most in educated society accepted it as simple common sense.

But why "interest"? Why make a general theory of human motivation out of a word that originally meant "penalty for late payment on a loan"?

Part of the term's appeal was that it derived from bookkeeping. It was mathematical. This made it seem objective, even scientific. Saying we are all really pursuing our own self-interest provides a way to cut past the welter of passions and emotions that seem to govern our daily existence, and to motivate most of what we actually observe people to do (not only out of love and amity, but also envy, spite, devotion, pity, lust, embarrassment, torpor, indignation, and pride) and discover that, despite all this, most really important decisions are based on the rational calculation of material advantage—which means that they are fairly predictable as well. "Just as the physical world is ruled by the laws of movement," wrote Helvétius, in a passage reminiscent of Lord Shang, "no less is the moral universe ruled by laws of interest."[57] And, of course, it was on this assumption that all the quadratic equations of economic theory could ultimately be built.[58]

The problem is that the origin of the concept is not rational at all. Its roots are theological, and the theological assumptions underpinning it never really went away. "Self-interest" is first attested to in the writings of the Italian historian Francesco Guicciadini (who was, in fact, a friend of Machiavelli), around 1510, as a euphemism for St. Augustine's concept of "self-love." For Augustine, the "love of God" leads us to benevolence toward our fellows; self-love, in contrast, refers to the fact that, since the Fall of Man, we are cursed by endless, insatiable desires for self-gratification—so much so that, if left to our own devices, we will necessarily fall into universal competition, even war. Substituting "interest" for "love" must have seemed an obvious move, since the assumption that love is the primary emotion was precisely what authors like Guicciadini were trying to get away from. But it kept that same assumption of insatiable desires under the guise of impersonal math, since what is "interest" but the demand that money *never cease* to grow? The same was true when it became the term for investments— "I have a twelve-percent interest in that venture"—it is money placed in the continual pursuit of profit.[59] The very idea that human beings are motivated primarily by "self-interest," then, was rooted in the profoundly Christian assumption that we are all incorrigible sinners; left to our own devices, we will not simply pursue a certain level of comfort and happiness and then stop to enjoy it; we will never cash in the chips, like Sindbad, let alone question why we need to buy chips to begin with. And as Augustine already anticipated, infinite desires in a finite world means endless competition, which in turn is why, as Hobbes insisted, our only hope of social peace lies in contractual arrangements and strict enforcement by the apparatus of the state.

■ ■ ■ ■ ■

The story of the origins of capitalism, then, is not the story of the gradual destruction of traditional communities by the impersonal power of the market. It is, rather, the story of how an economy of credit was converted into an economy of interest; of the gradual transformation of moral networks by the intrusion of the impersonal—and often vindictive—power of the state. English villagers in Elizabethan or Stuart times did not like to appeal to the justice system, even when the law was in their favor—partly on the principle that neighbors should work things out with one another, but mainly, because the law was so extraordinarily harsh. Under Elizabeth, for example, the punishment for vagrancy (unemployment) was, for first offense, to have one's ears nailed to a pillory; for repeat offenders, death.[60]

The same was true of debt law, especially since debts could often, if the creditor was sufficiently vindictive, be treated as a crime. In Chelsea around 1660,

> Margaret Sharples was prosecuted for stealing cloth, "which she had converted into a petticoat for her own wearing," from Richard Bennett's shop. Her defense was that she had bargained with Bennett's servant for the cloth, "but having not money sufficient in her purse to pay for it, took it away with purpose to pay for it so soon as she could: and that she afterwards agreed with Mr Bennett of a price for it." Bennett confirmed that this was so: after agreeing to pay him 22 shillings, Margaret "delivered a hamper with goods in it as a pawn for security of the money, and four shillings ninepence in money." But "soon after he disliked upon better consideration to hold agreement with her: and delivered the hamper and goods back," and commenced formal legal proceedings against her.[61]

As a result, Margaret Sharples was hanged.

Obviously, it was the rare shopkeeper who wished to see even his most irritating client on the gallows. As a result, decent people tended to avoid the courts entirely. One of the most interesting discoveries of Craig Muldrew's research is that the more time passed, the less true this became.

Even in the late Middle Ages, in the case of really large loans, it was not unusual for creditors to lodge claims in local courts—but this was really just a way of ensuring that there was a public record (remember that most people at the time were illiterate). Debtors were willing to go along with the proceedings in part, it would seem, because if there was any interest being charged, it meant that if they did default, the lender was just as guilty in the eyes of the law as they were. Less than one percent of these cases were ever brought to judgment.[62] The legalization of interest began to change the nature of the playing field. In the 1580s, when interest-bearing loans began to become common between villagers, creditors also began to insist on the use of signed, legal bonds; this led to such an explosion of appeals to the courts that in many small towns, almost every household seemed to be caught up in debt litigation of some sort or other. Only a tiny proportion of these suits were ever brought to judgment, either: the usual expedient was still to rely on the threat of punishment to encourage debtors to settle out of court.[63] Still, as a result, the fear of debtor's prison—or worse—came to hang over everyone, and sociability itself came to take on the color of crime. Even Mr. Coward, the kindly shopkeeper, was eventually laid low. His good credit itself became a problem, especially as he felt honor-bound to use it to help the less fortunate:

> He also dealt in merchandise with loose partners, and became concerned much with persons of declining circumstances, where neither profit nor credit could be got; and he gave uneasiness to his wife, by his frequenting some houses of no good character. And she was a very indolent woman, and drew money privately from him, and his circumstances became so burdensome that he daily expected to be made a prisoner. Which, with the shame of forfeiting his former reputation, it drew him into despair and broke his heart, so that he kept to his house for some time and died of grief and shame.[64]

It is perhaps not surprising, when one consults contemporary sources about what those prisons were like, particularly for those who were not of aristocratic origins. Mr. Coward would surely have known, as the conditions at the most notorious, like Fleet and Marshalsea, caused periodic scandals when exposed in parliament or the popular press, filling the papers with stories of shackled debtors "covered with filth and vermin, and suffered to die, without pity, of hunger and jail fever," as the aristocratic roués placed in the elite side of the same jails lived lives of comfort, visited by manicurists and prostitutes.[65]

The criminalization of debt, then, was the criminalization of the very basis of human society. It cannot be overemphasized that in a small community, everyone normally was both lender and borrower. One can only imagine the tensions and temptations that must have existed in communities—and communities, much though they are based on love, in fact, *because* they are based on love, will always also be full of hatred, rivalry, and passion—when it became clear that with sufficiently clever scheming, manipulation, and perhaps a bit of strategic bribery, they could arrange to have almost anyone they hated imprisoned or even hanged. What was it that Richard Bennett really had against Margaret Sharples? We'll never know the backstory, but it's a pretty safe bet there was one. The effects on communal solidarity must have been devastating. The sudden accessibility of violence really did threaten to transform what had been the essence of sociality into a war of all against all.[66] It's not surprising, then, that by the eighteenth century, the very notion of personal credit had acquired a bad name, with both lenders and borrowers considered equally suspect.[67] The use of coins—at least among those who had access to them—had come to seem moral in itself.

■ ■ ■ ■ ■

Understanding all this allows us to see some of the European authors considered in earlier chapters in an entirely new light. Take Panurge's encomium on debt: it turns out that the real joke is not the suggestion that debt ties communities together (any English or French peasant of the day would have simply assumed this), or even that *only* debt ties communities together; it is putting the sentiment in the mouth of a wealthy scholar who's really an inveterate criminal—that is, holding up popular morality as a mirror to make fun of the very upper classes who claimed to disapprove of it.

Or consider Adam Smith:

> It is not from the benevolence of the butcher, the brewer, or the baker, that we expect our dinner, but from their regard to their own interest. We address ourselves, not to their humanity but to their self-love, and never talk to them of our own necessities but of their advantages.[68]

The bizarre thing here is that, at the time Smith was writing, this simply wasn't true.[69] Most English shopkeepers were still carrying out the main part of their business on credit, which meant that customers appealed to their benevolence all the time. Smith could hardly have been unaware of this. Rather, he is drawing a utopian picture. He wants to imagine a world in which everyone used cash, in part because he agreed with the emerging middle-class consensus that the world would be a better place if everyone really did conduct themselves this way, and avoid confusing and potentially corrupting ongoing entanglements. We should all just pay the money, say "please" and "thank you," and leave the store. What's more, he uses this utopian image to make a larger point: that even if all businesses operated like the great commercial companies, with an eye only to self-interest, it wouldn't matter. Even the "natural selfishness and rapacity" of the rich, with all their "vain and insatiable desires" will still, through the logic of the invisible hand, lead to the benefit of all.[70]

In other words, Smith simply imagined away the role of consumer credit in his own day, just as he had his account of the origins of money.[71] This allowed him to ignore the role of both benevolence *and* malevolence in economic affairs, both the ethos of mutual aid that forms the necessary foundation of anything that would look like a free market (that is, one which is not simply created and maintained by the state), *and* the violence and sheer vindictiveness that had actually gone into creating the competitive, self-interested markets that he was using as his model.

Nietzsche, in turn, was taking up Smith's premises, that life is exchange, but laying bare everything (the torture, murder, mutilation) that Smith preferred not to have to talk about. Now that we have seen just a little of the social context, it's difficult to read Nietzsche's otherwise puzzling descriptions of ancient hunters and herdsmen keeping accounts of debts and demanding each others' eyes and fingers without immediately thinking of Casimir's executioner, who actually did present his master with a bill for gouged eyes and severed fingers. What he is really describing is what it took to produce a world in which the son of a prosperous middle-class reverend, such as himself, could simply assume that all human life is premised on calculated, self-interested exchange.

Part III:

Impersonal Credit-money

One reason that historians took so long to notice the elaborate popular-credit systems of Tudor and Stuart England is that when intellectuals of the time spoke about money in the abstract, they rarely mentioned them. For the educated classes, "money" soon came to mean gold and silver. Most wrote as if it could be taken for granted that gold and silver had always been used as money for all nations in history and, presumably, always would be.

This not only flew in the face of Aristotle; it directly contradicted the discoveries of European explorers of the time, who were finding shell money, bead money, feather money, salt money, and an endless variety of other currencies everywhere they went.[72] Yet all this just caused economic thinkers to dig in their heels. Some appealed to alchemy to argue that the monetary status of gold and silver had a natural basis: gold (which partook of the sun) and silver (which partook of the moon) were the perfected, eternal forms of metal toward which all baser metals tend to evolve.[73] Most, however, didn't feel that much explanation was required; the intrinsic value of precious metals was simply self-evident. As a result, when royal advisors or London pamphleteers discussed economic problems, the issues they debated were always the same: How do we keep bullion from leaving the country? What do we do about the crippling shortage of coin? For most, questions like, "How do we maintain trust in local credit systems?" simply did not arise.

This was even more extreme in Britain than on the Continent, where "crying up" or "crying down" the currency was still an option. In Britain, after a disastrous attempt at devaluation under the Tudors, such expedients were abandoned. Henceforth, debasement became a moral issue. For the government to mix base metal into the pure eternal substance of a coin was clearly wrong. So, to a lesser extent, was coin-clipping, a near-universal practice in England, which might be thought of as a kind of popular version of devaluation, since it involved secretly shaving silver off the edges of coins and then pressing them down so they seemed like they were still the original size.

What's more, those new forms of virtual money that began to emerge in the new age were firmly rooted in these same assumptions. This is critical, because it helps explain what might otherwise seem a bizarre contradiction: How is it that this age of ruthless materialism, in which the notion that money was a social convention was definitively rejected, also saw the rise of paper money, along with a whole host of new credit instruments and forms of financial abstraction that have become so typical of modern capitalism? True, most of these—checks, bonds, stocks, annuities—had their origins in the metaphysical world of the Middle Ages. Yet, in this new age, they underwent an enormous efflorescence.

If one looks at the actual history, though, it quickly becomes clear that all of these new forms of money in no way undermined the assumption that money was founded on the "intrinsic" value of gold and silver: in fact, they reinforced it. What seems to have happened is that, once credit became unlatched from real relations of trust between individuals (whether merchants or villagers), it became apparent that money could, in effect, be produced simply by saying it was there; but that, when this is done in the amoral world of a competitive marketplace, it would almost inevitably lead to scams and confidence games of every sort—causing the guardians of the system to periodically panic and seek new ways to latch the value of the various forms of paper back onto gold and silver.

This is the story normally told as "the origins of modern banking." From our perspective, though, what it reveals is just how closely
bound together war, bullion, and these new credit instruments were.
One need only consider the paths *not* traveled. For instance, there was
no intrinsic reason why a bill of exchange couldn't be endorsed over
to a third party, then become generally transferable—thus, in effect,
turning it into a form of paper money. This is how paper money first
emerged in China. In medieval Europe, there were periodic movements
in that direction, but for a variety of reasons, they did not go far.[74] Alternately, bankers can produce money by issuing book credits for more
than they have on cash reserve. This is considered the very essence of
modern banking, and it can lead to the circulation of private bank
notes.[75] Some moves were made in this direction as well, especially in
Italy, but it was a risky proposition, since there was always the danger
of depositors panicking and making a run, and most medieval governments threatened extremely harsh penalties on bankers unable to make
restitution in such cases: as witnessed by the example of Francesch
Castello, beheaded in front of his own bank in Barcelona in 1360.[76]

Where bankers effectively controlled medieval governments, it
proved safer and more profitable to manipulate the government's own
finances. The history of modern financial instruments, and the ultimate
origins of paper money, really begin with the issuing of municipal
bonds—a practice begun by the Venetian government in the twelfth
century when, needing a quick infusion of income for military purposes, it levied a compulsory loan on its taxpaying citizens, for which
it promised each of them five percent annual interest, and allowed the
"bonds" or contracts to become negotiable, thus creating a market in
government debt. The Venetians tended to be quite meticulous about
interest payments, but since the bonds had no specific date of maturity,
their market prices often fluctuated wildly with the city's political and
military fortunes, and so did resulting assessments of the likelihood
that they would be able to be repaid. Similar practices quickly spread
to the other Italian states and to northern European merchant enclaves
as well: the United Provinces of Holland financed their long war of independence against the Hapsburgs (1568–1648) largely through a series
of forced loans, though they floated numerous voluntary bond issues
as well.[77]

Forcing taxpayers to make a loan is, in one sense, simply demanding that they pay their taxes early; but when the Venetian state first
agreed to pay interest—and in legal terms, this was again *interesse*, a
penalty for late payment—it was in principle penalizing itself for not
immediately giving the money back. It's easy to see how this might

raise all sorts of questions about the legal and moral relation between people and government. Ultimately, the commercial classes in the mercantile republics that pioneered these new forms of financing did end up seeing themselves as owning the government more than they saw themselves as being in its debt. Not only the commercial classes: by 1650, a majority of Dutch households held at least a little government debt.[78] However, the true paradox only appears when one begins to "monetize" this debt—that is, to take government promises to pay and allow them to circulate as currency.

While already by the sixteenth century, merchants were using bills of exchange to settle debts, government debt bonds—*rentes*, *juros*, annuities—were the real credit money of the new age. It's here that we have to look for the real origins of the "price revolution" that hammered once-independent townsfolk and villagers into the ground and opened the way for most of them to ultimately be reduced to wage laborers, working for those who had access to these higher forms of credit. Even in Seville, where the treasure fleets from the New World first touched port in the Old, bullion was not much used in day-to-day transactions. Most of it was taken directly to the warehouses of Genoese bankers operating from the port and stored for shipment east. But, in the process, it became the basis for complex credit schemes whereby the value of the bullion was loaned to the emperor to fund military operations in exchange for papers entitling the bearer to interest-bearing annuities from the government—papers that could in turn be traded as if they were money. By such means, bankers could almost endlessly multiply the actual value of gold and silver they held. Already in the 1570s, we hear of fairs in places like Medina del Campo, not far from Seville, that had become "veritable factories of certificates," with transactions carried out exclusively through paper.[79] Since whether the Spanish government would actually pay their debts, or how regularly, was always slightly uncertain, the bills would tend to circulate at a discount—especially as *juros* began circulating throughout the rest of Europe—causing continual inflation.[80]

It was only with the creation of the Bank of England in 1694 that one can speak of genuine paper money, since its banknotes were in no sense bonds. They were rooted, like all the others, in the king's war debts. This can't be emphasized enough. The fact that money was no longer a debt owed *to* the king, but a debt owed *by* the king, made it very different than what it had been before. In many ways, it had become a mirror image of older forms of money.

The reader will recall that the Bank of England was created when a consortium of forty London and Edinburgh merchants—mostly already creditors to the crown—offered King William III a £1.2 million loan to help finance his war against France. In doing so, they also convinced him to allow them in return to form a corporation with a monopoly on the issuance of banknotes—which were, in effect, promissory notes for the money the king now owed them. This was the first independent national central bank, and it became the clearinghouse for debts owed between smaller banks; the notes soon developed into the first European national paper currency. Yet the great public debate of the time, a debate about the very nature of money, was about not paper but metal. The 1690s were a time of crisis for British coinage. The value of silver had risen so high that new British coins (the mint had recently developed the "milled edge" familiar from coins nowadays, which made them clip-proof) were actually worth less than their silver content, with predictable results. Proper silver coins vanished; all that remained in circulation were the old clipped ones, and these were becoming increasingly scarce. Something had to be done. A war of pamphlets ensued, which came to a head in 1695, one year after the founding of the bank. Charles Davenant's essay on credit, which I've already cited, was actually part of this particular pamphlet-war: he proposed that Britain move to a pure credit money based on public trust, and he was ignored. The Treasury proposed to call in the coinage and reissue it at a 20- to 25-percent lower weight, so as to bring it back below the market price for silver. Many who supported this position took explicitly Chartalist positions, insisting that silver has no intrinsic value anyway, and that money is simply a measure established by the state.[81] The man who won the argument, however, was John Locke, the Liberal philosopher, at that time acting as advisor to Sir Isaac Newton, then Warden of the Mint. Locke insisted that one can no more make a small piece of silver worth more by relabeling it a "shilling" than one can make a short man taller by declaring there are now fifteen inches in a foot. Gold and silver had a value recognized by everyone on earth; the government stamp simply attested to the weight and purity of a coin, and—as he added in words veritably shivering with indignation—for governments to tamper with this for their own advantage was just as criminal as the coin-clippers themselves:

> The use and end of the public stamp is only to be a guard and voucher of the quality of silver which men contract for; and the injury done to the public *faith*, in this point, is that which in clipping and false coining heightens the *robbery* into *treason*.[82]

Therefore, he argued, the only recourse was to recall the currency and restrike it at exactly the same value that it had before.

This was done, and the results were disastrous. In the years immediately following, there was almost no coinage in circulation; prices and wages collapsed; there was hunger and unrest. Only the wealthy were insulated, since they were able to take advantage of the new credit money, trading back and forth portions of the king's debt in the form of banknotes. The value of these notes, too, fluctuated a bit at first, but eventually stabilized once they were made redeemable in precious metals. For the rest, the situation only really improved once paper money, and, eventually, smaller-denomination currency, became more widely available. The reforms proceeded top-down, and very slowly, but they did proceed, and they gradually came to create the world where even ordinary, everyday transactions with butchers and bakers were carried out in polite, impersonal terms, with small change, and therefore it became possible to imagine everyday life itself as a matter of self-interested calculation.

It's easy enough to see why Locke would adopt the position that he did. He was a scientific materialist. For him, "faith" in government—as in the quote above—was not the citizens' belief that the government will keep its promises, but simply that it won't lie to them; that it would, like a good scientist, provide accurate information. Locke wanted to see human behavior as founded in natural laws that—like the laws of physics that Newton had so recently described—were higher than those of any mere government. The real question is why the British government agreed with him and resolutely stuck to this position despite all the immediate disasters. Soon afterward, in fact, Britain adopted the gold standard (in 1717) and the British Empire maintained it, and with it the notion that gold and silver *were* money, down to its final days.

True, Locke's materialism also came to be broadly accepted—even to be the watchword of the age.[83] Mainly, though, the reliance on gold and silver seemed to provide the only check on the dangers involved with the new forms of credit-money, which multiplied very quickly—especially once ordinary banks were allowed to create money too. It soon became apparent that financial speculation, unmoored from any legal or community constraints, was capable of producing results that seemed to verge on insanity. The Dutch Republic, which pioneered the development of stock markets, had already experienced this in the tulip mania of 1637—the first of a series of speculative "bubbles," as they came to be known, in which future prices would first be bid through the ceiling by investors and then collapse. A whole series of such bubbles hit the London markets in the 1690s, in almost every case built around a new joint-stock corporation formed, in imitation of the East India Company, around some prospective colonial venture. The famous South Sea Bubble in 1720—in which a newly formed trading company, granted a monopoly of trade with the Spanish colonies, bought up a considerable portion of the British national debt and saw its shares briefly skyrocket before collapsing in ignominy—was only the culmination. Its collapse was followed the next year by the collapse of John Law's famous Banque Royale in France, another central-bank experiment—similar to the Bank of England—that grew so quickly that within a few years it had absorbed all the French colonial trading companies, and most of the French crown's own debt, issuing its own paper money, before crashing into nothingness in 1721, sending its chief executive fleeing for his life. In each case, this was followed by legislation: in Britain, to forbid the creation of new joint-stock companies (other than for the building of turnpikes and canals), and in France, to eliminate paper money based in government debt entirely.

It's unsurprising, then, that Newtonian economics (if we may call it that)—the assumption that one cannot simply create money, or even, really, tinker with it—came to be accepted by almost everyone. Everyone concluded there had to be some solid, material foundation to all this, or the entire system would go insane. True, economists were to spend centuries arguing about what that foundation might be (was it really gold, or was it land, human labor, the utility or desirability of commodities in general?) but almost no one returned to anything like the Aristotelian view.

■ ■ ■ ■ ■

Another way to look at this might be to say that the new age came to be increasingly uncomfortable with the political nature of money. Politics, after all, is the art of persuasion; the political is that dimension of social life in which things really do become true if enough people believe them. The problem is that in order to play the game effectively, one can never acknowledge this: it may be true that, if I could convince everyone in the world that I was the King of France, I would in fact become the King of France; but it would never work if I were to admit that this was the only basis of my claim. In this sense, politics is very similar to magic—one reason both politics and magic tend, just about everywhere, to be surrounded by a certain halo of fraud. These suspicions were widely vaunted at the time. In 1711, the satirical essayist Joseph Addison penned a little fantasy about the Bank of England's—and as a result, the British monetary system's—dependence on public faith in the political stability of the throne. (The Act of Settlement of 1701 was the bill that guaranteed the royal succession, and a sponge was a popular symbol for default.) In a dream, he said,

> I saw Public Credit, set on her throne in the Grocer's Hall, the Great Charter over her head, the Act of Settlement full in her view. Her touch turned everything to gold. Behind her seat, bags filled with coin were piled up to the ceiling. On her right the door flies open. The Pretender rushes in, a sponge in one hand, and in the other a sword, which he shakes at the Act of Settlement. The beautiful Queen sinks down fainting. The spell by which she has turned all things around her into treasure is broken. The money bags shrink like pricked bladders. The piles of gold pieces are turned into bundles of rags or faggots of wooden tallies.[84]

If one does not believe in the king, then the money vanishes with him.

Thus kings, magicians, markets, and alchemists all fuse in the public imagination during this era, and so do we still talk about the "alchemy" of the market, or "financial magicians." In Goethe's *Faust* (1808), he actually has his hero—in his capacity as alchemist-magician—pay a visit to the Holy Roman Emperor. The Emperor is sinking under the weight of endless debts that he has piled up paying for the extravagant pleasures of his court. Faust and his assistant, Mephistopheles, convince him that he can pay off his creditors by creating paper money. It's represented as an act of pure prestidigitation. "You have plenty of gold lying somewhere underneath your lands," notes Faust. "Just issue notes promising your creditors you'll give it to them later. Since no one knows how much gold there really is, there's no limit to how much you can promise."[85]

Such magical language is almost unheard of in the Middle Ages.[86] It would appear that it's only in a resolutely materialist age that the ability to simply produce things by saying that they are there comes to be seen as scandalous, even diabolical. And the surest sign that one has entered such a materialist age is precisely the fact that it is seen so. We have already observed Rabelais, at the very beginning of the age, reverting to language almost identical to that used by Plutarch when he railed against moneylenders in Roman times—"laughing at those natural philosophers who hold that nothing can be made of nothing," as they manipulate their books and ledgers to demand back money they never actually had. Panurge just turned it around: no, it's by borrowing that I make something out of nothing and become a kind of god.

But consider the following lines, often attributed to Lord Josiah Charles Stamp, director of the Bank of England:

> The modern banking system manufactures money out of nothing. The process is perhaps the most astounding piece of sleight of hand that was ever invented. Banking was conceived in iniquity and born in sin. Bankers own the earth; take it away from them, but leave them with the power to create credit, and with the stroke of a pen they will create enough money to buy it back again . . . If you wish to remain slaves of Bankers, and pay the cost of your own slavery, let them continue to create deposits.[87]

Now, it seems extremely unlikely that Lord Stamp ever really said this, but the passage has been cited endlessly—in fact, it's probably the single most often-quoted passage by critics of the modern banking system. However apocryphal, it clearly strikes a chord, and apparently for the same reason: bankers are creating something out of nothing. They are not only frauds and magicians. They are evil, because they're playing God.

But there's a deeper scandal than mere prestidigitation. If medieval moralists did not raise such objections, it was not just because they were comfortable with metaphysical entities. They had a much more fundamental problem with the market: greed. Market motives were held to be inherently corrupt. The moment that greed was validated and unlimited profit was considered a perfectly viable end in itself, this political, magical element became a genuine problem, because it meant that even those actors—the brokers, stock-jobbers, traders—who effectively made the system run had no convincing loyalty to anything, even to the system itself.

Hobbes, who first developed this vision of human nature into an explicit theory of society, was well aware of this greed dilemma. It formed the basis of his political philosophy. Even, he argued, if we are all rational enough to understand that it's in our long-term interest to live in peace and security, our short-term interests are often such that killing and plundering are the most obviously profitable courses to take, and all it takes is a few to cast aside their scruples to create utter insecurity and chaos. This was why he felt that markets could only exist under the aegis of an absolutist state, which would force us to keep our promises and respect one another's property. But what happens when we're talking about a market in which it is state debts and state obligations themselves that are being traded; and where one cannot really speak of a state monopoly on force because one is operating in an international market where the primary currency is bonds that the state depends on for its very ability to marshal military force?

Having made incessant war on all remaining forms of the communism of the poor, even to the point of criminalizing credit, the masters of the new market system discovered that they had no obvious justification left to maintain even the communism of the rich—that level of cooperation and solidarity required to keep the economic system running. True, for all its endless strains and periodic breakdowns, the system has held out so far. But as 2008 dramatically testified, it has never been resolved.

Part IV:

So What Is Capitalism, Anyway?

We are used to seeing modern capitalism (along with modern traditions of democratic government) as emerging only later: with the Age of Revolutions—the industrial revolution, the American and French revolutions—a series of profound breaks at the end of the eighteenth century that only became fully institutionalized after the end of the Napoleonic Wars. Here we come face to face with a peculiar paradox. It would seem that almost all elements of financial apparatus that we've come to associate with capitalism—central banks, bond markets, short-selling, brokerage houses, speculative bubbles, securization, annuities—came into being not only before the science of economics (which is perhaps not too surprising), but also before the rise of factories, and wage labor itself.[88] This is a genuine challenge to familiar ways of thinking. We like to think of the factories and workshops as the "real economy," and the rest as superstructure, constructed on top of it. But if this were really so, then how can it be that the superstructure came first? Can the dreams of the system create its body?

All this raises the question of what "capitalism" is to begin with, a question on which there is no consensus at all. The word was originally invented by socialists, who saw capitalism as that system whereby those who own capital command the labor of those who do not. Proponents, in contrast, tend to see capitalism as the freedom of the marketplace, which allows those with potentially marketable visions to pull resources together to bring those visions into being. Just about everyone agrees, however, that capitalism is a system that demands constant, endless growth. Enterprises have to grow in order to remain viable. The same is true of nations. Just as five percent per annum was widely accepted, at the dawn of capitalism, as the legitimate commercial rate of interest—that is, the amount that any investor could normally expect her money to be growing by the principle of *interesse*—so is five percent now the annual rate at which any nation's GDP really ought to grow. What was once an impersonal mechanism that compelled people to look at everything around them as a potential source of profit has come to be considered the only objective measure of the health of the human community itself.

Starting from our baseline date of 1700, then, what we see at the dawn of modern capitalism is a gigantic financial apparatus of credit and debt that operates—in practical effect—to pump more and more labor out of just about everyone with whom it comes into contact, and as a result produces an endlessly expanding volume of material goods. It does so not just by moral compulsion, but above all by using moral compulsion to mobilize physical force. At every point, the familiar but peculiarly European entanglement of war and commerce reappears—often in startling new forms. The first stock markets in Holland and Britain were based mainly in trading shares of the East and West India companies, which were both military and trading ventures. For a century, one such private, profit-seeking corporation governed India. The national debts of England, France, and the others were based in money borrowed not to dig canals and erect bridges, but to acquire the gunpowder needed to bombard cities and to construct the camps required for the holding of prisoners and the training of recruits. Almost all the bubbles of the eighteenth century involved some fantastic scheme to use the proceeds of colonial ventures to pay for European wars. Paper money was debt money, and debt money was war money, and this has always remained the case. Those who financed Europe's endless military conflicts also employed the government's police and prisons to extract ever-increasing productivity from the rest of the population.

As everybody knows, the world market system initiated by the Spaniards and Portuguese empires first arose in the search for spices. It soon settled into three broad trades, which might be labeled the arms trade, the slave trade, and the drug trade. The last refers mostly to soft drugs, of course, like coffee, tea, and the sugar to put in them, and tobacco, but distilled liquor first appears at this stage of human history as well, and as we all know, Europeans had no compunctions about aggressively marketing opium in China as a way of finally putting an end to the need to export bullion. The cloth trade only came later, after the East India Company used military force to shut down the (more efficient) Indian cotton export trade. One need only take a glance at the book that preserves Charles Davenant's 1696 essay on credit and human fellowship: *The political and commercial works of that celebrated writer Charles D'Avenant: relating to the trade and revenue of England, the Plantation trade, the East-India trade and African trade.* "Obedience, love, and friendship" might suffice to govern relations between fellow Englishmen, then, but in the colonies, it was mainly just obedience.

As I've described, the Atlantic slave trade can be imagined as a giant chain of debt-obligations, stretching from Bristol to Calabar to the headwaters of the Cross River, where the Aro traders sponsored their secret societies; just as in the Indian Ocean trade, similar chains connected Utrecht to Capetown to Jakarta to the Kingdom of Gelgel, where Balinese kings arranged their cockfights to lure subjects to gamble their freedom away. In either case, the end product was the same: human beings so entirely ripped from their contexts, and hence so thoroughly dehumanized, that they were placed outside the realm of debt entirely.

The middlemen in these chains, the various commercial links of the debt chain that connected the stock-jobbers in London with the Aro priests in Nigeria, pearl divers in the Aru islands of Eastern Indonesia, owners of Bengali tea plantations, or Amazonian rubber-tappers, largely give the impression of having been sober, calculating, unimaginative men. At either end of the debt chain, the whole enterprise seemed to turn on the ability to manipulate fantasies, and to run a constant peril of slipping into what even contemporary observers considered varieties of phantasmagoric madness. On the one end were the periodic bubbles, propelled in part by rumor and fantasy and in part by the fact that just about everyone in cities like Paris and London with any disposable cash would suddenly become convinced that they would somehow be able to profit from the fact that everyone else was succumbing to rumor and fantasy.

Charles MacKay has left us some immortal descriptions of the first of these, the famous "South Sea Bubble" of 1710. Actually, the South Sea Company itself (which grew so large that at one point it bought up most of the national debt) was just the anchor for what happened, a giant corporation, its stock constantly ballooning in value, that seemed, to put it in contemporary terms, "too big to fail." It soon became the model for hundreds of new start-up offerings:

> Innumerable joint-stock companies started up everywhere.
> They soon received the name Bubbles, the most appropriate

imagination could devise . . . Some of them lasted a week or a fortnight, and were no more heard of, while others could not even live out that span of existence. Every evening produced new schemes, and every morning new projects. The highest of the aristocracy were as eager in this hot pursuit of gain as the most plodding jobber in Cornhill.[89]

The author lists, as arbitrary examples, eighty-six schemes, ranging from the manufacture of soap or sailcloth, the provision of insurance for horses, to a method to "make deal-boards out of sawdust." Each issued stock; each issue would appear, then be scooped up and avidly traded back and forth in taverns, coffee-houses, alleys, and haberdasheries across the city. In every case, their price was quickly bid through the ceiling—each new buyer betting, effectively, that he or she could unload them on some even more gullible sucker before the inevitable collapse. Sometimes people bid on cards and coupons that would allow them no more than the right to bid on other shares later. Thousands grew rich. Thousands more were ruined.

> The most absurd and preposterous of all, and which shewed, more completely than any other, the utter madness of the people, was one started by an unknown adventurer, entitled "*A company for the carrying on of an undertaking of great advantage, but nobody to know what it is.*"
>
> The man of genius who essayed this bold and successful inroad upon public credulity merely stated in his prospectus that the required capital was half a million, in five thousand shares of 100l. each, deposit 2l. per share. Each subscriber, paying his deposit, would be entitled to 100l. per annum per share. How this immense profit was to be obtained, he would not condescend to inform them at that time, but promised that in a month the full particulars would be duly announced, and call made for the remaining 98l. of the subscription. Next morning, at nine o'clock, this great man opened an office in Cornhill. Crowds beset his door, and when he shut up at three o'clock, he found that no less than one thousand shares had been subscribed for, and the deposits paid.
>
> He was philosopher enough to be contented with his venture, and set off that same evening for the Continent. He was never heard of again.[90]

If one is to believe MacKay, the entire population of London conceived the simultaneous delusion, not that money could really be manufactured out of nothing, but that other people were foolish enough to believe that it could—and that, for that very reason, they actually could make money out of nothing after all.

Moving to the other side of the debt chain, we find fantasies ranging from the charming to the apocalyptic. In the anthropological literature, we encounter everything from the beautiful "sea wives" of Aru pearl divers, who will not yield up the treasures of the ocean unless courted with gifts bought on credit from local Chinese shops,[91] to the secret markets where Bengali landlords purchase ghosts to terrorize insubordinate debt peons; to Tiv flesh-debts, a fantasy of human society cannibalizing itself; to finally, occasions at which the Tiv nightmare appears to have very nearly become true.[92] One of the most famous and disturbing was the great Putumayo scandal of 1909–1911, in which the London reading public was shocked to discover that the agents of the subsidiary of a British rubber company operating in the Peruvian rainforest had created their very own Heart of Darkness, exterminating tens of thousands of Huitoto Indians—who the agents insisted on referring to only as "cannibals"—in scenes of rape, torture, and mutilation that recalled the very worst of the conquest four hundred years earlier.[93]

In the debates that followed, the first impulse was to blame everything on a system whereby the Indians were said to have been caught in a debt trap, made completely dependent on the company store:

> The root of the whole evil was the so called *patron* or "peonage" system—a variety of what used to be called in England the "truck system"—by which the employee, forced to buy all his supplies at the employer's store, is kept hopelessly in debt, while by law he is unable to leave his employment until his debt is paid . . . The *peon* is thus, as often as not, a *de facto* slave; and since in the remoter regions of the vast continent there is no effective government, he is wholly at the mercy of his master.[94]

The "cannibals," who ended up flogged to death, crucified, tied up and used for target practice, or hacked to pieces with machetes for failure to bring in sufficient quantities of rubber, had, the story went, fallen into the ultimate debt trap; seduced by the wares of the company's agents, they'd ended up bartering away their very lives.

A later Parliamentary inquiry discovered that the real story was entirely different. The Huitoto had not been tricked into becoming debt peons at all. It was the agents and overseers sent into the region who were, much like the conquistadors, deeply indebted—in their case, to the Peruvian company that had commissioned them, which was ultimately receiving its own credit from London financiers. These agents had certainly arrived with every intention of extending that web of credit to include the Indians, but discovering the Huitoto to have no interest in the cloth, machetes, and coins they had brought to trade with them, they'd finally given up and just started rounding Indians up and forcing them to accept loans at gunpoint, then tabulating the amount of rubber they owed.[95] Many of the Indians massacred, in turn, had simply been trying to do what any reasonable person would do under the circumstances: which was to run away.

In reality, then, the Indians had been reduced to slavery; it's just that, by 1907, no one could openly admit this. A legitimate enterprise had to have some moral basis, and the only morality the company knew was debt. When it became clear that the Huitoto rejected the premise, everything went haywire, and the company ended up, like Casimir, caught in a spiral of indignant terror that ultimately threatened to wipe out its very economic basis.

■ ■ ■ ■ ■

It is the secret scandal of capitalism that at no point has it been organized primarily around free labor.[96] The conquest of the Americas began with mass enslavement, then gradually settled into various forms of debt peonage, African slavery, and "indentured service"—that is, the use of contract labor, workers who had received cash in advance and were thus bound for five-, seven-, or ten-year terms to pay it back. Needless to say, indentured servants were recruited largely from among people who were already debtors. In the 1600s, there were at times almost as many white debtors as African slaves working in southern plantations, and legally they were at first in almost the same situation, since, in the beginning, plantation societies were working within a European legal tradition that assumed slavery did not exist. Even Africans in the Carolinas were first classified as contract laborers.[97] Of course, this later changed when the idea of "race" was introduced. When African slaves were freed, they were replaced, on plantations from Barbados to Mauritius, with contract laborers again: though now ones recruited mainly in India or China. Chinese contract laborers built the North American railroad system, and Indian "coolies" built the South African mines. The peasants of Russia and Poland, who had been free landholders in the Middle Ages, were only made serfs at the dawn of capitalism, when their lords began to sell grain on the world market to feed the new industrial cities to the west.[98] Colonial regimes in Africa and Southeast Asia regularly demanded forced labor from their conquered subjects, or, alternately, created tax systems designed to force the population into the labor market through debt. British overlords in India, starting with the East India Company but continuing under Her Majesty's government, institutionalized debt peonage as their primary means of creating products for sale abroad.

This is a scandal not just because the system occasionally goes haywire, as it did in the Putumayo, but because it plays havoc with our most cherished assumptions about what capitalism really is— particularly that, in its basic nature, capitalism has something to do with freedom. For the capitalists, this means the freedom of the marketplace. For most workers, it means free labor. Marxists have questioned whether wage labor is ultimately free in any sense (since someone with nothing to sell but his or her body cannot in any sense be considered a genuinely free agent), but they still tend to assume that free wage labor is the basis of capitalism. Our dominant image of the origins of capitalism continues to be the English workingman toiling in the factories of the industrial revolution, and it is assumed this image can be traced forward to Silicon Valley, with a straight line in between. All those millions of slaves and serfs and coolies and debt peons disappear, or if we must speak of them, we write them off as temporary bumps along the road. Like sweatshops, they are assumed to represent a stage that industrializing nations had to pass through, just as it is still assumed that all those millions of debt peons and contract laborers and sweatshop workers who still exist, often in the same places, will surely live to see their children become regular wage laborers with health insurance and pensions, and *their* children, doctors and lawyers and entrepreneurs.

When one looks at the actual history of wage labor, even in countries like England, that picture begins to melt away. In most of medieval northern Europe, wage labor had been mainly a lifestyle phenomenon. From roughly the age of twelve or fourteen to roughly twenty-eight or thirty, everyone was expected to be employed as a servant in someone else's household—usually on a yearly contract basis, for which they received room, board, professional training, and usually a wage of some sort—until they accumulated enough resources to marry and set up a household of their own.[99] The first thing that "proletarianization" came to mean was that millions of young men and women across Europe found themselves effectively stuck in a kind of permanent adolescence. Apprentices and journeymen could never become "masters," and thus, never actually grow up. Eventually, many began to give up and marry early—to the great scandal of the moralists, who insisted that the new proletariat were starting families they could not possibly support.[100]

There is, and has always been, a curious affinity between wage labor and slavery. This is not just because it was slaves on Caribbean sugar plantations who supplied the quick-energy products that powered much of early wage laborers' work; not just because most of the scientific management techniques applied in factories in the industrial revolution can be traced back to those sugar plantations; but also because both the relation between master and slave, and between employer and employee, are in principle impersonal: whether you've been sold or you're simply rented yourself out, the moment money changes hands, *who* you are is supposed to be unimportant; all that's important is that you are capable of understanding orders and doing what you're told.[101]

This is one reason, perhaps, that in principle, there was always a feeling that both the buying of slaves and the hiring of laborers should really not be on credit, but should employ cash. The problem, as I've noted, was that for most of the history of British capitalism, the cash simply wasn't there. Even when the Royal Mint began to produce smaller-denomination silver and copper coins, the supply was sporadic and inadequate. This is how the "truck system" developed to begin with: during the industrial revolution, factory owners would often pay their workers with tickets or vouchers good only in local shops, with whose owners they had some sort of informal arrangement, or, in more isolated parts of the country, which they owned themselves.[102] Traditional credit relations with one's local shopkeeper clearly took on an entirely new complexion once the shopkeeper was effectively an agent of the boss. Another expedient was to pay workers at least partly in kind—and notice the very richness of the vocabulary for the sorts of things one was assumed to be allowed to appropriate from one's workplace, particularly from the waste, excess, and side products: cabbage, chips, thrums, sweepings, buggings, gleanings, potchings, vails, poake, coltage, knockdowns, tinge.[103] "Cabbage," for instance, was the cloth left over from tailoring, "chips" the pieces of board that dockworkers had the right to carry from their workplace (any piece of timber less than two feet long), "thrums" were taken from the warping-bars of looms, and so on. And, of course, we have already heard about payment in the form of cod and nails.

Employers had a final expedient: wait for the money to show up, and in the meantime, don't pay anything—leaving their employees to get by with *only* what they could scrounge from their shop floors, or what their families could finagle in outside employment, receive in charity, preserve in savings pools with friends and families, or, when all else failed, acquire on credit from the loan sharks and pawnbrokers who rapidly came to be seen as the perennial scourge of the working poor. The situation became such that, by the nineteenth century, any time a fire destroyed a London pawnshop, working-class neighborhoods would brace for the wave of domestic violence that would inevitably ensue when many a wife was forced to confess that she'd long since secretly hocked her husband's Sunday suit.[104]

We are, nowadays, used to associating factories eighteen months in arrears for wages with a nation in economic free-fall, such as occurred during the collapse of the Soviet Union; but owing to the hard-money policies of the British government, who were always concerned above all to ensure that their paper money didn't float away in another speculative bubble, in the early days of industrial capitalism, such a situation was in no way unusual. Even the government was often unable to find the cash to pay its own employees. In eighteenth-century London, the Royal Admiralty was regularly over a year behind in paying the wages of those who labored at the Deptford docks—one reason that they were willing to tolerate the appropriation of chips, not to mention hemp, canvas, steel bolts, and cordage. In fact, as Linebaugh has shown, the situation only really began to take recognizable form around 1800, when the government stabilized its finances, began paying cash wages on schedule, and therefore tried to abolish the practice of what was now relabeled "workplace pilfering"—which, meeting outraged resistance on the part of the dockworkers, was made punishable by whipping and imprisonment. Samuel Bentham, the engineer put in charge of reforming the dockyards, had to turn them into a regular police state in order to be able to institute a regime of pure wage labor—to which purpose he ultimately conceived the notion of building a giant tower in the middle to guarantee constant surveillance, an idea that was later borrowed by his brother Jeremy for the famous Panopticon.[105]

■ ■ ■ ■ ■

Men like Smith and Bentham were idealists, even utopians. To understand the history of capitalism, however, we have to begin by realizing that the picture we have in our heads—of workers who dutifully punch the clock at 8:00 a.m. and receive regular remuneration every Friday on the basis of a temporary contract that either party is free to break off at any time—began as a utopian vision, was only gradually put into effect even in England and North America, and has never, at any point, been the main way of organizing production for the market, ever, anywhere.

This is actually why Smith's work is so important. He created the vision of an imaginary world almost entirely free of debt and credit, and therefore, free of guilt and sin; a world where men and women were free to simply calculate their interests in full knowledge that everything had been prearranged by God to ensure that it will serve the greater good. Such imaginary constructs are of course what scientists refer to as "models," and there's nothing intrinsically wrong with them. Actually, I think a fair case can be made that we cannot think without them. The problem with such models—at least, it always seems to happen when we model something called "the market"—is that, once created, we have a tendency to treat them as objective realities, or even fall down before them and start worshipping them as gods. "We must obey the dictates of the market!"

Karl Marx, who knew quite a bit about the human tendency to fall down and worship our own creations, wrote *Das Capital* in an attempt to demonstrate that, even if we do start from the economists' utopian vision, so long as we also allow some people to control productive capital and, again, leave others with nothing to sell but their brains and bodies, the results will be in many ways barely distinguishable from slavery, and the whole system will eventually destroy itself. What everyone seems to forget is the "as if" nature of his analysis.[106] Marx was well aware that there were far more bootblacks, prostitutes, butlers, soldiers, pedlars, chimneysweeps, flower girls, street musicians, convicts, nannies, and cab drivers in the London of his day than there were factory workers. He was never suggesting that that's what the world was actually like.

Still, if there is anything that the last several hundred years of world history have shown, it's that utopian visions can be powerful. This is as true of Adam Smith's as of those ranged against it. The period from roughly 1825 to 1975 was a brief but determined effort on the part of a large number of very powerful people—with the avid support of many of the least powerful—to try to turn that vision into something like reality. Coins and paper money were, finally, produced in sufficient quantities that even ordinary people could conduct their daily lives without appeal to tickets, tokens, or credit. Wages started to be paid on time. New sorts of shops, arcades, and galleries appeared, where everyone paid in cash, or alternately, as time went on, by means of impersonal forms of credit like installment plans. As a result, the old puritanical notion that debt was sin and degradation began to take a profound hold on many of those who came to consider themselves the "respectable" working classes, who often took freedom from the clutches of the pawnbroker and loan shark as a point of pride, which separated them from drunkards, hustlers, and ditch-diggers as surely as the fact that they weren't missing teeth.

Speaking as someone brought up in that sort of working-class family (my brother died at the age of 53, having refused to his dying day to acquire a credit card), I can attest to the degree that, for those who spend most of their waking hours working at someone else's orders, the ability to pull out a wallet full of banknotes that are unconditionally one's own can be a compelling form of freedom. It's not surprising that so many of the economists' assumptions—most of those for which I have been taking them to task over the course of this book—have been embraced by the leaders of the historic workers' movements, so much so that they have come to shape our visions of what alternatives to capitalism might be like. The problem is not just—as I demonstrated in Chapter Seven—that it is rooted in a deeply flawed, even perverse, conception of human freedom. This is important to emphasize because one typical response to the sort of critical perspective I have presented here is to emphasize the political freedom, technological progress, and mass prosperity that this economic has also produced. There is no doubt that advances in productivity, hygiene, education, and the application of scientific understanding to everyday needs has produced an unprecedented improvement in the lives of billions in the 250 years or so since the industrial revolution, especially in their lives outside the workplace, but it is also by no means clear to me that all these improvements can be attributed to a single entity called "capitalism"—or whether it is more sensible to see capitalist economic relations, advances in scientific knowledge, and democratic politics as essentially independent phenomena, any one of which can occur in the absence of either of the others. But even if we grant capitalism the benefit of the doubt in this regard, one thing is clear: We could no more really have a universal world market than we could have a system in which everyone who wasn't a capitalist was somehow able to become a respectable, regularly paid wage laborer with access to adequate dental care. A world like that has never existed and never could exist. What's more, the moment that even the prospect that this might happen begins to materialize, the whole system starts to come apart.

Part IV:

Apocalypse

Let us return, finally, to where we began: with Cortés and the Aztec treasure. The reader might have asked herself, What did happen to it? Did Cortés really steal it from his own men?

The answer seems to be that by the time the siege was over, there was very little of it left. Cortés seems to have gotten his hands on much of it long before the siege even began. A certain portion he had won by gambling.

This story, too, is in Bernal Díaz, and it is strange and puzzling, but also, I suspect, profound. Let me fill in some of the gaps in our

story. After burning his boats, Cortés began to assemble an army of local allies, which was easy to do because the Aztecs were widely hated,
and then he began to march on the Aztec capital. Moctezuma, the Aztec emperor, who had been monitoring the situation closely, concluded
that he needed to at least figure out what sort of people he was dealing
with, so he invited the entire Spanish force (only a few hundred men)
to be his official guests in Tenochtitlán. This eventually led to a series
of palace intrigues during which Cortés's men briefly held the emperor
hostage before being forcibly expelled.

During the time when Moctezuma was being held captive in his
own palace, he and Cortés passed a good deal of their time playing
an Aztec game called *totoloque*. They played for gold, and Cortés, of
course, cheated. At one point, Moctezuma's men brought the matter
to the king's attention, but the king just laughed and made a joke of
it—neither was he concerned later when Pedro de Alvarado, Cortés's
chief lieutenant, began cheating even more flagrantly, demanding gold
for each point lost and, when he lost, paying only in worthless pebbles.
Why Moctezuma behaved so has remained something of an historical
mystery. Díaz took it as a gesture of lordly magnanimity, perhaps even
a way of putting the petty-minded Spaniards in their place.[107]

One historian, Inga Clenninden, suggests an alternate interpretation. Aztec games, she notes, tended to have a peculiar feature: there was
always a way that, by a freak stroke of luck, one could achieve total victory. This seems to have been true, for instance, of their famous ball
games. Observers always wonder, viewing the tiny stone hoops set high
above the court, how anyone could ever possibly have managed to score.
The answer seems to be: they didn't, at least not that way. Normally, the
game had nothing to do with the hoop. The game was played between two
opposing squads, attired as for battle, knocking the ball back and forth:

> The normal method of scoring was through the slow accumu-
> lation of points. But that process could be dramatically pre-
> empted. To send the ball through one of the rings—a feat, given
> the size of the ball and the ring, presumably rarer than a hole
> in one in golf—gave instant victory, ownership of all the goods
> wagered, and the right to pillage the cloaks of the onlookers.[108]

Whoever scored the point won everything, down to the audience's
clothing.

There were similar rules in board games, such as Cortés and Moctezuma were playing: if, by some freak stroke of luck, one of the dice
landed on its edge, the game was over, and the winner took everything.

This, Clenninden suggests, must have been what Moctezuma was really waiting for. After all, he was clearly in the middle of extraordinary events. Strange creatures had appeared, apparently from nowhere, with unheard-of powers. Rumors of epidemics, of the destruction of nearby nations, had presumably already reached him. If ever there was a time that some grandiose revelation was due from the gods, then surely this was it.

Such an attitude does seem to fit perfectly with the spirit of Aztec culture gleaned from its literature, which exuded a sense of impending catastrophe, perhaps astrologically determined, just possibly avoidable—but probably not. Some have suggested that Aztecs must have somehow been aware that they were a civilization skating on the brink of ecological catastrophe; others, that the apocalyptic tone is retrospective—since, after all, what we know of Aztec literature is almost entirely gleaned from men and women who actually did experience its complete destruction. Still, there does seem to be a certain frantic quality in certain Aztec practices—the sacrifice of as many as tens of thousands of war prisoners, most notably in the apparent belief that, were the Sun not continually fed with human hearts, it would die and the world with it—that it's hard to explain in any other way.

If Clenninden is right, for Moctezuma, he and Cortés were not simply gambling for gold. Gold was trivial. The stakes were the entire universe.

Moctezuma was above all a warrior, and all warriors are gamblers; but unlike Cortés, he was clearly in every way a man of honor. As we've also seen, the quintessence of a warrior's honor, which is a greatness that can only come from the destruction and degradation of others, is his willingness to throw himself into a game where he risks that same destruction and degradation himself—and, unlike Cortés, to play graciously, and by the rules.[109] When the time came, it meant being willing to stake everything.

He did. And as it turns out, nothing happened. No die landed on its edge. Cortés continued to cheat, the gods sent no revelation, and the universe was eventually destroyed.

If there's something to be learned here—and as I say, I think there is—it is that there may be a deeper, more profound relation between gambling and apocalypse. Capitalism is a system that enshrines the gambler as an essential part of its operation, in a way that no other ever has; yet at the same time, capitalism seems to be uniquely incapable of conceiving of its own eternity. Could these two facts be linked?

I should be more precise here. It's not entirely true that capitalism is incapable of conceiving of its own eternity. On the one hand, its exponents do often feel obliged to present it as eternal, because they insist that it is the only possible viable economic system: one that, as they still sometimes like to say, "has existed for five thousand years and will exist for five thousand more." On the other hand, it does seem that the moment a significant portion of the population begins to actually believe this and, particularly, starts treating credit institutions as if they really will be around forever, everything goes haywire. Note here how it was the most sober, cautious, responsible capitalist regimes—the seventeenth-century Dutch Republic, the eighteenth-century British Commonwealth—the ones most careful about managing their public debt—that saw the most bizarre explosions of speculative frenzy, the tulip manias and South Sea bubbles.

Much of this seems to turn on the nature of national deficits and credit money. The national debt is, as politicians have complained practically since these things first appeared, money borrowed from future generations. Still, the effects have always been strangely double-edged. On the one hand, deficit financing is a way of putting even more military power in the hands of princes, generals, and politicians; on the other, it suggests that government owes something to those it governs. Insofar as our money is ultimately an extension of the public debt, then whenever we buy a newspaper or a cup of coffee, or even place a bet on a horse, we are trading in promises, representations of something that the government will give us at some time in the future, even if we don't know exactly what it is.[110]

Immanuel Wallerstein likes to point out that the French Revolution introduced several profoundly new ideas in politics—ideas which, fifty years before the revolution, the vast majority of educated Europeans would have written off as crazy, but which, fifty years afterward, just about anyone felt they had to at least pretend they thought were true. The first is that social change is inevitable and desirable: that the natural direction of history is for civilization to gradually improve. The second is that the appropriate agent to manage such change is the government. The third is that the government gains its legitimacy from an entity called "the people."[111] It's easy to see how the very idea of a national debt—a promise of continual future improvement (at the very least, five percent annual improvement) made by government to people—might itself have played a role in inspiring such a revolutionary new perspective. Yet at the same time, when one looks at what men like Mirabeau, Voltaire, Diderot, Siéyes—the *philosophes* who first proposed that notion of what we now call "civilization"—were actually arguing about in the years immediately leading up to the revolution, it was even more about the danger of apocalyptic catastrophe, of the prospect of civilization as they knew it being destroyed by default and economic collapse.

Part of the problem was the obvious one: the national debt is, first, born of war; second, it is not owed to all the people equally, but above all to capitalists—and in France at that time, "capitalist" meant, specifically, "those who held pieces of the national debt." The more democratically inclined felt that the entire situation was opprobrious. "The modern theory of the perpetuation of debt," Thomas Jefferson wrote, around this same time, "has drenched the earth with blood, and crushed its inhabitants under burdens ever accumulating."[112] Most Enlightenment thinkers feared that it promised even worse. Intrinsic to the new, "modern" notion of impersonal debt, after all, was the possibility of bankruptcy.[113] Bankruptcy, at that time, was indeed something of a personal apocalypse: it meant prison, the dissolution of one's estate; for the least fortunate, it meant torture, starvation, and death. What national bankruptcy would mean, at that point in history, nobody knew. There were simply no precedents. Yet as nations fought greater and bloodier wars, and their debts escalated geometrically, default began to appear unavoidable.[114] Abbe Sieyés first put forward his great scheme for representative government, for instance, primarily as a way of reforming the national finances, to fend off the inevitable catastrophe. And when it happened, what would it look like? Would the money become worthless? Would military regimes seize power, regimes across Europe be likewise forced to default and fall like dominos, plunging the continent into endless barbarism, darkness, and war? Many were already anticipating the prospect of the Terror long before the revolution itself.[115]

It's a strange story because we are used to thinking of the Enlightenment as the dawn of a unique phase of human optimism, borne on assumptions that the advance of science and human knowledge would inevitably make life wiser, safer, and better for everyone—a naïve faith said to have peaked in the Fabian socialism of the 1890s, only to be annihilated in the trenches of World War I. In fact, even the Victorians were haunted by the dangers of degeneration and decline. Most of all, Victorians shared the near-universal assumption that capitalism itself would not be around forever. Insurrection seemed imminent. Many Victorian capitalists operated under the sincere belief that they might, at any moment, find themselves hanging from trees. In Chicago, for instance, a friend once took me on a drive down a beautiful old street, full of mansions from the 1870s: the reason, he explained, that it looked like that, was that most of Chicago's rich industrialists of the time were so convinced that the revolution was immanent that they collectively relocated along the road that led to the nearest military base. Almost none of the great theorists of capitalism, from anywhere on the political spectrum, from Marx to Weber, to Schumpeter, to von Mises, felt

that capitalism was likely to be around for more than another generation or two at the most.

One could go further: the moment that the fear of imminent social
revolution no longer seemed plausible, by the end of World War II, we
were immediately presented with the specter of nuclear holocaust.[116]
Then, when that no longer seemed plausible, we discovered global
warming. This is not to say that these threats were not, and are not,
real. Yet it does seem strange that capitalism feels the constant need
to imagine, or to actually manufacture, the means of its own imminent extinction. It's in dramatic contrast to the behavior of the leaders
of socialist regimes, from Cuba to Albania, who, when they came to
power, immediately began acting as if their system would be around
forever—ironically enough, considering they in fact turned out to be
something of an historical blip.

Perhaps the reason is because what was true in 1710 is still true.
Presented with the prospect of its own eternity, capitalism—or anyway, financial capitalism—simply explodes. Because if there's no end
to it, there's absolutely no reason not to generate credit—that is, future
money—infinitely. Recent events would certainly seem to confirm this.
The period leading up to 2008 was one in which many began to believe
that capitalism really was going to be around forever; at the very least,
no one seemed any longer to be able to imagine an alternative. The immediate effect was a series of increasingly reckless bubbles that brought
the whole apparatus crashing down.

Chapter Twelve

THE BEGINNING OF SOMETHING
YET TO BE DETERMINED

(1971 – PRESENT)

> *Look at all these bums: If only there*
> *were a way of finding out how much*
> *they owe.*
> —*Repo Man* (1984)

> *Free your mind of the idea of deserv-*
> *ing, of the idea of earning, and you will*
> *begin to be able to think.*
> —Ursula K. Le Guin, *The Dispossessed*

ON AUGUST 15, 1971, United States President Richard Nixon announced that foreign-held U.S. dollars would no longer be convertible
into gold—thus stripping away the last vestige of the international gold
standard.[1] This was the end of a policy that had been effective since
1931, and confirmed by the Bretton Woods accords at the end of World
War II: that while United States citizens might no longer be allowed
to cash in their dollars for gold, all U.S. currency held outside the
country was to be redeemable at the rate of $35 an ounce. By doing so,
Nixon initiated the regime of free-floating currencies that continues to
this day.

The consensus among historians is that Nixon had little choice. His
hand was forced by the rising costs of the Vietnam War—one that, like
all capitalist wars, had been financed by deficit spending. The United
States was in possession of a large proportion of the world's gold reserves in its vaults in Fort Knox (though increasingly less in the late
1960s, as other governments, most famously Charles de Gaulle's France,
began demanding gold for their dollars); most poorer countries, in contrast, kept their reserves in dollars. The immediate effect of Nixon's
unpegging the dollar was to cause the price of gold to skyrocket; it hit a
peak of $600 an ounce in 1980. This of course had the effect of causing

U.S. gold reserves to increase dramatically in value. The value of the dollar, as denominated in gold, plummeted. The result was a massive net transfer of wealth from poor countries, which lacked gold reserves, to rich ones, like the United States and Great Britain, that maintained them. In the United States, it also set off persistent inflation.

Whatever Nixon's reasons, though, once the global system of credit money was entirely unpegged from gold, the world entered a new phase of financial history—one that nobody completely understands. While I was growing up in New York, I would hear occasional rumors of secret gold vaults underneath the Twin Towers in Manhattan. Supposedly, these vaults contained not just the U.S. gold reserves, but those of all the major economic powers. The gold was said to be kept in the form of bars, piled up in separate vaults, one for each country, and every year, when the balance of accounts was calculated, workmen with dollies would adjust the stocks accordingly, carting, say, a few million in gold out of the vault marked "Brazil" and transferring them to the one marked "Germany," and so on.

Apparently, a lot of people had heard these stories. At least, right after the Towers were destroyed on September 11, 2001, one of the first questions many New Yorkers asked was: What happened to the money? Was it safe? Were the vaults destroyed? Presumably, the gold had melted. Was this the real aim of the attackers? Conspiracy theories abounded. Some spoke of legions of emergency workers secretly summoned to make their way through miles of overheated tunnels, desperately carting off tons of bullion even as rescue workers labored overhead. One particularly colorful conspiracy theory suggested that the entire attack was really staged by speculators who, like Nixon, expected to see the value of the dollar crash and that of gold to skyrocket—either because the reserves had been destroyed, or because they themselves had laid prior plans to steal them.[2]

The truly remarkable thing about this story is that, after having believed it for years, and then, in the wake of 9/11, having been convinced by some more knowing friends that it was all a great myth ("No," one of them said resignedly, as if to a child, "the United States keeps its gold reserves in Fort Knox"), I did a little research and discovered that, no, actually, it's true. The United States Treasury's gold reserves are indeed kept at Fort Knox, but the Federal Reserve's gold reserves, and those of more than one hundred other central banks, governments, and organizations, are stored in vaults under the Federal Reserve building at 33 Liberty Street in Manhattan, two blocks away from the Towers. At roughly five thousand metric tons (266 million troy ounces), these combined reserves represent, according to the Fed's own website, somewhere between one-fifth and one-quarter of all the gold that has ever been taken from the earth. Children are taken on tours of it:

"The gold stored at the Federal Reserve Bank of New York," according to the promotional literature, "is secured in a most unusual vault. It rests on the bedrock of Manhattan Island—one of the few foundations considered adequate to support the weight of the vault, its door, and the gold inside—eighty feet below street level and fifty feet below sea level . . . To reach the vault, bullion-laden pallets must be loaded into one of the Bank's elevators and sent down five floors below street level to the vault floor . . . If everything is in order, the gold is either moved to one or more of the vault's 122 compartments assigned to depositing countries and official international organizations or placed on shelves. 'Gold stackers,' using hydraulic lifts, do indeed shift them back and forth between compartments to balance credits and debts, though the vaults have only numbers, so even the workers don't know who is paying whom."[3]

There is no reason to believe, however, that these vaults were in any way affected by the events of September 11, 2001.

Reality, then, has become so odd that it's hard to guess which elements of grand mythic fantasies are really fantasy, and which are true. The image of collapsed vaults, the melted bullion, of secret workers scurrying deep below Manhattan with underground forklifts evacuating the world economy—all this turns out not to be. But is it entirely surprising that people were willing to consider it?[4]

What I would like to do in this chapter is, primarily, not so much to provide a detailed analysis of how the current system works, but to look at how the long-term patterns I've been examining so far can be seen as playing out at the present moment, and might provide us at least a hint of where it might be heading. Because this is definitely a moment of transition. No one is going to be able to have any chance of saying what all this really means for another generation, at the very least. On the other hand, as an anthropologist, I cannot help but see this confused play of symbols as important in and of itself, even, of playing a crucial role in maintaining the forms of power it claims to represent. In part, these systems work because no one knows how they really work.

In America, the banking system since the days of Thomas Jefferson has shown a remarkable capacity to inspire paranoid fantasies: whether centering on Freemasons, or Elders of Zion, or the Secret Order of the Illuminati, or the Queen of England's drug-money-laundering operations, or any of a thousand other secret conspiracies and cabals. It's the main reason why it took so long for an American central bank to be established to begin with. In a way there's nothing surprising here. The United States has always been dominated by a certain market populism, and the ability of banks to "create money out of nothing"—and even more, to prevent anyone else from doing so—has always been the bugaboo of market populists, since it directly contradicts the idea that markets are a simple expression of democratic equality. Still, since Nixon's floating of the dollar, it has become evident that it's *only* the wizard behind the screen who seems to be maintaining the viability of the whole arrangement. Under the free-market orthodoxy that followed, we have all been asked, effectively, to accept that "the market" is a self-regulating system, with the rising and falling of prices akin to a force of nature, and simultaneously to ignore the fact that, in the business pages, it is simply assumed that markets rise and fall mainly in anticipation of, or reaction to, decisions by Alan Greenspan, or Ben Bernanke, or whoever is currently the chairman of the Federal Reserve.[5]

■ ■ ■ ■ ■

One element, however, tends to go flagrantly missing in even the most vivid conspiracy theories about the banking system, let alone in official accounts: that is, the role of war and military power. There's a reason why the wizard has such a strange capacity to create money out of nothing. Behind him, there's a man with a gun.

True, in one sense, he's been there from the start. I have already pointed out that modern money is based on government debt, and that governments borrow money in order to finance wars. This is just as true today as it was in the age of King Phillip II. The creation of central banks represented a permanent institutionalization of that marriage between the interests of warriors and financiers that had already begun to emerge in Renaissance Italy and that eventually became the foundation of financial capitalism.[6]

Nixon floated the dollar in order to pay for the cost of a war in which, during the period of 1970–1972 alone, he ordered more than four million tons of explosives and incendiaries dropped on cities and villages across Indochina—causing one senator to dub him "the greatest bomber of all time."[7] The debt crisis was a direct result of the need to pay for the bombs, or, to be more precise, the vast military infrastructure required to deliver them. This was what was causing such an enormous strain on the U.S. gold reserves. Many hold that by floating the dollar, Nixon converted the U.S. currency into pure "fiat money"—mere pieces of paper, intrinsically worthless, that were treated as money only because the United States government insisted that they should be. In that case, one could well argue that U.S. military power was now the only thing backing up the currency. In a certain sense this is true, but the notion of "fiat money" assumes that money really "was" gold in the first place. Really we are dealing with another variation of credit money.

Contrary to popular belief, the U.S. government can't "just print money," because American money is not issued by the Federal government at all, but by private banks, under the aegis of the Federal Reserve System. The Federal Reserve, in turn, is a peculiar sort of public-private hybrid, a consortium of privately owned banks whose Governing Board is appointed by the U.S. president, with Congressional approval, but which otherwise operates autonomously. All dollar bills in circulation in America are "Federal Reserve Notes"—the Fed issues them as promissory notes and commissions the U.S. mint to do the actual printing, paying it four cents for each bill.[8] The arrangement is just a variation of the scheme originally pioneered by the Bank of England, whereby the Fed "loans" money to the United States government by purchasing treasury bonds, and then monetizes the U.S. debt by lending the money thus owed by the government to other banks.[9] The difference is that while the Bank of England originally loaned the king gold, the Fed simply whisks the money into existence by saying that it's there. Thus, it's the Fed that has the power to print money.[10] The banks that receive loans from the Fed are no longer permitted to print money themselves, but they are allowed to create virtual money by making loans ostensibly, at a fractional reserve rate established by the Fed—though in practice, even these restrictions have become largely theoretical.[11]

All this is a bit of a simplification: monetary policy is endlessly arcane and, it does sometimes seem, intentionally so. (Henry Ford once remarked that if ordinary Americans ever found out how the banking system really worked, there would be a revolution tomorrow.) There is no end to the smoke and mirrors here. For instance, while technically, the Fed cannot lend money directly to the government by buying Treasury Bonds, everyone knows that doing so indirectly is one of its primary reasons for being. And insofar as the government issues T-bonds, it actually is, in one sense, printing money: circulating debt tokens that—as one apparently paradoxical effect of Nixon's floating the dollar—have now themselves come to replace gold as the world's reserve currency: that is, as the ultimate store of value in the world, yielding the United States enormous economic advantages.[12]

Meanwhile, the U.S. debt remains, as it has been since 1790, a war debt: the United States continues to spend more on its military than do all other nations on earth put together, and military expenditures are

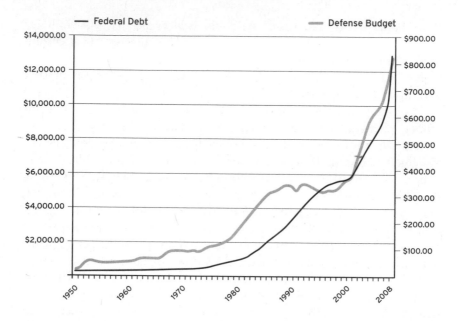

not only the basis of the government's industrial policy; they also take up such a huge proportion of the budget that by many estimations, were it not for them, the United States would not run a deficit at all.

The U.S. military, unlike any other, maintains a doctrine of global power projection: that it should have the ability, through roughly 800 overseas military bases, to intervene with deadly force absolutely anywhere on the planet. In a way, though, land forces are secondary; at least since World War II, the key to U.S. military doctrine has always been a reliance on air power. The United States has fought no war in which it did not control the skies, and it has relied on aerial bombardment far more systematically than any other military—in its recent occupation of Iraq, for instance, even going so far as to bomb residential neighborhoods of cities ostensibly under its own control. The essence of U.S. military predominance in the world is, ultimately, the fact that it can, at will, with only a few hours' notice, drop bombs at absolutely any point on the surface of the planet.[13] No other government has ever had anything remotely like this sort of capability. In fact, a case could well be made that it is this very cosmic power that holds the entire world monetary system, organized around the dollar, together.

Again, we are talking about symbolic power. In fact, it's a form of power that works largely insofar as it remains symbolic. In the days of the Cold War, the United States and USSR were considered superpowers largely because their leaders had the means, through their nuclear arsenals, to destroy humanity with the flick of a switch. Obviously this power could only be translated into political influence insofar as it wasn't actually exercised. In a more subtle way, this is still true of U.S. cosmic pretensions. They don't work by direct threat, but by creating a political environment defined by knowledge of utterly disproportionate access to the means of violence, and that sense of absolute power tends to be eroded the moment that violence is used in more than extremely sparing, and largely symbolic, ways.

How does it work economically?

Because of United States trade deficits, huge numbers of dollars circulate outside the country; and one effect of Nixon's floating of the dollar was that foreign central banks have little they can do with these dollars except to use them to buy U.S. treasury bonds.[14] This is what is meant by the dollar becoming the world's "reserve currency." These bonds are, like all bonds, supposed to be loans that will eventually mature and be repaid, but as economist Michael Hudson, who first began observing the phenomenon in the early '70s, noted, they never really do:

> To the extent that these Treasury IOUs are being built into the world's monetary base they will not have to be repaid, but are to be rolled over indefinitely. This feature is the essence of America's free financial ride, a tax imposed at the entire globe's expense.[15]

What's more, Hudson notes, over time, the combined effect of low interest payments and the inflation is that these bonds actually depreciate in value—adding to the tax effect, or, as I preferred to put it in the first chapter, "tribute." Economists prefer to call it "seigniorage." The effect, though, is that American imperial power is based on a debt that will never—can never—be repaid. Its national debt has become a promise, not just to its own people, but to the nations of the entire world, that everyone knows will not be kept.

At the same time, U.S. policy was to insist that those countries relying on U.S. treasury bonds as their reserve currency behaved in exactly the opposite way: observing tight money policies and scrupulously repaying their debts.

As I've already observed, since Nixon's time, the most significant overseas buyers of U.S. treasury bonds have tended to be banks in countries that were effectively under U.S. military occupation. In Europe, Nixon's most enthusiastic ally in this respect was West Germany, which then hosted more than three hundred thousand U.S. troops. In more recent decades the focus has shifted to Asia, particularly the central banks of countries like Japan, Taiwan, and South Korea—again, all U.S. military protectorates. In addition, the global status of the dollar is reinforced by the fact that it is, again since 1971, the only currency used to buy and sell petroleum, with any attempt by OPEC countries to begin trading in any currency stubbornly resisted by OPEC members Saudi Arabia and Kuwait—also U.S. military protectorates.[16] When Saddam Hussein made the bold move of singlehandedly switching from the dollar to the euro in 2000, followed by Iran in 2001, this was quickly followed by American bombing and military occupation.[17] How much did Hussein's decision to buck the dollar really weigh into the U.S. decision to depose him? It's impossible to say. His decision to stop using "the enemy's currency," as he put it, was one in a back-and-forth series of hostile gestures that likely would have led to war in any event; what's important here is that there were widespread rumors that this was one of the major contributing factors, and therefore, no policymaker in a position to make a similar switch can completely ignore the possibility. Much though their beneficiaries do not like to admit it, all imperial arrangements do, ultimately, rest on terror.[18]

■ ■ ■ ■ ■

The immediate effects of the advent of the free-floating dollar, then, marked not a break with the alliance of warriors and financiers on which capitalism itself was originally founded, but on something that looks a lot more like its ultimate apotheosis. Neither has the return to virtual money led to a great return to relations of honor and trust: quite the contrary. But we are talking about the very first years of what is likely to be a centuries-long historical era. By 1971, most of these changes had not even begun. The American Express card, the first general-purpose credit card, had been invented a mere thirteen years before, and the modern national credit-card system had only really come into being with the advent of Visa and MasterCard in 1968. Debit cards came later, creatures of the 1970s, and the current, largely cashless economy only came into being in the 1990s. All of these new credit arrangements were mediated not by interpersonal relations of trust but by profit-seeking corporations, and one of the earliest and greatest political victories of the U.S. credit-card industry was the elimination of all legal restrictions on what they could charge as interest.

If history holds true, an age of virtual money should mean a movement away from war, empire-building, slavery, and debt peonage (waged or otherwise), and toward the creation of some sort of overarching institutions, global in scale, to protect debtors. What we have seen so far is the opposite. The new global currency is rooted in military power even more firmly than the old was. Debt peonage continues to be the main principle of recruiting labor globally: either in the literal sense, in much of East Asia or Latin America, or in the subjective sense, whereby most of those working for wages or even salaries feel that they are doing so primarily to pay off interest-bearing loans. The new transportation and communications technologies have just made it easier, making it possible to charge domestics or factory workers thousands of dollars in transportation fees, and then have them work off the debt in distant countries where they lack legal protections.[19] Insofar as overarching grand cosmic institutions have been created that might be considered in any way parallel to the divine kings of the ancient Middle East or the religious authorities of the Middle Ages, they have not been created to protect debtors, but to enforce the rights of creditors. The International Monetary Fund is only the most dramatic case in point here. It stands at the pinnacle of a great, emerging global bureaucracy—the first genuinely global administrative system in human history, consisting not only of the United Nations, the World Bank, and the World Trade Organization, but also the endless host of economic unions and trade organizations and non-governmental organizations that work in tandem with them—created largely under U.S. patronage. All of them operate on the principle that (unless one is the United States Treasury, or perhaps American Insurance Group), "one has to pay one's debts"—since the specter of default by any country is assumed to imperil the entire world monetary system, threatening, in Addison's colorful image, to turn all the world's sacks of (virtual) gold into worthless sticks and paper.

All true. But again, we are speaking of a mere forty years here, in what is likely to a 400- or 500-year epoch. Nixon's gambit, what Hudson calls "debt imperialism," has already come under considerable strain. The first casualty was precisely the imperial bureaucracy dedicated to the protection of creditors (other than those that were owed money by the United States). IMF policies of insisting that debts be repaid almost exclusively from the pockets of the poor were met by an equally global movement of social rebellion (the so-called "anti-globalization movement"—though the name is profoundly deceptive), followed by outright fiscal rebellion in both East Asia and Latin America. By 2000, East Asian countries had begun a systematic boycott of the IMF. In 2002, Argentina committed the ultimate sin: they defaulted—and got away with it. Subsequent U.S. military adventures were clearly meant to reestablish the nation's symbolic, cosmological power—that is, to terrify and overawe (it didn't really matter whom)—but in that respect do not appear to have been very successful: partly because they demonstrated that the U.S. military was unable to totally overcome far weaker rivals; partly, too, because, to finance them, the United States had to turn not just to its military clients, but increasingly to China, its chief remaining military rival. After the near-total collapse of the U.S. financial industry, which despite having been very nearly granted rights to make up money at will, still managed to end up with trillions in liabilities it could not pay, brought the world economy to a standstill, the U.S. lost even the ability to argue that debt imperialism guaranteed stability.

Just to give a sense of how extreme a financial crisis we are talking about, here are some statistical charts culled from the pages of the St. Louis Federal Reserve web page.[20]

Here is the amount of U.S. debt held overseas:

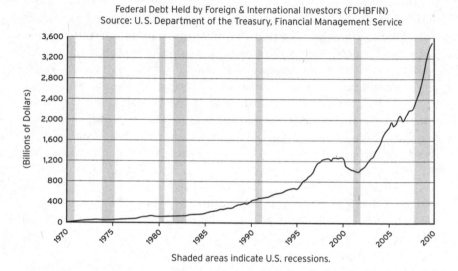

Federal Debt Held by Foreign & International Investors (FDHBFIN)
Source: U.S. Department of the Treasury, Financial Management Service

Shaded areas indicate U.S. recessions.

Meanwhile, private U.S. banks reacted to the crash by abandoning any pretense that we are dealing with a market economy, shifting all available assets into the coffers of the Federal Reserve itself:

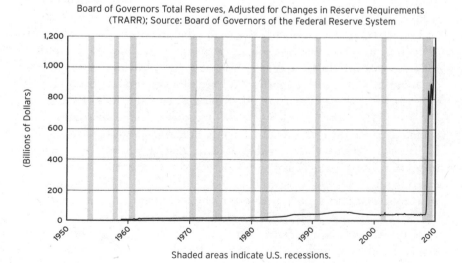

Board of Governors Total Reserves, Adjusted for Changes in Reserve Requirements
(TRARR); Source: Board of Governors of the Federal Reserve System

Shaded areas indicate U.S. recessions.

Allowing them, through yet another piece of arcane magic that none of us could possibly understand, to end up, after an initial near $400-billion dip, with far larger reserves in their own balance sheets than they had ever had before.

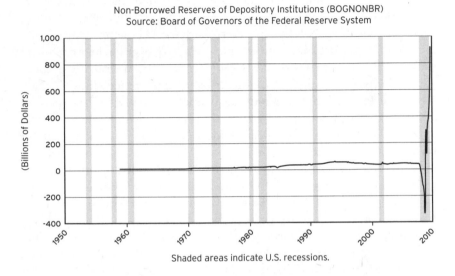

Non-Borrowed Reserves of Depository Institutions (BOGNONBR)
Source: Board of Governors of the Federal Reserve System

Shaded areas indicate U.S. recessions.

At this point, some U.S. creditors clearly feel they are finally in a position to demand that their own political agendas be taken into account.

CHINA WARNS U.S. ABOUT DEBT MONETIZATION

Seemingly everywhere he went on a recent tour of China, Dallas Fed President Richard Fisher was asked to deliver a message to Federal Reserve Chairman Ben Bernanke: "stop creating credit out of thin air to purchase U.S. Treasuries."[21]

Again, it's never clear whether the money siphoned from Asia to support the U.S. war machine is better seen as "loans" or as "tribute."[22] Still, the sudden advent of China as a major holder of U.S. treasury bonds has clearly altered the dynamic. Some might question why, if these really are tribute payments, the United States' major rival would be buying treasury bonds to begin with—let alone agreeing to various tacit monetary arrangements to maintain the value of the dollar, and hence, the buying power of American consumers.[23] But I think this is a perfect case in point of why taking a very long-term historical perspective can be so helpful.

From a longer-term perspective, China's behavior isn't puzzling at all. In fact, it's quite true to form. The unique thing about the Chinese empire is that it has, since the Han dynasty at least, adopted a peculiar sort of tribute system whereby, in exchange for recognition of the Chinese emperor as world-sovereign, they have been willing to shower their client states with gifts far greater than they receive in return. The technique seems to have been developed almost as a kind of trick when dealing with the "northern barbarians" of the steppes, who always threatened Chinese frontiers: a way to overwhelm them with such luxuries that they would become complacent, effeminate, and unwarlike. It was systematized in the "tribute trade" practiced with client states like Japan, Taiwan, Korea, and various states of Southeast Asia, and for a brief period from 1405 to 1433, it even extended to a world scale, under the famous eunuch admiral Zheng He. He led a series of seven expeditions across the Indian Ocean, his great "treasure fleet"—in dramatic contrast to the Spanish treasure fleets of a century later—carrying not only thousands of armed marines, but endless quantities of silks, porcelain, and other Chinese luxuries to present to those local rulers willing to recognize the authority of the emperor.[24] All this was ostensibly rooted in an ideology of extraordinary chauvinism ("What could these barbarians possibly have that we really need, anyway?"), but, applied to China's neighbors, it proved extremely wise policy for a wealthy empire surrounded by much smaller but potentially troublesome kingdoms. In fact, it was such wise policy that the U.S. government, during the Cold War, more or less had to adopt it, creating remarkably favorable terms of trade for those very states—Korea, Japan, Taiwan, certain favored allies in Southeast Asia—that had been the traditional Chinese tributaries; in this case, in order to contain China.[25]

Bearing all this in mind, the current picture begins to fall easily back into place. When the United States was far and away the predominant world economic power, it could afford to maintain Chinese-style tributaries. Thus these very states, alone amongst U.S. military protectorates, were allowed to catapult themselves out of poverty and into first-world status.[26] After 1971, as U.S. economic strength relative to the rest of the world began to decline, they were gradually transformed back into a more old-fashioned sort of tributary. Yet China's getting in on the game introduced an entirely new element. There is every reason to believe that, from China's point of view, this is the first stage of a very long process of reducing the United States to something like a traditional Chinese client state. And, of course, Chinese rulers are not, any more than the rulers of any other empire, motivated primarily by benevolence. There is always a political cost, and what that headline marked was the first glimmerings of what that cost might ultimately be.

■ ■ ■ ■ ■

All that I have said so far merely serves to underline a reality that has come up constantly over the course of this book: that money has no essence. It's not "really" anything; therefore, its nature has always been and presumably always will be a matter of political contention. This was certainly true throughout earlier stages of U.S. history, incidentally—as the endless nineteenth-century battles between gold-bugs, greenbackers, free bankers, bi-metallists, and silverites so vividly attest—or, for that matter, the fact that American voters were so suspicious of the very idea of central banks that the Federal Reserve system was only created on the eve of World War I, three centuries after the Bank of England. Even the monetization of the national debt is, as I've already noted, double-edged. It can be seen—as Jefferson saw it—as the ultimate pernicious alliance of warriors and financiers; but it also opened the way to seeing government itself as a moral debtor, and freedom as something literally owed to the nation. Perhaps no one put it so eloquently as Martin Luther King Jr., in his "I Have a Dream" speech, delivered on the steps of the Lincoln Memorial in 1963:

> In a sense we've come to our nation's capital to cash a check. When the architects of our republic wrote the magnificent words of the Constitution and the Declaration of Independence, they were signing a promissory note to which every American was to fall heir. This note was a promise that all men, yes, black men as well as white men, would be guaranteed the "unalienable Rights" of "Life, Liberty and the pursuit of Happiness." It is obvious today that America has defaulted on this promissory note, insofar as her citizens of color are concerned. Instead of honoring this sacred obligation, America has given the Negro people a bad check, a check which has come back marked "insufficient funds."

One can see the great crash of 2008 in the same light—as the outcome of years of political tussles between creditors and debtors, rich and poor. True, on a certain level, it was exactly what it seemed to be: a scam, an incredibly sophisticated Ponzi scheme designed to collapse in the full knowledge that the perpetrators would be able to force the victims to bail them out. On another level it could be seen as the culmination of a battle over the very definition of money and credit.

By the end of World War II, the specter of an imminent working-class uprising that had so haunted the ruling classes of Europe and North

America for the previous century had largely disappeared. This was because class war was suspended by a tacit settlement. To put it crudely: the white working class of the North Atlantic countries, from the United States to West Germany, were offered a deal. If they agreed to set aside any fantasies of fundamentally changing the nature of the system, then they would be allowed to keep their unions, enjoy a wide variety of social benefits (pensions, vacations, health care . . .), and, perhaps most important, through generously funded and ever-expanding public educational institutions, know that their children had a reasonable chance of leaving the working class entirely. One key element in all this was a tacit guarantee that increases in workers' productivity would be met by increases in wages: a guarantee that held good until the late 1970s. Largely as a result, the period saw both rapidly rising productivity and rapidly rising incomes, laying the basis for the consumer economy of today.

Economists call this the "Keynesian era," since it was a time in which John Maynard Keynes' economic theories, which already formed the basis of Roosevelt's New Deal in the United States, were adopted by industrial democracies pretty much everywhere. With them came Keynes' rather casual attitude toward money. The reader will recall that Keynes fully accepted that banks do, indeed, create money "out of thin air," and that for this reason, there was no intrinsic reason that government policy should not encourage this during economic downturns as a way of stimulating demand—a position that had long been dear to the heart of debtors and anathema to creditors.

Keynes himself had in his day been known to make some fairly radical noises, for instance calling for the complete elimination of that class of people who lived off of other people's debts—"the euthanasia of the rentier," as he put it—though all he really meant by this was their elimination through a gradual reduction of interest rates. As in so much of Keynesianism, this was much less radical than it first appeared. Actually, it was quite squarely in the great tradition of political economy, hearkening back to Adam Smith's ideal of a debtless utopia but especially David Ricardo's condemnation of landlords as parasites, their very existence inimical to economic growth. Keynes was simply proceeding along the same lines, seeing rentiers as a feudal holdover inconsistent with the true spirit of capital accumulation. Far from a revolution, he saw it as the best way of avoiding one:

> I see, therefore, the rentier aspect of capitalism as a transitional phase which will disappear when it has done its work. And with the disappearance of its rentier aspect much else in

it besides will suffer a sea-change. It will be, moreover, a great advantage of the order of events which I am advocating, that the euthanasia of the rentier, of the functionless investor, will be nothing sudden . . . and will need no revolution.[27]

When the Keynesian settlement was finally put into effect, after World War II, it was offered only to a relatively small slice of the world's population. As time went on, more and more people wanted in on the deal. Almost all of the popular movements of the period from 1945 to 1975, even perhaps revolutionary movements, could be seen as demands for inclusion: demands for political equality that assumed equality was meaningless without some level of economic security. This was true not only of movements by minority groups in North Atlantic countries who had first been left out of the deal—such as those for whom Dr. King spoke—but what were then called "national liberation" movements from Algeria to Chile, which represented certain class fragments in what we now call the Global South, or, finally, and perhaps most dramatically, in the late 1960s and 1970s, feminism. At some point in the '70s, things reached a breaking point. It would appear that capitalism, as a system, simply cannot extend such a deal to everyone. Quite possibly it wouldn't even remain viable if all its workers were free wage laborers; certainly it will never be able to provide everyone in the world the sort of life lived by, say, a 1960s auto worker in Michigan or Turin with his own house, garage, and children in college—and this was true even before so many of those children began demanding less stultifying lives. The result might be termed a crisis of inclusion. By the late 1970s, the existing order was clearly in a state of collapse, plagued simultaneously by financial chaos, food riots, oil shock, widespread doomsday prophecies of the end of growth and ecological crisis—all of which, it turned out, proved to be ways of putting the populace on notice that all deals were off.

The moment that we start framing the story this way, it's easy to see that the next thirty years, the period from roughly 1978 to 2009, follows nearly the same pattern. Except that the deal, the settlement, had changed. Certainly, when both Ronald Reagan in the United States and Margaret Thatcher in the UK launched a systematic attack on the power of labor unions, as well as on the legacy of Keynes, it was a way of explicitly declaring that all previous deals were off. Everyone could now have political rights—even, by the 1990s, most everyone in Latin America and Africa—but political rights were to become economically meaningless. The link between productivity and wages was chopped to bits: productivity rates have continued to rise, but wages have stagnated or even atrophied[28]:

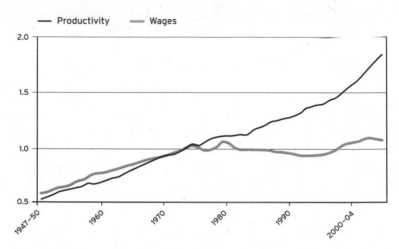

This was accompanied, at first, by a return to "monetarism": the doctrine that even though money was no longer in any way based in gold,
or in any other commodity, government and central-bank policy should
be primarily concerned with carefully controlling the money supply to
ensure that it acted *as if* it were a scarce commodity. Even as, at the
same time, the financialization of capital meant that most money being
invested in the marketplace was completely detached from any relation
to production or commerce at all, but had become pure speculation.

All this is not to say that the people of the world were not being offered something: just that, as I say, the terms had changed. In
the new dispensation, wages would no longer rise, but workers were
encouraged to buy a piece of capitalism. Rather than euthanize the
rentiers, *everyone* could now become rentiers—effectively, could grab
a chunk of the profits created by their own increasingly dramatic rates
of exploitation. The means were many and familiar. In the United
States, there were 401(k) retirement accounts and an endless variety
of other ways of encouraging ordinary citizens to play the market but
at the same time, encouraging them to borrow. One of the guiding
principles of Thatcherism and Reaganism alike was that economic reforms would never gain widespread support unless ordinary working
people could at least aspire to owning their own homes; to this was
added, by the 1990s and 2000s, endless mortgage-refinancing schemes
that treated houses, whose value it was assumed would only rise, "like
ATMs,"—as the popular catchphrase had it—though it turns out, in
retrospect, it was really more like credit cards. Then there was the
proliferation of actual credit cards, juggled against one another. Here,
for many, "buying a piece of capitalism" slithered undetectably into

something indistinguishable from those familiar scourges of the working poor: the loan shark and the pawnbroker. It did not help here that in 1980, U.S. federal usury laws, which had previously limited interest to between 7 and 10 percent, were eliminated by act of Congress. Just as the United States had managed to largely get rid of the problem of political corruption by making the bribery of legislators effectively legal (it was redefined as "lobbying"), so the problem of loan-sharking was brushed aside by making real interest rates of 25 percent, 50 percent, or even in some cases (for instance, for payday loans) up to 6,000 percent annually, the sort of numbers that would once have made the mafia blush, perfectly legal—and therefore, enforceable no longer by just hired goons and the sort of people who place mutilated animals on their victims' doorsteps, but by judges, lawyers, bailiffs, and police.[29]

Any number of names have been coined to describe the new dispensation, from the "democratization of finance" to the "financialization of everyday life."[30] Outside the United States, it came to be known as "neoliberalism." As an ideology, it meant that not just the market, but capitalism (I must continually remind the reader that these are not the same thing) became the organizing principle of almost everything. We were all to think of ourselves as tiny corporations, organized around that same relationship of investor and executive: between the cold, calculating math of the banker, and the warrior who, indebted, has abandoned any sense of personal honor and turned himself into a kind of disgraced machine.

In this world, "paying one's debts" can well come to seem the very definition of morality, if only because so many people fail to do it. For instance, it has become a regular feature of many sorts of business in America that large corporations or even some small businesses, faced with a debt, will almost automatically simply see what happens if they do not pay—complying only if reminded, goaded, or presented with some sort of legal writ. In other words, the principle of honor has thus been almost completely removed from the marketplace.[31] As a result, perhaps, the whole subject of debt becomes surrounded by a halo of religion.

Actually, one might even speak of a double theology, one for the creditors, another for the debtors. It is no coincidence that the new phase of American debt imperialism has also been accompanied by the rise of the evangelical right, who—in defiance of almost all previously existing Christian theology—have enthusiastically embraced the doctrine of "supply-side economics," that creating money and effectively giving it to the rich is the most Biblically appropriate way to bring about national prosperity. Perhaps the most ambitious theologian of the new creed was George Gilder, whose book *Wealth and Poverty* became a best-seller in 1981, at the very dawn of what came to be known

as the Reagan Revolution. Gilder's argument was that those who felt
that money could not simply be created were mired in an old fashioned,
godless materialism that did not realize that just as God could create
something out of nothing, His greatest gift to humanity was creativity itself, which proceeded in exactly the same way. Investors can indeed create value out of nothing by their willingness to accept the risk entailed
in placing their faith in others' creativity. Rather than seeing the imitation of God's powers of creation *ex nihilo* as hubris, Gilder argued that
it was precisely what God intended: the creation of money was a gift, a
blessing, a channeling of grace; a promise, yes, but not one that can be
fulfilled, even if the bonds are continually rolled over, because through
faith ("in God we trust" again) their value becomes reality:

> Economists who themselves do not believe in the future of
> capitalism will tend to ignore the dynamics of chance and faith
> that largely will determine that future. Economists who distrust
> religion will always fail to comprehend the modes of worship
> by which progress is achieved. Chance is the foundation of
> change and the vessel of the divine.[32]

Such effusions inspired evangelists like Pat Robertson to declare
supply-side economics "the first truly divine theory of money-creation."[33]

Meanwhile, for those who could not simply create money, there was
a quite different theological dispensation. "Debt is the new fat," Margaret Atwood recently remarked, struck by how much the advertisements
that surround her daily on the bus in her native Toronto had abandoned
their earlier attempts to make riders panic about the creeping terrors of
sexual unattractiveness, but instead turned to providing advice on how
to free oneself from the much more immediate terrors of the repo man:

> There are even debt TV shows, which have a familiar religious-
> revival ring to them. There are accounts of shopaholic binges du-
> ring which you don't know what came over you and everything
> was a blur, with tearful confessions by those who've spent them-
> selves into quivering insomniac jellies of hopeless indebtedness,
> and have resorted to lying, cheating, stealing, and kiting cheques
> between bank accounts as a result. There are testimonials by
> families and loved ones whose lives have been destroyed by the
> debtor's harmful behaviour. There are compassionate but severe
> admonitions by the television host, who here plays the part of
> priest or revivalist. There's a moment of seeing the light, fol-
> lowed by repentance and a promise never to do it again. There's

a penance imposed—*snip, snip* go the scissors on the credit cards—followed by a strict curb-on-spending regimen; and finally, if all goes well, the debts are paid down, the sins are forgiven, absolution is granted, and a new day dawns, in which a sadder but more solvent man you rise the morrow morn.[34]

Here, risk-taking is in no sense the vessel of the divine. Quite the opposite. But for the poor it's always different. In a way, what Atwood describes might be seen as the perfect inversion of the prophetic voice of Reverend King's "I Have a Dream" speech: whereas the first postwar age was about collective claims on the nation's debt to its humblest citizens, the need for those who have made false promises to redeem themselves, now those same humble citizens are taught to think of themselves as sinners, seeking some kind of purely individual redemption to have the right to any sort of moral relations with other human beings at all.

At the same time, there is something profoundly deceptive going on here. All these moral dramas start from the assumption that personal debt is ultimately a matter of self-indulgence, a sin against one's loved ones—and therefore, that redemption must necessarily be a matter of purging and restoration of ascetic self-denial. What's being shunted out of sight here is first of all the fact that *everyone* is now in debt (U.S. household debt is now estimated at on average 130 percent of income), and that very little of this debt was accrued by those determined to find money to bet on the horses or toss away on fripperies. Insofar as it was borrowed for what economists like to call discretionary spending, it was mainly to be given to children, to share with friends, or otherwise to be able to build and maintain relations with other human beings that are based on *something* other than sheer material calculation.[35] One must go into debt to achieve a life that goes in any way beyond sheer survival.

Insofar as there is a politics, here, it seems a variation on a theme seen since the dawn of capitalism. Ultimately, it's sociality itself that's treated as abusive, criminal, demonic. To this, most ordinary Americans—including Black and Latino Americans, recent immigrants, and others who were formerly excluded from credit—have responded with a stubborn insistence on continuing to love one another. They continue to acquire houses for their families, liquor and sound systems for parties, gifts for friends; they even insist on continuing to hold weddings and funerals, regardless of whether this is likely to send them skirting default or bankruptcy—apparently figuring that, as long as everyone now has to remake themselves as miniature capitalists, why shouldn't they be allowed to create money out of nothing too?

Granted, the role of discretionary spending itself should not be exaggerated. The chief cause of bankruptcy in America is catastrophic illness; most borrowing is simply a matter of survival (if one does not have a car, one cannot work); and for most, simply being able to go to college now means debt peonage for at least half of one's subsequent working life.[36] Still, it is useful to point out that for real human beings survival is rarely enough. Nor should it be.

By the 1990s, the same tensions had begun to reappear on a global scale, as the older penchant for loaning money for grandiose, state-directed projects like the Aswan Dam gave way to an emphasis on microcredit. Inspired by the success of the Grameen Bank in Bangladesh, the new model was to identify budding entrepreneurs in poor communities and provide them with small low-interest loans. "Credit," the Grameen Bank insisted, "is a human right." At the same time the idea was to draw on the "social capital"—the knowledge, networks, connections, and ingenuity that the poor people of the world are already using to get by in difficult circumstances—and convert it into a way of generating even more (expansive) capital, able to grow at 5 to 20 percent annually.

As anthropologists like Julia Elyachar discovered, the result is double-edged. As one unusually candid NGO consultant explained to her in Cairo in 1995:

> Money is empowerment. This is empowerment money. You need to be big, need to think big. Borrowers here can be imprisoned if they don't pay, so why be worried?
>
> In America we get ten offers for credit cards in the mail every day. You pay incredible real interest rates for that credit, something like 40 percent. But the offer is there, so you get the card, and stuff your wallet full of credit cards. You feel good. It should be the same thing here, why not help them get into debt? Do I really care what they use the money for, as long as they pay the loan back?[37]

The very incoherence of the quote is telling. The only unifying theme seems to be: people *ought* to be in debt. It's good in itself. It's empowering. Anyway, if they end up too empowered, we can also have them arrested. Debt and power, sin and redemption, become almost indistinguishable. Freedom is slavery. Slavery is freedom. During her time in Cairo, Elyachar witnessed young graduates of an NGO training program go on strike for their right to receive start-up loans. At the same time, just about everyone involved took it for granted that most of their fellow students, not to mention everyone else involved in the program, was corrupt and exploiting the system as their personal cash cow. Here too, aspects of economic life that had been based on longstanding relations of trust were, through the intrusion of credit bureaucracies, becoming effectively criminalized.

Within another decade, the entire project—even in South Asia, where it began—began to appear suspiciously similar to the U.S. sub-prime mortgage crisis: all sorts of unscrupulous lenders piled in, all sorts of deceptive financial appraisals were passed off to investors, interest accumulated, borrowers tried to collectively refuse payment, lenders began sending in goons to seize what little wealth they had (corrugated tin roofs, for example), and the end result has been an epidemic of suicides by poor farmers caught in traps from which their families could never possibly escape.[38]

Just as in the 1945–1975 cycle, this new one culminated in another crisis of inclusion. It proved no more possible to really turn everyone in the world into micro-corporations or to "democratize credit" in such a way that every family that wanted to could have a house (And if you think about it, if we have the means to build them, why shouldn't they? Are there families who don't "deserve" houses?) than it had been to allow all wage laborers to have unions, pensions, and health benefits. Capitalism doesn't work that way. It is ultimately a system of power and exclusion, and when it reaches the breaking point, the symptoms recur, just as they had in the 1970s: food riots, oil shock, financial crisis, the sudden startled realization that the current course was ecologically unsustainable, and attendant apocalyptic scenarios of every sort.

In the wake of the subprime collapse, the U.S. government was forced to decide who really gets to make money out of nothing: The financiers, or ordinary citizens. The results were predictable. Financiers were "bailed out with taxpayer money"—which basically means that their imaginary money was treated as if it were real. Mortgage holders were, overwhelmingly, left to the tender mercies of the courts, under a bankruptcy law that Congress had a year before (rather suspiciously presciently, one might add) made far more exacting against debtors. Nothing was altered. All major decisions were postponed. The Great Conversation that many were expecting never took place.

■ ■ ■ ■ ■

We live, now, at a genuinely peculiar historical juncture. The credit crisis has provided us with a vivid illustration of the principle set out in the last chapter: that capitalism cannot really operate in a world where people believe it will be around forever.

For most of the last several centuries, most people assumed that credit could not be generated infinitely because they assumed that the economic system itself was unlikely to endure forever. The future was likely to be fundamentally different. Yet, somehow, the anticipated revolutions never happened. The basic structures of financial capitalism largely remained in place. It's only now, at the very moment when it's becoming increasingly clear that current arrangements are not viable, that we suddenly have hit the wall in terms of our collective imagination.

There is very good reason to believe that, in a generation or so, capitalism itself will no longer exist—most obviously, as ecologists keep reminding us, because it's impossible to maintain an engine of perpetual growth forever on a finite planet, and the current form of capitalism doesn't seem to be capable of generating the kind of vast technological breakthroughs and mobilizations that would be required for us to start finding and colonizing any other planets. Yet, faced with the prospect of capitalism actually ending, the most common reaction—even from those who call themselves "progressives"—is simple fear. We cling to what exists because we can no longer imagine an alternative that wouldn't be even worse.

How did we get here? My own suspicion is that we are looking at the final effects of the militarization of American capitalism itself. In fact, it could well be said that the last thirty years have seen the construction of a vast bureaucratic apparatus for the creation and maintenance of hopelessness, a giant machine designed, first and foremost, to destroy any sense of possible alternative futures. At its root is a veritable obsession on the part of the rulers of the world—in response to the upheavals of the 1960s and 1970s—with ensuring that social movements cannot be seen to grow, flourish, or propose alternatives; that those who challenge existing power arrangements can never, under any circumstances, be perceived to win.[39] To do so requires creating a vast apparatus of armies, prisons, police, various forms of private security firms and military intelligence apparatus, and propaganda engines of every conceivable variety, most of which do not attack alternatives directly so much as create a pervasive climate of fear, jingoistic conformity, and simple despair that renders any thought of changing the world seem an idle fantasy. Maintaining this apparatus seems even more important to exponents of the "free market," even than maintaining any sort of viable market economy. How else can one explain what happened in the former Soviet Union? One would ordinarily have imagined that the end of the Cold War would have led to the dismantling of the army and the KGB and the rebuilding of the factories, but in fact what happened was precisely the other way around. This is just an extreme example of what has been happening everywhere. Economically, the apparatus is largely just a drag on the system; all those guns, surveillance cameras, and propaganda engines are extraordinarily expensive and don't really produce anything, and no doubt it's yet another element dragging the entire capitalist system down—along with producing the illusion of an endless capitalist future that laid the groundwork for the endless bubbles to begin with. Finance capital became the buying and selling of chunks of that future, and economic freedom, for most of us, was reduced to the right to buy a small piece of one's own permanent subordination.

In other words, there seems to have been a profound contradiction between the political imperative of establishing capitalism as the only possible way to manage anything, and capitalism's own unacknowledged need to limit its future horizons, lest speculation, predictably, go haywire. Once it did, and the whole machine imploded, we were left in the strange situation of not being able to even imagine any other way that things might be arranged. About the only thing we can imagine is catastrophe.

■ ■ ■ ■ ■

To begin to free ourselves, the first thing we need to do is to see ourselves again as historical actors, as people who can make a difference in the course of world events. This is exactly what the militarization of history is trying to take away.

Even if we are at the beginning of the turn of a very long historical cycle, it's still largely up to us to determine how it's going to turn out. For instance: the last time we shifted from a bullion economy to one of virtual credit money, at the end of the Axial Age and the beginning of the Middle Ages, the immediate shift was experienced largely as a series of great catastrophes. Will it be the same this time around? Presumably a lot depends on how consciously we set out to ensure that it won't be. Will a return to virtual money lead to a move away from empires and vast standing armies, and to the creation of larger structures limiting the depredations of creditors? There is good reason to believe that all these things will happen—and if humanity is to survive, they will probably have to—but we have no idea how long it will take, or what, if it does, it would really look like. Capitalism has transformed the world in many ways that are clearly irreversible. What I have been trying to do in this book is not so much to propose a vision of what, precisely, the next age will be like, but to throw open perspectives, enlarge our sense of possibilities; to begin to ask what it would mean to start thinking on a breadth and with a grandeur appropriate to the times.

Let me give an example. I've spoken of two cycles of popular movements since World War II: the first (1945–1978), about demanding the rights of national citizenship, the second (1978–2008), over access to capitalism itself. It seems significant here that in the Middle East, in the first round, those popular movements that most directly challenged the global status quo tended to be inspired by Marxism; in the second, largely, some variation on radical Islam. Considering that Islam has always placed debt at the center of its social doctrines, it's easy to understand the appeal. But why not throw things open even more widely? Over the last five thousand years, there have been at least two occasions when major, dramatic moral and financial innovations have emerged from the country we now refer to as Iraq. The first was the invention of interest-bearing debt, perhaps sometime around 3000 BC; the second, around 800 AD, the development of the first sophisticated commercial system that explicitly rejected it. Is it possible that we are due for another? For most Americans, it will seem an odd question, since most Americans are used to thinking of Iraqis either as victims or fanatics (this is how occupying powers always think about the people they occupy), but it is worthy of note that the most prominent working-class Islamist movement opposed to the U.S. occupation, the Sadrists, take their name from one of the founders of contemporary Islamic economics, Muhammad Baqir al-Sadr. True, much of what has since come to pass for Islamic economics nowadays has proved decidedly unimpressive.[40] Certainly in no sense does it pose a direct challenge to capitalism. Still, one has to assume that among popular movements of this sort, all kinds of interesting conversations about, say, the status of wage labor must be taking place. Or perhaps it's naïve to look for any new breakthrough from the puritanical legacy of the old patriarchal rebellion. Perhaps it will come out of feminism. Or Islamic feminism. Or from some as yet completely unexpected quarter. Who's to say? The one thing we can be confident of is that history is not over, and that wherever the most exciting new ideas of the next century come from, it will almost certainly be from someplace we don't expect.

■ ■ ■ ■ ■

The one thing that's clear is that such new ideas cannot emerge without our jettisoning of much of our accustomed categories of thought—which have become mostly sheer dead weight, if not intrinsic parts of the very apparatus of hopelessness—and formulating new ones. This is why I spent so much of this book talking about the market, but also about the false choice between state and market that so monopolized political ideology for the last centuries that it made it difficult to argue about anything else.

The real history of markets is nothing like what we're taught to think it is. The earlier markets that we are able to observe appear to be spillovers, more or less; side effects of the elaborate administrative systems of ancient Mesopotamia. They operated primarily on credit. Cash markets arose through war: again, largely through tax and tribute policies that were originally designed to provision soldiers, but that later became useful in all sorts of other ways besides. It was only the Middle Ages, with their return to credit systems, that saw the first manifestations of what might be called market populism: the idea that markets could exist beyond, against, and outside of states, as in those of the Muslim Indian Ocean—an idea that was later to reappear in China with the great silver revolts of the fifteenth century. It usually seems to arise in situations where merchants, for one reason or another, find themselves making common cause with common people against the administrative machinery of some great state. But market populism is always riddled with paradoxes, because it still does depend to some degree on the existence of that state, and above all, because it requires market relations to be founded, ultimately, in something other than sheer calculation: in the codes of honor, trust, and ultimately community and mutual aid, more typical of human economies.[41] This in turn means relegating competition to a relatively minor element. In this light, we can see that what Adam Smith ultimately did, in creating his debt-free market utopia, was to fuse elements of this unlikely legacy with that unusually militaristic conception of market behavior characteristic of the Christian West. In doing so he was surely prescient. But like all extraordinarily influential writers, he was also just capturing something of the emerging spirit of his age. What we have seen ever since is an endless political jockeying back and forth between two sorts of populism—state and market populism—without anyone noticing that they were talking about the left and right flanks of exactly the same animal.

The main reason that we're unable to notice, I think, is that the legacy of violence has twisted everything around us. It's not just that war, conquest, and slavery played such a central role in converting human economies into market ones; there is literally no institution in our society that has not been to some degree affected. The story told at the end of Chapter Seven, of how even our conceptions of "freedom" itself came to be transformed, through the Roman institution of slavery, from the ability to make friends, to enter into moral relations with others, into incoherent dreams of absolute power, is only perhaps the most dramatic instance—and most insidious, because it leaves it very hard to imagine what meaningful human freedom would even be like.[42]

If this book has shown anything, it's exactly how much violence it has taken, over the course of human history, to bring us to a situation where it's even possible to imagine that that's what life is really about. Especially when one considers how much of our own daily experience flies directly in the face of it. As I've emphasized, communism may be the foundation of all human relations—that communism that, in our own daily life, manifests itself above all in what we call "love"—but there's always some sort of system of exchange, and usually, a system of hierarchy built on top of it. These systems of exchange can take an endless variety of forms, many perfectly innocuous. Still, what we are speaking of here is a very particular type of exchange, founded on precise calculation. As I pointed out in the very beginning: the difference between owing someone a favor and owing someone a debt is that the amount of a debt can be precisely calculated. Calculation demands equivalence. And such equivalence—especially when it involves equivalence between human beings (and it always seems to start that way, because at first, human beings are always the ultimate values)—only seems to occur when people have been forcibly severed from their contexts, so much so that they can be treated as identical to something else, as in: "seven martin skins and twelve large silver rings for the return of your captured brother," "one of your three daughters as surety for this loan of one hundred and fifty bushels of grain" . . .

This in turn leads to that great embarrassing fact that haunts all attempts to represent the market as the highest form of human freedom: that historically, impersonal, commercial markets originate in theft. More than anything else, the endless recitation of the myth of barter, employed much like an incantation, is the economists' way of exorcising this uncomfortable truth. But even a moment's reflection makes it obvious. Who was the first man to look at a house full of objects and immediately assess them only in terms of what he could get for them in the market? Surely, he can only have been a thief. Burglars, marauding soldiers, then perhaps debt collectors, were the first to see the world this way. It was only in the hands of soldiers, fresh from looting towns and cities, that chunks of gold or silver—melted down, in most cases, from some heirloom treasure, that like the Kashmiri gods, or Aztec breastplates, or Babylonian women's ankle bracelets, was both a work of art and a little compendium of history—could become simple, uniform bits of currency, with no history, valuable precisely for their lack of history, because they could be accepted anywhere, no questions asked. And it continues to be true. Any system that reduces the world to numbers can only be held in place by weapons, whether these are swords and clubs, or, nowadays, "smart bombs" from unmanned drones.

It can also only operate by continually converting love into debt. I know my use of the word "love" here is even more provocative, in its own way, than "communism." Still, it's important to hammer the point home. Just as markets, when allowed to drift entirely free from their violent origins, invariably begin to grow into something different, into networks of honor, trust, and mutual connectedness, so does the maintenance of systems of coercion constantly do the opposite: turn the products of human cooperation, creativity, devotion, love, and trust back into numbers once again. In doing so, they make it possible to imagine a world that is nothing more than a series of cold-blooded calculations. Even more, by turning human sociality itself into debts, they transform the very foundations of our being—since what else are we, ultimately, except the sum of the relations we have with others— into matters of fault, sin, and crime, and make the world into a place of iniquity that can only be overcome by completing some great cosmic transaction that will annihilate everything.

Trying to flip things around by asking, "What do we owe society?" or even trying to talk about our "debt to nature" or some other manifestation of the cosmos is a false solution—really just a desperate scramble to salvage something from the very moral logic that has severed us from the cosmos to begin with. In fact, if anything, it is the culmination of the process, the process brought to a point of veritable dementia, since it's premised on the assumption that we're so absolutely, thoroughly disentangled from the world that we can just toss all other human beings—or all other living creatures, even, or the cosmos—in a sack, and then start negotiating with them. It's hardly surprising that the end result, historically, is to see our life itself as something we hold on false premises, a loan long since overdue, and therefore, to see existence itself as criminal. Insofar as there's a real crime here, though, it's fraud. The very premise is fraudulent. What could possibly be more presumptuous, or more ridiculous, than to think it would be possible to negotiate with the grounds of one's existence? Of course it isn't. Insofar as it is indeed possible to come into any sort of relation with the Absolute, we are confronting a principle that exists outside of time, or human-scale time, entirely; therefore, as medieval theologians correctly recognized, when dealing with the Absolute, there can be no such thing as debt.

Conclusion:

Perhaps the World Really Does Owe You a Living

Much of the existing economic literature on credit and banking, when it turns to the kind of larger historical questions treated in this book, strikes me as little more than special pleading. True, earlier figures like Adam Smith and David Ricardo were suspicious of credit systems, but already by the mid–nineteenth century, economists who concerned themselves with such matters were largely in the business of trying to demonstrate that, despite appearances, the banking system really was profoundly democratic. One of the more common arguments was that it was really a way of funneling resources from the "idle rich," who, too unimaginative to do the work of investing their own money, entrusted it to others, notably, to the "industrious poor"—who had the energy and initiative to produce new wealth. This justified the existence of banks, but it also strengthened the hand of populists who demanded easy money policies, protections for debtors, and so on—since, if times were rough, why should the industrious poor, the farmers and artisans and small businessmen, be the ones to suffer?

This gave rise to a second line of argument, that no doubt the rich were the major creditors in the ancient world, but now the situation has been reversed. So Ludwig von Mises, writing in the 1930s, around the time when Keynes was calling for the euthanasia of the rentiers:

> Public opinion has always been biased against creditors. It identifies creditors with the idle rich and debtors with the industrious poor. It abhors the former as ruthless exploiters and pities the latter as innocent victims of oppression. It considers government action designed to curtail the claims of the creditors as measures extremely beneficial to the immense majority at the expense of a small minority of hardboiled usurers. It did not notice at all that nineteenth-century capitalist innovations have wholly changed the composition of the classes of creditors and debtors. In the days of Solon the Athenian, of ancient Rome's agrarian laws, and of the Middle Ages, the creditors were by and large the rich and the debtors the poor. But in this age of bonds and debentures, mortgage banks, saving banks, life insurance policies, and social security benefits, the masses of people with more moderate income are rather themselves creditors.[43]

Whereas the rich, with their leveraged companies, are now the principal debtors. This is the "democratization of finance" argument and it too is nothing new: whenever there are some people calling for the elimination of the class that lives by collecting interest, there will be others to object that this will destroy the livelihood of widows and pensioners.

The remarkable thing is that, nowadays, defenders of the financial system are often prepared to use both arguments, appealing to one or the other according to the rhetorical convenience of the moment. On the one hand, we have "pundits" like Thomas Friedman, celebrating the fact that "everyone" now owns a piece of Exxon or Mexico and that rich debtors are therefore answerable to the poor. On the other, Niall Ferguson, author of *The Ascent of Money*, published in 2009, can still announce as one of his major discoveries that:

> Poverty is not the result of rapacious financiers exploiting the poor. It has much more to do with the lack of financial institutions, with the absence of banks, not their presence. Only when borrowers have access to efficient credit networks can they escape from the clutches of loan sharks, and only when savers can deposit their money in reliable banks can it be channeled from the idle rich to the industrious poor.[44]

Such is the state of the conversation in the mainstream literature. My purpose here has been less to engage with it directly than to show how it has consistently encouraged us to ask the wrong questions. Let's take this last paragraph as an illustration. What is Ferguson really saying here? Poverty is caused by a lack of credit. It's only if the industrious poor have access to loans from stable, respectable banks—rather than to loan sharks, or, presumably, credit card companies, or payday loan operations, which now charge loan-shark rates—that they can rise out of poverty. So actually Ferguson is not really concerned with "poverty" at all, just with the poverty of some people, those who are industrious and thus do not deserve to be poor. What about the non-industrious poor? They can go to hell, presumably (quite literally, according to many branches of Christianity). Or maybe their boats will be lifted somewhat by the rising tide. Still, that's clearly incidental. They're undeserving, since they're not industrious, and therefore what happens to them is really beside the point.

For me, this is exactly what's so pernicious about the morality of debt: the way that financial imperatives constantly try to reduce us all, despite ourselves, to the equivalent of pillagers, eyeing the world simply for what can be turned into money—and then tell us that it's only those who are willing to see the world as pillagers who deserve access to the resources required to pursue anything in life *other* than money. It introduces moral perversions on almost every level. ("Cancel all student loan debt? But that would be unfair to all those people who struggled for years to pay back their student loans!" Let me assure the reader that, as someone who struggled for years to pay back his student loans and finally did so, this argument makes about as much sense as saying it would be "unfair" to a mugging victim not to mug their neighbors too.)

The argument might perhaps make sense if one agreed with the underlying assumption—that work is by definition virtuous, since the ultimate measure of humanity's success as a species is its ability to increase the overall global output of goods and services by at least 5 percent per year. The problem is that it is becoming increasingly obvious that if we continue along these lines much longer, we're likely to destroy everything. That giant debt machine that has, for the last five centuries, reduced increasing proportions of the world's population to the moral equivalent of conquistadors would appear to be coming up against its social and ecological limits. Capitalism's inveterate propensity to imagine its own destruction has morphed, in the last half-century, into scenarios that threaten to bring the rest of the world down with it. And there's no reason to believe that this propensity is ever going to go away. The real question now is how to ratchet things down a bit, to move toward a society where people can live more by working less.

I would like, then, to end by putting in a good word for the non-industrious poor.[45] At least they aren't hurting anyone. Insofar as the time they are taking off from work is being spent with friends and family, enjoying and caring for those they love, they're probably improving the world more than we acknowledge. Maybe we should think of them as pioneers of a new economic order that would not share our current one's penchant for self-annihilation.

■ ■ ■ ■ ■

In this book I have largely avoided making concrete proposals, but let me end with one. It seems to me that we are long overdue for some kind of Biblical-style Jubilee: one that would affect both international debt and consumer debt. It would be salutary not just because it would relieve so much genuine human suffering, but also because it would be our way of reminding ourselves that money is not ineffable, that paying one's debts is not the essence of morality, that all these things are human arrangements and that if democracy is to mean anything, it is the ability to all agree to arrange things in a different way. It is significant, I think, that since Hammurabi, great imperial states have almost invariably resisted this kind of politics. Athens and Rome established the paradigm: even when confronted with continual debt crises, they insisted on legislating around the edges, softening the impact, eliminating obvious abuses like debt slavery, using the spoils of empire to throw all sorts of extra benefits at their poorer citizens (who, after all, provided the rank and file of their armies), so as to keep them more or less afloat—but all in such a way as never to allow a challenge to the principle of debt itself. The governing class of the United States seems to have taken a remarkably similar approach: eliminating the worst abuses (e.g., debtors' prisons), using the fruits of empire to provide subsidies, visible and otherwise, to the bulk of the population; in more recent years, manipulating currency rates to flood the country with cheap goods from China, but never allowing anyone to question the sacred principle that we must all pay our debts.

At this point, however, the principle has been exposed as a flagrant lie. As it turns out, we don't "all" have to pay our debts. Only some of us do. Nothing would be more important than to wipe the slate clean for everyone, mark a break with our accustomed morality, and start again.

What is a debt, anyway? A debt is just the perversion of a promise. It is a promise corrupted by both math and violence. If freedom (real freedom) is the ability to make friends, then it is also, necessarily, the ability to make real promises. What sorts of promises might genuinely free men and women make to one another? At this point, we can't even say. It's more a question of how we can get to a place that will allow us to find out. And the first step in that journey, in turn, is to accept that in the largest scheme of things, just as no one has the right to tell us our true value, no one has the right to tell us what we truly owe.

Afterword

2014

WHEN I FIRST set out to write this book, in mid-2008, the upcoming financial meltdown was very much on my mind. Most people who were interested in such matters recognized that some kind of crash was inevitable—except, that is, for those who had a professional interest in claiming otherwise. It was this larger political context that transformed what I had originally conceived as a theoretically oriented academic book into something much larger: an attempt to see if it was still possible to use the intellectual tools available to someone like myself—historical, ethnographic, theoretical—to actually influence public debate on issues that really mattered.

Partly for that reason, I also decided I wanted to write a big, sprawling, scholarly book—the kind that people don't write anymore. This is especially true of anthropologists like myself. I've always felt there was a tragic irony about the way that anthropologists have come to position themselves in the academy. For at least a century, anthropologists have largely played the role of gadflies: whenever some ambitious European or American theorist appears to make some grandiose generalizations about how human beings go about organizing political, economic, or family life, it's always the anthropologist who shows up to point out that there are people in Samoa or Tierra del Fuego or Burundi who do things exactly the other way around. But for this very reason, anthropologists are also the only people in a position to make broad generalizations that actually could stand up to the evidence. Yet increasingly, we have come to feel it is somehow wrong to do so. It is seen to smack of a kind of arrogance, even an intellectual imperialism.

It struck me, however, that such a grand, comparative effort was precisely what the times were calling for. There were two reasons that led me to feel this way. First (and most obvious): there had been, as I noted, a certain collapse of our collective imaginations. It's almost as if people had been led to believe that the era's technological advances and its greater overall social complexity had had the effect of *reducing* our political, social, and economic possibilities, rather than expanding them. Instead of unleashing visions, it had made visionary politics of any sort impossible. A work taking in the broad sweep of human history would necessarily reveal just how many different ways humans had found to arrange their political and economic lives in the past and, in doing so, help open up our sense of the future.

The second reason—and this is why I thought a five-thousand-year history would be especially useful—was more subtle. It was clear that 2008 marked a historical watershed of some sort—the real question was one of scale. After all, when one is in the middle of dramatic historical events that seem to represent some kind of break, the most important thing one has to do is to get a sense of the larger rhythmic structure. Is this crisis some kind of generational phenomenon, or a mere movement of capitalism's boom-or-bust cycle, or the inevitable unfolding of some sixty-year Kondratieff curve of technological innovation and decline? Or is it something even grander or more epochal? How do all these rhythms weave in and out of each other? Is there one core rhythm pushing the others along? How do they sit inside one another, syncopate, concatenate, harmonize, clash?

The more I puzzled over the question, the more I decided that this was a break on the broadest possible historical scale, and that in order to understand it, we needed to completely rethink our sense of the rhythms of economic history.

Now, an anthropologist might not seem the obvious candidate for this job, but in fact, we are pretty much perfectly positioned here as well. This is because historians and economists tend to go astray in opposite directions. Economists tend to come at history with their mathematical models—and the assumptions about human nature that come along with them—already fully in place: it's largely a matter of arranging the data around the equations. Historians, in contrast, are so resolutely empirical that they often refuse to extrapolate at all; in the absence of direct evidence for, say, democratic popular assemblies in the European Bronze Age, they will not ask whether it is reasonable to assume such assemblies existed, or whether they would have left a trace in the available evidence had they existed. Instead, they simply act as if these assemblies did not exist and could not have existed, and therefore speak of the "birth of democracy" as having taken place in Iron Age Greece. This is why we can have so many "histories of money" that are actually histories of coinage: since coins leave obvious traces, and credit records often don't, historians often ignore the possibility of their existence entirely. Anthropologists in contrast are empirical—they don't just apply preset models—but they also have such a wealth of comparative material at their disposal they can actually speculate about what village assemblies in Bronze Age Europe or credit systems in ancient China were likely to be like. And they can reexamine the evidence to see if it confirms or contradicts their assessment.

Finally, anthropologists are keenly aware that one cannot speak of "economic life" as an a priori category. Even three hundred years ago, there was no such thing as "the economy," at least in the sense of something people could talk about as an entity unto itself, with its own laws and principles. For the vast majority of people who have ever lived, "economic affairs" were just one aspect of what we'd call politics, law, domestic life, or even religion. Economic language has always been—and still is—fundamentally moral, even when it insists that it is not (as in the cutthroat realpolitik of the Axial Age, or the "rational" cost-benefit analysis of economists today), and a genuine economic history must therefore also be a history of morality. This is why the chapter on transactional logics—communism, exchange, and hierarchy—has such a central place in the book. Any argument about economic affairs, about rights of access to or the disposition of valuable products or resources, let alone about debt, is always going to be a tangle of different moral discourses clashing in a dozen different ways.

In all this, probably my greatest inspiration was the early twentieth-century French anthropologist Marcel Mauss—both because he was perhaps the first to recognize that all societies are such a jumble of contradictory principles, and also, much more specifically, because he was one of the first to try to combine the insights of ancient history with those of contemporary ethnography, in order to unmask the bizarre assumptions about human life and human nature on which modern economics is constructed. Above all, he tried to provide an alternative to the "myth of barter," which he correctly identified as in most important ways, the founding myth of our contemporary civilization.

Mauss is a curious figure in the history of anthropology. Even though he never conducted fieldwork and never even wrote a proper book (he died surrounded by unfinished writing projects), the stream of occasional essays that he did produce was incredibly influential—just about every one of them has inspired a whole body of subsequent literature. Mauss had an extraordinary knack for asking the most interesting questions—about the meaning of sacrifice, the nature of the magic or the gift, the way cultural assumptions are inscribed in posture and other techniques of the body, or the very idea of the self. These questions have come to define what anthropology is basically about, so as a theorist, he has found his work to be enormously successful. But Mauss was also a political activist, a cooperativist, and an avid contributor to socialist newspapers and magazines who very much sought to apply the insights of social theory to political problems, and here his efforts met with almost no success at all. His best-known work, *The Gift*, was meant to put to rest for all time the notion that primitive economies operated on barter, and despite its fame in intellectual circles, it had virtually no effect whatsoever on the way economics was taught, or on popular understandings of the issue.

When I was writing this book, I sometimes told myself I wanted to write the sort of book Mauss might have written—had he ever managed to overcome his perpetual disorganization and actually write one. I'm not sure I succeeded—I'm not even sure that it would have been a good thing if I had—but I am extremely gratified that there is one way in which I have actually helped realize one of his lifelong goals: to finally put to rest the myth of barter. Incidentally, this isn't just Mauss's goal—it's been a kind of pet peeve of anthropologists for more than a century. When it comes to this myth, most of us have felt like we were smashing our heads against the wall as we've watched this same, just-so story repeated ad nauseam by economists, seen it reappear in textbooks, cartoons, and heard it retold as common knowledge everywhere, no matter how many times we demonstrated that it simply couldn't have been true. Obviously, it will take some time to see how deep or enduring the change really is, but it does seem that the success of *Debt* might have finally made an impact. Just this year, the Bank of England issued a statement on "The Role of Money in the Modern Economy," accompanied by a video and text explaining the origins of money, which starts as if it were about to tell the myth of barter ("Imagine there was a primitive fisherman, and a farmer, who wanted to exchange with one another . . .") but instead launches into a story about improvised IOUs that could have easily been taken directly from my book. Indeed, one or two of my friends strongly suspect that it actually was. I wouldn't know about that—it could equally well have been inspired by proponents of Modern Money Theory—but I must admit my first reaction was to pop a bottle of champagne on behalf of anthropologists everywhere: after a century's work, we may well have finally managed to do it!

This is not the only way I've been surprised—even startled—by the impact this book has had. Of course, a lot of its success is simply due to extreme serendipity of timing. There is no small irony here, because before *Debt*, my intellectual career had been marked by some of the worst timing imaginable. I had written a long, detailed, novelistic ethnography (*Lost People*) at just the moment that publishing long ethnographies became almost impossible; I had produced a work of anthropological theory (*Toward an Anthropological Theory of Value*) at just the moment the discipline decided it was no longer interested in theory books; I came out as a proponent of direct action immediately before 9/11. Then, in 2011, it was as if all the good timing I'd missed over the past decade and a half decided to catch up with me. Not only did my book on debt appear just when people had abandoned the idea that 2008 represented a momentary blip—and when they seemed ready to start asking serious questions about what debt-based politics really meant—I also showed up in New York to promote it at exactly the moment that a social movement was beginning to take form that would sweep the nation, and indeed the world, on exactly that basis.

Obviously, I did have something to do with Occupy Wall Street. When I returned to New York in June of 2011, I went looking for an activist project of some sort, and ended up one of the eighty-odd activists who worked to plan the occupation of Zuccotti Park. But at the time, I didn't really see the two things as much connected. In fact, I worked hard to keep them separate—after all, I didn't want to become some vanguardist intellectual imposing his ideological vision on a movement; I also thought it would be rather sleazy to use a social movement to promote one's book. I tried to avoid talking about the book, or the arguments in it, during activist meetings and events. But I came to find this increasingly difficult. Every time I gave a book talk with any number of young people in the crowd, at least one of them—and often several—would approach me afterward to inquire about the prospects of creating some sort of movement around the issue of student debt. Then, when the occupation of Zuccotti began—and we had no idea who, if anyone, was actually going to show up to the occupation—we discovered that the largest contingent by far were debt refugees. After the suppression of the camps, we began a series of popular assemblies to explore where people wanted us to take the movement, and the assemblies around debt were far and away larger and more enthusiastic than the others. Before long, I had joined up with Strike Debt!—a working group of Occupy that I had actually avoided getting involved with in its early days, for precisely the reasons outlined earlier—and helped formulate the strategy for the *Debt Resistors' Operations Manual*, the Rolling Jubilee, and other projects.

Where all this will ultimately go remains to be seen. Neither the ultimate intellectual legacy of the book nor the ultimate political meaning of the movements of 2011 and subsequent debt mobilizations are likely to be clear for some time to come. I suspect—at least I like to think—that most interesting debates about the questions raised in the book lie in the future as well. Most of the initial response was pretty much what one might expect for a book that tries to reframe longstanding problems in unfamiliar and somewhat unsettling terms. Many American liberals, for instance, accepted the basic premise (that there has for thousands of years been an intimate connection between the organization of empires and other forms of state violence, debt, and forms of money-creation) as a fascinating historical revelation—and then reacted with outrage when I went on to suggest that this continued to be the case even after 1945. (We are supposed to believe that the old system has now been replaced with a purely voluntary and non-imperial system that just happens to look and operate in almost exactly the same way.) Many radicals simply chided me for writing this book rather than some other book (on Marxian value theory, perhaps, or maybe neoclassical economic history). While there have been some brilliant exceptions—Benjamin Kunkel, George Caffentzis, Silvia Federici come most immediately to mind—we're going to have to wait awhile, I think, before the really important conversations actually begin.

What I would like best of all, of course, would be to see this book contribute, in some small way, to a broader moral reassessment of the very idea of debt, work, money, growth, and "the economy" itself. As I say, the very notion that there is something called "the economy" is relatively new. Is it possible that children born today might live to see the day when there is no longer an "economy," when we can examine these matters in completely different terms? What would such a world even look like? From our current vantage, it's very hard for us to even imagine. But if we are going to create a world that does not threaten to wipe out humanity every generation or so, this is exactly the scale on which we're going to have to start reimagining things. And in the process, many of our most cherished assumptions—about the value of work, for instance, or the virtue of paying debts—are likely to be stood on their heads.

It was with such thoughts in the back of my mind that I decided to end the book the way that I did, with words of praise for the world's non-industrious poor.

Let me end this afterword, then, in a similar vein, with a bow to Adam Smith. Now, I know that the great Scottish moral philosopher does not come off particularly well in this book. This is partly because I have only talked about one side of his philosophy—his dedication to imagining a kind of utopian vision in which everyone could simply trade fairly with one another, each seeking their best advantage and then walking away without owing anyone anything. But all of this rested on a theory of human motivations that assumed that people, in general, were motivated above all to be the object of others' sympathetic attentions. People seek wealth because they know that others care more about the well-to-do. This is why he thought a free market could work to the betterment of all: because he was convinced ordinary human beings would *not* be so industrious, and so self-aggrandizing, as to continue pursuing their advantage once a certain comfortable prominence was achieved: that is, that they would not continue amassing more and more wealth simply for the sake of doing so. For Smith, the pursuit of wealth beyond a point where one had achieved such a comfortable position was pointless, even pathological. Hence, in his *Theory of Moral Sentiments*, he recounts this story from Plutarch:

> What the favourite of the King of Epirus said to his master may be applied to all men in the ordinary situations of human life. When the king had recounted to him, in their proper order, all the conquests which he proposed to make, and had come to the last of them;
>
> "And what does your Majesty propose to do then?" said the Favourite.
>
> "I propose then," said the King, "to enjoy myself with my friends, and endeavour to be good company over a bottle."
>
> "And what hinders your Majesty from doing so now?" replied the Favourite.[1]

The funny thing about this incident is that the moment I read it, I realized it was basically the same joke that my graduate school adviser, the anthropologist Marshall Sahlins, used to tell—though in his case, it's been transformed into a fanciful meeting between a missionary and a Samoan, whom he discovered lying on the beach:

> MISSIONARY: Look at you! You're just wasting your life away, lying around like that.
> SAMOAN: Why? What do you think I should be doing?
> MISSIONARY: Well, there are plenty of coconuts all around here. Why not dry some copra and sell it?

SAMOAN: And why would I want to do that?

MISSIONARY: You could make a lot of money. And with the money you make, you could get a drying machine, and dry copra faster, and make even more money.

SAMOAN: Okay. And why would I want to do that?

MISSIONARY: Well, you'd be rich. You could buy land, plant more trees, expand operations. At that point, you wouldn't even have to do the physical work anymore, you could just hire a bunch of other people to do it for you.

SAMOAN: Okay. And why would I want to do that?

MISSIONARY: Well, eventually, with all that copra, land, machines, employees, with all that money—you could retire a very rich man. And then you wouldn't have to do anything. You could just lie on the beach all day.

NOTES

Chapter One

1. With the predictable results that they weren't actually built to make it easier for Malagasy people to get around in their own country, but mainly to get products from the plantations to ports to earn foreign exchange to pay for building the roads and railways to begin with.

2. The United States, for example, only recognized the Republic of Haiti in 1860. France doggedly held on to the demand and the Republic of Haiti was finally forced to pay the equivalent of $21 billion between 1925 and 1946, during most of which time they were under U.S. military occupation.

3. Hallam 1866 V: 269–70. Since the government did not feel it appropriate to pay for the upkeep of improvidents, prisoners were expected to furnish the full cost of their own imprisonment. If they couldn't, they simply starved to death.

4. If we consider tax responsibilities to be debts, it's the overwhelming majority— and if nothing else the two are closely related, since over the course history, the need to assemble money for tax payments has always been the most frequent reason for falling into debt.

5. Finley 1960:63; 1963:24; 1974:80; 1981:106; 1983:108. And these are only the ones I managed to track down. What he says for Greece and Rome would appear to be equally true of Japan, India, or China.

6. Galey 1983.

7. Jacques de Vitry, in Le Goff 1990:64.

8. Kyokai, *Record of Miraculous Events in Japan* (c. 822 AD), Tale 26, cited in LaFleur 1986:36. Also Nakamura 1996:257–59.

9. ibid:36

10. ibid:37.

11. Jan Hoffman, "Shipping Out of the Economic Crisis" (www.relooney.fatcow .com/0_New_7594.pdf). About the only shipping-related industry that expanded in the immediate wake of 2008 was that centered on breaking cargo ships down for scrap metal.

12. Simon Johnson, the IMF's chief economist at the time, put it concisely in a recent article in *The Atlantic*: "Regulators, legislators, and academics almost all assumed that the managers of these banks knew what they were doing. In retrospect, they didn't. AIG's Financial Products division, for instance, made $2.5 billion in pretax profits in 2005, largely by selling underpriced insurance on complex, poorly understood securities. Often described as 'picking up nickels in front of a steamroller,' this strategy is profitable in ordinary years, and catastrophic in bad ones. As of last fall, AIG had outstanding insurance on more than $400 billion in securities. To date, the U.S. government, in an effort to rescue the company, has committed about $180 billion in investments and loans to cover losses that AIG's sophisticated risk modeling had said were virtually impossible." (Johnson 2010) Johnson of course passes over the possibility that

AIG knew perfectly well what was eventually going to happen, but simply didn't
care, since they knew the steamroller was
going to flatten someone else.

13. In contrast, England already had a
national bankruptcy law in 1571. An attempt to create a U.S. federal bankruptcy
law in 1800 foundered; there was one
briefly in place between 1867 and 1878,
aimed to relieve indebted Civil War veterans, but it was eventually abolished
on moral grounds (see Mann 2002 for a
good recent history). Bankruptcy reform
in America is more likely to make the
terms harsher than the other way around,
as with the 2005 reforms, which Congress
passed, on industry urgings, just before
the great credit crash.

14. The mortgage relief fund set up
after the bailout, for example, has only
provided aid to a tiny percentage of claim-
ants, and there has been no movement
toward liberalization of bankruptcy laws
that had, in fact, been made far harsher,
under financial industry pressure, in 2005,
just two years before the meltdown.

15. "In Jail for Being in Debt," Chris
Serres and Glenin Howatt, Minneapolis–
St. Paul *Star Tribune*, June 9, 2010, www
.startribune.com/local/95692619.html. See
"In for a Penny: The Rise of America's
New Debtor's Prisons," American Civil
Liberties Union, October 2010, www.aclu
.org/files/assets/InForAPenny_web.pdf.

16. "IMF warns second bailout
would 'threaten democracy.'" Angela
Jameson and Elizabeth Judge, business
.timesonline.co.uk/tol/business/eco
nomics/article6928147.ece#cid=OTC
-RSS&attr=1185799, accessed November
25, 2009

Chapter Two

1. Case, Fair, Gärtner, & Heather
1996:564. Emphasis in the original.
2. Op cit.

3. Begg, Fischer, and Dornbuch
(2005:384); Maunder, Myers, Wall, and
Miller (1991:310), Parkin & King (1995:65).

4. Stiglitz and Driffill 2000:521. Emphasis again in the original.

5. Aristotle *Politics* I.9.1257

6. Neither is it clear we are really
speaking of barter here. Aristotle used the
term *métadosis*, which in his day normally
meant "sharing" or "sharing out." Since
Smith, this has usually been translated
"barter," but as Karl Polanyi (1957a:93)
has long since emphasized, this is probably
inaccurate, unless Aristotle was introducing an entirely new meaning for the term.
Theorists of the origin of Greek money
from Laum (1924) to Seaford (2004) have
emphasized that customs of apportioning
goods (e.g., war booty, sacrificial meat),
probably did play a key role in the development of Greek currency. (For a critique
of the Aristotelian tradition, which does
assume Aristotle is talking about barter,
see Fahazmanesh 2006.)

7. See Jean-Michel Servet (1994, 2001)
for this literature. He also notes that in
the eighteenth century, these accounts suddenly vanished, to be replaced by endless
sightings of "primitive barter" in accounts
of Oceania, Africa, and the Americas.

8. *Wealth of Nations* I.2.1–2. As we'll
see, the line seems to be taken from much
older sources.

9. "If we should enquire into the principle of human mind on which this disposition of trucking is founded, it is clearly
the natural inclination every one has to
persuade. The offering of a shilling, which
to us appears to have so plain and simple
meaning, is in reality offering an argument
to persuade one to do so and so as it is for
his interest" (*Lectures on Jurisprudence*,
56) It's fascinating to note that the assumption that the notion that exchange
is the basis of our mental functions, and
manifests itself both in language (as the
exchange of words) and economics (as the
exchange of material goods) goes back to
Smith. Most anthropologists attribute it
to Claude Levi-Strauss (1963:296).

10. The reference to shepherds implies he may be referring to another part of the world, but elsewhere his examples, for instance of trading deer for beaver, make it clear he's thinking of the Northeast woodlands of North America.

11. Wealth of Nations I.4.2.

12. Wealth of Nations I.4.3.

13. Wealth of Nations I.4.7.

14. The idea of an historical sequence from barter to money to credit actually seems to appear first in the lectures of an Italian banker named Bernardo Davanzati (1529–1606; so Waswo 1996); it was developed as an explicit theory by German economic historians: Bruno Hildebrand (1864), who posited a prehistoric stage of barter, an ancient stage of coinage, and then, after some reversion to barter in the Middle Ages, a modern stage of credit economy. It took canonical form in the work of his student, Karl Bücher (1907). The sequence has now become universally accepted common sense, and it reappears in at least tacit form in Marx, and explicitly in Simmel—again, despite the fact that almost all subsequent historical research has proved it wrong.

15. Though they did make an impression on many others. Morgan's work in particular (1851, 1877, 1881), which emphasized both collective property rights and the extraordinary importance of women, with women's councils largely in control of economic life, so impressed many radical thinkers—included Marx and Engels—that they became the basis of a kind of counter-myth, of primitive communism and primitive matriarchy.

16. Anne Chapman (1980) goes if anything further, noting that if pure barter is to be defined as concerned only with swapping objects, and not with rearranging relations between people, it's not clear that it has ever existed. See also Heady 2005.

17. Levi-Strauss 1943; the translation is from Servet 1982:33.

18. One must imagine the temptation for a sexual variety must be fairly strong, for young men and women accustomed to spending almost all of their time with maybe a dozen other people the same age.

19. Berndt 1951:161, cf. Gudeman 2001: 124–25, who provides an analysis quite similar to my own.

20. Berndt 1951:162.

21. Though as we will note later, it's not exactly as if international business deals now never involve music, dancing, food, drugs, high-priced hookers, or the possibility of violence. For a random example underlining the last two, see Perkins 2006.

22. Lindholm 1982:116.

23. Servet 2001:20-21 compiles an enormous number of such terms.

24. The point is so obvious that it's amazing it hasn't been made more often. The only classical economist I'm aware of who appears to have considered the possibility that deferred payments might have made barter unnecessary is Ralph Hawtrey (1928:2, cited in Einzig 1949:375). All others simply assume, for no reason, that all exchanges even between neighbors must have necessarily been what economists like to call "spot trades."

25. Bohannan 1955, Barth 1969. cf. Munn 1986, Akin & Robbins 1998. A good summary of the concept can be found in Gregory 1982:48–49. Gregory gives one example of a highland Papua New Guinea system with six ranks of valuables, with live pigs and cassowary birds on the top rank, "pearl-shell pendants, pork sides, stone axes, cassowary-plume headdresses, and cowrie-shell headbands" on the second, and so on. Ordinarily items of items of consumption are confined to the last two, which consist of luxury foods and staple vegetable foods, respectively.

26. See Servet 1998, Humphries 1985.

27. The classic essay here is Radford 1945.

28. In the 1600s, at least, actually called the old Carolingian denominations "imaginary money"—everyone persisting in using pounds, shillings, and pence (or livres, deniers, and sous) for the intervening 800

years, despite the fact that for most of that period, actual coins were entirely different, or simply didn't exist (Finandi 1936).

29. Other examples of barter coexisting with money: Orlove 1986; Barnes & Barnes 1989.

30. One of the disadvantages of having your book become a classic is that often, people will actually check out such examples. (One of the advantages is that even if they discover you were mistaken, people will continue to cite you as an authority anyway.)

31. Innes 1913:378. He goes on to observe: "A moment's reflection shows that a staple commodity could not be used as money, because *ex hypothesi*, the medium of exchange is equally receivable by all members of the community. Thus if the fishers paid for their supplies in cod, the traders would equally have to pay for their cod in cod, an obvious absurdity."

32. The temples appear to have come first; the palaces, which became increasingly important over time, took over their system of administration.

33. Smith was not dreaming about these: the current technical term for such ingots is "hacksilber" (e.g., Balmuth 2001).

34. Compare Grierson 1977:17 for Egyptian parallels.

35. e.g., Hudson 2002:25, 2004:114

36. Innes 1913:381

37. Peter Spufford's monumental *Money and Its Use in Medieval Europe* (1988), which devotes hundreds of pages to gold and silver mining, mints, and debasement of coinage, makes only two or three mentions of various sorts of lead or leather token money or minor credit arrangements by which ordinary people appear to have conducted the overwhelming majority of their daily transactions. About these, he says, "we can know next to nothing" (1988:336). An even more dramatic example is the tally-stick, of which we will hear a good deal: the use of tallies instead of cash was widespread in the Middle Ages, but there has been almost no systematic

research on the subject, especially outside England.

Chapter Three

1. Heinsohn & Steiger (1989) even suggest the main reason their fellow economists haven't abandoned the story is that anthropologists have not yet provided an equally compelling alternative. Still, almost all histories of money continue to begin with fanciful accounts of barter. Another expedient is to fall back on pure circular definitions: if "barter" is an economic transaction that does not employ currency, then any economic transaction that doesn't involve currency, whatever its form or content, must be barter. Glyn Davies (1996:11–13) thus describes even Kwakiutl potlatches as "barter."

2. For my own take on the labor theory of value, see Toward an Anthropological Theory of Value (Graeber, 2001).

3. We often forget that there was a strong religious element in all this. Newton himself was in no sense an atheist—in fact, he tried to use his mathematical abilities to confirm that the world really had been created, as Bishop Ussher had earlier argued, sometime around October 23, 4004 BC.

4. Smith first uses the phrase "invisible hand" in his *Astronomy* (III.2), but in *Theory of Moral Sentiments* IV.1.10, he is explicit that the invisible hand of the market is that of "Providence." On Smith's theology in general see Nicholls 2003:35–43; on its possible connection to Medieval Islam, see chapter 10 below.

5. Samuelson 1948:49. See Heinsohn and Steiger 1989 for a critique of this position; also Ingham 2004.

6. Pigou 1949. Boianovsky 1993 provides a history of the term.

7. "We do not know of any economy in which systematic barter takes place without the presence of money" (Fayazmanesh

2006:87)—by which he means, in the sense of money of account.

8. On the government role of fostering the "self-regulating market" in general, see Polanyi 1949. The standard economic orthodoxy, that if the government just gets out of the way, a market will naturally emerge, without any need to create appropriate legal, police, and political institutions first, was dramatically disproved when free-market ideologues tried to impose this model in the former Soviet Union in the 1990s.

9. Innes as usual puts it nicely: "The eye has never seen, nor the hand touched a dollar. All that we can touch or see is a promise to pay or satisfy a debt due for an amount called a dollar." In the same way, he notes, "All our measures are the same. No one has ever seen on ounce or a foot or an hour. A foot is the distance between two fixed points, but neither the distance nor the points have a corporeal existence" (1914:155).

10. Note that this does assume some means of calculating such values—that is, that money of account of some sort already exists. This might seem obvious, but remarkable numbers of anthropologists seem to have missed it.

11. To give some sense of scale, even the relatively circumscribed commercial city-state of Hong Kong currently has roughly $23.3 billion in circulation. At roughly 7 million people, that's more than three thousand Hong Kong dollars per inhabitant.

12. "State theory may be traced to the early nineteenth century and to [Adam] Muller's New Theory of Money, which attempted to explain money value as an expression of communal trust and national will, and culminated in [G.F.] Knapp's State Theory of Money, first published in German in 1905. Knapp considered it absurd to attempt to understand money 'without the idea of the state.' Money is not a medium that emerges from exchange. It is rather a means for accounting for and settling debts, the most important

of which are tax debts" (Ingham 2004:47.) Ingham's book is an admirable statement of the Chartalist position, and much of my argument here can be found in much greater detail in it. However, as will later become apparent, I also part company with him in certain respects.

13. In French: livres, sous, and deniers.

14. Einaudi 1936. Cipolla (1967) calls it "ghost money."

15. On tallies: Jenkinson 1911, 1924; Innes 1913; Grandell 1977; Baxter 1989; Stone 2005.

16. Snell (1919:240) notes that kings while touring their domains would sometimes seize cattle or other goods by right of "preemption" and then pay in tallies, but it was very difficult to get their representatives to later pay up: "Subjects were compelled to sell; and the worst of it was that the King's purveyors were in the habit of paying not in cash down, but by means of an exchequer tally, or a beating . . . In practice it was found no easy matter to recover under this system, which lent itself to the worst exactions, and is the subject of numerous complaints in our early popular poetry."

17. It is also interesting to note, in this regard, that the Bank of England still kept their own internal accounts using tally sticks in Adam Smith's time, and only abandoned the practice in 1826.

18. See Engels (1978) for a classic study of this sort of problem.

19. Appealing particularly to debtors, who were understandably drawn to the idea that debt is simply a social arrangement that was in no sense immutable but created by government policies that could just as easily be reshuffled—not to mention, who would benefit from inflationary policies.

20. On the tax, Jacob 1987; for the Betsimisaraka village study, Althabe 1968; for analogous Malagasy case studies, Fremigacci 1976, Rainibe 1982, Schlemmer 1983, Feeley-Harnik 1991. For colonial tax policy in Africa more generally, Forstater 2005, 2006.

21. So, for instance, Heinsohn & Steiger 1989:188–189.

22. Silver was mined in the Midwest itself, and adopting bi-metallism, with both gold and silver as potential backing for currency, was seen as a move in the direction of free credit money, and to allow for the creation of money by local banks. The late nineteenth century saw the first creation of modern corporate capitalism in the United States and it was fervently resisted, with the centralization of the banking system being a major field of struggle, and mutualism—popular democratic (not profit oriented) banking and insurance arrangements—one of the main forms of resistance. The bi-metallists were the more moderate successors of the Greenbackers, who called for a currency detached from metal altogether, such as Lincoln briefly imposed in wartime (Dighe (2002) provides a good summary of the historical background.)

23. They only became ruby slippers in the movie.

24. Some have even suggested that Dorothy herself represents Teddy Roosevelt, since syllabically, "dor-o-thee" is the same as "thee-o-dor", only backwards.

25. See Littlefield 1963 and Rockoff 1990 for a detailed argument about *The Wizard of Oz* as "monetary allegory." Baum never admitted that the book had a political subtext, and it is quite possible this interpretation emerged only after the book's publication (so says Parker 1994; cf. Taylor 2005), but the fact remains that the book developed this reputation at some point, so it's really just a question of whether Baum created the myth or others did.

26. Reagan could as easily be argued to be a practitioner of extreme military Keynesianism, using the Pentagon's budget to create jobs and drive economic growth; anyway, monetary orthodoxy was abandoned very quickly even rhetorically among those actually managing the system.

27. See Ingham 2000.

28. Keynes 1930: 4–5

29. The argument is referred to as the paradox of banking. To provide an extremely simplified version: say there was only one bank. Even if that bank were to make you a loan of a trillion dollars based on no assets of its own of any kind whatever, you would ultimately end up putting the money back into the bank again, which would mean that the bank would now have one trillion in debt, and one trillion in working assets, perfectly balancing each other out. If the bank was charging you more for the loan than it was giving you in interest (which banks always do), it would also make a profit. The same would be true if you spent the trillion—whoever ended up with the money would still have to put it into the bank again. Keynes pointed out the existence of multiple banks didn't really change anything, provided bankers coordinated their efforts, which, in fact, they always do.

30. I might note that this assumption echoes the logic of neoclassical economic theory, which assumes that all basic institutional arrangements that define the context of economic activity were agreed to by all parties at some imaginary point in the past, and that since then, everything has and will always continue to exist in equilibrium. Interestingly, Keynes explicitly rejected this assumption in his theory of money (Davidson 2006). Contemporary social contract theorists incidentally make a similar argument, that there's no need to assume that this actually happened; it's enough to say it could have and act as if it did.

31. Aglietta is a Marxist, and one of the founders of the "Regulation School," Orléans, an adherent of the "economics of convention" favored by Thevenot and Boltanski. Primordial debt theory has been mainly developed by a group of researchers surrounding economists Michel Aglietta and André Orléans, first in *La Violence de la Monnaie* (1992), which employed a psychoanalytic, Giradian framework, and then in a volume called *Sovereignty, Legitimacy and Money* (1995) and a collection

called *Sovereign Money* (Aglietta, Andreau, etc. 1998), co-edited by eleven different scholars. The latter two volumes abandon the Girardian framework for a Dumontian one. In recent years the main exponent of this position has been another Regulationist, Bruno Théret (1992, 1995, 2007, 2008). Unfortunately almost none of this material has ever been translated into English, though a summary of many of Aglietta's contributions can be found in Grahl (2000).

32. For instance, Randall Wray (1990, 1998, 2000) and Stephanie Bell (1999, 2000) in the United States, or Geoffrey Ingham (1996, 1999, 2004) in the United Kingdom. Michael Hudson and others in the ISCANEE group have taken up elements of the idea, but have never to my knowledge fully embraced it.

33. **Rna*. Malamoud (1983:22) notes that already in the earliest text it had both the meaning of "goods received in return for the promise to hand back either the goods themselves or something of at least equivalent value", as well as "crime" or "fault." So also Olivelle 1993:48, who notes **rna* "can mean fault, crime, or guilt—often at the same time." It is not however the same as the word for "duty." For a typical example of early prayers for release from debt, see Atharva Veda Book 6 Hymns 117, 118, and 119.

34. *Satapatha Brahmana* 3.6.2.16

35. As Sylvain Lévi, Marcel Mauss's mentor, remarked, if one takes the Brahmanic doctrine seriously, "the only authentic sacrifice would be suicide" (1898:133; so also A.B. Keith 1925:459). But of course no one actually took things that far.

36. More precisely, it offered the sacrificer a way to break out of a world in which everything, including himself, was a creation of the gods, to fashion an immortal, divine body, ascend into heaven, and thus be "born into a world he made himself" (*Satapatha Brahmana* VI:2.2.27) where all debts could be repaid, buy back his abandoned mortal body from the gods

(see, i.e., Lévi 1898:130–32, Malamoud 1983:31–32). This is certainly one of the most ambitious claims ever made for the efficacy of sacrifice, but some priests in China around that time were making similar ones (Puett 2002).

37. Translated "saints" in the text with which I began the chapter, but since it refers to the authors of the sacred texts, the usage seems appropriate.

38. I am fusing here two slightly different versions: one in *Tattiriya Sarphita* (6.3.10.5), which says that all Brahmans are born *with* a debt, but only lists gods, Fathers, and sages, leaving out the duty of hospitality, and the other in *Satapatha Brahmana* (1.7.2.1–6) that says all men are born *as* a debt, listing all four—but which seems really to be referring to males of twice-born castes. For a full discussion: see Malamoud 1983 and Olivelle 1993:46-55, also Malamoud 1998.

39. Théret 1999:60–61

40. "The ultimate discharge of this fundamental debt is sacrifice of the living to appease and express gratitude to the ancestors and deities of the cosmos" (Ingham 2004:90).

41. op cit. He cites Hudson 2002:102–3, on the terms for "guilt" or "sin," but as we'll see the point goes back to Grierson (1977:22–23).

42. Laum 1924. His argument about the origin of money in Greece in temple distributions is intriguing and has found contemporary exponents in Seaford (2004) and partly in Hudson (e.g., 2003) but is really a theory of the origin of coinage.

43. More than I would ever dream of trying to cite. There are two standard survey works on "primitive money," by Quiggin and by Einzig, both of which, curiously, came out in 1949. Both are outdated in their analysis but contain a great deal of useful material.

44. English "pay" is from French *payer*, which in turn is derived from Latin *pacare*, "to pacify," "to make peace with." *Pacare* in turn is related to *pacere*,

"to come to terms with an injured party" (Grierson 1977:21).

45. Grierson 1977:20.

46. In fact, as Grierson notes, the authors often seemed to be intentionally making fun of themselves, as in the Irish text that specifies that one can demand compensation for a bee-sting, but only if one first deducts the cost of the dead bee (Grierson 1977:26).

47. We have plenty of myths and hymns from ancient Mesopotamia, too, for instance—but most were discovered in the ruins of ancient libraries that were also full of records of court trials, business contracts, and personal correspondence. In the case of the oldest Sanskrit texts, religious literature is all we have. What's more, since these were texts passed on verbatim from teacher to student for thousands of years, we can't even say with any precision when and where they were written.

48. Interest-bearing loans certainly existed in Mesopotamia, but they only appear in Egypt in Hellenistic times, and in the Germanic world even later. The text speaks of "the tribute that I owe to Yama," which *could* refer to "interest," but the comprehensive review of early Indian legal sources in Kane's *History of Dharmasastra* (1973 III:411–461) comes to no clear conclusion on when interest first appeared; Kosambi (1994:148) estimates that it might have appeared in 500 BC but admits this is a guess.

49. Mesopotamia, Egypt, and China come most immediately to mind. The notion that life is a loan from the gods does occur elsewhere: it seems to crop up spontaneously in ancient Greece, around the same time as money and interest-bearing loans do. "We are all owed as a debt to death," wrote the poet Simonides, around 500 BC. "The sentiment that life was a loan to be repaid by death [became] an almost proverbial saying" (Millet 1991a:6). No Greek author to my knowledge connects this explicitly to sacrifice, though one could conceivably argue that Plato's character Cephalus does so implicitly in one passage of the *Republic* (331d).

50. Hubert and Mauss (1964) provide a good survey of the ancient literature in this regard.

51. Finley 1981:90

52. This was something of a legalistic distinction; what it really meant in practice was that funds levied in Persia were technically considered "gifts," but it shows the power of the principle (Briant 2006:398–99)

53. Pharaonic Egypt and imperial China certainly did levy direct taxes, in money, kind, or labor, in different proportions at different times. In early India, the *gana-sangha* republics do not seem to have demanded taxes of their citizens, but the monarchies that ultimately replaced them did (Rhys Davies 1922:198–200). My point is that taxes were not inevitable and were often seen as marks of conquest.

54. I am following what I believe is still the predominant view; though at least in some places Palaces were in charge of pretty much everything from quite early on, and Temples quite subordinate (see Maekawa 1973–1974). There is lively debate about this, as with the balance of temple, palace, clan, and individual holdings in different times and places, but I have avoided going into such debates, however interesting, unless they have a direct bearing on my argument.

55. I am following Hudson's interpretation (2002), though others—e.g. Steinkeller 1981, Mieroop 2002:64—suggest that interest may have instead originated in rental fees.

56. For a good summary, Hudson 1993, 2002. The meaning of *amargi* is first noted in Falkenstein (1954), see also Kramer (1963:79, Lemche (1979:16n34).

57. In ancient Egypt there were no loans at interest, and we know relatively little about other early empires, so we don't know how unusual this was. But the Chinese evidence is at the very least suggestive. Chinese theories of money were always resolutely Chartalist; and in the

standard story about the origins of coinage, since at least Han times, the mythic founder of the Shang dynasty, upset to see so many families having to sell their children during famines, created coins so that the government could redeem the children and return them to their families (see chapter 8, below).

58. What is sacrifice, after all, but a recognition that an act such as taking an animal's life, even if necessary for our sustenance, is not an act to be taken lightly, but with an attitude of humility before the cosmos?

59. Unless the recipient is owed money by the creditor, allowing everyone to cancel their debts in a circle. This might seem an extraneous point, but the circular cancellation of debts in this way seems to have been quite a common practice in much of history: see, for instance, the description of "reckonings" in chapter 11 below.

60. I am not ascribing this position to the authors of the Brahmanas necessarily; only pursuing what I take to be the internal logic of the argument, in dialogue with its authors.

61. Malamoud 1983:32.

62. Comte 1891:295

63. In France, particularly by political thinkers like Alfred Fouillé and Léon Bourgeois. The latter, leader of the Radical Party in the 1890s, made the notion of social debt one of the conceptual foundations for what his philosophy of "solidarism"—a form of radical republicanism that, he argued, could provide a kind of middle-ground alternative to both revolutionary Marxism and free-market liberalism. The idea was to overcome the violence of class struggle by appealing to a new moral system based on the notion of a shared debt to society—of which the state, of course, was merely the administrator and representative (Hayward 1959, Donzelot 1994, Jobert 2003). Emile Durkheim too was a Solidarist politically.

64. As a slogan, the expression is generally attributed to Charles Gide, the late-nineteenth-century French cooperativist, but became common in Solidarist circles. It became an important principle in Turkish socialist circles at the time (Aydan 2003), and, I have heard, though I have not been able to verify, in Latin America.

Chapter Four

1. Hart 1986:638.

2. The technical term for this is "fiduciarity," the degree to which its value is based not on metal content but public trust. For a good discussion of the fiduciarity of ancient currencies, see Seaford 2004:139–146. Almost all metal coins were overvalued. If the government set the value below that of the metal, of course, people would simply melt them down; if it's set at exactly the metal value, the results are usually deflationary. As Bruno Théret (2008:826–27) points out, although Locke's reforms, which set the value of the British sovereign at exactly its weight in silver, were ideologically motivated, they had disastrous economic effects. Obviously, if coinage is debased or the value otherwise set too high in relation to the metal content, this can produce inflation. But the traditional view, where, say, the Roman currency was ultimately destroyed by debasement, is clearly false, since it took centuries for inflation to occur (Ingham 2004:102–3).

3. Einzig 1949:104; similar gambling chits, in this case made of bamboo, were used in Chinese towns in the Gobi desert (ibid: 108).

4. On English token money, see Williamson 1889; Whiting 1971; Mathias 1979b.

5. On cacao, Millon 1955; on Ethiopian salt money, Einzig 1949:123–26. Both Karl Marx (1857:223, 1867:182) and Max Weber (1978:673–74) were of the opinion that money had emerged from barter between societies, not within them. Karl Bücher

(1904), and arguably Karl Polanyi (1968), held something close to this position, at least insofar as they insisted that modern money emerged from *external* exchange. Inevitably there must have been some sort of mutually reinforcing process between currencies of trade and the local accounting system. Insofar as we can talk about the "invention" of money in its modern sense, presumably this would be the place to look, though in places like Mesopotamia this must have happened long before the use of writing, and hence the history is effectively lost to us.

6. Einzig (1949:266), citing Kulischer (1926:92) and Ilwof (1882:36).

7. *Genealogy of Morals*, 2.8.

8. As I remarked earlier, both Adam Smith and Nietzsche thus anticipate Levi-Strauss's famous argument that language is the "exchange of words." The remarkable thing here is that so many have managed to convince themselves that in all this, Nietzsche is providing a radical alternative to bourgeois ideology, even to the logic of exchange. Deleuze and Guattari, most embarrassingly, insist that "the great book of modern ethnology is not so much Mauss' *The Gift* as Nietzsche's *On the Genealogy of Morals*. At least it should be," since, they say, Nietzsche succeeds in interpreting "primitive society" in terms of debt, where Mauss still hesitates to break with the logic of exchange (1972:224–25). On their inspiration, Sarthou-Lajus (1997) has written philosophy of debt as an alternative to bourgeois ideologies of exchange, that, she claims, assume the prior autonomy of the person. Of course what Nietzsche proposes is not an alternative at all. It's another aspect of the same thing. All this is a vivid reminder of how easy it is to mistake radicalized forms of our own bourgeois tradition as alternatives to it (Bataille [1993], who Deleuze and Guattari also praise as an alternative to Mauss in the same passage, is another notorious example of this sort of thing).

9. *Genealogy of Morals* 2.5.

10. Nietzsche had clearly been reading too much Shakespeare. There is no record of the mutilation of debtors in the ancient world; there was a good deal of mutilation of slaves, but they were by definition people who could not be in debt. Mutilation for debt is occasionally attested to in the Medieval period, but as we'll see, Jews tended to be the victims, since they were largely without rights, and certainly not the perpetrators. Shakespeare turned the story around.

11. *Genealogy of Morals* 2.19.

12. *Genealogy of Morals* 2.21.

13. Freuchen 1961:154. It's not clear what language this was said in, considering that Inuit did not actually have an institution of slavery. It's also interesting because the passage would not make sense unless there were *some* contexts in which gift exchange *did* operate, and therefore, debts accrued. What the hunter is emphasizing is that it was felt important that this logic did not extend to the basic means of human existence, such as food.

14. To take an example, the Ganges Valley in the Buddha's time was full of arguments about the relative merits of monarchical and democratic constitutions. Gautama, though the son of a king, sided with the democrats, and many of the decision-making techniques used in democratic assemblies of the time remain preserved in the organization of Buddhist monasteries (Muhlenberger & Paine 1997.) Were it not for this we would not know anything about them, or even be entirely sure that such democratic polities existed.

15. For instance, buying back one's ancestral land (Leviticus 25:25, 26) or anything one had given to the Temple (Leviticus 27).

16. Here too, in the case of complete insolvency, the debtor might lose his own freedom as well. See Houston (2006) for a good survey of the contemporary literature on economic conditions in the time of the prophets. I here follow a synthesis of his and Michael Hudson's (1993) reconstruction.

17. See for instance, Amos 2.6, 8.2, and Isaiah 58.

18. Nehemiah 5:3–7.

19. There continues to be intense scholarly debate about whether these laws were in fact invented by Nehemiah and his priestly allies (especially Ezra), and whether they were ever actually enforced in any period: see Alexander 1938; North 1954; Finkelstein 1961, 1965; Westbrook 1971; Lemke 1976, 1979; Hudson 1993; Houston 1996 for a few examples. At first there were similar debates about whether Mesopotamian "clean states" were actually enforced, until overwhelming evidence was produced that they were. The bulk of the evidence now indicates that the laws in Deuteronomy were enforced as well, though we can never know for certain how effectively.

20. "Every seventh year you shall make a cancellation. The cancellation shall be as follows: every creditor is to release the debts that he has owing to him by his neighbor" (Deuteronomy 15:1–3). Those held in debt bondage were also freed. Every 49 (or in some readings 50) years came the Jubilee, when all family land was to be returned to its original owners, and even family members who had been sold as slaves set free (Leviticus 25:9).

21. Unsurprisingly, since the need to borrow was most often sparked by the need to pay taxes imposed by foreign conquerors.

22. Hudson notes in Babylonian, clean slates were "called hubullum (debt) masa'um (to wash), literally 'a washing away of the debt [records],' that is, a dissolving of the clay tablets on which financial obligations were inscribed" (1993:19).

23. Matthew 18: 23–34.

24. To give a sense of the figures involved, ten thousand talents in gold is roughly equivalent to the entire Roman tax receipts from their provinces in what's now the Middle East. A hundred denarii is 1/60 of one talent, and therefore worth 600,000 times less.

25. *Opheilēma* in the Greek original, which meant "that which is owed," "financial debts," and by extension, "sin." This was apparently used to translate the Aramaic *hoyween*, which also meant both "debt" and, by extension, "sin." The English here (as in all later Bible citations) follows the King James version, which in this case is itself based on a 1381 translation of the Lord's prayer by John Wycliffe. Most readers will probably be more familiar with 1559 Book of Common Prayer version that substitutes "And forgive us our trespasses, as we forgive them that trespass against us." However, the original is quite explicitly "debts."

26. Changing these to "spiritual debts" doesn't really change the problem.

27. The prospect of sexual abuse in these situations clearly weighed heavily on the popular imagination. "Some of our daughters are brought unto bondage already" protested the Israelites to Nehemiah. Technically, daughters taken in debt bondage were not, if virgins, expected to be sexually available to creditors who did not wish to marry them or marry them to their sons (Exodus 21:7–9; Wright 2009:130–33) though chattel slaves were sexually available (see Hezser 2003), and often the roles blurred in practice; even where laws theoretically protected a man's daughter, he must often have had little means to protect her or ensure those laws were actually enforced. This was also true of sons. The Roman historian Livy's account of the abolition of debt bondage in Rome in 326 BC, for instance, featured a handsome young man named Caius Publilius placed in bondage for a debt he'd inherited from his father, and who was savagely beaten for refusing the sexual advances of his creditor (Livy 8.28). When he appeared on the streets and announced what had happened to him, crowds gathered and marched on the Senate to demand that they abolish the institution.

28. Particularly if the slaves were foreigners captured in war. As we'll see, the

common belief that there were no moral objections to slavery in the ancient world is false. There were plenty. But aside from certain radicals such as the Essenes, the institution was accepted as an unfortunate necessity.

29. Hudson (2002:37) cites the Greek historian Diodorus Siculus (i.79) who attributes this motive to the Egyptian pharaoh Bakenranef, though he too emphasizes that military considerations were not the only ones, but that cancellations reflected broader feelings about justice.

30. Oppenheim 1964:88. Oppenheim suggests that interest-free loans were more common in the Levant, and that in Mesopotamia social equals were more likely to charge each other interest but on easier terms, citing an Old Assyrian merchant who speaks of "the rate one brother charges another" (op cit). In ancient Greece, friendly loans between social equals were known as *eranos* loans, usually of sums raised by an impromptu mutual-aid society and not involving the payment of interest (Jones 1956:171–73; Vondeling 1961; Finley 1981:67–68; Millet 1991:153–155). Aristocrats often made such loans to one another, but so did groups of slaves trying to pool money to buy back their freedom (Harrill 1998:167). This tendency, for mutual aid to be most marked at the very top and very bottom of the social scale is a consistent pattern to this day.

31. Hence the constant invocation of the phrase "your brother," particularly in Deuteronomy, e.g., "you shall not lend at interest to your brother" (23:20).

Chapter Five

1. As we'll see in chapter seven, Plato begins *The Republic* in exactly the same way.

2. For a polite but devastating assessment, see Kahneman 2003.

3. Homans 1958, also Blau 1964; Levi-Strauss 1963:296. In anthropology, the first to propose reciprocity as a universal principle was Richard Thurnwald (1916), but it was made famous by Malinowski (1922).

4. One reason no known law code has ever been known to enforce the principle; the penalty was always there to be commuted to something else.

5. Atwood (2008:1). The author then proceeds to explore the nature of our sense of economic morality by comparing the behavior of caged apes with middle-class Canadian children so as to argue that all human relations are indeed either exchange or forcible appropriation (ibid:49). Despite the brilliance of many of its arguments, the result is a rather sad testimony to how difficult it is for the scions of the North Atlantic professional classes not to see their own characteristic ways of imagining the world as simple human nature.

6. Seton's father, a failed shipping magnate turned accountant, was, Seton later wrote, so cold and abusive that his son spent much of his youth in the woods trying to avoid him; after paying the debt—which incidentally came to $537.50, a tidy but not insurmountable sum in 1881—he changed his name and spent much of the rest of his life trying to develop more healthy child-rearing techniques.

7. Rev. W.H. Beatley in Levy-Bruhl 1923:411

8. Rev. Fr. Bulléon, in Levy-Bruhl 1923:425

9. This phrase was not coined by Marx, incidentally, but was apparently a slogan current in the early French workers' movement, first appearing in print in the work of socialist Louis Blanc in 1839. Marx only took up the phrase in his *Critique of the Gotha Programme* in 1875, and even then used it in a rather idiosyncratic way: for the principle he imagined could apply on the level of society as a whole once technology had reached the point of guaranteeing absolute material abundance. For Marx, "communism"

was both the political movement aiming to bring about such a future society, and that society itself. I am drawing here more on the alternate strain of revolutionary theory, evident most famously perhaps in Peter Kropotkin's *Mutual Aid* (1902).

10. At least, unless there is some specific reason not to—for instance, a hierarchical division of labor that says some people get coffee and others do not.

11. What this means of course is that command economies—putting government bureaucracies in charge of coordinating every aspect of the production and distribution of goods and services within a given national territory—tends to be much less efficient than other available alternatives. This is obviously true, though if it "just doesn't work" at all, it's hard to imagine how states like the Soviet Union could have existed, let alone maintain themselves as world powers, in the first place.

12. Evans-Pritchard 1940:182

13. Similarly, a middle-class pedestrian would be unlikely to ask a gang member for directions, and might even run in fear if one approached him to ask for the time, but this is again because of an assumption of a tacit state of war existing between them.

14. Ibid, p. 183.

15. Richards 1939:197. Max Gluckman, remarking on such customs, concludes that insofar as it is possible to speak of "primitive communism," it exists in consumption, rather than production, which tends to be much more individually organized (1971:52).

16. A typical example: "if a cabin of hungry people meets another whose provisions are not entirely exhausted, the latter share with the newcomers the little which remains to them without waiting to be asked, although they expose themselves thereby to the same danger of perishing as those whom they help . . ." Lafitau 1974 Volume II:61.

17. Jesuit Relations (1635) 8:127, cited in Delâge 1993:54.

18. This is a common arrangement in certain parts of the world (particularly the Andes, Amazonia, insular Southeast Asia, and Melanesia), and invariably there is some rule whereby each half is dependent on the other for something considered essential to human life. One can only marry someone from the other side of the village, or maybe one can only eat pigs raised on the other side, or perhaps one side needs people from the other side to sponsor the rituals that initiate its male children into manhood.

19. As I have suggested elsewhere, Graeber 2001:159–60; cf. Mauss 1947: 104–5.

20. I'm side-stepping the whole question of one-sided examples discussed in Graeber 2001:218.

21. Marshall Sahlins (1972) coined the phrase "generalized reciprocity" to describe this sort of relation, on the principle that if everything circulates freely, eventually, all accounts will balance out. Marcel Mauss was already making such an argument in lectures back in the 1930s (1947), but he also recognized the problems: while this might be true of Iroquois moieties, some relationships never balance out—for instance, between mother and child. His solution, "alternating reciprocity"—that we repay our parents by having children ourselves—is clearly drawn from his study of the Vedas, but it ultimately demonstrates that if one has already decided that all relations are based on reciprocity, one can always define the term so broadly as to make it true.

22. *Hostis*: see Benveniste 1972:72. The Latin terminology concerning hospitality emphasizes the absolute mastery of the house by its (male) owner as the precondition of any act of hospitality; Derrida (2000, 2001) argues that this points to a central contradiction in the very concept of hospitality, since it implies an already-existing absolute dominium or power over others, the kind that might be seen as taking its most exploitative form in Lot's offering his own daughters up to

a crowd of Sodomites to dissuade them from raping his houseguests. However, this same principle of hospitality can be equally well documented in societies—such as the Iroquois—that were anything but patriarchal.

23. Evans-Pritchard 1940:154, 158.

24. This is of course one reason why the very rich like to associate mainly with one another.

25. In a less hostile vein one can speak of an exchange of prisoners, notes, or compliments.

26. A good source on haggling: Uchendo 1967.

27. Bohannan 1964:47.

28. Not even a real business deal, since these may often involve a great deal of collective wining and dining and giving of presents. More the sort of imaginary business deal that appears in economics textbooks.

29. One need only glance at the vast anthropological literature on "competitive feasting": e.g., Valeri 2001.

30. Bourdieu 1965 is the key text, but he repeats the main points in Bourdieu 1990:98–101.

31. Onvlee 1980:204.

32. Petronius 51; Pliny *Natural History* 36.195; Dio 57.21.5–7.

33. "This king is of all men the most addicted to the making of gifts and the shedding of blood. His gate is never without some poor man enriched or some living man executed."

34. Or even the very rich. Nelson Rockefeller, for example, used to pride himself on never carrying a wallet. He didn't need one. Every now and then when he was working late and wanted cigarettes, he would borrow some from the security people at the desk at Rockefeller Center, who would then be able to boast that they had lent a Rockefeller money and would rarely ask for it back. In contrast, "the sixteenth-century Portuguese monarch Dom Manuel, newly rich from the Indies trade, adopted the title 'Lord of the Conquest, Navigation, and Commerce of Ethiopia, Arabia, Persia, and India.' Others called him the "grocer king." (Ho 2004:227).

35. See Graeber 2001:175–76.

36. Even between strangers it's a bit unusual: as Servet (1981, 1982) has emphasized, most "primitive trade" takes place through trade partnership and specialized regional middlemen.

37. I frame things this way because I am mainly interested here in economics. If we were thinking simply of human relations, I suppose one might say that at one extreme is killing, and at the other, giving birth.

38. In fact, it seems essential to the nature of charity that, like a gifts to a king, it can never lead to reciprocity. Even if it turns out that the pathetic-looking beggar is really a god wandering the earth in mortal form, or Harun al-Rashid, your reward will be entirely disproportionate. Or consider all those stories about drunken millionaires on a binge who, when they got their life back together, hand out fancy cars or houses to their earlier benefactors. It's easier to imagine a panhandler giving you a fortune than returning an exact equivalent to the dollar that you gave him.

39. Xenophon *Cyropedia* VIII.6, Herodotus 3.8.9; see Briant 2006:193–194, 394–404, who acknowledges that something broadly along these lines probably did take place, with a more impromptu gift system under Cyrus and Cambyses being systematized under Darius.

40. Marc Bloch (1961:114–15), who adds "every act, especially if it was repeated three or four times, was likely to be transformed into a precedent—even if in the first instance it had been exceptional or even frankly unlawful."

41. The approach is often identified with British anthropologist A.M. Hocart (1936). The important thing is that this does not necessarily mean that these became their main or exclusive occupations: most of the time, such people remained simple farmers like everybody else. Yet

what they did for the king, or later, on ritual occasions, for the community, was seen as defining their essential nature, their identity within the whole.

42. In fact, we may become indignant at her for an act of stinginess we would never even consider stingy in anyone else—especially, ourselves.

43. "'The Missing White Girl Syndrome': Disappeared Women and Media Activism," Sarah Stillman, *Gender and Development*, Vol. 15, No. 3, Media (November 2007), pp. 491–502.

44. Karatani (2003:203–205) makes this point compellingly. The Kwakiutl and other First Nations of the Northwest Coast are something of an intermediary case—aristocratic, but at least in the period we know about, using non-coercive means to gather resources (though Codere 1950.)

45. Georges Duby (1980) provides the definitive history of this concept, which goes back to much older Indo-European ideas.

46. For a typical example of imaginary reciprocity between father and son, see Oliver 1955:230. Anthropological theory buffs will notice that I am here endorsing Edmund Leach's (1961) position on the "circulating connubium" problem. He later applied the same argument to the famous "kula chain" (1983).

47. Actually, there are hierarchical relations that are explicitly self-subverting: the one between teacher and student, for example, since if the teacher is successful in passing her knowledge to the student, there is no further basis for inequality.

48. Freuchen 1961: 154. It's not clear what the original language was here, considering that the Inuit did not have an institution of slavery. Also, the passage would not make sense unless there were *some* contexts in which gift exchange did operate, and therefore, in which debts accrued. What the hunter is emphasizing is that it was felt important that this logic did not extend to basic needs like food.

49. Firth 1959:411–12 (also in Graeber 2001:175). His name was Tei Reinga.

50. For one famous example: Chagnon 1996:170–76.

51. Similarly, two groups might form an alliance by contracting a "joking relation," in which any member of one could at least in theory make similar outrageous demands of the other (Hébert 1958).

52. Marcel Mauss, in his famous "Essay on the Gift" (1924), often did, and the results have sometimes confused debate for generations to come.

53. Mauss 1925, the Greek source being Posidonius. As usual one does not know how literally to take this account. Mauss thought it likely accurate; I suspect it might at best have happened once or twice.

54. As retold by William Ian Miller (1993:15–16). The first quote is directly from the original, Egil's Saga, chapter 78. Egil remained ambivalent about the shield: he later took it to a wedding party and contrived to drop it into a vat of sour whey. Afterward, concluding it was ruined, he stripped it for its raw materials.

55. See, for instance, Wallace-Hadrill 1989.

56. Blaxter 1971:127–28.

57. Another anthropologist, for instance, defines patron-client relations as "long-term contracted relations in which the client's support is exchanged for the patron's protection; there is an ideology which is morally charged and appears to rule out strict, open accounting, but both parties keep some tacit rough account; the goods and services exchanged are not similar, and there is no implication of fair exchange or balance of satisfactions, since the client is markedly weaker in power and needs the patron more than he is needed by him" (Loizos 1977:115). Again, it both is and isn't an exchange, it's both a matter of accounting and not a matter of accounting.

58. It's exactly the same if one takes a job at a doughnut shop; legally, it must be a free contract between equals, even if

in order to be able to say this we have to maintain the charming legal fiction that one of them is an imaginary person named "Krispy Kreme."

59. For instance the word "should," in English, originally derives from German *schuld*, meaning "guilt, fault, debt." Benveniste provides similar examples from other Indo-European languages (1963:58). East Asian languages such as Chinese and Japanese rarely conflate the actual words, but a similar identification of debt with sin, shame, guilt, and fault can be easily documented (Malamoud 1988).

60. Plutarch *Moralia* 303 B, also discussed in Finley 1981:152, Millett 1991a:42. Similarly, St. Thomas Aquinas made it a matter of Catholic doctrine that sins were "debts of punishment" owed to God.

61. This is one reason why it's so easy to dress up other sorts of relationships as debts. Say one wishes to help out a friend in desperate need of money but doesn't want to embarrass her. Usually, the easiest way to do it is to provide the money and then insist that it's a loan (and then let both parties conveniently forget it ever happened). Or think of all the times and places where the rich acquire servants by advancing what is ostensibly a loan.

62. One could argue that some equivalent of "please" and "thank you" could be identified in any human language, if one were determined to find them, but then the terms you find are often used so differently—for instance, only in ritual contexts, or to hierarchical superiors—that it's hard to attach much significance to the fact. It is significant that over the last century or so just about every human language that is used in offices or to make transactions in shops has had to create terms that do function as an exact equivalent of the English "please," "thank you," and "you're welcome."

63. In Spanish one first asks a favor (*por favor*), and then says *gracias*, in order affirm you recognize one has been done for you, since it derives from the Latin word *gratia*, meaning "influence, or favor." "Appreciate" is more monetary: if you say "I really appreciate your doing that for me," you are using a word that derives from Latin *appretiare*, "to set a price."

64. "You're welcome," first documented in Shakespeare's time, derives from Old English *wilcuma*, *wil* being "pleasure" and *cuma* being "guest." This is why people are still welcomed into a house. It is thus like "be my guest," implying that, no, if there is an obligation it's on my part, as any host is obliged to be generous to guests, and that dispatching such obligations is a pleasure in itself. Still, it's significant that moralists rarely chide anyone for failure to say "you're welcome"—that one is much more optional.

65. Book I.12. This and other quotes are from the 2006 Penguin Screech translation, in this case, p. 86.

66. Compare the Medieval Arab philosopher Ibn Miskaway: "The creditor desires the well-being of the debtor in order to get his money back rather than because of his love for him. The debtor, on the other hand, does not take great interest in the creditor." (in Hosseini 2003:36).

67. Appropriate, since Panurge's entire discourse is nothing but a comical elaboration of Marcelo Ficino's argument that the entire universe is driven by the power of love.

Chapter Six

1. From: Peter Carlson, "The Relatively Charmed Life of Neil Bush," *The Washington Post*, Sunday December 28, 2003, Page D01.

2. Grierson 1977:20.

3. To be fair to Grierson, he does later suggest that slavery played an important part in the origins of money—though he never speculates about the gender, which seems significant: slave girls also served as the highest denomination of currency in Medieval Iceland (Williams 1937), and in

the Rig Veda, great gifts and payments are regularly designated in "gold, cattle, and slave girls" (Chakravarti 1985:56–57). By the way, I say "young" because elsewhere, when slaves are used as monetary units, the unit is assumed to be a slave about 18–20 years old. A *cumal* was considered the equivalent in value of three milch cows or six heifers.

4. On *cumal* see Nolan 1926, Einzig 1949:247–48, Gerriets 1978, 1981, 1985, Patterson 1982:168–69, Kelly 1998:112–13. Most merely emphasize that *cumal* were just used as units of account and we don't know anything about earlier practices. It's notable, though, that in the law codes, when several different commodities are used as units of account, they will include that country's most significant exports, and trade currency (that's why in Russian codes, the units were fur and silver). This would imply a significant trade in female slaves in the period just before written records.

5. So Bender 1996.

6. Here I am drawing on the detailed ethnographic survey work of Alain Testart (2000, 2001, 2002). Testart does a magnificent job synthesizing the evidence, though he too—as we'll see in the next chapter—has some equally strange blind spots in his conclusions.

7. "Although the rhetorical phrase 'selling one's daughter into prostitution' has wide currency . . . the actual arrangement is more often presented as either a loan to the family or an advance payment for the girl's (usually unspecified or misrepresented) services. The interest on these 'loans' is often 100 percent, and the principal may be increased by other debts—for living expenses, medical care, bribes to officials—accrued once the girl has begun work" (Bishop & Robinson 1998:105).

8. So Michael Hudson (cited in Wray 1999), but it's clear enough if one looks at the language of the original: "Thou shalt not covet thy neighbour's house, thou shalt not covet thy neighbour's wife, nor his manservant, nor his maidservant, nor his ox, nor his ass, nor any thing that is thy neighbour's" (Exodus 20:17, Deuteronomy 5:21).

9. Wampum is a good example: Native Americans never seem to have used it to buy things from other members of the same community, although it was regularly used in conducting trade with settlers (see Graeber 2001:117–150). Others, like Yurok shell money or some Papuan currencies, are widely used as currencies in addition to their social functions, but the first seems to have emerged from the second.

10. The most important texts on the "brideprice debate": Evans-Pritchard 1931, Raglan 1931, Gray 1968, Comaroff 1980, Valeri 1994. One reason why Evans-Pritchard originally proposed to change the name from "brideprice" to "bridewealth" because the League of Nations had in 1926 outlawed the practice as a form of slavery (Guyer 1994).

11. On Tiv kinship and economy: Duggan 1932; Abraham 1933; Downes 1933; Akiga 1939; L. Bohannan 1952; P. Bohannan 1955, 1957, 1959; P. & L. Bohannan 1953, 1968, Tseayo 1975; Keil 1979.

12. Akiga Sai 1939:106 for a good analysis of how this could happen. For a later comparative reanalysis in regional perspective, see Fardon 1984, 1985.

13. Paul Bohannan puts it: "The *kem* relationship of debt between a man and his wife's guardian is never broken, because *kem* is perpetual, the debt can never be fully paid." (1957:73.) Otherwise the account is from Akiga (1939:126–127).

14. Rospabé 1993:35.

15. Evans-Pritchard 1940:153.

16. As the ethnographer puts it, "that they are accepting the cattle only in order to honour him and not because they are ready to take cattle for the life of their dead kinsman." (1940:153)

17. Op cit 154–155.

18. Morgan 1851:332. Morgan, a lawyer by training, is using a technical term here, "condonation," which the Oxford

English Dictionary defines as "the voluntary overlooking of an offence."

19. Morgan 1851:333. The baseline was
five fathoms for a man, ten for a woman, but other factors might intervene (T.
Smith 1983:236; Morgan 1851:331–34; Parker 1926). On "mourning wars" see Richter
1983; the expression "putting his name
upon the mat" is from Fenton 1978:315.
Incidentally I am assuming it's a man who
dies, since these are the examples in the
sources. It's not clear if the same was done
for women who died naturally.

20. Evans-Pritchard 1940:155, 1951:109–
11; Howell 1954:71–80, Gough 1971,
Hutchinson 1996:62, 175–76.

21. Rospabe 1995:47–48, citing Peters
1947.

22. On mourning war: Richter 1983.
Interestingly, something similar occurred
among the Nambikwara. I mentioned in
chapter 3 that the feasts held after barter
could lead to seductions and jealous murders; Levi-Strauss adds that the ordinary
way of resolving such murders is for the
killer to marry the victim's wife, adopt his
children, and thus, effectively, become the
person the victim used to be (1943:123).

23. Though people did use them to
commission certain fancy craft goods (say,
musical instruments) from specialists in
other villages (1963:54–55).

24. Douglas 1958: 112; also 1982:43.

25. Douglas (1963:58) estimates that a
successful man will have spent at minimum 300 raffia cloths in payments, and
given away at least 300 more as gifts, by
the time he reached full social maturity.

26. As anthropologists often note, the
fact that one traces descent through the
female line does not necessarily mean that
women themselves have a lot of power.
It can; it did among the Iroquois, and it
does among Minangkabau right now. But
it doesn't necessarily.

27. Douglas 1963:144–45, which is an
adoption of 1960:3–4.

28. She was in fact a conservative
Catholic and Tory who tended to look
with disdain on liberal concerns.

29. As if to hammer this home, a man
was actually considered to be owed a life-
debt for fathering female children (Douglas 1963:115)—that could only be paid
by allowing him to take one of his own
daughters' daughters as a pawn. This only
makes sense if we assume a principle that
only men can be owed a life, and therefore, in the case of women, the creation
of life was assumed to be given free. Men,
as noted, could be pawns and many were,
but they were never traded.

30. Douglas 1966:150.

31. On "village-wives," see particularly
Douglas 1951, also 1963:128–40.

32. Douglas 1963:76; compare 1951:11.
The author is clearly simply repeating her
informants' explanation for the custom:
the Lele didn't "have to" make such an
arrangement; in fact, most African societies did not.

33. Some village wives were literally
princesses, since chiefs' daughters invariably chose to marry age-sets in this way.
The daughters of chiefs were allowed to
have sex with anyone they wanted, regardless of age-set, and also had the right
to refuse sex, which ordinary village wives
did not. Princesses of this sort were rare:
there were only three chiefs in all Lele territory. Douglas estimates that the number
of Lele women who became village wives,
on the other hand, was about 10 percent
(1951).

34. For instance: 1960:4, 1963:145–46,
168–73, 1964:303. Obviously, men could
sometimes put a great deal of physical
pressure on women, at least, if everyone
else agreed they had a moral right to do
so, but even here Douglas emphasizes
most women had a good deal of room for
maneuver.

35. On peacefulness, particularly,
1963:70–71.

36. 1963:170.

37. 1963:171.

38. Cost of slaves: 1963:36, 1982:46–47.

39. Partly, though, this was because
the main purpose of male slaves was to

be sacrificed at important men's funerals (1963:36).

40. See Graeber 2001, chapter 4. The great exception might seem to be the cattle money of the Nuer, and similar pastoral peoples. Yet even these were arguably adornment of the person of a sort.

41. Akiga Sai 1939: 121, 158–60.

42. So too when Tiv practiced marriage by capture: Akiga Sai (1939:137–41).

43. Here I'm drawing on the classic "spheres of exchange" analysis by Paul Bohannan (1955, 1959), supplemented by Dorward (1976) and Guyer (2004:27–31).

44. So Akiga Sai 1939:241; P. Bohannan 1955:66, P. & L. Bohannnan 1968:233, 235. As charisma in general: East in Akiga Sai 1939:236, Downes 1971:29.

45. See Abraham 1933:26; Akiga Sai 1939:246; P. Bohannan 1958:3; Downes 1971:27.

46. On witches in general: P. Bohannan 1957:187–88, 1958; Downes 1971: 32–25. On flesh debts (or ikipindi): Abraham 1933:81–84; Downes 1971:36–40.

47. Akiga Sai 1939:257.

48. Akiga Sai 1939:260.

49. Following here Wilson 1951.

50. Paul Bohannan (1958:4) makes a similar but not identical argument.

51. Tiv migration stories (e.g. Abraham 1933:17–26; Akiga & Bohannan 1954; P. Bohannan 1954) do not explicitly say this, but they could easily be read this way. Akiga's story (1939:137) about Tiv migrants painting what looked like sores on their women's bodies so raiders would not take them is particularly suggestive. Despite their lack of government, Tiv did have a notoriously effective war organization, and as Abrahams notes (1933:19), managed to successfully play the Fulani and Jukun against each other by intervening in their own wars with each other.

52. Some of these raids were not entirely unsuccessful. For a while, it would appear, the nearby Jukun kingdom, which made several efforts to incorporate the Tiv in the eighteenth century, all of which ultimately failed, appear to have been selling Tiv captives to slave dealers operating on the coast (Abraham 1933:19; Curtin 1965:255, 298; Latham 1973:29; Tambo 1976: 201–3.) It's doubtless significant here that many Tiv insisted in the 1930s that the Jukun were themselves cannibals, and that the origins of the mbatsav "organization" lay in certain chiefly titles that Tiv acquired from them when they finally came to a political rapprochement (Abraham 1933:33–35).

53. Jones 1958; Latham 1971; Northrup 1978:157–64; Herbert 2003:196. The famous Medieval Arab traveler Ibn Battuta, who we've already met at the court of the King of Singh in chapter 2, saw people using them as money in the Niger region, not far away, in the 1340s.

54. Herbert (2003:181) estimates that Europeans imported about 20,000 tons of English brass and copper into Africa between 1699 and 1865. It was manufactured in Bristol, Cheadle, and Birmingham. The vast majority was exchanged for slaves

55. I base this number on the fact that 152,076 slaves are known to have been exported from the Bight of Biafra as a whole in those years (Eltis, Behrent, Richardson & Klein 2000). The slave trade at Old Calabar lasted roughly from 1650 to 1841, during which time the port was by far the largest in the Bight, and the exports from the Bight itself during its height represent about 20 percent of all Africa (Lovejoy & Richardson 1999:337).

56. Sheridan 1958, Price 1980, 1989, 1991.

57. A larger variety of beads.

58. Barbot in Talbot 1926 I: 185–186.

59. Inkori (1982) demonstrates that in the late eighteenth century, British ships docking in Old Calabar brought on average 400 muskets each, and that between 1757 and 1806, the total number imported into the Calabar-Cameroons region was 22,986. Rum and other liquor was, however, a very minor import.

60. One common expedient, especially in the early years, was for merchants to arrive at village markets with canoes full

of wares, exchange them for slaves, and then, if they didn't come up to quota, wait until nightfall and simply attack homesteads along the river, carrying off anyone they could find (Clarkson in Northrup 1978:66, also cited in Noah 1990:94.)

61. The existing scholarly literature is of little help in reconstructing the history of how one form was transformed into the other, since there are only works treating pawnship *either* as a matter of kinship (e.g., Douglas 1964, Fardon 1985, 1986), or of commerce (e.g., Falola & Lovejoy 1994), but never comparing the two. As a result, many basic questions remain unasked. Falola and Lovejoy, for instance, suggest that pawns' labor functions as interest, but the book contains no information on whether interest-bearing loans even existed in the parts of Africa where pawnship was practiced.

62. It's also clear that this sort of pawnship must have developed from something like the Lele institution. Many of the rules are the same: for instance, much as among the Lele, if a girl was pledged, the creditor often had the option of marrying her when she reached maturity, thus canceling the debt.

63. Lovejoy & Richardson 1999:349–51; 2001.

64. Equiano 1789:6–13.

65. Others included the Akunakuna, and the Efik, who were based in Calabar itself. The Aro were Igbo-speakers, and the region a patchwork of speakers of Igbo and Ibibio languages.

66. On the Aro in general, see Jones 1939; Ottenberg 1958; Afigbo 1971; Ekejiuba 1972; Isichei 1976; Northrup 1978; Dike & Ekejiuba 1990; Nwauwa 1991.

67. Dike and Ekejiuba (1990:150) estimate that 70 percent of the slaves sold to Europeans in the Bight of Biafra came from the Aro. Most of the rest came from the other merchant societies.

68. One twentieth-century elder recalled, "a woman who commited adultery would be sold by her husband and the husband kept the money. Thieves were

sold, and the money went to the elders whose responsibility it was to make the decision." (Northrup 1978: 69)

69. Northrup 1978:73

70. On Ekpe as debt enforcement in Calabar itself: Jones 1968, Latham 1973:35–41, Lovejoy & Richardson 1999:347–49. On the spread of Ekpe to Arochukwe and throughout the region: Ruel 1969:250–258, Northrup 1978:109–110, Nwaka 1978, Ottenberg & Knudson 1985. Nwaka (1978:188) writes: "The Ekpe society, the most widespread in the Cross River area, formed the basis of local government. It performed executive and judicial functions in areas where it operated. Through the agency of its members, punishments were administered to public offenders, customs enforced and the authority of the elders upheld. Ekpe laws to some extent regulated the lives of most members of the community in such matters as the cleaning of towns and streets, collection of debts and other measures of public benefit."

71. Latham 1963:38.

72. Taken from Walker 1875:120

73. Ottenberg & Ottenberg 1962:124.

74. Partridge 1905:72.

75. If one were seeking a pawn, one couldn't simply take a random child from a neighboring village, as his or her parents would quickly track the child down.

76. In Lovejoy & Richardson 2001:74. For a parallel case in Ghana, see Getz 2003:85.

77. Remarkably, Akiga Sai (1939:379–80) insists that, among the Tiv, this was the origin of slavery: the seizing of hostages from the same lineage as someone who refused to pay a debt. Say, he says, the debtor still refuses to pay. They will keep their hostage fettered for a while, then, finally, sell them in another country. "This is the origin of slavery."

78. So Harris 1972:128 writing of another Cross River district, Ikom: one of the major suppliers of slaves for Calabar. There, she notes, debtors were often obliged to pawn themselves when maternal and paternal kin intervened to prevent

them from selling off any more of their relatives, with the result that they were finally enslaved and sent to Calabar.

79. We do not know what proportion. King Eyo II told a British missionary that slaves "were sold for different reasons— some as prisoners of war, some for debt, some for breaking their country's laws and some by great men who hated them" (in Noah 1990:95). This suggests that debt was not insignificant, especially since as Pier Larson (2000:18) notes, all sources at the time would list "war," since it was considered the most legitimate. Compare Northrup (1978:76–80).

80. Reid 1983:8

81. op cit.

82. Reid 1983:10

83. Vickers (1996) provides an excellent history of Bali's image in the North Atlantic imagination, from "savage Bali" to terrestrial paradise.

84. Geertz & Geertz 1975; Boon 1977:121–24. Belo (1936:26) cites informants in the 1920s that insisted that marriage by capture was a fairly recent innovation, which emerged from gangs of young men stealing women from enemy villages and, often, demanding that their fathers pay money to get them back.

85. Boon 1977:74

86. Covarrubias (1937:12) notes that as early as 1619, Balinese women were in great demand in slave markets in Reunion.

87. Boon 1977:28, van der Kraan 1983, Wiener 1995:27

88. Vickers 1996:61. I need only remark that the anthropological literature on Bali, most notably Clifford Geertz's famous essay on the Balinese cockfight as "deep play" (1973), a space where Balinese people can express their inner demons and tell stories about themselves, or his conception of pre-colonial governments as "theater states" (1980) whose politics centered around gathering the resources to create magnificent rituals, might well be rethought in the light of all of this. There is a peculiar blindness in this literature. Even Boon, after the above quote about

men hiding their daughters, proceeds on the very next page (1977:75) to refer to that government's "subjects" as really just a "slightly taxed audience for its rituals," as if the likely prospect of the rape, murder and enslavement of one's children didn't really matter, or, anyway, was not of explicitly political import.

89. All this is meant in part as a critique of Louis Dumont's arguments (1992) that the only truly egalitarian societies are modern ones, and even those only by default: since their ultimate value is individualism, and since each individual is valuable above all for the degree to which he or she is unique, there can be no basis for saying that anyone is intrinsically superior to anybody else. One can have the same effect without any doctrine of "Western individualism" at all. The entire concept of "individualism" needs to be seriously rethought.

90. Beattie 1960: 61.

91. True, in many traditional societies, penalties are given to men who beat their wives excessively. But again, the assumption is that *some* such behavior is at least par for the course.

92. On charivari, see for instance Davis 1975, Darnton 1984. Keith Thomas (1972:630), who cites this very Nyoro story in an account of English villages of that time, recounts a whole series of social sanctions, such as dunking the "village scold," that seem almost entirely aimed at the violent control of women, but oddly, he claims that charivari were directed at *men* who beat their wives, despite the fact that all other sources say the opposite.

93. Not quite all. Again, one might cite Iroquois society of the same period as an example: it was in many senses a matriarchy, particularly on the everyday household level, and women were not exchanged.

94. Taken from Trawick 2000:185, figure 11.

95. The diagram is reproduced from P. Bohannan 1957:87.

96. Akiga Sai 1939:161.

97. So too among the Lele, where Mary Douglas (1963:131) remarks that it was considered acceptable to whip a village wife for refusing work or sex, but this was no reflection on her status, since the same was true of Lele wives married to just one man, too.

Chapter Seven

1. sumerianorg/prot-sum.htm, from a "Proto-Sumerian dictionary"

2. Florentius in Justinian's Institutes (1.5.4.1). It is interesting to note that when attempts are made to justify slavery, starting with Aristotle, they generally focus not on the institution, which is not in itself justifiable, but on the inferior qualities of some ethnic group being enslaved.

3. Elwahid 1931. Clarence-Smith (2008:17n56) notes that al-Wahid's book itself emerged from within lively debates in the Middle East about the role of slavery in Islam that had been going on at least since the mid-nineteenth century.

4. Elwahid 1931: 101–10, and passim. An analogous list appears in Patterson 1982:105.

5. The sale of children was always felt to be a sign of economic and moral breakdown; even later Roman emperors like Diocletian, notes al-Wahid, supported charities aimed to provide relief for poor families explicitly so they would not have to resort to things like this (Elwahed 1931: 89–91).

6. Mitamura 1970.

7. Debt slavery, he notes, was practiced in early Roman history, but this is because according to the laws of the twelve tablets, insolvent debtors could actually be killed. In most places, where this was not possible, debtors were not fully enslaved by reduced to pawns or peons (see Testart 2000, 2002, for a full explanation of the different possibilities).

8. Al-Wahid cites examples from Athenaeus of Greek patients who offered themselves as slaves to doctors who had saved their lives (op cit:234)

9. Ulpian is precise: "In every branch of the law, a person who fails to return from enemy hands is regarded as having died at the moment when he was captured." (Digest 49.15.18) The Lex Cornelia of 84–81 BC specifies the need for remarriage.

10. Meillassoux 1996:106

11. Patterson 1982. "Slavery," as he defines it, "is the permanent, violent domination of natally alienated and generally dishonored persons." (1982:13)

12. He quotes Frederick Douglass here to great effect: "A man without force is without the essential dignity of humanity. Human nature is so constituted that it cannot honor a helpless man, although it can pity him; and even that it cannot do long, if the signs of power do not arise." (in Patterson 1982:13)

13. Presumably an honorable woman as well, though in the case of women, as we shall see, the question became inextricably caught up in questions of fidelity and chastity.

14. Paul Houlm (in Duffy, MacShamhráin and Moynes 2005:431.) True, the balance of trade seems to have shifted back and forth; at some periods Irish ships were raiding English shores, and after 800 AD the Vikings carried off thousands, briefly making Dublin the largest slave market in Europe. Still, by this time, cumals do not appear to any longer have been used as actual currency. There are some parallels here with Africa, where in certain times and places affected by the trade, debts were tallied up in slaves as well (Einzig 1949:153).

15. St. Patrick, one of the founders of the Irish church, was one of the few of the early Church Fathers who was overtly and unconditionally opposed to slavery.

16. Doherty 1980:78–83.

17. Gerriets 1978:128, 1981:171–72, 1985:338. This was in dramatic contrast, incidentally, to Welsh laws from only two or three centuries later, where the prices of all such objects are fastidiously specified

(Ellis 1926:379–81). The list of items is a random selection from the Welsh codes.

18. Doherty 1980:73–74

19. This was true in Irish and in Welsh, and apparently, other Celtic languages as well. Charles-Edwards (1978:130, 1993:555) actually translates "honor price" as "face value."

20. The one exception being an early ecclesiastical text: Einzig 1949:247–48, Gerriets 1978:71.

21. The main source on the monetary system is Gerriets (1978), a dissertation that unfortunately was never published as a book. A table of standard rates of exchange between cumal, cows, silver, etc, are also to be found in Charles-Edwards 1993:478–85.

22. Gerriets 1978:53.

23. If you had lent a man your horse or sword and he didn't return it in time for a battle, causing loss of face, or even if a monk lent his cowl to another monk who didn't return it in time, causing him not to have proper attire for an important synod, he could demand his honor price (Fergus 1988:118).

24. The honor price of Welsh kings was far higher (Ellis 1926:144).

25. Provincial kings, who ranked higher, had an honor price of 14 cumals, and in theory there was a high king at Tara who ruled all Ireland, but the position was often vacant or contested (Byrne 1973).

26. All of this is a simplification of what's in fact an endlessly complicated system, and some points, especially concerning marriage, of which there are several varieties, with different integrations of brideprice and dowry, remain obscure. In the case of clients, for example, there were two initial payments by the lord, the honor price being one of them; with "free clients," however, the honor price was not paid and the client was not reduced to servile status, (See Kelly 1988 for the best general summary.)

27. Dimetian Code II.24.12 (Howel 2006:559). A similar penalty is specified for the killing of public officials from certain districts (Ellis 1926:362).

28. "There is no evidence that goods themselves could be assigned prices. That is, while Irish moneys could quantify the status of an individual, they were not used to quantify the value of goods." (Gerriets 1985:338).

29. Sutton 2004:374.

30. Gallant 2000. One might also consider here the phrase "affair of honor," or for that matter, "honor killing"—which also make clear that such sentiments are hardly confined to rural Greece.

31. In fact, one could just as easily turn the question around, and ask: Why is it so insulting to suggest that a man's sister is trading sex for money in the first place? This one reason I say that concepts of honor still shape our perceptions in ways we're not aware of—there are plenty of places in the world where the suggestion that a man's wife is trading sex for profit, or that his sister is engaged with multiple partners, is more likely to be greeted with bemused good humor than with murderous rage. We've already seen examples in the Gunwinggu and the Lele.

32. Obviously I am distinguishing the term here from the broader sense of patriarchy used in much feminist literature, of any social system based on male subordination of women. Clearly the origins of patriarchy in this broader sense must be sought in a much earlier period of history in both the Mediterranean and Near East.

33. The "Semitic infiltration" model is already to be found in such classic sources as Saggs (1962). Generally speaking, the pattern seems to be one of periodic urban crisis, the near-breakdown of riverine society being followed by revival, apparently after the advent of a new wave of Semitic pastoralists (Adams et al. 1974).

34. Rohrlich 1980 is a compelling example.

35. This is of course a vast simplification of a thesis mainly identified with the anthropologist Jack Goody (1976, 1983, 1990). The basic principle is that dowry

is not so much a payment by the bride's father (it might come equally from both sides) but a kind of premature inheritance. Goody has had very little to say about Mesopotamia, though, and that little (1990:315–17) focuses almost exclusively on upper-class practice.

36. Wilcke 1985, Westbrook 1988, Greengus 1990, Stol 1995:125–27. For Mari: Lafont 1987; for Old Babylonian practice: Greengus 1966, 1969; for Nuzi, Grosz 1983, 1989.

37. Our best sources are from the city of Nuzi c1500 BC, though Nuzi was atypical in certain ways, mainly due to Hurrian influence. There, marriage payments appear to have been made in stages, for instance, at the birth of a first child (Grosz 1981:176)—a pattern familiar to anthropologists from Melanesia, Africa, and numerous other parts of the world.

38. Finkelstein 1966, VerSteeg 2000:121, 153n91. A father could claim monetary damages against someone who falsely claimed that his daughter was not a virgin, presumably because it would lower the bride-price (Cooper 2002:101).

39. Bottéro 1992:113.

40. Stol 1995:126.

41. Cardascia 1959 on "matrimonial adoption" (also Mendelsohn 1949:8–12, Greengus 1975). During times of famine, sometimes even the brideprice was dispensed with, and a starving family might turn over their daughter to a rich household in exchange for a promise to keep her alive.

42. Evans-Prichard 1931, Raglan 1931. It's a little ironic that the debate was occurring in England, since this was one of the few places where it was, technically, legal to sell or even auction off one's wife (Menefee 1981; Stone 1990:143–48; see Pateman 1988). Stone notes that while public "wife-sales" in English villages were apparently really prearranged divorces, "the details of the ritual were designed to emphasize the final nature of the transfer of property, by imitating as closely as possible the sale of a cow or

a sheep. A halter was used to lead the wife from her home to the market, and from the market to the house of her purchaser." (1990:145) The practice, confined to the popular classes, caused a scandal when documented in Hardy's *Mayor of Casterbridge*, but it was only completely abandoned in 1919.

43. Finley 1981:153–55; Stienkeller 2003; Mieroop 2005:27–28. Mieroop notes that the earliest such contract is documented from twenty-first-century Babylonia. This is an interesting example for the early history of wage labor. As I've written elsewhere (Graeber 2006:66–69; 2007:91–94), wage-labor contracts in the ancient world were primarily a matter of the rental of slaves—a practice that in Mesopotamia is first documented only in neo-Babylonian times (Oppenheim 1964:78, VerSteeg 2000:70–71; for an Egyptian parallel VerSteeg 2002:197).

44. The entire issue has been complicated by Herodotus' claim (1.199) that all Babylonian women other than daughters of the elite were expected to prostitute themselves at temples, once, to earn the money for their dowries. This was certainly false, but it has caused the terms of debate to become rather confused between people insisting on the importance of "hierodules" or even claiming that all prostitution was effectively sacred (e.g., Kramer 1969, Lambert 1992) and those rejecting the entire notion as Orientalist fantasy (Arnaud 1973, Westenholz 1989, Beard & Henderson 1997, Assante 2003). However, recently published texts from Kish and Sippar make clear that sexual rituals involving temple women, at least some of whom were paid for their services, definitely did take place (Gallery 1980; Yoffee 1998; Stol 1995:138–39) The devadasi analogy incidentally was first to my knowledge proposed in Yoffee 1998:336. On devadasis in general: Orr 2000, Jordan 2003, Vijaisri 2004.

45. Kramer 1963:116, Bahrani 2001: 59–60.

46. A similar reading can be found in Bottéro 1992:96, but without the ambivalence, which Lerner (1980:247) emphasizes.

47. See Lerner 1980, Van Der Toorn 1989, Lambert 1992.

48. Also, in many places, small-scale female traders are likened to or confused with prostitutes, simply because they have multiple ongoing relationships with unrelated men (for a contemporary Kazakh example: Nazpary 2001)—and the roles can sometimes overlap.

49. Diakonoff (1982). Loose bands of pastoral nomads or refugees, who also sometimes doubled as soldiers, were often referred to generically as *hapiru* or *habiru*, both in Mesopotamia and to the West. This might be the origin of the term "Hebrew," another group that according to their own histories had fled from bondage, wandered with their flocks in the desert, and eventually descended as conquerors on urban society.

50. Herodotus 1.199, also Strabo 16.1.20.

51. Revelations 17.4–5. Revelations seems to follow the perspective of the followers of Peter more than those of Paul. I observe in passing that Rastafarianism, the main prophetic voice today that makes use of the image of Babylon as corruption and oppression—though it does tend to play down the imagery of sexual corruption—has in practice been very much about the reassertion of patriarchal authority among the poor.

52. 1980:249–54; 1989:123–40. The main textual source is Driver & Miles 1935; also Cardascia 1969.

53. In Sumerian weddings, a bride's father would cover her with a veil, and the groom would remove it—it was by this act that he made her his wife (Stol 1995:128). Not only does this demonstrate the degree to which the veil was a symbol of encompassment in some man's domestic authority; it might also have been the source from which the later Assyrian practice was eventually adopted.

54. My take on Confucianism follows Deng's (1999) somewhat unconventional approach. See Watson 1980 on the commoditization of women; Gates 1989 on its relation to general decline of women's freedoms during the Song; there seems to have been another major setback during the Ming dynasty—for a recent overview, Ko, Haboush, and Piggott (2003). Testart (2000, 2001:148–49, 190) emphasizes that the case of China confirms his "general sociological law," that societies that practice brideprice will also allow debt slavery (Testart, Lécrivain, Karadimas & Govoroff 2001), since this was a place where the government vainly tried to stop both. Another aspect of Confucianism was that male slavery was seen as much more dubious than female slavery; though it never went as far as in Korea, where after the invasion of Hideyoshi, a law was passed decreeing that *only* women could be enslaved.

55. Tambiah (1973, 1989) was the first to make what is now the standard critique of Goody's argument. Goody prefers to see these as indirect dowry payments since they were normally passed to the family (1990:178–97).

56. On Homeric honor: Finley 1954:118–19, Adkins 1972:14–16 Seaford 1994:6–7. Cattle are again the main unit of account, and silver. Is also apparently used As Classicists have noted, the only actual acts of buying and selling in the Homeric epics are with foreigners (Von Reden 1995:58–76, Seaford 2004:26–30, Finley 1954:67–70). Needless to say, Homeric society lacked the legalistic precision of the Irish notion of "honor price" but the principles were broadly the same, since *tīme* could mean not only "honor" but "penalty" and "compensation."

57. *Tīme* is not used for the "price" of commodities in the *Iliad* or the *Odyssey*, but then prices of commodities are barely mentioned. It is, however, used for "compensation," in the sense of wergeld or honor-price (Seaford 2004:198n46). The first attested use of *time* as purchase price

is in the slightly later Homeric Hymn to Demeter (132) where, as Seaford notes, it seems significant that in fact it refers to a slave.

58. Aristotle, *Constitution of the Athenians* 2.2. He is referring to the great crisis leading to Solon's reforms, the famous "shaking off of burdens" of c. 594 BC.

59. Greek chattel slavery was in fact much more extreme than anything that appears to have existed in the ancient Near East at the time (see e.g., Westermann 1955; Finley 1974, 1981; Wiedemann 1981; Dandamaev 1984; Westbrook 1995), not only because most Near Eastern "slaves" were not technically slaves at all but redeemable debt pawns, who therefore at least in theory could not be arbitrarily abused, but because even those who were absolute private property had greater rights.

60. "Self-sufficiency is an end and what is best" (Aristotle *Politics* 1256–58; see Finley 1974:109–11, Veyne 1979, for classic discussions of what this meant in practice.)

61. The argument here follows Kurke 2002. On the public brothels, see Halperin 1990, Kurke 1996. There actually were Temple prostitutes in Greece too, mostly famously in Corinth, where Strabo (8.6.20) claimed that the Temple of Aphrodite owned a thousand of them, apparently, slaves who had been dedicated to the temple by pious worshippers.

62. As noted in the quote from David Sutton (2004) above. For a sampling of the anthropological literature on honor in contemporary Greek society, see: Campbell 1964, Peristiany 1965, Schneider 1971, Herzfeld 1980, 1985, Just 2001.

63. On the impropriety of women's work outside the household, see Brock 1994. On segregation of women in general: Keuls 1985, Cohen 1987, Just 1989, Loraux 1993.

64. The evidence is overwhelming, but until recently has been largely ignored. Llewellyn-Jones (2003) notes that the practice began as an aristocratic affection, but that by the fifth century, all

respectable women "were veiled daily and routinely, at least in public or in front of non-related men" (ibid:14).

65. van Reden 1997:174, referencing Herodotus 7.233, Plutarch's Pericles, 26.4.

66. A woman who one of them, Achilles, had personally reduced to slavery. Briseis was from the Trojan town of Lyrnessus, and after Achilles killed her husband and three brothers in the Greek attack on the town, she was awarded to him as a prize. (On learning of this, her father later hanged himself.) In the Iliad, Achilles insists he loves her. Briseis' opinions were not considered worth recording, though later poets, uncomfortable with the idea that the greatest epic of antiquity was a celebration of simple rape, concocted a story whereby Briseis had actually long been in love with Achilles from afar, and somehow manipulated the course of events so as to cause the battle to begin with.

67. Homeric warriors weren't really aristocrats at all, or if they were, as Calhoun puts it (1934:308) they were aristocrats "only in the loosest sense of the word." Mostly they were just a collection of local chieftains and ambitious warriors.

68. See Kurke 1997:112–13, 1999:197–98 for Greek elaborations on the theme. So too Seaford: "Whereas the Homeric *gift* is invested with the personality of its heroic donor, the only kind of person that *money* resembles is the prostitute. For Shakespeare it is 'the common whore of all mankind'" (2002:156, emphasis in the original. For what it's worth, Seaford is slightly off here: Shakespeare described the *earth* as the "common whore of all mankind," whose womb produces gold, which is money [*Timon of Athens* 4.3.42–45].)

69. Seaford 2002 in his review of Kurke notes that Greek sources regularly go back and forth on this.

70. In the *Odyssey* (11.488–91), famously, Achilles, when trying to invoke the lowest and most miserable person he can possibly imagine, invokes not a slave

but a *thete*, a mere laborer unattached to any household.

71. Free *porne* were always the daughters of foreigners or resident aliens. So, incidentally, were the aristocrats' courtesans.

72. The reader will observe that even in the anecdotes that follow, women simply don't appear. We have no idea who Polemarchus' wife was.

73. Recall here that pederasty was technically against the law. Or, to be more exact, for a man to submit to the passive role in sodomy was illegal; one could be stripped of one's citizenship for having done so. While most adult men were involved in love affairs with boys, and most boys with men, all did so under the pretense that no intercourse was actually taking place; as a result, almost anyone could be accused of former impropriety. The most famous case here is Aeschines' *Against Timarchus* (see van Reden 2003:120–23, also Dillon 2003:117–28.) Exactly the same dilemmas resurface in Rome, where Cicero, for instance, accused his rival Marc Antony of having once made his living as a male prostitute (*Philippics* 2.44–45), and Octavian, the later Augustus, was widely reputed to have "prostituted" himself, as a youth, to Julius Caesar, among other powerful patrons (Suetonius *Augustus* 68).

74. The most famous cases were Athens, Corinth, and Megara (Asheri 1969; St. Croix 1981; Finley 1981:156–57.)

75. The law was called the *palintokia* and is known mainly from Plutarch (*Moralia* 295D, apparently drawing on a lost Aristotelian *Constitution of the Megarians*.) Almost everything about it is at issue in current scholarship (Asheri 1969:14–16; Figueria 1985:149–56, Millettt 1989: 21–22; Hudson 1992:31; Bryant 1994:100-044). Hudson for instance argues that since the event is said to have happened around 540 BC, at a time when interest-bearing loans might not even have existed, the whole story is likely to be later propaganda. Others suggest that

it really happened much later. It's interesting that all Greek sources treat this as a most radical and outrageous populist measure—despite the fact that similar measures became standard Catholic policy during most of the European Middle Ages.

76. It is entirely unclear whether loans at interest even existed in this early period, since the first apparent reference to interest is from roughly 475 BC, and the first utterly clear ones from the later part of that same century (Bogaert 1966, 1968; Finley 1981; Millett 1991a: 44–45; Hudson 1992).

77. Compare for example Leviticus 25:35–37, which stipulates that it is permissible to make an impoverished "fellow countryman" a client or tenant, but *not* to give him an interest-bearing loan.

78. As Hesiod emphasizes in *Works and Days* (II 344–63); he's our main source on such matters. Paul Millett (1991a:30–35) provides a close reading of this passage, to illustrate the ambiguities between gifts and loans. Millett's book *Lending and Borrowing in Ancient Athens* (op cit) is the basic work on that topic. Scholarship on the Greek economy has long been preoccupied by what's still (rather anachronistically) called the Primitivist-Modernist debate; Millett takes a strong Primitivist position and has taken predictable heat from the other side (e.g., Cohen 1995, Shipley 1997, 2001). Most of the debate, though, turns on the prevalence of commercial lending, which is tangential to my present concerns.

79. The story is so striking because Nasruddin almost never elsewhere behaves in a way that a contemporary audience would consider unfair or exploitative. Those stories that do always focus on his relations with his neighbor the miser—the listener is presumed to know that being a miser, he must, necessarily, be up to no good.

80. "Against Nicostratus" (Demosthenes 53). My version largely follows Millet (1991a:53–59) but also draws on

Trevett 1992, Dillon 2002:94–100, Harris 2006:261–63). The interpretation of Nicostratus' motives is my own; Dillon, for example, suspects that the entire story of his kidnapping and ransom at Aegina was made up—though if that were the case, one would imagine Apollodorus would have eventually found out and told the jurors. The text doesn't explicitly say that Nicostratus was an aristocrat, but this seems the most plausible explanation of why someone might have a comfortable country estate but no money. Apollodorus, though, was known, from other contexts, to have feared that his fellow citizens would have contempt for his lowly background, and tried to compensate by lavish—and some felt, over-lavish—generosity (see Ballin 1978; Trevett 1992).

81. Athenians when trying to be high-minded at least spoke as if fellow citizens should behave this way to one another; to loan money at interest to a citizen in dire need was treated as obviously reprehensible behavior (Millett 1991a:26). All philosophers who touched on the subject, starting with Plato (*Laws* 742c, 921c) and Aristotle (*Politics* 1258c) denounced interest as immoral. Obviously not everyone felt that way. Here as in the Middle East, from whence the custom had spread (Hudson 1992), the dilemma was that charging interest made obvious sense in the case of commercial loans, but easily became abusive in the case of consumer loans.

82. It's not clear whether debt slavery, or at least debt peonage, was anywhere entirely eliminated, and debt crises continued to occur at regular intervals in cities other than Athens (Asheri 1969; St. Croix 1981). Some (Rhodes 1981:118–27; Cairns 1991; Harris 2006:249–80) believe that debt bondage was not even entirely eliminated in Athens. Millett (1991a:76) is probably right to say that imperial capitals like Athens, and later Rome, fended off the dangers of debt crises and resulting unrest less by forbidding the practice than by funneling tribute money into social programs that provided a constant source of

funds for the poor, making usury largely unnecessary.

83. Millett 1991b:189–92. The same was true in Roman Galilee (Goodman 1983:55), and presumably in Rome as well (Howgego 1992:13).

84. the Furies, who pursue Orestes to avenge his killing of his mother, insist that they are collecting a debt due in blood (Aeschylus, Eumenides 260, 319.) Millett (1991a:6–7) compiles a number of examples. Korver (1934, cf. Millet 1991:29–32) demonstrates that there was never any formal distinction between "gift" and "loan"; the two continually shaded into each other.

85. The two were seen to be connected: Herodotus, famously, argued that for the Persians, the greatest crime was to lie, and that they therefore forbade the loaning of money at interest since it would necessarily give rise to untruthful behavior (1.138).

86. Plato *Republic* 331c.

87. Plato Republic 345d. My reading is strongly influenced here by that of Marc Shell (1978). Shell's essay is important, but sadly neglected, as Classicists only seem to cite each other (at least, on the subject of the Classics).

88. What Polemarchus is invoking of course is the logic of the heroic gift, and of the feud. If someone helps or harms you, you pay them back the same or better. Polemarchus actually says that there are two circumstances when it's easiest to do this: in war, and in banking.

89. The Republic was written in 380 BC, and these events took place in 388/7. See Thesleff 1989:5, DuBois 2003:153–54, for the dates and references to ancient and contemporary scholarship on the issue, which concur that these events did take place. It's not entirely clear if Plato was taken in an act of piracy, sold on the orders of an angry ex-patron, or seized as a prisoner of war (Aegina—Plato's birthplace, incidentally—was then at war with Athens.) But the lines blurred. Curiously, Diogenes the Cynic, a younger

contemporary of Plato, was also captured by pirates on a trip to Aegina around the same time. In his case no one came to his aid (unsurprising considering that he rejected all worldly attachments and tended to insult everyone he met). He ended up spending the rest of his life as a slave in Corinth (Diogenes Laertius, 4.9). Plato, Aristotle, and Diogenes were the three most famous philosophers of the fourth century; the fact that two of the three had the experience of standing on an auction block demonstrates that such things really could happen to anyone.

90. Plato recounts the events in his *Seventh Letter to Dion*, but Annikeris only appears in Diogenes Laertius 3.19–20.

91. Ihering 1877.

92. Rights *"in rem,"* or "in the thing," are considered to be held "against all the world," since "a duty is incumbent on all persons whatsoever to abstain from acts injurious to the right"—this is opposed to rights *"in personem,"* which are held against a specific individual or group of individuals (Digby & Harrison 1897:301). Garnsey (2007:177–178) notes that Proudhon (1840) was correct in insisting that the "absolute" nature of property rights in the French Civil Code and other paradigmatic modern legal documents goes back directly to Roman law, *both* to the notion of absolute private property, and to that of the emperor's absolute sovereignty.

93. The idea that Roman property was not a right goes back to Villey (1946), and became mainstream in English scholarship with Tuck (1979:7–13) and Tierney (1997), though Garnsey (2007:177–95) has recently made a convincing case that Roman jurists did see property as a right (*ius*) in the sense that one had a right of alienation, and to defend one's claims in court. It's an interesting debate, largely turning on one's definition of "right," but somewhat tangential to my own argument.

94. "The paradigmatic relation between a person and a thing is that of ownership, yet the omans themselves seemed never to have defined it. To them, it was

a power relation—a form of *potestas*—directly exercised over the physical thing itself" (Samuel 2003:302).

95. In earliest Roman law (the Twelve Tablets of c450 BC) slaves were still people, but of diminished worth, since injuries against them counted as 50 percent those of a free person (Twelve Tablets VIII.10). By the late Republic, around the time of the emergence of the concept of dominium, slaves had been redefined as *res*, things, and injuries to them had the same legal status as injuries to farm animals (Watson 1987:46)

96. Patterson: "it is difficult to understand why the Romans would want to invent the idea of a relation between a person and a thing (an almost metaphysical notion, quite at variance with the Roman way of thinking in other areas) . . . unless we understand that, for most purposes, the 'thing' on their minds was a slave" (1982:31).

97. It does not appear in the Twelve Tablets or early legal documents.

98. *Dominus* first appears in III BC, *dominium*, sometime later (Birks 1985:26). Keith Hopkins (1978) estimates that by the end of the Republic, slaves made up between 30 and 40 percent of the Italian population, perhaps the highest proportion of any known society.

99. *Digest* 9.2.11 pr., Ulpian in the 18th book on the Edict.

100. The examples are from *Digest* 47.2.36 pr., Ulpian in the 41st book on Sabinus, and *Digest* 9.2.33 pr, Paulus' second book to Plautius, respectively.

101. See Saller (1984) on *domus* versus *familia*. The word *familia*, and its various later European cognates, *famille* in French, *family* in English, and so on, continued to refer primarily to a unit of authority and not necessarily of kinship until at least the 18th century (Stone 1968, Flandrin 1979, Duby 1982:220–23, Ozment 1983; Herlihy 1985)

102. Westbrook 1999:207 goes through the three known cases of this really happening. It would seem that the father's

authority here was considered identical to that of the state. If a father was found to have executed his child illegitimately, he could be punished.

103. Or to enslave them. In fact the Law of the Twelve Tablets (III.1) itself seems to be an attempt to reform or moderate even harsher practices, as al-Wahid (Elwahed 1931:81–82) was perhaps the first to point out.

104. Finley notes that the sexual availability of slaves "is treated as a commonplace in the Graeco-Roman literature" (1980:143; see Saller 1987:98–99, Glancey 2006:50–57).

105. There is a lively debate about whether breeding slaves was ever extensively practiced in Rome: one common theory of slavery (e.g., Meillassoux 1996, Anderson 1974) arguing that it is never profitable to do so, and when a supply of new slaves is cut off, slaves will ordinarily be converted into serfs. There seems no reason to weigh in on this here, but for a summary, see Bradley 1987.

106. True, Roman citizens could not legally enslave one another; but they could be enslaved by foreigners, and pirates and kidnappers rarely put too fine a point on such things.

107. The Chinese emperor Wang Mang was so fastidious on this point, for instance, that he once ordered one of his own sons put to death for the arbitrary murder of a slave (Testart 1998:23.)

108. The *lex Petronia*. Technically it bans owners from ordering slaves to "fight the wild beasts," a popular public entertainment: "fight," though, is usually a euphemism, since those fighting hungry lions were provided with no weapons, or obviously inadequate ones. It was only a century later, under Hadrian (117–138 AD), that owners were forbidden to kill their slaves, maintain private dungeons for them or practice other cruel and excessive punishments. Interestingly, the gradual limitation of the power of slave-owners was accompanied by increasing state power, expansion of citizenship, but also the return of various forms of debt-bondage and the creation of dependent peasantry (Finley 1972:92–93; 1981:164 65).

109. Thus Livy (41.9.11) notes in 177 BC the senate actually passed a law to prevent Italians who were not Roman citizens from selling relatives into slavery in this way in order to become citizens.

110. The phrase is preserved in the work of the elder Seneca (*Controversias* 4.7) and noted by Finley (1980:96), among others. There is a detailed discussion in Butrica 2006:210–23.

111. Wirszubski 1950. On the etymology, see Benveniste 1963:262–72. Similarly Kopytoff and Miers (1977) emphasize that in Africa, "freedom" always meant incorporation into some kin group—only slaves were "free" (in our sense) of all social relations.

112. Florentius in Justinian's Institutes (1.5.4.1). Some suggest that the word "natural" in the first sentence was only inserted in later editions, perhaps in the fourth century. The position that slavery is a product of force enshrined in law, contrary to nature, however, goes back at least to the fourth century BC, when Aristotle (Politics 1253b20–23) explicitly takes issue with it (see Cambiano 1987).

113. Already in the that century, lawyers like Azo and Bracton began asking: If this is true, wouldn't that mean a serf is a free man too? (Harding 1980:424 note 6; see also Buckland 1908:1, Watson 1987).

114. Ulpian wrote that "everyone was born free under the law of nature" and that slavery was a result of the *ius gentium* ("law of nations"), the common legal usages of mankind. Some later jurists added that property was originally common and the *ius gentium* was responsible for kingdoms, property, and so on (Digest 1.1.5). As Tuck notes (1979:19), these were really scattered ideas, only systematized by Church thinkers like Gratian much later, during the twelfth-century revival of Roman law.

115. *Princeps legibus solutus est* ("the sovereign is not bound by the laws"), a

phrase initially coined by Ulpian and repeated by Justinian (1.3 pr.) This was a very new notion in the ancient world; the Greeks, for instance, had insisted that while men could do as they liked with their women, children, and slaves, any ruler who exploited their own subjects in the same way was the definition of a tyrant. Even the basic principle of modern sovereignty, that rulers hold the ultimate power of life and death over their subjects (which modern heads of state still hold in their power to grant pardons), was looked on with suspicion. Similarly, under the Republic, Cicero argued that rulers who insisted on holding the power of life and death were by definition tyrants, "even if they prefer to be called kings" (*De Re Publica* 3.23, Westbrook 1999:204.)

116. In the Chronicle of Walter of Guisborough (1957:216); see Clanchy 1993:2–5.

117. Aylmer 1980.

118. To be fair, a classical liberal would insist that this is the logical conclusion with starting out from the notion of freedom as active instead of passive (or as philosophers put it, that there are "subjective rights")—that is, seeing freedom not just as others' obligations to allow us to do whatever the law or custom says we can do, but to do anything that is not specifically forbidden, and that this has had tremendous liberating effects. There is certainly truth in this. But historically, these have been something of a side effect, and there are many other ways to come to the same conclusion that do not require us to accept the underlying assumptions about property.

119. Tuck 1979:49, cf. Tully 1993:252, Blackburn 1997:63–64.

120. Note here that in this period, the justification was not based on any assumption of racial inferiority—racial ideologies came later—but rather on the assumption that African laws were legitimate and should be considered binding, at least on Africans.

121. I've made the argument that wage labor is rooted in slavery extensively in the past—see e.g., Graeber 2006.

122. This is the reason, as C.B. MacPherson (1962) explained, that when "human rights abuses" are evoked in the newspapers, it is only when governments can be seen as trespassing on some victim's person or possessions—say, by raping, torturing, or killing them. The Universal Declaration of Human Rights, like just about all similar documents, also speaks of universal rights to food and shelter, but one never reads about governments committing "human rights abuses" when they eliminate price supports on basic foodstuffs, even if it leads to widespread malnutrition, or for razing shantytowns or kicking the homeless out of shelters.

123. One can trace the notion back as least as far back as Seneca, who in the first century AD, argued that slaves could be free in their minds, since force only applied to the "prison of the body" (*De beneficiis* 3.20)—this appears to have been a key point of transition between the notion of freedom as the ability to form moral relations with others, and freedom as an internalization of the master's power.

124. See Roitman 2003:224 for one author who explicitly relates this to debt. For objects as unique points in a human history, there is a vast literature, but see Hoskins 1999, Graeber 2001.

125. One can tell how unusual slavery was by informants' assumptions that slaves would have no idea that this was to be their fate.

126. Significantly, at the very moment when his social existence was the only existence he had left. The mass killing of slaves at the funerals of kings, or grandees, has been documented from ancient Gaul, to Sumer, China, and the Americas.

127. *Iliad* 9:342–44.

128. Evans-Pritchard 1948:36; cf., Sahlins 1981. For a good example of identification of kings and slaves, Feeley-Harnik 1982. Obviously, everyone is well aware

that kings do have families, friends, lovers, etc—the point is that this is always seen as something of a problem, since he should be king to all his subjects equally.

129. Regarding the influence of Roman law on the liberal tradition, it is fascinating to note that the very earliest author we have on record who laid out something like Smith's model, where money, and ultimately coinage, is invented as an aid to commerce, was another Roman jurist, Paulus: *Digest* 18.1.1.

130. But it has by no means been eliminated. (If anyone is inclined to doubt this, I recommend they take a stroll through their neighborhood ignoring all property rights, and see just how long it takes for the weapons to come out.)

Chapter Eight

1. "Debt, n. An ingenious substitute for the chain and whip of the slavedriver," wrote the notorious cynic Ambrose Bierce (*The Devil's Dictionary*, 1911:49). Certainly for those Thai women who appeared at Neil Bush's door, the difference between having been sold by one's parents, and working off one's parents' debt contract, was as much a technicality as it would have been two thousand years ago.

2. One of the few authors I know who's confronted the question head-on is Pierre Dockés (1979), who makes a convincing statement that it has to do with the power of the state: at least, slavery as an institution was briefly revived under the Carolingian empire and then vanished again afterward. It is certainly interesting that since the nineteenth century at least, the "transition from feudalism to capitalism" has become our historical paradigm for epochal social change, and no one much addresses the transition from ancient slavery to feudalism, even though there is reason to believe that whatever is happening now may much more closely resemble it.

3. Robin Blackburn makes this argument quite convincingly in *The Making*

of New World Slavery (1997). There were some exceptions, notably the Italian city-states. The story is of course more complicated than I'm representing it: one reason for the hostility was that during much of the Middle Ages, Europeans were largely victims of slave-raiders rather than their beneficiaries, with many captives marketed in North Africa and the Middle East.

4. The Aegean coins were stamped; the Indian, punched; and the Chinese, cast. This suggests that we are not talking about diffusion here. Speaking of Indian coins, for instance, one historian remarks: "If there is one thing that seems clear from a punch-marked coin, it is that the person who thought it up had never seen a Greek coin—or if he had seen one, it had not impressed him. The punch-marked coin is made by an entirely different metallurgical process" (Schaps 2006:9).

5. Pruessner (1928) was perhaps the first to point this out.

6. They appear to have been widely used by Old Assyrian merchants operating in Anatolia (Veenhof 1997).

7. Powell (1978, 1979, 1999:14–18) provides an excellent assessment of the evidence, emphasizing that Babylonians did not produce scales accurate enough to measure the tiny amounts of silver they would have had to use to make ordinary household purchases like fried fish or cords of firewood in cash. He concludes that silver was largely used in transactions between merchants. Market vendors therefore presumably acted as they do in small-scale markets in Africa and Central Asia, today, building up lists of trustworthy clients to whom they could extend credit over time (e.g., Hart 1999:201, Nazpary 2001).

8. Hudson 2002:21–23, who hypothesizes that the time element was important as merchants would presumably otherwise delay to employ the funds as long as possible. See Renger 1984, 1994; Meiroop 2005.

9. I'm referring here to *Qirad* and *Mudaraba* arrangements, similar to the ancient and Medieval Mediterranean *Commenda* (Udovitch 1970, Ray 1997).

10. Herodotus 1.138.

11. Herodotus 3.102–5.

12. Mieroop 2002:63, 2005:29. He notes that Enmetena's total grain income in any one year was roughly 37 million liters, making the sum he claims to be owed more than one thousand times his own palace's annual revenue.

13. Lambert 1971; Lemche 1979:16.

14. Hudson 1993 provides the most detailed overview of this literature.

15. Hudson 1993:20.

16. Grierson 1977:17, citing Cerny 1954:907.

17. Bleiberg 2002

18. One authority states categorically: "I do not know of debt-annulment decrees issued by any Pharaoh" (Jasnow 2001:42), and adds that there is no evidence for debt-bondage until the very late Demotic period. This is the same period when Greek sources begin to speak of both.

19. VerSteeg 2002:199; see Lorton 1977:42–44.

20. This in certain ways resembles the legal loopholes created in both the Medieval Christian and Islamic worlds, where interest was formally banned: see chapter 10 below.

21. Diodorus Siculus 1.79. See Westermann 1955:50–51 for a comparison of Greek and Egyptian sources on the subject.

22. The history of the dissemination of interest-bearing debt is only beginning to be reconstructed. It does not yet appear in Ebla (c. 2500 BC), in Old or Middle Kingdom Egypt, or in Mycenaean Greece, but it eventually becomes common in the Levant in the late Bronze Age, and also in Hittite Anatolia. As we'll see, it came quite late to Classical Greece, and even later to places like Germany.

23. In Chinese historiography, in fact, this whole epoch is known as "the feudal period.")

24. The *Guanzi*, cited in Schaps 2006:20.

25. Yung-Ti (2006) has recently argued that they weren't, though we wouldn't really know. Thierry (1992:39–41) simply assumes they were, providing much evidence of their use both as units of account and means of payment, but none of their use for buying and selling.

26. At any rate, cowries were definitely being used as the equivalent of coins in later periods, and the government periodically either suppressed their use or reintroduced them (Quiggin 1949, Swann 1950, Thierry 1992:39–41, Peng 1994.) Cowrie money survived, alongside tally sticks, as a common form of currency in Yunnan province in the far south until relatively recent times (B. Yang 2002), and detailed studies exist, but—as far as I can tell—only in Chinese.

27. Scheidel 2004:5.

28. Kan 1978:92, Martzloff 2002:178. I note in passing that a study of the Inca *khipu* system itself would itself be quite fascinating in this regard; the strings were used to record both obligations we would consider financial, and others we would consider ritual, since as in so many Eurasian languages, the words "debt" and "sin" were the same in Quechua as well (Quitter & Urton 2002:270).

29. L. Yang (1971:5) finds the first reliable literary reference to loans at interest in the fourth century BC. Peng (1994:98–101) notes that the earliest surviving records (the oracle bones and inscriptions) do not mention loans, but there's no reason they would; he also assembles most of the available literary references, finds many references to loans in early periods, and concludes that there's no way to know whether to take them seriously. By the Warring States period, however, there is abundant evidence for local usurers, and all the usual abuses.

30. *Yan tie lun* I 2/4b2–6, in Gale (1967):12.

31. Guanzi (73 12), Rickett (1998:397)

32. So around 100 BC, "when flood and drought come upon them . . . those who have grain sell at half value, while those who have not borrow at exorbitant usury. Then paternal acres change hands; sons and grandsons are sold to pay debts; merchants make vast profits, and even petty tradesmen set up business and realize

unheard of gains" (in Duyvendak 1928:32). Loans at interest are first documented in the fourth century BC in China but may have existed before that (Yang 1971:5). For a parallel case of child-selling for debt in early India, Rhys Davids 1922:218.

Chapter Nine

1. Jaspers 1949.

2. Parkes 1959:71.

3. Or, if one must be even more precise, we should probably end it in 632 AD, with the death of the Prophet.

4. Obviously Vedic Hinduism is earlier; I am referring to Hinduism as a self-conscious religion, which is generally seen as having taken shape in reaction to Buddhism and Jainism around this time.

5. The date used to be set much earlier, at 650 or even 700 BC, but recent archaeology has called this into question. Lydian coins still seem to be the earliest, though, as most of the others have been seem to be the earliest though.

6. Prakash & Singh 1968, Dhavalikar 1974, Kosambi 1981, Gupta & Hardaker 1995. The latest accepted dates for the appearance of coinage in India, based on radiocarbon analysis, is circa 400 BC (Erdosy 1988:115, 1995:113).

7. Kosambi (1981) notes that there seems to be a direct connection between the first of these and Bronze Age Harappan cities: "even after the destruction of Mohenjo Daro, which is entirely a trade city as shown by its fine weights and poor weapons, the traders persisted, and continued to use the very accurate weights of that period." (ibid:91). Given what we know of Mesopotamia, with which the Harappan civilization was in close contact, it also seems reasonable to assume that they continued to employ older commercial techniques, and, indeed, "promissory notes" do appear as familiar practices in our earliest literary sources, such as the Jakatas (Rhys Davids 1901:16, Thapar

1995:125, Fiser 2004:194), even if these are many centuries later. Of course, in this case, the marks were presumably meant to confirm the accuracy of the weight, to show that it hadn't been further trimmed, but the inspiration of earlier credit practices seems likely. Kosambi later confirms this: "The marks would correspond to modern countersignatures on bills or cheques cleared through business houses." (1996:178–79)

8. Our first literary record of coinage in China is of a kingdom that reformed its currency system in 524 BC—which means that it already had a currency system, and presumably had for some time (Li 1985:372).

9. Schaps 2006:34. For a similar recent argument, Schoenberger 2008.

10. Of course the very first coins were of fairly high denominations and quite possibly used for paying taxes and fees, and for buying houses and cattle more than for everyday purchases (Kraay 1964, Price 1983, Schaps 2004, Vickers 1985). A real market society in Greece, for instance, could only be said to exist when, as in the fifth century, ordinary citizens went to the market carrying minuscule coins of stamped silver or copper in their cheeks.

11. First proposed by Cook (1958), the explanation has since lost favor (Price 1983, Kraay 1964, Wallace 1987, Schaps 2004:96–101; though cf. Ingham 2004:100)—largely, on the argument that one cannot pay soldiers with coins unless there are already markets with people willing to accept the coins. This strikes me as a weak objection, since the absence of coinage does not imply the absence of either money or markets; almost all parties to the debate (e.g., Balmuth [1967, 1971, 1975, 2001) who argues that irregular pieces of silver were already in wide use as currency, and Le Rider (2001), Seaford (2004:318–37) or for that matter Schaps (2004:222–35), who argue that they were not numerous enough to be a viable everyday currency, seem to give much

consideration to the possibility that most market trade took place on credit. Anyway, as I've noted earlier, it would be easy enough for the state to ensure that the coins became acceptable currency simply by insisting that they were the only acceptable means of payment for obligations to the state itself.

12. Most of the earliest known Greek bankers were of Phoenician descent, and it's quite possible that they first introduced the concept of interest there (Hudson 1992).

13. Elayi & Elayi 1992.

14. Starr 1977:113; see Lee 2000.

15. It's interesting to note that, to our knowledge, the great trading nations did not produce much in the way of great art or philosophy.

16. The great exception was of course Sparta, which refused to issue its own coinage but developed a system whereby aristocrats adopted a strict military lifestyle and trained permanently for war.

17. Aristotle himself noted the connection when he emphasized that the constitution of a Greek state could be predicted by the main army of its military: aristocracies if they relied on cavalry (since horses were very expensive), oligarchies in the case of heavy infantry (since armor was not cheap), democracy in the case of light infantry or navies (since anyone could wield a sling or row a boat) (*Politics* 4.3.1289b33–44, 13.1297b16–24, 6.7.1321a6–14).

18. Keyt (1997:103) summarizing *Politics* 1304b27–31.

19. Thucydides (6.97.7) claimed that 20,000 escaped from the mines in 421 BC, which is probably exaggerated, but most sources estimate at least 10,000 for most of that century, generally working shackled and under atrocious conditions (Robinson 1973).

20. Ingham 2004:99–100.

21. MacDonald 2006:43.

22. On Alexander's armies monetary needs, Davies 1996:80 in turn, 83; on his logistics more generally, Engels 1978. The figure 120,000 includes not only actual troops but servants, camp-followers, and so forth.

23. Green 1993:366.

24. The Roman institution was called *nexum*, and we don't know entirely how it worked: i.e., whether it was a form of labor contract, whereby one worked off the debt for a fixed term, or something more like African pawn systems, where the debtor—and his or her children—served in conditions roughly like those of a slave until redemption (see Testart 2002 for the possibilities). See Buckler 1895, Brunt 1974, Cornell 1994:266–67, 330–32.

25. Hence, most of the scandalous stories that sparked uprisings against debt bondage centered on dramatic cases of physical or sexual abuse; of course, once debt bondage was abolished and household labor was instead supplied by slaves, such abuse was considered normal and acceptable.

26. The first bronze coins paid to soldiers seem to have been coined around 400 BC (Scheidel 2006), but this was the traditional date according to Roman historians.

27. What I am arguing flies in the face of much of the conventional scholarly wisdom, summed up best perhaps by Moses Finley when he wrote "in Greece and Rome the debtor class rebelled; whereas in the Near East they did not"—and therefore reforms like those of Nehemiah were at least minor, temporary palliatives. Near Eastern rebellion took a different form; moreover, Greek and Roman solutions were both more limited and more temporary than he supposed.

28. Ioannatou 2006 for a good example. Cataline's conspiracy of 63 BC was an alliance of indebted aristocrats and desperate peasants. On continued Republican debt and land redistribution campaigns: Mitchell 1993.

29. Howgego makes this point: "If less is heard of debt under the Principate it may well be because political stability removed the opportunity for the expression

of discontent. This argument is supported by the way in which debt re-emerges as an issue at times of open revolt" (1992:13).

30. Plutarch, *Moralia*, 828f–831a.

31. There is, needless to say, a vast and conflicting literature, but probably the best source is Banaji (2001). He emphasizes in the late empire, "debt was the essential means by which employers enforced control over the supply of labour, fragmenting the solidarity of workers and 'personalizing' relations between owners and employees" (ibid:205), a situation he compares interestingly to India.

32. Kosambi 1966, Sharma 1968, Misra 1976, Altekar 1977:109–38. Contemporary Indian historians, who refer to them as gana-sanghas ("tribal assemblies"), tend to dismiss them as warrior aristocracies supported by populations of helots or slaves, though of course, Greek city-states could be described the same way.

33. In other words, they looked more like Sparta than like Athens. The slaves were also collectively owned (Chakravarti 1985:48–49.) Again, one has to wonder how much this was really the general rule, but I yield to the predominant scholarly opinion on such matters.

34. *Arthasastra* 2.12.27. See Schaps 2006:18 for a nice comparative commentary.

35. Thapar 2002:34, Dikshitar 1948.

36. There were also taxes, of course, usually ranging from 1/6 to 1/4 of total yield (Kosambi 1996:316; Sihag 2005), but taxes also served as a way to bring goods to the market.

37. So Kosambi 1966:152–57.

38. And wage labor, two phenomena that, as so often in the ancient world, largely overlapped: the common phrase for workers used in texts from the period was *dasa-karmakara*, "slave-hireling" with the assumption that slaves and laborers worked together and were barely distinguishable (Chakravarti 1985). On the predominance of slavery, see Sharma 1958, Rai 1981. The extent is contested, but early Buddhist texts do seem to assume that any wealthy family would normally have domestic slaves—which certainly wasn't true in other periods.

39. Punch-marked coins were also eventually replaced, after Alexander's brief conquest of the Indus Valley and his establishment of Greek colonists in Afghanistan, by Aegean-style coins, ultimately causing the entire Indian tradition to disappear (Kosambi 1981, Gupta & Hardaker 1985.)

40. It's referred to as the "Pillar Edict" (Norman 1975:16).

41. There's a good deal of debate as to when: Schopen (1994) emphasizes there is little evidence for substantial Buddhist monasteries until the first century AD, perhaps three centuries later. This has a great deal of bearing on monetarization too, as we'll see.

42. "The private trader was regarded as a thorn (*kantaka*), a public enemy just short of a national calamity, by Arth. 4.2, taxed and fined for malpractices of which many are taken for granted" (Kosambi 1996:243).

43. Those wishing to become monks had to first affirm that they were not themselves debtors (just as they also had to promise they weren't runaway slaves); but there was no rule saying the monastery itself could not lend money. In China, as we'll see, providing easy credit terms for peasants came to be seen as a form of charity.

44. Similarly, Buddhist monks are not allowed to see an army, if they can possibly avoid it (Pacittiya, 48–51).

45. Lewis 1990.

46. Wilbur 1943, Yates 2002. The state of Qin, during the Warring States period, not only allowed for army officers to be allocated slaves by rank, but for merchants, craftsmen, and the "poor and idle" to themselves be "confiscated as slaves" (Lewis 1990:61–62).

47. Scheidel (2006, 2007, 2009) has considered the matter at length and concluded that Chinese currency took the unusual form that it did for two maibn

reasons: (1) the historical coincidence that Qin (which used bronze coins) defeated Chu (which used gold) in the civil wars, and subsequent conservatism, and (2) the lack of a highly paid professional army, which allowed the Chinese state to act like the early Roman republic, which also limited itself to bronze coins for peasant conscripts—but unlike the Roman republic, was not surrounded by states accustomed to other forms of currency.

48. Pythagoras was, as far as we know, the first to take the latter course, founding a secret political society that for a while had control over the levers of political power in the Greek cities of southern Italy.

49. Hadot 1995, 2002. In the ancient world, Christianity was recognized as a philosophy largely because it had its own forms of ascetic practice.

50. On the Tillers: Graham 1979, 1994:67–110. They seem to have flourished around the same time as Mo Di, the founder of Mohism (roughly 470–391 BC). The Tillers ultimately vanished, leaving behind mainly a series of treatises on agricultural technology, but they had a tremendous influence on early Taoism—which, in turn, became the favorite philosophy for peasant rebels for many centuries to come, starting with the Yellow Turbans of 184 AD. Eventually, Taoism was displaced by messianic forms of Buddhism as the favorite ideology of rebellious peasants.

51. Wei-Ming 1986, Graham 1989, Schwartz 1986.

52. Legend has it that after one Pythagorean mathematician discovered the existence of irrational numbers, other members of the sect took him on a cruise and dropped him overboard. For an extended discussion of the relation of early Pythagoreanism (530–400 BC) to the rise of a cash economy, see Seaford 2004:266–75).

53. At least if my own experience in Madagascar is anything to go on.

54. War is quite similar: it's also an area in which it's possible to imagine everyone as playing a game where the rules and stakes are unusually transparent. The main difference is that in war one does care about one's fellow soldiers. On the origins of our own notion of "self-interest," see chapter 11 below.

55. Not to be confused with the unrelated Confucian term *li*, meaning "ritual" or "etiquette." Later, *li* became the word for "interest"—that is, not only "self-interest," but also "interest payment" (e.g., Cartier 1988:26–27). I should note that my argument here is slightly unconventional. Schwartz (1985:145–51) notes that in Confucius, "profit" has a purely pejorative meaning, and he argues that it was subversively reinterpreted by Mo Di. I find it unlikely that Confucius represents conventional wisdom at this time; while his writings are the earliest we have on the subject, his position was clearly marginal for centuries after his death. I am assuming instead that the Legalist tradition reflected the common wisdom even before Confucius—or certainly, Mencius.

56. *Zhan Guo Ce* ("Strategies of the Warring States") no. 109, 7.175

57. *Annuals of Lü Buwei*, 8/5.4.

58. See Ames (1994) for a discussion of key terms: *si li* (self-interest), *shi* (strategic advantage), and *li min* (public profit).

59. Book of Lord Shang 947–48, Duyvendak 1928:65.

60. Kosambi's translation (1965:142); the Encyclopedia Britannica prefers "handbook on profit" (entry for "Cārvāka"); Altekar (1977:3), "the science of wealth."

61. Nag & Dikshitar 1927:15. Kosambi argues that the Mauryan polity was thus based on a fundamental contradiction: "a moral law-abiding population ruled by a completely amoral king" (1996:237). Yet such a situation is hardly unusual, before or since.

62. Thucydides 5.85-113 (cf. 3.36–49). The event took place in 416 BC, around the same time that Lord Shang and Kautilya were writing. Significantly, Thucydides' own objections to such behavior are not explicitly moral but center

on showing that it was not to the "long-term profit" of the empire (Kallet 2001:19). On Thucydides' own utilitarian materialism more generally, see Sahlins 2004.

63. Mozi 6:7B, in Hansen 2000:137

64. Mencius 4.1, in Duyvendak 1928:76–77. He appears to be referring to a distinction originally made by Confucius himself: "the superior person understands what is right while the inferior person only understands what is personally profitable" (*Analects* 7.4.16).

65. The Mohist path—overtly embrace financial logic—was the less well trodden. We've already seen how in India and Greece, attempts to frame morality as debt went nowhere: even the Vedic principles are ostensibly about liberation from debt, which was also, as we've seen, a central theme in Israel.

66. Leenhardt 1979:164.

67. This interpretation does fly fairly directly in the face of the main thrust of scholarship on the issue, which tends instead to emphasize the "transcendental" nature of Axial Age ideas (e.g., Schwartz 1975, Eisenstadt 1982, 1984, 1986, Roetz 1993, Bellah 2005).

68. The Greek system actually began with Fire, Air, and Water, and the Indian with Fire, Water, and Earth, though in each case there were numerous elaborations. The Chinese elemental system was fivefold: Wood, Fire, Earth, Metal, Water.

69. In Christianity, at least in the Augustinian tradition, this is quite explicit: the material world does not in any sense partake of God; God is not in it; it was simply made by Him (*De civitate dei* 4.12)—this radical separation of spirit and nature being—according to Henri Frankfort (1948:342–44)—a peculiarity of the Judaeo-Christian tradition. That same Augustinian tradition, though, also drew on Plato to insist that reason, on the other hand—the abstract principle which allows us to understand such things, and which is entirely separate from matter—*does* partake of the divine (see Hoitenga

1991:112–14, for the conflict in Augustine's own ideas here).

70. Shell's essay "The Ring of Gyges" (1978) has already been cited in the last chapter, in my discussion of Plato; Seaford 1998, 2004.

71. This is based on the fact that Miletus was one of the cities, if not the first city, to produce coins of small enough denominations that they could be used for everyday transactions (Kraay 1964:67).

72. Heraclitus was from the nearby Ionian city of Ephesus and Pythagoras originally from the Ionian island of Samos. After Ionia was incorporated into the Persian empire, large numbers of Ionians fled to southern Italy, which then became the center of Greek philosophy, again, at just the period when the Greek cities there became thoroughly monetarized. Athens became the center of Greek philosophy only in the fifth century, which is also when Athens was militarily dominant and the Athenian "owl" coinage became the main international currency of the Eastern Mediterranean.

73. Or as Seaford (2004:208) puts it, echoing Anaximander's description of his primal substance, "a distinct, eternal, impersonal, all-embracing, unlimited, homogeneous, eternally moving, abstract, regulating substance, destination for all things as well as their origin" (or, at least, "all things" that were available for purchase.)

74. Seaford 2004:136–46; see Picard 1975; Wallace 1987; Harris 2008a:10. Purely "fiduciary" money is of course what a metallist would call "fiat" or "token" money, or a Keynesian, "chartal money." Despite Finley's arguments to the contrary (1980:141, 196), just about all ancient money was fiduciary to some extent. It's easy to see why coins would ordinarily circulate at a higher face value than their weight in gold or silver, since the price of the latter would tend to fluctuate, but the moment the coin's face value was lower than that of its metal content, there would be no reason not to melt it down.

75. In the case of truly large states like the Roman or Mauryan empires, inflation did eventually result, but the full effects were not felt for at least a century (see Ingham 2002:101–4, Kessler & Temin 2008, Harris 2008b for some good discussions of the Roman situation.)

76. Seaford 2004:138–39.

77. I am partly inspired here by Marcel Mauss's arguments about of the concept of substance (Allen 1998).

78. Hence, as we'll see Aristotle's position that a coin was only a social convention (*Nicomachean Ethics* 1133a29–31) remained very much a minority view in the ancient world. It did become the predominant view later, in the Middle Ages.

79. He is known as Pāyāsi in the Buddhist scriptures, Paesi in the Jaina (see Bronkhorst 2007:143–159 for a good discussion of these earliest Indian materialists; for the later materialist school, to which Kautilya is said to belong, see Chattopadhyaya 1994. Jaspers (1951:135), writing of India, notes the appearance of "all philosophical trends, including skepticism and materialism, sophistry and nihilism"—a significant list, since it's obviously not a list of "all" philosophical trends at all, but only the most materialist.

80. In *The Republic* it is rejected out of hand. In India, as I've argued, the Hindu tradition only appears to embrace it. Buddhists, Jains, and other oppositional philosophies didn't use the term at all.

81. Philo of Alexandria, writing around the time of Christ, says of the Essenes: "not a single slave is to be found among them, but all are free, exchanging services with each other, and they denounce the owners of slaves, not merely for their injustice in outraging the law of equality, but also for their impiety in annulling the statute of nature" (*Quod omnis probus liber sit* 79). The Therapeutae, another Jewish group, group rejected all forms of property, but looked on slavery "to be a thing absolutely and wholly contrary to nature, for nature has created all men free" (*De Vita*

Contemplativa 70). The similarity to Roman law ideas is notable. Jewish groups are unusually well documented; if similar sects existed in, say, Thrace, or Numidia, we probably wouldn't know.

82. Later legend had it that his father was a king and he grew up in a palace, but the Sakya "king" of the time was in fact an elected and rotating position (Kosambi 1965:96).

Chapter Ten

1. Coins produced by the barbarian successor states generally did not have a great deal of gold or silver in them; as a result they tended to circulate only within the principality of the king or baron who issued them and were largely useless for trade.

2. Dockés (1979:62–70) provides a good overview of the situation—literally, since current understandings of the extent of Roman slave estates in France are based largely on aerial photography. Over time even the free communities largely ended up in debt peonage of one sort or another, or bound to the land as serfs (in Latin, *coloni*).

3. As we've seen, Kosambi saw Magadha as a peak of monetarization. R.S. Sharma (2001:119–62) argues that coinage remained commonplace under the Guptas (280 to 550 AD) but then abruptly disappeared almost everywhere thereafter. However, even if he is right that the total number of coins in circulation did not diminish until then, he himself points out (ibid:143) that the total population of the Ganges Plain almost tripled over this period, so even this would mark a steady decline.

4. For an overview: R.S. Sharma 1965, Kane 1968 III:411–61, Chatterjee 1971. Schopen (1994) especially emphasizes that the techniques grow more sophisticated over the course of the Middle Ages, for

instance, developing bookkeeping techniques for combining compound interest with partial repayments.

5. Documents on the regulation of monastic affairs pay a great deal of attention to the details: how when the money was lent out, contracts would be signed, sealed, and deposited in the temple before witnesses; how a surety or pledge worth twice the amount of the loan should be turned over, how "devout lay brothers" should be assigned to manage the investment, and so forth (Schopen 1994).

6. From the Arab *dinar*, which in turn derives from the Roman *denarius*. It is unclear whether such sums were actually paid in coins at this point: one early monastic manual, for example, speaking of objects that might be relegated to the Inexhaustible Treasuries and thus put out at interest, mentions "gold and silver, whether in the form of coins, finished or raw, in large or small quantities, pure or alloyed, or whether in the form of utensils, finished or unfinished" (Mahāsāmghika Vinaya, in Gernet 1956 [1995:165]).

7. Fleet 1888: 260–62, as translated in Schopen 1994:532–33. One need hardly remark on the irony of this emphasis on eternity emerging within Buddhism, a religion founded on the recognition of the impermanence of all worldly attachments.

8. The commercial loans are documented from an inscription at the West Indian monastery at Karle (Levi 1938: 145; Gernet 1956 [1995:164]; Barreau 1961:444–47), the assemblies from later Tamil temples (Ayyar 1982:40–68, R.S. Sharma 1965.) It is not clear whether some of these were commercial loans, or more like the later Buddhist custom of *jisa* still current in Tibet, Bhutan, and Mongolia, where an individual, or collective, or group of families wishing to support a specific ceremony or, say, an educational project might receive a 500-rupee loan "in perpetuity" and then be expected to provide 800 rupees a year to organize the ceremony. The responsibilities are then inherited, though

the "loan" can be transferred (Miller 1961, Murphy 1961).

9. Kalhana, *Rajatarangini* 7.1091–98; see Basham 1948, Riepe 1961:44n49.) The monks were apparently Ajivkas, who still existed at this time.

10. Naskar 1996, R.S. Sharma 2001:45–66, on the Puranic description of the "Kali age," which seems to be the way later Brahmins referred to the period from roughly Alexander's reign to the early Middle Ages, a period of insecurity and unrest when foreign dynasties ruled much of India, and caste hierarchies were widely challenged or rejected.

11. Manusmṛti 8.5.257. Significantly, the debt to other humans vanishes entirely in these texts.

12. Manusmṛti 8.5.270–72. A Sudra's tongue would also be cut off for insulting a member of the twice-born castes (8.270).

13. R.S. Sharma 1958, 1987, Chauhan 2003.

14. "A Sudra, though emancipated by his master, is not released from a state of servitude, for a state which is natural to him, by whom can he be divested?" (Manusmṛti, Yājñavalkya Smṛti 8.5.419), or even "Sudras must be reduced to slavery, either by purchase or without purchase, because they were created by God for the sake or serving others (8.5.413).

15. Kautilya allowed 60 percent for commercial loans, 120 percent "for enterprises that involve journeys through forests," and twice that for those that involve shipping goods by sea (*Arthasastra* 3.11; one later code, Yājñavalkya Smṛti 2.38 follows this.)

16. Yājñavalkya Smṛti 2.37, Manusmṛti 8.143, Viṣnusmṛti 5.6.2, see Kane 1968 III:421.

17. R.S. Sharma 1965:68. Similarly, early law-codes specified that anyone who defaulted on a debt should be reborn as a slave or even a domestic animal in their creditor's household: one later Chinese Buddhist text was even more exact, specifying that for each eight wen defaulted, one must spend one day as an ox, or for

each seven, one day as a horse (Zhuang Chun in Peng 1994:244n17)

18. Dumont (1966).

19. Gyan Prakash (2003:184) makes this point for the colonial period: when one-time caste hierarchies began to be treated instead as matters of debt bondage, subordinates turned into persons who had equal rights, but whose rights were temporarily "suspended."

20. To be fair, one could also argue that indebted peasants are also likely to be in command of more resources, and thus be more capable of organizing a rebellion. We know very little about popular insurrections in Medieval India (though see Guha (1999). Palat (1986, 1988:205–15; Kosambi 1996:392–93), but the total number of such revolts seems to have been relatively low in comparison to Europe and certainly in comparison to China, where rebellion was almost ceaseless.

21. "No one knows just how many rebellions have taken place in Chinese history. From the official record there were several thousand incidents within just three years from 613 to 615 AD, probably one thousand events a year (Wei Z. AD 656: ch. "Report of the Imperial Historians"). According to Parsons, during the period 1629–44, there were as many as 234,185 insurrections in China, averaging 43 events per day, or 1.8 outbreaks per hour" (Deng 1999:220).

22. Following Deng (1999).

23. Huang 1999:231.

24. These loans appear to have been an extension of the logic of the state granaries, which stockpiled food; some to sell at strategic moments to keep prices low, some to distribute free in times of famine; some to loan at low interest to provide an alternative to usurers.

25. Huang op cit; cf. Zhuoyun & Dull 1980:22–24. For his complex currency reforms: Peng 1994:111–14.

26. Generally, interest rates were set at a maximum of 20 percent and compound interest was banned. Chinese authorities eventually also adopted the Indian principle that interest should not be allowed to exceed the principal (Cartier 1988:28; Yang 1971:92–103).

27. Braudel 1979; Wallerstein 1991, 2001.

28. I am here especially following the work of Boy Bin Wong (1997, 2002; also Mielants 2001, 2007.) Granted, most Braudelans only see later dynasties like the Ming as fully embodying this principle, but I think it can be projected backwards.

29. So, for instance, while markets themselves were considered beneficial, the government also systematically intervened to prevent price fluctuations, stockpiling commodities when they were cheap and releasing them if prices rose. There were periods of Chinese history when rulers made common cause with merchants, but the result was usually a major popular backlash (Deng 1999:146).

30. Pommeranz 1998, Goldstone 2002 for an introduction to the vast literature on comparative standards of living. India was actually doing rather well also for most of its history.

31. Zürcher 1958:282.

32. Gernet 1956 (1999: 241–42); for the following discussion see Gernet 1960, Jan 1965, Kieschnick 1997, Benn 1998, 2007.

33. Tsan-ning (919-1001 AD) quoted in Jan 1965:263. Others appealed to the history of bodhisattvas and pious kings who had made gifts of their own bodies, such as the king who, in time of famine, leapt to his death to be transformed into a mountain of flesh, replete with thousands of heads, eyes, lips, teeth, and tongues, which for ten thousand years only grew larger no matter how much of it humans and animals ingested (Benn 2007:95, 108; cf. Ohnuma 2007).

34. Tu Mu, cited in Gernet 1956 (1995:245).

35. This might come as something of a surprise, since the phrase is used so often in contemporary Western popular usage, "karmic debt" becoming something of a New Age cliché. But it seems to strike a much more intuitive chord with

Euro-Americans than it ever did in India. Despite the close association of debt and sin in the Indian tradition, most early Buddhist schools avoided the concept—largely because it implied a continuity of the self, which they saw as ephemeral and ultimately illusory. The exception were the Sammitiya, called "personalists" as they did believe in an enduring self, who developed the notion of aviprāṇaśa, whereby the results of good or bad actions—karma—"endure like a sheet of paper on which a debt is inscribed" as an unconscious element of the self that passes from one life to another (Lamotte 1997:22–24, 86–90; Lusthaus 2002:209–10). The idea might have died with that sect had it not been taken up by the famous Mahayana philosopher Nāgārjuna, who compared it to an "imperishable promissory note" (Kalupahana 1991:54–55, 249; Pasadika 1997). His Mādhyamaka school in turn became the Sanlun or "Three Treatise" school in China; the notion of karmic debt was taken up in particular by the "Three Stages" or "Three Levels" school created the monk Hsin-Hsing (540–94 AD) (Hubbard 2001).

36. *Commentary on the Dharma of the Inexhaustible Storehouse of the Mahayana Universe*, as translated by Hubbard (2001:265), with a few changes based on Gernet (1956 [1995:246]).

37. In Hubbord 2001:266.

38. Dao Shi, in Cole 1998:117. Cole's book provides an excellent summary of this literature (see also Ahern 1973, Teiser 1988, Knapp 2004, Oxfeld 2005). Some Medieval texts focus exclusively on the mother, others on parents generally. Interestingly, the same notion of an infinite and unpayable "milk-debt" to one's mother also appears in Turkey (White 2004:75–76).

39. *Sutra for the Recompense of Gratitude* cited in Baskind 2007:166. My "four billion years" translates "kalpa," which is technically 4.32 billion years. I also changed "them" for parents to "her" for mother since the context refers to a man who cut his own flesh specifically for his mother's sake.

40. Chinese Buddhists did not invent the pawnshop, but they appear to have been the first to sponsor them on a large scale. On the origins of pawnbroking in general, see Hardaker 1892, Kuznets 1933. On China specifically: Gernet 1956 [1995:170–73], Yang 1971:71–73, Whelan 1979. In a remarkable parallel, the first "formal" pawnshops in Europe also emerged from monasteries for similar purposes: the *monti di pieta* or "banks that take pity" created by the Franciscans in Italy in the fifteenth century. (Peng 1994:245, also makes note of the parallel.)

41. Gernet 1956 [1995:142–86], Ch'en 1964:262–65; Collins 1986:66–71; Peng 1994:243–45. It would seem that Taoist monasteries, which also multiplied in this period, banned making loans (Kohn 2002:76), perhaps in part to mark a distinction.

42. Gernet 1956 [1995:228], where he famously wrote, "the donors to the Inexhaustible Treasuries were shareholders, not in the economic domain but that of religion." As far as I know, the only contemporary scholar who has fully embraced the premise that this was indeed an early form of capitalism is Randall Collins (1986) who sees similar monastic capitalism in later Medieval Europe as well. The accepted Chinese historiography has tended to see the first "shoots of capitalism" developing later, in the Song, which was much less hostile to merchants than other dynasties, followed by a full embrace of the market—but firm rejection of capitalism—in the Ming and Qing. The key question is the organization of labor, and in Tang times this remains somewhat opaque, since even if statistics were available, which they're not, it's difficult to know what terms like "serf," "slave," and "wage-laborer" actually meant in practice.

43. Gernet 1956 [1995:116–39], Ch'en 1964:269–71, on land reclamation and monastic slaves.

44. "It is claimed that the purpose of this generosity is to relieve the poor and

orphans. But in fact there is nothing to it but excess and fraud. This is not a legitimate business" Gernet 1956 (1995:104–5, 211).

45. Gernet 1956 [1995:22].

46. See Adamek 2005, Walsh 2007.

47. This is probably why abstractions like Truth, Justice, and Freedom are so often represented as women.

48. Marco Polo observed the practice in the southern province of Yunnan in the thirteenth century: "But when they have any business with one another, they take a round or square piece of stick, and split it in two; and one takes one half and the other takes the other half. But before they split it, they make two or three notches in it, or as many as they wish. So, when one of them comes to pay another, he gives him the money or whatever it is, and gets back the piece of stick the other had" (Benedetto 1931:193). See also Yang 1971:92, Kan 1978, Peng 1994:320, 330, 508, Trombert 1995:12–15. Tallies of this sort seem, according to Kan, to have preceded writing; and one legend claims that the same man, a minister to the Yellow Emperor, invented both writing and tally contracts simultaneously (Trombert 1995:13).

49. Graham 1960:179.

50. Actually the similarity was noticed in antiquity as well: Laozi (*Daodejing* 27) speaks of those who can "count without a tally, secure a door without a lock." Most famously, he also insisted "when wise men hold the left tally pledge, they do not press their debtors for their debts. Men of virtue hold on to the tally; men lacking virtue pursue their claims" (stanza 79).

51. Or one might better say, turning them at one snap from monetary debts to moral ones, since the very fact that we know the story implies he was eventually rewarded (Peng 1994:100). It is probably significant that the word *fu*, meaning "tally," also could mean "an auspicious omen granted to a prince as a token of his appointment by Heaven" (Mathews 1931:283). Similarly, Peng notes a passage from *Strategems of the Warring States*,

about a lord attempting to win popular support: "Feng hurried to Bi, where he had the clerks assemble all those people who owed debts, so that his tallies might be matched against theirs. When the tallies had been matched, Feng brought forth a false order to forgive these debts, and he burned the tallies. The people all cheered" (ibid:100n9). For Tibetan parallels, see Uebach 2008.

52. Similar things happened in England, where early contracts were also broken in half in imitation of tally sticks: the phrase "indentured servant" derives from this practice, since these were contract laborers; the word actually derives from the "indentations" or notches on the tally stick used as a contract (Blackstone 1827 I:218).

53. L. Yang 1971:52; Peng 1994:329–31. Peng perceptively notes "this method of matching tallies to withdraw cash was actually an outgrowth of the process used in borrowing money, except that the movement over time of loans was transformed into a movement over space" (1994:330).

54. They were called "deposit shops"— and L. Yang (1971:78–80) calls them "proto-banks." Peng (1994:323–27) notes something along these lines was already operating, at least for merchants and travelers, under the Tang, but the government had strict controls preventing bankers from reinvesting the money.

55. The practice began in Sichuan, which had its own peculiar form of cash, in iron, not bronze, and therefore much more unwieldy.

56. Peng 1994:508, also 515, 833. All this is very much like the token money that circulated in much of Europe in the Middle Ages.

57. The most important scholarly exponent of this view is von Glahn (1994, though Peng [1994] holds to something close), and it seems the prevailing one among economists, popular and otherwise.

58. Diagram from MacDonald 2003:65.

59. One of the favorite images employed when remembering the rule of

the Legalists, under the much-hated First Dynasty, was that they constructed great brass cauldrons, in which each law was openly and explicitly spelled out—then used them to boil criminals alive.

60. See Bulliet 1979 (also Lapidus 2003:141–46) on the process of conversion. Bulliet also emphasizes (ibid:129) that the main effect of mass conversion was to make the ostensible justification of government, as protector and expander of the faith, seem increasingly hollow. Mass popular support for caliphs and political leaders only reemerged in periods, like the Crusades or during the *reconquista* in Spain, when Islam itself seemed under attack; as of course, for similar reasons, it has in much of the Islamic world today.

61. "Most of the time the lower circles paid their taxes through their heads, and looked after themselves. Similarly the government received the taxes and provided some sort of security, and apart from this, occupied itself with matters of concern to itself: external war, patronage of learning and the arts, a life of luxurious ostentation" (Pearson 1982:54).

62. The proverb appears, attributed to the Prophet himself, in al-Ghazali's *Ihya', kitab al-'Ilm*, 284, followed by a long list of similar statements: "Sa'id Bin Musaiyab said, 'When you see a religious scholar visiting a prince, avoid him, for he is a thief.' Al-Auza'i said, 'There is nothing more detestable to Allah than a religious scholar who visits an official' . . ." etc. This attitude has by no means disappeared. A strong majority of Iranian ayatollahs, for example, oppose the idea of an Islamic state, on the grounds that it would necessarily corrupt religion.

63. Lombard 1947, Grierson 1960. This is often represented as a wise policy of refusal to "debase" the coinage, but it might equally be read as meaning that the caliph's signature added no additional value. An experiment with Chinese-style paper money in Basra in 1294 failed, as no one was willing to accept money backed only by state trust (Ashtor 1976:257).

64. MacDonald 2003:64. Gradually this became unsupportable and Muslim empires adopted the more typically Medieval *iqta'* system, whereby soldiers were granted the tax revenues from specific territories.

65. Neither have slaves been employed as soldiers since, except in temporary and anomalous circumstance (e.g., by the Manchus, or in Barbados).

66. It seems significant that (1) the "inquisition" of 832, the failed Abbasid attempt to take control of the ulema; (2) the most important mass conversion of the Caliphate's subjects to Islam, peaking around 825–850; and (3) the definitive ascent of Turkish slave soldiers in Abbasid armies, often dated to 838, all roughly corresponded in time.

67. Elwahed 1931:111–35. As he puts it (ibid:127), "the *inalienability of liberty* is one of the fundamental and uncontested principles of Islam." Fathers do not have the right to sell their children, and individuals do not have the right to sell themselves—or at least, if they do, no courts will recognize any resultant ownership claims. I note that this is the diametrical opposite of the "natural law" approach that later developed in Europe.

68. There is a certain controversy here: some scholars, including some contemporary Muslim scholars opposed to the Islamic economics movement, insist that *riba*, which is unequivocally condemned in the Koran, did not originally refer to "interest" in general, but to a pre-Islamic Arabian practice of fining late payment by doubling the money owed, and that the blanket condemnation of interest is a misinterpretation (e.g., Rahman 1964, Kuran 1995). I am in no position to weigh in but, if true, this would suggest that the ban on usury really emerged in Iraq itself as part of the process of the creation of grassroots Islam, which would actually reinforce my general argument.

69. The best records we have are actually from a community of Jewish merchants in Geniza, in twelfth-century Egypt,

who observed the ban on interest even in dealings with one another. The one area where we regularly hear of interest being charged is the one area where coercion was also regularly employed: that is, in dealings with kings, viziers, and officials, who often borrowed large sums of money at interest—especially, but not exclusively, from Jewish or Christian bankers—to pay their troops. Obliging a request for such an illegal loan was a dangerous business, but refusing even more so (for Abbasid examples, see Ray 1997:68–70, mainly drawing from Fischel 1937).

70. There were also a whole host of legal subterfuges (called *hiyal*) that one might undertake if one were absolutely determined to charge interest: for instance, buying one's debtor's house for the amount of the loan, charging them rent for it, and then allowing them to buy it back for the same sum; having one's debtor agree to buy a certain product monthly and sell it to one at a discount, and so forth. Some schools of Islamic law banned these outright; others merely disapproved. It used to be assumed that these methods were widely employed, since most economic historians assumed interest to be a necessary element of credit, but recent research provides no evidence that they were especially common (for the older view: Khan 1929, for the new: Ray 1997:58–59).

71. Mez 1922:448, quoted in Labib 1969:89. Note that Basra, the city where everyone in the market paid by check, was also the city where, a century later, Mongol attempts to introduce government-issue paper money were so doggedly resisted. The word *sakk* is incidentally the origin of the English "check." The ultimate origins of *sakk* are contested: Ashtor (1972:555) suggests they were Byzantine; Chosky (1988), Persian.

72. Goitein (1966, 1967, 1973) provides a detailed summary of financial practices among Jewish merchants in twelfth-century Egypt. Almost every transaction involved credit to some degree. Checks,

remarkably similar even in appearance to the kind used today, were in common usage—though sealed bags of metal coins were even more common in everyday transactions.

73. Though apparently governments sometimes paid wages by check (Tag El-Din 2007:69.) I am no doubt underplaying the government role in all this: there were, for instance, attempts to set up central government banks, and certainly usually a commitment in principle that the government should enforce commercial standards and regulations. It seems, however, that this rarely came to much in practice.

74. Udovitch 1970:71–74.

75. Sarakhsi in Udovitch 1975:11, who has a good discussion of the issues involved. Likewise Ray 1997:59–60.

76. This should surely also be of interest to students of Pierre Bourdieu, who made a famous argument, based on his study of Kabyle society in Algeria, that a man's honor in such a society is a form of "symbolic capital," analogous to but more important than economic capital, since it is possible to turn honor into money but not the other way around (Bourdieu 1977, 1990). True, the text above does not quite say this, but one does wonder how much this is Bourdieu's own insight, and how much simply reflects the common sense of his informants.

77. Following K.N. Chaudhuri (1985:197). The expansion of Islam was spearheaded by both Sufi brotherhoods and legal scholars; many merchants doubled as either or both. The scholarly literature here is unusually rich. See, for instance: Chaudhuri 1985, 1990; Risso 1995; Subrahmanyam 1996; Barendtse 2002; Beaujard 2005.

78. In Goody 1996:91.

79. M. Lombard 2003:177–79.

80. Burton's translation; 1934 IV:2013.

81. And what's more, officials employed their own person bankers, and themselves made extensive use of credit instruments such as *suftaja* both for transfer of tax payments, and the secreting

away of ill-gotten gains (Hodgson 1974 I:301, Udovitch 1975:8, Ray 1994:69–71.)

82. "For Mohammed this natural regulation of the market corresponds to a cosmic regulation. Prices rise and fall as night follows day, as low tides follow high, and price imposition is not only an injustice to the merchant, but a disordering of the natural order of things" (Essid 1995:153).

83. Only very limited exceptions were made, for instance in times of disaster, and then most scholars insisted it was always better to provide direct relief to the needy than to interfere with market forces. See Ghazanfar & Islahi 2003, Islahi 2004:31–32; for a fuller discussion of Mohammed's views on price formation, see Tuma 1965, Essid 1988, 1995.

84. Hosseini 1998:672, 2003:37: "Both indicate that animals, such as dogs, do not exchange one bone for another."

85. Hosseini 1998, 2003. Smith says he visited such a factory himself, which may well be true, but the example of the eighteen steps originally appears in the entry "Épingle" in Volume 5 of the French *Encyclopedie*, published in 1755, twenty years earlier. Hosseini also notes that "Smith's personal library contained the Latin translations of some of the works of Persian (and Arab) scholars of the medieval period" (Hosseini 1998:679), suggesting that he might have lifted them from the originals directly. Other important sources for Islamic precedents for later economic theory include: Rodison 1978, Islahi 1985, Essid 1988, Hosseini 1995, Ghazanfar 1991, 2000, 2003, Ghazanfar & Islahi 1997, 2003. It is becoming more and more clear that a great deal of Enlightenment thought traces back to Islamic philosophy: Descartes' *cogito*, for example, seems to derive from Ibn Sina (a.k.a. Avicenna), Hume's famous point that the observance of constant conjunctions does not itself prove causality appears in Ghazali, and I have myself noticed Immanuel Kant's definition of enlightenment in the mouth of a magic bird in the fourteenth-century Persian poet Rumi.

86. Tusi's *Nasirean Ethics*, in Sun 2008:409.

87. Ghazanfar & Islahi 2003:58; Ghazanfar 2003:32–33.

88. So for example among Ghazali's ethical principles, we find "the buyer should be lenient when bargaining with a poor seller and strict when transacting with a rich seller," and "a person should be willing to sell to the poor who do not have the means and should extend credit to them without the expectation of repayment" (Ghazali *Ihya Ulum al Din* II:79–82, cited in Ghazanfar & Islahi 1997:22)—the latter of course recalling Luke 6:35.

89. Ghazali in Ghazanfar & Islahi 1997:27.

90. Ibid:32.

91. Ibid:32.

92. Ibid:35. On postmen in Medieval Islam: Goitein 1964. Ghazali's position here recalls and is no doubt influenced by Aristotle's *Nicomachean Ethics* (1121b): that since money is a social convention meant to facilitate exchange, diverting it into usury defies its purpose; but its ultimate thrust is quite different, closer to Thomas Aquinas' argument that money is basically a measure and that usury distorts it, and Henry of Ghent's argument that "money is a medium in exchange and not a terminus"—unsurprisingly, since Aquinas was likely directly influenced by him (Ghazanfar 2000).

93. It's hard to overstate this. Even the famous "Laffer Curve," by which the Reagan Administration in the 1980s tried to argue that cutting taxes would increase government revenue by stimulating economic activity, is often called the Khaldun-Laffer curve because it was first proposed, as a general principle, in Ibn Khaldun's 1377 *Muqaddimah*.

94. Goitein 1957 for the rise of the "Middle Eastern bourgeoisie."

95. "Crying down" acted as a de facto tax increase, since one would now need to pay more ecus to make up a tax rate fixed in shillings. Since wages were fixed in pounds, shillings, and pence, this also

had the effect of raising their value, and hence it was usually popular. "Crying up" by contrast had the effect of lowering the effective value of the units of account. This could be useful to reduce a king's— or his allies'—personal debt measured in such units, but it also undercut the income of wage-earners and those on any sort of fixed income and so was often protested.

96. Langholm 1979, Wood 2002:73–76.

97. On the patristic literature on usury: Maloney 1983; Gordon 1989; Moser 2000; Holman 2002:112–26; Jones 2004:25–30.

98. Matthew 5:42

99. St Basil of Caesarea, *Homilia II in Psalmum XIV* (PG 29, 268–69).

100. op cit.

101. op cit.

102. Ambrose *De Officiis* 2.25.89.

103. Ambrose *De Tobia* 15:51. See Nelson 1949:3–5, Gordon 1989:114–118.

104. Though not entirely. It's worthy to note that the main supply of slaves to the empire at this time came from Germanic barbarians outside the empire, who were acquired *either* through war or debt.

105. "If each one," he wrote, "after having taken from his personal wealth whatever would satisfy his personal needs, would leave what was superfluous to those who lack every necessity, there would be no rich or poor" *(In Illiud Lucae* 49D)—Basil himself had been born an aristocrat, but he had sold off his landed estates and distributed the proceeds to the poor.

106. *Homilia II in Psalmum XIV* (PG 29, 277C). The reference is to Proverbs 19.17.

107. *Summa* 8.3.1.3: "since grace is freely given, it excludes the idea of debt . . . In [no] sense does debt imply that God owes anything to another creature."

108. Clavero (1986) sees this as a basic conflict over the nature of the contract, and hence the legal basis of human relations in European history: usury, and by extension profit, was denounced, but rent, the basis of feudal relations, was never challenged.

109. Gordon 1989:115. "What is commerce," wrote Cassiodorus (485–585), "except to want to sell dear that which can be bought cheap? Therefore those merchants are detestable who, with no consideration of God's justice, burden their wares more with perjury than value. Them the Lord evicted them from the Temple saying, 'Do not make my Father's house into a den of thieves" (in Langholm 1996:454).

110. On the Jewish legal tradition concerning usury, see Stein 1953, 1955; Kirschenbaum 1985.

111. Poliakov 1977:21.

112. Nelson (1949) assumed that the "Exception" was often held to apply to relations between Christians and Jews, but Noonan (1957:101–2) insists that it was mainly held to apply only to "heretics and infidels, particularly the Saracens," and by some, not even to them.

113. Up to 52 percent with security, up to 120 percent without (Homer 1987:91).

114. Debtor's prisons, in the sense of prisons exclusively for debtors, existed in England only after 1263, but the imprisonment of debtors has a much longer history. Above all, Jewish lenders seem to have been employed as the means of transforming virtual, credit money into coinage, collecting the family silver from insolvent debtors, and turning it over to royal mints. They also won title to a great deal of land from defaulting debtors, most of which ended up in the hands of barons or monasteries (Singer 1964; Bowers 1983; Schofield & Mayhew 2002).

115. Roger of Wendower, *Flowers of History* 252–53. Roger doesn't name the victim; in some later versions his name is Abraham, in others, Isaac.

116. Matthew Prior, in Bolles 1837:13.

117. Or even, for that matter, Nietzsche's fantasies of the origins of justice in mutilation. Where one was a projection onto Jews of atrocities actually committed against Jews, Nietzsche was writing in an age where actual "savages" were often punished by similar tortures and mutilations for failure to pay their debts to the

colonial tax authorities, as later became a most notorious scandal in Leopold's Belgian Congo.

118. Mundill (2002), Brand (2003).

119. Cohn 1972:80.

120. Peter Cantor, in Nelson 1949:10–11.

121. It was a firm from Cahors, for instance, who received the property of the English Jews when the latter were finally expelled in 1290. Though for a long time, Lombards and Cahorsins were themselves dependent on royal favor and hardly in much better position than the Jews. In France, the kings seemed to expropriate and expel Jews and Lombards alternately (Poliakov 1977:42).

122. Noonan 1957:18–19; Le Goff 1990:23–27.

123. "There are two sorts of wealth-getting, as I have said; one is a part of household management, the other is retail trade: the former necessary and honorable, while that which consists in exchange is justly censured; for it is unnatural, and a mode by which men profit from one another. The most hated sort, and with the greatest reason, is usury, which makes a profit out of money itself, and not from the natural object of it. For money was intended to be used in exchange, but not to increase at interest. And this term 'interest' (*tokos*), which means the birth of money from money, is applied to the breeding of money because the offspring resembles the parent. Wherefore of all modes of getting wealth this is the most unnatural" (Aristotle, *Politics* 1258b). *The Nicomachean Ethics* (1121b) is equally damning. For the best general analysis of the Aristotelean tradition on usury: Langholm 1984.

124. Noonan 1957:105–12; Langholm 1984:50.

125. The technical term for the lost income is *lucrum cessans*: see O'Brien 1920: 107–10, Noonan 1957:114–28, Langholm 1992:60–61; 1998:75; Spufford 1989:260.

126. As German merchants also did in the Baltic cities of the Hanseatic alliance.

On the Medici bank as a case in point, see de Roover 1946, 1963, Parks 2005.

127. The situation in Venice, a pioneer in these matters, is telling: there was no merchant guild, but only craft guilds, since guilds were essentially created as protection against the government, and in Venice, the merchants *were* the government (MacKenney 1987; Mauro 1993:259–60).

128. They were accused of both heresy and sodomy: see Barber 1978.

129. One cannot "prove" the Islamic inspiration of European bills of exchange, but considering the amount of trade between the two sides of the Mediterranean, denying it seems bizarre. Braudel (1995:816–17) proposes that the idea must have reached Europe through Jewish merchants, who we know to have long been using them in Egypt.

130. On bills of exchange: Usher 1914; de Roover 1967; Boyer-Xambeu, Deleplace, and Gillard 1994; Munro 2003b:542–46; Denzel 2006. There were innumerable currencies, any of which might at any time be "cried up," "cried down," or otherwise fluctuate in value. Bills of exchange also allowed merchants to effectively engage in currency speculation, and even get around usury laws, once it became possible to pay for one bill of exchange by writing a different bill of exchange, due in several months' time, for a slightly higher sum. This was called "dry exchange" (de Roover 1944), and over time the Church became increasingly skeptical, causing yet another round of financial creativity to get around the laws. It's worthy of note that the rates of interest on such commercial loans were generally quite low: twelve percent at the highest, in dramatic contrast to consumer loans. This is a sign of the increasingly lower risk of such transactions (see Homer 1987 for a history of interest rates).

131. Lane 1934.

132. "In very many respects, such as the organization of slave labor, management of colonies, imperial administration, commercial institutions, maritime technology

and navigation, and naval gunnery, the Italian city-states were the direct forerunners of the Portuguese and Spanish empires, to the shaping of which the Italians contributed so heavily, and in the profits of which they so largely shared" (Brady 1997:150).

133. They appear to have used Greek serfs at first, and sometimes Arabs captured in the Crusades, and only later, Africans. Still, this was the economic model that was eventually transported by Portuguese merchants to Atlantic islands like the Canaries, then eventually to the Caribbean (Verlinden 1970, Phillips 1985:93–97, Solow 1987, Wartburg 1995).

134. Scammell 1981:173–75.

135. Spufford 1988:142

136 On the notion of adventure: Auerbach 1946, Nerlich 1977.

137. Duby (1973) makes this point. The "round table" was originally a type of tournament, and especially in the 1300s, it became common to make such tournaments explicit imitations of King Arthur's court, with knights entering the contests taking on roles from them: Galahad, Gawain, Bors, etc.

138. Also at a time when technological changes, especially the invention of the crossbow and the rise of professional armies, were beginning to render knights' role in combat increasingly irrelevant (Vance 1973).

139. Kelly 1937:10.

140. See Schoenberger 2008 for a recent and compelling take: comparing the role of war mobilization in creating markets in Greece and Rome to Western Europe in the High Middle Ages.

141. Wolf 1954.

142. A point originally made by Vance (1986:48). The similarity is more obvious in the German poet Wolfram von Eschenbach's *Parzifal*, written perhaps twenty years later, in which knights "roam freely over Spain, North Africa, Egypt, Syria, to Baghdad, Armenia, India, Ceylon" (Adolf 1957:113)—and Islamic references are legion (Adolf 1947, 1957)—that is, areas known to Europeans of the time only through trade. The fact that actual merchants, on those rare occasions when they appear, are never sympathetic characters has little bearing.

143. Wagner, *Die Wibelungen: Weltgeschichte aus der Sage* (1848)—which in English is "World History as Told in Saga." I am taking my account of Wagner's argument from another wonderful, if sometimes extravagant, essay by Marc Shell called "Accounting for the Grail" (1992:37–38). Wagner's argument is really more complicated: it centers on the failed attempt by the Holy Roman Emperor Frederick Barbarossa to subdue the Italian city-states and the abandonment of his principle that property can only flow from the king; instead, we have the rise of mercantile private property, which is echoed by financial abstraction.

144. Shell sees the Grail as a transformation of the older notion of the cornucopia or inexhaustible purse in an age "just beginning to be acquainted with checks and credit"—noting the connection of the legend with the Templars, and fact that Chretien—whose name means "Christian"—was likely, for that reason, to have been a converted Jew. Wolfram also claimed that he got the legend from a Jewish source (Shell 1992:44–45).

145. Even China was often split and fractured. Just about all the great empire-building projects of the Middle Ages were the work not of professional armies, but of nomadic peoples: the Arabs, Mongols, Tatars, and Turks.

146. *Nicomachean Ethics* 1133a29–31.

147. He compares money not only to a postman, but also, to a "ruler," who also stands outside society to govern and regulate our interactions. It's interesting to note that Thomas Aquinas, who might have been directly influenced by Ghazali (Ghazanfar 2000), did accept Aristotle's argument that money was a social convention that humans could just as easily change. For a while, in the late Middle

Ages, this became the predominant Catholic view.

148. As far as I know, the only scholar to have pointed out the connection is Bernard Faure, a French student of Japanese Buddhism: Faure 1998:798, 2000:225.

149. Later still, as cash transactions became more common, the term was applied to small sums of cash offered as downpayment, rather in the sense of English "earnest money." On *symbola* in general: Beauchet 1897; Jones 1956:217; Shell 1978:32–35.

150. Descat 1995:986.

151. Aristotle *On Interepretation* 1.16–17. Whitaker (2002:10) thus observes that for Aristotle, "the meaning of a word is fixed by convention, just as the importance attached to a tally, token, or ticket depends on agreement between the parties concerned."

152. *Nicomachean Ethics* 1133a29–31.

153. But they believed that these formulae summed up or "drew together" the essence of those secret truths that the Mysteries revealed—"symbolon," being derived the verb *symballein*, meaning "to gather, bring together, or compare."

154. Müri 1931, Meyer 1999. The only knowledge we have of such *symbola* comes from Christian sources; Christians later adopted their own symbolon, the Creed, and this remained the primary referent of the term "symbol" throughout the Middle Ages (Ladner 1979).

155. Or pseudo-Dionysius, since the real Dionysius the Areopagite was a first-century Athenian converted to Christianity by St. Paul. Pseudo-Dionysius' works are an attempt to reconcile neo-Platonism, with its notion of philosophy as the process of the liberation of the soul from material creation and its reunification with the divine, with Christian orthodoxy. Unfortunately, his most relevant work, *Symbolic Theology*, has been lost, but his surviving works all bear on the issue to some degree.

156. In Barasch 1993:161.

157. Pseudo-Dionysius, *On the Celestial Hierarchy* 141A–C. On Dionysius'

theory of symbolism in general, and its influence, see Barasch 1993:158–80, also Goux 1990:67, Gadamer 2004:63–64.

158. He calls them, like communion, "gifts that are granted to us in symbolic mode." *On the Celestial Hierarchy* 124A.

159. Mathews 1934:283. Compare the definition of symbolon:

A. *tally*, i.e. each of two halves or corresponding pieces of a knucklebone or other object, which two guest friends, or any two contracting parties, broke between them, each party keeping one piece, in order to have proof of the identity of the presenter of the other.

B. of other devices having the same purpose, e.g. a seal-impression on wax,
1. any token serving as proof of identity
2. guarantee
3. token, esp. of goodwill

After Liddell and Scott 1940:1676–77, without the examples, and with the Greek words for "knucklebone" and "guest-friend" rendered into English.

160. Rotours 1952:6. On *fu* (or *qi*, another name for debt tallies that could be used more generally for "tokens") more generally: Rotours 1952, Kaltenmark 1960, Kan 1978, Faure 2000:221–29: Falkenhausen 2005.

161. There is a curious tension here: the will of heaven is also in a certain sense the will of the people, and Chinese thinkers varied on where they placed the emphasis. Xunzi, for instance, assumed that the authority of the king is based on the confidence of the people. He also argued that while confidence among the people is maintained by contracts ensured by the matching of tally sticks, under a truly just king, social trust will be such that such objects will become unnecessary (Roetz 1993:73–74).

162. Kohn 2000:330. Similarly in Japan: Faure 2000:227.

163. In the *Encyclopedia of Taoism* they are described as "diagrams, conceived as a form of celestial writing, that derive their power from the matching celestial counterpart kept by the deities who bestowed them" (Bokenkamp 2008:35). On Taoist *fu*: Kaltenmark 1960; Seidel 1983; Strickmann 2002:190—91; Verellen 2006; on Buddhist parallels, see Faure 1998; Robson 2008.

164. Sasso 1978; the origins of the yin-yang symbol remain obscure and contested but those Sinologists I've consulted find this plausible. The generic word for "symbol" in contemporary Chinese is *fúhào*, which is directly derived from fu.

165. Insofar as I'm weighing in on the "Why didn't the Islamic world develop modern capitalism?" debate, then, it seems to me that both Udovitch's argument (1975:19–21) that the Islamic world never developed impersonal credit mechanisms, and Ray's objection (1997:39–40) that the ban on interest and insurance was more important, carry weight. Ray's suggestion that differences in inheritance laws might play a role also deserves investigation.

166. Maitland 1908:54.

167. Davis 1904.

168. In the Platonic sense: just as any particular, physical bird we might happen to see on a nearby fruit tree is merely a token of the general idea of "bird" (which is immaterial, abstract, angelic), so do the various physical, mortal individuals who join together to make up a corporation become an abstract, angelic Idea. Kantorowicz argues that it took a number of intellectual innovations to make the notion of the corporation possible: notably, the idea of the aeon or aevum, eternal time, that is, time that lasts forever, as opposed to the Augustinian eternity which is outside of time entirely and was considered the habitation of the angels, to the revival of the works of Dionysius the Areopagite (1957:280–81).

169. Kantorowicz 1957:282–83.

170. Islamic law, for instance, not only did not develop the notion of fictive persons, but steadfastly resisted recognizing corporations until quite recently (Kuran 2005).

171. Mainly Randall Collins (1986:52–58), who also makes the comparison with China; cf. Coleman 1988.

172. See Nerlich 1987:121–24.

Chapter Eleven

1. On English wages, see Dyer 1989; on English festive life, there is a vast literature, but a good recent source is Humphrey 2001. Silvia Federici (2004) provides a compelling recent synthesis.

2. For a very small sampling of more recent debates over the "price revolution," see Hamilton 1934, Cipolla 1967, Flynn 1982, Goldstone 1984, 1991, Fisher 1989, Munro 2003a, 2007. The main argument is between monetarists who continue to argue that increase in the amount of specie is ultimately responsible for the inflation, and those who emphasize the role of rapid population increase, though most specific arguments are considerably more nuanced.

3. Historians speak of "bullion famines"—as most active mines dried up, such gold and silver that wasn't sucked out of Europe to pay for eastern luxuries was increasingly hidden away, causing all sorts of difficulties for commerce. In the 1460s, the shortage of specie in cities like Lisbon had been so acute that merchant ships visiting with cargoes full of wares often had to return home without selling anything (Spufford 1988:339–62).

4. Brook 1998. Needless to say, I'm simplifying enormously: another problem was the growth of landlordism, with many smallholders falling in debt to landlords for inability to pay. As members of the ever-increasing royal family and other favored families gained tax exemptions

from the state, the tax burden on small-holders became so heavy that many felt forced to sell their lands to the powerful families in exchange for tenancy agreements to free those lands from taxes.

5. Chinese historians count 77 different "miners' revolts" during the 1430s and '40s (Harrison 1965:103–4; cf. Tong 1992:60–64; Gernet 1982:414). Between 1445 and 1449 these became a serious threat as silver miners under a rebel leader named Ye Zongliu made common cause with tenant farmers and the urban poor in overpopulated Fujian and Shaxian, sparking an uprising that spread to a number of different provinces, seizing a number of cities and expelling much of the landed gentry.

6. Von Glahn (1996:70–82) documents the process. Gernet (1982:415–16) documents how between 1450 and 1500, most taxes became payable in silver. The process culminated in the "single lash of the whip" method: tax reforms put into place between 1530 and 1581 (Huang 1974, see Arrighi, Hui, Hung and Seldon 2003:272–73).

7. Wong 1997, Pomeranz 2000, Arrighi 2007, among many others who make this point.

8. Pomeranz 2000:273.

9. The value of silver in China (as measured in gold) remained, through the sixteenth century, roughly twice what it was in Lisbon or Antwerp (Flynn & Giráldez 1995, 2002).

10. von Glahn 1996b:440; Atwell 1998.

11. Chalis 1978:157.

12. China had its own "age of exploration" in the early fifteenth century, but it was not followed by mass conquest and enslavement.

13. It's possible that they were wrong. Generally populations did decline by 90 percent even in areas where no direct genocide was taking place. But in most places, after a generation or so, populations started recovering; in Hispaniola and many parts of Mexico and Peru, around the mines, the ultimate death rate was more like 100 percent.

14. Todorov 1984:137–38; for the original, Icazbalceta 2008:23–26.

15. One historian remarks: "By the close of the sixteenth century bullion, primarily silver, made up over 95 percent of all exports leaving Spanish America for Europe. Nearly that same percentage of the indigenous population had been destroyed in the process of seizing those riches" (Stannard 1993:221).

16. Bernal Díaz 1963:43.

17. Bernal Díaz: the quote is a synthesis of the Lockhart translation (1844 II:120) and Cohen translation (1963:412), though these appear to be based on slightly different originals.

18. Bernal Díaz op cit.

19. Cortés 1868:141.

20. Most of the conquistadors had similar stories. Balboa came to the Americas to flee his creditors; Pizarro borrowed so heavily to outfit his expedition to Peru that after early reverses, it was only the fear of debtor's prison that prevented his return to Panama; Francisco de Montejo had to pawn his entire Mexican possessions for an eight-thousand-peso loan to launch his expedition to Honduras; Pedro de Alvarado too ended up deeply in debt, finally throwing everything into a scheme to conquer the Spice Islands and China—on his death, creditors immediately tried to put his remaining estates to auction.

21. e.g., Pagden 1986.

22. Gibson 1964:253. All this is disturbingly reminiscent of global politics nowadays, in which the United Nations, for example, will urge poor countries to make education free and available to everyone, and then the International Monetary Fund (which is, legally, actually a part of the United Nations) will insist that those same countries do exactly the opposite, imposing school fees as part of broader "economic reforms" as a condition of refinancing the country's loans.

23. Following William Pietz (1985:8), who studied early merchant adventurer's

accounts of West Africa; though Todorov (1984:129–31) on the very similar perspective of the conquistadors.

24. Some did go bankrupt—for instance, one branch of the Fuggers. But this was surprisingly rare.

25. Martin Luther, *Von Kaufshandlung und Wucher*, 1524, cited in Nelson 1949:50.

26. In Luther's time the main issue was a practice called *Zinskauf*, technically rent on leased property, which was basically a disguised form of interest-bearing loan.

27. In Baker 1974:53–54. The reference to Paul is in Romans 13:7.

28. He argued that the fact that Deuteronomy allows usury under any circumstances demonstrates that this could not have been a universal "spiritual law," but was a political law created for the specific ancient Israeli situation, and therefore, that it could be considered irrelevant in different ones.

29. And in fact, this is what "capital" originally meant. The term itself goes back to Latin *capitale*, which meant "funds, stock of merchandise, sum of money, or money carrying interest" (Braudel 1992:232). It appears in English in the mid–sixteenth century largely as a term borrowed from Italian bookkeeping techniques (Cannan 1921, Richard 1926) for what remained when one squared property, credits, and debts; though until the nineteenth century, English sources generally preferred the word "stock"—in part, one suspects, because "capital" was so closely associated with usury.

30. Nations that, after all, also practiced usury on one another: Nelson 1949:76.

31. Ben Nelson emphasized this in an important book, *The Idea of Usury: From Tribal Brotherhood to Universal Otherhood.*

32. Midelfort 1996:39.

33. Zmora 2006:6–8. Public financing at this period largely meant disguised interest-bearing loans from the minor nobility, who were also the stratum from which local administrators were drawn.

34. On church lands: Dixon 2002:91. On Casimir's gambling debts: Janssen 1910 IV:147. His overall debt rose to half a million guilders in 1528, and over three quarters of a million by 1541 (Zmora 2006:13n55.)

35. He was later accused of conspiring with Count Wilhelm von Henneburg, who had gone over to the rebels, to become secular Duke of the territories then held by the Bishop of Wurzburg.

36. From "Report of the Margrave's Commander, Michel Gross from Trockau," in Scott & Scribner 1991:301. The sums are based on a promise of 1 florin per execution, ½ per mutilation. We do not know if Casimir ever paid this particular debt.

37. For some relevant accounts of the revolt and repression: Seebohm 1877:141–45; Janssen 1910 IV:323–26; Blickle 1977; Endres 1979; Vice 1988; Robisheaux 1989:48–67, Sea 2007. Casimir is said to have ultimately settled into exacting fines, eventually demanding some 104,000 guldens in compensation from his subjects.

38. Linebaugh (2008) makes a beautiful analysis of this sort of phenomenon in his essay on the social origins of the Magna Carta.

39. It is telling that despite the endless reprisals against commoners, none of the German princes or nobility, even those who openly collaborated with the rebels, was held accountable in any way.

40. Muldrew 1993a, 1993b, 1996, 1998, 2001; cf. MacIntosh 1988; Zell 1996, Waswo 2004, Ingram 2006, Valenze 2006, Kitch 2007. I find myself strongly agreeing with most of Muldrew's conclusions, only qualifying some: for instance, his rejection of MacPherson's possessive individualism argument (1962) strikes me as unnecessary, since I suspect that the latter does identify changes that are happening on a deeper structural level less accessible to explicit discourse (see Graeber 1997).

41. Muldrew (2001:92) estimates that in c. 1600, eight thousand London merchants might have possessed as much as one-third of all the cash in England.

42. Williamson 1889; Whiting 1971; Mathias 1979b; Valenze 2006:34–40.

43. Gold and silver were a very small part of household wealth: inventories reveal on average fifteen shillings of credit for every one in coin (Muldrew 1998).

44. This principle of a right to livelihood is key to what E.P. Thompson famously called "moral economy of the crowd" (1971) in eighteenth-century England, a notion that Muldrew (1993a) thinks can be applied to these credit systems as a whole.

45. Stout 1742:74–75, parts of the same passage are cited in Muldrew 1993a:178, and 1998:152.

46. To be more precise, either piety (in the Calvinist case) or good natured sociality (in the case of those that opposed them in the name of older festive values)—in the years before the civil war, many parish governments were divided between the "godly" and "good honest men" (Hunt 1983:146)

47. Shepherd 2000, Walker 1996; for my own take on "life-cycle service" and wage labor, see, again, Graeber 1997.

48. Hill 1972:39–56, Wrightson & Levine 1979, Beier 1985.

49. Muldrew 2001:84.

50. For a classic statement on the connection of Tudor markets, festivals, and morality, see Agnew (1986).

51. Johnson 2004:56–58. On the two conceptions of justice: Wrightson 1980. Bodin's essay was widely read. It drew on Aquinas' view of love and friendship as prior to the legal order, which, in turn, harkens back to Aristotle's *Nicomachean Ethics*, which reached Europe through Arab sources. Whether there was also a direct influence from the Islamic sources themselves we do not know, but considering the degree of general mutual engagement (Ghazanfar 2003) it seems likely.

52. Gerard de Malynes's *Maintenance of Free Trade* (1622), cited in Muldrew 1998:98, also Muldrew 2001:83.

53. Chaucer is full of this sort of thing: the Wife of Bath has much to say about conjugal debts (e.g., Cotter 1969). It was really in the period of about 1400–1600 that everything came to be so framed as debt, presumably reflecting the first stirrings of possessive individualism, and attempts to reconcile it to older moral paradigms. Guth (2008), a legal historian, thus calls these centuries "the age of debt," one which was then replaced after 1600 by an "age of contract."

54. Davenant 1771:152.

55. Marshall Sahlins (1996, 2008) has been emphasizing the theological roots of Hobbes for some time. Much of the following analysis draws on his influence.

56. Hobbes himself doesn't use the term "self-interest" but does speak of "particular," "private," and "common" interests.

57. *De L'Esprit* 53, cited in Hirschman 1986:45. Exploring the contrast between Shang's "profit" and Helvétius' "interest" would be a telling history in itself. They are not the same concept.

58. "Interest" (from *interesse*) comes into common usage as a euphemism for usury in the fourteenth century, but it only comes to be used in its more familiar, general sense in the sixteenth. Hobbes doesn't use "self-interest," though he speaks of "private" and "common" interests; but that term was already current, having appeared in the work of Machiavelli's friend Francesco Guicciadini in 1512. It becomes commonplace in the eighteenth century (see Hirschman 1977, 1992, especially chapter 2, "on the concept of interest"; Dumont 1981; Myers 1983, Heilbron 1998).

59. Sée (1928:187) notes that until around 1800, "interesse" was the common word for "capital" in French; in English the preferred word was "stock." It is curious to note that Adam Smith, for one, actually returns to the Augustinian usage, "self-love," in his famous passage about

the butcher and the baker (*Wealth of Nations* 1.2.2).

60. Beier 1985:159–63; cf. Dobb 1946:234. Consorting with gypsies was also a capital crime. In the case of vagrancy, justices found it so difficult to find anyone willing to press charges against vagrants that they were eventually forced to reduce the penalty to public whipping.

61. In Walker 1996:244.

62. Helmholtz 1986, Brand 2002, Guth 2008.

63. Helmholz 1986, Muldrew 1998:255, Schofield & Mayhew 2002, Guth 2008).

64. Stout 1742:121.

65. "The horrors of the Fleet and Marshalsea were laid bare in 1729. The poor debtors were found crowded together on the 'common side,'—covered with filth and vermin, and suffered to die, without pity, of hunger and jail fever . . . No attempt was made to distinguish the fraudulent from the unfortunate debtor. The rich rogue—able, but unwilling to pay his debts—might riot in luxury and debauchery, while his poor unlucky fellow-prisoner was left to starve and rot on the 'common side'" (Hallam 1866 V:269–70.)

66. I do not want to argue that the more familiar narrative of "primitive accumulation," of the enclosure of common lands and rise of private property, the dislocation of thousands of one-time cottagers who became landless laborers, is false. I simply highlight a less familiar side of the story. It's especially helpful to highlight it because the degree to which the Tudor and Stuart periods were actually marked by a rise of enclosures is a heated matter of debate (e.g., Wordie 1983). The use of debt to split communities against themselves is meant in the same vein as Silvia Federici's (2004) brilliant argument about the role of witchcraft accusations in reversing popular gains of the late Middle Ages and opening the way to capitalism.

67. "Personal credit received a bad press in the eighteenth century. It was frequently said that it was wrong to go into debt simply to pay for everyday consumption goods. A cash economy was celebrated and the virtues of prudent housekeeping and parsimony extolled. Consequently retail credit, pawnbroking, and moneylending were all attacked, with both borrowers and lenders the targets" (Hoppit 1990:312–13.)

68. *Wealth of Nations* 1.2.2.

69. Muldrew makes this point: 1993:163.

70. *Theory of Moral Sentiments* 4.1.10.

71. "The man who borrows in order to spend will soon be ruined, and he who lends to him will generally have occasion to repent of his folly. To borrow or to lend for such a purpose, therefore, is in all cases, where gross usury is out of the question, contrary to the interest of both parties; and though it no doubt happens sometimes that people do both the one and the other; yet, from the regard that all men have for their own interest, we may be assured that it cannot happen so very frequently as we are sometimes apt to imagine" (*Wealth of Nations* 2.4.2). He does occasionally acknowledge the existence of retail credit, but he grants it no significance.

72. Reeves 1999. Reeves, like Servet (1994, 2001) shows that many were aware of the variability of money-stuffs: Puffendorf, for example, made a long list of them.

73. When we attribute value to gold, then, we simply recognize this. The same argument was usually invoked to solve the old Medieval puzzle about diamonds and water: Why is it that diamonds are so expensive, though useless, and water, which is useful in all sorts of ways, hardly worth anything at all? The usual solution was: diamonds are the eternal form of water. (Galileo, who objected to the entire premise, at one point suggested that those who make such claims should really be turned into statues. That way, he suggested, in inimitable Renaissance style, everyone would be happy, since (1) they would be eternal, and (2) the rest of us would no longer have to listen to their

stupid arguments.) See Wennerlind 2003, who notes, interestingly, that most European governments employed alchemists in the seventeenth century in order to manufacture gold and silver for coins; it's only when these schemes definitively failed that the governments moved to paper currency.

74. Kindleberger 1984; Boyer-Xambeu, Deleplace, & Gillard 1994; Ingham 2004:171. Rather, this path eventually led to the creation of stock markets: the first public bourses, in fifteenth-century Bruges and Antwerp, began not by trading shares in joint-stock ventures, which barely existed at the time, but by "discounting" bills of exchange.

75. Usher (1934, 1944) originally introduced the distinction between "primitive banking," where one simply lends out what one has, and "modern banking," based on some sort of fractional reserve system—that is, one lends more than one has, thus effectively creating money. This would be another reason why we have now moved to something other than "modern banking"—see below.

76. Spufford 1988:258, drawing on Usher 1943:239–42. While deposit notes were used, private bank notes, based on credit, only appear quite late—from London goldsmiths, who also acted as bankers, in the seventeenth and eighteenth centuries.

77. See Munro 2003b for a useful summary.

78. MacDonald 2006:156.

79. Tomas de Mercado in Flynn 1978:400.

80. See Flynn 1979; Braudel 1992:522–23; Stein & Stein 2000: 501–05, 960–62; Tortella & Comín 2002. The number of *juros* in circulation went from 3.6 million ducats in 1516 to 80.4 million in 1598.

81. The most famous exponent of this position was Nicholas Barbon (1690), who argued that "money is a value made by law" and a measure in just the same manner as inches or hours or fluid ounces. He also emphasized that most money was credit anyway.

82. Locke (1691:144) also cited in Caffentzis 1989:46–47, which remains the most insightful summary of the debate and its implications. Compare Perlman & McCann 1998:117–20; Letwin 2003:71–78; Valenze 2006:40–43.

83. We tend to forget that the materialism of the Marxist tradition is not some radical departure—Marx was, like Nietzsche, taking bourgeois assumptions (though in his case, different ones) and pushing them in directions that would outrage their original proponents. Anyway, there is good reason to believe that what we now call "historical materialism" is really Engels' addition to the project—Engels being himself nothing if not bourgeois in background and sensibilities (he was a stalwart of the Cologne stock exchange).

84. Macaulay 1886:485—the original essay was published in the Spectator, March 1, 1711.

85. *Faust* II, Act 1—see Shell 1992, Binswanger 1994 for a detailed analysis. The connection with alchemy is revealing. When in 1300 Marco Polo had remarked that the Chinese emperor "seemed to have mastered the art of alchemy" in his ability to turn mere paper into something as good as gold, this was clearly meant as a joke; by the seventeenth century most European monarchs actually did employ alchemists to try to produce gold from base metals; it was only their failure that led to the adoption of paper money (Wennerlend 2003).

86. It's not as if suspicions about money didn't exist—but they tended to focus, instead, on moral and metaphysical issues (e.g., "the theft of time").

87. Said to have been given at a talk at the University of Texas in 1927, but in fact, while the passage is endlessly cited in recent books and especially on the internet, it cannot be attested to before roughly 1975. The first two lines appear to actually derive from a British investment advisor named L.L.B. Angas in 1937: "The modern Banking system manufactures money

out of nothing. The process is perhaps the most astounding piece of sleight of hand that was ever invented. Banks can in fact inflate, mint and unmint the modern ledger-entry currency" (Angas 1937:20–21). The other parts of the quote are probably later inventions—and Lord Stamp never suggested anything like this in his published writings. A similar line, "the bank hath benefit of all interest which it creates out of nothing" attributed to William Patterson, the first director of the Bank of England, is likewise first attested to only in the 1930s, and is also almost certainly apocryphal.

88. Joint-stock corporations were created in the beginning of the colonial period, with the famous East India Company and related colonial enterprises, but they largely vanished during the period of the industrial revolution and were mainly revived only at the end of the nineteenth century, and then principally, at first, in America and Germany. As Giovanni Arrighi (1994) has pointed out, the heyday of British capitalism was marked by small family firms and high finance; it was America and Germany, who spent the first half of the twentieth century battling over who would replace Great Britain as hegemon, that introduced modern bureaucratic corporate capitalism.

89. MacKay 1854:52.

90. MacKay 1854:53–54.

91. Spyer 1997.

92. Prakash 2003:209–16.

93. Hardenburg & Casement 1913; the story has been analyzed most famously, and insightfully, by Mick Taussig (1984, 1987).

94. Encyclopedia Britannica, 11th edition (1911): entry for "Putumayo."

95. As Taussig notes (1984:482), when the head of the company was later asked what he actually meant by "cannibal" he said, simply, that it meant the Indians refused to trade with anybody else.

96. This is a point demonstrated in great detail in an important book by Yann Moulier-Boutang (1997), which

unfortunately has never been translated into English.

97. Davies 1975:59. "Indentured" comes from the "indentations" or notches on a tally again, since these were widely used as contracts for those who, like most indentured servants, couldn't read (Blackstone 1827 I:218).

98. Immanuel Wallerstein (1974) provides the classic analysis of this "second serfdom.

99. This was true, incidentally, across the class spectrum: everyone was expected to do this, from lowly milkmaids and apprentices to "ladies in waiting" and knight's pages. This was one reason, incidentally, why indentured-service contracts did not seem like much of a jump in the seventeenth century: they were simply lengthening the term of contracted employment from one to five or seven years. Even in Medieval times there were also adult day-laborers, but these were often considered indistinguishable from simple criminals.

100. The very word "proletariat" in a way alludes to this, as it's taken from a Roman term for "those who have children."

101. C.L.R. James 1938; Eric Williams 1944.

102. "Many devices were available by which businessmen economized in the use of cash in wage payments—payment could be made only at long intervals; payment might consist in giving claims on others (truck payment, tickets or vouchers to authorize purchasing from shops, etc., the provision of private notes and tokens)"—Mathias 1979a:95.

103. Actually the full list is: "cabbage, chips, waxers, sweepings, sockings, wastages, blessing, lays, dead men, onces, primage, furthing, dunnage, portage, wines, vails, tinge, buggings, colting, rumps, birrs, fents, thrums, potching, scrapings, poake, coltage, extra, tret, tare, largess, the con, nobbings, knockdown, boot, tommy, trimmings, poll, gleanings, lops, tops, bontages, keepy back, pin money"

(Linebaugh 1993:449; see also Linebaugh 1982, Rule 1986:115–17).

104. Tebbutt 1983:49. On pawnbroking in general: Hardaker 1892, Hudson 1982, Caskey 1994, Fitzpatrick 2001.

105. Linebaugh 1993: 371–404.

106. Usually in order to conclude that today, of course, we are living in an entirely different world, because clearly that's not true any more. It might help here to remind the reader that Marx saw himself as writing a "critique of political economy"—that is, of theory and practice of economics of his day.

107. See the Lockhart translation of Bernal Díaz (Díaz 1844 II:396), which gives several versions of the story, drawn from different sources.

108. Clenninden 1991:144.

109. It is on these grounds that Testart distinguishes slavery owing to gambling, where the gambler stakes his own person, and debt slavery, even if these are ultimately gambling debts. "The mentality of the gambler who directly stakes his person in the game is closer to that of the warrior, who risks losing his life in war or being taken into slavery, than to that of the poor person willing to sell himself to survive" (Testart 2002:180).

110. This is incidentally why complaints about the immorality of deficits are so profoundly disingenuous: since modern money effectively *is* government debt, if there was no deficit, the results would be disastrous. True, money can also be generated privately, by banks, but there would appear to be limits to this. This is why U.S. financial elites, led by Alan Greenspan, panicked in the late 1990s when the Clinton administration began to run budget surpluses; the Bush tax cuts appear to have been designed specifically to ensure that the deficit was maintained.

111. Wallerstein 1989.

112. 1988:600.

113. Britain passed its first bankruptcy law in 1542.

114. This is no doubt what Goethe was getting at when he had Faust, specifically, tell the emperor to pay his debts with IOUs. After all, we all know what happened to him when his time came due.

115. Sonenscher (2007) gives a long and detailed history of these debates.

116. One might trace a religious element here: in the time of Augustus, a group of religious cultists in the Middle East conceived the idea that fire was about to come from the sky and consume the planet. Nothing seemed less likely at the time. Leave them in charge of a corner of the world for two thousand years, they figure out a way to do it. But still, this is clearly part of a larger pattern.

Chapter Twelve

1. I was first put on to the significance of the date by fellow anthropologist Chris Gregory (1998: 265–96; also Hudson 2003a). U.S. citizens had not been able to cash in dollars for gold since 1934. The analysis that follows is inspired by both Gregory and Hudson.

2. One plausible-sounding version, which cites rather small amounts of bullion, can be found at: www.rediff.com/money/2001/nov/17wtc.htm. For a more entertaining, fictional version: www.rense.com/general73/confess.htm.

3. "The Federal Reserve Bank of New York: the Key to the Gold Vault" (new yorkfed.org/education/addpub/goldvaul.pdf).

4. As a minor aside, I remember from the time also reading news reports noting that there were, in fact, a number of expensive jewelry shops in the arcades directly beneath the Towers, and that all the gold in them did in fact disappear. Presumably they were pocketed by rescue workers, but considering the circumstances, it would seem there were no serious objections—at least, I've never heard anything about the matter being further investigated, let alone prosecuted.

5. It's no coincidence, certainly, that William Greider decided to name his great history of the Federal Reserve (1989) *The*

Secrets of the Temple. This is actually how many of its own officials privately describe it. He quotes one: "The System is just like the Church . . . It's got a pope, the chairman; and a college of cardinals, the governors and bank presidents; and a curia, the senior staff. The equivalent of the laity is the commercial banks . . . We even have different orders of religious thought like Jesuits and Franciscans and Dominicans only we call them pragmatists and monetarists and neo-Keynesians" (ibid:54).

6. This is hardly a new claim, and it rests in part on the Braudelian (world-systems) school, for instance, the recent work of Mielants (2007). For a more classically Marxist version developing the connection since Nixon's time, see Custers 2007. For a more mainstream neoclassical treatments of the connection, see Mac-Donald & Gastman 2001, MacDonald 2006.

7. Senator Fullbright, in McDermott 2008:190.

8. I note that this flies directly in the face of the intent of the United States Constitution (1.8.5), which specifies that only Congress was relegated the power "to coin money, [and] regulate the value thereof"—no doubt at the behest of the Jeffersonians, who were opposed to creating a central bank. The United States still observes the letter of the law: United States coins are issued directly by the Treasury. United States paper money, while signed by the head of the Treasury, is not issued by the Treasury but by the Federal Reserve. They are technically banknotes, though as with the Bank of England, one bank is granted a monopoly in issuing them.

9. For those who don't know how the Fed works: technically, there are a series of stages. Generally the Treasury puts out bonds to the public, and the Fed buys them back. The Fed then loans the money thus created to other banks at a special low rate of interest, so that those banks can then lend at higher ones. In its capacity as regulator of the banking system, the

Fed also establishes the fractional reserve rate: just how many dollars these banks can "lend"—effectively, create—for every dollar they borrow from the Fed, or have on deposit, or can otherwise count as assets. Technically this is 10 to 1, but a variety of legal loopholes allow banks to go considerably higher.

10. Which does raise the rather interesting question of what its gold reserves are actually for.

11. The exact role of Central Banks in money-creation is a matter of no little political debate at the moment. Some insist the Fed really is, or should be, an extension of government policy; others insist it is effectively the autonomous voice of the investor class. Its role in money-creation, and the status of fractional reserve banking, is all much contested, as recent debates between Paul Krugman, representing the neoclassical approach, and Steve Keen, an advocate of the Modern Monetary Theory (MMT) approach, illustrate. The Bank of England weighed in on the debate in a recent report called "Money Creation in the Modern Economy," where, surprisingly, they explicitly endorsed the MMT position that most money is indeed created by private banks and that the fractional reserve system does not, effectively, limit their ability to do so. This is a very dramatic statement—essentially an admission that almost all the language used to justify austerity programs is simply wrong.

12. As it happens, there is one way that the U.S. government can, in fact, print money, though it has not availed itself of the option. That is by printing high-denomination coins. Since the constitution stipulates that only the Federal Government can "coin" money, metal currency continues to be produced directly by the Treasury, even as paper money is produced by the Fed. While the highest denomination coin currently produced by the government is a dollar coin, there's no legal reason it couldn't, say, produce a "Platinum Coin" worth a trillion dollars and use it to pay down its debts. This was actually proposed by Modern Monetary

Theory advocates during the deficit crisis of 2010, and discussed in the media; but it apparently was never seriously considered by the Obama administration.

13. Indeed, perhaps the greatest compromise to United States global power in recent years is the fact that there is now one place—the region of China facing Taiwan—where air defenses are now so dense and sophisticated that the United States Air Force is no longer certain that it can penetrate at will. The inability to blow up Osama bin Laden is, of course, the most dramatic limit to this power.

14. Or, to put the money in the United States stock market, which ultimately has a similar effect. As Hudson notes, "American diplomats have made it clear that to buy control of U.S. companies or even to return to gold would be viewed as an unfriendly act" (2002a:7), so, unless they want to move out of dollars entirely, which would be considered an even more unfriendly act, there is little alternative.

15. Hudson 2002a:12.

16. As many have remarked, the three countries that switched to the euro around this time—Iraq, Iran, and North Korea—were precisely those singled out by Bush as his "Axis of Evil." Of course we can argue about cause and effect here. It's also significant that the core euro-using states such as France and Germany uniformly opposed the war, while U.S. allies were drawn from euro-skeptics like the UK.

17. For a few representative takes on the relation of dollar and empire: from a conservative, neoclassical perspective, Ferguson (2001, 2004), from a post-Keynesian perspective, Hudson (2003a), from a Marxist one, Brenner (2002).

18. There is also some debate among both mainstream and heterodox economists over whether the fact that oil sales are denominated in dollars really does confer any seigniorage advantages to the U.S. For present purposes what really matters is that U.S. policymakers seem to feel the fact that they are symbolically important and resist any attempt to alter this.

19. Even the CIA now ordinarily refers to such arrangements as "slavery," though technically debt peonage is different.

20. Compare this to the deficit/military chart above, on page 366—the curve is effectively identical.

21. See dailybail.com/home/china-warns-us-about-debt-monetization.html, accessed December 22, 2009. The story is based on a piece from the *Wall Street Journal*, "Don't Monetize the Debt: The president of the Dallas Fed on inflation risk and central bank independence" (Mary Anastasia O'Grady, *WSJ*, May 23, 2009.) I should add that in popular usage nowadays, "to monetize the debt" is generally used as a synonym for "printing money" to pay debt. This usage has become almost universal, but it's not the original sense of the term, which is to turn the debt itself into money. The Bank of England did not print money to pay the national debt; it turned the national debt itself into money. Here too there is a profound argument going on about the nature of money itself.

22. The arrangement is sometimes referred to as Bretton Woods II (Dooley, Folkerts-Landau & Garber 2004, 2009): effectively, an agreement since the 1990s at least to use various unofficial means to keep the dollar's value artificially high, and East Asian currencies—particularly the Chinese—artificially low, in order to expedite cheap Asian exports to the United States. Since real wages in the United States have either stagnated or retreated continually since the 1970s, this, and the accumulation of consumer debt, is the only reason living standards in the United States have not precipitously declined.

23. On Zheng He, see Dreyer 2006, Wade 2004, Wake 1997. On the tribute trade in general: Moses 1967, Yü 1967, Hamashita 1994, 2003; Di Cosmo & Wyatt 2005.

24. The argument here follows Arrighi, Hui, Hung and Selden 2003, some

elements of which were echoed in Arrighi's last work, *Adam Smith in Beijing* (2007).

25. Giovanni Arrighi, for example, has argued that the U.S. did try to turn its debt into a tribute system, but that this was ultimately unsustainable: "the U.S economic revival of the 1990s, and the continuing dependence of the world economy on a growing U.S. economy, have been based on an increase in U.S. foreign indebtedness that has no precedent in world history. A situation of this kind can hardly be reproduced for any length of time without transforming into an outright tribute, or "protection payment," the more than $2 billion (and counting) that the United States needs daily to balance its current accounts with the rest of the world. And yet . . . U.S. attempts to make the extraction of such a tribute the foundation of a new, and for the first time in history, truly universal empire, have failed miserably, creating a situation of global political instability with no precedent since the 1920s and 1930s." (2009:164). Arrighi argued it was this very attempt that led to the financial crisis of 2008.

26. Japan of course was something of an exception, since it had arguably achieved something like First World status even before this.

27. Keynes 1936:345.

28. See www.irle.berkeley.edu/events/spring08/feller/.

29. The key legislation was the "Depository Institutions Deregulation and Monetary Control Act" of 1980, which struck down all federal usury laws: ostensibly, in reaction to the rampant inflation of the late 1970s, though of course they were never restored when inflation was brought back under control, as it has in the last quarter-century. It left state interest ceilings in place, but institutions like credit-card companies were allowed to observe the laws of the state in which they are registered, no matter where they operated. This is why most are registered

in South Dakota, which has no maximum interest rate.

30. The first is from Thomas Friedman (1999) in a cocky and vacuous book called *The Lexus and the Olive Tree*, the second from Randy Martin (2002) in a book of the same name.

31. In America this "universal otherness" is accomplished above all through racism. This is why most small retailing in the United States is conducted on ethnic lines: say, Korean grocers or dry-cleaners, who pool credit with one another, whose clients, however, are sufficiently socially distant that there is no question of extending credit outside, or even expecting basic relations of trust—since they themselves ordinarily expect electricians, locksmiths, contractors of various sorts who provide services to at least attempt to shaft them. Essentially the market across racial or ethnic lines becomes one where everyone is assumed to be Amalek.

32. Gilder 1981:266, cited in Cooper 2008:7. Cooper's essay is a brilliant exploration of the relation between debt imperialism—a phrase she seems to have coined, inspired by Hudson—and evangelical Christianity, and it is heartily recommended. See also Naylor 1985.

33. Robertson 1992:153. In Cooper again: op cit.

34. Atwood 2008:42.

35. This is, incidentally, also the best response to conventional critiques of the poor as falling into debt because they are unable to delay gratification—another way in which economic logic, with all its human blind spots, skews any possible understanding of "consumers'" actual motivations. Rationally, since CDs yield around 4 percent annually, and credit cards charge 20 percent, consumers should save as a cushion and only go into debt when they absolutely have to, postponing unnecessary purchases until there's a surplus. Very few act this way, but this is rarely because of improvidence (can't wait to get that flashy new dress) but because human relations can't actually be put off in the same way

as imaginary "consumer purchases": one's daughter will only be five once, and one's grandfather has only so many years left.

36. There are so many books on the subject that one hesitates to cite, but a couple of outstanding examples are Anya Kamentz's *Generation Debt* (2006), and Brett William's *Social History of the Credit Trap* (2004). The larger point about demands for debt as a form of class struggle is in large part inspired by the Midnight Notes collective, who argue that, however paradoxically, "neoliberalism has thrown open a new dimension of struggle between capital and the working class within the domain of credit" (2009:7). I have followed this analysis to a degree, but tried to move away from the economistic framing of human life as "reproduction of labor" that hobbles so much Marxist literature—the emphasis on life beyond survival might be distantly Vaneigem-influenced (1967), but largely falls back on my own work on value theory (Graeber 2001).

37. Elyachar 2002:510.

38. See for instance, "India's microfinance suicide epidemic," Soutik Biswas, BBC News South Asia, 16 December 2010, bbc.co.uk/news/world-south-asia-11997571.

39. I have observed this first hand on any number of occasions in my work as an activist: police are happy to effectively shut down trade summits, for example, just to ensure that there's no possible chance that protestors can feel they have succeeded in doing so themselves.

40. In practice, it mainly consists of "interest-free" banking arrangements that pay lip service to the notion of profit-sharing but in reality operate in much the same way as any other bank. The problem is that if profit-sharing banks are competing with more conventional ones in the same marketplace, those who anticipate that their enterprises will yield high profits will gravitate toward the ones offering fixed-interest loans, and only those who anticipate lower profits will turn to the profit-sharing option (Kuran 1995:162). For a transition to no-interest banking to work, it would have to be total.

41. Under the Caliphate, to guarantee the money supply; in China, through systematic intervention to stabilize markets and prevent capitalistic monopolies; later, in the United States and other North Atlantic republics, through allowing the monetization of its own debt.

42. True, as I showed in chapter 5, economic life will always be a matter of clashing principles, and thus might be said to be incoherent to a certain extent. Actually I don't think this is in any way a bad thing—at the very least, it's endlessly productive. The distortions born of violence strike me as uniquely insidious.

43. von Mises 1949:540–41. The original German text was published in 1940 and presumably composed a year or two previous.

44. Ferguson 2007:iv.

45. I can speak with some experience here; I am well known by my friends to be a workaholic—to their often justifiable annoyance—and keenly aware that such behavior is at best slightly pathological, and certainly in no sense makes one a better person.

Afterword

1. *Theory of Moral Sentiments* 3.36. The story is about Pyrrhus, King of Epirus, who really should have listened to his friend's advice.

BIBLIOGRAPHY

Abraham, Roy Clive. 1933. *The Tiv People*. Lagos: Government Printer.

Abu Lughod, Janet. 1989. *Before European Hegemony* Oxford: Oxford University Press.

Adamek, Wendi L. 2005. "The Impossibility of the Given: Representations of Merit and Emptiness in Medieval Chinese Buddhism." *History of Religions* 45 (2): 135–80.

Adams, Robert McC,. C. Lamberg-Karlovsky, William L. Moran. 1974. "The Mesopotamian Social Landscape: The View from the Frontier." *Bulletin of the American Schools of Oriental Research. Supplementary Studies* No. 20, Reconstructing Complex Societies: An Archaeological Colloquium, pp. 1–20.

Adkins, Arthur W. H. 1972. *Moral Values and Political Behaviour in Ancient Greece: From Homer to the End of the Fifth Century*. New York: Norton.

Adolf, Helen. 1947. "New Light on Oriental Sources for Wolfram's Parzival and Other Grail Romances." *PMLA* 62 (2): 306–24.

———. 1957. "Christendom and Islam in the Middle Ages: New Light on 'Grail Stone' and 'Hidden Host.'" *Speculum* 32 (1): 103–15.

Afigbo, Adiele Eberechukwu. 1971. "The Aro of southeastern Nigeria: a socio-historical analysis of legends of their origins." *African Notes* 6: 31–46.

Aglietta, M. and Orlean, A. 1992. *La Violence de la monnaie*. Paris: Presses Universitaires de France.

———. 1995. *Souveraineté, légitimité de la monnaie*. Paris: Association d'Économie Financière (Cahiers finance, éthique, confiance).

———. 1998. *La Monnaie souveraine*. Paris: Odile Jacob.

Aglietta, M., et al. 1998. "Introduction." In: *La monnaie souveraine* (M. Aglietta & A. Orléan, eds.), pp. 9–31. Paris: Odile Jacob.

Aglietta, M., & Orléan, A. (Eds.). 1995. *Souveraineté, légitimité de la monnaie*. Paris: Association d'Économie Financière (Cahiers finance, éthique, confiance).

Agnew, Jean-Christophe. 1986. *Worlds Apart: The Market and the Theater in Anglo-American Thought*. Cambridge: Cambridge University Press.

Ahern, Emily. 1973. *The Cult of the Dead in a Chinese Village*. Stanford: Stanford University Press.

Akiga Sai, B. 1939. *Akiga's story; the Tiv tribe as seen by one of its members. Translated and annotated by Rupert East*. London, New York, Published for the International African Institute by the Oxford University Press.

———. 1954. "The 'Descent' of the Tiv from Ibenda Hill" (translated by Paul Bohannan.) *Africa: Journal of the International African Institute* 24 (4): 295–310.

Akin, David and Joel Robbins,. 1998. "An Introduction to Melanesian Currencies: Agencies, Identity, and Social Reproduction". In *Money and Modernity: State and Local Currencies in Melanesia* (David Akin and Joel Robbins, ed.), pp. 1–40. Pittsburgh: University of Pittsburgh Press.

Alexander, John B. 1938. "A Babylonian Year of Jubilee?" *Journal of Biblical Literature* 57: 55–79.

Allen, N. J. 1998. "The category of substance: a Maussian theme revisited." In Marcel Mauss: A Centenary Tribute (Wendy James, N. J. Allen, eds.), pp. 175–191. London: Berghahn Books.

Altekar, Anant Sadashiv. 1977. *State and Government in Ancient India*. Delhi: Motilal Banar-
    sidass.

———. 1983. *The Position of Women in Hindu Civilization*. Delhi: Motilal Banarsidass.

Althabe, Gérard. 1968. "La circulation monétaire dans un village Betsimisaraka." *Tany Gasy*
    8: 35–46.

Ames, Roger. 1994. *The Art of Rulership: A Study of Ancient Chinese Political Thought*. Al-
    bany: State University of New York Press.

Anderson, Perry. 1974. *Passages from Antiquity to Feudalism*. London: Verso Press.

Angas, Lawrence Lee Bazley. 1937. *Slump Ahead in Bonds*. New York: Somerset Pub. Co

Arnaud, Daniel. 1973. "La prostitution sacrée en Mésopotamie, un mythe historique?" *Revue
    de l'histoire des religions* 183: 111–15.

Arrighi, Giovanni. 1994. *The Long Twentieth Century: Money, Power, and the Origins of Our
    Times*. London: Verso.

———. 2007. *Adam Smith in Beijing: Lineages of the Twenty-First Century*. London: Verso.

Arrighi, Giovanni, Po-Keung Hui, Ho-Fung Hung and Mark Selden,. 2003. "Historical Capi-
    talism, East and West". In *The Resurgence of East Asia: 500, 150, and 50 year perspectives*.
    (Giovanni Arrighi, Takeshi Hamashita and Mark Selden, eds.) London: Routledge, pp.
    259–333.

Asheri, David. 1969. "Leggi greche sul problema dei debiti." *Studii classici e orientali* 18:
    5–122.

Ashtor, Eliahu. 1972. "Banking instruments between the Muslim East and the Christian
    West." *Journal of European Economic History* 1: 559–73.

———. 1976. *A Social and Economic History of the Middle East*. Berkeley: University of
    California Press.

Assante, Julia. 2003. "From Whores to Hierodules: The Historiographic Invention of Meso-
    potamian Female Sex Professionals." In *Ancient Art and Its Historiography* (edited A.A.
    Donahue and Mark D. Fullerton), 13-47. Cambridge: Cambridge University Press.

Atwood, Margaret. 2008. *Payback: Debt and the Shadow Side of Wealth*. London: Blooms-
    bury.

Auerbach, Erich. 1946 [2003]. *Mimesis: The Representation of Reality in Western Literature*.
    Princeton: Princeton University Press.

Aydan, Ertan. 2003. *The Peculiarities of Turkish Revolutionary Ideology in the 1930s: the
    ülüku version of Kemalism, 1933-1936*. Ph.D. dissertation, Bilkent University, Ankara
    (www.thesis.bilkent.edu.tr/0002416.pdf).

Aylmer, G. E. 1980. "The Meaning of Property in Seventeenth-Century England." *Past and
    Present* 86: 87–97.

Ayyar, P. V. Jagadisa. 1982. *South Indian Shrines: Ilustrated*. New Delhi: Apex.

Bahrani, Zainab. 2001. *Women of Babylon: Gender and Representation in Mesopotamia*. Lon-
    don: Routledge.

Baker, J. Wayne. 1974. "Heinrich Bullinger and the Idea of Usury." *The Sixteenth Century
    Journal* 5 (1): 49–70.

Baker, Jennifer. 2005. *Securing the commonwealth: debt, speculation, and writing in the mak-
    ing of early America*. Baltimore: Johns Hopkins University Press.

Ballin, Theodore N. 1978. 'A Commentary on [Demosthenes] 50.' Doctoral Dissertation:
    University of Washington, Seattle.

Balmuth, Miriam S. 1967. "The Monetary Forerunners of Coinage in Phoenicia and Pal-
    estine," in Aryeh Kindler,ed., *International Numismatic Convention, Jerusalem, 27-31
    December 1963: The Patterns of Monetary Development in Phoenicia and Palestine in An-
    tiquity, Proceedings* (Shocken, Tel Aviv, pp. 25–32.

———. 1971. "Remarks on the Appearance of the Earliest Coins", in David G. Mitten, John
    Griffiths Pedley, and Jane Ayer Scott, eds., *Studies Presented to George M. A. Hanfmann*
    (Philipp von Zabern, Mainz), pp. 1–7.

———. 1975. "The Critical Moment: the Transition from Currency to Coinage in the Eastern
    Mediterranean." *World Archeology* 6: 293-9.

————. 2001. Hacksilber to Coinage: New Insights into the Monetary History of the Near East and Greece. *Numismatic Studies* No. 24. New York: American Numismatic Society,

Banaji, Jairus. 2001. *Agrarian change in late antiquity: gold, labour, and aristocratic dominance.* Oxford: Oxford University Press.

Barasch, Moshe. 1993. *Icon: studies in the history of an idea.* New York: NYU Press.

Barber, Malcolm. 1978. *The Trial of the Templars.* Cambridge: Cambridge University Press.

Barendse, Rene J. 2002. *The Arabian Seas: The Indian Ocean World of the Seventeenth Century.* Armonk: M. E. Sharpe.

Barnes, Robert Harrison and Ruth Barnes. 1989. "Barter and Money in an Indonesian Village Economy." *Man (New Series)* 24 (3): 399–418.

Barreau, Andre. 1961. "Indian and Ancient Chinese Buddhism: Institutions Analogous to the Jisa." *Comparative Studies in Society and History* 3 (4): 443–51.

Barth, Frederick. 1969. "Economic Spheres in Darfur." Themes in Economic Anthropology, ASA Monographs no. 6, pp. 149-174. London: Tavistock.

Basham, Arthur Llewellyn. 1948. "Harsa of Kashmir and the Iconoclast Ascetics." *Bulletin of the School of Oriental and African Studies, University of London* 12 (3/4): 668–99.

Baskind, James. 2007. "Mortification Practices in the Obaku School." In *Essays on East Asian Religion and Culture, Festschrift in honour of Nishiwaki Tsuneki on the occasion of his 65th birthday* (edited by Christian Wittern and Shi Lishan). Kyoto: Kyoto University.

Bataille, George. 1993. "The Accursed Share Volume III, Sovereignty, Part One: 'What I Understand by Sovereignty;" pp. 197–257. In *The Accursed Share Volumes II & III*, New York: Zone Books.

Baxter, W. T. 1989. "Early accounting: The tally and checkerboard." *Accounting Historians Journal* 16 (2): 43–83.

Beard, Mary and John Henderson. 1997. "With This Body I Thee Worship: Sacred Prostitution in Antiquity." *Gender & History* 9: 480–503.

Beattie, John. 1960. *Bunyoro: an African Kingdom.* New York: Holt, Rinehart and Winston.

Beauchet, Ludovic. 1897. *Histoire du droit privé de la République athénienne.* Paris: Chevalier-Maresoq.

Beaujard, Philippe. 2005. "The Indian Ocean in Eurasian and African World-Systems before the Sixteenth Century." *Journal of World History* 16 (4): 411–65.

Begg, David, Stanley Fischer, and Rudiger Dornbusch. 2005. *Economics* (Eighth Edition). Maidenhead, Berkshire: McGraw-Hill.

Beier, A. Lee. 1985. *Masterless men: the vagrancy problem in England 1560–1640.* London: Routledge.

Bell, Stephanie. 1999. "Do taxes and bonds finance government spending?" *Journal of Economic Issues* 34: 603–20.

————. 2000. "The role of the state and the hierarchy of money." *Cambridge Journal of Economics* 25: 149–63.

Bell, Stephanie and John F. Henry. 2001. "Hospitality versus Exchange: the Limits of Monetary Economics." *Review of Social Economics* 54 (2): 203–26.

Bellah, Robert N. 2005. "What is Axial About the Axial Age?" *Archives of European Sociology* 46 (1): 69–87.

Belo, Jane. 1936. "A Study of the Balinese Family." *American Anthropologist* 38 (1):12–31.

Benedetto, Luigi Foscolo. 1994. *The Travels of Marco Polo the Venetian* (Aldo Ricci's translation). London: Routledge.

Benn, James A. 1998. "Where Text Meets Flesh: Burning the Body as an Apocryphal Practice in Chinese Buddhism." *History of Religions* 37 (4): 295–322.

————. 2007. *Burning for the Buddha: Self-Immolation in Chinese Buddhism.* Honolulu: University of Hawaii Press.

Benveniste, Emile. 1963. *Indo-European Language and Society* (2 volumes). London: Faber & Faber.

————. 1972. "Don et échange dans le vocabulaire indo-européen." In *Problèmes de linguistique générale* (Paris: Galimard).

Berndt, Ronald M. 1951. "Ceremonial Exchange in Western Arnhem Land." *Southwestern Journal of Anthropology* 7 (2): 156–76.

Binswanger, Hans Christoph. 1994. *Money and Magic: A Critique of the Modern Economy in the Light of Goethe's Faust*. Chicago: University of Chicago Press.

Birks, Peter. 1985. "The Roman Law Concept of Dominium and the Idea of Absolute Ownership." *Acta Juridica* 7: 1–37.

Bishop, Ryan and Lilian S. Robinson. 1998. *Night Market: Sexual Cultures and the Thai Economic Miracle*. New York: Routledge.

Blackburn, Robin. 1997. *The Making of New World Slavery: From the Baroque to the Modern, 1492-1800*. London: Verso.

Blackstone, Sir William. 1827. *Commentaries on the laws of England*. London: E. Duyckinck.

Blanc, Louis. 1839. *L'organisation du travail*. Paris: Au Bureau de Nouveau Monde.

Blau, Peter. 1964. *Exchange and Power in Social Life*. New York: Wiley.

Blaxter, Lorraine. 1971. "*Rendre service* and *Jalouisie*." In *Gifts and Poison* (F. G. Bailey, ed.). London: Basil Blackwell, pp. 119–30.

Bleiberg, Edward. 2002. "Loans, Credit and Interest in Ancient Egypt." In *Debt and Economic Renewal in the Ancient Near East* (Hudson, Michael and Marc Van de Mieroop, eds.), pp. 257–76. Bethesda: CDL Press.

Blickle, Peter. 1977. *The Revolution of 1525: The German Peasant's War from a New Perspective*. (Thomas Brady and Erik Midelfort, translators.) Baltimore: Johns Hopkins.

Bloch, Marc. 1961. *Feudal Society*. (2 volumes). Chicago: University of Chicago Press.

Bogaert, Raymond. 1966. *Les Origines antiques de la banque de dépôt*. Leiden: Sijthoff.

———. 1968. *Banques et banquiers dans les cités grecques*. Leiden: Sijthoff

Bohannan, Laura. 1952. "A Genealogical Charter." *Africa: Journal of the International African Institute* 22:301–15.

———. 1958. "Political Aspects of Tiv Social Organization." In *Tribes Without Rulers* (John Middleton and David Tait, eds.), pp. 33-66. London: Routledge & Kegan Paul.

———. 1964. *Return to Laughter, An Anthropological Novel*. (As "Elenore Bowen Smith"). New York: Praeger.

Bohannan, Paul. 1954. "The Migration and Expansion of the Tiv." *Africa: Journal of the International African Institute* 24 (1): 2–16.

———. 1955. "Some Principles of Exchange and Investment among the Tiv." *American Anthropologist* 57:60–67.

———. 1957. *Justice and Judgment among the Tiv*. London: Oxford University Press.

———. 1958. "Extra-processual events in Tiv Political Institutions." *American Anthropologist* 60:1–12.

———. 1959. "The Impact of Money on an African Subsistence Economy." *Journal of Economic History* 19:491–503.

Bohannan, Paul and Laura Bohannan. 1953. *The Tiv of Central Nigeria*. London: International African Institute.

———. 1968. *Tiv Economy*. Evanston: Northwestern University Press.

———. 1969. *A Source Notebook on Tiv Religion*. 5 volumes. New Haven: Human Relations Area Files.

Boianovsky, Mauro. 1993. "Böhm-Baewerk, Irving Fisher, and the Term 'Veil of Money.'" *History of Political Economy* 25 (4):725–38.

Bokenkamp, Stephen R. 2008. "*Fu*: Talisman, Tally, Charm." In *The Encyclopedia of Taoism* (Fabrizio Pregadio, ed.), pp. 35–38. London: Routledge.

Bolles, John Augustus. 1837. *A treatise on usury and usury laws*. Boston: James Munroe.

Boon, James. 1975. *The anthropological romance of Bali, 1597–1972: dynamic perspectives in marriage and caste, politics, and religion*. Cambridge: Cambridge University Press.

Bottéro, Jean. 1961. "Desordre économique et annulation des dettes en Mesopotamie à l'epoque paleo-babylonienne." *Journal of the Economic and Social History of the Orient* 4:113–64.

————. 1992. *Everyday Life in Ancient Mesopotamia.* (Translated by Antonia Nevill.) Baltimore: Johns Hopkins.

Bourdieu, Pierre. 1965. "The Sentiment of Honor in Kabyle Society." In J. G. Peristiany, editor, *Honour and Shame: the Values of Mediterranean Society.* London: Trinity Press, pp. 191–242.

————. 1977. *Outline of a Theory of Practice.* Cambridge: Cambridge University Press.

————. 1990. *The Logic of Practice* (Translated by Richard Nice.) Cambridge: Polity Press.

Bowers, Richard H. 1983. "From Rolls to Riches: King's Clerks and Moneylending in Thirteenth-Century England." *Speculum* 58 (1): 60–71.

Boyer-Xambeu, Marie-Thérèse, Ghislain Deleplace, and Lucien Gillard. 1994. *Private Money & Public Currencies: the 16th Century Challenge.* (Azizeh Azodi, translator). Armonk: M. E. Sharpe.

Bradley, Keith R. 1987. "On the Roman Slave Supply and Slavebreeding." In *Classical Slavery* (M. I. Finley, ed.), pp. 42–64. London: Routledge.

Brady, Thomas A., Jr. 1997. "The Rise of Merchant Empires, 1400-1700. A European Counterpoint." In *The political economy of merchant empires* (James D. Tracy, ed.), pp. 117–60. Cambridge: Cambridge University Press.

Brand, Paul. 2002. "Aspects of the Law of Debt, 1189-1307." In *Credit and debt in medieval England, c.1180-c.1350* (Schofield, Phillipp R. and N. J. Mayhew, eds.), pp. 19–41. London: Oxbow.

————. 2003. "The Jewish Community of England in the Records of the English Royal Government." In *The Jews in medieval Britain: historical, literary, and archaeological perspectives* (Patricia Skinner, ed.), pp. 73–96. Woodbridge: Boyden and Brewer.

Braudel, Fernand. 1979. *Civilisation matérielle, économie et capitalisme, XVe-XVIIIe siècle, 3: Le temps du monde.* Paris: A. Colin.

————. 1992. *Civilization and Capitalism, 15th–18th Century: The wheels of commerce.* Berkeley: University of California Press.

————. 1995. *The Mediterranean and the Mediterranean world in the age of Philip II* (two volumes). Berkeley: University of California Press.

Brenner, Robert. 2002. *The Boom and the Bubble: The US in the World Economy.* London and New York: Verso.

Briant, Paul. 2006. *From Cyrus to Alexander: A History of the Persian Empire.* New York: Eisenbrauns.

Brock, Roger. 1994. "The Labour of Women in Classical Athens." *The Classical Quarterly* (new series) 44 (2): 336–46.

Bronkhorst, Johannes. 2007. *Greater Magadha: Studies in the Culture of Early India.* Leiden: Brill.

Brook, Timothy. 1998. *The Confusions of Pleasure: Commerce and Culture in Ming China.* Berkeley: University of California Press.

Brunt, P. A. 1974. *Social Conflicts in the Roman Republic.* New York: Norton.

Bryant, Joseph M. 1996. *Moral Codes and Social Structure in Ancient Greece: A Sociology of Greek Ethics from Homer to the Epicureans and Stoics.* Albany: SUNY.

Bücher, Karl. 1907. *Industrial Evolution.* (S. Morley Wickett, trans.) New York: Holt.

Buckland, William Warwick. 1908. *The Roman Law of Slavery.* Cambridge: Cambridge University Press.

Buckler, W. H. 1896. *The Origin and History of Contract in Roman Law down to the End of the Republican Period.* London: C. J. Clay & Sons.

Bulliet, Richard W. 1979. *Conversion to Islam in the Medieval Period: An Essay in Quantitative History.* Cambridge: Harvard University Press.

Burton, Sir Richard F. 1934. *The Book of a Thousand Nights and a Night* (6 volumes). New York: Heritage Press.

Butrica, James L. 2006. "Some Myths and Anomalies in the Study of Roman Sexuality." In *Same-Sex Desire and Love in Greco-Roman Antiquity and in the Classical Tradition of the West* (Beert C. Verstraete and Vernon Provencal, eds.), pp. 209–70. Berkeley: University of California Press.

Byrne, Frances. 1971. "Tribes and Tribalism in early Ireland." *Ériu* 22: 128–66.

———. 1973. *Irish Kings and High Kings*. London: Batsford.

Caffentzis, Constantine George. 1989. *Clipped Coins, Abused Words, and Civil Government: John Locke's Philosophy of Money*. New York: Autonomedia.

Cairns, Francis. 1991. "The 'Laws of Eretria' ("IG" XII. 9 1273 and 1274): Epigraphic, Legal, Historical, and Political Aspects." *Phoenix* 45 (4): 296–313.

Calhoun, George W. 1934. "Classes and Masters in Homer." *Classical Philology* 29:192-206, 301–16.

Cambiano, Guiseppe. 1987. "Aristotle and the Anonymous Opponents of Slavery." In *Classical Slavery* (M. I. Finley, ed.), pp. 28–53. London: Frank Cass.

Campbell, John Kennedy. 1964. *Honour, family and Patronage: A Study of Institutions and Moral Values in a Greek Mountain Community*. Oxford: Oxford University Press.

Cannan, Edwin. 1921. "Early History of the Term Capital." *Quarterly Journal of Economics* 35 (3): 469–81.

Cardascia, Guillaume. 1959. "L'adoption matrimonlale à Babylone et à Nuzi." *Revue historique de droit français et étranger* 37: 1–16.

———. 1969. *Les lois assyriennes*. Littératures Anciennes du Proche-Orient 2. Paris: Cerf.

Cartier, Michel. 1988. "Dette et propriété en Chine." In *Lien de Vie: Noued Mortel: les representations de la dette en Chine, au Japan, et dans le monde Indien* (Charles Malamoud, ed.), pp. 17–29. Paris: Editions de l'Ecole des Hautes Études en Science Sociales.

Case, Karl E., Ray C. Fair, Manfred Gärtner, and Ken Heather. 1996. *Economics*. London: Prentice Hall.

Caskey, John P. 1994. *Fringe Banking: Check-Cashing Outlets, Pawnshops, and the Poor*. New York: Russell Sage Foundation.

Cerny, Jaroslav. 1954. "Prices and wages in Egypt in the Ramesside period." *Cahiers d'histoire mondiale* 4: 903–21.

Chakravarti, Uma. 1985. "Of dasas and karmakaras: servile labor in ancient India." In *Chains of Servitude: Bondage and Slavery in India* (Utsa Patnaik, Manjari Dingwaney, eds.), pp. 35–75. Reno: University of Nevada Press.

Chapman, Anne. 1980. "Barter as a Universal Mode of Exchange." *L'Homme* 22 (3): 33–83.

Charles-Edwards, T. M. 1978. "Honour and Status in Some Irish and Welsh Prose Tales." *Eriu* 29: 123–41.

———. 1993. *Early Irish and Welsh kinship*. Oxford: Oxford University Press.

Chatterjee, Heramba. 1971. *The Law of Debt in Ancient India*. Calcutta: Sanskrit College.

Chattopadhyaya, Debiprasad. 1994. *Carvaka/Lokayata: An Anthology of Source Materials and Some Recent Studies*. New Delhi: Mrinal Kanti Gangopadhyaya.

Chaudhuri, Kirti N. 1985. *Trade and Civilisation in the Indian Ocean: An Economic History from the Rise of Islam to 1750*. Cambridge: Cambridge University Press.

———. 1990. *Asia Before Europe: Economy and Civilization of the Indian Ocean from the Rise of Islam to 1750*. Cambridge: Cambridge University Press.

Chauhan, Gian Ghand. 2003. *An Economic history of early medieval northern India*. New Delhi: Atlantic Publishers.

Ch'en, Kenneth K.S. 1964. *Buddhism in China: A Historical Survey*. Princeton: Princeton University Press.

Choksy, Jamsheed K. 1988. "Loan and sales contracts in ancient and early medieval Iran." *Indo-Iranian Journal* 31(3: 191–218.

Cipolla, Carlo M. 1967. *Money, Prices and Civilisation in the Mediterranean World: Fifth to Seventeenth Centuries*. Princeton: Princeton University Press.

Clanchy, M. T. 1993. *From memory to written record, England 1066–1307*. Oxford: Blackwell.

Clarence-Smith, William G. 2008. "Islamic Abolitionism in the Western Indian Ocean from c. 1800." Presented at the conference, *Slavery and the Slave Trades in the Indian Ocean and Arab Worlds: Global Connections and Disconnections*, Yale University, November 7–8, 2008. www.yale.edu/glc/indian?ocean/clarence?smith.pdf.

Clavero, Bartolomé. 1986. "The jurisprudence on usury as a social paradigm in the history of Europe." In *Historische Soziologie der Rechtswissenschaft* (Erik Volkmar Heyen, ed.), pp. 23–36. Frankfurt: Vittorio Klostermann.

Codere, Helen. 1950. *Fighting with Property: A Study of Kwakiutl Potlatching and Warfare 1792-1930*. Monograph 18. New York: American Ethnological Society.

Cohen, David. 1987. "Seclusion, separation and the status of women in classical Athens." *Greece and Rome* 36.(1): 1–15.

Cohen, Edward E. 1995. Review of 'Lending and Borrowing in Ancient Athens', Bryn Mawr Classical Review 3 (4): (hegel.lib.ncsu.edu/stacks/serials/bmcr/bmcr-v3n04-cohen-lending)

Cohn, Norman. 1972. *The pursuit of the millennium: revolutionary millenarians and mystical anarchists of the Middle Ages*. New York: Oxford University Press.

Cole, Alan. 1998. *Mothers and Sons in Chinese Buddhism*. Palo Alto: Stanford University Press.

Coleman, Janet. 1985. "Dominium in 13th and 14th Century Political Thought and its 17th Century Heirs: John of Paris and Locke." *Political Studies* 33: 73-100.

———. 1988. "Property and Poverty." In *The Cambridge History of Medieval Political Thought, c1350-1450* (J. H. Barnes, ed.), pp. 607-648. Cambridge: Cambridge University Press.

Collins, Randall. 1986. *Weberian Social Theory*. Cambridge: Cambridge University Press.

———. 1989. *The Sociology of Philosophies: A Global Theory of Intellectual Change*. Cambridge: Harvard University Press.

Cook, Robert Manuel. 1958. "Speculations on the Origins of Coinage." *Historia* 7: 257–67.

Cooper, Frederick. 1979. "The Problem of Slavery in African studies." *Journal of African History* 20:103–25.

Cooper, Jerrold S. 1986. *Sumerian and Akkadian Royal Inscriptions, Volume 1: Presargonic Inscriptions*. New Haven: American Oriental Society.

———. 2002. "Virginity in Ancient Mesopotamia." *Compte rendu, Rencontre Assyriologique Internationale* 47: 91–112.

Cooper, Melinda. 2006. "The Unborn Born Again: Neo-Imperialism, the Evangelical Right and the Culture of Life." *Postmodern Culture* (PMC) 17.1: #3.

———. 2008. *Life as surplus: biotechnology and capitalism in the neoliberal era*. Seattle: University of Washington Press.

Cornell, Tim. 1995. *The beginnings of Rome: Italy and Rome from the Bronze Age to the Punic Wars (c. 1000–264 BC)*. London: Routledge.

Cortés, Hernan. 1868. *The fifth letter of Hernan Cortes to the Emperor Charles V: containing an account of his expedition to Honduras*. London: Hakluyt Society.

Cotter, James Finn. 1969. "The Wife of Bath and the Conjugal Debt." *English Language Notes* 6: 169–72.

Covarrubias, Miguel. 1937. *Island of Bali*. London: Kegan Paul.

Curtin, Phillip D. 1969. *The Atlantic Slave Trade: A Census*. Madison: University of Wisconsin Press.

Curtin, Phillip D., and Jan Vansina,. 1964. "Sources of the Nineteenth Century Atlantic Slave Trade." *Journal of African History* 5 (2): 185–208.

Custers, Peter. 2006. *Questioning Globalized Militarism: Nuclear and Military Production and Critical Economic Theory*. Monmouth: Merlin Press.

Dandamaev, Muhammed. 1984. *Slavery in Babylonia, from Nabopolasser to Alexander the Great (626–331 BC)*. De Kalb: Northern Illinois University Press.

Darnton, Robert. 1984. *The Great Cat Massacre*. New York: Vintage Books.

Davenant, Charles. 1771. "Discourses on the Public Revenues and on Trade. Discourse II: Concerning Credit, and the Means and Methods by which it may be restored." In *The political and commercial works of that celebrated writer Charles D'Avenant: relating to the trade and revenue of England, the Plantation trade, the East-India trade and African trade* (Sir Charles Whitworth, ed.), pp. 150–206. London: R. Horsefeld.

Davidson, Paul. 2006. "Keynes and Money."In *A Handbook of Alternative Monetary Economics* (Philip Arestis and Malcolm Sawyer, eds.), pp. 139–53. Cheltenham: Edward Elgar.

Davies, Glynn. 1996. *A History of Money*. Cardiff: University of Wales Press.

Davies, Kenneth Gordon. 1975. *The North Atlantic world in the seventeenth century*. St. Paul: University of Minnesota Press.

Davis, John. 1904. *Corporations*. New York: Capricorn.

Delâge, Denys. 1993. *Bitter Feast: Amerindians and Europeans in Northeastern North America, 1600–64*. Vancouver: University of British Columbia Press.

Deleuze, Giles and Felix Guattari. 1972. *Anti-Oedipe*. Translated into English as *Anti-Œdipus*. (Robert Hurley, Mark Seem and Helen R. Lane, translators.) New York: Continuum, 2004.

Deng, Gang. 1999. *The Premodern Chinese Economy: Structural Equilibrium and Capitalist Stagnation*. London: Routledge.

Denzel, Markus A. 2006. "The European bill of exchange." Paper presented at the XIV International Economic History Congress, Helsinki, Finland, 21 to 25 August 2006. www .helsinki.fi/iehc2006/papers1/Denzel2.pdf.

Derrida, Jacques. 2000. *Of Hospitality: Anne Dufourmantelle Invites Jacques Derrida to Respond*. (Trans. Rachel Bowlby), Stanford: Stanford University Press.

———. 2001. *Acts of Religion*. London: Routledge.

Descat, Raymond. 1995. "L'économie antique et la cité grecque: Un modèle en question." Annales. Histoire, Sciences Sociales, 50e Année, No. 5: 961–89.

Dhavalikar, Madhukar Keshav. 1975. "The Beginning of Coinage in India." *World Archaeology* 6 (3):330–38.

Di Cosmo, Nicola & Don J. Wyatt, editors. 2005. *Political frontiers, ethnic boundaries, and human geographies in Chinese history*. London: Routledge Curzon.

Diakonoff, Igor. 1982. "The Structure of Near Eastern Society before the Middle of the 2nd Millennium BC." *Oikumene* 3: 7–100.

Diaz, Bernal. 1844. *The memoirs of the conquistador Bernal Diaz del Castillo, Written by Himself, Containing a True and Full Account of the Discovery and Conquest of Mexico and New Spain*. (John Ingram Lockhart, translator.) Boston: J. Hatchard and Son.

———. 1963. *The Conquest of New Spain*. (J. M. Cohen, translator.) New York: Penguin Books.

Digby, Kenelm Edward, and William Montagu Harrison. 1897. *An Introduction to the History of the Law of Real Property with Original Authorities*. Fifth Edition. Oxford: Clarendon Press.

Dighe, Ranjit, editor. 2002. *The historian's Wizard of Oz: reading L. Frank Baum's classic as a political and monetary allegory*. Westport: Greenwood Publishing Group.

Dike, K. Onwuka and Felicia Ekejiuba. 1990. *The Aro of south-eastern Nigeria, 1650–1980: a study of socio-economic formation and transformation in Nigeria*. Ibadan: University Press.

Dikshitar, V. R. Ramachandra. 1948. *War in Ancient India*. Delhi: Motilal Banarsidass.

Dillon, John M. 2004. *Morality and Custom in Ancient Greece*. Bloomington: Indiana University Press.

Dixon, C. Scott. 2002. *The Reformation and Rural Society: The Parishes of Brandenburg-Ansbach-Kulmbach, 1528–1603*. Cambridge: Cambridge University Press.

Dockés, Pierre. 1979. *Medieval Slavery and Liberation* (Arthur Goldhammer, translator). Chicago: University of Chicago Press.

Doherty, Charles. 1980. "Exchange and Trade in Early Medieval Ireland." *Journal of the Royal Society of Antiquaries of Ireland* 110: 67–89.

Donzelot, Jacques. 1994. *L'invention du social: essai sur le déclin des passions politiques*. Paris: Seuil

Dorward, David C. 1976. "Precolonial Tiv Trade and Cloth Currency." *International Journal of African Historical Studies* 9 (4):576–591.

Douglas, Mary. 1951. "A form of polyandry among the Lele of the Kasai." *Africa: Journal of the International African Institute* 21 (1):1–12. (As Mary Tew.)

———. 1958. "Raffia Cloth Distribution in the Lele Economy." *Africa: Journal of the International African Institute* 28 (2): 109–122.

———. 1960. "Blood-Debts and Clientship Among the Lele." *Journal of the Royal Anthropological Institute of Great Britain and Ireland* 90 (1): 1–28.

———. 1962. "The Lele Compared with the Bushong: A Study in Economic Backwardness." In *Markets in Africa* (Paul Bohannan and George Dalton, eds.), pp. 211–23. Chicago: Northwestern University Press.

———. 1963. *The Lele of the Kasai.* London: Oxford University Press.

———. 1964. "Matriliny and Pawnship in Central Africa." *Africa: Journal of the International African Institute* 34 (4): 301–13.

———. 1966. *Purity and Danger: An Analysis of Concepts of Pollution and Taboo.* London: Routledge and Kegan Paul.

———. 1982. *In the Active Voice.* London: Routledge and Kegan Paul.

———. 1999. "Sorcery Accusations Unleashed: the Lele Revisited, 1987." *Africa: Journal of the International African Institute* 69 (2): 177–93.

Downes, Rupert Major. 1933. *The Tiv Tribe.* Kaduna: Government Printer.

———. 1977. *Tiv Religion.* Ibadan: Ibadan University Press.

Dreyer, Edward L. 2006. *Zheng He: China and the Oceans in the Early Ming Dynasty, 1405–1433.* Library of World Biography (editor, Peter N. Stearns). New York: Pearson Longman, 2006.

Driver, Godfrey Rolles. and John C. Miles. 1935. *The Assyrian Laws.* Oxford: Clarendon Press.

Dubois, Page. 2003. *Slaves and Other Objects.* Chicago: University of Chicago Press.

Duby, Georges. 1973. *Guerriers et paysans, VIIe–XIIe sècle: Premier essor de l'économie européenne.* Paris: Gallimard.

———. 1980. *The Three Orders: Feudal Society Imagined* (translated by Arthur Goldhammer). Chicago: University of Chicago Press.

———. 1982. *Rural Economy and the Country Life in the Medieval West.* New York: Routledge and Kegan Paul.

Duffy, Seán, Ailbhe MacShamhráin, and James Moynes, editors. 2005. *Medieval Ireland: an encyclopedia.* Dublin: CRC Press.

Duggan, E. de C. 1932. "Notes on the Munshi Tribe." *Journal of the African Society* 31: 173–82.

Dumont, Louis. 1966. *Homo Hierarchicus: Essai sur le système des castes.* Paris: Gallimard.

———. 1981. *From Mandeville to Marx: the Genesis and Triumph of Economic Ideology.* Chicago: University of Chicago Press.

———. 1992. *Essays on Individualism: Modern Ideology in Anthropological Perspective.* Chicago: University of Chicago Press.

Duyvendak, Jan Julius Lodewijk. 1928. *The Book of Lord Shang.* London: Arthur Probsthain.

Dyer, Christopher. 1989. *Standards of living in the later Middle Ages: social change in England, c.* 1200–1520. Cambridge: Cambridge University Press.

Einaudi, Luigi. 1936. "The Theory of Imaginary Money from Charlemagne to the French Revolution", in F. C. Lane and J. C. Riemersma (eds.), *Enterprise and Secular Change,* London: Allen & Unwin, 1956.

Einzig, Paul. 1949. *Primitive Money in its Ethnological, Historical, and Ethnographic Aspects.* New York: Pergamon Press.

Eisenstadt, Shmuel N. 1982. "The Axial Age: The Emergence of Transcendental Visions and the Rise of Clerics." *European Journal of Sociology* 23(2):294–314.

———. 1984. "Heterodoxies and Dynamics of Civilizations." *Proceedings of the American Philosophical Society* 128 (2): 104–13.

———. 1986. *The Origins and Diversity of Axial Age Civilizations.* Albany: State University of New York Press.

Ekejiuba, Felicia Ifeoma. 1972. "The Aro trade system in the nineteenth century." *Ikenga* 1 (1):11-26, 1 (2):10–21.

Elayi, Josette and A. G. Elayi. 1993. *Trésors de monnaies phéniciennes et circulation monétaire (Ve-IVe siècle avant J.-C.)*. Paris: Gabalda.

Ellis, Thomas Peter. 1926. *Welsh Tribal Law and Custom in the Middle Ages*. Oxford: Oxford University Press.

Eltis, David, Stephen D. Behrent, David Richardson, Herbert S. Klein. 2000. *The Transatlantic Slave Trade: A Database*. Cambridge: Cambridge University Press.

Elwahed, Ali Abd. 1931. *Contribution à une théorie sociologique de l'esclavage. Étude des situations génératrices de l'esclavage. Avec appendice sur l'esclavage de la femme et bibliographie critique*. Paris: Éditions Albert Mechelinck.

Elyachar, Julia. 2002. "Empowerment Money: The World Bank, Non-Governmental Organizations, and the Value of Culture in Egypt." *Public Culture* 14 (3): 493–513.

———. 2005. *Markets of Dispossession: NGOs, Economic Development, and the State in Cairo*. Durham: Duke University Press.

Endres, Rudolf. 1979. "The Peasant War in Franconia." In *The German Peasant War of 1525—New Viewpoints* (Bob Scribner & Gerhard Benecke, eds.), pp. 63–83. London: Allen & Unwin.

Engels, Donald W. 1978. *Alexander the Great and the Logistics of the Macedonian Army*. Berkeley: University of California Press.

Equiano, Olaudah. 1789. *The Interesting Narrative of the Life of Olaudah Equiano: or, Gustavus Vassa, the African*. Modern Library Edition, New York, 2004.

Erdosy, George. 1988. *Urbanisation in Early Historic India*. Oxford: British Archaeological Reports.

———. 1995. "City states in North India and Pakistan at the time of the Buddha." In *The archaeology of early historic South Asia: the emergence of cities and states* (Frank Allichin and George Erdosy, eds.), pp. 99–122. Cambridge: Cambridge University Press.

Essid, Yassine. 1988. "Islamic Economic Thought." In *Preclassical Economic Thought: From the Greeks to the Scottish Enlightenment* (edited by Todd Lowry), pp. 77–102. Boston: Kluwer.

———. 1995. *A critique of the origins of Islamic economic thought*. Leiden: E. J. Brill.

Evans-Pritchard, E. E. 1931. "An Alternative Term for 'Bride-Price'." *Man* 31: 36–39.

———. 1940. *The Nuer: a Description of the Modes of Livelihood and Political Institutions of a Nilotic People*. Oxford: Clarendon Press.

———. 1948. *The Divine Kingship of the Shilluk of the Nilotic Sudan. The Frazer Lecture for 1948*. Cambridge: Cambridge University Press.

———. 1951. *Kinship and Marriage among the Nuer*. Oxford: Clarendon Press.

Falkenhausen, Lothar von. 2005. "The E Jun Qi Metal Tallies: Inscribed Texts and Ritual Contexts." In *Text and Ritual in Early China* (edited by Martin Kern), pp. 79–123. Seattle: University of Washington Press.

Falkenstein, Adam. 1954. "La cité-temple sumérienne." *Cahiers d'histoire mondiale* 1: 784–814.

Falola, Toyin and Paul E. Lovejoy, editors. 1994. *Pawnship in Africa: Debt Bondage in Historical Perspective*. Boulder: University of Colorado Press.

Fardon, Richard. 1985. "Sisters, Wives, Wards and Daughters: A Transformational Analysis of the Political Organization of the Tiv and their Neighbors. Part I: The Tiv. *Africa: Journal of the International African Institute* 54 (4): 2–21.

———. 1986. "Sisters, Wives, Wards and Daughters: A Transformational Analysis of the Political Organization of the Tiv and their Neighbors. Part II: The Transformations." *Africa: Journal of the International African Institute* 55 (1): 77–91.

Faure, Bernard. 1998. "The Buddhist Icon and the Modern Gaze." *Critical Inquiry* 24 (3): 768–813.

———. 2000. *Visions of Power: Imagining Medieval Japanese Buddhism*. Princeton: Princeton University Press.

Fayazmanesh, Sasan. 2006. *Money and Exchange: Folktales and Reality*. New York: Routledge.

Federal Reserve Bank of New York. 2008. "The Key to the Gold Vault." www.newyorkfed .org/education/addpub/goldvaul.pdf.

Federici, Silvia. 2004. *Caliban and the Witch: Women, the Body and Primitive Accumulation.* New York: Autonomedia.

Feeley-Harnik, Gillian. 1982. "The King's Men in Madagascar: Slavery, Citizenship and Saka-lava Monarchy." *Africa: Journal of the International African Institute* 52 (2): 31–50.

Fenton, William N. 1978 "Northern Iroquois Culture Patterns." In *Handbook of the North American Indians, volume 15, Northeast* (W. Sturtevant and B. Trigger, eds.), pp. 296–321. Washington D.C.: Smithsonian Institute Press.

Ferguson, Niall. 2001. *The Cash Nexus: Money and Power in the Modern World, 1700–2000.* London: Allen Lane.

———. 2004. *Colossus: the price of America's empire.* London: Penguin.

———. 2007. *The Ascent of Money: A Financial History of the World.* London: Penguin.

Finkelstein, Jacob J. 1961. "Ammisaduqa's Edict and the Babylonian 'Law Codes.'" *Journal of Cuneiform Studies* 15: 91–104.

———. 1965. "Some New Misharum Material and Its Implications." *Assyriological Studies* 16: 233–46.

———. 1966. "Sex Offenses in Sumerian Laws." *Journal of the American Oriental Society* 86:355–72.

Finley, Moses I. 1954. *The World of Odysseus.* New York: Viking Press.

———. 1960. *Slavery in classical antiquity: views and controversies.* Cambridge: W. Heffer & Sons.

———. 1963. *The ancient Greeks: an introduction to their life and thought.* New York: Viking Press.

———. 1964. "Between Slavery and Freedom" *Comparative Studies in Society and History* 6 (3): 233–49.

———. 1974. *The Ancient Economy.* Berkeley: University of California Press.

———. 1980. *Ancient Slavery and Modern Ideology.* London: Penguin

———. 1981. *Economy and Society in Ancient Greece.* New York: Penguin.

———. 1983. *Politics in the Ancient World.* Cambridge: Cambridge University Press.

———. 1985. *Studies in land and credit in ancient Athens, 500–200 B.C.: the horos inscriptions.* New Brunswick: Transaction Publishers.

Firth, Raymond. 1959. *Economics of the New Zealand Maori.* Wellington, New Zealand: R. E. Owen.

Fischel, Walter J. 1937. *Jews in the Economic and Political Life of Medieval Islam.* London: Royal Asiatic Society.

Fiser, Ivo. 2004. "The Problem of the Setthi in Buddhist Jatakas." In *Trade in Early India* (Ranabir Chakravarti, ed.), pp. 166-198. Oxford: Oxford University Press.

Fisher, Douglas. 1989. "The Price Revolution: A Monetary Interpretation." *Journal of Economic History* 49 (1):884–902.

Fitzpatrick, Jim. 2001. *Three Brass Balls: the Story of the Irish Pawnshop.* Dublin: Collins Press.

Flandrin, Jean-Louis. 1979. *Families in Former Times.* Cambridge: Cambridge University Press.

Fleet, John Faithful. 1888. *Inscriptions of the Early Gupta Kings and Their Successors, Corpus Inscriptionium Indicarum, vol. III.* Calcutta: Government Printer.

Flynn, Dennis. 1978. "A New Perspective on the Spanish Price Revolution: The Monetary Approach to the Balance of Payments." *Explorations in Economic History* 15:388-406.

———. 1979. "Spanish-American Silver and World Markets in the Sixteenth Century." *Economic Forum* 10: 46-71.

———. 1982. "The Population Thesis View of Sixteenth-Century Inflation Versus Economics and History." In *Munzpragung, Geldumlauf und Wechselkurse/Mintage, Monetary Circulation and Exchange Rates. Akten der C7-Section des 8th International Economic History Congress Budapest 1982.* (F. Irsigler and E. H.G. Van Cauwenberghe, editors.), pp. 361–82. Trier: THF-Verlag.

Flynn, Dennis and Arturo Giráldez. 1995. "Born with a 'Silver Spoon': the Origin of World
   Trade in 1571." *Journal of World History* VI (2): 201–11.
———. 2002. "Cycles of Silver: Global Economic Unity through the Mid-Eighteenth Century." *Journal of World History*, vol. 13, no. 2, pp. 391–427.
Forstater, Mathew. 2005. 'Taxation and Primitive Accumulation: The Case of Colonial Africa,' *Research in Political Economy*, 22, 51–64.
———. 2006. 'Taxation: Additional Evidence from the History of Thought, Economic His-
   tory, and Economic Policy,' in M. Setterfield (ed.), *Complexity, Endogenous Money, and
   Exogenous Interest Rates*, Chetlenham, UK: Edward Elgar.
Frankfort, Henri. 1948. *Kingship and the Gods: A Study of Ancient Near Eastern Religion as
   the Integration of Society and Nature*. Chicago: University of Chicago Press.
Freuchen, Peter. 1961. *Book of the Eskimo*. Cleveland, Ohio: World Publishing Co.
Friedman, Thomas L. 1999. *The Lexus and the Olive Tree*. New York: Farrar, Straus and
   Giroux.
Gadamer, Hans-Georg. 2004. *Truth and Method* (Joel Weinsheimer; Donald G Marshall,
   translators). London: Continuum.
Gale, Esson McDowell. 1967. *Discourse on Salt and Iron: a debate on state control of com-
   merce and industry in ancient China* (by Huan K'uan). Taipei: Ch'eng-Wen.
Galey, Jean-Claude. 1983. "Creditors, Kings and Death: determinations and implications of
   bondage in Tehri-Gathwal (Indian Himalayas)." In *Debts and Debtors* (Charles Mala-
   moud, ed.), pp. 67–124. London: Vikas.
Gallant, Thomas W. 2000. "Honor, Masculinity, and Ritual Knife Fighting in Nineteenth-
   Century Greece." *American Historical Review* 105 (2): 359–82.
Gardiner, Geoffrey. 2004. "The Primacy of Trade Debts in the Development of Money." In
   Credit and State Theories of Money: The Contributions of A. Mitchell Innes (L. Randall
   Wray, ed.). Cheltingham, Edward Elgar.
Garnsey, Peter. 1996. *Ideas of Slavery from Aristotle to Augustine*. Cambridge: Cambridge
   University Press.
———. 2008. *Thinking about Property: From Antiquity to the Age of Revolution*. Cambridge:
   Cambridge University Press.
Gates, Hill. 1989. "The Commoditization of Women in China." *Signs* 14 (4): 799–832.
Geertz, Clifford. 1973. "Deep play: notes on the Balinese cockfight." In *The Interpretation of
   Culture*. New York: Basic Books.
Geertz, Hildred, and Clifford Geertz. 1975. *Kinship in Bali*. Chicago: University of Chicago
   Press.
Gernet, Jacques. 1956. *Les aspects economiques du bouddhisme dans la societe chinoise du Ve
   au Xe siècle*. Paris: Ecole francaise d'Extreme-Orient. English version: *Centuries* (Francis-
   cus Verellen, translator). New York: Columbia University Press, 1995.
———. 1960. "Les suicides par le feu chez les bouddhiques chinoises de Ve au Xe siecle,"
   Melange publies par l'Institut des Hautes Études II: 527–58.
———. 1982. *A History of Chinese Civilization*. Cambridge: Cambridge University Press.
Gerriets, Marilyn. 1978. *Money and Clientship in the Ancient Irish Laws*. Ph.D. dissertation,
   University of Toronto.
———. 1981. "The Organization of Exchange in Early Christian Ireland." *Journal of Eco-
   nomic History* 41 (1): 171–76.
———. 1985. "Money in Early Christian Ireland according to the Irish Laws." *Comparative
   Studies in Society and History* 27 (2): 323–39.
———. 1987. "Kinship and Exchange in Pre-Viking Ireland." *Cambridge Medieval Celtic
   Studies* 13: 39–72.
Getz, Trevor R. 2003. "Mechanisms of Slave Acquisition and Exchange in Late Eighteenth
   Century Anomabu: Reconsidering a Cross-Section of the Atlantic Slave Trade." *African
   Economic History* 31: 75–89.
Ghazanfar, Shaikh M. 1991. "Scholastic Economics and Arab Scholars: The 'Great Gap'
   Thesis Reconsidered." *Diogenes: International Review of Humane Sciences*; No.154:
   117–33.

———. 2000. "The Economic Thought of Abu Hamid Al-Ghazali and St. Thomas Aquinas: Some Comparative Parallels and Links." *History of Political Economy*, 32 (4): 857–88.

———. 2003. *Medieval Islamic economic thought: filling the "great gap" in European economics*. New York: Routledge.

Ghazanfar, Shaikh M., and Abdul Azim Islahi,. 1997. *The Economic Thought of al-Ghazali (450–505 A.H. / 1058–1111 A.D.)* Jeddah: Scientific Publishing Centre King Abdulaziz University.

———. 2003. "Explorations in Medieval Arab-Islamic Thought: Some Aspects of Ibn Taimiyah's Economics." In *Medieval Islamic economic thought: filling the "great gap" in European economics* (S. Ghazanfar, ed.), pp. 53–71. New York: Routledge.

Gibson, Charles. 1964. *The Aztecs under Spanish rule: a history of the Indians of the Valley of Mexico, 1519–1810*. Stanford: Stanford University Press.

Gilder, George. 1981. *Wealth and Poverty*. New York: Basic Books.

———. 1990. *Microcosm: the quantum revolution in economics and technology*. New York: Simon & Schuster.

Glahn, Richard Von. 1996a. *Fountain of Fortune: Money and Monetary Policy in China, 1000–1700*. Berkeley: University of California Press.

———. 1996b. "Myth and Reality of China's Seventeenth Century Monetary Crisis." *Journal of Economic History* 56, no. 2, pp. 429–54.

Glancey, Jennifer A. 2006. *Slavery in Early Christianity*. Oxford: Oxford University Press.

Gluckman, Max. 1971. *Politics, Law and Ritual in Tribal Society*. London: Basil Blackwell.

Goldstone, Jack A. 1984. "Urbanization and Inflation: Lessons from the English Price Revolution of the Sixteenth and Seventeenth Centuries." *American Journal of Sociology* 89 (5): 1122–60.

———. 1991. "Monetary Versus Velocity Interpretations of the 'Price Revolution': A Comment." *Journal of Economic History* 51 (1): 176–81.

———. 2002. "Efflorescences and Economic Growth in World History: Rethinking the 'Rise of the West' and the Industrial Revolution." *Journal of World History* 13 (2): 323–89.

Goodman, Martin. 1983. *State and Society in Roman Galilee, A.D. 132–212*. London: Valentine Mitchell.

Goody, Jack. 1976. *Production and reproduction: a comparative study of the domestic domain*. Cambridge: Cambridge University Press.

———. 1983. *Development of Marriage and the Family in Europe*. Cambridge: Cambridge University Press.

———. 1990. *The Oriental, the Ancient, and the Primitive: Systems of Marriage and the Family in the Pre-Industrial Societies of Eurasia*. Cambridge: Cambridge University Press.

———. 1996. *The East in the West*. Cambridge: Cambridge University Press.

Goody, Jack and Stanley J. Tambiah. 1973. *Bridewealth and Dowry*. Cambridge: Cambridge University Press.

Goitein, Shelomo Dov. 1954. "From the Mediterranean to India: Documents on the Trade to India, South Arabia, and East Africa from the Eleventh to Twelfth Centuries." *Speculum* 29: 181–97.

———. 1957. "The Rise and Fall of the Middle Eastern bourgeoisie in early Islamic times." *Journal of World History* 3: 583–603.

———. 1964. "The commercial mail service in medieval Islam." *Journal of the American Oriental Society* 84: 118–23.

———. 1966. "Banker's Accounts from the Eleventh Century A.D." *Journal of the Economic and Social History of the Orient* 9: 28–66.

———. 1967. *A Mediterranean Society, The Jewish Communities of the Arab World as Portrayed in the Documents of the Cairo Geniza*. Berkeley: University of California. Press.

———. 1973. *Letters of Medieval Jewish Traders*. Princeton: Princeton University Press.

Gordon, Barry. 1982. "Lending at interest: some Jewish, Greek, and Christian approaches, 800 BC–AD 100." *History of Political Economy* 14 (3):406–26.

———. 1989. *The economic problem in biblical and patristic thought*. Leiden: E. J. Brill.

Gough, Kathleen. 1971. "Nuer Kinship: a Reexamination." In *The Translation of Culture: Essays to E. E. Evans-Pritchard* (T. Beidelman, ed.), pp. 79–123. London: Tavistock Publications.

Goux, Jean-Joseph. 1990. *Symbolic Economies: After Marx and Freud* (Jennifer Curtiss Gage, translator.) Ithaca: Cornell University Press.

Graeber, David. 1997. "Manners, Deference and Private Property: the Generalization of Avoidance in Early Modern Europe." *Comparative Studies in Society and History* 39 (4): 694–728.

———. 2001. *Toward an Anthropological Theory of Value: The False Coin of Our Own Dreams.* New York: Palgrave.

———. 2005. "Fetishism and Social Creativity, or Fetishes are Gods in Process of Construction." *Anthropological Theory* 5 (4): 407–38.

———. 2006. "Turning Modes of Production Inside Out: Or, Why Capitalism Is a Transformation of Slavery (short version)." *Critique of Anthropology* 26 (1): 61–81.

———. 2007. *Possibilities: Essays on Hierarchy, Rebellion and Desire.* Oakland: AK Press.

———. 2009. "Debt, Violence, and Impersonal Markets: Polanyian Meditations." In *Market and Society: The Great Transformation today* (Chris Hann and Keith Hart, eds.), pp. 106–32. Cambridge: Cambridge University Press.

Graham, Angus Charles. 1960. *The Book of Lieh-Tzu.* London: John Murray.

———. 1979. "The Nung-Chia 'School of the Tillers' and the Origin of Peasant Utopianism in China." *Bulletin of the School of Oriental and African Studies, University of London*, Vol. 42 no. 1, pp. 66–100.

———. 1989. *Disputers of the Tao: Philosophical Argument in Ancient China.* La Salle, Illinois: Open Court Press.

———. 1994. Studies in Chinese philosophy and philosophical literature. *SUNY series in Chinese philosophy and culture.* Albany: SUNY.

Grahl, John. 2000. "Money as Sovereignty: the Economics of Michel Aglietta." *New Political Economy* 5 (2): 291–316.

Grandell, Axel. 1977. "The reckoning board and tally stick." *Accounting Historians Journal* 4 (1): 101–105.

Gray, Robert F. 1968. "Sonjo Bride-Price and the Question of African 'Wife Purchase.'" *American Anthropologist* 62: 34–47.

Greengus. Samuel. 1966. "Old Babylonian Marriage Ceremonies and Rites." *Journal of Cuneiform Studies* 20: 57–72.

———. 1969. "The Old Babylonian marriage contract." *Journal of the American Oriental Society* 89: 505–32.

———. 1975. "Sisterhood Adoption at Nuzi and the 'Wife-Sister' in Genesis." *Hebrew Union College Annual* 46: 5–31.

———. 1990. "Bridewealth in Sumerian sources." *Hebrew Union College Annual* 61: 25–88.

Gregory, Christopher A. 1982. *Gifts and Commodities.* New York: Academic Press.

———. 1998. *Savage Money: The Anthropology and Politics of Commodity Exchange.* Amsterdam: Harwood Academic Publishers.

Green, Peter. 1993. *Alexander to Actium: the historical evolution of the Hellenistic age.* Berkeley: University of California Press.

Greider, William. 1989. *Secrets of the Temple: How the Federal Reserve Runs the Country.* New York: Simon & Schuster.

Grierson, Phillip. 1959. "Commerce in the Dark Ages: a critique of the evidence." *Transactions of the Royal Historical Society*, 5th series 9: 123–40.

———. 1960. "The monetary reforms of 'Abd al-Malik: their metrological basis and their financial repercussions." *Journal of the Economic and Social History of the Orient* 3: 241–64.

———. 1977. *The Origins of Money.* London: Athlone Press.

———. 1978. "The Origins of Money." In *Research in Economic Anthropology Vol. I.* Greenwich: Journal of the Anthropological Institute Press.

———. 1979. *Dark Age Numismatics.* London: Variorium Reprints.

Grosz, Katarzyna. 1983. "Bridewealth and Dowry in Nuzi." In *Images of Women in Antiquity* (A. Cameron and A. Kuhrt, eds.), pp. 193–206. Detroit: Wayne State University Press.

———. 1989. "Some aspects of the position of women in Nuzi." In *Women's Earliest Records From Ancient Egypt and Western Asia* (Barbara S. Lesko, ed.), pp. 167–80. Atlanta: Scholar's Press.

Gudeman, Stephen. 2002. *The Anthropology of Economy.* London: Blackwell.

Guha, Ranjanit. 1999. *Elementary Aspects of Peasant Insurgency in Colonial India.* Durham: Duke University Press.

Guisborough, William of. 1954. *The Chronicle of William of Guisborough.* (H. Rothwell, editor.) London: Camden.

Gupta, Parameshwari Lal and T. R. Hardaker,. 1985. *Indian Silver Punchmarked Coins: Magadha-Maurya Karshapana Series.* Nashik: Indian Institute of Research in Numismatic Studies.

Guth, Delloyd J. 2008. "The Age of Debt: the Reformation and English Law." In *Tudor Rule and Revolution: Essays for G. R. Elton from His American Friends* (Delloyd J. Guth and John W. McKenna, eds.), pp. 69–86. Cambridge: Cambridge University Press.

Guyer, Jane I. 1994. "Brideprice." In The Encyclopedia of Social History (Peter N. Stearns, ed.), p. 84. London: Taylor & Francis.

———. 2004. *Marginal Gains: Monetary Transactions in Atlantic Africa.* Chicago: University of Chicago Press.

Hadot, Pierre. 1995. *Philosophy as a Way of Life: Spiritual Exercises from Socrates to Foucault.* (Michael Chase, translator). Oxford: Blackwell.

———. 2002. *What Is Ancient Philosophy?* Cambridge: Belknap Press.

Hallam, Henry. 1866. *The constitutional history of England, from the accession of Henry VII to the death of George II.* London: Widdelton.

Halperin, David. 1990. "The Democratic Body: Prostitution and Citizenship in Classical Athens." In *One Hundred Years of Homosexuality and Other Essays on Greek Love* (David Halperin, ed.), pp. 88–112. New York: Routledge.

Hamashita, Takeshi. 1994. "Tribute Trade System and Modern Asia." In *Japanese Industrialization and the Asian Economy* (A.J.H. Latham and H. Kawakatsu, ed), pp. 91–107. London and New York: Routledge.

———. 2003 "Tribute and treaties: maritime Asia and treaty port networks in the era of negotiations, 1800–1900. In *The resurgence of East Asia: 500, 150 and 50 year perspectives* (Giovanni Arrighi, et al., eds.), pp. 15–70. London; New York: Routledge.

Hamilton, Earl J. 1934. *American Treasure and the Price Revolution in Spain, 1501–1650.* Cambridge: Harvard University Press.

Hardaker, Alfred. 1892. *A Brief History of Pawnbroking.* London: Jackson, Ruston and Keeson.

Hardenburg, Walter Ernest, and Sir Roger Casement. 1913. *The Putumayo: the devil's paradise; travels in the Peruvian Amazon region and an account of the atrocities committed upon the Indians therein.* London: T. F. Unwin.

Harding, Alan. 1980. "Political Liberty in the Middle Ages." *Speculum* 55 (3): 423–43.

Harrill, J. Albert. 1998. *The manumission of slaves in early Christianity.* Tübingen: Mohr Siebek.

Harris, Edward M. 2006. *Democracy and the Rule of Law in Classical Athens: Essays on Law, Society, and Politics.* Cambridge: Cambridge University Press.

Harris, William Vernon, editor. 2006. "A Revisionist View of Roman Money." *Journal of Roman Studies* 96: 1–24.

———. 2008a. "Introduction." In *The monetary systems of the Greeks and Romans* (W. V. Harris, ed.), pp. 1–12. Oxford: Oxford University Press.

———. 2008b. "The Nature of Roman Money." In *The monetary systems of the Greeks and Romans* (W. V. Harris, ed.), pp. 174–207. Oxford: Oxford University Press.

Harris, Rosemary. 1972. "The History of Trade at Ikom, Eastern Nigeria." *Africa: Journal of the International African Institute* Vol. 42 (2): 122–39.

Harrison, James P. 1965. "Communist Interpretations of the Chinese Peasant Wars." *The China Quarterly*, no. 24. pp. 92–118.

Hart, Keith. 1986. "Heads or Tails? Two Sides of the Coin." *Man* (N.S.) 21: 637–56.

———. 1999. *The Memory Bank: Money in an Unequal World*. London: Perpetua Books

Huang, Ray. 1974. *Taxation and Governmental Finance in Sixteenth-Century China*. Cambridge: Cambridge University Press.

———. 1999. *Broadening the horizons of Chinese history: discourses, syntheses, and comparisons*. Amonk: M. E. Sharpe.

Hawtrey, Ralph G. 1928. *Currency and Credit*. 3rd edition. London: Longmans, Green and Co.

Hayward, Jack. 1959. "Solidarity: The Social History of an Idea in Nineteenth-Century France." *International Review of Social History* 4: 261–84.

Heady, Patrick. 2005. "Barter." In *Handbook of Economic Anthropology* (James Carrier, ed.), pp. 262–74. Cheltenham: Edward Elgar.

Hébert, Jean-Claude. 1958. "La Parenté à Plaisanterie à Madagascar: Étude d'Ethnologie Juridique." *Bulletin de Madagascar* No. 142–143 (April–May 1958): 122–258.

Heilbron, Johan. 1998. "French Moralists and the Anthropology of the Modern Era: On the Genesis of the Notions of 'Interest' and 'Commercial Society.'" In *The rise of the social sciences and the formation of modernity: conceptual change in context, 1750–1850* (Björn Wiitrock, Johan Heilbron, & Lars Magnusson, eds.), pp. 77–106. Dordrecht: Kluwer Academic Publishers.

Heinsohn, Gunnar and Otto Steiger. 1989. "The Veil of Barter: The Solution to 'The Task of Obtaining Representations of an Economy in which Money is Essential." In *Inflation and Income Distribution in Capitalist Crisis: Essays in Memory of Sidney Weintraub*. Edited by J. A. Kregel. New York: NYU Press, pp. 175–202.

Helmholz, Richard H. 1986. "Usury and the Medieval English Church Courts." *Speculum* 56: 364–80.

Herbert, Eugenia W. 2003. *Red Gold of Africa: Copper in Precolonial History and Culture*. Madison: University of Wisconsin Press.

Herlihy, David. 1985. *Medieval Households*. Cambridge: Harvard University Press.

Herzfeld, Michael. 1980. "Honour and Shame: Problems in the Comparative Analysis of Moral Systems." *Man* 15:339–51.

———. 1985. *The Poetics of Manhood*. Princeton: Princeton University Press.

Hezser, Catherine. 2003. "The Impact of Household Slaves on the Jewish Family in Roman Palestine." *Journal for the Study of Judaism* 34 (4): 375–424.

Hildebrand, Bruno. 1864. "Natural-, Geld- und Creditwirtschaft." *Jahrbuch Nationalökonomie* 1864.

Hill, Christopher. 1972. *The World Turned Upside Down*. New York: Penguin.

Hirschman, Albert O. 1977. *The Passions and the Interests: Political Arguments for Capitalism Before its Triumph*. Princeton: Princeton University Press.

———. 1992. *Rival views of market society and other recent essays*. Cambridge: Harvard University Press.

Hocart, Alfred M. 1936. *Kings and Councillors: an essay in the comparative anatomy of human society*. Chicago: University of Chicago Press.

Hodgson, Marshall G. S. 1974. *The Venture of Islam: Conscience and History in a World Civilization*. Chicago: University of Chicago Press.

Hoitenga, Dewey J. 1991. *Faith and reason from Plato to Plantinga: an introduction to Reformed epistemology*. Albany: SUNY Press.

Holman, Susan R. 2002. *The hungry are dying: beggars and bishops in Roman Cappadocia*. New York: Oxford University Press.

Homans, George. 1958. "Social Behavior as Exchange." *American Journal of Sociology* 63 (6): 597–606.

Homer, Sydney. 1987. *A History of Interest Rates* (2nd edition). New Brunswick: Rutgers University Press.

Hopkins, Keith. 1978. *Conquerors and Slaves: Sociological Studies in Roman History*. Cambridge: Cambridge University Press.

Hoppit, Julian. 1990. "Attitudes to Credit in Britain, 1680–1790." *The Historical Journal* 33 (2): 305–22.

Hoskins, Janet. 1999. *Biographical Objects: How Things Tell the Stories of People's Lives*. New York: Routledge.

Hosseini, Hamid S. 1995. "Understanding the market mechanism before Adam Smith: economic thought in Medieval Islam." *History of Political Economy* 27 (3): 539–61.

———. 1998. "Seeking the roots of Adam Smith's division of labor in medieval Persia." *History of Political Economy* 30 (4): 653–81.

———. 2003. "Contributions of Medieval Muslim Scholars to the History of Economics and their Impact: A Refutation of the Schumpeterian Great Gap." In *The Blackwell Companion to Contemporary Economics, III: A Companion to the History of Economic Thought* (Warren J. Samuels, Jeff Biddle, and John Bryan Davis, eds.), pp. 28–45. London: Wiley-Blackwell.

Houston, Walter J. 2006. *Contending for Justice: Ideologies and Theologies of Social Justice in the Old Testament*. London: T & T Clark.

Howel, King. 2006. *Ancient laws and institutes of Wales: Laws Supposed to Be Enacted by Howel the Good*. Clark, New Jersey: The Lawbook Exchange, Ltd.

Howell, Paul P. 1954. *A Manual of Nuer Law*. International Africa Institute. London: Oxford University Press.

Howgego, Christopher. 1992. "The Supply and Use of Money in the Roman World 200 B.C. to A.D. 300." *Journal of Roman Studies* 82: 1–31.

Hubbard, Jamie. 2001. *Absolute Delusion, Perfect Buddhahood: The Rise and Fall of a Chinese Heresy*. Honolulu: University of Hawaii.

Hubert, Henri and Marcel Mauss. 1964. *Sacrifice: Its Nature and Function*. Translated by W.D. Halls. London: Cohen and West.

Hudson, Kenneth. 1982. *Pawnbroking: An Aspect of British Social History*. London: The Bodley Head.

Hudson, Michael. 1992. "Did the Phoenicians Introduce the Idea of Interest to Greece and Italy—And if So, When?" In *Greece Between East and West: 10th–8th Centuries BC* (Günter Kopcke and Isabelle Tokumaru, eds.), pp. 128–43. Mainz: Verlag Philipp von Zabern.

———. 1993. "The Lost Tradition of Biblical Debt Cancellations." Research paper presented at the Hentry George School of Social Science, 1992 (www.michael-hudson.com/articles/debt/Hudson,LostTradition.pdf).

———. 2002. "Reconstructuring the Origins of Interest-Bearing Debt and the Logic of Clean Slates." In *Debt and Economic Renewal in the Ancient Near East* (Hudson, Michael and Marc Van de Mieroop, eds.), pp. 7–58. Bethesda: CDL Press.

———. 2003a. *Super Imperialism: The Origins and Fundamentals of U.S World Dominance*. London: Pluto Press.

———. 2003b. "The creditary/monetarist debate in historical perspective." *The State, the Market, and Euro: chartalism versus metallism in the theory of money*. (edited by Stephanie Bell and Edward Nell), pp. 39–76. Cheltenham: Edward Elgar Press.

———. 2004a. "The archeology of money: debt vs. barter theories of money." In *Credit and State Theories of Money* (Randall Wray, ed.), pp. 99–127. Cheltenham: Edward Elgar Press.

———. 2004b. "The Development of Money-of-Account in Sumer's Temples." In *Creating Economic Order: Record-Keeping, Standardization and the Development of Accounting in the Ancient Near East* (Michael Hudson and Cornelia Wunsch, eds.), pp. 303–29. Baltimore: CDL Press.

Hudson, Michael and Marc Van de Mieroop, editors. 2002. *Debt and Economic Renewal in the ancient Near East*. Bethesda, MD: CDL Press.

Humphrey, Caroline. 1985. "Barter and Economic Disintegration." *Man* 20: 48–72.

————. 1994. "Fair Dealing, Just Rewards: the Ethics of Barter in North-East Nepal." In *Barter, Exchange, and Value: An Anthropological Approach* (Caroline Humphrey and Stephen Hugh-Jones, eds.), pp. 107–41. Cambridge: Cambridge University Press.

Humphrey, Chris. 2001. *The politics of carnival: festive misrule in medieval England*. Manchester: Manchester University Press.

Hunt, William. 1983. *The Puritan moment: the coming of revolution in an English county*. Cambridge: Harvard University Press.

Hutchinson, Sharon. 1996. *Nuer Dilemmas: Coping with Money, War, and the State*. Berkeley: University of California Press.

Ibn Battuta. 1354 [1929]. *Travels in Asia and Africa, 1325–1354* (translated by H.A.R. Gibb). London: Routledge and Kegan Paul.

Icazbalceta, Joaquin Garcia. 2008. Memoriales de Fray Toribio de Motolinia. Charleston: BiblioBazaar.

Ihering, Rudolf von. 1877. *Geist des Romischen Rechts auf den verschieden en Stufen seiner Entwicklung*. (Republished 2003 by Adamant Media Corporation, Berlin.)

Ilwof, Franz. 1882. *Tauschhandel und Geldsurrogate in alter und neuer Zeit*. Graz.

Ingham, Geoffrey. 1996. "Money as a Social Relation." *Review of Social Economy* 54 (4): 507–29.

————. 1999. "Capitalism, Money, and Banking: a critique of recent historical sociology." *British Journal of Sociology* 5 (1): 76–96.

————. 2000. "'Babylonian Madness': on the historical and sociological origins of money." in *What Is Money?* (edited by John Smithin), New York: Routledge, pp. 16–41.

————. 2004. *The Nature of Money*. Cambridge: Polity Press.

Ingram, Jill Phillips. 2006. *Idioms of Self-Interest: Credit, Identity and Property in English Renaissance Literature*. New York: Routledge.

Inkori, Joseph E. 1982. "The Import of Firearms into West Africa, 1750 to 1807: a quantative analysis." In *Forced Migration: The Impact of the Export Slave Trade on African Societies* (J. E. Inkori, ed.), pp. 126–53. London: Hutchinson University Library.

Innes, A. Mitchell. 1913. "What Is Money?" *Banking Law Journal* (May1913): 377–408.

————. 1914. "The Credit Theory of Money." *Banking Law Journal* (January 1914): 151–68.

Ioannatou, Marina. 2006. *Affaires d'argent dans la correspondance de Cicéron: l'aristocratie sénatoriale face à ses dettes*. Paris: De Boccard.

Isichei, Elizabeth. 1976. *A History of the Igbo People*. London: Basingstoke.

Islahi, Abdul Azim. 1985. "Ibn Taimiyah's Concept of Market Mechanism." *Journal of Research in Islamic Economics2* (2): 55–65.

————. 2003. *Contributions of Muslim Scholars to Economic Thought and Analysis* (11-905 A. H./632–1500 A.D.) Jeddah: Islamic Research Center.

Jacob, Guy. 1987. "Gallieni et 'l'impot moralisateur' a Madagascar: théorie, pratiques et conséquences (1901–1905)." *Revue Francaise d'Histoire d'Outre-mer* 74 (277): 431–73.

James, C. L. R. 1938. *The Black Jacobins: Toussaint L'Ouverture and the San Domingo Revolution*. London: Secker and Warburg.

Jan, Yun-hua. 1964. "Buddhist Self-Immolation in Medieval China." *History of Religions* (4) 2: 243–68.

Janssen, Johannes. 1910. *A History of the German People at the Close of the Middle Ages*. (A. M. Christie, translator.) London: Kegan Paul.

Jasnow, Richard Lewis. 2001. "Pre-demotic Pharaonic sources." In *Security for debt in Ancient Near Eastern law* (Westbrook, R. & Jasnow, R, eds.), pp. 35–45. Leiden, Boston & Köln: Brill.

Jaspers, Karl. 1949. *Vom Ursprung und Ziel der Geschichte*. München: Piper Verlag.

————. 1951. *Way to Wisdom: An Introduction to Philosophy*. New Haven: Yale University Press.

Jefferson, Thomas. 1988. *Political Writings*. (Joyce Oldham Appleby, Terence Ball, eds.). Cambridge: Cambridge University Press.

Jenkinson, C. Hilary. 1911. "Exchequer Tallies." *Archaeologia* 62: 367–80.

————. 1924. "Medieval Tallies, Public and Private." *Archaeologia* 74: 289–324.

Jevons, W. Stanley. 1871. *Theory of Political Economy.* New York: Macmillan & Co.

———. 1875. *Money and the Mechanism of Exchange.* New York: Appleton and Company.

Jobert, Bruno. 2003. "De la solidarité aux solidarités dans la rhétorique politique française." In C. Becc and G. Procacci, ed., *De la responsabilité solidaire,* pp. 69–83. Paris: Syllepses.

Johnson, Lynn. 2004. "Friendship, Coercion, and Interest: Debating the Foundations of Justice in Early Modern England." *Journal of Early Modern History* 8 (1): 46–64.

Johnson, Simon. 2009. "The Quiet Coup." Atlantic Monthly, May 2009, www.theatlantic .com/doc/200905/imf-advice.

Jones, David. 2004. *Reforming the morality of usury: a study of differences that separated the Protestant reformers.* Lanham: University Press of America.

Jones, G. I. 1939. "Who are the Aro?" *Nigerian Field* 8: 100–103.

———. 1958. "Native and Trade Currencies in Southern Nigeria during the Eighteenth and Nineteenth Centuries." *Africa: Journal of the International African Institute* 28 (1): 43–56.

———. 1968. "The Political Organization of Old Calabar." In *Efik Traders of Old Calabar* (D. Forde, ed.). London: International African Institute.

Jones, J. Walter. 1956. *The Law and Legal Theory of the Greeks.* Oxford: Clarendon Press.

Jordan, Kay E. 2003. *From Sacred Servant to Profane Prostitute: A History of the Changing Legal Status of Devadasis in India, 1857–1947.* New Delhi: Manohar.

Just, Roger. 1989. *Women in Athenian Law and Life.* London: Routledge.

———. 2001. "On the Ontological Status of Honour." In *An anthropology of indirect communication* (Joy Hendry, C. W. Watson, eds.), pp. 34–50. ASA Monographs 37. London: Routledge.

Kahneman, Daniel. 2003. "A Psychological Perspective on Economics." *American Economic Review* 93 (2): 162–68.

Kallet, Lisa. 2001. *Money and the corrosion of power in Thucydides: the Sicilian expedition and its aftermath.* Berkeley: University of California Press.

Kaltenmark, Max. 1960. "Ling pao: Notes sur un terme du taoîsme religieux." *Mélanges publiés par l'Institut des Hautes Études Chinoises* 2: 559–88.

Kalupahana, David. 1991. *Mulamadhyamakakarika of Nagarjuna: the Philosophy of the Middle Way.* Delhi: Motilal Banarsidas.

Kamentz, Anya. 2006. *Generation Debt: Why Now is A Terrible Time to Be Young.* New York: Riverhead Books.

Kan, Lao. 1978. "The Early Use of the Tally in China." In *Ancient China: Studies in Early Civilization* (edited by David T. Roy and Tsuen-hsuin Tsien), pp. 91–98. Hong Kong: Chinese University Press.s

Kane, Pandurang Vaman,. 1968. *History of Dharmasastra Volume III.* Poona: Bhandarkar Oriental Research Institute.

Kantorowicz, Ernst H. 1957. *The King's Two Bodies: a Study in Medieval Political Theology.* Princeton: Princeton University Press.

Karatani, Kojin. 2003. *Transcritique: On Kant and Marx.* Cambridge: MIT Press.

Keil, Charles. 1979. *Tiv Song.* Chicago: University of Chicago Press.

Keith, Arthur Berriedale. 1925. *The Religion and Philosophy of the Veda and Upanishads.* Cambridge: Harvard University Press.

Kelly, Amy. 1937. "Eleanor of Aquitaine and Her Courts of Love." *Speculum* 12 (1): 3–19.

Kelly, Fergus. 1988. *A Guide to Early Irish Law.* Dublin: Dublin Institute for Advanced Studies.

Kessler, David & Peter Temin. 2008. "Money and Prices in the Early Roman Empire." In *The monetary systems of the Greeks and Romans* (W. V. Harris, ed.), pp. 137–60. Oxford: Oxford University Press.

Keuls, Eva. 1985. *The Reign of the Phallus: Sexual Politics in Ancient Athens.* Cambridge: Harper & Row.

Keynes, John Maynard. 1930. *A Treatise on Money.* London: MacMillan.

———. 1936. The General Theory of Employment, Interest and Money.

Keyt, David. 1997. *Aristotle: Politics Books VII and VIII.* Oxford: Clarendon Press.

Khan, Mir Siadat Ali. 1929. "The Mohammedan Laws against Usury and How They Are Evaded." *Journal of Comparative Legislation and International Law*, Third Series 11 (4): 233–24.

Kieschnick, John. 1997. *The eminent monk: Buddhist ideals in medieval Chinese hagiography*. Honolulu: University of Hawaii Press.

Kim, Henry S. 2001. "Archaic Coinage as Evidence for the Use of Money," in, A. Meadows and K. Shipton, eds., Money and Its Uses in the Ancient Greek World (Oxford: Oxford University Press), 7–21.

———. 2002. "Small Change and the Moneyed Economy." In *Money, Labour and Land: Approaches to the economies of ancient Greece* (Paul Cartledge, Edward E. Cohen and Lin Foxhall, eds.). New York: Routledge.

Kindleberger, Charles P. 1984. *A Financial History of Western Europe*. London: MacMillan.

———. 1986. *Manias, Panics, and Crashes: A History of Financial Crises*. London: Mac-Millan.

Kirschenbaum, Aaron. 1985. "Jewish and Christian Theories of Usury in the Middle Ages." *The Jewish Quarterly Review* 75 (1): 270–89.

Kitch, Aaron. 2007. "The Character of Credit and the Problem of Belief in Middleton's City Comedies." *Studies in English Literature* 47 (2): 403–26.

Klein, Martin A. 2000. "The Slave Trade and Decentralized Societies." *Journal of African History* 41 (1): 49–65.

Knapp, Georg Friedrich. 1905. *Staatliche Theorie des Gelde*. Leipzing: Dunker and Humblot. [English edition, *The State Theory of Money*. London: MacMillan, 1925.]

Knapp, Keith N. 2004. "Reverent Caring: the parent-son relation in early medieval tales of filial offspring." In *Filial Piety in Chinese Thought and History* (Alan Kam-leung Chan, and Sur-hoon Tan, eds.), pp. 44–70. London: Routledge.

Ko, Dorothy, JaHyun Kim Haboush, and Joan R. Piggott, editors. 2003. *Women and Confucian cultures in premodern China, Korea, and Japan*. Berkeley: University of California Press.

Kohn, Livia. 2000. *Daoism handbook*. Leiden: E. J. Brill.

———. 2002. *Monastic life in medieval Daoism: a cross-cultural perspective*. Honolulu: University of Hawaii Press.

Kopytoff, Igor and Suzanne Miers. 1977. "African 'Slavery' as an Institution of Marginality." In *Slavery in Africa: Historical and Anthropological Perspectives* (edited by Suzanne Miers and Igor Kopytoff), pp. 1–84. Madison: University of Wisconsin Press.

Korver, Jan. 1934. *Die terminologie van het crediet-wezen en het Grieksch*. Amsterdam: H. J. Paris.

Kosambi, Damodar Dharmanand. 1965. *The Culture and Civilisation of Ancient India in Historical Outline*. London: Routledge & Kegan Paul.

———. 1966. *Ancient India: A History Of Its Culture And Civilization*. New York: Pantheon Books.

———. 1981. *Indian Numismatics*. Hyderabad: Orient Longman.

———. 1996. *An introduction to the study of Indian history*. Bombay: Popular Prakashan.

Kraan, Alfons van der. 1983. "Bali: Slavery and Slave Trade." In *Slavery, Bondage and Dependence in Southeast Asia* (Anthony Reid, ed.), pp. 315–340. New York: St. Martin's Press

Kraay, Colin M. 1964. "Hoards, Small Change and the Origin of Coinage," *Journal of Hellenic Studies*, 84, pp. 76–91.

Kramer, Samuel Noah. 1963. *The Sumerians: Their History, Culture, and Character*. Chicago: University of Chicago Press.

———. 1969. *The Sacred Marriage: Aspects of Faith, Myth and Ritual in Ancient Sumer*. Bloomington: Indiana University Press.

Kropotkin, Peter. 1902. *Mutual Aid: A Factor of Evolution*. London: William Heinemann.

Kulischer, Joseph. 1926. *Allgemeine Wirtschaftsgeschichte des Mittelalters und der Neuzeit*. Munich.

Kuran, Timur. 1995. "Islamic Economics and the Islamic Subeconomy." *Journal of Economic Perspectives* 9 (4): 155–73.

———. 2005. "The Absence of the Corporation in Islamic Law: Origins and Persistence." *American Journal of Comparative Law* 53 (4): 785–834.

Kurke, Leslie. 1995. "Pindar and the Prostitutes, or Reading Ancient 'Pornography.'" *Arion*, Third Series 4 (2): 49–57.

———. 1997. "Inventing the 'Hetaira': Sex, Politics, and Discursive Conflict in Archaic Greece." *Classical Antiquity* 16 (1):106–50.

———. 2002. *Coins, bodies, games, and gold: the politics of meaning in archaic Greece.* Princeton: Princeton University Press.

Kuznets, Solomon. 1933. "Pawnbroking." In *Encyclopaedia of the Social Sciences* (Edwin R. A. Seligman, ed.), VII:38. New York: MacMillan.

Labib, Subhi Y. 1969. "Capitalism in Medieval Islam." *The Journal of Economic History* 29 (1): 79–96.

Ladner, Gerhardt B. 1979. "Medieval and Modern Understanding of Symbolism: A Comparison." *Speculum* 54 (2): 223–56.

Lafitau, Joseph François. 1974. *Customs of the American Indians Compared with the Customs of Primitive Times* (edited and translated by William N. Fenton and Elizabeth L. Moore). Toronto: Champlain Society.

LaFleur, William R,. 1986. *The karma of words: Buddhism and the literary arts in medieval Japan.* Berkeley: University of California Press.

Lafont, Bertrand. 1987. "Les filles du roi de Mari." In *La femme dans le Proche-orient antique* (J.-M. Durand, ed.), pp. 113–23. Paris: ERC.

Lambert, Maurice. 1971. "Une Inscription nouvelle d'Entemena prince de Lagash." *Revue du Louvre* 21:231–36.

Lambert, Wilfried G. 1992. "Prostitution." In *Aussenseiter und Randgruppen: Beitrage zu einer Sozialgeschichte des Alten Orients* (edited V. Haas), 127–57. Konstanz: Universitatsverlag

Lamotte, Etienne. 1997. *Karmasiddhi Prakarana: The Treatise on Action by Vasubandhu.* Freemont: Asian Humanities Press.

Lane, Frederic Chapin. 1934. *Venetian ships and shipbuilders of the Renaissance.* Baltimore: Johns Hopkins.

Langholm, Odd. 1979. *Price and Value in the Aristotelian Tradition.* Oslo: Universitetsforlaget.

———. 1984. *The Aristotelian Analysis of Usury.* Bergen: Universitetsforlaget.

———. 1992. *Economics in the Medieval Schools: Wealth, Exchange, Value, Money and Usury According to the Paris Theological Tradition, 1200–1350:* 29 (Studien Und Texte Zur Geistesgeschichte Des Mittelalters). Leiden: E. J. Brill.

———. 1996. "The Medieval Schoolmen, 1200–1400." In *Ancient and Medieval Economic Ideas and Concepts of Social Justice* (edited by S. Todd Lowry and Barry Gordon), pp. 439–502. Leiden: E. J. Brill.

———. 1998. *The Legacy of Scholasticism in Economic Thought: Antecedents of Choice and Power.* Cambridge: Cambridge University Press.

———. 2002. *The Merchant in the Confessional: Trade and Price in the Pre-Reformation Penitential Handbooks.* Leiden: E. J. Brill.

Lapidus, Ira. 1995. "State and Religion in Islamic Societies." *Past and Present* 151: 3–27.

———. 2002. *A History of Islamic Societies* (2nd edition.) Cambridge: Cambridge University Press.

Larson, Pier. 2000. *History and Memory in the Age of Enslavement: Becoming Merina in Highland Madagascar, 1770–1822.* Portsmouth: Heinemann.

Latham, A. J. H. 1971. "Currency, Credit and Capitalism on the Cross River in the Precolonial Era." *Journal of African History* 12 (4): 599–605.

———. 1973. *Old Calabar 1600–1891: The Impact of the International Economy Upon a Traditional Society.* Oxford: Clarendon Press.

———. 1990. "The Pre-Colonial Economy; The Lower Cross Region." In *A History of the Cross River Region of Nigeria.* (Monday B. Abasiattai, ed.), pp. 70–89. Calabar: University of Calabar Press.

Laum, Bernard. 1924. *Heiliges Geld: Eine historische Untersuchung ueber den sakralen Ursprung des Geldes.* Tübingen: J.C.B. Mohr.

Law, Robin. 1994. "On Pawning and Enslavement for Debt in the Pre-colonial Slave Coaast." *Pawnship in Africa: Debt Bondage in Historical Perspective* (Falola, Toyin and Paul E. Lovejoy, eds.), pp. 61–82. Boulder: University of Colorado Press.

Le Guin, Ursula. 1974. *The Disposessed.* New York: Avon.

Leach, Edmund R. 1961. *Rethinking Anthropology.* London: Athlone Press.

———. 1983. "The kula: an alternative view." In *The Kula: New Perspectives on Massim Exchange* (Jerry Leach, ed.), pp. 529–38. Cambridge: Cambridge University Press.

Le Goff, Jacques. 1990. *Your Money or Your Life: Economy and Religion in the Middle Ages.* (Translated by Patricia Ranum.) New York: Zone Books.

Le Rider, George,. 2001. *La naissance de la monnaie: pratiques monétaires de l'Orient ancient.* Paris: Presses universitaires de France.

Lee, Ian. 2000. "Entella: the silver coinage of the Campanian mercenaries and the site of the first Carthaginian mint, 410–409 BC." *Numismatic Chronicle* 160: 1–66.

Leenhardt, Maurice. 1967. *Do Kamo: Person and Myth in the Melanesian World.* Chicago: University of Chicago Press.

Lemche, Niels Peter. 1975. "The 'Hebrew Slave': Comments on the Slave Law, Ex. Xxi 2–11." *Vetus Testamentum* 25: 129–44.

———. 1976. "The Manumission of Slaves: The Fallow Year, The Sabbatical Year, The Jobel Year." *Vetus Testamentum* 26: 38–59.

———. 1979. *Andurarum* and *Misharum*: Comments on the Problems of Social Edicts and their Application in the Ancient Near East," *Journal of Near Eastern Studies* 38:11–18.

———. 1985. *Ancient Israel: A New History of Israelite Society.* Sheffield: Sheffield Academic Press.

Lerner, Abba P. 1947. "Money as a Creature of the State." *American Economic Review, Papers and Proceedings* 37 (2): 312–17.

Lerner, Gerda. 1983. "Women and Slavery." *Slavery and Abolition: A Journal of Comparative Studies* 4 (3): 173–98.

———. 1980. "The Origin of Prostitution in Ancient Mesopotamia." *Signs* 11 (2): 236–54.

———. 1989. *The Creation of Patriarchy.* New York: Oxford University Press.

Letwin, William. 2003. *Origins of Scientific Economics: English Economic Thought, 1660–1776.* London: Routledge.

Lévi, Sylvain. 1898. *La Doctrine du Sacrifice dans les Brâhmanas.* Paris: Ernest Leroux.

———. 1938. *L'Inde civilisatrice.* Paris: Institut de Civilisation Indienne.

Levi-Strauss, Claude. 1943. "Guerre et commerce chez les Indiens d'Amérique du Sud." *Renaissance.* Paris: Ecole Libre des Hautes Études, vol, 1, fascicule 1 et 2.

———. 1963. *Structural Anthropology.* (C. Jacobson and B. G. Schoepf, translators.) New York: Basic Books.

Lévy-Bruhl, Lucien. 1923. *Primitive Mentality.* London: Allen & Unwin.

Lewis, Mark Edward. 1990. *Sanctioned Violence in Early China.* Albany: State University of New York Press.

Li, Xueqin. 1985. *Eastern Zhou and Qin Civilizations.* (translated by K. C. Chang). New Haven: Yale University Press.

Liddell. Henry George and Robert Scott. 1940. *A Greek-English Lexicon, revised and augmented throughout by Sir Henry Stuart Jones with the assistance of Roderick McKenzie.* Oxford. Clarendon Press.

Lindholm, Charles. 1982. *Generosity and Jealousy: the Swat Pukhtun of Northern Pakistan.* New York: Columbia University Press.

Linebaugh, Peter. 1982. "Labour History without the Labour Process: A Note on John Gast and His Times." *Social History* 7 (3): 319–28.

———. 1993. *The London Hanged: Crime and Civil Society in the Eighteenth Century.* Cambridge: Cambridge University Press.

———. 2008. *The Magna Carta Manifesto: Liberties and Commons for All.* Berkeley: University of California Press.

Littlefield, Henry. 1963. "The Wizard of Oz: Parable on Populism." *American Quarterly* 16 (1): 47–98.

Llewellyn-Jones, Lloyd. 2003. *Aphrodite's Tortoise: the veiled woman of ancient Greece.* Swansea: Classical Press of Wales.

Locke, John. 1680–1690. *Two Treatises on Government.* Cambridge: Cambridge University Press edition, 1988.

———. 1691. "Further Considerations Concerning Raising the Value of Money." In The Works of John Locke Volume 5, pp. 131-206. London: W. Otridge & Son, 1812.

Loizos, Peter. 1977. "Politics and patronage in a Cypriot village, 1920–1970." In Ernest Gellner and John Waterbury, editors, *Patrons and Clients* (London: Duckworth), pp. 115–35.

Lombard, Maurice. 1947. 'Les bases monétaires d'une suprématie économique: l'or musulman du VIIe au XIe siècle', *Annales* 2:143–60.

———. 2003. *The Golden Age of Islam.* Princeton: Markus Wiener Publishers.

Loraux, Nicole. 1993. *The Children of Athena: Athenian Ideas About Citizenship and the Division Between the Sexes.* Princeton: Princeton University Press.

Lorton, David. 1977. "The Treatment of Criminals in Ancient Egypt: Through the New Kingdom." *Journal of the Economic and Social History of the Orient* 20 (1): 2–64.

Lovejoy, Paul F. and David Richardson. 1999. "Trust, Pawnship, and Atlantic History: The institutional foundations of the Old Calabar slave trade." *American Historical Review* 104: 333–55.

———. 2001. "The Business of Slaving: Pawnship in Western Africa, c. 1600-1810." *Journal of African History* 42 (1) 67–84.

———. 2004. "'This Horrid Hole': Royal Authority, Commerce and Credit at Bonny, 1690-1840." *Journal of African History* 45 (3): 363–92.

Lusthaus, Dan. 2002. *Buddhist phenomenology: a philosophical investigation of Yogācāra Buddhism and the Ch?eng Wei-shih lun.* Volume 13 of Curzon critical studies in Buddhism. New York: Routledge.

Macaulay, Baron Thomas Babington. 1886. *The history of England, from the accession of James the Second.* London: Longmans, Green and co.

MacDonald, James. 2006. *A free nation deep in debt: the financial roots of democracy.* Princeton: Princeton University Press.

MacDonald, Scott B. and Albert L. Gastmann. 2001. *A History of Credit & Power in the Western World.* New Brunswick: Transaction Publishers.

MacIntosh, Marjorie K. 1988. "Money Lending on the Periphery of London, 1300–1600." *Albion* 20 (4): 557–71.

Mackay, Charles. 1854. *Memoirs of extraordinary popular delusions: and the madness of crowds, Volumes 1-2.* London: G. Routledge and sons.

MacKenney, Richard. 1987. *Tradesmen and Traders: The World of the Guilds in Venice and Europe (c. 1250–c. 1650).* Totowa: Barnes & Noble.

MacPherson, Crawford Brough. 1962. *The political theory of possessive individualism; Hobbes to Locke.* Oxford: Clarendon Press.

Maekawa, Kazuya. 1974. "The development of the É-MÍ in Lagash during Early Dynastic III." *Mesopotamia* 8–9: 77–144.

Maitland, Frederick William. 1908. *The Constitutional History of England: A Course of Lectures Delivered.* Cambridge: Cambridge University Press.

Malamoud, Charles. 1983. "The Theology of Debt in Brahmanism." In *Debts and Debtors* (Charles Malamoud, ed.), pp. 21–40. London: Vices.

———. 1988. "Présentation." *In Lien de vie, noeud mortel. Les représentations de la dette en Chine, au Japon et dans le monde indien* (Charles Malamoud, ed.), pp. 7–15. Paris: EHESS.

———. 1998. "Le paiement des actes rituals dans l'Inde védique." In *La Monnaie Suzerain* (Michael Aglietta and André Orlean, eds.), pp. 35–54. Paris: Editions Odile Jacob.

Malinowski, Bronislaw. 1922. *Argonauts of the Western Pacific: An Account of Native Enterprise and Adventure in the Archipelagoes of Melanesian New Guinea.* London: Routledge.

Maloney, Robert P. 1983. "The Teaching of the Fathers on Usury: An Historical Study on the Development of Christian Thinking." *Vigiliae Christianae* 27 (4):241–65.

Mann, Bruce H. 2002. *Republic of Debtors: Bankruptcy in the Age of American Independence.* Cambridge: Harvard University Press.

Martin, Randy. 2002. *The Financialization of Everyday Life.* Philadelphia: Temple University Press.

Martzloff, Jean-Claude. 2006. *A history of chinese mathematics.* Berlin: Springer Verlag.

Marx, Karl. 1853. "The British Rule in India." *New-York Daily Tribune*, June 25, 1853.

———. 1857 [1973]. *The Grundrisse.* New York: Harper and Row.

———. 1858 [1965]. *Pre-Capitalist Economic Formations.* (Jack Cohen, trans.) New York: International Publishers.

———. 1867 [1967]. *Capital.* New York: New World Paperbacks. 3 volumes.

Mathews, Robert Henry. 1931. *Mathews' Chinese-English dictionary.* Cambridge: Harvard University Press.

Mathias, Peter. 1979a. "Capital, Credit, and Enterprise in the Industrial Revolution." In *The transformation of England: essays in the economic and social history of England in the eighteenth century* (Peter Mathias, ed.), pp. 88-115. London: Taylor & Francis.

———. 1979b. "The People's Money in the Eighteenth Century: The Royal Mint, Trade Tokens and the Economy." In *The transformation of England: essays in the economic and social history of England in the eighteenth century* (Peter Mathias, ed.), pp. 190–208. London: Taylor & Francis.

Maunder, Peter, Danny Myers, Nancy Wall, Roger LeRoy Miller,. 1991. *Economics Explained (Third Edition).* London: Harper Collins.

Mauro, Frédéric. 1993. "Merchant Communities, 1350–1750." In *The Rise of merchant empires: long-distance trade in the early modern world, 1350–1750* (James D. Tracy, ed.), pp. 255–86. Cambridge: Cambridge University Press.

Mauss, Marcel. 1924. Essai sur le don. Forme et raison de l'échange dans les sociétés archaïques." *Annee sociologique*, 1 (series 2):30–186.

———. 1925. "Commentaires sur un texte de Posidonius. Le suicide, contre- prestation supreme." *Revue celtique* 42: 324–29.

———. 1947. *Manuel d'ethnographie.* Paris: Payot.

Meillassoux, Claude. 1996. *The Anthropology of Slavery: The Womb of Iron and Gold* (Alide Dasnois, translator). Chicago: University of Chicago Press.

Menefee, Samuel Pyeatt. 1981. *Wives for Sale: an Ethnographic Study of British Popular Divorce.* Oxford: Blackwell.

Mendelsohn, Isaac. 1949. *Slavery in the Ancient Near East: A Comparative Study of Slavery in Babylonia, Assyria, Syria and Palestine from the Middle of the Third Millennium to the End of the First Millennium.* Westport: Greenwood Press.

Menger, Karl. 1892. "On the origins of money." *Economic Journal* 2 no 6, pp. 239–55.

Meyer, Marvin W. 1999. *The ancient mysteries: a sourcebook: sacred texts of the mystery religions of the ancient Mediterranean world.* Philadelphia: University of Pennsylvania Press.

Midelfort, H. C. Erik. 1996. *Mad princes of renaissance Germany.* Charlottesville: University of Virginia Press.

Midnight Notes Collective. 2009. "Promissory Notes: From Crises to Commons." www .midnightnotes.org/Promissory_Notes.pdf.

Mielants, Eric. 2001. "Europe and China Compared." *Review* XXV, no. 4, pp. 401-49.

———. 2007. *The Origins of Capitalism and the "Rise of the West."* Philadelphia: Temple University Press.

Mieroop, Marc Van De. 2002. "A History of Near Eastern Debt?" In *Debt and Economic Renewal in the Ancient Near East* (Hudson, Michael and Marc Van de Mieroop, eds.), pp. 59–95. Bethesda: CDL.

———. 2005. "The Invention of Interest: Sumerian Loans." In *The Origins of Value: The Financial Innovations That Created Modern Capital Markets* (William N. Goetzmann and K. Geert Rouwenhorst, eds.), pp. 17–30. Oxford: Oxford University Press.

Mez, Adam. 1932. *Die Renaissance des Islams.* Heidelberg: C. Winter.

Miller, Joseph. 1988. *Way of Death: Merchant Capitalism and the Angolan Slave Trade 1730– 1830.* Madison: University of Wisconsin Press.

Miller, Robert J. 1961. "Monastic Economy: The Jisa Mechanism." *Comparative Studies in Society and History* 3 (4): 427–38.

Miller, William. 1993. *Humiliation : and other essays on honor, social discomfort, and violence*. Ithaca: Cornell University Press.

———. 2006. *An Eye for an Eye*. Ithaca: Cornell University Press.

Millett, Paul. 1989. "Patronage and its Avoidance." In *Patronage in Ancient Society* (A. Wallace-Hadrill, ed.), pp. 15–47. London: Routledge.

———. 1991a. *Lending and Borrowing in Classical Athens*. Cambridge: Cambridge University Press.

———. 1991b. "Sale, Credit and Exchange in Athenian Law and Society." In *Nomos* (P. Cartiledge, P. C. Millett and S. C. Todd, eds.), pp. 167–94. Cambridge: Cambridge University Press.

Millon, Frances. 1955. *When money grew on trees: a study of cacao in ancient Mesoamerica*. Ph.D dissertation, Columbia University.

Mises, Ludwig von. 1949. *Human Action: A Treatise on Economics*. New Haven: Yale University Press.

Misra, Shive Nandan. 1976. *Ancient Indian Republics: from the Earliest Times to the 6th Century A.D.* Delhi: Upper India Publishing House.

Mitamura, Taisuke. 1970. *Chinese eunuchs: the structure of an intimate politics*. Rutland: Charles E. Tuttle Company.

Mitchell, Richard E. 1993. "Demands for Land Redistribution and Debt Reduction in the Roman Republic." In *Social Justice in the Ancient World* (K. D. Irani and Morris Silver, eds.), pp. 199–214. Westport: Greenwood Press.

Morgan, Lewis Henry. 1851. *League of the Ho-de-no-sau-nee, or Iroquois*. Secaucus: Citadel Press.

———. 1877. *Ancient Society*. New York: Henry Holt.

———. 1881. *Houses and House-Life of the American Aborigines*. [1965 edition] Chicago: University of Chicago Press.

Moser, Thomas. 2000. "The Idea of Usury in Patristic Literature." In *The canon in the history of economics: critical essays* (edited by Michalēs Psalidopoulos), pp. 24–44. London: Routledge.

Moses, Larry W. 1976. "T'ang tribute relations with the Inner Asian barbarian." In *Essays on T'ang society: the interplay of social, political and economic forces* (Perry, John C. and Bardwell L. Smith, eds.), pp. 61–89. Leiden: Brill.

Moulier-Boutang, Yann. 1997. *De l'esclavage au salariat: économie historique du salariat bridé*. Paris : Presses universitaires de France.

Muhlenberger, Steven, and Phil Paine. 1997. "Democracy in Ancient India." World History of Democracy site, www.nipissingu.ca/department/history/histdem.

Muldrew, Craig. 1993a. "Interpreting the Market: The Ethics of Credit and Community Relations in Early Modern England." *Social History* 18 (2): 163–83.

———. 1993b. "Credit and the Courts: Debt Litigation in a Seventeenth-Century Urban Community." *The Economic History Review*, New Series, 46 (1): 23–38.

———. 1996. "The Culture of Reconciliation: Community and the Settlement of Economic Disputes in Early Modern England." *The Historical Journal* 39 (4): 915–42.

———. 1998. *The Economy of Obligation: The Culture of Credit and Social Relations in Early Modern England*. New York: Palgrave.

———. 2001. "'Hard Food for Midas': Cash and its Social Value in Early Modern England." *Past and Present* 170: 78–120.

Mundill, Robin R. 2002. *England's Jewish Solution: Experiment and Expulsion, 1262–1290*. Cambridge: Cambridge University Press.

Munn, Nancy. 1986. *The Fame of Gawa: A Symbolic Study of Value Transformation in a Massim (Papua New Guinea) Society*. Cambridge, Cambridge University Press.

Munro, John H. 2003a. "The Monetary Origins of the 'Price Revolution': South German Silver Mining, Merchant Banking, and Venetian Commerce, 1470-1540." In *Global Con-*

nections and Monetary History, 1470–1800 (D. Flynn, A. Giráldez, and R. Von Glahn eds.), pp. 1–34. Burlington: Ashgate.

———. 2003b. "The Medieval Origins of the Financial Revolution: Usury, Rents, and Negotiability." *International History Review* 25 (3): 505–62.

———. 2007. "Review of Earl J. Hamilton, *American Treasure and the Price Revolution in Spain,* 1501–1650." EH.Net Economic History Services, Jan 15 2007. eh.net/bookreviews/library/munro.

Müri, Walter. 1931. *Symbolon: Wort- und sachgeschichtliche Studie.* Bern: Beilage zum Jahresbericht über das städtische Gymnasium Bern.

Murphy, George. 1961. "[Buddhist Monastic Economy: The Jisa Mechanism]: Comment." *Comparative Studies in Society and History* 3 (4): 439–42.

Myers, Milton L. 1983. *The Soul of Modern Economic Man: Ideas of Self-Interest, Thomas Hobbes to Adam Smith.* Chicago: University of Chicago Press.

Nag, Kalidas and V. R. Ramachandra Dikshitar. 1927. "The Diplomatic Theories of Ancient India and the *Arthashastra.*" *Journal of Indian History* 6 (1): 15–35.

Nakamura, Kyōko Motomochi. 1996. *Miraculous stories from the Japanese Buddhist tradition: the Nihon ryōiki of the monk Kyōkai.* London: Routledge.

Naskar, Satyendra Nath. 1996. *Foreign impact on Indian life and culture (c.* 326 B.C. *to c.* 300 A.D.*)* New Delhi: Abhinav Publications.

Naylor, Robin Thomas. 1985. *Dominion of debt: centre, periphery and the international economic order.* London: Black Rose Books.

Nazpary, Jomo. 2001. *Post-Soviet Chaos: Violence and Dispossession in Kazakhstan.* London: Pluto.

Nelson, Benjamin. 1949. *The Idea of Usury: From Tribal Brotherhood to Universal Otherhood.* Oxford: Oxford University Press.

Nerlich, Michael. 1987. *Ideology of adventure: studies in modern consciousness,* 1100–1750. (translation by Ruth Crowley). Minneapolis: University of Minnesota Press.

Nicholls, David. 2003. *God and Government in an "Age of Reason."* New York: Routledge.

Noah, Monday Efiong. 1990. "Social and Political Developments: The Lower Cross Region, 1600-1900." In *A History of the Cross River Region of Nigeria.* (Abasiattai, Monday B., ed.), pp. 90–108. Calabar: University of Calabar Press.

Nolan, Patrick. 1926. *A Monetary History of Ireland.* London: King.

Noonan, John T. 1957. *The Scholastic Analysis of Usury.* Cambridge: Harvard University Press.

Norman, K. R. 1975. "Aśoka and Capital Punishment: Notes on a Portion of Aśoka's Fourth Pillar Edict, with an Appendix on the Accusative Absolute Construction." *The Journal of the Royal Asiatic Society of Great Britain and Ireland* 1: 16–24.

North, Robert. 1954. *Sociology of the Biblical Jubilee.* Rome: Pontifical Biblical Institute.

Northrup, David. 1978. *Trade Without Rulers: Pre-Colonial Economic Development in South-Eastern Nigeria.* Oxford: Clarendon Press.

———. 1995. *Indentured labor in the age of imperialism,* 1834–1922. Cambridge: Cambridge University Press.

Nwaka, Geoffrey I. 1978. "Secret Societies and Colonial Change: A Nigerian Example (Sociétés secrètes et politique coloniale: un exemple nigerian)." Cahiers d'Études Africaines, Vol. 18(69/70): 187–200.

Nwauwa, Apollos Okwuchi. 1991. "Integrating Arochukwu into the Regional Chronological Structure." *History in Africa* 18: 297–310.

O'Brien, George. 1920. *An Essay on Medieval Economic Teaching.* London: Longmans, Green & Co.

Ohnuma, Reiko. 2007. *Head, eyes, flesh, and blood: giving away the body in Indian Buddhist literature.* New York: Columbia University Press.

Olivelle, Patrick. 1992. *The Asrama System: The History and Hermeneutics of a Religious Institution.* Oxford: Oxford University Press.

———. 2005. *Manu's Code of Law: A Critical Edition and Translation of the Mānava-Dharmaśāstra.* Oxford: Oxford University Press.

———. 2006. "Explorations in the Early History of Dharmaśāstra." In *Between the Empires: Society in India 300 BC to 400 CE* (Patrick Olivelle, ed.), pp. 169–90. New York: Oxford University Press.

———. 2009. "Dharmaśāstra: A Literary History." In *The Cambridge Handbook of Law and Hinduism* (T. Lubin and D. Davis, eds.), pp. 112–43. Cambridge: Cambridge University Press.

Oliver, Douglas. 1955. *A Solomon Island Society.* Cambridge: Harvard University Press.

Onvlee, Louis. 1980. "The Significance of Livestock on Sumba." In *The Flow of Life: Essays on Eastern Indonesia* (James J. Fox, ed.), pp. 195–207. Cambridge: Harvard University Press.

Oppenheim, Leo. 1964. *Ancient Mesopotamia: Portrait of a Dead Civilization.* Chicago: University of Chicago Press.

Orléan, André. 1998. "La monnaie autoréférentielle." In: M. Aglietta & A. Orléan (eds.), *La monnaie souveraine*, pp. 359–86. Paris: Odile Jacob.

Orlove, Benjamin. 1986. "Barter and Cash Sale on Lake Titicaca: A Test of Competing Approaches." *Current Anthropology* 27 (2): 85–106.

Orr, Leslie C. 2000. *Donors, Devotees, and Daughters of God: Temple Women in Medieval Tamilnadu.* Oxford: Oxford University Press.

Ottenberg, Simon. 1958. "Ibo Oracles and Intergroup Relations." *Southwestern Journal of Anthropology* 14 (3): 295–317.

Ottenberg, Simon and Phoebe Ottenberg. 1962. "Afikpo Markets: 1900-1960." In *Markets in Africa* (Paul Bohannan and George Dalton, eds.), pp. 118–69. Chicago: Northwestern University Press.

Ottenberg, Simon and Linda Knudsen. 1985. "Leopard Society Masquerades: Symbolism and Diffusion." *African Arts* 18 (2): 37–44.

Oxfeld, Ellen. 2004. "'When You Drink Water, Think of its Source': Morality, Status, and Reinvention in Chinese Funerals." *Journal of Asian Studies* 63 (4): 961-990.

Ozment, Steven. 1983. *When Fathers Ruled.* Harvard University Press, Cambridge: Cambridge University Press.

Pagden, Anthony. 1986. *The Fall of Natural Man: the American Indian and the origins of comparative ethnology.* Cambridge: Cambridge University Press.

Palat, Ravi Arvind. 1986. "Popular Revolts and the State in Medieval South India: A Study of the Vijayanagara Empire (1360–1565)," *Bijdragen tot de taal-, Land-, en Volkenkunde*, CXII, pp. 128–44.

———. 1988. *From World-Empire to World-Economy: Southeastern India and the Emergence of the Indian Ocean World-Economy (1350–1650).* Ph. D. Dissertation, State University of New York at Binghamton.

Parker, Arthur. 1926. *An Analytical History of the Seneca Indians.* Researches and Transactions of the New York State Archaeological Association. Rochester, NY.

Parker, David B. 1994. "The Rise and Fall of The Wonderful Wizard of Oz as a 'Parable on Populism.'" *Journal of the Georgia Association of Historians* 15: 49–63.

Parkes, Henry Bamford. 1959. *Gods and Men: The Origins of Western Culture.* New York: Vintage Books.

Parkin, Michael and David King. 1995. *Economics (Second Edition).* London: Addison-Wesley Publishers.

Parks, Time. 2005. *Medici Money: Banking, Metaphysics, and Art in Fifteenth-Century Florence.* New York: Norton.

Partridge, Charles. 1905. *Cross River Natives: Being Some Notes on the Primitive Pagans of Obubura Hill District, Southern Nigeria.* London: Hutchinson & Co.

Pasadika, Bhikkhu. 1997. "The concept of avipranāśa in Nāgārjuna." In *Recent Researches in Buddhist Studies: Essays in Honour of Y. Karunadasa*, pp. 516–23. Kuala Lumpur: Y. Karunadasa Felicitation Committee. & Chi Ying Foundation.

Pateman, Carole. 1988. *The Sexual Contract.* Stanford: Stanford University Press.

Patterson, Orlando. 1982. *Slavery and Social Death: A Comparative Study.* Cambridge: Harvard University Press.

Pearson, Michael N. 1982. "Premodern Muslim Political Systems." *Journal of the American Oriental Society* vol. 102 (no. 1):47–58.

Peng, Xinwei. 1994. *A monetary history of China (Zhongguo Huobi Shi)*. Two Volumes. (Edward H. Kaplan, translator). Bellingham: Western Washington University.

Perkins, John. 2006. *Confessions of an Economic Hit Man*. New York: Plume.

Perlman, Mark and Charles Robert McCann. 1998. *The pillars of economic understanding: ideas and traditions*. Ann Arbor: University of Michigan Press.

Peters, E. L. 1967. "Some Structural Aspects of the Feud Among the Camel-Herding Bedouins of Cyrenaica." *Africa* 37: 261–82.

Phillips, William D. 1985. *Slavery From Roman Times to the Early Transatlantic Trade*. Minneapolis: University of Minnesota Press.

Picard, Olivier. 1975. "La 'fiduciarité' des monnaies métalliques en Grèce." *Bulletin de la Société Française de Numismatique* 34 (10): 604–609.

Pietz, William. 1985. . "The Problem of the Fetish I." *RES: Journal of Anthropology and Aesthetics* 9:5–17.

Pigou, Arthur Cecil. 1949. *The Veil of Money*. London: Macmillan.

Polanyi, Karl. 1949. The Great Transformation. New York: Rinehart.

———. 1957a. "Aristotle Discovers the Economy." In K. Polanyi, C. Arensberg and H. Pearson (eds.), *Trade and Market in the Early Empires*, pp. 64-94. Glencoe: The Free Press.

———. 1957b. "The economy as an instituted process." In K. Polanyi, C. Arensberg and H. Pearson (eds.), *Trade and Market in the Early Empires*, pp. 243–69. Glencoe: The Free Press.

———. 1968. "The Semantics of Money Uses." In *Primitive, Archaic, and Modern Economies: Essays of Karl Polanyi*. (George Dalton, ed.) New York: Anchor.

Poliakov, Léon. 1977. *Jewish bankers and the Holy See from the thirteenth to the seventeenth century*. London: Routledge.

Pomeranz, Kenneth. 1998. *The Great Divergence: China, Europe, and the Making of the Modern World Economy*. Princeton: Princeton University Press.

Powell, Marvin A. 1978. "A Contribution to the History of Money in Mesopotamia prior to the Invention of Coinage." In *Festschrift Lubor Matous* (B. Hruska and G. Comoroczy, eds.) Budapest) II, pp. 211–43.

———. 1979. "Ancient Mesopotamian Weight Metrology: Methods, Problems and Perspectives." In *Studies in Honor of Tom B. Jones* (M. A. Powell and R. H. Sack, eds.), pp. 71–109. Amsterdam: Kevelaer/Neukirchen-Vluyn.

———. 1999. "*Wir mussen unsere nisch Nutzen*: Monies, Motives and Methods in Babylonian economics." In *Trade and Finance in Ancient Mesopotamia, Proceedings of the First Mos Symposium (Ledien 1997)*, (J. G. Derksen, ed.), pp. 5–24. Istanbul: Nederlands Historich-Archeologisch Instiuut.

Prakash, Gyan. 2003. *Bonded Histories: Genealogies of Labor Servitude in Colonial India*. Cambridge: Cambridge University Press.

Prakash, Satya and Rajendra Singh,. 1968. *Coinage in Ancient India* New Delhi: Research Institute of Ancient Scientific Studies.

Price, Jacob M. 1980. *Capital and Credit in British Overseas Trade: the View from the Chesapeake, 1700–1776*. Cambridge: Harvard University Press.

———. 1989. "What Did Merchants Do? Reflections on British Overseas Trade, 1660–1790." *The Journal of Economic History* 49 (2): 267-284.

———. 1991. "Credit in the Slave Trade and Plantation Economies." In Barbara L. Solow, editor, *Slavery and the Rise of the Atlantic System*, pp. 313–17. Cambridge: Cambridge University Press.

Price, Martin Jessop,. 1983. "Thoughts on the beginnings of coinage." In *Studies in Numismatic Method Presented to Philip Grierson* (C.N.L. Brooke et al., eds.,), pp. 1–10. Cambridge: Cambridge University Press.

Proudhon, Pierre-Joseph. 1840. *Qu'est-ce que la propriété? Recherche sur le principe du droit et du gouvernement. Premier mémoire*. Paris : J.-F. Brocard.

Puett, Michael J. 2002. *To Become a God: Cosmology, Sacrifice, and Self-Divinization in Early China.* Cambridge: Harvard University Press.

Quiggin, A. Hingston. 1949. *A Survey of primitive money; the beginning of currency* London: Methuen.

Quilter, Jeffrey and Gary Urton. 2002. *Narrative threads: accounting and recounting in Andean Khipu.* Austin: University of Texas.

Radford, R. A. 1945. "The Economic Organization of a POW Camp." *Economica* 12 (48): 189—201.

Raglan, FitzRoy Richard Somerset, Baron. 1931. "Bride Price." *Man* 31: 75.

Rahman, Fashur. 1964. "Riba and Interest." *Islamic Studies* 3:1–43.

Rai, G. K. 1981. *Involuntary Labour in Ancient India.* Allahabad: Chaitanya Press.

Ray, Nicholas Dylan. 1997. "The Medieval Islamic System of Credit and Banking: Legal and Historical Considerations." *Arab Law Quarterly* 12 (1): 43—90.

Reden, Sitta von. 1997. "Money, Law and Exchange: Coinage in the Greek Polis." *Journal of Hellenic Studies* 117: 154–76.

———. 2003. *Exchange in Ancient Greece.* London: Duckworth.

Reeves, Eileen. 1999. "As Good as Gold: The Mobile Earth and Early Modern Economics." *Journal of the Warburg and Courtauld Institutes* 62: 126–66.

Reid, Anthony. 1983. *Slavery, Bondage and Dependence in Southeast Asia.* New York: St. Martin's Press.

Renger, Johannes. 1983. "Patterns of Non-Institutional Trade and Non-Commercial. Exchange in Ancient Mesopotamia at the Beginning of the Second Millennium B.C." In *Circulation of Goods in Non-palatial Contexts in the Ancient Near East* (A. Archi, ed.), pp. 31–123. Rome: Edizioni dell'Ateneo

———. 1994. "On Economic Structures in Ancient Mesopotamia." *Orientalia* 18:157–208.

Retours, Robert de. 1952. "Les insignes en deux parties (fou) sous la dynastie des T'ang (618–907)." *T'oung Pao* 41 (1/3): 1–148.

Rhys Davids, Caroline A. F. 1901. "Economic Conditions in Ancient India." *The Economic Journal* 11 (43): 305-320

———. 1922. "Economic Conditions According to Early Buddhist Literature." In *The Cambridge History of India Volume I: Ancient India* (E. J. Rapson, ed.), pp. 198–219. Cambridge: Cambridge University Press.

Richard, R. D. 1926. "Early History of the Term Capital." *Quarterly Journal of Economics* 40 (2): 329–38.

Richards, Audrey. 1939. *Land, Labour and Diet in Northern Rhodesia.* London: Oxford University Press.

Richter, Daniel K. 1983. "War and Culture: the Iroquois Experience." *William and Mary Quarterly*, 3d Series, 40:528–59.

Rickett, W. Allyn. 1998. *Guanzi: Political, Economic, and Philosophical Essays from Early China* (2 volumes). Princeton: Princeton University Press.

Riepe, Dale Maurice. 1961. *The Naturalistic Tradition in Indian Thought.* Seattle: University of Washington Press.

Risso, Patricia. 1995. *Merchants and Faith: Muslim Commerce and Culture in the Indian Ocean.* Boulder: Westview Press.

Robertson, Pat. 1992. *The Secret Kingdom.* Dallas and London: Word Publishing.

Robinson, Rachel Sargent. 1973. *The size of the slave population at Athens during the fifth and fourth centuries before Christ.* Westport: Greenwood Press.

Robisheaux, Thomas. 1989. *Rural society and the search for order in early modern Germany.* Cambridge: Cambridge University Press.

Rockoff, Hugh. 1990. "The 'Wizard of Oz' as a Monetary Allegory." *Journal of Political Economy* 98 (4): 739–60.

Rodinson, Maxine. 1978. *Islam and Capitalism.* Austin: University of Texas Press.

Roetz, Heiner. 1993. *Confucian ethics of the axial age: a reconstruction under the aspect of the breakthrough toward postconventional thinking.* Albany: SUNY.

Rohrlich, Ruby. 1980. "State Formation in Sumer and the Subjugation of Women." *Feminist Studies* 6 (1): 76–102.

Roitman, Janet. 2003. "Unsanctioned Wealth; or, the Productivity of Debt in Northern Cameroon." *Public Culture* 15 (2): 211–37.

Roover, Raymond de. 1944. "What is Dry Exchange? A Contribution to the Study of English Mercantilism." *Journal of Political Economy* 52: 250–66.

———. 1946. "The Medici Bank." *Journal of Economic History* 6: 24–52, 153–72.

———. 1948. *Money, Banking, and Credit in Mediæval Bruges.* Cambridge: Mediaeval Academy of America.

———. 1963. *The Rise and Decline of the Medici Bank: 1397–1494.* New York: W.W. Norton.

———. 1967. "The Scholastics, Usury and Foreign Exchange." *Business History Review* 41 (3): 257–71.

Rospabé, Philippe. 1993. "Don Archaïque et Monnaie Sauvage." In *MAUSS: Ce Que Donner Vuet Dire: Don et Intéret.* Paris: Éditions la découverte, pp. 33–59.

———. 1995. *La Dette de Vie: aux origines de la monnaie sauvage.* Paris: Editions la Découverte/MAUSS.

Rotours, Robert de. 1952. "Les insignes en deux parties (fou) sous la dynastie des T'ang (618–907)." *T'oung Pao* 41: 1–148.

Ruel, Malcolm. 1969. *Leopards and Leaders.* London: Tavistock

Rule, John. 1986. *The Labouring Classes in Early Industrial England, 1750–1850.* London: Longman.

Saggs, Henry William Frederick. 1962. *The Greatness That Was Babylon.* New York: Mentor Books.

Sahlins, Marshall. 1972. *Stone Age Economics.* Chicago: Aldine.

———. 1981. "The stranger-king or Dumézil among the Fijians." *Journal of Pacific History* 16: 107–32.

———. 1988. "Cosmologies of Capitalism." *Proceedings of the British Academy* 74:1–51.

———. 1996. "The Sadness of Sweetness: The Native Anthropology of Western Cosmology." *Current Anthropology*, Vol. 37 (3): 395–428.

———. 2004. *Apologies to Thucydides: Understanding History as Culture and Vice Versa.* Chicago: University of Chicago Press.

———. 2008. *The Western Illusion of Human Nature.* Chicago: Prickly Paradigm Press.

Saller, Richard P. 1984. "'Familia, Domus', and the Roman Conception of the Family." *Phoenix* 38 (4): 336–55.

———. 1987. "Slavery and the Roman family." In *Classical Slavery* (Moses Finley, ed.), pp. 82-110. London: Frank Cass.

Samuel, Geoffrey. 2003. "Property, Obligations: Continental and Comparative Perspectives." In *New Perspectives on Property Law, Human Rights, and the Home* (Alastair Hudson, ed.), pp. 295–318. London: Cavendish Publications.

Samuelson, Paul A. 1948. *Economics.* New York: McGraw Hill.

———. 1958. "An exact consumption-loan model of interest with or without the social contrivance of money." In *The Collected Scientific Papers of Paul A. Samuelson*, volume 1 (J. Stiglitz, ed.), pp. 219–33. Cambridge: MIT Press.

Sarthou-Lajous, Nathalie. 1997. *L'ethique de la dette.* Paris: Presses Universitaires de France.

Sasso, Michael. 1978. "What is the Ho-Tu?" *History of Religions* 17 (314): 399–416.

Scammel, Jeffrey Vaughan. 1981. *The world encompassed: the first European maritime empires c.800-1650.* London: Taylor & Frances.

Schaps, David. 2004. *The Invention of Coinage and the Monetization of Ancient Greece.* Ann Arbor : University of Michigan Press.

———. 2006. "The Invention of Coinage in Lydia, in India, and in China." Helsinki: XIV International Economic History Congress.

Scheidel, Walter. 2006. "The Divergent Evolution of Coinage in Eastern and Western Eurasia." Princeton/Stanford Working Papers in Classics (April 2006): www.princeton.edu/~pswpc/pdfs/scheidel/040603.pdf

————. 2007. "The Monetary Systems of the Han and Roman Empires." Available at www .princeton.edu/~pswpc/pdfs/scheidel/110505.pdf.

————. 2009. *Rome and China: Comparative Perspectives on Ancient World Empires*. Oxford: Oxford University Press.

Schlemmer, Bernard. 1983. *Le Menabe: histoire d'une colonization*. Paris: ORSTOM.

Schneider, Jane. 1971. "Of Vigilance and Virgins: Honor, Shame, and Access to Resources in Mediterranean Societies." *Ethnology* 10:1–24.

Schoenberger, Erica. 2008. "The Origins of the Market Economy: State Power, Territorial Control, and Modes of War Fighting." *Comparative Studies in Society and History* 50 (3): 663–91.

Schofield, Phillipp R. and N. J. Mayhew, editors. 2002. *Credit and debt in medieval England, c.1180–c.1350*. London: Oxbow.

Schopen, Gregory. 1994. "Doing Business for the Lord: Lending on Interest and Written Loan Contracts in the Mūlasarvāstivāda-vinaya." *Journal of the American Oriental Society* 114 (4): 527–54.

————. 1995. "Monastic Law Meets the Real World: A Monk's Continuing Right to Inherit Family Property in Classical India." *History of Religions* 35 (2): 101–23.

————. 1997. *Bones, stones, and Buddhist monks: collected papers on the archaeology, epigraphy, and texts of monastic Buddhism in India*. Honolulu: University of Hawaii Press.

————. 2004. *Buddhist monks and business matters: still more papers on monastic Buddhism in India*. Honolulu: University of Hawaii Press.

Schumpeter, Joseph. 1934. *History of Economic Analysis*. New York: Oxford University Press.

Schwartz, Benjamin I. 1975. "The Age of Transcendence." *Daedalus* 104:1–7.

————. 1986. *The World of Thought in Ancient China*. Cambridge: Harvard University Press.

Scott, Tom, and Bob Scribner, editors. 1991. *The German Peasants' War: A History in Documents*. Atlantic Highlands: Humanities Press.

Sea, Thomas F. 2007. "The German Princes' Responses to the Peasants' Revolt of 1525." *Central European History* 40 (2): 219–40.

Seaford, Richard. 1994. *Reciprocity and Ritual. Homer and Tragedy in the Developing City-State*. Oxford: Oxford University Press.

————. 1998. "Tragic Money." *Journal of Hellenic Studies* 110: 76–90.

————. 2002. "Review: Reading Money: Leslie Kurke on the Politics of Meaning in Archaic Greece." *Arion*, Third Series 9 (3):145–65.

————. 2004. *Money and the Early Greek Mind: Homer, Philosophy, Tragedy*. Cambridge: Cambridge University Press.

Sée, Henri Eugène. 1928. *Modern capitalism: its origin and evolution*. New York: Adelphi.

Seebohm, Frederic. 1877. *The Era of the Protestant Revolution*. London: Longmans, Green.

Seidel, Anna. 1983. "Imperial Treasures and Taoist Sacraments: Taoist Roots in Apocrypha." In *Tantric and Taoist Studies in Honor of Rolf A. Stein* (Michel Strickmann, ed.), II, pp. 291-371. Bruxelles: Institute Belge des Hautes Études Chinoises.

Servet, Jean-Michel. 1981. "Primitive Order and Archaic Trade. Part I" *Economy and Society* 10 (4): 423–50.

————. 1982. "Primitive Order and Archaic Trade. Part II." *Economy and Society* 11 (1): 22–59.

————. 1994. "La fable du troc," numero spécial de la revue *XVIIIe siècle, Economie et politique* (sous la direction Gerard Klotz, Catherine Larrere et Pierre Retat), no. 26: 103–15.

————. 1998. "Demonétarisation et remonétarisation en Afrique-Occidentale et Équatoriale (XIXe-XXe siècles)." In *La Monnaie souveraine* (Aglietta and Orleans, eds.), pp. 289–324. Paris: Odile Jacob.

————. 2001. "Le troc primitif, un mythe fondateur d'une approche économiste de la monnaie." *Revue numismatique* 2001: 15–32.

Sharma, J. P. 1968. *Republics in Ancient India: c 1500–c. 500 BC*. Leiden: E. J. Brill.

Sharma, Ram Sharan. 1958. *Sudras in Ancient India*. Delhi: Mohtial Banarsidas.

————. 1965. "Usury in Medieval India (A.D. 400–1200)." *Comparative Studies in Society and History* 8 (1): 56–77.

————. 1987. *Urban Decay in India c. 300–c.1000*. Delhi: Munshiram Manoharlal.

————. 2001. *Early medieval Indian society: a study in feudalisation*. Hyderbad: Orient Longman.

Shell, Marc. 1978. *The Economy of Literature*. Baltimore: Johns Hopkins University Press.

————. 1992. *Money, Language, and Thought*. Baltimore: Johns Hopkins University Press.

Sheridan, R. B. 1958. "The Commercial and Financial Organization of the British Slave Trade, 1750–1807." *The Economic History Review*, New Series 11 (2): 249–63.

Silver, Morris. 1985. *Economic structures of the ancient Near East*. London: Taylor & Francis.

Singer, Sholom A. 1964. "The Expulsion of the Jews from England in 1290." *The Jewish Quarterly Review*, New Series, 55 (2): 117–36.

Skinner, Quentin. 1998. *Liberty before Liberalism*. Cambridge: Cambridge University Press.

Smith, Adam. 1761. *Theory of moral sentiments*. Cambridge: Cambridge University Press (2002 edition).

————. 1762. *Lectures on Jurisprudence*. Glasgow Edition of the Works and Correspondence of Adam Smith Vol. 5. Indianapolis: Liberty Fund (1982 edition).

————. 1776. *An Inquiry into the nature and causes of the wealth of nations*. Oxford: Clarendon Press (1976 edition).

Smith, Edwin, and Andrew Murray Dale. 1968. *The Ila Speaking Peoples Of Northern Rhodesia*. Two Volumes. London: Kessinger.

Smith, Timothy. 1983. "Wampum as Primitive Valuables." *Research in Economic Anthropology* 5: 225–46.

Snell, F. J. 1919. *The Customs of Old England*. London: Methuen.

Solow, Barbara. 1987. "Capitalism and Slavery in the Exceedingly Long Run." *Journal of Interdisciplinary History* 17 (4): 711–37.

Sonenscher, Michael. 2007. *Before the Deluge: Public Debt, Inequality, and the Intellectual Origins of the French Revolution*. Princeton: Princeton University Press.

Spufford, Peter. 1988. *Money and Its Use in Medieval Europe*. Cambridge: Cambridge University Press.

Spyer, Patricia. 1997. "The Eroticism of Debt: Pearl Divers, Traders, and Sea Wives in the Aru Islands of Eastern Indonesia." *American Ethnologist* 24 (3): 515–38.

Ste. Croix, Geoffrey Ernest Maurice De. 1981. *The Class Struggle in the Ancient Greek World: from the Archaic Age to the Arab Conquests*. Ithaca: Cornell University Press.

Stannard, David E. 1993. *American holocaust: the conquest of the New World*. New York: Oxford University Press.

Starr, Chester G. 1977. *The Economic and Social Growth of Early Greece. 800-500 BC*. New York: Oxford University Press.

Stein, Siegfried. 1953. "Laws of Interest in the Old Testament." *Journal of Theological Studies* 4: 161–70.

————. 1955. "The Development of the Jewish Law of Interest from the Biblical Period to the Expulsion of the Jews from England." *Historia Judaica* 17:3–40.

Stein, Stanley J., and Barbara H. Stein. 2000. *Silver, trade, and war: Spain and America in the making of early modern Europe*. Baltimore: Johns Hopkins University Press.

Steinkeller, Piotr. 1980. "The Renting of Fields in early Mesopotamia and the Development of the Concept of 'Interest' in Sumerian." *Journal of the Economic and Social History of the Orient* 24: 113–45.

————. 2003. "Money-Lending Practices in Ur III Babylonia: the question of economic motivation." In *Debt and Economic Renewal in the Ancient Near East* (Hudson, Michael and Marc Van de Mieroop, eds.), pp. 109–37. Bethesda: CDL.

Stiglitz, Joseph, and John Driffill. 2000. *Economics*. New York: W. W. Norton.

Stol, Marten. 1995. "Women in Mesopotamia." *Journal of the Economic and Social History of the Orient* 38 (2): 123–44.

Stone, Lawrence. 1968. *The Family, Sex and Marriage in England 1500–1800*. London: Unwin.

————. 1990. *Road to Divorce: England 1530-1987*. Oxford: Oxford University Press.

Stone, Willard E. 2005. "The Tally: An Ancient Accounting Instrument." *Abacus* 11 (1): 49–57.

Stout, William. 1742 [1967]. *The Autobiography of William Stout of Lancaster 1665–1752*. (John Duncan Marshall, editor.) Manchester: Manchester University Press.

Strickmann, Michel. 2002. *Chinese magical medicine*. Stanford: Stanford University Press.

Subrahmanyam, Sanjay. 1996. "Of Imarat and Tijarat: Asian Merchants and State Power in the Western Indian Ocean, 1400 to 1750." *Comparative Studies in Society and History* Vol. 37 no. 4, pp. 750–80.

Sun, Guang-Zhen. 2008. "Fragment: Nasir ad-Din Tusi on social cooperation and the division of labor: Fragment from The Nasirean Ethics." *Journal of Institutional Economics* 4 (3): 403–13.

Sutton, David. 2004. "Anthropology's value(s)." *Anthropological Theory* 4(3): 373–79.

Swann, Nancy Lee. 1950. *Food and Money in Ancient China: The earliest economic history of China to A. D. 25. Han Shu 24 with related texts. Han Shu 91 and Shih-chi 129*. Princeton: Princeton University Press.

Tag El-Din, Saif I. 2007. "Capital and Money Markets of Muslims: The Emerging Experience in Theory and Practice." Kyoto Bulletin of Islamic Area Studies, 1–2: 54–71.

Tambiah, Stanley J. 1973. "Dowry and Bridewealth and the Property Rights of Women in South Asia." In *Bridewealth and Dowry* (Jack Goody and S. J. Tambiah, eds.), pp. 59–169. Cambridge: Cambridge University Press.

————. 1989. "Bridewealth and Dowry Revisited: The Position of Women in Sub-Saharan Africa and North India." *Current Anthropology* 30 (4): 413–34.

Tambo, David C. 1976. "The Sokoto Caliphate Slave Trade in the Nineteenth Century." *International Journal of African Historical Studies* 9 (2): 187–217.

Taussig, Michael. 1984. "Culture of Terror—Space of Death. Roger Casement's Putumayo Report and the Explanation of Torture." *Comparative Studies in Society and History* 26 (3): 467–97.

————. 1987. *Shamanism, Colonialism, and the Wild Man*. Chicago: University of Chicago Press.

Taylor, Quentin P. 2005. "Money and Politics in the Land of Oz." *The Independent Review* 9 (3): 413–26.

Tebbutt, Melanie. 1983. *Making Ends Meet: Pawnbroking and Working-Class Credit*. New York: St. Martin's Press.

Teiser, Stephen F. 1988. *The Ghost Festival in Medieval China*. Princeton: Princeton University Press.

Testart, Alain. 1997. "Le mise en gage de personnes: sociologie comparative d'une institution." *Archives Européenes de Sociologie* 38: 38–67.

————. 1998. "Pourquoi la condition de l'esclave s'ameliore-t-elle en regime despotique?" *Revue française de sociologie* 39 (1): 3–38.

————. 2000. "L'Esclavage pour dettes en Asie Orientale." *Moussons* 2: 3–29.

————. 2001. *Esclave, la dette et le pouvoir: études de sociologie comparative*. Paris : Errance

————. 2002. "The extent and significance of debt slavery." *Revue Française de Sociologie* 43: 173–204.

Testart, Alain, Valerie Lécrivain, Dimitri Karadimas and Nicolas Govoroff. 2001. "Prix de la fiancée et esclavage pour dettes: Un exemple de loi sociologique." *Études rurales* No. 159/160: 9–33.

Thapar, Romila. 1995. "The First Millennium BC in Northern India." In *Recent perspectives of early Indian history* (R. Thapar, ed.) pp. 87–150. New Delhi: Book Review Trust.

————. 2002. "The Role of the Army in the Exercise of Power in Ancient India." In *Army and power in the ancient world. Volume 37 of Heidelberger althistorische Beiträge und epigraphische Studien* (Ángelos Chaniótis, Pierre Ducre, eds.), pp. 25–39. Heidelberg: Franz Steiner Verlag.

Thesleff, Holgar. 1989. "Platonic Chronology." *Phronesis* 34 (1): 1–26.

Théret, Bruno. 1992. *Régimes économiques de l'ordre politique : esquisse d'une théorie régulationniste des limites de l'Etat.* Paris: Presses Universitaires de France,.

———. 1995. *L'État, la finance et le social. Souveraineté nationale et construction européenne* (direction de publication). Paris: Éditions la Découverte.

———. 1999. "The Socio-Cultural Dimensions of the Currency: Implications for the Transition to the Euro." *Journal of Consumer Policy* 22: 51–79.

———. 2007. *La monnaie dévoilée par ses crises* (direction de publication). Paris: Editions de l'EHESS, 2 volumes: volume 1, "Monnaies métalliques, volume 2 "Monnaies autoréférentielles. Les autres monnaies en Allemagne et en Russie au XXème siècle.

———. 2008. "Les trios états de la monnaie: approche interdisciplinaire du fait monétaire." *Revue Economique* 59 (4): 813–42.

Thierry, François. 1992. *Monnaies de Chine.Paris*: Bibliothèque nationale.

———. 2001. "Sur les spécifités fondamentales de la monnaie chinoise." In *Aux origines de la monnaie* (Alain Testart, ed.), pp. 109-44. Paris: Éditions Errance.

Thomas, Keith. 1972. *Religion and the Decline of Magic: Studies in popular beliefs in sixteenth and seventeenth century England.* New York: Scribners.

Thompson, Edward Palmer. 1971. "The Moral Economy of the English Crowd in the 18th Century." *Past & Present* 50: 76–136.

Thurnwald, Richard C. 1916. "Banaro Society: Social Organization and Kinship System of a Tribe in the Interior of New Guinea." *Memoirs of the American Anthropological Association* 8:251–391.

Tierney, Brian. 1997. *The Idea of Natural Rights: Studies on Natural Rights, Natural Law and Church Law 1150–1625.* (Emory University Studies in Law and Religion, number 5). Atlanta: Scholars Press.

Todorov, Tzvetan. 1984. *The conquest of America: the question of the other.* Chicago: University of Chicago Press.

Tong, James W. 1989. *Disorder Under Heaven: Collective Violence in the Ming Dynasty.* Stanford: Stanford University Press.

Tortella, Gabriel and Francisco Comîn. 2002. "Fiscal and Monetary Institutions in Spain, 1600–1900." In *Transferring wealth and power from the old to the new world: monetary and fiscal institutions in the 17th through the 19th century* (Michael D. Bordo and Robert Cortés Conde, eds.), pp. 140-186. Cambridge: Cambridge University Press.

Trawick, Margaret. 1992. *Notes on Love in a Tamil Family.* Berkeley: University of California Press.

Trevett, Jeremy. 1992. *Apollodoros the Son of Pasion.* Oxford: Clarendon Press.

———. 2001. "Coinage and Democracy at Athens," in A. Meadows and K. Shipton, eds., *Money and Its Uses in the Ancient Greek World* (Oxford: Oxford University Press), pp. 23–34.

Trombert, Eric. 1995. *Le crédit à Dunhuang: Vie matérielle et société en Chine médiévale.* Paris: Ihec/Inst.Hautes Etudes.

Tseayo, Justin Iyorbee. 1975. *Conflict and Incorporation in Nigera: the Integration of the Tiv.* Zaria Nigeria: Gaskiya.

Tuck, Richard. 1979. *Natural rights theories: their origin and development.* Cambridge: Cambridge University Press.

Tull, Herman Wayne. 1989. *The Vedic Origins of Karma: cosmos as man in ancient Indian myth and ritual.* Albany: SUNY.

Tully, James. 1993. *An Approach to Political Philosophy: Locke in Contexts.* Cambridge: Cambridge University Press.

Tuma, Elias. 1965. "Early Arab Economic Policies, 1st/7th–4th/10th Centuries." *Islamic Studies* 4 (1): 1–23.

Uchendo, Victor. 1967. "Some Principles of Haggling in Peasant Markets." *Economic Development and Cultural Change* 16 (1): 37–50.

Udovitch, Abraham L. 1970. *Partnership and Profit in Medieval Islam.* Princeton: Princeton University Press.

———. 1975. "Reflections on the Institutions of Credit and Banking in the Medieval Islamic Near East." *Studia Islamica* 41: 5–21.

Uebach, Helga. 2008. "From Red Tally to Yellow Paper: the official introduction of paper in Tibetan administration in 744/745." *Revue d'Etudes Tibétaines* 14: 57–69.

Usher, Abbot Payson. 1914. "The Origin of the Bill of Exchange." *Journal of Political Economy* 22: 566–76.

———. 1934. "The Origins of Banking: The Primitive Bank of Deposit, 1200–1600." *Economic History Review* 4 (4): 399–428.

———. 1943. *The Early History of Deposit Banking in Mediterranean Europe*. Cambridge: Harvard University Press.

Valenze, Deborah M. 2006. *The social life of money in the English past*. Cambridge: Cambridge University Press.

Valeri, Valerio. 1994. "Buying Women but no Selling Them: Gift and Commodity Exchange in Huaulu Alliance." *Man* (n.s.) 29:1–26.

———. 2001. "Feasts." In *Fragments from Forests and Libraries*, pp. 1–27. Durham: Carolina Academic Press.

Van Der Toorn, Karel. 1989. "Female Prostitution in Payment of Vows in Ancient Israel." *Journal of Biblical Literature* 108 (2): 193–205.

Vance, Eugene. 1973. "Signs of the City: Medieval Poetry as Detour." *New Literary History* 4 (3): 557–74.

———. 1986. "Chrétien's Yvain and the Ideologies of Change and Exchange." *Yale French Studies* 70: 42–62.

Vaneigem, Raoul. 1967. *Traité de savoir-vivre à l'usage des jeunes générations*. Paris, Gallimard.

Veenhof, Karl. 1997. "'Modern' Features in Old Assyrian Trade." *Journal of the Economic and Social History of the Orient* 40: 336–66.

Verellen, Franciscus. 2006. "The Dynamic Design: Ritual and Contemplative Graphics in Daoist Scriptures." In *Daoism in History: Essays in Honor of Liu Rs'un-yan* (Quanlen Liu, Benjamin Penny, eds.), pp. 159–82. London: Routledge.

Verlinden, Charles. 1970. *The Beginnings of Modern Colonization: Eleven Essays with an Introduction*. Ithaca: Cornell University Press.

VerSteeg, Russ. 2000. *Early Mesopotamian Law*. Durham: Carolina Academic Press.

———. 2002. *Law in Ancient Egypt*. Durham: Carolina Academic Press.

Veyne, Paul-Marie. 1979. "Mythe et réalité de l'autarcie à Rome." *Revue des études anciennes* 81: 261–80.

Vice, Roy L. 1988. "Leadership and Structure of the Tauber Band during the Peasants' War in Franconia." *Central European History* 24 (2): 17595.

Vickers, Adrian. 1996. *Bali: a paradise created*. Singapore: Periplus Editions.

Vickers, Michael J. 1985. "Early Greek Coinage, a Reassessment." *Numismatic Chronicle* 145:1–44.

Vijaisri, Priyadarshini. 2004. *Recasting the Devadasi: Patterns of Sacred Prostitution in Colonial South India*. New Delhi: Kanishka.

Villey, Michel. 1946. "L'Idee du droit subjectif et les systemes juridiques romains." Revue historique de droit, series 4: 201–27.

Vondeling, Jan. 1961. *Eranos* (with a summary in English). Amsterdam: Gron.

Wade, Geoffrey. 2004. "The Zheng He Voyages: A Reassessment." *Asia Research Institute Working Paper Series* No. 31, Oct 2004.

Wake, Christopher. 1997. "The Great Ocean-going Ships of Southern China in the Age of Chinese Maritime Voyaging to India, Twelfth to Fifteenth Centuries," *International Journal of Maritime History* 9 (2): 51–81.

Walker, Garthene. 1996. "Expanding the Boundaries of Female Honour in Early Modern England." *Transactions of the Royal Historical Society*, Sixth Series, 8:235–45.

Walker, James Broom. 1875. "Notes on the Politics, Religion, and Commerce of Old Calabar." *The Journal of the Anthropological Institute of Great Britain and Ireland* 6: 119–24.

Wallace, Robert B. 1987. "The Origin of Electrum Coinage." *American Journal of Archaeology* 91: 385–97.

Wallace-Hadrill, Andrew, editor. 1989. *Patronage in Ancient Society* (Leicester-Nottingham Studies in Ancient Society, Volume 1) London: Routledge.

Wallerstein, Immanuel. 1974. *The Modern World System, volume I.* New York. Academic Press.

———. 1989. "The French Revolution as a World-Historical Event." *Social Research* 56 (1): 33–52.

———. 1991. "Braudel on Capitalism, or Everything Upside Down." *Journal of Modern History* 63 (2): 354–61.

———. 2001. *The End of the World as We Know It: Social Science for the Twenty-First Century.* Minneapolis: University of Minnesota Press.

Walsh, Michael J. 2007. "The Economics of Salvation: Toward a Theory of Exchange in Chinese Buddhism." *Journal of the American Academy of Religion* 75 (2): 353–82.

Warburton, David. 2000. "Before the IMF: The Economic Implications of Unintentional Structural Adjustment in Ancient Egypt." *Journal of the Economic and Social History of the Orient* 43 (2): 65–131.

———. 2001. "State and economy in ancient Egypt." In *World System History: the social science of long-term change* (Robert Denemark, Jonathan Friedman, Barry Gills, and George Modelski, eds.), pp. 169–84. New York: Routledge.

Wartburg, Marie Louise von. 1995. "Production de sucre de canne à Chypre." In *Coloniser au Moyen Age* (Michel Balard and Alain Ducellier, eds.), Paris: A. Colon, pp. 126–31.

Waswo, Richard. 1996. "Shakespeare and the Formation of the Modern Economy." *Surfaces* Vol. 6. 217 (v.1.0A), www.pum.umontreal.ca/revues/surfaces/vol6/waswo.html.

———. 2004. "Crises of Credit: Monetary and Erotic Economies in the Jacobean Theater." In *Plotting early modern London: new essays on Jacobean City comedy* (Dieter Mehl, Angela Stock, Anne-Julia Zwierlein, eds.), pp. 55–74. London: Ashgate Publishing.

Watson, Alan. 1987. *Roman Slave Law.* Baltimore: Johns Hopkins University Press.

Watson, James L. 1980. "Transactions in People: The Chinese Market in Slaves, Servants, and Heirs." In *Asian and African Systems of Slavery* (James L. Watson, ed.), pp. 223–50. Cambridge: Cambridge University Press.

Weber, Max. 1924. *Gesammelte Aufsätze zur Soziale- und Wirtschaftegeschichte.* Tubingen. English version: *The Agrarian Sociology of Ancient Civilizations.* (R. I. Frank, trans.) London: Verso.

———. 1961. *General Economic History.* New York: Collier Books.

———. 1978. *Economy and Society: An Outline of Interpretive Sociology.* (Ephrain Fischoff, trans.) Berkeley: University of California Press.

Wennerlind, Carl. 2003. "Credit-money as the Philosopher's Stone: Alchemy and the Coinage Problem in Seventeenth-century England." *History of Political Economy* 35:234–61.

Westbrook, Raymond. 1971. "Jubilee Laws." *Israel Law Review* 6: 209-26.

———. 1984. "The enforcement of morals in Mesopotamian law." *Journal of the American Oriental Society* 104: 753-756.

———. 1988. *Old Babylonian Marriage Law.* Archiv für Orientforschung, Beiheft 23. Horn: F. Burger.

———. 1990. "Adultery in Ancient Near Eastern Law." *Revue biblique* 97: 542–80.

———. 1991. *Property and the Family in Biblical Law.* Sheffield: Sheffield Academic Press.

———. 1995. "Slave and Master in Ancient Near Eastern Law." *Chicago-Kent Law Review* 70: 1631–76.

———. 1999. "Vitae Necisque Potestas." *Historia: Zeitschrift für Alte Geschichte* 48 (2): 203–23.

Westenholz, Joan Goodnick. 1989. "Tamar, *Qedesa, Qadistu,* and Sacred Prostitution in Mesopotamia." *Harvard Theological Review* 82: 245–265.

Westermann, William L. 1955. *The Slave Systems of Greek and Roman Antiquity.* Philadelphia: American Philosophical Society.

Whelan, T. S. 1979. *The Pawnshop in China*. Ann Arbor: Centre for Chinese Studies, University of Michigan.

Whitaker, C. W. A. 2002. *Aristotle's De interpretatione: contradiction and dialectic*. Oxford: Oxford University Press.

White, Jenny Barbara. 2004. *Money makes us relatives: women's labor in urban Turkey*. London: Routledge.

Whiting, John Roger Scott. 1971. *Trade Tokens: A Social and Economic History*. London: Newton Abbot.

Wiedemann, Thomas. 1981. *Greek and Roman Slavery*. New York: Routledge.

Wiener, Margaret J. 1995. *Visible and invisible realms: power, magic, and colonial conquest in Bali*. Chicago: University of Chicago Press.

Wilbur, C. Martin. 1943. *Slavery in China during the Former Han Dynasty*. Anthropological Series, volume 34. Chicago: Chicago Field Museum of Natural History.

Wilcke, Claus. 1985. "Familiengründung im alten Babylonien." In *Geschlechtsreife und Legitimation zur Zeugung* (E.W Müller, ed.), pp. 213–317. Freiburg and München: Alber.

Williams, Brett. 2004. *Debt for Sale: A Social History of the Credit Trap*. Philadelphia: University of Pennsylvania Press.

Williams, Carl O. 1937. *Thraldom in Ancient Iceland: A Chapter in the History of Class Rule*. Chicago: University of Chicago Press.

Williams, Eric. 1944. *Capitalism and Slavery*. Chapel Hill: University of North Carolina Press.

Williamson, George Charles. 1889. *Trade tokens issued in the seventeenth century in England, Wales, and Ireland, by corporations, merchants, tradesmen, etc. Illustrated by numerous plates and woodcuts, and containing notes of family, heraldic, and topographical interest respecting the various issuers of the tokens*. London: E. Stock.

Wilson, Monica Hunter. 1951. "Witch Beliefs and Social Structure." *The American Journal of Sociology* 56 (4): 307–31.

Wink, André. 2002. *Al-Hind: Early medieval India and the expansion of Islam, 7th-11th centuries*. Leiden: E. J. Brill.

Wirszubski, Chaim. 1950. *Libertas as a Political Ideal at Rome During the Late Republic and Early Principate*. Cambridge: Cambridge University Press.

Wolf, Robert L. 1954. "The Mortgage and Redemption of an Emperor's Son: Castile and the Latin Empire of Constantinople." *Speculum* 29: 45–85.

Wong, Roy Bin. 1997. *China Transformed: Historical Change and the Limits of European Experience*. Ithaca: Cornell University Press.

———. 2002. "Between Nation and World: Braudelian Regions in Asia." *Review* 26 (1): 1–45.

Wood, Diana. 2002. *Medieval Economic Thought*. Cambridge: Cambridge University Press.

Wordie, J. R. 1983. "The Chronology of English Enclosure, 1500-1914." Economic History Review, 2nd ser. 26:483–505.

Wray, L. Randall. 1990. *Money and Credit in Capitalist Economies*. Aldershot: Edward Elgar.

———. 1998. *Understanding Modern Money: the key to full employment and price stability*. Edward Elgar: Cheltenham.

———. 1999. "An Irreverent Overview of the History of Money from the Beginning of the Beginning to the Present." *Journal of Post Keynesian Economics*. 21 (4): 679–87.

———. 2000. *Credit and State Theories of Money*. Cheltenham: Edward Elgar.

Wright, David P. 2009. *Inventing God's Law: How the Covenant Code of the Bible Used and Revised the Laws of Hammurabi*. Oxford: Oxford University Press.

Wrightson, Keith. 1980. "Two concepts of order: justices, constables and jurymen in seventeenth-century England," in *An Ungovernable People: The English and their Law in the Seventeenth and Eighteenth Centuries* (John Brewer and John Styles, eds.), pp. 21–46. London: Hutchinson.

Wrightson, Keith, and David Levine. 1979 *Poverty and Piety in an English Village*. Cambridge: Cambridge University Press.

Xu, Zhuoyun, and Jack L. Dull. 1980. *Han agriculture: the formation of early Chinese agrarian economy, 206 B.C.–A.D. 220*. Seattle: University of Washington Press.

Yang, Bin. 2002. "Horses, Silver, and Cowries: Yunnan in Global Perspective." *Journal of World History*, vol. 15 no 3:281–322.

Yang, Lien-sheng. 1971. *Money and Credit in China: A Short History*. Harvard-Yenching Institute Monographs 12. Cambridge: Harvard University Press.

Yates, Robin D. S. 2002. "Slavery in Early China: A Socio-Cultural Approach." *Journal of East Asian Archaeology* 3 (1/2): 283–31.

Yoffee, Norman. 1998. "The Economics of Ritual at Late Babylonian Kish." *Journal of the Economic and Social History of the Orient* 41 (3): 312–43.

Yü, Ying-shih. 1967. *Trade and Expansion in Han China. A Study in the Structure in Sino-Barbarian Economic Relations*. Berkeley: University of California Press.

Yung-Ti, Li. 2006. "On the Function of Cowries in Shang and Western Zhou China." *Journal of East Asian Archaeology* 5: 1–26.

Zell, Michael. 1996. "Credit in the Pre-Industrial English Woollen Industry." *The Economic History Review*, New Series, 49 (4): 667–91.

Zmora, Hillay. 2006. "The Princely State and the Noble Family: Conflict and Co-operation in the Margraviates Ansbach-Kulmbach in the Early Sixteenth Century." *The Historical Journal* 49: 1–21.

Zürcher, Erik. 1958. *The Buddhist conquest of China: the spread and adaptation of Buddhism in early medieval China*. Volume 11 of Sinica Leidensia. Leiden: E. J. Brill.

INDEX

A

Abbasid Caliphate, 169, 272–275, 303
abolitionism, 166–167
absolute power
    in property rights, 198–201, 421n92, 421n96
    of state and monarchs, 205–207, 325, 331, 385
    (abuse/destruction), 199
Abyssinia, 26
"Accounting for the Grail" (Shell), 441nn143–144
Achilles, 189, 209, 418n66, 418n70
Act of Settlement of 1701, 243
adal-badal (give and take), 33–34
Addison, Joseph, 242, 368
adultery
    biblical view of, 129, 409n8
    in Lele culture, 138
advantage, concept of, 239
Aeschines, 418–419n73
"affair of honor," 177, 415n30
Africa
    barter systems in, 24, 394n7
    cloth money in, 129
    colonialism in, 350
    currency in, 150, 152, 411n53, 411nn53–54
    Islam in, 272, 273
    Kabyle Berber men (Algeria), 106
    negative image of, 156
    reciprocity, examples of in, 92–94
    slave trade in, 148–155
    See also Lele people; slavery; Tiv people
African slavery laws, 169
Against Timarchus (Aeschines), 418–419n73
Agamemnon, 189

age of debt, 446n53
age of exploration, 308, 444n12
Age of Revolutions, 345
Aglietta, Michel, 55, 56, 398n30
Agni (god), 56
ahimsa, principles of, 234, 255
AIG (American International Group, Inc.), 18, 393n11
Akiga, Sai, 132, 161–162, 410n42, 411n51, 412n77
Akkadian language, 178
Akunakuna people, 412n65
alchemy, 336, 343, 448n85
Alexander the Great, 219, 227, 229–230, 233, 427n22, 428n39, 432n10
Algeria
    Kabyle Berber men in, 106, 277, 437n76
    national liberation movements in, 374
al-Sadr, Muhammud Baqir, 384
"alternating reciprocity," 405n21
"alternative tradition," 54, 55
Althabe, Gerard, 51
Alvarado, Pedro de, 356, 444n20
al-Wahid, Ali ibn `Abd, 168–169, 274, 414nn3–8, 421n103
amargi (freedom), 65, 216
Amazonia, burial customs in, 99, 405n18
Ambrose, Saint, 282, 284–285, 286, 287
American dream, ideals of, 374–375, 381
American Express, 368
Americas, European conquest of, 314–318, 350
Amorite language, 178
Amos, 73
Anaximander/Anaximenes, 230n73, 245
ancient Greece. See Greece
ancient Rome. See Rome
Angas, L.L.B., 448n87

copper, 27

copper bars, as currency, 150, 152, 411nn53–54

corporations
bailouts for, 16–17, 381, 393n11
"fictive person" *(persona ficta),* 304, 443n170
in India, 346
joint-stock companies, 292, 305, 320, 342, 347, 449n88
legal idea of, 304
legal recognition of, 304–306, 443n170
medieval corporations, 303–305
motives of, 368
start-up companies, 347
structure of, 320

corpus intellectuale (intellectual body), 304

Cortes, Hernan, 309, 316–317, 320–321, 325–326, 355–357, 444n20

coveting, biblical view of, 409n8

Coward, Henry, 328, 334

cowries, 60, 131, 220, 225, 425n25, 425n26

credit, as human right, 380–381

credit, as meaning "reputation," 328

credit, economic history and, 38–40

credit-card companies, 367, 452n25

credit cards
creation of, 367–368
debit cards, 368
interest charged by, 379, 453n31
offers for, 380

credit money. *See* virtual money

credit money system, U.S. dollar and, 361–362

creditors, societal views of, 388

credit systems
checks and promissory notes, 269–270, 275–276, 435n54, 437n71
debit and credit cards, 368
as extension of human society, 330–331
Inca *khipu* system, 220, 425n28
microcredit, 379–381
Muslim *suftaja,* 201, 276, 291, 437n81
negative views of, 335, 447n66

private bank notes, 338, 448n75, 449n102
proverbs about, 326
shopkeepers and, 352
tally sticks, 48, 268, 396n37, 397n16, 425n26, 435nn48–53, 442n161
trust in, 73, 328–329, 337, 340–341, 347
utopian ideals about, 335–336
vs. coins/coinage, 40, 213
See also interest-bearing loans; virtual money

credit systems, origins of
ancient systems, 18, 37–38
in China, 219–221, 269–270, 425n25, 425n28, 428n43, 435n54
destruction of ancient systems and, 327
in Greece, 231
in India, 255–257
in Mesopotamia, 214–217
in Middle East, 215, 275–277, 424n9, 436–437nn68–74

Credit Theory of money, 46–52

credtit trap, 453n32

Creed, the (symbol), 442n154

crime
debt-default as, 17, 329
gift by stealth, 109–111
hierarchy and, 109–111
redemption and exchange, 19
societal debt of criminals, 121–122

criminalization, as debt, 334, 446n60

criminals, punishments for, 435n59

"crisis," etymology of, 177

Critique of the Gotha Programme (Marx), 404n9

Cross River societies. *See* merchant societies, slave trade

Crusades, 291, 318

"crying down/crying up," 282, 337, 438n95, 440n130

Cuba, communism in, 94

cumals, 171, 173, 408nn3–4, 414n14, 414n21, 415n25
bondmaids, 61, 128

cuneiform documents, Mesopotamian, 38, 54

currency. *See* coinage; coins/coinage; currency; money; primitive money

ABOUT THE AUTHORS

DAVID GRAEBER (1961–2020) was an American professor of anthropology at the London School of Economics, who also taught at Goldsmiths College and Yale University. One of the original organizers of Occupy Wall Street, Graeber was also the author of *Utopia of Rules* and numerous other books, as well as for magazines and newspapers including *The Guardian*, *Harper's*, *The Baffler*, *n+1*, *The Nation*, *The New Inquiry* and *The New Left Review*.

THOMAS PIKETTY is professor of economics at the School for Advanced Studies in the Social Sciences, associate chair at the Paris School of Economics, and Centennial Professor of Economics in the International Inequalities Institute at the London School of Economics. His book, *Capital in the Twenty-First Century*, reached number one on the *New York Times* bestseller list.